NAPO PROBATION DIRECTORY 2001

Compiled by Owen Wells

R. W. M.

Shaw & Sons Limited

Published for NAPO by
Shaw & Sons Limited
Shaway House
21 Bourne Park
Bourne Road
Crayford
Kent DA1 4BZ

tel 01322 621100
fax 01322 550553

Published January 2001

ISBN 0 7219 1553 1

ISSN 0142–1328

Page make-up by Groundwork, Skipton
Printed in Great Britain

A CIP catalogue record for this book is available from the British Library

The Editor

The NAPO Probation Directory is compiled by a full time probation officer, Owen Wells. If you have any suggestions or questions about the directory, he can be contacted on:

(01943) 602270
07951 436126 (mobile)
fax (01943) 816732

Introduction

The NAPO Probation Directory is compiled each October. Wherever possible changes that occur after October are included in the text up to 31st December. The very short time between compilation and publication means that the NAPO Probation Directory is probably the most up-to-date book of its kind published anywhere. Errors will, of course, occur; any that are notified to the publisher will normally be published in the Probation Bulletin.

Probation Service Reorganisation

At the time of going to press the Probation Service was undergoing substantial reorganisation. The Directory represents the structure of the Service as it will be on publication (31.1.2001), and where possible draws attention to the new structures that will come into being on 1.4.2001. From this date a number of Probation Areas will amalgamate and the Children and Family Court Advisory and Support Service will take over the functions formerly fulfilled by Probation Officers working as Family Court Welfare Officers. With such massive changes, the Directory in 2001 represents something of a compromise. But readers should note: nearly all main grade staff will be working from the same offices, with the same phone numbers. The Directory will therefore be as useful as ever for contacting practitioners, even though it will not necessarily show the management structure from 1.4.2001.

Acknowledgement

Without the help of the Chief Probation Officers and their administrative staff, the Home Office Probation and Prison Departments, and many others this directory could not have been produced. The publisher wishes to thank them all.

Abbreviations

acpo	Assistant Chief Probation Officer
aco	Assistant Chief Officer
cclo	Crown Court Liaison Officer
cpo	Chief Probation Officer
csa	Community Service Assistant
cso	Community Services Officer
dcpo	Deputy Chief Probation Officer
fcwo	Family Court Welfare Officer
fso	Fine Supervision Offlicer
js	Job-sharing
mclo	Magistrates' Court Liaison Officer
p	Part-time
pao	Principal Administrative Officer
psco	Probation Service Court Officer
psa	Probation Service Assistant
scwo	Senior Court Welfare Officer
spo	Senior Probation Officer
ssw	Senior Social Worker
sw	Social Worker

CONTENTS

PROBATION SERVICE & PROFESSIONAL ORGANISATIONS

NAPO

4 Chivalry Road
London SW11 1HT
020-7223 4887
fax 020-7223 3503

General Secretary: Judy McKnight
Assistant General Secretary (campaign & pr): Harry Fletcher
Assistant General Secretary (negotiating & tuo): Kathleen Jones
Assistant General Secretary (er, training, prof): Cordell Pillay
Research and Information Officer: Pete Bowyer (p)
Office Manager: Annie Kearns

Admin worker (journal & publications): Jeannie Ah-Fong (p)
Admin worker (gen sec): Jenetta Haley
Admin worker (resources & reception): Ivor Jones
Admin worker (ags, neg & tuo): Colleen Reynolds
Admin worker (ags, er, tr, pr): Gaenor Kyffin
Admin worker (ags, cam & pr): Olive Kinlock
Admin worker (membership): Simitie Lavaly (p)
Admin worker (nec & officers): Chris McGarry
Admin worker (reception): Jacqueline Paryag (p)
Admin worker (finance): Jean Tagg
Admin worker (membership): Lee Walker

Chair: Jonathan Ledger
Home 020-8882 0762

Vice Chair: Rob Thomas
Vice Chair: Christine Winters
Vice Chair: Duncan Moss
Treasurer: Mike McClelland

Association of Chief Officers of Probation

4th Floor, 8/9 Grosvenor Place, London SW1X 7SH
020-7823 2551 *fax 020-7823 2553*

Gen Mgr Communications: George Barrow
Office Administrator: Perminder Purewal
Clerical Assistant: Jaki Anderson
PA to Policy Devpt Advisor: Paul Cooper
PA/Admin Asst: Gretha Albertyn

Chair: Gill Mackenzie (cpo, Gloucestershire)
Vice Chair: Peter Sampson (acting cpo Avon)
Vice Chair: Christine Knott (cpo G Manchester)
Treasurer: David Hancock (cpo, Nottinghamshire)

Gen Mgr Administration: Jill Thomas
(01924) 387801
fax (01924) 372837
Resources Officer: Alison Thompson
(01943) 604224
fax (01943) 604211
Administration Officer: Lynn Stephenson
(01924) 387804
fax (01924) 372837

Policy Devpt Advisor (Service Delivery): Stuart McPhillips
tel/fax (01995) 606639
Policy Devpt Advisor (Enforcement): Steve Hemming
tel/fax (01452) 613184
Policy Devpt Advisor (Race Equality): Diane Baderin
tel/fax 0151-727 5262

Central Probation Council

4th Floor, 8/9 Grosvenor Place, London SWlX 7SH
020-7245 9364/9480
fax 020-7245 9045

e mail by individual name on NPSIS Lotus Notes or: cpc.cpc@talk21.com

Director: Martin Wargent
Deputy Director: Rodney Carroll
Assistant Director: Sarah Gore Langton
Administration Officer: Liz Hogan
Clerical Asst: Jasmin Jankowski-Doyle
Accountant: Brian Jelley (p)

National Association of Probation and Bail Hostels

The national organisation working to support and promote all Home Office approved probation and bail hostels with particular responsibility for the voluntary managed sector. Approved hostels provide enhanced supervision in order to protect the public and reduce risk. The association works alongside other bodies concerned with residential facilities for offenders and tackling crime.

2 New Walk, Totnes, Devon TQ9 5HA
(01803) 864781
fax (01803) 866265

General Secretary: Eunice Dunkley

Association of Black Probation Officers

The Association's definition of Black is a political one, which emphasises the common experiences and common determination of people of African, African-Caribbean and Asian origin to oppose the effects of racism.

217a Balham High Road, London SW17 7BP
020-8682 9322 *fax 020-8682 2087*

Chair: Glenda Joseph 020-8682 9322
Vice Chair: John Wilson (01227) 769345
Treasurer: Claudia Lewis-Moore 020-8682 9322
Info Officer: Makeda James-Goodridge (01332) 340047
Logistics Mgr: Susan Royle 020-8682 9322
N. Regional Convenor: Hyacinth Williams 0161-795 1777
Midlands Regional Convenor: Marilyn Owens-Rawle (01509) 212904 or 0116-251 6008
S. Regional Convenor: Stephen Benamaisia 020-8681 5039

National Association of Asian Probation Staff

Encourages and maintains a support group of members promoting an Asian perspective on professional issues. Initiates and campaigns for changes within the CJ System to adjust the imbalance of disadvantage suffered by all minority ethnic groups.

General Secretary: Shamin Khan, Middlesex Probation Service, Crown Court, Woodhall House, Lordship Lane, Wood Green, London N22 5LF. 020-8881 1400 *fax 020-8881 2665*
Chair: Gurdev Singh 0115-916 9500
Vice Chair: Cookie Oliver (01923) 240144
Treasurer: Surinder Dillon (01384) 455351
Info Officer: Mohammed Mustafa (01733) 746546
Nat Co-ord for partnership issues: Inderbir Kaur 0121-357 2727
Midlands Regional co-ordinator: Inderbir Kaur 0121-357 2727
Northern Regional co-ordinator: Azra Sharif (01924) 464171
Southern Regional co-ordinator: Cookie Oliver (01923) 240144
and Shamin Khan 020-8881 1400 ext 2189
Project Mgr: Mohammed Dhullah (01332) 553572

Lesbians and Gay Men in Probation

National Convenors: Julie Virgin & Francesca McGarrigle, 401 St John Street, London EC1V 4RN. 020-7837 9223 and Graham Johnston, Longsight District Centre, 521 Stockport Road, Manchester M12 4NE. 0161-248 6273
Treasurer: Andrea Crosby-Josephs, 1-5 Dorset Close, Marylebone, London NW1 5AN. 020-7724 1531
Regional contacts:
Andrew Chandler, W Yorks, Lancs (01977) 791357
Katherine Rix, NE London 020-8472 5412
Elaine Delmar, Beds (01582) 418200
Graeme Vaughan, E Anglia, (01603) 724000
Stevie Lishman, Northants (01604) 604707

The Edridge Fund

The Edridge Fund of the National Association of Probation Officers is a Registered Charity that gives financial help to those in need. All members of the service who are members of NAPO, or are eligible to be members of NAPO can benefit, as can retired staff and bereaved partners and dependants of either of the above. Each NAPO Branch has its own Edridge Representative. Applications are generally made through those Representatives and passed on to the Trustees who sit about 6/7 times a year to consider applications. These applications have to be based on financial need. The Secretary of the Fund is:

Richard Martin, The Limes, Lynn Road, Gayton, King's Lynn, Norfolk PE32 1QJ
(01553) 636570

IMPACT Probation & Welfare Officers' Branch (Irish Republic)

Probation & Welfare Officers in the Republic of Ireland are a branch of IMPACT, the Public Services Trade Union

N.B. When dialling from UK dial 00 353 and omit first 0 of Irish dialling code

IMPACT, Nerney's Court, Dublin 1
01-8171512
fax 01-8171501
Asst Gen Secy (working with the branch): Peter Nolan

Branch Officers
Chair: Brian Horgan, c/o Smithfield Chambers, Smithfield, Dublin 7, 01-8173600

Vice Chair: Carmell Donnelly, c/o Crumlin Probation Office, Clonard Road, Dublin 12, 014925625
Secretary: Joe Fay, c/o Smithfield Chambers, Smithfield, Dublin 7, 01-8173600
Treasurer: Vanessa McCarthy, 7 Ashe Street, Tralee, Co Kerry, 066-22666
PR Officer: Patrick O'Dea, 101 Clontarf Road, Dublin 3, 01-8333838

Association of Family Court Welfare Officers

An independent professional association, AFCWO is concerned to promote an effective court welfare service that is appropriately resourced, whose practitioners are well trained and who work to agreed national standards.

York Court, Unit 9, Wilder Street, Bristol BS2 8QH
0117-923 2070 *fax 0117-923 2075*

Chair: Jim Lawson 0117-954 1224
Treasurer: Michael Bullock (01482) 351192

Central Council for Education and Training in Social Work

CCETSW is a UK wide organisation, established by Parliament to promote and approve education and training for social work and social care staff. CCETSW regulates social work and post-qualification education and training for staff in the criminal justice services in Scotland and Northern Ireland. There are information services at London, Cardiff, Edinburgh & Belfast offices. Due to be replaced by the General Social Care Council in 2001.

Central Office: Derbyshire House, St Chad's Street, London WC1H 8AD. 020-7278 2455 *fax 020-7278 2934*

London Office: Caledonia House, 223-231 Pentonville Road, London N1 9NG 020-7833 8090 *fax 020-7833 5955*

England (main) Office: 21 Princes Street, Bristol BS1 4PH 0117-929 3888 *fax 0117-929 4456*

Northern Ireland Office: 6 Malone Road, Belfast BT9 5BN. (01232) 665390 fax (01232) 669469

Scotland Office: c/o Scottish Executive, James Craig Walk, Edinburgh EH1 3BA. 0131-244 1949 *fax 0131-244 3494*

Wales/Cymru Office: 2nd Floor, West Wing, South Gate House, Wood Street, Cardiff CF1 1EW (01222) 226257 *fax (01222) 384764*

The National Organisation for Practice Teaching

NOPT is an organisation created to provide quality practice teaching in social work. Membership of about 250. Provides members for several national committees and influences social work education. Annual, workshop based, conference plus regional workshops

Administrator: Janet Sewart, 227 Bramhall Moor Lane, Hazel Grove, Stockport SK7 5JL 0161-483 3788

International Social Service of the United Kingdom

International Social Service (ISS) is a voluntary organisation, staffed by social workers, linking social services around the world. It exists to help individuals and families with problems requiring social work intervention in more than one country. ISS is used regularly by family court welfare officers who require reports from abroad.

If service is required, it is helpful if ISS can be consulted as early as possible. A duty officer is available to discuss cases on the telephone and to estimate the time required to obtain a report. A referral guide is available on request. ISS works through its overseas network of branches and correspondents - thus the service is normally provided by a national social worker of the overseas country. A charge is levied for the service

International Social Service of the UK, Cranmer House, 39 Brixton Road, London SW9 6DD 020-7735 8941 *fax 020-7582 0696*

Promotion of Community Penalties

Payback is a campaign to increase public confidence in community punishments, as a way of reducing the number of non violent offenders in prison and increasing their constructive input to their communities.

Payback, 356 Holloway Road, London N7 6PA. 020-7700 8123 *fax 020-7700 0099* e mail betterways@payback.org.uk

REGIONAL TRAINING CONSORTIA

1. **East of England Probation Training & Development Consortium**
   Crowland House
   Withersfield Road
   Haverhill, Suffolk CB9 9LA
   (01440) 705875
   fax (01440) 703413

   Stephen Pestell (director)
   Philip, Tristram (nvq co-ord)
   Ruth Searle (devpt mgr)
   Tillie, Prowse (prog mgr)
   Lisa Buttery (admin)

2. **Greater London Training Consortium**
   Mitre House, 223-237 Borough High Street,
   London SE1 1JD
   020-7740 8500
   fax 020-7740 8448

   Stephen Fox (director)
   Brown, Angela C (nvq assessment centre mgr)
   Mike Jones (devpt mgr)
   Martin Fenlon (devpt mgr)
   Sarah Anderson (assessment & devpt mgr)
   Tracy Hopkins (admin mgr)
   Jo Horlock (temp admin)

3. **North East Probation Training & Development Consortium**
   c/o Teesside Probation Service
   Probation House
   2-3 Longlands Road
   Middlesborough TS4 2JL
   (01642) 230533
   fax (01642) 220083

4. **Probation North West Consortium**
   Sefton House, 1 Molyneux Way
   Old Roan, Liverpool L10 2JA
   0151-526 1346
   fax 0151-526 0692

   Tom McQuillan (aco reg staff devpt)
   Irene Doyle (consortium admin)

   Regional Development & Assessment Centre
   107 Towngate, Leyland
   Preston PR5 1LQ
   (01772) 621160
   fax (01772) 621160

   Lesley Thompson (rdac mgr)
   Margaret Costello (rdac admin)

5. **South East Regional Probation Training Consortium**
   College House, Woodbridge Road
   Guildford, Surrey GU1 4RS
   (01483) 304963
   fax (01483) 440601

   Paula Cairney (director)
   Pearl McMullen (nvq mgr)
   Angela Warner (co-ord)
   Susie Williams (co-ord)

6. **Probation South West Training & Development Consortium**
   The Lonsdale Centre
   Blake Street
   Bridgwater TA6 3NB
   (01278) 727139
   fax (01278) 727145

   Mark Green (mgr)
   Linda Sage (programme & nvq devpt mgr)
   Elizabeth Corsie (admin)

7. **Midlands Training Assessment & DevelopmentConsortium**
   Tamworth Probation Centre
   Moor Street, Tamworth B79 7QZ
   (01827) 314479
   fax (01827) 69533
   e mail mtac_birmingham@hotmail.com

   Ian Macnair (director),
   Nikki Moule (prog mgr)
   Rob Canton (prog mgr)
   Ellen Wallace (ops mgr)
   Claire Chudleigh (proj mgr/'what works?')
   Jo Fairclough (nvq devpt off)

8. **Yorkshire & Humberside Consortium**
   Devonshire House
   38 York Place, Leeds LS1 2ED
   0113-244 6044
   fax 0113-245 1394
   e mail yhpcgen@yhpc.co.uk

   Mike Ashe (director)
   Cosgrove, Steve (prog mgr)
   Kirkpatrick, Helen (nvq centre co-ord)
   David Atkinson (training mgr)

9. **Wales Probation Staff Development Consortium**
   c/o S Glamorgan Probation Service
   33 Westgate Street
   Cardiff CF10 1JE
   (02920) 785010
   fax (02920) 230384
   e mail consort.wales@talk21.com

Tudor Williams (consortium mgr)
Penelope John (admin)

TRAINING ORGANISATIONS

It is hoped to expand this section in future years. Organisations that feel they should be included in this section are invited to contact the Editor. The descriptions included are those of the organisations. The Editor accepts no responsibility for any statements made in this section.

TOPSS England National Training Organisation for Social Care

TOPSS England is the employer's body consulting on the skills mix and training strategies for social care workers. Licensed by DfEE as a National Training Organisation, TOPSS became independent of CCETSW in April 2000.

26 Park Row, Leeds LS1 5QB. 0113-245 1716 *fax 0113-243 6417* www.topss.org.uk

CJNTO Community Justice National Training Organisation

Promotes education, training and development for those in the community justice sector

344-354 Grays Inn Road, London WC1X 8BP. 020-7278 1366 *fax 020-7278 2462* e mail info@cjnto.demon.co.uk

Community Justice Training College

A specialist, non-profit, national college of further and adult education. CJTC aims to significantly contribute to the development of capacity, competence and professionalism across the community justice service sector by providing relevant, accessible, cost effective and high quality learning experiences through supported open learning and work-based delivery and assessment.

Staff Development Further and Higher Academic, Vocational and Professional Development programmes, including: diversity at work, PSO induction, working with diverse communities, and management development.

Consultancy/Organisational Development project management and evaluation, change management, communication, human resource planning, training design, modelling and evaluation

Offenders/at risk Design of CS accreditation schemes, hostel programmes, post-custody assessment and support, advice and guidance, ETE, education and funding partnerships

Area of operation national through regional satellites

Administration and Management Located Manchester and London
Information freephone 0800 083 0353
e mail: cjtc@ukonline.co.uk

The Community Justice Training College
Ridgefield House, 14 John Dalton Street, Manchester M2 6JR

MPTC Midlands Probation Training Consortium

1 Printing House Street, Birmingham B4 6DE
0121-248 6325 *fax 0121-236 6384*
e mail enquiries@mptc.demon.co.uk or on NPSISS system @MPTC

Peter Lewis (director),
Linda Gast (asst director)
Roger Clare (asst director)

MPTC is a not-for-profit training organisation wholly owned by the ten Midlands Probation Services (but able to work in other regions too) providing training, consultancy. mentoring and conferences. It runs an academically accreditted management development programme, designs training materials and is able to work in-house in partnership with service staff or to bring in external Associate Trainers.

PROBLINK

Problink is a consortium of Further Education Colleges which may undertake work in the criminal justice sector. Many members are providers of prison education services. Some colleges work with other agencies on specific programmes such as New deal.

Membership varies from time to time according to the activities/interests of colleges.

For further information on local links contact: problink@ccm.ac.uk

Delight Training Servives

93 Ryles Park Road, Macclesfield, Cheshire SK11 8AL

(01625) 421045 *fax (01625) 262686*
e mail admin@delight.co.uk

Groupwork skills, motivational interviewing, presentation/facilitation skills. Training on evidence based programmes for general offending, substance use, and violence, using one-to-one/groupwork with adult/juvenile offenders.

AFTA Thought Training Consultancy

Unit C8, 10 Brunswick Business Centre, Brunswick Dock, Liverpool L3 4BD
0151-708 7774 *fax 0151-709 3416*
e mail info@aftathought.co.uk.
www.aftathought.co.uk

Works in collaboration with probation services to provide training to probation officers and clients. Use specialised training techniques, incorporating drama with skilled actors to bring issues to life: specialised areas of work include domestic violence, managing challenging behaviour, child protection assessment of risk.

CJC Consultancy

3 Beckside Gardens, Huddersfield, W Yorks HD5 8RS
(01484) 304800 *fax (01484) 304801*
e mail info@cjc.co.uk www. cjc.co.uk

CJC Consultancy has many years experience in working with probation services across the country providing stress management training courses. Also specialises in employee well being schemes, stress audits, health profiles, exercise programmes, ergonomics, risk assessment, dietary analysis, and relaxation techniques. Member of Association for Workplace Health promotion (AWHP); International Stress Management Association (Validated Trainer); Confederation of Stress Managers.

GM Associates

GM Associates, PO Box 60, Waterlooville, Hants PO7 7TP
023-9225 3380
fax: 023-9226 5595

e mail: davidgodson@gm-associates.co.uk

GM Associates specialise in the provision of enforcement training for probation and youth offending teams. Courses include community sentences, youth justice, early release, as well as the procedural aspects of enforcement. Training is provided at national, regional and area level depending upon end user requirements using leading academics, legal practitioners and specialist probation staff. There are courses covering the process of effective supervision, sound legal practice and work in the court setting aimed at a range of staff from those new to the enforcement task, to those holding specialist enforcement roles. Contact David Godson

Groupwork Consultation & Training

PO Box 363, Southsea, Hants PO4 0YB
phone/fax 02392 750030
e mail: dave@groupct.demon.co.uk
www.groupct.demon.co.uk

GCT was established in 1987 to provide social groupwork training to groupworkers in the public sector, Probation Services, Social Services, Health Authorities and voluntary organisations. Courses are held at various venues (and also in-service). They include training in foundation, intermediate and advanced level groupwork. Also short courses e.g. cognitive behavioural groupwork, anger management, and various other offending behaviour groups.

GCT is a CNJTO endorsed training provider

LMT Training and Consultancy

17 High House Drive, Lickey, Birmingham B45 8ET
0121-445 6688 *fax 0121-445 6388*
e mail info@lmt.uk.com

A well established provider of high quality team and individual performance development opportunities for practitioners and managers involved in providing effective services to address offending behaviour.

LMT is a CNJTO endorsed training provider.

New Leaf Training and Counselling

PO Box 4, Wellington, Somerset TA21 0YU
tel & fax (01823) 660426
Specialises in peer education, Dealing with Conflict & Anger Courses for offenders (usually in Probation Hostels). An accredited Assertiveness and Drug Alcohol Course for use in prisons and probation.

Alison Rudin

176 Aylsham Drive, Ickenham, Middx UB10 8UF
phone & fax 01895 675130
e mail arudin@aol.co.uk

People progression seeks to provide practical, tailored development solutions. Training areas: presentation skills, team building, assertion skills, meetings management, coaching, personal effectiveness, training the trainer.

Tuklo Orenda Associates

15 Kinveachy Gardens, Charlton, London SE7 8EE
020-8317 *fax 020-8317 9323*
e mail info@Tuklo.co.uk

Tuklo Associates have been working in the CJ system since 1987, extensively in the probation service. Has a commitment and expertise in the field of equal opportunities and change management. Interested in working in holistic but effective ways that engage with the spirit, intellect and emotion of an organisation and the individuals within it. Provides consultancy, training, mediation, conferences, etc to all levels of staff.

Unicorn Consultancy Services Ltd

Caversham House, 13-17 Church Road, Caversham, Reading RG7 7AA
01189 464048 *fax 01189 464101*
e mail bill.paterson@unicornworks.co.uk
www. unicornworks.co.uk

Provides health and safety services to national and local government organisations including the Inner London Probation Service. These services extend from conducting risk assessments, workplace/property inspections, policy development, auditing, through to providing health and safety training to staff ensuring that clients fulfil their legal duties.

PRISONS OMBUDSMAN from 1.4.01 Prisons & Probation Ombudsman

Ashley House, 2 Monck Street, London SW1P 2BQ
020-7276 2876 *fax 020-7276 2860*

Function

To provide independent investigation of prisoners' complaints for those who have failed to obtain complete satisfaction through the Service's internal Requests and Complaints system and to make recommendations to the Home secretary and Prison Service to help resolve justified complaints.

With effect from 1.4.01 will also deal with complaints about the Probation Service (exact terms of reference to be defined)

Staff

Prisons Ombudsman
Stephen Shaw 020-7276 2850

Assistant Ombudsman
David Barnes 020-7276 2866

Assistant Ombudsman
Tony Heal 020-7276 2863

Assistant Ombudsman
Barbara Stow 020-7276 2852

Personal Secretary
Jennifer Buck 020-7276 2851

Investigators

Stewart Greer 020-7276 2858

Hilary Howard 020-7276 2861

John Maggi 020-7276 2854

Rebecca Mulcahy 020-7276 2859

Nick Woodhead 020-7276 2865

Administrative Support

Office Manager
Geoff Hubbard 020-7276 2855

Executive Officer
Sarah Range 020-7276 2857

Nazma Begum 020-7276 2868

Margaret Holt 020-7276 2862

Nicola Jeffrey 020-7276 2853

Tracey Wright 020-7276 2856

HOME OFFICE

50 Queen Anne's Gate, London SW1H 9AT, 020-7273 4000

CRIMINAL POLICY GROUP

Director	Sue Street	020-7273 2178 *fax 020-7273 4395*
Senior Personal Secretary	Sue Chapman	020-7273 3903

NATIONAL PROBATION DIRECTORATE

Horseferry House, Dean Ryle Street
London SW1P 2AW
020-7217 6000 (for the operator) fax 020-7217 0660

The National Directorate will exercise, on behalf of the Home Secretary, all his responsibilities for the probation service in England and Wales. The National Probation Service for England and Wales will consist of a National Directorate and 42 local Probation Boards.

National Director	Eithne Wallis	020-7217 0650
Personal Secretary	Christine Tyne	020-7217 0651
Interin Head of Unit	Tony Woolfenden	020-7217 0776
Personal Secretary	Christine Tyne	020-7217 0651

Secretariat

The Head of Secretariat is mainly responsible for providing support to Eithne Wallis and Tony Woolfenden
* Management of Unit and Senior Management Team meetings.
* Responsibility for the following main unit management functions:
    Accommodation, co-ordination of briefings for Ministers, organisation of Chairs and Chiefs conferences, first point of contact for general enquiries, co-ordination of the issuing and filing of Probation Circulars, stationery, health and safety.

Head of Secretariat	John MacGregor	020-7217 0652
Unit Manager	Jill Naylor	020-7217 0653
Deputy Unit Manager	Lesley Smith	020-7217 0654
Asst Unit Manager	David Gire-Mooring	020-7217 0655
Unit Support	Syed Ali	020-7217 0656
Communications Officer	new post	020-7217 0658

Modernisation Team

Modernisation of the Probation Service (until 31.3.01)
Policy for the new National Probation Service; policy and exit strategy for Family Court Welfare.

HO member of CAFCASS

Project Team	Joan Bonelle	020-7217 0736
FCW Officer	Violet Huggins	020-7217 0738
Modernisation Team Support	Jewell Jackman-Jones	020-7217 0741

Seconded Staff

National Directorate Devpt Adviser	John Scott	020-7217 0740
Probation Committee Adviser	David Chantler	020-7217 0743
Adviser for Wales	Ian Fox	020-7217 0737
(c/o FCW Service, 3rd Floor, 37 The Kingsway, Swansea SA1 5LF)		
Personal Secretary	Marie Malone	020-7217 0742
		fax 020-7217 0796

Finance & Estates

Head of Finance & Estates — to be appointed

Finance

Financial Spending Review 2000		
Group Accountant	Mike DuBock	020-7217 0713
Personal Secretary		020-7217 0714
Local Services Accountant	Janet Dowding	020-7217 0724
Accountant (NAO)	Stephen Wright	020-7217 0726

Revenue and capital grant payments, co-ordination of SR 2000, cash allocation formula, management of unit budgets, invoice payments.

Central Services Accountant	Peter Bellerby	020-7217 0715
Personal Secretary	Vacancy	020-7217 0705
Accountant (Planning)	Neil Hope	020-7217 0723
Personal Secretary	Vacancy	020-7217 0705
Payments Manager	Bunmi Abidoye	020-7217 0717
Budgets Manager	David Gosling	020-7217 0718
Grant Payment Officer	Peter Sully	020-7217 0716
Grant Payment Officer	Elsa Campbell	020-7217 0722
Payments Officer	Michelle Garland	020-7217 0721
Payments Officer	Stephen Lott	020-7217 0720
Payments Officer	Yvonne Arthur	020-7217 0719

Estates

Strategic planning of probation estate, capital funding of hostels and probation estate,and implementation of PFI.

Estate Development Adviser	Sebert Cox	020-7217 0704
Personal Secretary	Vacancy	020-7217 0705
Estate Development Co-ordinator	Monty Farrow	020-7217 0707
Estate Development Co-ordinator	Ann Boshell (p)	020-7217 0706
Estate Development Co-ordinator	Mike Hamburger	020-7217 0709
Estate Development Assistant	Carole Sylvester	020-7217 0708
Estate Support Officer	Eleanor McCurdy	020-7217 0710
Estate Support Assistant	Amanda Meyer	020-7217 0711
		fax 020-7217 0712

Planning

Head of Planning, Perfomance Management and Regional Co-ord	to be appointed
Regional Managers	to be appointed

Activity sampling, performance measures, probation service national plan, Unit plan.

Strategic Planning Manager	Ed Stradling	020-7217 0758
Deputy Strategic Planning Manager	Lulu Robbani (p)	020-7217 0757

Human Resources

Head of Human Resources	to be appointed	

Human Resources Management

Trainee probation officer scheme, enquiries and administrative support, equal opportunities, pay and conditions of service, complaints, Honours, industrial relations, training budget management, Charter Marks, Freemasonry, freedom of information, HREU liaison, general recruitment enquiries.

Head of HR Management	Dave Rigby	020-7217 0728
Personal Secretary	to be appointed	020-7217 0729
Team Leader	George Barnes	020-7217 0732
HR Manager	Roger Davis	020-7217 0730
Co-ordinator	Simone Sheppard	020-7217 0731
Co-ordinator	Suzanne Jones	020-7217 0733
General enquiries		020-7217 0735 *fax 020-7217 0734*

Human Resource Management Advisers

Trainee probation officer scheme and HR projects, service delivery training, manager training.

HR Management Adviser	Jo Langdale	020-7217 0788
Personal Secretary	to be appointed	020-7217 0729
HR Management Adviser	Su Gambling	020-7217 0791
HR Management Adviser	Vacancy	
HR Management Adviser	Sue Roberts	01782 712730

c/o Queen's Garden Business Centre, 31 Ironmarket, Newcastle under Lyme ST5 1RP
fax (01782) 712731

Policy

Head of Policy Innovation, Reasearch and Sentencing Framework	to be appointed	
Head of Policy Group	Keir Hopley	020-7217 0774
Personal Secretary	Agnes Harris	020-7217 0760 *fax 020-7217 0799*

Criminal Law & Supervision

Legislation, policy and procedures on: community sentences; post-release supervision; PSR sand court duty; enforcement; National Standards; bail information; drugs/alcohol; Drug Treatment & Testing Orders; Human Rights Act; relevant criminal provisions of the Criminal Justice and Court Services Act. Policy and associated casework on serious incidents reporting.

Policy Developer	Alison Foulds	020-7217 0745
Policy Developer	Stephen Bailey	020-7217 0761
Policy Developer	Robert Stanbury	020-7217 0767
Policy Developer	Christine Micallef	020-7217 0762
Policy Administrator	Paul Beaufond	020-7217 0770
Policy Administrator	Mose Oginni	020-7217 0769

Resettlement
Policy and procedures on: victims; throughcare; partnerships; accommodation; resettlement; approved hostels; and ETE

Head of Resettlement	Felicity Hawksley	020-7217 0773
Policy Developer	Kelly Egan	020-7217 0764
Policy Developer	Marcus Smart	020-7217 0766
Policy Developer	Michael Dewey	020-7217 0763
Policy Administrator	Mark Chidwick	020-7217 0765
Policy Developer	John Russell	020-7217 0772
Policy Administrator	Uche Oji	020-7217 0771

Dangerous Offenders
Policy on dangerous offenders and their supervision in the community; liaison with local agencies on dangerous offenders' release plans.

Head of Unit	Carol Kellas	020-7217 0744
Casework Team Manager	Sheran Ridge	020-7217 0748
Policy Developer	Mark Warren	020-7217 0752
Caseworker	Denise Herman	020-7217 0750
Caseworker	Susan Mehmet	020-7217 0749
Casework Administrator	Yvonne Tijani	020-7217 0751
Policy Administrator	Liz Barley	020-7217 0753

Dangerous Offenders Unit Seconded Staff

Paddy Doyle (Northumbria Probation Service)	020-7217 0746
Helen Jebb (Nottinghamshire Police Service)	020-7217 0747
	fax 020-7217 0756

Interventions Programmes & Process Development

Head of Interventions Programmes & Process Development	to be appointed	
Head of 'What Works' and Offending Behaviour Programmes	David Perry	020-7217 0775
'What Works' Programme Manager	Roger Stevens	020-7217 0688
Offending Behaviour Programme Implementation Adviser	Jill Shackleton	020-7217 0678
Programme Devpt Manager	Meg Blumson	020-7217 0673
Programme Devpt Mgr (ETS & violence)	Danny Clark	020-7217 0675
Prog Devpt Mgr (Priestley 1:1 and R&R)	Sandra Fieldhouse	020-7217 0674
Programme Devpt Mgr (subst misuse)	new post	
Programme Devpt Mgr (RMOs)	Kate Law	020-7217 0676
Programme Devpt Mgr (SOTPs)	Claire Wiggins	020-7217 0672
Programme Devpt Administrator	Gerard Guildharry	020-7217 0677
Programme Devpt Administrator	Neal Thorley	020-7217 0679
Head of Community Reintegration	Chris Johnson	020-7217 0695
Programme Devpt Mgr (CS)	new post	
Implementation Adviser (community reintegration)	new post	
Programme Devpt Mgr (basic skills)	Laura Fairweather	020-7217 0680

Development Adviser (basic skills)	new post	
Programme Devpt Mgr (resettlement)	Steve Pitts	020-7217 0682
Voluntary Sector/Partnerships Adviser	George Burns	020-7217 0683
Programme Development Administrator	Damian Laurence	020-7217 0685
Personal Secretary	Margaret Quin	020-7217 0686
Head of Offender Assessment	Sarah Mann	020-7217 0694
Personal Secretary	Judith Purssell	020-7217 0689
OASys Implementation Manager	Julia Stephens-Row	020-7217 0697
OASys PDM	Trish Borrows	020-7217 0696
Project Secretary	Vacancy	
Senior Research Officer	Natasha Garnham	020-7217 0699
Research Officer	Vicky Tunbridge	020-7217 0698
Research Officer	Kathryn Dodgson	020-7217 0701
Personal Secretary	Marjorie Baker	020-7217 0700
Governor V	Nigel Foote	020-7217 0703
OASys Project Assistant	Claire Medder	020-7217 0692
'What Works' Communications Officer	Mark Slater	020-7217 0687
'What Works' Assistant Project Manager	Hyacinth Robinson	020-7217 0690
'What Works' Administrator	Rosemary Howell	020-7217 0691 *fax 020-7217 0693*

Information Services Group (ISG)

Head of IS/IT	Robin Pape	020-7217 0661

Programme Office; Strategy and Policy Management; Service Management

Head of Strategic & Policy & Service Management	Lorraine Rogerson	020-7217 0777
Personal Secretary	Angela Larbie	020-7217 0662
Service Delivery Manager	Stephanie Lester	020-7217 0778
Programme Office Support	Chi Cryer	020-7217 0668
Programme Office Manager	Jackie Fowler	020-7217 0664
Communications Officer	Eleanor Marshall	020-7217 0670
Senior Programme Planner	Rebecca Baty	020-7217 0666
Contract Manager	Irene Morris	020-7217 0792
ISPB Secretary	Jane Hummerston (p)	020-7217 0669
Programme Office Support	Ranti Salami	020-7217 0667
Programme Office Support	Alpna Shah	020-7217 0665

Secondees

Project manager	Kevin Cartwright	020-7217 0784 & 01543 877875
Service Delivery Manager	Janine Williams	020-7217 0779 & 01462 681281 or 07957 113899 (mobile)
Implementation Project Manager	Vincent Barron	020-7217 0217 & 07770 841765

Implementation Project Manager	Ann Maughan	020-7217 0783 *fax 020-7217 0663*

Senior Management Team

Peter Bellerby
Mike DuBock
Keir Hopley
John MacGregor (Secretary)
Sarah Mann
Robin Pape
David Perry
Dave Rigby
Lorraine Rogerson
Eithne Wallis
Tony Woolfenden

plus new Strategic Heads when appointed

HER MAJESTY'S INSPECTORATE OF PROBATION

Functions
General inspection and liaison with Probation Service in England and Wales, including probation hostels and probation service work in prison service establishments. The promotion of high quality and effectiveness in probation services. Advises the Home Offfice about probation service matters.

Staff

H M Chief Inspector of Probation	Graham Smith	020-7273 3766
Senior Personal Secretary	Eileen Waters	020-7273 3906
Statistician	Peter Ramell	020-7273 3791
Secretariat		
EO	Mary Taylor	020-7273 2320
AO	Edward Brucey	020-7273 3747
AO Enquiries	Michelle Berry	020-7273 3955
AA Enquiries	Paul Cockburn	020-7273 2815
Personal Secretary	Jean Baker	020-7273 3721

Inspectors based at 50 Queen Anne's Gate, London SW1H 9AT *fax 020-7273 2131*

H M Asst Chief Inspector	Joe Kuipers	020-7273 3145
H M Asst Chief Inspector	Jane Furniss	020-7273 2778
H M Inspectors	Di Askwith	020-7273 3657
	Ged Bates	020-7273 3257
	Pat Edwards	020-7273 3926
	John Hutchings	020-7273 3364
	Martin Copsey	020-7273 3951
	Claudia Lewis-Moore	020-7273 2389

Inspectors based at Grove House, Skerton Road, Old Trafford, Manchester M16 0WJ 0161-848 0566 (with ansaphone for out of hours messages). *fax 0161-872 4570*

H M Asst Chief Inspector	Frances Flaxington
H M Inspectors	Liz Calderbank
	Mary Fielder
	Philip Lockett
	Roger McGarva

EO	Andrew Bonny
AO/Enquiries	Deborah Moore
Temporary Personal Secretary	Jean Hartington
Typist	Serina Khan

Accreditation Programme Audit Manager Alan MacDonald

MENTAL HEALTH UNIT

Functions The Mental Health Unit has responsibility for casework and policy in respect of the Home Secretary's responsibilities under the Mental Health Act 1983 for mentally disordered offenders.

Casework on restricted patients is allocated by initial letter of patient's surname. All enquiries should be addressed to EO caseworkers. In an emergency outside office hours a 24 hour messenger service at the Home Office can be contacted on 020-7273 4000 who will contact a member of the Mental Health Unit's staff at home.

Staff

Telephone: dial 020-7273 plus extension for individual officers. *fax 020-7273 2172/4311/2937/4517*

			Room No	*Tel Extn*
Head of Unit		Mike Boyle	208	2455
Personal Secretary		Jan Allison-Norman	210	2927
Snr Policy Advisor		Dr Dilys Jones	207	4583
Personality Disorder Policy, Clinical Advice on Forensic Psychiatry				
SCS		Jonathan Sedgwick	204	4528
Personality Disorder Policy				
Grade 7	Pam Lutterloch	C, D, Q, X, Y, Z (S47/S48 A-K)	217	3394
	Ros Johnson	E, I, J, K, O, V (S47/S48 L-R, T)	211	2603
	Arch Mantle	A, G, H, Williams-Wing	218	3004
	Helen McKinnon	B, F, R, N	209	3233
	Jennifer Morris	S, T, Wa-William, Winh-Wz (S47-S48 S, U-Z)	206	2654
	Nigel Shackleford	L, M, P, U	217	3021
	Andrew Morley	Personality Disorder Policy	204	2384
Personal Secretaries				
	Mavis Treen/Mary Morley (R Johnson, A Mantle, N Shackleford)		212	4157
	Carolyn Bunn (H McKinnon, A Morley, J Morris, J Sedgwick)		204	2662
SEOs	Heidi Parris	Personality Disorder Policy	204	4384
	Gail Winter	Personality Disorder Policy	204	3874
HEOs	Ros Arnold	I, N, S, T	230	4153
	Geoff Burton	B, R	215	3613
	Jean Bushell	P, Wa-Williamr (S48 P, S-X, Z)	229	3232
	Wayne Jones	A, F	227	3691
	Rob Moseley	C, Winh-Wing (S48 D, E, G-K)	224	3438
	Dave Pearson	G, H, Q, X-Z	227	3717
	Caroline Smith	L, M, U	214	2910
	Brenda Storey	D, E, Williams-Wing (S48 A-C, F)	224	3118
	Marie Wall	J, K, O, V (S48 L-O, Q, R, Y)	224	3406
EOs	Allison Allen	Cog-Cz, Q, X-Z (S47 F, H, J)	224	4004
	Matthew Armer	Hoh-Hz, Brog-Bz	227	3464

Nigel Battson	A, Ba-Barrn	227	3231
Mandi Connor	P, U	229	4029
Linda Doran (p)	Ma-McBeam	214	2213
Pat Durnwell	Ha-Hog	227	3261
Jacqui Frankum	Barro-Brof	215	2394
Kevin Gilzean	F, Williams-Wing	227	3934
Martin Green	McBean-Moser	214	2213
Lyndel Grover	I, Wa-Williamr	229	2673
Jane Kirkby	N, Sa-Skot	230	3752
Al Lama	Ca-Cof (S47 K, L, M)	224	3358
James Lowe	T, Winh-Wz	230	2374
Beverley Pimm	Da-Dou (S47 A, B, E, I, N)	224	2395
Colin Pocock	R	215	3908
Jane Stearman	Skou-Sz	230	3074
Lee Stephen	Dou-Dz, E, V (S47 C, D, G)	224	3190
Mike Turner	K, Oa-Oz (S47 O, R, S)	224	3575
Vacancy	G	227	3789
Nicky Westbrook	J, O'A-O'Z (S47 P, Q, T-Z)	224	4225
Sylvia Williams	L, Moses-Mz	214	4187
Amanda Smitherman	Personality Disorder Policy	204	2384
George Goodwin	Personality Disorder Policy	204	2156
Hot Desk	Personality Disorder Policy	204	3954

RESEARCH DEVELOPMENT AND STATISTICS DIRECTORATE

Director of Research, Development and Statistics — Paul Wiles
Senior Personal Secretary — Michelle Washer — 020-7273 2616

Offenders & Corrections Unit
50 Queen Anne's Gate, London SW1H 9AT

Chief Statistician — Chris G Lewis
Personal Secretary — Sue Shelley — 020-7273 2842

Functions probation, criminality and international.

Grade 6 — Patrick Collier
Personal Secretary — Sue Shelley — 020-7273 3012

Functions probation statistics for England and Wales

Statistician — Peter Sheriff
Higher Executive Officers — Gary Renshaw
Executive Officers — Nick Couchman, Keith Ward
Enquiries — 020-7273 3419/2571

Functions reconvictions

Statistician — Julian Prime
Executive Officer — Andrew Kalinski
Enquiries — 020-7273 3608

Functions probation research

Grade 7 — Vacancy
Senior Research Officers — Vacancy
Research Officers — Darren Sugg, Sarah Partridge
Enquiries — 020-7273 2899/2580/2696

Functions offenders in prison

Grade 6 Maureen Colledge
Grade 7/Senior Research Officers John Ditchfield, Ed Mortimer
Enquiries 020-7217 5875/5456

DRUGS PREVENTION ADVISORY SERVICE (DPAS)

Home Office, Horseferry House, Dean Ryle Street, London SW1P 2AW

Head of DPAS

Head of Unit	Jim Nicholson	020-7217 8055
Personal Secretary	Carolyn Bunn	020-7217 8582
Enquiries		020-7217 8631

fax 020-7217 8422
e mail jim.nicholson@homeoffice.gsi.gov.uk

The Drugs Prevention Advisory Service, an England wide service established 1.4.99, provides advice to Drug Action Teams and their member agencies on tackling drug misuse and prevention policies and programmes. DPAS also works across Government and in collaboration with local, regional and national partners, to expand the evidence-base for tackling drug misuse and help deliver national drugs strategy aims.

The initial focus for DPAS was on the first two of the four national strategy aims - to help young people resist drug misuse and to protect communities from drug related anti-social and criminal behaviour. However, in order to broaden the support available to DATs the Government quickly agreed that DPAS should also take on responsibility for advising on the third and fourth strategy aims - helping people who already have drug problems to overcome them through treatment; and stifling the availability of illegal drugs on the streets.

DPAS manages the Government's £20 million Arrest Referral Joint Funding Initiative and is a key source of advice on the implementation of interventions in the criminal justice system to tackle drug misuse. DPAS has published guidance manuals on such interventions in both the adult and youth justice systems. Regional enquiries should be addressed to the appropriate team. Sheena Sadiq (01483 459018) and John Dunworth (020-7217 8298) take the DPAS lead on national policy issuses relating to drugs and the criminal justice system

DPAS has an ongoing role in facilitating the implementation of Drug Treatment and Testing orders on a national level by working with the Probation Unit and, locally, by supporting probation services and Drug Action Teams via it's regional network. Contact Nino Maddalena (020-7217 3433)

DPAS REGIONAL TEAMS

DPAS Eastern 2nd Floor, Block A1, Westbrook Centre, Milton Road, Cambridge CB4 1YG
(01223) 345740 e mail ruth.joyce@homeoffice.gsi.gov.uk

covers: Bedfordshire, Cambridgeshire, Essex, Hertfordshire, Norfolk, Suffolk

Ruth Joyce (regional mgr)

DPAS East Midlands The Belgrave Centre, Stanley Place, Talbot Street, Nottingham NG1 7EG
0115-971 2733 e mail robin.burgess@homeoffice.gsi.gov.uk

covers: Derbyshire, Leicestershire, Lincolnshire, Northamptonshire, Nottinghamshire

Robin Burgess (regional mgr)

DPAS London Riverwalk House, 157-161 Millbank, London SW1P 4RR
020-7217 3462 e mail steve.tippell@homeoffice.gsi.gov.uk

covers: Metropolitan and City of London

Steve Tippell (regional mgr)

DPAS North East 11th Floor, Wellbar House, Gallowgate, Newcastle upon Tyne NE1 4TD
0191-233 1972 e mail fiona.young@homeoffice.gsi.gov.uk

covers: Cleveland, Durham, Northumbria

Fiona Young (regional mgr)

DPAS North West Room 2105, Sunley Tower, Piccadilly Plaza, Manchester M1 4BE
0161-237 9634 e mail mike.ryan@homeoffice.gsi.gov.uk

covers: Cheshire, Cumbria, Greater Manchester, Lancashire, Merseyside

Mike Ryan (regional mgr)

DPAS South East 1 Walnut Tree Close, Guildford GU1 4GA
(01483) 459018 e mail shereen.sadiq@homeoffice.gsi.gov.uk

covers: Hampshire, Kent, Surrey, Sussex, Thames Valley

Shereen Sadiq (regional mgr)

DPAS South West 5th Floor, The Pithay, Bristol BS1 2PB
0117 922 7997 e mail ian.clements@homeoffice.gsi.gov.uk

covers: Avon & Somerset, Devon & Cornwall, Dorset, Gloucestershire, Wiltshire

Ian Clements (regional mgr)

DPAS West Midlands 2nd Floor, 77 Paradise Circus, Queensway, Birmingham B1 2DT
0121 212 5131 e mail nick.lawrence@homeoffice.gsi.gov.uk

covers: Staffordshire, Warwickshire, West Mercia, West Midlands

Nick Lawrence (regional mgr)

DPAS Yorkshire & the Humber 12th Floor, City House, New Station Street, Leeds LS1 4JD
0113 283 5257 e mail phil.willan@homeoffice.gsi.gov.uk

covers: Humberside, North Yorkshire, South Yorkshire, West Yorkshire

Phil Willan (regional mgr)

PAROLE BOARD OF ENGLAND AND WALES

Abell House, John Islip Street, London SW1P 4LH

Chairman	D Hatch
Senior Personal Secretary	Mrs C Stimson
Secretariat	
Grade 6, Chief Executive	J Casey
SEOs	T McCarthy, M Stevens
HEOs	P Boshell, S Powell, D Saarbrucken, F Saeed

Enquiries
Enquiries about Discretionary Conditional Release cases and Discretionary Lifer panels should be directed to the Parole Board Secretariat

Discretionary Conditional Release cases	
Pre Panel	020-7217 5840/5512 (A-K)
	020-7217 5939/5387 (L-Z)
Post Panel	020-7217 5222 (A-Z)
Discretionary Lifer Panels	020-7217 5340
General Enquiries	020-7217 5314
fax DLP	*020-7217 5677*
fax DCR	*020-7217 5488*

H M PRISON SERVICE

Abell House, John Islip Street, London SW1P 4LH
020-7217 6000

SENTENCE MANAGEMENT GROUP

Head of Group	Nigel Newcomen	020-7217 5711 *fax 020-7217 5865*
Personal Secretary	Michelle Reid	020-7217 5693

LIFER UNIT

Functions: Lifer tariffs, review, release, supervision and recall of *all* life sentence prisoners, including Her Majesty's Pleasure detainees and those sentenced to life under Sectn 2 Crime (Sentences) Act 1997.

Head of Unit	Jeremy Page	020-7217 5181 *fax 020-7217 5865*
Out of hours enquiries		020-7273 4000
Jim Watts is responsible for First Stage Teams 1 & 2 and Review Team 3		020-7217 5226 *fax 020-7217 5865*

First Stage Team 1 Room 112
Dealing with both review and management work
This team will be responsible for all C and L cases and will be working to a common queue

Lynda Morley	
John Boorman	020-7217 5622
Toni Jowett	020-7217 5601
Judy Weldon	020-7217 5084
Nicky Halse	020-7217 5691
Dave Norris	020-7217 5251
Mark Ferrigan	020-7217 5893

First Stage Team 2 Room 113
Dealing with both review and management work
This team wll be responsible for all G and W cases, but with a specific allocation to the EOs

Howard Smith	020-7217 5299	
Lisa Burrell	020-7217 5594	Wa-Wh
Helen Corduff	020-7217 5216	Ga-Gre
Chris Hughes	020-7217 2040	Gri-Gz, Wi-Wz
Justin Kelly	020-7217 2023	
Bins Powar	020-7217 5804	
Agency AA		

All Review Teams will continue to have specific caseload allocations for each EO

Nikki Penfold is responsible for Review Teams 1, 2 & 4		020-7217 5742 *fax 020-7217 5865*
Review Team 1 Room 115		
Simon Greenwood	020-7217 5007	
Siju Anibaba	020-7217 5579	D & Y
Jeff D'Cruz	020-7217 5555	S-Sot
Lee Freitas	020-7217 5518	
Agency AA	020-7217 5415	
Review Team 2 Room 131		
Hazel Dixon	020-7217 5699	
Janice Carolan	020-7217 5794	E & T
Sonia Octave	020-7217 5518	A & Pa-Pin
Jan Ivens	020-7217 5897	
Agency AA	020-7217 5415	
Review Team 3 Room 117		
Christine Foulger	020-7217 5468	
Jason Nurden	020-7217 5896	O R & Z
Lesley Storer	020-7217 5501	Ha-Holly
Barbara Griffiths	020-7217 5471	
Agency AA	020-7217 5415	
Review Team 4 Room 131		
John Freeth	020-7217 5287	
Erika Dyke	020-7217 5284	Holn-Hz Sou-Sz
Gilian Osborn	020-7217 5460	F & J
Pauline Savage	020-7217 5792	
Agency AA		
Tim Morris is responsible for Review Teams 5 & 6		020-7217 5701 *fax 020-7217 5865*
Review Team 5 Room 118		
John Mills	020-7217 5288	
Akile Osman		Bro-Bz Mj-MZ
Anne Lund	020-7217 5595	I K Pio-Pz Q U V X
Vacancy AO		
Agency AA		
Review Team 6 Room 120		
John Dwyer	020-7217 5432	
Katherine McIlwee	020-7217 5761	Ma-Mi
Vicky Bassill	020-7217 5554	B-Bri
Tony Turrell	020-7217 5526	
Agency AA		

The 126 N cases will be divided up equally among the six review teams and will be centrally managed by Simon Greenwood and Lee Freitas to whom initial contact should be made.

Management Section

Function: management and allocation of non category A life sentence prisoners
Michael Loughlin is Head of Section 020-7217 5478
Ian Truffet is his deputy 020-7217 5712

Team 1 Room 131	
Heather Miller	020-7217 5700

Bobbi Ingram	020-7217 5703
Mark Lee	020-7217 5812
Kevin Hampton	020-7217 5071
D M N O X	

Team 2 Room 131	
Valerie Navato	020-7217 5015
Matt Jenkins	020-7217 5009
Philip Ranson	020-7217 5524
H I S	

Team 3 Room 131	
Alistair Albosh	020-7217 5493
Joss Mistry/Dominic Smith	020-7217 5795
Vacancy	020-7217 5071
Agency AA	020-7217 5333
A E K P Q R Y Z	

Team 4 Room 131	
Maggie Wilson	020-7217 2039
Andrew Collymore	020-7217 5483
Agency AA	020-7217 5416
B F J T U V	

Policy Team Room 120	
Paul Jackson	020-7217 5785
Nick Newton	020-7217 2084
Tony Turrell	020-7217 5526

Tariff Section Room 135	
John Courtney	020-7217 5753
Simon Alderman	020-7217 5405
Jeremy Dixon	020-7217 5205
Anne Hailstone	020-7217 5902
Agency AA	020-7217 5389

SENTENCE ENFORCEMENT UNIT

Functions: policy in relation to parole and release of determinate sentence prisoners under the Criminal Justice Act 1991 including responsibility for the overall parole process; co-ordination of Prison Service interests in sentencing policy; co-ordination of Prison Service interests in dangerous offenders and severe personality disordered offenders; policy on prison Service therapeutic communities; enforcement of release licences, including Home Detention Curfew; administration of compassionate release cases; transfer of prisoners under the Mental Health Acts; discretionary release for deportation.

Head of Unit	Nicole Smith	020-7217 5263
Policy section	Alistair McMurdo	020-7217 5186
HDC casework	GSSC & Securicor areas	020-7217 5124
	Premier areas	020-7217 5120
Other casework	Team 1 A-K	020-7217 5102
	Team 2 L-Z	020-7217 5563
Unit fax		*020-7217 5223*
Out of hours (emergency recall requests)		020-7273 4000

'WHAT WORKS' IN PRISON UNIT

Functions: development of policy and strategy in relation to 'what works' with prisons, development and policy on regimes and resettlement; prison/probation issues; prisoner assessment, sentence management and planning; prisoner's information book.

Heads of Unit	Elizabeth Barnard	020-7217 5086
	Trish Wincote	020-7217 5141

DRUGS STRATEGY UNIT

Functions: Implementation of the Prison Service Drug Strategy; treatment; mandatory drug testing; voluntary testing; supply reduction; research.

Head of Unit	Digby Griffith	020-7217 5431
Personal Secretary	Denise Gayle	020-7217 5898
Head of Supply Reduction & Testing	Martin Lee	020-7217 5798
Head of Treatment	Liz Hogarth	020-7217 5798
Head of Alcohol & Hostels	Richard Mason	020-7217 5834
Head of Finance, Marketing, Briefing	Vacancy	020-7217 5767

OFFENDING BEHAVIOUR PROGRAMMES UNIT

Functions: provision and development of offending behaviour programmes.

Head of Unit	Dr David Thornton	020-7217 5370
Personal secretary	Rita Palmer	020-7217 5928
		fax 020-7217 5871
Sex offender treatment programme team	Ruth Mann	020-7217 5059
Throughcare Manager	Andy Rooke	020-7217 2037
		fax 020-7217 2005
Living skills team	Dr Linda Blud	020-7217 5648
Psychopathology team	Gill Attrill	020-7217 5029
Cognitive self change programme team	Jenny Bunton	020-7217 5119
CALM anger & emotion mgmnt team	Dr Mia Debidin	020-7217 5261
Domestic violence programme team	Anya McHayle	020-7217 5905
Cognitive skills programmes	Arlene Kerrigan	020-7217 5660
	Claire Hunt	020-7217 5070
Throughcare manager	Jim Cowley	020-7217 5180
Short-term offender programmes	Sue James	020-7217 5051
Juvenile programmes	Christine Nichols	020-7217 5434
		fax 020-7217 5392
Long term evaluation team	Caroline Friendship	020-7217 5347
Policy & administration	Gabriel Denvir	020-7217 5921
		fax 020-7217 5824

MANAGEMENT UNIT

Head of Unit	Adrian Scott	020-7217 5912
		fax 020-7217 5865
Enquiries		020-7217 5271

LORD CHANCELLOR'S DEPARTMENT

CHILDREN & FAMILY COURT ADVISORY & SUPPORT SERVICE

3rd Floor, Southside, 105 Victoria Street
London SW1E 6QT

Project Team
telephone: dial 020-7210 plus extension for individual
fax 020-7210 0749

Project Director	David Lye	0745
PS to Project Manager	Joyce Connell	0733
Project Manager		
Service Issues & Communications	Helen Hartwell	0720
Communications &		
Conference Co-ord	Vinice Morris	0722
Communications Support Officer	Adil Anwar	0722
Project Manager Legislation & IT	Bridget Ogden	1984
Support Infrastructure		
Project Manager	Howard Evans	1742
Support Infrastructure		
Business Analyst	Susan Kirkwood	1742
Business Infrastructure Office Mgr	Toby Martin	0713
Business Infrastructure Officer	Katie Learman	0713
Legislation Officer	Femi Ogulende	1273
Project Manager HR,		
Accom & Finance	Wendy Mason	1951
HR Co-ord	Charlotte McNeil	0726
HR Consultant	Lynda Anderson	
HR Consultant	Lesley Nicholls	
Accom Project Mgr & BLO	Mary Grant	1783
Office Mgr & Deputy BLO	Judith Laurent	
Meetings Co-ord	Jayne Foster	1932
Admin Officer	Charles Sanders	1932
Finance Consultant	David O'Doinnell	1272
Liaison with Dept of Health	Arran Poyser	020-7972 4261
Liaison with Home Office	Joan Bonelle	020-7273 2638

ASSISTED PRISON VISITS UNIT, PRISONER LOCATION SERVICE, AND VICTIM HELPLINE

Assisted Prison Visits Unit, PO Box 2152, Birmingham B15 1SD

Head of Unit	Alan K Jones	0121-626 2208
Assisted Prison Visits		
Team Leader	North Section	0121-626 3700
	South Section	0121-626 2772
		fax 0121-626 3474
General enquiries & customer services	(10.15-11.45 am, 2.15-3.45pm)	0845 300 1423
Prisoner Location Service		
General enquiries	9.30-12noon, 2.00pm-4.00pm	0121-626 2773

Probation enquiries	0121-626 2742/2839 (24 hr ansaphone)
All fax enquiries	*0121-626 3474*
Prison Service Victim Helpline	Mon-Fri 9am-4pm 08457 585112 (24hr ansaphone)

ELECTRONIC MONITORING SERVICES

The three Home Office contractors are responsible for the management and enforcement of Home Detention Curfew, Curfew Orders and other applications of electronic monitoring within the criminal justice system of England and Wales.

GSSC OF EUROPE

Frankland Road, Blagrove, Swindon SN5 8YF (01793) 438300
fax (1793) 438342
0800 9171691

Areas covered
Avon, Berkshire, Cornwall, Devon, Dorset, Gloucestershire, Hampshire, Kent, Oxfordshire & Buckinghamshire, Somerset, Surrey, East & West Sussex, Wiltshire

Regional Manager	Simon Noble	(01793) 438308
Monitoring Centre Manager	Adam Brooks	(01793) 438327
Monitoring Centre		(01793) 438300 08080 100120
Liaison & Marketing Manager	Graham Shepherd	07899 926342
Case Managers	Karen Fowler	07769 883446
	John Williamson	07769 883470

Avon, Cornwall, Devon, Dorset, Gloucestershire, Somerset, Wiltshire

	Lisa Carter	07899 926340
	Stephanie Redford	07899 926338

Berkshire, Hampshire, Kent, Oxfordshire & Buckinghamshire, Surrey, East & West Sussex

PREMIER MONITORING SERVICES LTD

Austin House, Stannard Place, St Crispin's Road, Norwich NR3 1YF (01603) 428300
fax (01603) 428311

Director	Mike Webb	01603 428300
Asst Dir Monitoring (Operations)	Terry Harris	01603 428300
Asst Dir Operations Support (Liaison)	Andy Homer	01603 428300
Asst Dir Finance & Admin	Paul Reed	01603 428300
Control Centre Managers (24hrs)	(01603) 428399	
Control Operators (24hrs)	(01603) 428410/6	
Legal/Enforcement Officers	(01603) 428390	
Area Manager London & East	Jane Ensor	020-8364 4756

Areas Covered
Derbyshire, Dyfed, Gwent, Hereford & Worcester, Leicestershire, Lincolnshire, Northamptonshire, N Wales, Nottinghamshire, Powys, Shropshire, Staffordshire, Warwickshire, Mid, South & West Glamorgan, West Midlands

Croydon Base Manager	Vacancy	020-8689 1681
Enfield Base Manager	David Weston	020-8364 4756
Ipswich Base Manager	Adam Oxbury	(01473) 215828
Huntingdon Base Manager	Tim Millington	(01480) 451451

Area Manager Midlands & Wales	Eric Garbett	0121-236 4208

Areas Covered
Bedfordshire, Cambridgeshire, Essex, Hertfordshire, Inner London, Middlesex, Norfolk, NE & SE & SW London, Suffolk, parts of Surrey

Birmingham Base Manager	Barry Ashcroft	0121-236 4208
Nottingham Base Manager	Rob Marlow	0115-941 4768
Shrewsbury Base Manager	Kevin Gooch	(01743) 851 243
Cardiff Base Manager	Steve Woodward	029-2046 5187

SECURICOR CUSTODIAL SERVICES
205-207 Mallard Court, Salford, Manchester M5 2UE 0161-868 3000
fax 0161-877 0364

Areas Covered
Cheshire, Cumbria, Durham, Greater Manchester, Humberside, Lancashire, Merseyside, Northumbria, N & S & W Yorkshire, Teesside

Control Centre	0161-868 2300	
Interagency Manager	Claire Sims	0161-877 0364

WEB SITES RELATING TO CRIME AND PENAL ISSUES

Compiled by Prison Service HQ Library

UK SITES

Aftermath
http://www.soft.net.uk/turner/aftermath.htm
Charity for the offender's family. History and work of Aftermath. Counselling help.

Board of Visitors (BOV)
http://www.homeoffice.gov.uk/bov.htm
Describes the purpose of the BOV, including details of the job, how to apply and a list of local BOVs. Full text newsheets, annual reports 97 & 98, brief history of BOV 1898-1998 and speeches.

The British Journal of Criminology
http://www.oup.co.uk/crimin
Journal contents and abstracts from issue 1, 1996 -

British Society of Criminology
http://info.lut.ac.uk/departments/ss/bsc/homepage/homepage.htm
E-journal 'British Criminology Conferences : selected proceedings'. Code of ethics for researchers of criminology.

Cambridge Institute of Criminology
http://www.law.cam.ac.uk/crim/iochpg.htm
Listings of seminars / conferences. Online library catalogue. Research papers by the Institute. Institute publications.

HM Inspectorate of Prisons
http://www.homeoffice.gov.uk/hmipris/hmipris.htm
Details of the Inspectorate. Inspection programme. Full list of Inspectorate reports. Full text thematic reviews and annual reports.

HM Prison Service
http://www.hmprisonservice.gov.uk
Full list of HM Prison establishments with descriptions and addresses. News releases. Corporate information (annual reports, vision etc.). Statistics (prison population, staffing levels). Charities and organisations giving advice for offenders and families. Prison service Orders (selected), Prison Service Journal, Prison Rules, Prison Service Standards, Prison Service News. Information on prison life.

HM Prison Enterprises
http://www.hmpenterprises.co.uk
Online brochures. Details of setting up business links.

Home Office
http://www.homeoffice.gov.uk
Press releases. Aims and Objectives. Bills before Parliament. Directorates and Units. Publications (annual report, business plan).

Howard League for Penal Reform
http://www.howardleague.org
Details of their work. Reports, briefing papers and fact sheets. Press releases and forthcoming publications.

ISTD: The Centre for Crime and Justice Studies
http://www.kcl.ac.uk/istd
List of publications with abstracts and bibliographies. Research programs. Criminal justice resources. Details of conferences / seminars / courses.

Insight Arts Trust
http://www.penlex.org.uk/pages/insight.html
Details of the Trust. Drama workshops. Multi-arts projects. Touring Theatre Programmes. Anger management and Life Skills. History and funding.

Inside Art
http://www.inside-art.co.uk
Details of art education programs. Gallery of artists' work. Prisoner's views.

Inside Arts Trust - New life maps (drama in prison projects)
http://www.newlifemaps.com
Details of drama projects. Reading list.

Inside Out Trust
http://www.inside-out.org.uk
Activities for offenders and ex-offenders in order to integrate them into the community. Project details. Reports.

International Centre for Prison Studies (King's College London)
http://www.prisonstudies.org
Advises on the development of policies on prisons and use of imprisonment. Aims and objectives. Work and current projects.

NACRO (National Association for the Care and Resettlement of Offenders)
http://www.nacro.org
(Website under construction)

National Criminal Intelligence Service (NCIS)
http://www.ncis.co.uk
Details of the work of the NCIS, UK Division, Intelligence Development Division and International Division. Links to Interpol and Europol.

National Probation Research and Information Conference Web Site
http://www.gm.associates.co.uk
The official website for the conference, up-dated each year. The site give details of the conference and will enable visitors to download copies of the report of proceedings of the conferences from 1999 onwards. GM Associates are the conference administrators.

Northern Ireland Prison Service
http://www.niprisonservice.gov.uk
Mission statement. Information on establishments. Weekly updated statistics on prison populations. Major historical events concerning the NI Prison Service. Publications (annual report, business plan etc.)

Parole Board
http://www.paroleboard.gov.uk
Annual reports 97/98, 98/99. Release directions. Press releases.

Penal Lexicon
http://www.penlex.org.uk
Online catalogue. Penal structure in England and Wales. UK Legislation. UK Case Law. European Prison Rules. Annual reports for BOV, Ombudsman. Information on a range of penal issues.

Prison Governor's Association (PGA)
http://www.wavespace.waverider.co.uk/~prisgovuk/in
History of PGA. Manifesto. Constitution.

Prison! Me! No Way! Trust
http://www.curdev.hull.ac.uk/prison/index.html
Details of the Trust's work. Descriptions of video, tape and information packs aimed at discouraging young people from criminal activities. Gallery of photographs of prison life. Education and effectiveness study research by Hull University.

Police
http://www.police.uk
Full list of Police Services in the UK with links to homepages.

Prisons Ombudsman
http://www.homeoffice.gov.uk/prisomb.htm
Annual report 96 & 97. Structure and responsibilities of Prisons' Ombudsman.

Prisons Over Two Centuries
http://www.homeoffice.gov.uk/prishist.htm
Extract from *Home Office 1782-1982* written to commemorate the Bicentenary of the Home Office in 1982.

Prison Rules
http://www.hmso.gov.uk/si/si1999/19990728.htm
Full text version of the Prison Rules 1999

Scarman Centre for the Study of Public Order (Leicester University)
http://www.le.ac.uk/cp/cp.html
Publications. Research Projects.

Scottish Prison Service
http://www.sps.gov.uk
Overview of SPS. Research Papers. Press releases. Members of SPS Board. List of prison establishments. Charter Standards for prisoners and visitors. Prison population figures. Visiting arrangements. Prison transport service. Information Line for families.

Unit for the Arts and Offenders
http://www.a4offenders.org.uk
Creative arts opportunities for offenders and ex-offenders. Research projects. Publications.

Unlock (National Association of Ex-offenders)
http://www.tphbook.dircon.co.uk/unlock.html
Details of Unlock program and discharge packs. Short biographies of founding members.

OVERSEAS SITES

American Corrections Association (ACA)
http://www.corrections.com/aca/
Details the history of the ACA. ACA officers. Selected articles from Corrections Compendium and Corrections Today.

American Jail Association (AJA)
http://www.corrections.com/aja/
Details of the AJA, Board of Directors. American Jails Magazine and Bulletins.

Australian Institute of Criminology
http://www.aic.gov.au
Library database. Publications. Research. Statistical information. Directories. News releases.

Bureau of prisons library
http://bop.library.net
Resources cover corrections, criminology, sociology, psychology and business, also listings of periodicals

The Corrections Connection
http://www.corrections.com
Resources and links to information on Corrections, including education, juveniles, industries, healthcare etc. News items.

Federal Bureau of Prisons
http://www.bop.gov
Press releases. Statistics. Historical documents. List of offices. Inmate information. Freedom of Information Act/ Privacy Act. Publications.

Justice Information Center
http://www.ncjrs.org
Documents, websites and listervs on corrections, courts, crime prevention, Criminal Justice Statistics, drugs and crime, juvenile justice, law enforcements, research, victims. Abstract database.

Justice Network (Canada)
http://www.acjnet.org
Legislative documents. Information on a range of topics to do with justice issues.

National Archive of Criminal Justice Data
http://www.icpsr.edu/NACJD/index.html
Research on crime and criminal justice system.

National Institute of Corrections Information Center
http://nicic.org
Publications and current research projects.

National Institute of Justice
http://www.ojp.usdoj.gov/nij
Details of programs. Publications. Journal archive.

Office of International Criminal Justice
http://www.acsp.uic.edu/index.htm
Monthly newsmagazine of criminal justice news, views and trends (whole articles). Journal of the International Association for the study of Organised Crime (brief abstracts). Journal of the International Association of Correctional Officers (brief abstracts).

Penal Reform International
http://www.penalreform.org/home/home.htm
Objectives. PRI activities. Newsletter. Policy documents and reports. Articles from seminars.

Prison Zone
http://www.prisonzone.com
Prison art in America. Comprehensive list of websites covering prisons (US). Prisoners' writing and poetry. Guide to plea bargaining. Michael Pardue case. Haunting of Sante Fe Prison.

Sourcebook of criminal justice statistics
http://www.albany.edu/sourcebook
Sourcebook available in PDF Format.

United Nations Crime & Justice Information Network
http://www.uncjin.org
Description of Centre for International Crime Prevention, including its global programmes and research. List of institutes concerned with crime. UN rules. UN publications list. Statistics. Details of Constitutions, Treaties and Laws.

US Department of Justice
http://www.usdoj.gov/
Department of Justice organisations list. Press releases, speeches and statements. Freedom of Information Act. Annual Reports. Community support and grants. Fugitives and missing persons. Juvenile justice.

WHO Health in Prisons Project
www.hipp-europe.org
Project description. World resources on health in prisons.

World Criminal Justice Library Network
http://newark.rutgers.edu/~wcjlen/WCJ/
New publications in criminal justice research.

NORTHUMBRIA
DURHAM
1
CUMBRIA
NORTHERN IRELAND
YORKSHIRE NORTH
LANCASHIRE
HUMBER-SIDE
YORKS WEST
3
2
YORKS SOUTH
CHESHIRE
DERBY-SHIRE
4
LINCOLN-SHIRE
NORTH WALES
STAFFORD-SHIRE
NORFOLK
SHROP-SHIRE
LEICESTER-SHIRE
5
CAMBRIDGE-SHIRE
6
7
SUFFOLK
POWYS
HEREFORD & WORCESTER
8
DYFED
10
ESSEX
14
9
11
GWENT
12
LONDON
13
AVON
WILT-SHIRE
BERKSHIRE
KENT
SURREY
HAMPSHIRE
SOMERSET
SUSSEX WEST
SUSSEX EAST
DEVON
DORSET
CORNWALL
1 TEESSIDE
2 MERSEYSIDE
3 GREATER MANCHESTER
4 NOTTINGHAMSHIRE
5 WEST MIDLANDS
6 WARWICKSHIRE
7 NORTHAMPTONSHIRE
8 BEDFORDSHIRE
9 OXFORDSHIRE & BUCKINGHAMSHIRE
10 HERTFORDSHIRE
11 WEST GLAMORGAN
12 MID GLAMORGAN
13 SOUTH GLAMORGAN
14 GLOUCESTERSHIRE
LONDON AREAS
INNER
NORTH EAST
SOUTH EAST
SOUTH WEST
MIDDLESEX

AVON PROBATION SERVICE from 1.4.01 amalgamating with Somerset Probation Service

Probation Officers in Avon are divided into case managers and programme providers

Offices

1. **Head Office**
Brunel House, 83 Newfoundland Road
Bristol BS2 9LU
0117-983 0000
direct dial 0117-9151 + no
fax 0117-983 0052

Sampson, Peter (acting cpo) 303
Redfern, Gary (aco) 311
Jones, Phil (aco) 305
Wakefield, Robert (aco) 307
Phillips, Shirley (info mgr) 325
Thompson, Bruce (syst mgr) 350
Clark, Jane (finance mgr) 321
Pomphrey, Christopher (finance off) 322
Mayhew, Nicola (personnel mgr) 315
Ockenden, Caroline (personnel off) (js) 316
Cathy Stuart (personnel off) (js) 318
Scott, Robin (spo, dtto) 348

Training Unit
Jakiro, Dinah (spo) 331
Ackerman, Sarah (pract devpt assessor) 332
Edwards, Rosie (pract devpt assessor) 339
Sage, Linda 310
Wilson, Jim 310

Hitchens, Andrew (crime/disorder mgr) (based at Create Centre 0117-925 0505)

2. **Family Court Welfare**
from 1.4.01 part of Children & Family Court Advisory & Support Service
York Court, Unit 9
Wilder Street
Bristol BS2 8QH
0117-923 2070
fax 0117-923 2075

Simpson, Trevor (spo)
Dunford, Gene (js)
Jarvie, Jeanette
Jones, E Miriam (js)
Lawson, Jim
Liddle, Christine
O'Neill, Dara
West, Sarah

3. Bridewell Street
Bristol BS1 2JX
0117-929 0671
fax 0117-925 5488

O'Connor, Dan (spo, crt assessment team)
Perry, Stephanie (snr pract, crt assessment team)

Case Managers
Bristol, Tiggy
Burford, Gwen
Farrelly, Richard
Nabi, Ishrat (pso)

Programme Providers
Almond, Tracy (home office secondment)
Austin, Rachel
Vacancy (js)
Cormack, Rita
Goedhart, Adriana (home office secondment)
Haines, Liz
Hutchinson, Stuart
Smith, Helen (js)
Ashby, Paul (pso)
Banfield, Rosemary (pso)
Cooper, Carla (pso)
Duncan, Melanie (pso)
Harper, Sandra (pso)
Holmes, Tim (pso)
Nevin, Arnold (pso)
Parrington, Diana (pso)
Smart, Charmiane (pso)
van der Eerden, Barbara (pso)

Court Assessment Team
Atchinson, Jane
Clements, Pip (js)
Fagg, Pat
Harrison, Marilyn (js)
Hawkin, Sheila
Hunt Allason
McFeeley, Jane
Price, Hal
Thompson, Suzanne (js)
Thompson, Steve
Walsh, Jonathan
Cook, Bev (pso) (js)
Cox, Stephen (pso)
Jackson, Caroline (pso) (js)
Hinkins, Stuart (pso)
Searle, Alison (pso)
Yates, Ina (pso)
Yeomans, Rebecca (pso)

Administration
Shelley, Mike (office mgr)
Thomas, Alex (office mgr)

4. **Crown Court**
The Law Courts, Small Street
Bristol BS1 1DA
0117-976 3071/2
fax 0117-976 3073

Harris, Avril (pso)
Phillips, Beth (pso)

5. 31-45 Lower Ashley Road
St Agnes Bristol BS2 9PZ
0117-954 1311
fax 0117-935 1660

Sanyasi, Marcia (spo, cse mgmnt)

Case Managers
Boswell, Sief
Rich, Val
van Bergan, Paula (p)
Williams, Paul

Programme Provider
Parker, Lesley (p, pso)

Employment & Training
East, John (pso)
Farrell, Nicky (pso)
Hawkins, Catherine (pso)
Williams, Mike (pso)

Community Service
Dunstan, Nicky (com safety proj off)

Administration
Cornelius, Sally (office mgr)

6. Devon House, 123 Whitehall Road
Easton Bristol BS5 9BJ
0117-954 1224
fax 0117-935 0174

Wise, Mair (spo, com protectn team)

Case Managers
Vacancy
Wallace, Paulette

Community Protection Team
John, Gareth
Hodge, Liz
Watson, Sybil

Community Service
Madams, Jim (cso)

Administration
Smith, Angela (office mgr)

7. Greystoke Avenue
Westbury on Trym
Bristol BS10 6AD
0117-950 9105
fax 0117-959 1933

Allum, Jim (spo, prog providers)
Lane, Keith (spo, vlounteers, victims, etc)
Jenner, Sue (snr pract, prog provider)

Case Managers
Gordon, Caroline (js)
Moreton, Amanda
O'Connel, Michael
Parsons, Steve
Sutton, Caroline (js)
Thomas, Sally
Daly, Clare (pso)

Programme Provider
Galena, Cherry (pso, volunteers)
Kent-Probert, Fleur (pso, volunteers)

Community Protection Team
Hurcom, Maureen
Miners, David

Community Service
Green, Jackie (cso)
Wellman, Stuart (cso)

Administration
Pellow, Patricia (office mgr)

8. 70 Crossways Road
Knowle Park Bristol BS4 2SP
0117-983 0050
fax 0117-983 0051

Day, Kevin (cs mgr)
Etherton, Sue (cs mgr)
Ellery, Mark (ptnrshps mgr)

Case Managers
Cragg, Rachel
O'Brien, Cathy
Palmer, Vicky (p)
Lawson, James (pso)

Programme Provider
Britton, Jessica (pso)
McGreevy, Lisa (pso)

Community Service
Campbell, Mary (cso)
Hook, Mike (cso)

Administration
Reed, Liz (office mgr)

9. Willow House
Three Wells Road
Withywood Bristol BS13 8PB
0117-964 9523
fax 0117-935 8588

Edwards, Judi (spo case mgmnt)

Case Managers
Clark, Helen (p)
Copple, Lesley
Henderson, Richard
Ring, Lisa (pso)

Community Service
Higgins, Frank (cso)

Administration
Beeson, Lesley (office mgr)

10. 24 High Street
Staple Hill Bristol BS16 5HW
0117-956 9021
fax 0117-957 3559

Hull, Sue (spo, psrs) (js) (11)
Teniola, Wendy (spo, psrs) (js) (11)

Case Managers
Leary, Michaela
Neubert, Chris
Sole, Stuart

Court Assessment Team
Pasco, Mark
Tiernan, Joseph
Hancock, Sue (pso) (js)
Oakes, Tracey (pso) (js)

Community Service
Britton, Jeremy (cso)
Merchant, Ellaine (cso)
Merchant, Ron (cso)

Administration
Shellard, Helen (office mgr)

11. The Old Convent
35 Pulteney Road **Bath** BA2 4JE
Bath (01225) 460673
fax (01225) 480404

Hull, Sue (spo, case mgmnt) (js) (10)
Teniola, Wendy (spo, case mgmnt) (js) (10)

Case Managers
Barnett, Paul (p)
Crowhurst, Annie
Smith, Robert
Love, Di (pso)
Quinn, Lorraine (p, pso)

Programme Providers
Friend, Ann
Mountford, Guy (pso)
Vacancy (pso)

Court Assessment Team
Brazier, Tony
Breckenridge, Allyson
Parsons, Dave (pso) (js)
Smith, Elaine (pso) (js)

Community Protection Team
Davis, Paul
Rakoczi, Jenny (p)

Family Court Welfare
Pennell, Owen
Rentall, Jane

Community Service
Wilkinson, Clive (cso)

Administration
Toombs, Chris (office mgr)

12. 50 The Boulevard
Weston-super-Mare BS23 1NF
Weston-super-Mare (01934) 623526
fax (01934) 621111

Cornelius, Simon (spo case mgmnt)

Case Managers
Hays, John
Madani, Nasser
Woods, Doug
Coveney, Helen (pso) (js)

Programme Providers
Burnett, Laurence
Camish, Marilyn
Harris, Andrew

Court Assessment Team
Bates, Julie
D'Rozario, Sue (p)
Edwards, David (pso)

Community Protection Team
Thatcher, Sally

Community Service
Edwards, Tony (cso)
Griffin, Annie (cso)

Administration
Clarke, Annette (office mgr)

Youth Offending Teams

13. Kenham House
Wilder Street **Bristol** BS2 8PD
0117-903 6506
fax 0117-903 6481

Simpson, Howard
Robinson, Anne
Trundley, Katy

14. 180 Frome Road
Bath BA2 5FR
Bath (01225) 396966

Mallaney, Anthea

15. Youth Justice Social Services Department
Weston super Mare Police Station
Walliscote Road
Weston super Mare N Somerset
(01934) 638201

Shaw, Paul

16. 48-50 Elm Park
Filton Bristol BS34 7PH
0117-945 4814

Hassett, Tracey

Hostels

15. **Ashley House Probation Hostel**
14 Somerset Street, Bristol BS2 8NB
0117-924 9697
fax 0117-944 4290

Gough, Nick (spo mgr)
Preston, Boyce (po deputy)
Ashby, Richard (asst mgr)
Hooper, June (asst mgr)
Romain, Maria (asst mgr)
Whittaker, John (asst mgr)
Wilde, Sally (asst mgr)

Administration
Garner, Paul (office mgr)

16. Probation and Bail Hostel
6 **Brigstocke Road** Bristol BS2 8UB
0117-942 5851
fax 0117-944 5945

Holden, Garry (spo)
Vacancy (po)
Booth, Simon (asst mgr)
Fox, Darren (asst mgr)
Francis, Ian (pso, prog prov)
Samura, Dino (asst mgr)
Warren, Martin (asst mgr)
Wells, Tracy (asst mgr)

Administration
Jacobs, Gillian (office mgr)

17. **Bridge House**
78 Filton Road Bristol BS7 0PD
0117-969 3123
fax 0117-931 2167

Miller, Jennie (po)
Champagnie, Cynthia (asst mgr)
Bryant, Richard (asst mgr)
Dunkley, Tracy (asst mgr)
McEneaney, Bernard (asst mgr)
Orchard, Patrick (asst mgr)

Administration
Lane, Jenny (office mgr) (js)
Dolores, Gonsales (office mgr) (js)

Institutions

18. H M Prison, Cambridge Road,
Horfield **Bristol** BS7 8PS
0117-980 8100
Direct dial 0117-9808+ext
fax 0117-980 8153
probn fax 0117-980 8239

Probn admin ext 239
Discipline ext 290
Special visits ext 271

McCoid, Ingrid (spo) ext 219
Edward, Sheila ext 219
Fraser, Rosemarie ext 226
Glass, Katrina ext 145
Hall, Lesley ext 226
Lane, Russell ext 297
McMillan, John (p) ext 337
Maynard, Sally ext 353
Sherwood, Angie (pso) ext 200

17. H M Prison **Leyhill**
Wotton-under-Edge GL12 8HL
Falfield (01454) 260681
fax (01454) 261398
probn/sentence planning fax (01454) 261629

Probn admin ext 255/6
Discipline ext 243

Shevlin, Mike (spo) ext 300
Brice, Tish ext 354
Pattman, Mike ext 302
Peckham, Zoe ext 439
Perry, Roger ext 303
Vacancy ext 278

20. H M Women's Remand Centre
Eastwood Park Falfield
Wotton under Edge, Glos GL12 8DB
Falfield (01454) 262100
fax (01454) 262101
probn fax (01454) 262120

Special Visits (01454) 262088

King, Anne (spo) (js) 262046
Spencer, Elizabeth (spo) (js) 262046
Fegredo, June (remand) 262127

Garrett, Tina (drugs th'care) 262048
Hothersall, Anna (adult sentenced women) (js) 262126
Vacancy (adult sentenced women) (js) 262126
Tonkinson, Claire (adult sentenced women) 262034
Lambert, Pam (yoi) (js) 262126

21. HM Prison & YOI **Ashfield**
Shortwood Road
Pucklechurch BS16 9QG
0117-303 8000
fax (0117) 303 8001

Munn, Graham
Willding, Gary

Petty Sessional Areas

3-9 Bristol
11 Bath & Wansdyke
10 Northavon
12 Woodspring

Crown Court

4 Bristol

Area Code 11

BEDFORDSHIRE PROBATION SERVICE

Offices

1. **Head Office**
3 St Peter's Street
Bedford MK40 2PN
Bedford (01234) 213541
fax (01234) 327497

Scott, John R M (cpo)
Pace, Elisabeth (acpo)
Deverson, Tony (aco)
Williams, John (acpo)
Emm, Ben (info services mgr)
Morrison, Audrey (admin services mgr)
Anderson, Yvonne (info officer, statistics)
Coster, Brenda (info devpt off)
Mainwaring, Mick (netwk sup off)

1a. **Staffing Devpt & Training**
23-27 Napier Road
Luton LU1 1RF
Luton (01582) 735153
fax (01582) 451536

Munday, Mal (spo) (3)

Community Supervision

2. 41 Harpur Street
Bedford MK40 1LY
Bedford (01234) 350401
fax (01234) 328658

Harding, Alison (spo)
Kemp, Jan (spo)
Powell, Andrew (spo)
Scott, Martin (spo)
Breaky, Paul
Brenton, Steve
Church, Paula
Ciuro, Mark
Holley, Gerald
Maisfield, Sue
Mitchell, Rosemary (p)
Munro, Valerie
O'Shea, Melanie
Powell, Malgorzata
Prescott, Karrie
Price, Louise
Smith, Leslie
Wain, Lynda
Wale, Richard
White, Kate (snr pract)
Wildman, Les
Cairncross, Sarah (trainee)
Harrington, Ruth (trainee)
Judge, Gabriel (trainee)
Kerr, Jennifer (trainee)
Wilson, Gwen (emplt) (3)
McNicholls, Dave (ps0)

Forster, Linda (cso)
Hudson, Shaun (cso)
Peddar, Alan (work suprvr)

County Victim Contact Service
(01234) 358978
Doughty, Alan (p, vlo)
Desquesnes, Janet (pso)

2a. **Bedfordshire Youth Offending Service**
N Bedfordshire Team
7 Ashburnham Road
Bedford MK40 1BX
Bedford (01234) 316400
fax (01234) 349238

Mercer, Andrew (hd of yth offending)
Williams, Sue (po)
Corbett, Sue (team leader)
Austin, David (yth & com wrkr)
Anderson, Tony (crt duty off)

3. Frank Lord House
72 Chapel Street
Luton LU1 5DA

Luton (01582) 413172
fax (01582) 418279

Corcoran, Janet (spo) (1a)
de Souza, Chris (spo)
Sheldon, Julie (spo)
Stott, John (spo)
Abbotts, Phillip
Andrews, Debra
Barton, Jon
Brimble, Pat
Brown, Jennifer
Burnell, Karen (snr pract)
Cobb, Stuart
Collier, Peter
Davis, Barbara
Edward, Max
Fisher, Valerie
Francis-Quinton, Minnette
Fraser, Mark
Harris, Dave
Hodkinson, Denise
Hooper, Stephen
Jackson, Gordon
Johnson, Morris
Kirkby, Ros
Lightfoot, Jennifer
Messam, David
Miller, Ashley
Neimantas, Linda
Nickels, Kate
Oliver, Samantha
Sherlock, Helen
Sparke, Jacky (p)
Stowe, Noleania (p)
Whitehurst, Nicole
Khaliq, Roswana (trainee)
Smith, Teresa (trainee)
Wilson, Gwen (emplt) (2)
McFarlane, Gillian (pso)

Joynes, Karen (p, cso)
Stow, Jan (cso)
Samsuddin, Khadeja (cso)
Day, Chris (csa)

3a. **Luton Youth Offending Team**
16 Rothsay Road, Luton LU1 1QX
Luton (01582) 547900
fax (01582) 547901
e mail
lutonyouthoffendingteam@luton.gov.uk

Thomas, Mike (hd of yth offending)
Briddon, Anita (team ldr)
O'Connor, John (dep team ldr)
Burke, Ronald (yth wrkr)
Garrett, Janet (ewo)
Gordon-Jackson, Denise (yjo)
Headington, Melanie (bail supvn off)
Hull, Liz (yjo)
Lazell, Eddie (yjo)
Moth, Tony (police constable)
Potter, Sally (yjo)
Reimann, Rod (po)
Robinson, Dawn (yjo)
Wren, Carol (health visitor)
Vacancy (yjo)
Vacancy (bail supvn off)

3b. **Bedfordshire Youth Offending Service Mid Bedfordshire Team**
39 Oakwood Avenue
Dunstable LU5 4AS
Dunstable (01582) 524420
fax (01582) 424421

Vacancy (p, po)
Murray, Gerard (team leader)
Zaheed, Alyla (yth & com wrkr)
Tait, Chris (ewo)

Court Services

4. Magistrates' Court Liaison Office
Shire Hall **Bedford** MK40 1SQ
Bedford (01234) 358402
fax (01234) 358070

Purkiss, Anita (mclo)

4a. **Crown Court Liaison Office**
Luton Crown Court
7-9 George Street, Luton LU1 2AA
Luton (01582) 452079

Crown Court Switchboard
(01582) 452846
fax (01582) 485529

Stott, Jonathan (spo) (3)
Vacancy

4b. Magistrates' Court Liaison Office
The Court House
Stuart Street, **Luton** LU1 5DL
Luton (01582) 482710
fax (01582) 457261

Berg, Gillian (p)
Gritton, Phillipa (pso)
Vacancy (pso)
Saunders, John (pso)

Family Court Service
from 1.4.01 part of Children & Family Court Advisory & Support Service

5. 23-27 Napier Road
Luton LU1 1RF
Luton (01582) 735265
fax (01582) 451536

Rouse, Mike (spo)
Baker, Sylvia
Bentley, Sandra
Jones, Wendy
Lesley, Jane (p)
Lowe, Gillian (p)
Plater, Christina (p)
Sherlock, Philip

Offender Accomodation

6a. 36-40 Napier Road
Luton LU1 1RG
Luton (01582) 418200
fax (01582) 737391

Hazeltine, Mike (mgr)
Delmar, Elaine (dep mgr)
Allen, Carol(asst warden)
Barras, Peter (asst mgr)
Flavin, Pat (asst warden)
Morris, John (asst warden)

6b. 80 Chaucer Road
Bedford MK40 2AP
Bedford (01234) 340501
fax (01234) 351715

Vacancy (mgr)
Nichols, Magdalena (dep mgr)
Gorry, Sally (asst warden)
Lewis, Mitchelle (asst warden)
Saunders, Andrew (asst warden)
Tate, David (asst warden)
Wheatley, Gary (asst warden)

Institution

7. H M Prison, St Loyes
Bedford MK40 1HG
Bedford (01234) 358671
fax (01234) 273568
probn fax (01234) 326243
bail info fax (01234) 347268

Burrows, Matthew (spo)
Bell, George
Hart, Gordon
Ireland, Deborah (pso)

Petty Sessional Areas

2 Bedford
2 Ampthill
2 Biggleswade
3 Dunstable
3 Leighton Buzzard
3 Luton

Crown Court

4a Luton

Area Code 12

BERKSHIRE PROBATION SERVICE from 1.4.01 amalgamating with Oxfordshire & Buckinghamshire Probation Service

CHASE Services stands for Contact, Health, Accommodation, Substance misuse, Employment

Out of hours emergency contact point
St Leonards Hostel
0118-957 3171

Offices

1. **Head Office**
145 Friar Street
Reading RG1 1EX
Reading 0118-957 4091
fax 0118-958 8394

from 1.4.01 at
Kingsclere Road
Bicester, Oxon OX26 23QD
(01869) 255300
fax (01869) 255355

* staff moving to Bicester

Bridges, Andrew (cpo)
Simpkins, Valerie (pa to cpo)
Brooks, Susan (aco) *
Coker, Pip (aco) *
Rolley, Tony (aco) *
Malster, Nicola (communications)
Evans, Rosemary (personnel) *
Tompkins, Josie (finance)
Reynolds, Mike (spo staff devpt)
Lewis, Denise (po practice devpt)
Warwick, Leah (po practice devpt)
Hills, Ann (training & nvq)
Boylan, Tracey (po training)
Scaife, Adrian (info systems)

2. James Glaisher House
Grenville Place
Bracknell RG12 1BP
Bracknell (01344) 420446
fax (01344) 301274

Smith, Alison (spo)
Albon, Tony
Bliss, Valerie
Harris, Rowan
Nagib-Ali, Abdulla
Rice, Scott
Black, Jo (psa)

CHASE Services (East)
Blakesley, Clive (p)
Harris, Steve (psa)
Wilkinson, Emma (psa)
Joss, Maureen (basic skills)

Cooper, Ann (office services)

3. Bridge Road
Maidenhead SL6 8PB
Maidenhead (01628) 770858
fax (01628) 788675

Windsor Court (01753) 853533
fax (01753) 866891

Maidenhead & Windsor Team
Morgan, Carol (spo)
Hardwicke, Dee
Jones, Kevin
McClone, Ann
McGregor-Paterson, Colin
Powell, Vivian
Haines, Mark (psa)

CHASE Services (East)
Walsh, Angela (psa)

Khanum, Naheed (office services)

4. Mill Lane
Newbury RG14 5QS
Newbury (01635) 43535
fax (01635) 42103

Pearson, Jocelyn (spo)
Aldridge, Richard
Castle, Alan
Donald, Nick (p)
Griffiths, Suzanne
Randle, Gillian
Mullen, Barbara (psa crt)

CHASE Services (West)
Baron, Sally (psa)
Rutterford, Kate (psa)

Lawes, Carole (office services)

5. Crown House, Crown Street
Reading RG1 2SE
Reading 0118-956 0466
fax 0118-962 0301

Adult Case Management
Sceeny, Wendy (spo)
Fane, Dian
Greenwood, Judy
Jones, Simon (p)
Kasozimusoke, Sozzie
Kueberuwa, Norma
Lambert, Ian
Martin, Ross
Millar, Melanie
Russell, Jan
Stephens, Beryl
Rowlands, Jonathan (psa)
Spilstead, Helen (psa)

YO & Restorative Justice
Chilvers, Jo (spo)
Downing, Vanessa
Hafling, Juliet (p)
Large, Anne (p)
Llewellyn, Heather (p)
Martin, Sarah (p)
Manders, Gary
Griffith, Barbara (psa)

County Groupwork
Roberts, John (spo)
Acteson, Doreen
Fry, Chris
Kelly, Vince
Mayston, Greg (p)
Willmer, Clare (p)
Thorpe, Catherine (psa)

CHASE Services (West)
Wilson, Gillian (mgr)
Gothard, Ann
Smith, Paul (p)
Howard, Margaret (psa)
Leahy, Mike (psa)
Phillips, Madeleine (psa)
Stoddart, Gary (psa)

Blower, Barbara (mgr dtto)
Blakesley, Clive (p)
Smith, Paul (p)

Brincat, Jackie (office services)

6. **Reading Crown Court**
The Old Shire Hall, The Forbury
Reading RG1 3EH
0118-967 4420
fax 0118-967 4431

Evans, Grant (spo) (7)
Aslett, Alec (psa)
Chrisp, Linda (psa)
Heath, Jim (psa)
Morris, Delia (psa)

7. **Reading Magistrates' Court**
18a Castle Street, Reading RG1 7SD
Reading 0118-958 6141
fax 0118-958 6119

Evans, Grant (spo) (6)
Bywater, Matt
Goodliffe, Joy (psa)
Humphreys, Andrew (psa)
Bhatti, Jasvir (psa)

Mentally Disordered Offenders Diversion
0118-956 1904
Evans, Grant (spo project mgr)
Howard, Kay (co-ord)
Leighton, Jay (admin)

County Administration
Eaton, Sue (mgr)
Smith, Karen (office services)
Wilkinson, Sharon (facilities)

8. **Family Courts Welfare Service**
from 1.4.01 part of Children & Family Court Advisory & Support Service
Glasson Centre, 319 Oxford Road
Reading RG30 1AU
Reading 0118-956 6322
fax 0118-950 2618

Jones, Alison (spo)
Boundy, Margaret
Breeze, Janet
Budd, Janet
Harrington, Brian
Mitchell, Mollie
Pratt, Rosalind
Stuart, Sue
Wright, Sue (team admin)

9. Revelstoke House, Chalvey Park
Slough SL1 2HF
Slough (01753) 537516
fax (01753) 552169

Courts
Rymer, Julia (spo)
de Silva, Maureen (psa crt)
Lock, Jan (psa crt)
Marggetson, Carolyn (p, psa)
Whyte, Peter (psa)

Case Management
Wootton, Lynne (spo)
Amahwe, Gabriel
Bradley, Felicity
Carmichael, Jane
Cooke, Sue (p)
Holland, Sarah
Lord, Helen
Oztemel, Deniz
Smith, Melanie
Onyeaka, Jude (psa)

CHASE Services (East)
Openshaw, Jim (mgr)
Bull, Richard
Fethers, Cathy (psa)
Harvie, Debbie (psa)
Newton, Mary (psa)
Parash, Varda (p, psa)

Hamilton, Val (office services)

10. **Community Service**

(Bracknell, Maidenhead, Slough & Windsor)
James Glaisher House
Grenville Place
Bracknell RG12 1BP
Bracknell (01344) 452516
fax (01344) 304330

Cleary, John (spo mgr) (based at Reading)
Eldridge, Andrew (dep cs mgr)
Fletcher, Amy (cso)
Hamblin, Emma (cso)
Kiff, Glenys (cso)
Mondaye, Andrew (cso)
Palmer, Christopher (cso)
Pickless, S Mike (cso)

(Reading and Newbury)
18a Castle Street
Reading RG1 7SD
Reading 0118-958 6141
fax 0118-959 6880

Cleary, John (spo mgr)
Clements, Jeremy (dep cs mgr)
Adams, Lynne (cso)
Kendrick, Emma (cso)
Mould, Adam (cso)
Quinn, Tom (cso)
Titcomb, Fiona (cso)
Smith, Karen (office services)

11. **Community Service Workshop**
Unit C1, Reading Small Business Centre
Weldale Street
Reading RG1 7BX

Reading 0118-959 7447

Finan, Mick (psa)

12. **Youth Offending Teams**
Reading & Wokingham
(01189) 390420
Turney, Bob

Maidenhead & Bracknell
(01628) 627364
Reilly, Sheila

Newbury
(01635) 264759/264752
Donald, Nick (p)

Slough
(01753) 522702
Vacancy

Hostels

13. **St Leonard's Probation Hostel**
2 Southcote Road, Reading RG30 2AA
Reading 0118-957 3171
fax 0118-956 0677

Roberts, Karen (spo mgr)
Yapp, Liam (po deputy)
Ademefun, Ade (asst warden)
Bailey, Ian (asst warden)
Hutchins, Lucy (asst warden)
Mundy, Pam (asst warden)
Pencavel, Katharine (asst warden)
Smith, Margaret (asst warden)
Parkes, Margo (team admin)

14. **Manor Lodge Probation Hostel**
8 Straight Road, Old Windsor SL4 2RL
Windsor (01753) 868807
fax (01753) 620466

Pearce, Clive (spo mgr)
Blower, Mike (po deputy)
Cooper, Ian (asst warden)
Duval-Hall, Sarah (asst warden)
Isabelle, Eddy (asst warden)
Oni, Ade (asst warden)
President, Liz (asst warden)
Stewart, Alan (asst warden)
Tajima, Shula (asst warden)
Lang, Anne (team admin)

15. **Elizabeth Fry Probation Hostel**
(Voluntary Managed)
6 Coley Avenue, Reading RG1 6LQ
Reading 0118-957 2385
fax 0118-951 0340

Kebby, Shirley (mgr)
Oke, Caroline (asst mgr)
Vacancy (p, mental health)
Blake, Richard (proj wrkr)
Flanagan, Nicola (proj wrkr)
Marchant, Nicola (proj wrkr)
Skinner, Madeleine (proj wrkr)
Snape, Jan (proj wrkr)
Goddard, Mary (gp wrkr)
Webb, Emma (drugs)
Yapp, Anita (asst warden)
Lammas, Jan (team admin)

Institution

16. H M Young Offender Institution
and Remand Centre
Forbury Road
Reading RG1 3HY
Reading 0118-958 7031
fax 0118-959 4581

Treeby, Lionel (spo) ext 297
Cowan, Sally
Brown, Tara (psa hdc) ext 205
Sitton, Jeanette (psa, remands & bail) ext 421
Cook, Vicky (psa, convicted & pre release) ext 300
Giles, Debbie (admin) ext 248

Petty Sessional Areas

5-7 Reading & Sonning
10 Slough (covers Bracknell, Windsor & Maidenhead)
4 West Berkshire

Crown Court

6 Reading

Area Code 13

CAMBRIDGESHIRE PROBATION SERVICE

Out of hours emergency contact point
Wesleyan Road Hostel
(01733) 551678

1. **Head Office**
1 Brooklands Avenue
Cambridge CB2 2BB
Cambridge (01223) 712345
direct dial (01223) 71+ext
fax (01223) 568822

Hughes, John (cpo) ext 2358
Lowe, Margaret (acpo) ext 2350

Clarke, Dot (acpo) ext 2352
Smith, Andy (acpo) ext 2376
Johnstone, Fran (p, marketing/pr) ext 2370
Seaton, Paul (p, finance) ext 2354

1a. **Support Services Unit**
Grammar School Walk
Huntingdon PE18 6LF
(01223) 712345
direct dial (01480) 37+ext
fax (01480) 375769

English, Doreen (staff devpt mgr) ext 5765
Vacancy (p, staff devpt off) ext 5766
Thornley, Ste (info analyst) ext 5759
Black, Cathy (p, info officer) ext 5763
Corfield, Helen (admin services mgr) ext 5764
Marshall, Bernard (it sup mgr) ext 5767
Sedzikowski, Sue (personnel mgr) ext 5762
Warren, Janet (facilites mgr) ext 5770

2. Warkworth Lodge
Warkworth Street
Cambridge CB1 1EG
Cambridge (01223) 712271
fax (01223) 712700

McGhee, John (spo)
Wallace, David (spo)
Beale, Julie
Crewes, Geraldine (p)
Farren, Niamh
Flack, Julia
Foreman, Fran
French, Gill (p)
Harding, Michael
Lowes, Julie
Parmar-Poynter, Bhavna
Phelps, Daniel
Pink, Matthew (yot)
Shadbolt, Maureen
Shember, John
Simons, Philippa
Tasker, Christopher
Smith, Val
Wilson, Claire
Hunt, Alice (trainee)
Marsh, Linsey (trainee)
Hillyer, Sheila (psa)
Jenkins, Brian (psa)
Austin, Joan (com resource co-ord)
Gooch, Baden (scso)
Pease, Adrian (cso)
Steel, Rodney (p, cso)
Kedge, Susan (emplt asst)
Taylor, Carole (p, emplt)

3. Sessions House, Lynn Road
Ely Cambridge CB6 1DA
Ely (01353) 663523
fax (01353) 669047

Open Tues & Thurs only
all mail to office 2

Harding, Michael (supvn)
Hillyer, Sheila (psa crts)

4. Old County Buildings
Grammar School Walk
Huntingdon PE18 6LF
Huntingdon (01480) 376100
fax (01480) 376123

Webster, Nicki (spo) (11)
Bale, David (p)
Coyle, Eric
Hill, Anne (p)
Landeryou, Minty
Lawson, Alexandra
Ogden, Clare
Pender-Johns, Rosemary (p)
Seddon, Graeme
Wallace, Lesley
Morse, Mike (trainee)
Dominey, Jane (p, pract devpt assessor)

Mawditt, Marilyn (psa)
Barr, Lynn (scso)
Woodham, Jackie (cso)
Kedge, Susan (emplt asst)

County Groupwork Team
Huntingdon (01480) 376111/2
Hopkinson, Jonathan (spo)
Dawkins, Ellwyn
Hayden, Alan
Sengendo, Janeen
Tomlin, Laura
von Rabenau, Elisabeth (p)

5. Castle Lodge, 1 Museum Square
Wisbech PE13 1ES
Wisbech (01945) 461451
fax (01945) 476350

Jarvis, Andy (p, spo)
Bell, Nicola (p)
Drury, Adrienne
Johnson, Verity
Lewis, Bob
Parmar-Poynter, David
Malloy, Val (p, psa)
Makey, Pauline (p, emplt)
Jones, Pat (p, emplt asst)

Community Service Unit
Mackett, Chris (spo)
Simmons, Gordon (scso)
Stokes, Paula (cso)

5a. The Court House
Market Place **March** PE15 9JF
March (01354) 650677

all mail to office 5

6. Magistrates Court, Bridge Street
Peterborough PE1 1ED
Peterborough (01733) 564367
fax (01733) 315758

Ashford, Carol (spo)
Goffrey, Mark (spo)
Bennett, Jasmine
Block, Nigel
Chapman, Denise
Fish, Michael
Howard, Kate
Leeming, Su (p)
Ludlam, Mel (p)
Maguire, Marian (p)
Maxwell, Christopher
Strowbridge, David (p, yot)
Wallis, Stuart
Walsh, Patrick
Westerbury, Sofi (psa)
Sargent, Rebecca (psa)
Makey, Pauline (empl)
Jones, Pat (emplt asst)

Crown Court
Peterborough (01733) 352763
fax (01733) 565284

Fish, Michael
Kelly, Liz (psa)

7. Gloucester House, 23a London Road
Peterborough PE2 8AP
Peterborough (01733) 348828
fax (01733) 313765

Ryder-Whish, Matthew (spo)
Benn, Colin
Curry, Devinder (p)
Dawkins, Ellwyn
Oliver, Mick
Providence, Belinda
Supper, Lisa
Webb, Martin
Wood, Philip
Fiddy, Anita (trainee)
Lange, Nicola (trainee)
Wiles, Anita (psa)

Harris, Martin (scso)
Bird, Betty (cso)
Shearer, David (cso)
Spruce, Jenny (p, cso)

Family Court Welfare Service
from 1.4.01 part of Children & Family Court Advisory & Support Service

8. 71 London Road
Peterborough PE2 9BB
Peterborough (01733) 312159
fax (01733) 344138

North Team
Kirby, Brian (spo)
Brown, Paul
Green, Martin
Oliver, Jess
Oliver, Joe
Nelson, Michael
Timson, Maureen (p, psa)

9. 1 Brooklands Avenue
Cambridge CB2 2BB
Cambridge (01223) 712345
fax (01223) 568822

South Team
Floyd, Judy
Radnor, Philip

Hostel

10. Probation and Bail Hostel
5 Wesleyan Road
Peterborough PE1 3RW
Peterborough (01733) 551678
fax (01733) 345161

Crews, Teri (spo, warden)
English, Mike (po deputy)
Beech, Garry (asst warden)
Butler, Cindy (asst warden)
Johnson, Richard (asst warden)
Vacancy (asst warden)

Institutions

11. H M Prison **Littlehey**
Perry, Huntingdon
Cambs PE18 0SR
Huntingdon (01480) 812202
fax (01480) 812151

Webster, Nicki (p, spo) (4)
Brown, Niel
Crawford, Tom
Furner, Keith

Miller, Karen (p)
Whelan, Paula

12. H M Prison **Whitemoor**
Longhill Road, March PE15 0AF
March (01354) 660653
fax (01354) 650783

Probn clerk ext 216
Custody/Sentence Management ext 259

Jeary, Katharine (spo)
Baxter, Gill
McDonald, Charles
Miller, Iain
Walker, Mick

Petty Sessional Areas

2 Cambridge
3 East Cambridgeshire
4 Huntingdon
3 Newmarket
5 Fenland
6,7 Peterborough

Crown Courts

2 Cambridge
6 Peterborough

Area Code 15

CHESHIRE PROBATION SERVICE

Out of hours emergency contact number
0589 044623

Offices

1. **Head Office**
17 Cuppin Street
Chester CH1 2BN
Chester (01244) 312333
fax (01244) 317318

Taylor, Andrew (cpo)
Link, Sandra (acpo comm sentences, th'care, cty practice team)
Ingram, Keith (acpo prisons/fcw/ com sentences)
Orrell, Maria (acpo residential/cs/crt services)
Evans, Christine (aco management services)

Chester (01244) 313990
Plumridge, Elaine (hr mgr)
Parker, Jon (hr officer)
Evans, Becky (hr asst)

Chester (01244) 312333
mobile 07740 613008
Sutton-Thompson, Andy (isu mgr)

Chester (01244) 322204
Gaughran, Liz (property & safety mgr)

Community Service
Johnson, Mary (cs area mgr)
Crawford, Karen (p, cso)
Marland, John (p, cso)
Millington, Grenville (cso)
Shone, Jenny (p, cso)

2. 1 Stanley Place
off Lower Watergate Street
Chester CH1 2LU
Chester (01244) 324493
fax (01244) 346112

Case Management - West Cheshire
Heath, Bernie (spo) (3)
Kyle, Tim (spo)
Longshaw, Vivienne
Middleton, Susan
Nolan-Beattie, Cathy
Orr, Rosie
Ramsdale, Sue (p, th'care)
Robertson, Kerry Ann
Scott, Christine
Sykes, Janet (th'care)
Webster, Frances
Bradshaw, Frank (p, psa)
Breen, Linda (p, psa th'care)
Osbourne, Louise(psa)

Webber, Sue (area admin) (also 3, 7)

Partnership Contracts/ Purchased Accommodation Services
Chester (01244) 340310
fax (01244) 350061

Millington, Dianne
Robinson, Wendy
Slavin, Jim
Atkinson, Sue (p, psa)

Chester Community Drugs/ Alcohol Unit
Chester (01244) 344999
Mordue, George

Court Liaison Unit
Chester (01244) 312757
fax (01244) 317612

Berry, Julian (spo)
McAlea, Carol

McDonagh, Chris
Ashfield, Sherry-Ann (pa)
Buckley, Rachel (crt off) (3)
Head, Mavis (crt off) (2)
Holmes, Bea (crt off) (10)
Law, Anne (p, crt off) (7)
Palin, Julie (p, crt off) (7)
Parry, Angie (crt off) (2)
Percival, Jane (crt off) (4)
Simpson, Richard (crt off) (7)
Telford, Sue (crt off) (9)
Townley, Norma (crt off) (8)
Wroe, Lindsay (crt off) (7)

also at
Crown and County Court
Legh Street, **Warrington** WA1 1UR
Warrington (01925) 570766
fax (01925) 570767

and
Knutsford Crown Court
Knutsford (01565) 755486
fax (0565) 652454

3. Marshall Memorial Hall
Woodford Lane **Winsford** CW7 2JS
Winsford (01606) 551166
fax (01606) 861267

Case Management - Winsford
McDermott, Gerry (spo) (5)
Blackham, Caroline
Challis, Emma
Jones, Brian
Mountford, John (dtto)
Smith, Tom (th'care)
Dickenson, Janet (psa)
Stewart, Christine (p, psa th'care)

Community Service
Winsford (01606) 593574
Bentley, Margot (cso) (9)
McKeown, Michael (cso)
Turner, Jill (csso)

4. 150 London Road
Northwich CW9 5HH
Northwich (01606) 43192
fax (01606) 43212

Training & Development
Denton,Mike (spo, training mgr)
Hamilton, Marie (training admin)

County Practice Support Unit
Skynner, David (spo)

Cheshire Victim Liaison
phone/fax (01606) 352020

Roscoe, Claire (p, co-ord)
Frith, Fiona (p, admin)

5. **Family Court Welfare Service**
from 1.4.01 part of Children & Family Court Advisory & Support Service
10 Congleton Road
Sandbach CW11 1WJ
Sandbach (01270) 753502
fax (01270) 759462

McKee, David (spo)
Pemberton, Jackie (p, psa)

Sandbach (01270) 760658
Longson, Margaret
McGrath, Maurice
Waite, Ian

5a. 55 Hoole Road
Chester CH2 3NJ
Chester (01244) 348201
fax (01244) 400427

Edwards, Carol (p)
Horsefield, Alan
Hughes, Beryl (p)

5b. 1st Floor, Norton House
Crown Gate **Runcorn** WA7 2UR
Runcorn (01928) 701255
fax (01928) 717899

Bennett, Christine (p)
Bowman, Pauline
Cheadle, Tom
Jones, Nancy (p)
Smith, Keith (p)
Taylor, Mike

6. Howard House, 10a Friars Gate
Warrington WA1 2RW
Warrington (01925) 650613
fax (01925) 445109

Case Management - Warrington
Edmondson, Lorna (spo)
Hay, Keith (spo th'care)
Bootherstone, Kate
Chamber, Angela
Jackson, Helen
Keatley, Sahra
Kernahan, Chris (th'care)
Mikulin, Ellen-Marie (th'care)
Parkinson, Hilary
Walsh, Chris (dtto)
Woodruff, John
Yunus, Mohammed (th'care)
Gibbons, Julie-Ann (psa, th'care)

Hayes, Tracy (p, psa)
Hedge, Ernie (p, psa)

Community Service
(01925) 419709
Wilson, Bernard (cs area mgr)
Blennerhassett, Marjorie (cso)
Gibson, Tony (p, cso)
Jones, Sahra (cso)
McGregor, Sheila (cso)
Rutter, Barry (proj off)
Couzens, Denise (csso)
Jones, Ann (csso)
Nixon, Janice (csso)

7. Norton House, Crown Gate
Runcorn WA7 2UR
Runcorn (01928) 713555
fax (01928) 701985

Case Management - Halton
Maskell, Colin (spo)
Barnett, Sharon
Brayshaw, Alana
Davies, Lesley-Ann
Harris, Angela
Jones, Peter (th'care)
Lamb, Mary
Lawlor, Jim
Taylor, Karen
Thorndon, Kim
Yates, Peter (th'care)
Dundon, Chris (p, psa)
Riccio, Marian (psa th'care)

Community Service
(01928) 791951
Wilson, Bernard (cs area mgr) (7)
Blennerhassett, Marjorie (cso)
Jones, Sarah (p, cso)

Iremonger, Gordon (area admin) (also 6, 6a, 6b)

Practice Support Unit
Skyner, David (spo)
Alison, Emily (6)
Bennett, Susan (9a)
Edwards, Chris (8)
McDonough, Katie (2)
Rowntree, Rosie (3)
Thorne, Anna (psa) (7)

Information Services Unit
Runcorn (01928) 712202
fax (01928) 710220
Vernon, Eileen (i.s.u. mgr)

Partnership Contracts/ Purchased Accommodation Services
Runcorn (01928) 713555
fax (01928) 701985
Slavin, Jim (p, psa)

8. 47 Delamere Street
Crewe CW1 2DS
Crewe (01270) 257781
fax (01270) 251181

Carruthers, Jim (spo)
McDemott, Gerry (spo, th'care)
Baldham, Sharon
Bale, Ruth
Donnelly, Paul (th'care)
Grey, Garnett
Pazio, John
Peacock, Liz
Pritchard, Carol
Sanders, Francis (th'care)
Sloyan, Fiona (p)
Harding, Eve (psa)
Nuttall, Christine (p, psa th'care)
Sheldon, Kerry (psa, drug treatment)
Woby, Robert (p, psa bail)

Community Service
Hart, Jan (cs area mgr) (10, 10a)
Bentley, Margot (cso) (4)
Brunt, Geoff (p, cso)
Scragg, Bill (cso)
Turner, Ruth (p, cso) (10)

Garner, Liz (area admin) (also 4, 5, 10)

9. Bradshaw House
45 Cumberland Street
Macclesfield SK10 1BY
Macclesfield (01625) 423974
fax (01625) 421345

Meade, Donna (spo) (9a)
Haines, Rebecca
Pearce, Cynthia
Sergeant, David
Spiers, Dorothy
Thomas, Wyn
Byrne, Sally (p, psa th'care)
MacKenzie, Norma (p, psa, bail info)
Norris, Val (p, psa)

Community Service
Hart, Jan (cs area mgr) (9, 10a)
Collins, Shirley (p, cso)
Sutton, Mike (cso)
Turner, Ruth (p, cso) (9)

9a. 6 Parkway
Wilmslow SK9 1LS
Wilmslow (01625) 530881
fax (01625) 549353

Meade, Donna (spo)
Maude, Manjit (p)
Hart, Jan (cs area mgr) (9)

Youth Offending Team

10. Broughton Hall
Filkins Lane
Broughton, Chester CH3 5EJ
Broughton (01244) 310007

Davies, Lesley-Ann (seconded)

11. The Mayo Centre
Byron Road
Macclesfield SK11 7QA
Macclesfield (01625) 433257

Peacock, Liz (seconded)

12. Rutland House
Halton Lea
Runcorn

Yates, Peter (seconded)

Hostels

13. Linden Bank Bail Hostel
40 London Road
Elworth **Sandbach** CW11 9JA
Sandbach (01270) 759181
fax (01270) 759579

Scally, Christine (spo)
Bushill, Graham (dep warden)

14. Bunbury House Bail Hostel
Alnwick Drive, Stanney Grange
Ellesmere Port L65 9HE
phone & fax 0151-357 3551

Vacancy (spo & bail info)
Connolly, Kay (dep warden)

Institutions

15. H M Prison & Young Offender Institution
Styal Wilmslow SK9 4HR
Wilmslow (01625) 532141
fax (01625) 524156

Probn Office/Special Visits ext 289
Discipline/Sentence Planning/Parole Clerk ext 304/351/301
Messages to be left on exts 403 or 405

Brotherston, Sheila (spo) ext 378
Ashfield, Sherry-Anne ext 411
Benbrook, Maureen ext 413
Graham, Diane ext 411
Moscrop, Tony ext 408
Neary, Jackie ext 407 (or 274)
Thurlbeck, Gail (p) ext 417
Watson, Mary ext 407 (or 274)
Lancaster, Phil (bail info)
Lowe, Dianne (psa) ext 410

16. H M Prison
Warrington Road **Risley**
via Warrington WA3 6BP
Warrington (01925) 763871
fax (01925) 764103
probn fax (01925) 766975

McLaughlin, Marie (spo) ext 303
Biddle, Malveen
Crawford, Ann
Croker, Gwen
Day, Julie
Elsworth, Val
McIntyre, Kevin
Nixon, Annette
Price, David
Morrey, Carol (psa)
O'Neil, Fiona (psa)
Wyatt, Susan (psa)

17. H M Young Offender Institution
Thorn Cross Appleton Thorn
via Warrington WA4 4RL
Warrington (01925) 605100
Direct dial (01925) 605+ext
fax (01925) 605101

home detention curfew *fax (01925) 605212*
probn clerk ext 219

all enquiries about individual prisoners to Personal Officer on the Unit

Selby, Anastasia (spo) ext 201
Woods, Denise (spo) ext 237
Martin, Peter ext 219
Probert, Julie (psa) ext 232

Training Consortium

18. **Probation North West Training Consortium**
2 Candleford Road
Withington, Manchester M2 9JH
0161-434 3049/3039
mobile 017713 214776

Summerfield, Julia (prog co-ord)
Rowe, Peter (pract devpt assessor) (7)

Petty Sessional Areas

2 Chester
2 Ellesmere Port
3 Vale Royal
7 Warrington
8 Halton
8 Crewe, Nantwich and Congleton
9 Macclesfield

Crown Court

2 Chester, Knutsford and Warrington

Area Code 16

CORNWALL PROBATION SERVICE from 1.4.01 amalgamating with Devon Probation Service

Offices

1. **Head Office**
22 Lemon Street
Truro TR1 2LS
Truro (01872) 260032
or direct dial (01872) 265 + ext
fax (01872) 272349

Bridges, Colin (cpo) ext 767
Pascoe-Buchanan, Jane (pa to cpo) ext 766
Menary, Rob (acpo) ext 756
Evered, Stuart (aco/treasurer) ext 758
Jenner, Janice (research) ext 768
Keenan, Alice (external funding) ext 761
Linscott, Cris (proj mgr) ext 757
Belert, Naomi (partnerships) ext 763
Harris, Lucy (personnel) ext 765
Orchard, Susie (finance) ext 753
Overend, Mark (systems mgr) ext 752

2. Tremorvah Wood Lane
off Mitchell Hill **Truro** TR1 1HZ
Truro (01872) 261293
fax (01872) 261311

Levay, Gill (office mgr)

Courts & Assessment
also at Truro Combined Court
Truro (01872) 260691
fax (01872) 260717
Malekin, Shelagh (spo mgr)
Davies, Jenny

Programmes
Cousins, John (spo, mgr)
Coley, Helen (p)
McDonald, Joe
Stanley, Paul
Collier, Maxine (gpwk tutor)
Robinson, Simon (gpwk tutor)

Family Court Welfare
Henry, Roger

2a. The Court House, Park Terrace
Falmouth TR11 2DJ
Falmouth (01326) 313313
fax (01326) 212653

Courts & Assessment
Fisher, Carol
Connock, Darren (p, psa)

Case Management
Bray, Brydie
Murdock, Joanna (psa)

3. Endsleigh House, Roskear
Camborne TR14 8DN
Camborne (01209) 612006
fax (01209) 612551

Davey, Gill (office mgr)
Beddow, Jon (trainee)
Stubbings, Pauline (trainee)

Courts & Assessment
Bellamy, Jane
Lewis, Mary
May, Terry

Case Management
Allison, Sarah (p)
Richards, Mike (psa)
Skinner, Julie (admin)

Programmes
King, Carol
Lawrence, Josette

Resettlement
Whalley, Ian (spo mgr)
Field, Geoffrey
Haslam, Jane
Robinson, Helen
Wells, Peter (psa)

Family Court Welfare
Mallinson, John
Peacock, Leighton (p)

3a. 1 Guildhall Road
Penzanze TR18 2Qj
Penzanze (01736) 363934
fax (01736) 330690

Case Management
Brown, Tony
Hooper, Kay (psa)

4. 3 Kings Avenue
St Austell PL25 4TT
St Austell (01726) 72654
fax (01726) 63553

Jesson, Kathy (office mgr)
Thomas, Hannah (trainee)
Wilson, Gail (trainee)

Courts & Assessment
Ciocci, Tony
Turner, Mary

Case Management
Hall, Bob
Wilson, David (psa)

Resettlement
Frazer, Mark
Morgan, David (psa)

Community Service
St Austell (01726) 76282
fax (01726) 76982
Davies, Gareth (spo mgr)
Bishop, Sue (projects off)
Maxwell, Mike (projects off)
Gomersall, Anne Marie (cso enforcement)
Richards, Geoff (cso logistics)

5. Culverland Road
Liskeard PL14 6RF
Liskeard (01579) 348544
fax (01579) 340277

Shaw, Doreen (office mgr)

Courts & Assessment
Lloyd, David (p)
Montague, Graham (p)

Case Management
Liskeard (01579) 345668
Allen, Graham (spo mgr)
Lynch, Gill
Huggins, Paul (psa)

Programmes
Toms, Min

Resettlement
Stapleton, David

6. **Family Court Welfare**
from 1.4.01 part of Children & Family Court Advisory & Support Service
7 Greenbank Lane
Likeard PL14 3LA
Liskeard (01579) 344844
fax (01579) 344020

Golding, Liz
Jensen, Ellie
Meanwell, Rosemary

7. **Youth Offending Team**
Chiltern House
City Road **Truro** TR1 2JL
Truro (01872) 274567
fax (01872) 242436

Witworth, Tom (mgr)
Myer, Mark (seconded po)

Hostel

8. **Meneghy House**
East Hill, Tuckingmill
Camborne TR14 8NQ
Camborne (01209) 715050
fax (01209) 612595

Pascoe, Nigel (mgr)
Bennett, Mrs Sheila (office mgr)
Coad, Steve (dep mgr)
Aldridge, Kevin (p, asst mgr)
Dyer, Dick (asst mgr)
French, Jenny (asst mgr)
Reseigh, Nic (asst mgr)

Petty Sessional Areas

2 Truro and South Powder
3 Penwith
3 Isles of Scilly
2a Falmouth and Kerrier
3 East Penwith
4 East Powder (St Austell)
4 Pydar (Newquay, St Columb)
5 Bodmin
5 Dunheved and Stratton
5 South East Cornwall

Crown Court

2 Truro

Area Code 18

CUMBRIA PROBATION SERVICE

Out of hours emergency contact point
Bowling Green Hostel
(01228) 340024

Teams in Cumbria are known as Case Management Units. Officers in Cumbria are specialised. SPOs are responsible for specialist officers in different offices.

Shown below is a list of units and SPOs

Community Supervision	Chris Jones (6)
CS	Ted Montague (2)
Courts	Paul Kimberley (4)
Family CourtWelfare	Adrian Swenson (3)
Hostel	Richard Watson (9)
Prison	Caroline Green (10)
Programmes	Pat Herman (7)
Resettlement	Stuart Hamilton (2)

1. **Head Office**
Lime House, The Green
Wetheral, Carlisle CA4 8EW
Carlisle (01228) 560057
fax (01228) 561164

White, Ian S (cpo)
Maiden, Mike (acpo)
Gadman, Alan (acpo)
Brown, Michelle (aco admin)
Quille, Mike (devpt mgr)
Cleminson, Christine (info mgr)
Kelleher, Anne (info systems)
Hartley, Hazel S (finance mgr)
Martin, Gillian (personnel mgr)
French, Andrea (support services mgr)

2. 10 Lawson Street
Barrow-in-Furness LA14 2LW
Barrow-in-Furness (01229) 820870
fax (01229) 834029

Hamilton, Stuart (spo, resettlement)
Montague, Ted (spo cs)

Courts
Hubbard, Stephen (snr pract)
Buttery, Rob
Carruthers, Brian (psa)

Resettlement
King, Caroline (snr pract)
Reed, Emily
Keightley, Ian (psa)

Community Supervision
Fields, David (snr pract)
Anderton, Ralph
Eacott, Sue
Haslam, Jean (p)
McNicol, Pat (psa)

Programmes
Norris, Sue
Kelly, Trish (psa)
Childs, David (psa)

Family Court Welfare
from 1.4.01 part of Children & Family Court Advisory & Support Service
Cooper, Colin

CS
Huddart, Lynn (cso)
Burgess, Alan (css)

NW Consortium
Hodgson, Gill (pract devpt assessor)

3. Georgian House, Lowther Street
Carlisle CA3 8DR
Carlisle (01228) 522333
fax (01228) 512674

Kimberley, (spo, crts)

Courts
Irwin, Derek (snr pract)
Haynes, Chris
Hope, Val
Murray, Phil (p)
Gilbertson, Jean (psa)
McNeish, Jean (psa)

Resettlement
Mears, David (snr pract)
Loy, Helen
Maynard, Paul
Brough, Katherine (psa)

Community Supervision
Kendal, Paul (snr pract)
Bloomfield, Margaret
Farrier, Jill
Kacedan, Alyson
Vacancy
Walkingshaw, Sue (psa)

Programmes
Vacancy (p)
Muller, Karl (psa)
Quigley, Sandra (psa)

Family Court Welfare
from 1.4.01 part of Children & Family Court Advisory & Support Service
Dooley, Penny
Downie, Julia (p)
Gopsill, Ian

3a. **Community Service Office**
Stanley Way, off Botchergate
Carlisle CA1 1RZ
Carlisle (01228) 515994
fax (01228) 511670

Fawcus, Alan (cso)
Dobson, David (css)
Vevers, Paul (css)

4. Busher Lodge, 149 Stricklandgate
Kendal LA9 4RF
Kendal (01539) 723126
fax (01539) 733486

Swenson, Adria (spo, fcw from 1.4.01 pt of CAFCASS)
Herman, pat (spo, progs)

Courts
Helliwell, Brian
Robinson, Jane
Teasdale, Bob (psa)

Resettlement
Carter, Roger

Community Supervision
Gallagher, Ken
Haslam, Jean (p)

Family Court Welfare
from 1.4.01 part of Children & Family Court Advisory & Support Service
Pratt, Mary

NW Consortium
Brown, Christine (pract devpt assessor)

4a. **Community Service Office**
Unit 13, Kendal Business Park
Appleby Road, **Kendal** LA9 6ES
Kendal (01539) 721580
fax (01539) 733130

Clough, Stephen (css)

5. First Floor, Clint Mill
Cornmarket
Penrith CA11 7HW
Penrith (01768) 864928
fax (01768) 891034

Resettlement
Murray, Phil (p)

CS
Hedley, Janet (p, css)

NW Consortium
Penrith (01768) 892579
Davidson, Chris (prog co-ord)
Lear, Jon (prog mgr 'What Works')
Bell de Zarza, Moray (acc natl trainer 'Think First')

6. The Court House, Catherine Street
Whitehaven CA28 7PA
Whitehaven (01946) 64244/5
fax (01946) 590302

Jones, Chris (spo, cs)

Courts
Hogan, Alison
Connor, Susan (psa)

Resettlement
Hayward, Judith (snr pract)

Community Supervision
Holmes Sue (snr pract)
Craven, Michael
Hodgson, John
Howes, Linda (p, psa)

Family Court Welfare
from 1.4.01 part of Children & Family Court Advisory & Support Service
Flynn, Peter
Quigley, Mark (p)

CS
Ashmore, Tom (css)

7. Hall Park, Ramsay Brow
Workington CA14 4AR
Workington (01900) 604691
fax (01900) 603572

Courts
MacKenzie, Barbara (snr pract)
Hallam Davies, Steve
Arrowsmith, Noreen (psa)

Resettlement
Barrett, Vivien
Bowker, Pam (p)
Simpson, John (psa)

Community Supervision
Moore, Philip
Howes, Linda (p, psa)

Programmes
Miles, Clive (snr pract/treatment mgr)

CS
Arnold, Steve (cso)
Martin, Derek (css)

8. 41 Curzon Street
Maryport CA15 6LW
Maryport (01900) 812467
fax (01900) 815152

Programmes
Grant, Steven (psa)
Brinnicombe, Pat (psa)
Chisnall, Lindsay (psa)

Cumbria Youth Offending Team

9. **North Division**
5 Brunswick Street

Carlisle CA1 1PB
(01228) 607090
fax (01228) 607094

Hawkeswell, Fiona (team leader)
Downie, Jack (p)

10. **West Division**
67 Wood Street
Maryport CA15 6LD
(01900) 813531
fax (01900) 812636

Monnelly, Wendy (team leader)
Albon, Audrey (p)

11. **South Division**
Newbridge House
Ewan Close, Barrow in Furness LA13 9ED
(01229) 826080
fax (01229) 824165

Gallagher, Jane

Hostel

12. **Bowling Green Probation Hostel**
90 Lowther Street, Carlise CA3 8DP
Carlisle (01228) 534024
fax (01228) 590967

Watson, Richard (spo warden)
Vacancy (po deputy)
Vacancy (asst warden)
Harrison, Stuart (asst warden)
Schollick, Peter (asst warden)
Thwaites, Ray (asst warden)

Institution

13. H M Prison **Haverigg**
Millom LA18 4NA
Barrow in Furness (01229) 772131
fax (01229)770011

Green, Caroline (spo)
Vacancy
Vacancy
Hutt, Robin
Raynor, Barry
Sutton, Emma (psa)
Tosh, Jenny (psa)

Petty SessionalAreas

2 Furness District
3 Carlisle District
3 Wigton
4 South Lakes
4 Kendal
5 Appleby
5 Penrith and Alston
6 Whitehaven
7 West Allerdale
7 Keswick

Crown Court

3 Carlisle

Area Code 19

DERBYSHIRE PROBATION SERVICE

Out of hours emergency contact point
Burdett Lodge
(01332) 341324

Offices

1. **Head Office**
18 Brunswood Road
Matlock Bath, Matlock DE4 3PA
Matlock (01629) 55422
fax (01629) 580838

(01629) 582692
Goode, Dr Steve (cpo)

(01629) 57692
Campbell, Ms Hilary (aco)
Boocock, Ms Helen (aco)

(01629) 57691
Perry, David (aco) (seconded to Home Office)
O'Sullivan, David (aco)
Allsop, John (aco admin)
Webster, Ian (property services & safety mgr)
Gillham-Hardy, Mrs Sandy (personnel mgr)
Radford, Gary (finance off)
Browne, John (proj mgr)
Marshall, Dominic (research & eval off)
Slade, Michael (info mgr)
Parkin, Mark (info off)

1a. **Training Centre**
1 Institute Lane
Alfreton DE55 7BQ
Alfreton (01773) 833247
fax (01773) 831944

James-Goodridge, Ms Mareka (spo training)

2. **Derby Combined Court Centre**
Morledge, Derby DE1 2XE
Derby (01332) 622549
fax (01332) 622548

Crown Court Liaison
Pearne, William (cclo)
Maguire, Helen (probn asst)

3. 2 Siddals Road
Derby DE1 2PB
Derby (01332) 340018
fax (01332) 340056

Derby Magistrates' Court Team
Taylor, Paul (spo) (4)
Fisher, Pauline (dep divnl off mgr)
Fitch, Adrian
Morgan, Byron (mclo)
Ottewell, Roy
Buckley, Wendy (probn asst)
Francis, Ms Deanna (probn asst)
Rose, Jean (probn asst)
Singh, Emma (probn asst)

Intake Team
Taylor, Paul (spo) (4)
Roberts, Ms Sîan
Self, Mark
Bastien, Ms Jackie (probn asst)

Derby Community Supvn Teams
Derby (01332) 340047
Bocock, Caroline (spo)
Morrison, Des (spo)
Watson, Jane (divnl off mgr)
Barkley, Alison
Carter, Sharon
Dames, Ms Ann
Flint, Ms Lesley
Gandy, Zephaniah
Machennan, Rachel
Powell, Ann
Purser, Ms Alison
Sealey, Lois
Smith, Nicola
Squire, Shirley
Townsend, Kirsty
Turner, Phillip
Ullyatt, Hugh
Unwin, David
Aspden, Paul (trainee)
Payne, Ms Emma (trainee)
Smith, Catrin (trainee)
Burton, Nicki (probn asst)
Else, Paul (probn asst)
Gordon, Marlene (probn asst)
Stevens, Pete (probn asst)

Adult Throughcare (N&S Derby)
Derby (01332) 340029
MacLachlan, Iain (spo)
Amberley, Rosetta
Belk, John (p)
Clarke, David
Dosanjh, Michael
Draper, Jeremy
Ferguson, Tom
Green, Kate
Boyer, Su (probn asst)
Davey, Clare (probn asst)
Lowde, Clare (probn asst)
Smith, Marie (probn asst)

Derby Community Service Office
Derby (01332) 340053
Burgess, Ms Sheila (divnl cs mgr)
Adler, Ms Keren (p, cso)
McDonald, David (cso)
Morrison, David (cso)
Sheldon, George (cso)
Tibbert, Ms Julie (cso)
Smith, Paul (placement supr)
Adams, Robert (placement supr)

4. The Court House, Civic Way
Swadlincote DE11 0AH
Burton on Trent (01283) 221372
fax (01283) 221141

Taylor, Paul (spo) (3)
Emslie, Ann
Henderson, Jean
Tansey, Susan (probn asst)
Wilson, Marion (probn asst)

5. **Derby Probation Centre**
Willow House, la Willow Row
Derby DE1 3NZ
Derby (01332) 361200
fax (01332) 294011

Programmes (Groupwork)
Hodgson, Robert
Rees, Ms Angela (p)
Parker, Ms Susan (p)
Elliott, Gill (cs & persistent offender initiative)
Buckley, Helen (core prog co-ord)
Gillon, Richard (info asst)
Wright, peter (info asst)

Drug Treatment & Testing Orders
Plang, Rosemary (spo)
Graham, Jamie

Practice Devpt Assessors
Baptiste, Ms Toni
Vacancy

6. 3 Brimington Road
Chesterfield S41 7UG
Chesterfield (01246) 276171

fax (01246) 556505

Nuttall, Brian (spo) (7)
Williams, Trevor (spo crts)
Vardy, Brenda (divnl off mgr)
Anderson, Ms Christine (p)
Cornell, Phil (mclo)
Fitton, Brian (p)
Heathcote, Michael
Kenny, Paul (core prog co-ord)
Massey, Michael
Millard, Lynne
Parry, Chris (p)
Robinson-Day, Mandy
Schreder, Mark
Simpson, Howard
Sloan, Sue
Spendlove, Rod
Wray, Ms Shelagh
Egginten, Matthew (trainee)
McCormick, Ms Ros (trainee)
Bramley, Ms Hayley (probn asst)
Lunn, Ms Jayne (p, probn asst)
Northedge, June (p, probn asst)
Small, Chloë (probn asst)
Reynolds, Rebecca (probn asst)
Sampson, Ms Adrienne (p probn asst)
Whitworth, Ms Julia (p, probn asst)
Woolliscroft, Danny (info asst)

Drug Treatment & Testing Orders
Higgins, Jane

Family Court Welfare Service
from 1.4.01 part of Children & Family Court Advisory & Support Service
(01246) 221082
fax (01246) 278118
Coe, Ms Elizabeth (spo) (12)
Graham, Ms Elaine
Jones, Gareth
Moss, Ms Karen (p)
Ward, Ms Janice

Community Service
Hickey, Janet (spo)
Wagstaff, Neil (divnl cs mgr)
Clay, Stephen (cso)
Coupland, Bill (cso)
Rowland, Ms Viv (p, cso)
Weston, Dave (cso)
Freeman, Gaynor (pps)
Lennon, Bevin (pps)
Holland, Maurice (pps)

7. 40/42 Town End
Bolsover S44 6DT
Bolsover (01246) 240404
fax (01246) 241382

Connor, Peter (spo, prog mgr)
Hobson, Ms Teijha
Westnidge, Peter
Birkett, Mrs Laraine (p)
Reynolds, Rebecca (probn asst)

8. 1 Institute Lane
Alfreton DE55 7BQ
Alfreton (01773) 833074
fax (01773) 831944
weekends only

Martin, Marjory (cso)

9. 2d Dale Road
Matlock DE4 3LT
Matlock (01629) 582148/55665
fax (01629) 57872

Woods, Joe (spo) (10)
Chapman, Ms Louise (p)
Longson, Roy
Woodcock, Terry
Arlow, Shelley (probn asst)

Small, John (cs unit mgr)
Beresford, John (cso)

10. Chesterfield House
24 Hardwick Street
Buxton SK17 6DH
Buxton (01298) 25558
fax (01298) 79132

Woods, Joe (spo) (9)
Clitheroe, Pat (divnl off mgr)
Calvino, Caroline
Conte, Lara
Duffy, Cath
Galligan, Ms Ellen
Whitehill, Jim
Jeanmaire, Mrs Liz
Coleman, Sheree (trainee)
Cornish, Ms carole (probn asst)
Cottrell, David (probn asst)
Lee, Ms Catherine (p, probn asst)
King, Lynne (cso)
Ashenden, Luke (info asst)

11. 34 South Street
Ilkeston DE7 5QJ
Ilkeston 0115-930 1123
fax 0115-930 2503

Cartledge, Isobel (spo)
Marjoram, Ms Sandra (spo)
Nicholson, Barbara (divnl off mgr)
Bower, Mark
Brittain, Mick
Cheyne, Jenny

Fidkin, Rebecca
Flewitt, Ms Wendy
Galea, Ms Yvonne (p)
Gee, Ms Di
Gooch, Daniel
Machin, Helen
Mortimer, Susan
Neville, Bill
Penman, Linda
Purewal, Harjit
Riley, Steven
Smith, Ms Jeanne (p)
Stack, Pat (p)
Humphrey, Sheridan (trainee)
Walker, Ms Karen (trainee)
Barnes, Ms Sharon (p, probn asst)
Brown, Claire (probn asst)
Buxton, Vanessa (probn asst)
Murphy, Ms Gill (p, probn asst)
Raven, Mark (probn asst)
Sfar-Gandoura, Ms Nina (probn asst)
Dymond, Laura (probn asst)
Tutin, Doug (cso)
Cooke, Kevin (info asst)

Family Court Welfare Service
from 1.4.01 part of Children & Family Court Advisory & Support Service

12. 12 The Strand
Derby DE1 1BA
Derby (01332) 290214
fax (01332) 292268

Burns, Mrs Margaret
Edwards, Ms Claudette
Tydeman, Mrs Jill
Wilson, Ms Janet

Hostel

13. **Burdett Lodge**
6 Bass Street, Derby DE22 3BR
Derby (01332) 341324
fax (01332) 202089

Ellicott, David (spo mgr)
Cashin, Sean (po, dep mgr)
Woodhaouse, Sharon (p, bursar)
Andrews, Kerry (p, hostel sup wrkr)
Gordon, Fitzroy (p, hostel sup wrkr)
Nicholson, Shirley (p, hostel sup wrkr)
Bremner, Carol (hostel asst)
Burton, Kevin (hostel asst)
Farry, Christine (hostel asst)
Gilligan, Dominic (hostel asst)
Robinson, Fred (hostel asst)
Robinson, Gary (hostel asst)
Garmory, Richard (mentor sup off)
Woollen, Len (mentor sup off)
Sheldon, Sue (p, admin asst)

Institution

14. H M Prison **Sudbury**
Ashbourne DE6 5HW
Sudbury (01283) 585511
fax (01283) 585736

Probn clerk (inc probn visits) ext 477
Discipline ext 311/459

Mason, Glenn (spo) ext 456
Addis, Ms Veronica ext 303
Arthur, Terry ext 455
Beck, Ms Laura ext 470
Beardmore, Diane ext 401
Bolton, Nicola ext 404
Green, Ms Carolyn (probn asst) ext 401

15. H M Prison **Foston Hall**
Foston, Derby DE65 5DN
Derby (01283) 585802
fax (01283) 585826

Page-Smith, Marion (p, spo) ext 466
Cammack, Jane ext 374
Fisher, Stephen
Wheater, Paul ext 373
Hill, Sharon (probn asst) ext 474
Maguire, Helen (p, probn asst)

Petty Sessional Areas

9 West Derbyshire
6, 7 Chesterfield
3, 4, 5 Derby & South Derbyshire
10 Glossop and High Peak
8, 11 East Derbyshire

Crown Court

2 Derby

Area Code 20

DEVON PROBATION SERVICE from 1.4.01 amalgamating with Cornwall Probation Service

Out of hours emergency contact point
Lawson House (01752) 568791
Offices

1. **Head Office**
Queen's House
Little Queen Street
Exeter EX4 3LJ
Exeter (01392) 474100
fax (01392) 413563

Shepherd, Mrs D E (cpo)
Clewlow, I (acpo)
Morris, Mrs K (acpo)
Vallis, P (temp acpo)
Wooderson, Mrs L J (acpo)
Barnett, C (business systems mgr)
Macklin, N (personnel mgr)
Warrick, Miss J (finance mgr)
Annison, K (staff training & effectiveness mgr)
Addicott, Mrs M L (personnel off)
Wright, Miss A (snr finance off)
Cheetham, Miss L (corporate finance asst)
Cupit, J P S (info systems off)

1a. 49 Polsloe Road
Exeter EX1 2DT
Exeter (01392) 218273
fax (01392) 431843

Family Court Welfare Team
from 1.4.01 part of Children & Family Court Advisory & Support Service
Robey, Ms J (p, temp spo until 30.3.01)
Burrows, J (p)
Flack, Mrs R (p)
Johnson, Ms J
Leveridge, Mrs I
Robey, Ms J (p)
Williams, S

Programmes
Exeter (01392) 421122

Bown, G (spo) (based at 1)
Benden, M (p) (based at 2)
Stammers, Ms J (p) (based at 2)
Willett, Ms R (based at 2)
Dawson, Ms L (prog tutor) (based at 2)
Leech, Miss H (p, prog co-ord) (based at 2)

Practice Development Unit
Exeter (01392) 410962

Greenslade, T p, pract devpt assessor)
Raitt, A (p, pract devpt assessor)
Gaywood, A (trainee)
Haslam, Miss J (trainee)
Rayfield, M (trainee)
Steele, Mrs K (trainee)

2. 3/5 Barnfield Road
Exeter EX1 1RD
Exeter (01392) 421122
fax (01392) 434839

Exeter Integrated Probation Team
Mitchell, Ms M (spo)
Clapinson, C (p, spo)
Edwards, R (spo)
Adcock, Mrs A (p, temp)
Bailey, Mrs R
Benbow, Mrs L
Birchnall, Mrs O
Caddick, Ms C
Gaunt, A
Greenslade, T (p)
Leete, Mrs D
Lynch, R (+napo duties)
Maltby, Ms C (p)
Nation, D
Octigan, Ms K (p, temp)
Stammers, Mrs J (p)
Thomas, Ms V
Thorpe, B
Vickers, Miss J
Watkis-Smith, Mrs L
Weeks, D
Vacancy
Wilson, Miss L J (p)
Bennett, Miss S (pso)
Corney, Mrs E (pso, seconded to W Country Training)
Williams, Ms S (pso)

Community Service
(01392) 455419
Moss, D (p, spo cty mgr) (based at 1a)
Rogan, D (p, spo cty mgr) (based at 1a)
Vacancy (cs unit mgr)
Champion, Ms D (pso supvr)
Emmerson, Mrs L (pso supvr)
Trask, B (pso supvr)
Robson, Mrs L (pso supvr) (temp)
Vacancy (pso supvr)
Dan, Ms S (cs proj off)
Wallis, G P (cs proj off)

3. **New Devon Youth Offending Team**
Ivybank, 45 St David's Hill
Exeter EX4 4DN
Exeter (01392) 384933
fax (01392) 384985

Grose, K
Kennett, P

4. 100 Chapel Street
Tiverton EX16 9BU
Tiverton (01884) 254618
fax (01884) 254888

Exeter Integrated Probation Team
Coker, Mrs C
Welland, Mrs S (pso)

5. **North Devon Team**
Kingsley House, Castle Street
Barnstaple EX31 1DR
Barnstaple (01271) 321681
fax (01271) 329864

List, T (spo)
Ballam, Ms S
Coker, J (p)
Marshall, Ms B
Milton, M
Raitt, A (p)
Wells, Mrs J A
Feesey, Miss S (pso)
Thompson, Ms J (p, pso)
Vacancy (pso supvr)
Rayfield, M (pso supvr)

Community Service
Moss, D (p, spo cty mgr) (based at 1a)
Rogan, D (p, spo cty mgr) (based at 1a)
Ford, Ms G (cs unit mgr/cs proj mgr)
Ashford, Ms G (p, temp cs proj off)
Turner-Hewson, Mrs C (cs proj off)

Family Court Welfare (North)
Hipkiss, D

Programmes
Rosser, P (p)
Hannis, Ms F (p, prog tutor)
Knight, Ms L (p, pso)

6. **Practice Development Unit**
Greville House
Budshead Way, Crownhill
Plymouth PL6 5ER
Plymouth (01752) 766327
fax (01752) 766319

Nason, J (spo) (based at 15)
Benden, M (p, pract devpt assessor) (based at 2)
Ross, Mrs L (p, pract devpt assessor)
Davies, Ms D (trainee)
Dunbar, Ms S (trainee)
Glascock, Miss J (trainee)
Hooper, Miss S (trainee)

7. **Family Court Welfare Team**
from 1.4.01 part of Children & Family Court Advisory & Support Service
8 Ford Park Lane
Mutley, Plymouth PL4 6RR
Plymouth (01752) 229124
fax (01752) 254919

Forsythe Mrs P (temp spo until 30.3.01) (based at 2)
Bishop, P
Dennison, C
Judge, Mrs M
Schleh, W K
Williams, Ms J (p)

8. Compton House
11 & 14 Gibbon Lane
Sherwell **Plymouth** PL4 8BR
Plymouth (01752) 672260
fax (01752) 254918

Mitchell, Ms D (p, spo)
Wilson, Mrs H (temp spo)

Programmes
Gates, Mrs E A (p)
Tamlyn, Mrs A (p)
Dane, Mrs L (prog tutor)
Price, Mrs S (prog tutor)
Vacancy (prog tutor)
Peros, D (pso)

Service Delivery
Plymouth (01752) 672260

Fyfe, Mrs L
Gates, Mrs E A (p)
Falkingham, P
Hart, Miss B (pso)
Kingshott, Mrs F (pso)
Sinnott, Mrs E (pso, seconded to W Country Training)
Theisinger, Miss J (pso)
Williams, R (pso)
Saunders, Mrs J (pso temp)
Wilson, Mrs C (pso temp)

Community Service
Plymouth (01752) 672212

Moss, D (p, spo cty mgr) (temp) (based at 1a)
Rogan, D (p, spo cty mgr) (temp) (based at 1a)
Wakley, R (cs unit mgr)
Haskell, N (cs supvr)
Warrington, S (cs supvr)
Tricker P (cs supvr)
Nicholl, M (cs supvr)
Allen, S (pso supvr)

Adams, B (pso supvr)
Bishop, G (pso supvr)
Darrian, Mrs E (pso supvr)
Ham, Mrs D (pso supvr)
Corrigan, Mrs M P (cs proj off)
Caulfield, M (cs proj off)
Farley, J (cs proj off)
Leeming, Mrs V (cs proj off)

9. **Elizabeth Court**
Higher Lane, Plymouth PL1 2AN
Plymouth (01752) 671075
fax (01752) 254917

Courts Team
Lockett, P (spo)
Bennellick, A T
Carew, Ms L
Casey, C (p)
Hopkins, Mrs L
Johnston, Mrs P
Lister, Mrs M
Phillips, G
Sanigar, B (p, temp)
Wooler, A (p, temp)
Taylor-Jones, Miss L (bail info off)
Rowe, Ms D (pso)
Thorne, P G (pso)

Case Management & Public Protection
Plymouth (01752) 671075
Chown, P (spo)
Cookson, A (temp spo)
Roesner, Ms S (spo)
Barlow, Ms P
Dale, Mrs J
Craddock, F
Millin, G
Read, Ms M
Reilly, J
Shirley, I
Stewart, Mrs V
van Waterschoot, Ms L
Bellinger, Mrs S (pso)
Willmott, P, pso)
Tooth, R (pso)
Narin, Mrs J (p, pso)
Patheyjohns Miss K (temp pso)
Orr, Mrs J (temp pso)

10. **Plymouth Youth Offending Team**
Compton House
11 & 14 Gibbon Lane
Sherwell, Plymouth PL4 8BR
Plymouth (01752) 673626
fax (01752) 254914

Grant, D

11. ThurlowHouse
Thurlow Road **Torquay** TQ1 3EQ
Torquay (01803) 213535
fax (01803) 290871

Ruffles, M (spo ptnrship/Plymouth)

Torbay Integrated Probation Team
Clapinson, C (p, spo)
Johnson, Ms E A (spo)
McGregor, I J (spo)
Dowling, Ms J
Durie, D
Vacancy
McTiernan, S
Moore, Mrs P
Nunn, Ms M
Pearson, A
Richards, Mrs M
Robinson, D
Rogers, A
Unwin, M
Winter, Ms D
Wescott, P
Dark, Mrs J (bail info off)
Hughes, W (pso)
Noble, Mrs V (pso)
Randle, Miss H (pso)

Programmes
Torquay (01803) 297322

Swinfen-Styles, Ms M (p)
Wheeler, Miss V (prog tutor)
Babbage, Miss C (prog co-ord)
Lewis, Ms M (p, prog co-ord)

Family Court Welfare Team
Torquay (01803) 200194
fax (01803) 290871

Forsythe, Mrs P (p, temp spo)
Bell, Mrs E
Meteyard, B

Community Service Office
Torquay (01803) 213530

Moss, D (p, spo cty mgr) (based at 1a)
Rogan, D (p, spo cty mgr) (based at 1a)
Drennan, A (cs unit mgr)
Broad, R (pso supvr)
Gray, C (pso supvr)
Harding, Mrs L (pso supvr)
Pitt, B (pso supvr)
Wickham, F (pso supvr)
Busby, Mrs E (cs proj off)
Horsefield, S (cs proj off)

12. **Torbay Youth Offending Team**
75 Abbey Road
Torquay TQ2 5NN
Torquay (01803) 201655

Dubash, D

13. **Amalgamation Unit**
49 Polsloe Road
Exeter EX1 2DT
Exeter (01392) 430321
fax (01392) 427600

Howard, J (proj mgr)

14. **Legal Proceedings Team**
Rogan, D (p, spo) (based at 1a)
Jennings, Ms R (legal proceedings off) (based at 9)
Delany, Mrs C (legal proceedings off) (based at 9)
Gilbert, Mrs R (legal proceedings off) (based at 11)
Taylor, Mrs C (legal proceedings off) (based at 2)
Thompson, Ms J (p, legal proceedings off) (based at 5)

Hostel

15. **Lawson House**
13/14 Paradise Place
Stoke, Plymouth PL1 5QE
Plymouth (01752) 568791
fax (01752) 606815

Nason, J (spo, manager)
Lacey, H (po deputy)
Huckstepp, Mrs M WJ (asst mgr)
Lamerton, M (asst mgr)
Ross, Miss B (asst mgr)
Taylor, Mrs O (asst mgr)
Whiteoak, MrsA (asst mgr)

Institutions

16. H M Prison **Channings Wood**
Denbury, Newton Abbot TQ12 6DW
Ipplepen (01803) 812361
fax (01803) 813175

Janus-Harris, C (spo)
Bull, Ms J
Chamberlain, Ms S
Clark, Ms D
Ingram, Ms J
Jones, C
Kippax, A
Austen, Miss N (prog co-ord)

17. H M Prison **Dartmoor**
Yelverton PL20 6RR
Princetown (01822) 890261
fax (01822) 890569

Metherell, Mrs C (spo)
Vacancy (p, spo)
Birt, Ms J
Burgess, Ms L
Carey, J
McFarlane, A
McVey, Ms J
Parks, Miss R J
Squire, Ms L
Ward, R
Foster, Ms A (prog co-ord)
Measures, Ms D (prog co-ord)
Creasy, Ms P (pso)
Mellows, Ms J (pso)

18. H M Prison, New North Road
Exeter EX4 4EX
Exeter (01392) 278321
fax (01392) 214684
hospital fax (01392) 495339

Douglas, P (spo)
Forsythe, Mrs P (p)
Fuller, Ms M (p)
Godfrey, R
Hodge, Ms C
Mallon, R
Savage, Ms V
Burns, Ms M (pso)
English, B (pso)

Petty Sessional Areas

2, 4 Central Devon
5 North Devon
9 Plymouth
11 South Devon

Crown Court

2 Exeter
6 Barnstaple
9 Plymouth

Area Code 21

DORSET PROBATION SERVICE

Out of hours emergency contact points
Weston Probation Hostel
Weymouth (01305) 775742
The Pines Bail & Probation Hostel
Bournemouth (01202) 391757

Officers in Dorset are specialised. SPOs are responsible for specialist officers in different offices.

Shown below is a list of teams and SPOs

ct central team
Julian Kohn (4)
bft Bournemouth field team
Margaret Harris (3)
fcw family court welfare
Mike Reynolds (10)
pct probn centre team
Alan Yelling (4)
vpr victim & pre release team
Mike Thomas (3)
wft west field team
David Webb (9)

Offices

1. **Head Office**
Wadham House
50 High West Street
DorchesterDT1 1UT
Dorchester (01305) 224786
fax (01305) 225097

Crook, B D (cpo) 224669
Hutchinson, A (acpo field teams, crts, cs, probn centre, effective practice, research & info) 224413
Best, Mrs P (acpo, finance & admin, ete, personnel, training, nvq, it, quality assurance, health & safety, equal opps) 224675
Drew, D (finance & admin mgr) 224670
Curtis, Mrs Glo (finance off) 224666
McCann, Miss L (personnel mgr) 224787
Southam, Miss V (personnel off) 224918
Morgan, A (info tech) 224674
Bowers, R (it support) 224674
Cox, M R (research/info) 224800

1a. acpo based at office 3
(01202) 228006

Rudenko, M (acpo Bournemouth, risk assmnt [inc pdo's], prisons, hostels, resettlement, sex offenders, mentally disordered offenders, ptnrships, accom, youth just, responsibility for crim pract sub cttee)

2. Law Courts, Salisbury Road
Blandford DT11 7DW
Blandford (01258) 452567
fax (01258) 459597

Fox, Beth (devpt mgr)
Mabey, Phil (devpt off)
(mobile 07779 255752)

Kohn, Julian (spo) (4)
Green, Mrs L (ct)
Russell, Mrs J (ct)
Rubie, Ms (vpr)

3. 7 Madeira Road
Bournemouth BH1 1QL
Bournemouth (01202) 228000
fax (01202) 228080

Rudenko, M (acpo) 228006
Thomas, Mike (spo vpr/com resources) 228037
Harris, Mrs M (spo bft) 228025
Dempsey, Ms A (bft) 228038
Dixon, James (bft) 228015
Dunlavey, Jennifer (bft) 228026
Evans, Mrs A (bft) 228040
Harris, Ms A (vpr) 228044
Jerman, P (vpr) 228042
Molyneux, Ms E (bft) 228021
Newman, Mrs R (vpr) 228034
Owen, B (bft) 228031
Porter, Ms V (bft) 228032
Reynolds, Mrs D (bft) 228032
Shepherd, Ms S (bft) 228023
Watkins, Mrs Liz (bft) 228024

McDonald, P (duty asst, vpr) 228010
Taylor, Wendy (accom off) 228048
McGrath, D (psa) 228019
Matthias, K (psa) 228018
Price, M (psa) 228048

4. **Poole Probation Centre**
63 Commercial Road, Parkstone
Poole BH14 0JB
Bournemouth (01202) 724053
fax (01202) 724060

Fieldwork Team
Kohn, Julian (spo, ct) 724001
Chambers, Mrs J (ct) 724068
Hopkins, T (ct) 724067
Jones, Ann (ct) 724066
Openshaw, Ms H (vpr) 724099
Psaradelli, M (ct) 724065
Webb, Mrs Jackie (ct) 7324066
Woolridge, M (ct) 724058
Woolf, Chris (ct) 724056

Zakrzewski, A (ct) 724056
Boyle, T (pso) 724057

Probation Centre
Yelling, Alan (spo) 724051
Feaver, N (pct) 724008
Holroyde, B (pct) 724016
Kennedy, Ms K (pct) 724013
Phillips, Ms E (pct, cn) 724025
Pietrosanti, Ms A (pct) 724015
Ives, Mrs G (psa) 724015
Potts, T (pso, pct) 4004
Francis, Miss M (pso, pct) 724030
Pollard, J (pso, follow up officer) 724059
Shepherd, Miss T (pso) 724025

5. **Magistrates' Court Liaison Office**
The Law Courts, Stafford Road
Bournemouth BH1 1LE
fax (01202) 789468

(01202) 291392 (court matters)
(01202) 291392 (administration)

6. **Crown Court Liaison Office**
The Courts of Justice
Deansleigh Road
Bournemouth BH7 7DS
fax (01202) 430522 (bft)
fax (0102) 430525 (fcw)

Rutland, Mrs M (fcw) (01202) 430616

7. Little Keep, Bridport Road
Dorchester DT1 1SJ
Dorchester (01305) 224471
fax (01305) 225122

Webb, David (spo, wft) (9) 224742
Duxbury, Mrs T (wft) 224467
Evans, Mrs J (wft) 224469
Fremantle, S (fcw) 224468
Humphries, Terri (cadas) 225054
Miller, Ms C (wft) 224469
Ireland, D (wft) 224470

8. **Cygnet Training**
Court Buildings, Worgret Road
Wareham BH20 6BE
Wareham (01929) 553333
fax (01929) 554045
e mail office@cygnet.idps.co.uk

Cooney, Barry (pract devpt assessor/trainer)
Lane, Terri (it officer)
Smith, Kitty (admin asst)

9. Law Courts, Westwey Road
Weymouth DT4 8SU
Weymouth (01305) 774921
fax (01305) 780102

Webb, David (spo, wft) 752606
Cotgrove, D (vpr) 752611
Dawson, A (vpr/nspcc) 752614
Eccleston, Ms A (fcw) 752607
Lye, K (wft) 752610
Mills, L (pso, wft) 752613
Staddon, Ms L (wft) 752609
Tessler, Elana (wft) 752612
Wernick, Ms S (wft) 752613

10. **Family Court Welfare Service**
from 1.4.01 part of Children & Family Court Advisory & Support Service
Hanham Road
Wimborne BH21 1AS
Wimborne (01202) 881416
fax (01202) 840876

Reynolds, M (spo, fcw, purchasing & health)
Dixon, Ms B (fcw)
Jennings, N (fcw)
Owen, B (fcw)
Welch, D (fcw)
Wood, M (fcw)

11. **Community Service Office**
Unit 19, Sandford Lane
Wareham BH20 4JH
Wareham (01929) 556513
fax (01929) 553756

Ridge, Mrs T (spo)
Humphreys, P (po)
Matthews, M (dep mgr/cso)
Dark, N (cso)
Drewson, M (cso)
Jones, Miss D (cso)
Richardson, Mrs R (cso)
Gascoyne, Mrs P (cso)
Goss, N (cso)
Jones, Ms J (cso)
Payne, K (cso)

12. **CADAS**
28 High West Street
Dorchester DT1 1UP
Dorchester (01305) 265635

Humphries, Ms T (based at 7)

13. **Community Drugs Team**
Park Lodge
Kings Park Community Hospital
Gloucester Road
Bournemouth BH7 6JF
Bournemouth (01202) 397003

Ennis, J
Finch, Ms A

14. **Youth Justice Service (West)**
Southwinds
Cranford Avenue
Weymouth DT4 7TL
Weymouth (01305) 760336
fax (01305) 761423

Dolder, J

15. **Youth Justice Service (East)**
Bournemouth Central Local Office
9 Madeira Road
Bournemouth BH1 1QN
Bournemouth (01202) 555844
fax (01202) 446605

Tohill, Ms A
Shepherd, Mrs S

Hostels

16. **Weston Probation Hostel**
(Self Catering)
2 Westwey Road
Weymouth DT4 8SU
Weymouth (01305) 775742
fax (01305) 766510

Harknett, P (spo mgr) (17)
Friday, Ms B (po deputy)
Butterworth, Mrs S (asst mgr)
Goss, Mrs S (asst mgr)
Fisher, C (p, asst mgr)
Hamilton, I (asst mgr)
Koscikiewicz, M (p, asst mgr)
Wallis, Mrs C (asst mgr)

17. **The Pines Bail & Probation Hostel**
11 Cecil Road, Boscombe
Bournemouth BH5 1DU
Bournemouth (01202) 391757
fax (01202) 391867

Harknett, P (spo mgr) (16)
Allsop, Sarah (po deputy)
Eames, D (asst mgr)
Freemantle, Mrs K (p, asst mgr)
Morrell, P (asst mgr)
Molavi, Mrs S (p, asst mgr)
Norton, P (asst mgr)

Institutions

18. H M Prison
7 North Square
Dorchester DT1 1JD
Dorchester (01305) 266021
fax (01305) 267379

Gaubert, I (spo)
Newall, Mrs S (hdc)
Dryer, Miss L (pso)
Gulliford, D (pso)

19. H M Prison **The Verne**
Portland DT5 1EQ
Portland (01305) 820124
fax (01305) 823724
Probn Office fax (01305) 820487

Harris, Ms Dee (spo)
Brown, Mrs M
Hartsilver, Ms J
Henderson, Mrs K
Russell, Ms K
Walker, Ms S (hdc)

20. H M Prison **The Weare**
Rotherham Road
Castletown, Portland DT5 1PZ
Portland (01305) 822100
fax (01305) 820792

Minty, Ms Sharon (spo)
Morgan, M
Stroud, Ms A (hdc)

21. H M Young Offender Institution
The Grove, Easton
Portland DT5 1DL
Portland (01305) 820301
fax (01305) 860794

Leadley, S (spo)
Parker, L

22. H M Young Offender Institution & Prison
Guys Marsh Shaftesbury SP7 8AH
Shaftesbury (01747) 853344
fax (01747) 850217

Th'care desk ext 381/382

Atkinson, D (spo, th'care mgr) ext 374
Harris, Ms D ext 386
Pugh, Mrs L (hdc) ext 379
Garland, Miss S (pso)

Petty Sessional Areas

3, 5, 6 Bournemouth & Christchurch
2, 8, 10 Central Dorset
4 Poole
7 West Dorset
9 Weymouth and Portland

Crown Court

5 Bournemouth

Area Code 22

DURHAM PROBATION SERVICE

Abbreviations:

assmt	assessment
com sen	community sentence
pcsa	probation community service assistant
pcso	probation community service officer
ppu	public protection unit
resmt	resettlement
vlo	victim liaison officer

Out of hours emergency contact number
01523 157154

Offices

1. **Head Office**
Forest House
Aykley Heads Business Centre
Durham City DH1 5TS
0191-383 9083
fax 0191-374 6958/6959

McPhee, Pam (cpo)
Winn, Allison (divnl sup mgr)
Bruce, Russell (aco, inf, resettlement, ppu, pr)
Hill, Roger (aco, com sen, admin, pmu)
McLoughlin Pauline (aco , crts, fcw, yot, finance)
Norman, Keith (aco, prisons, pathfinder, human resources)
Bewley, Mary (comm mgr) (seconded tsde)
Butler, Jodie (psychologist)
Pearson, Dominic (psychologist)

Holdhusen, Barbara (aco, hr) (based in Teesside)

Pathfinder Project
Egglestone, David (spo)
D'Souza, Nikki (spo)
Robinson, Lisa (pso)
Stoddart, Kathryn (pso)

2. **Family Court Welfare (North)**
from 1.4.01 part of Children & Family Court Advisory & Support Service
38 Saddler Street
Durham City DH1 3NU
0191-386 9426
fax 0191-386 6211

Walker, Tony (spo) (3)
Brinkman, Jeannette
Cooper, John
Ditchburn, Laura
Woodhouse, John

3. **Family Court Welfare (South)**
4 Adelaide Street
Bishop Auckland DL14 7BD
Bishop Auckland (01388) 450066
fax (01388) 606242

Walker, Tony (spo) (2)
Hunter, Stephanie
Spivey, Jenny
Turner, Matt
Waldron, Catherine

4. Highfield House, Parliament Street
Consett DH8 5DH
Consett (01207) 502821
fax (01207) 583989

North West Team
Blackburn, Karen (spo) (mat leave)
Thomson, Lynn (spo, com sen)
Barker, Anne (com sen)
Carey, Carina (assmt)
Reynard, Rob (com sen)
Visram, Ann (assmt)
Cayton, Laura (pso com sen)
Joyce, Ian (pso com sen)
Brandy, Shawn (pcsa) (temp)
Thompson, Keith (csa)

5. Oakdale House, Oakdale Terrace
West Lane **Chester-le-Street** DH3 3DH
0191-388 7951
fax 0191-388 1252

North Team
Askew, Sheila (spo, res, ppu)
Buckingham, Howard (ppu)
Firbank, David (res)
McDermott, Linda (assmt)
Ryland, Mark (res)
Tyers, Jean (res)
Trotter, Jeanne (vlo)

Duncan, Lynn (psa, vlo)
McHugh, Maureen (pso, res)
Metherell, Janet (pso, res)
Neale, Gay (pso, com sen)
Proudlock, Susan (pso ppu)
Hounan, Ken (pcso)
Pears, Derek (pcsa)

6. 84 Claypath
Durham DH1 1RG
0191-386 1265
fax 0191-386 4668

North Team
Lambert, Steve (spo, com sen)
Bagley, John G (com sen)
Creaby-Atwood, Ann (assmt)
Charlton, Claire (assmt)
Gray, Eileen (pso, com sen)
Knox, Amanda (pso, com sen)
Hood, Jacqui (pcsa)
Lawson, Rachel (pcsa)
Moore, Andrew (pcsa)

7. **Durham Crown Court**
Old Elvet, Durham DH1 3HW
0191-384 8130
fax 0191-386 2695

Douglas, Stewart (cclo)
Luke, Lindy (pso)

8. Durham House
60 Yoden Way
Peterlee SR8 1PS
0191-586 2480
fax 0191-586 3442

North Team
Leishman, John (spo, com sen)
Thomas, Neil (spo, cs)
Balmain, Wendy (spo, dtto)
Bligh, Carolyn (assmt)
Byrne, Ben (com sen)
Douglas, Lynn (com sen)
Furniss, Paul (com sen)
Griffin, Anne (assmt)
North, Saphron (pso, com sen)
Payne, Hillary (pso, accom, com sen)
Wood, Heather (pso, com sen)

Hounan, Ken (pcso)
Walton, Andy (pcso)
Brightwell, James (pcsa)
Burr, Jean (pcsa)

9. 9 Corporation Road
Darlington DL3 6TH
Darlington (01325) 486231
fax (01325) 382760

South Team
Albuquerque-Neale, Maria (spo, com sen)
Attenborough, Rachel (com sen)
Collins, Helen (com sen)
Hosie, Isabel (com sen)
Howard, Andrew (assmt)
Mills, Alan (com sen)
Place, Shirley (assmt)
Rafiq, Mohammed (com sen)
Ramsey, Marian (aasmt)
Harland, David (pso com sen)
Zacharias, Anna (pso, com sen)

Strike, Martyn (spo resmt)
Liivand, Ann (resmt)
Langthorne, Chris (resmt)
McEvoy, Siobhan (resmt)
Passmore, Barbara (ppu)
Tregonning, Susan (pso, resmt)
Brown, Diane (pso, resmt)

Heath Deborah (pract devpt assessor)

Crosby, Helen (pcso)
Jones, Stephen (pcsa)
Iceton, Julie (pcsa)
Playfor, Duncan (pcsa)
Rose, Eric (pcsa)

10. Probation Office, Greenwell Road
Newton Aycliffe DL5 4DH
Darlington (01325) 315444
fax (01325) 301208

South West Team
Anderson, Diane (spo, assmt)
Creedon, Mike (spo, assmt, dtto)
Hobbs, Sue (spo, com sen)
Hamalainen, Kerry (com sen)
Landon, Ray (assmt)
Cuthbertson, Hayley (pso, Narey crt team)
Green, Sandra (pso, com sen)
Hunter, Beryl (pso, com sen)
Milburn, Susan (pso, accom, com sen)
Sibert, Maureen (pso, dtto)

Howard, Joe
Graves, Isabella (snr prj wrkr)
Franks, Jill (proj wrkr)
Bell, John (pcsa)

11. Beechburn House, 8 Kensington
Cockton Hill Road
Bishop Auckland DL14 6HX
Bishop Auckland (01388) 602182
fax (01388) 458403

South West Team
Auckland, Mary (com sen)
Durrans, Elizabeth (assmt)
Leighton, Rhonda (com sen)
Malaby, Jeanette (pso, com sen)
Makinson, Margaret (probn cs off)

Banham, Steve (pcsa)
Denton, John (pcsa) (temp)
Moore, Andrew (pcsa)
Scott, Rachel (pcsa)
Walton, David (pcsa)
Bryson, Jean (pso)

12. **Youth Offending Team**
(jointly with Durham Social Services)
County Hall, Durham DH1 5UG
0191-383 3478
Armstrong, Val

Central House, Gladstone Street
Darlington DL3 6JX
Darlington (01325) 346267
Casswell, Glynn

Aycliffe Young People's Centre
Newton Aycliffe DL5 6JE
(01325) 372808
Stockeld, Keith

Andhill House, North Road
Catchgate, Consett DH9 8UW
(01207) 291400
Wetherall, Alan

Institutions

13. H M Prison, Old Elvet
Durham DH1 3HU
0191-386 2621
fax 0191-386 2524

Cope, Mike A (spo)
Bell, George
Haberfield, Lee
Harrison, Linda
Hodgson, Jean
Irving, Derek
Parker, Judith
Sanderson, Diana
Vallente, Claire
Davison, Olwyn (pso)
Fisher, Clare (pso)
Hamilton, Diane (pso)
Merrick, Janet (pso)
Mulligan, Michael (pso)
Pratt, Kathleen (pso)

14. H M Prison **Frankland**
Finchale Avenue, Brasside
Durham DH1 5YD
0191-384 5544
special visits 0191-383 2484
fax 0191-384 9203

Probn clerk ext 221
Discipline ext 311, 309, 441, 446
Sentence mgmnt ext 256, 308, 439, 440

Mooney, Jenny (spo) ext 218
Ghosh, Marc (spo)
Anderson, Keith
Booker, Howard ext 450
Gilmore, Maureen ext 451
Hancock, Derek
Marr, Anne
Penzer, Anne-Marie
Pattison, Ian ext 451

15. H M Remand Centre **Low Newton**
Brasside, Durham DH1 5SE
0191-386 1141
fax 0191-386 1408

Probn clerk ext 298
Discipline ext 308/309
Special visits: switchboard

Banecki, Bronia (spo) ext 296
Capstick, Anna
Seymour, Sandra
Cawson, Sheena (pso pathfinder)
Cook, Susan (pso)
Kendall, Susan (pso)
Walls, Angie (pso)

16. H M Young Offender Institution
Deerbolt Bowes Road
Barnard Castle DL12 9BG
Barnard Castle (01833) 637561
fax (01833) 630878

Probn clerl ext 281
Discipline ext 310/311
Th'care office ext 327
Th'care clerk ext 232
Special visits ext 374

Spencer, John (spo)
Thomas, Jenny
Ware, Bruce
Elland, Maureen (pso)

Petty Sessional Areas

4 Chester-le-Street
9 Darlington
5 Derwentside
6 Durham
8 Easington
10 Sedgefield
10 Wear Valley and Teesdale

Crown Court
7 Durham

Area Code 23

ESSEX PROBATION SERVICE

Central Bail Referral telephone number
(01268) 557550

Out of hours emergency contact point
Basildon Hostel (01268) 557550

Essex has a new grade 'divisional manager' who are intermediate between spo and acpo grades.

Offices

1. **Head Office**
Cullen Mill
49 Braintree Road, Witham CM8 2DD
Witham (01376) 501626
fax (01376) 501174

Hill, Liz (cpo) ext 244
Budd, John (acpo) ext 246
Gould, Phil (acpo) ext 248
Jones, Peter (acpo) ext 264
Fisher, Toni (aco human resources) ext 233
McCann, Helen (training & staff devpt mgr) ext 271
Simpson, Mrs Jenny (p, head of finance) ext 251
Wilson, Stephen (cttee secy) ext 252
Piccolo, Mrs Diana (personnel & training mgr) ext 269
Frost, Mrs Dawn (property mgr) ext 272
Gorrie, Paul (finance mgr) ext 222
Lawden, Sue (admin mgr) ext 400
Thompson, Bill (info & systems mgr) ext 235
McKay, Mrs Lynne (communications officer) ext 250
Hayes, Mrs Elizabeth (p, spo pract devpt) ext 267
Rickman, Penny (spo effective pract) ext 247
Juniper, Ms Laurel (spo contracts unit) ext 266
Forrest, Richard (spo, dtto) ext 265
Green, Jim (divnl mgr) ext 340
Jarvis, Marion (fund raising) ext 236

2. Ryegate House, 23 St Peter's Street
Colchester CO1 1HL
Colchester (01206) 768342
fax (01206) 768348

Bamber, Alex (divnl mgr)
Haxton, Liz (spo)
Mead, David (spo)
Woodhouse, Miss Karen (admin mgr)
Allister, Helen
Barford, Geoff
Duffett, Miss Emma
Duffy, Ms Andrea
Fitzpatrick, John
Kennedy, Mandy
Lloyd, Steve
Lovelock, Ms Jo
Napier, Mrs Gill
Pryke, Steven
Rodway, Ms Deborah
Ross, David
Tweed, Nigel
Williams, Bill
Bell, Linda (pso)
Bevis, Mrs Michele (pso)
Cook, Mrs Dorothy (pso)
Evans, Harvy (pso)
Hever, Mrs Helen (p, pso)
Lane, Val (pso)
Paterson, Michelle (pso)
Robinson, Mrs Sheila (pso)

Community Service
Baldwin, Mrs Iris (cso)
Minns, John (cso)
Rowlands, Mrs Gill (cso)
Thorne, Des (cso)

N E Essex Youth Offending Team
Colchester (01206) 573188
Vacancy

3. Ashby House, Brook Street
Chelmsford CM1 1UH
Chelmsford (01245) 287154
fax (01245) 491321

Webb, Tessa (divnl mgr)
Button, Brian(spo)
Johnson-Proctor, Steve (spo)
Wallace, Mrs Caroline (admin mgr)
Brun, Heather
Bryan, Malcolm
Chittenden, Mrs Gloria
Fairchild, Christine
Finch, Ms Martine
Hall, Mrs Joanna
Hepworth, Mrs Fay
Lees, Ms Ann
McPhillips, Anthony
Parker, Ian
Stevenson, Pauline (p)
Teather, Mrs Carole

Tozer, Neil
Whiteman, Ms Eileen
Woulfe, Mick
Clark, Roland (pso accom)
Coker, Steven (pso)
Corbett, Joanne (pso)
Haggerty, Mrs Sheila (p, pso)
Redman, Mrs Deborah (p, pso)
Roache, Kerry (pso)
Skingle, Peter (pso)
Watson, Sarah (pso)

Community Service
Chelmsford (01245) 491808
Cruickshank, Mrs Sandra (cso)
Hill, Mrs Adele (cso)
Jones, David (p, cso)

Mid Essex Youth Offending Team
Chelmsford (01245) 358092
Bird, Lise (p)

4. **Crown Court Liaison Office**
Crown Court, New Street
Chelmsford CM1 1EL
Chelmsford (01245) 358833
fax (01245) 258136

Wills, Andy (p, spo cclo)
Gamble, Ray
Jarman, Miss Gail
Seager, Mrs Marija
Hopkins, Jeanette (pso)
Shelford, Valerie (pso)

5. 13 Market House, Stone Cross
Harlow CM20 1BL
Harlow (01279) 410692
fax (01279) 454116

Bishop, Neeve (spo)
Stiles, Min (spo)
Wolstencroft, Derek (spo)
Prowse, Tillie (pract devpt ass)
Bald, Caroline
Bradbury, Richard
Buckland, Mrs Susan
Chinnery, Tony
Howes, Cliff (p)
Kelly, Francis
Lamont, Alison
Storar, Bill
Dixon, Doreen (pso)
Mason, Frances (pso accom)
Matthewman, Stephen (pso)
Howard, Neal (pso)
Jannert, Natalia (pso)
Sampson, Mrs Carol (pso)

Community Service
Cowie, Ms Lorraine (cso)
Rogers, Jerry (cso)
Sapwell, Steve (cso)
Skinner, Frances (cso)

W Essex Youth Offending Team
Harlow (01279) 427495
Neill, Lorraine (p)

6. Warrior House
42-82 Southchurch Road
Southend-on-Sea SS1 2LZ
Southend (01702) 461641
fax (01702) 612139

Crown Court enquiries to office 4

Dewitt, Nigel (divnl mgr)
Butlin, Miss Carolyn (p, spo)
Parker, Carole (spo)
Werry, Malcolm (spo)
Burrell, Pauline (admin mgr)
Bacon, Mrs Sue
Britt, Therese
Burr, Stephen (p)
Cherrett, Andy
Dowden, Clive
Frost, Russell
Gower, Alun
Green, Josie (p)
Jess, Michael
Martinson, Dawn
Moore, Bruce
Osler, Ms Alex
Payne, Philip
Routh, Jo Ann
Smith, Patrick
Titchner, Colin
Ward, Ms Gill (p)
Watts, Mrs Janice (p)
Brand, Sarah-Jane (pso)
Brining, Mrs Janice (pso)
Coates, Kim (pso)
Collins, Mrs Ann (pso)
Hobart, Ms Toni (pso)
Manley, Sarah (pso)
Laycock, Mrs Linda (pso)
Woollard, Peter (pso)
Arnold, Rhiannon (pso accom)
Williams, Jonathon (pso accom)

Community Service
Southend (01702) 470734
Cock, Jacqueline (cso)
Farrow, George (cso)
Godfrey, John (cso)
Kinder, Richard (cso)
Owens, Jan (cso)

SE Essex Youth Offending Team
Southend (01702) 330464
Dent, Julie

7. Carraway House, Durham Road
Laindon **Basildon** SS15 6PH
Basildon (01268) 412241
fax (01268) 544241

Crown Court enquiries to office 4

Dewitt, Jane (spo)
Evans, Lisa (spo)
Wild, Tracy (spo)
Parratt, Mrs Margaret (admin mgr)
Birchmore, Alan
Culliton, Bob
Kennedy, Miss Mandy
Linahan, Ms Rosan
Marangos, Helen
Meadows, Max
Robinson, Peter
Titcomb, Hugh
West, Miss Kim
Beney, Kim (pso)
King, Clive (pa accom)
Levy, Marion (pso)

Community Service
Basildon (01268) 532345
Felice, Paul (cso)
Gordon, Mrs Linda (cso)
Laycock, Terry (cso)
Norman, Stacey (cso)
Rate, Peter (p, cso)
Sadler, Mrs Norma (cso)

7a. **SW Essex Youth Offending Team**
31 Battleswick
Basildon SS14 3LA
Basildon (01268) 520612
fax (01268) 270924

Peto, Ms Jose

8. Five Wells, West Street
Grays Thurrock RM17 6XR
Grays Thurrock (01375) 382285
fax (01375) 394715

Russell, Diane (spo)
Allan, Mrs June
Baker, Ms Karen (p)
Crook, Harry (p)
Franklin, Mrs Gill
Montague, Miss Mary
Mozzanica, Louise (p)
Phillips, Mrs Lesley
Surtees, Brian
Toper, Sue
Blaker, Sarah (pso)
Horvath, Eddie (pso)
Howard, Jean (pso)
Lucas, Andrew
Stowers, Mrs Susan (pso)

8a. **Thurrock Youth Offending Team**
Quarry Hill Bungalow
Orsett Road
Grays Thurrock RM17 5TY
Grays Thurrock ()1375) 392495
fax (01375) 393376

Lewis, Florence

9. **Family Courts' Service**
from 1.4.01 part of Children & Family Court Advisory & Support Service
7 St Peter's Court
Middleborough
Colchester CO1 1WD
(01206) 540885
fax (01206) 366886

Critchley, Alan (p, spo)
Barry, Mick
Burr, Ms Chris
Coatalen, Ms Jill
Eagle, Russell
Hamilton, Ms Halcyon (p)
Kettlewell, Ms Sue
Lawrance, Fred
Legg, Ms Pat (p)
Jennings, Mrs Deborah
Marshall, Brian
Ould, Mrs Sylvia
Shaffer, Ray

Hostels

10. **Basildon Bail Hostel**
1 Felmores, Basildon SS13 1RN
Basildon (01268) 557550/557600
fax (01268) 558661

Kent, Harry (spo mgr)
Franklin, Arlita (sp deputy)
Bavin, Belinda (hostel off)
Cupid, Kenny (hostel off)
Gales, Annette (hostel off)
Jamieson, Mrs Kathy (hostel off)
Mallin, Mrs Jean (hostel off)
Sturch, Tony (hostel off)
Gambier, Mrs Pauline (p, finance asst)
Wood, Mrs Anne (p, finance asst)

Institutions

11. H M Young Offender Institution & Prison
Bullwood Hall
High Road, Hockley SS5 4TE
Southend (01702) 202515
fax (01702) 207464

Heining, Duncan (spo)
Osler, Alex
Perkins, Cheryl
Leeding, Chris (pso)

12. H M Prison Springfield Road
Chelmsford CM2 6LQ
Chelmsford (01245) 268651
fax (01245) 493041

Probn admin ext 301
Bail Info scheme ext 444
Health care ext 338
Reception ext 280
Discipline ext 311
Special visits ext 329

Scofield, Roger (spo) ext 300
Glen, Gill ext 459
James, Pat ext 299
Cranley, Mrs Chris ext 297
Redford, Mrs Debbie (pso) ext 298

Petty Sessional Areas

7 Basildon
8 Brentwood
3 Braintree, & Halstead
3 Chelmsford
2 Colchester
5 Dunmow & Saffron Walden
5 Epping & Ongar (Epping)
5 Harlow
2 Harwich
3 Maldon & Witham
6 Southend-on-Sea & Rochford
2 Tendring
9 Thurrock

Crown Courts

4 Basildon
4 Chelmsford
4 Southend

Area Code 24

GLOUCESTERSHIRE PROBATION SERVICE

Out of hours emergency contact point
Ryecroft Hostel (01452) 380268

Offices

1. Head Office
Bewick House
1 Denmark Road
Gloucester GL1 3HW
Gloucester (01452) 426250
fax (01452) 426239

Carter, John (acting cpo)
Cryer, Naomi (acpo)
Weaver, Christine (acpo)
Smith, Martin (acting acpo)
Fogarty Tim (business syste & info mgr)
Allen, Brian (it officer)
Bircher, Jane (it training officer)
Leese, Ann (personnel)
Maloney, Debra (finance officer)
Westhead, Chris (office services mgr)
Gash, Brian (Single Regeneration Board scheme co-ord)

East Division

2. County Offices
St George's Road
Cheltenham GL50 3EW
Cheltenham (01242) 532425
fax (01242) 532448

Risk Team
Reynolds, Kate (spo)
Knight, Tony
Sedgley, Pat
Rousseau, Pauline

Courts & Community Team
Foden, Anthea(spo) (3)
Clarke, Anita
Cox, David
Harris, Andrea
Kerr-Rettie, Kathy (pract devpt assessor)
Vacancy

Intensive Supervision Team
Goodhall, Margaret
Hands, Angela
Hughes, Joanna (p)
Pearson, Pauline

Trainees
Fairman, Andrea
Green, Jenny
Gough, Will

Lear, Margaret (education)
Smeaton, Christine (divnl admin)

3. 40a Dyer Street
Cirencester GL7 2PF
Cirencester (01285) 652981
fax (01285) 658835

Courts & Community Team
Spouse, M

4. 118 Cainscross Road
Stroud GL5 4HN
Stroud (01453) 760100
fax (01453) 760107

Risk Team
O'Kelly, Sheelagh

Intensive Supervision Team
Barrett, Keith (spo) (3)
Lewis-Henry, Beverley
Rose, Nick

Courts & Community Team
Buxton, Sally (p)
Foreman, Siobhan
Pritchard, Clive

Goldsmith, Joan (education)

West Division

5. Barbican House
31 Barbican Road
Gloucester GL1 2JF
Gloucester (01452) 426300
fax (01452) 427130

Risk Team
John Bensted (spo)
Mason, Richard
Matchett, Chris
Scully, Mark
Shaw, Mary

Courts & Community Team
Sharma, Ushma (spo) (7)
Vacancy
Cooke, Elizabeth (p)
Kennedy, Catherine
McBride, Stephanie
Sleigh-Smith, Celia
Toor, Haramandeep

Trainees
Mills, Lisa
Wilson, Julie

Jones Denise (education)
Herniman, Sally (divnl admin)

6. Oakes House
55-57 London Road
Gloucester GL1 3HF
Gloucester (01452) 551200
fax (01452) 522181

Intensive Supervision Team
Pearce, Sue (spo)
Jones, Rhiannon
Richards, Jonquil
Temple, Richard
Vacancy
Worsley, Andrew
Windsor, Lindy (pso)

7. Coleford Magistrates' Court
Gloucester Road
Coleford GL16 8BL
Coleford (01594) 837090
fax (01594) 837256

Courts & Community Team
Anderson, Bob
Coombs, Sue
Cousins, Terry

8. **Crown Court/Victim Enquiry**
Longsmith Street
Gloucester GL1 2TS
Gloucester (01452) 426327
fax (01452) 381249

Oulton, Julia (spo, based at 9)
Boroughs, Vicky
Jones, Barbara

9. **Community Service Unit**
Unit 26, Morelands Trading Estate
off Bristol Road
Gloucester GL1 5PL
Gloucester (01452) 426330
fax (01452) 387913

Oulton, Julia (spo, victim enquiry, crown crt) (8)
Boughton, Angie (cso)
Cobb, Julia (cso)
Grant-Jones, Pauline (cso)
Havard, Patricia (cso)
Leibbrandt, Stephanie (cso)
Morgan, Greg (cso)
Purcell, Angie (cso)
Worrall, Sian (cso)
Thompson, Allan (projects)

10. **Family Courts Service**
from 1.4.01 part of Children & Family Court Advisory & Support Service
Northgate House, 19 London Road
Gloucester GL1 3HB
Gloucester (01452) 311888
fax (01452) 386474

Tate, Sarah (sfco)
Anderson, Dawn
Beard, Angela
Moorby, Elizabeth (p)
Penaliggon, Victoria (p)
Pickering-Pick, David (p)
Spry, Paul
Stephenson, Christine (p)

11. **Criminal Justice Drugs Team**
Oakes House, 55-57 London Road
Gloucester GL1 3HF
Gloucester (01452) 551200
fax (01452) 522181

Yates, Ted (spo)
Arch, Michael (p)
Cooper, Anne (p)
Maddock, Claire (p)
McIlvaney, Helen
Ashton, Steve (cpn)
Hughes, John (cpn)
Vacancy
Wood, Andy (drugs worker)
Gill, Dawn (drugs worker)
Taylor, Paul (drugs worker)

12. **Youth Offending Team**
Windsor House
40 Brunswick Road
Gloucester GL1 1HG
(01452) 547540
fax (01452) 551114

Desmond, Lulu
Hann, Kevin
Simon, Cynthia

Hostel

13. **Ryecroft Approved Probation & Bail Hostel**
78 Ryecroft Street, Tredworth
Gloucester GL1 4LY
Gloucester (01452) 380268
fax (01452) 302969

Snell, Christina (spo mgr)
Gibbs, Rupert (po deputy)
Griffiths, Richard (asst mgr)
Hannaford, Keith (asst mgr)
Hill, Susan (p, asst mgr)
Pellant, Christine (asst mgr)
Fisher, Mary (hostel sup)
Golding, Cleon (hostel sup)
Fletcher, James (hostel sup)

Institution

14. HM Prison, Barrack Square
Gloucester GL1 1JN
Gloucester (01452) 529551
special visits (01452) 308218
fax (01452) 310302

Mead, Gary (spo)
Kenyon, Judith
Sivley, Angela (p)
Wadcock, Mike (p)
Baker, Jacqui (prison play co-ord)

Petty Sessional Areas

2 North Gloucestershire
5 Gloucester
3 Cirencester (incorporating Fairford and Tetbury)
4 South Gloucestershire
7 Forest of Dean

Crown Court

8 Gloucester

Area Code 25

HAMPSHIRE PROBATION SERVICE

Out of hours contact point:
The Grange Probation Hostel
023 9236 3474

Offices

1. **Head Office**
Friary House
Middle Brook Street
Winchester S023 8DQ
Winchester (01962) 842202
Direct dial (01962) 842 + ext
fax (01962) 865278

Scott, David (cpo) ext 203
Holland, Jack (acpo) ext 207
Liz Ashton (acpo) ext 206
Pearce, Richard (acpo) ext 210
Hooper, Brian (cao) ext 202

Vacancy (head of human resources)

Mary Kenny (hr adviser, training & devpt) ext 202
Ogburn, Janet (hr adviser, employee relations) ext 202
Rowe, Barbara (hr adviser recruitment) ext 202
Witt, Margaret (hr training) ext 205
Hunter, Karen (hr admin) ext 204
Reavey, Diane (sao) ext 202

Hale, Elizabeth (info resources team mgr) ext 202
Hacker, John (info officer) ext 202
Collins, Nicki (info resources sup off) ext 202
Higgins, Sarah (i.t. & data admin) ext 202

Kirkham, Alex (premises off) ext 202
Savage, Lisa (snr finance off) ext 202
Bates, Carol (finance off) ext 202
Scott, Barry (finance off) ext 202
Townsend-Brown, Angela (office mgr) ext 208

2. Imperial House, 2 Grosvenor Road
Aldershot GU11 1DP
Aldershot (01252) 324288
fax (01252) 329515

Humphrey, Miss Jean (spo) (3, 9)
Alderton, Judith
Despitch, Kathy
Duff, Tony (breach prosecution officer)
Etherington, Kate (seconded to ACORN project)
Griffiths, Jean
Regan, Cliff
Smailes, Alison
Murray, Melissa (pso)
Ward, Maggie (pso)

Hill, Robbie (support services off) (3, 9)

3. 25 Normandy Street
Alton GU34 1DQ
Alton (01420) 84155/88134
fax (01420) 542375

Humphrey, Miss Jean (spo) (2, 9)
Boddy, Pat
Fisher, Claire
Jolly, Ann
Morgan, Catherine

4. The Court House
West Street **Andover** SP10 1QP
Andover (01264) 364411
fax (01264) 335457

Caswell, Paul (spo) (23)
Elliott, Joanna
Williams, J David
Cummins, Suzanne (com links off)

Hannington, Jill (support services off) (5, 6, 26)

5. The Court House, London Road
Basingstoke RG21 4AA
Basingstoke (01256) 464272124824
fax (01256) 812374

Walker, Laura (spo) (6)
Chantrill, Judith
Faulkner, John
Evans, Linda
Lambert, Penny
Roomes, Mel
Everson, Terry (com links off)
Wheeler, Stephen (breach prosecution off)

6. **Regional Resource Unit**
The Baring Centre,
35 Sarum Hill Basingstoke RG21 1SS
Basingstoke (01256) 816004
fax (01256) 357292

Walker, Laura (spo) (5)
Caren, Ian (partnership devpt adviser)
Engelbrecht, Jill
Fry, Christine
Hardy, Susan

7. The Court House
Leigh Road **Eastleigh** S050 9ZP
Eastleigh 023-8061 2163/2923
fax 023-8067 0294

Pascoe, Tony (spo) (13, 21)
Lawrence-Jones, Jill
Hale, Louise
Marshall, Richard
Andrews, Natalie (com links off / pso)

Orman, Lin (support services off) (13, 21)

8. 20 High Street **Fareham** P016 7AF
Fareham (01329) 235888
fax (01329) 825023

Sleeman, Sylvia (spo)
Vacancy
Crooks, Avril (p)
Gagliardini, John M
Green, Jim
Herbert, Lorraine
Lester, Gwyneth (p)
Vacancy
Scarbro, Paul

Joslin, Susie
Winkworth, Jane
Pickering, Deborah (p, com links off)
Starbuck, Theresa (p, com links off)
Burns, Jill (p, psa crt)
Hartman, Jennifer (cso)
Smith, Penny (cso)
Taylor, Peter (cs supvr)

Lloyd, Julie (support services off)

9. 46-48 Victoria Road
Farnborough GU14 7PG
Farnborough (01252) 513020
fax (01252) 370246

Humphrey, Miss Jean (spo) (2, 3)
Briggs, Susan
Hall, Louise
Harpham-Salter, Andrew
James, Rebecca

10. Probation Office
Elmleigh Road **Havant** P09 2AS
Havant 023-9247 3011
fax 023-9249 8275

Hall, Jacqueline (spo)
Blackwell, Sheila
Carnegie, Joan
Dillon, Barbara
Doherty, Anne
Duncan, John (PSO)
Hahn, Colin
Kennard, Simon
Leishman, Angela (p) (Shift Project)
McDuff, Helen
Tomlinson, Chris
Strong, Lynne (p) (Shift Project)
Wells, Andy (p)
Ward, Julie (p)

Richards, Teresa (support services off)

11. **Community Service Office (SE Region)**
Spring Gardens
Portsmouth PO1 2BT
Portsmouth 023-9287 1441
fax 023-9287 1183

Davies, John (unit mgr)
Bareham, N (cso)
Baxter, J (cso)
Birch, E (cso)
Fountain, Richard (cso)
Hadden, Karen (cso)
Hogben, Christine (cso)
Richards, Ian (cso)
Samways, L (cso)
Aylott, (project sup)
Dumper, D (project sup)
Patterson, S (project sup)
Saunders-Brown, Ian (project sup)
Balloch, Anne (admin asst)
Dopico, M C (admin asst)
Stedman, R (admin asst)

12. 8 Sea Street, Newport
Isle of Wight P030 5BN
Newport (01983) 523265
fax (01983) 528994

Kiely, David (spo)
Charlesworth, Brian
Clarke, George
Dugard-Craig, Barbara
Owen, Bryony
Scott, Michael W
Scott, Wendy
Svendsen, Jo Inge
Lagdon, Geoff (cso)
Lewis, Amanda (cso)
Greenhalgh, Barrie (cs supr)
Nelson, Robert (cs supr)
Pritchard, Martin, (cs supr)
Lewis, Stephen (com links off)
Newnham, Francis (com links off)
Leighton, Jenny (pso)

Campbell, Ann (support services off)

13. Island House, Priestlands Place
Lymington S041 9GA
Lymington (01590) 673107/677462
fax (01590) 671521

Pascoe, Tony (spo) (7, 21)
Rynne, Martin
Smyth, Joan
Black, Janet (pso / clo)
Cash, Zoe (pso Lyndhurst Court)

Community Service (Solent)
(01590) 675359

James, Nigel (unit mgr)
Emans, Trevor (cso) (13)
Howell, Steve (cso) (13)
Hartman, Jennifer (cso) (8)
Smith, Penny (cso) (8)
Lagdon, Geoff (cso) (12)
Lewis, Amanda (cso) (12)
Morris, Julie (admin asst) (8)
Spain, Rebecca (admin asst) (13)
Greenhalgh, B (project supvr)
Mothersole, B (project supvr)
Nelson, R (project supvr)
Painter, J (project supvr)

Parker, W (project supvr)
Pritchard, M (project supvr)
Taylor, P (project supvr)

14. Probation Office
52 Isambard Brunel Road
Portsmouth POI 2BD
Portsmouth 023-9282 9044
fax 023-9285 1618

Adult Supervision (26 years +)
Holt, Sarah (spo)
Bridden, Dave
Gough, Dennis
Kirby, Gloria
Plant, Louise (p)
Simpson, Sandra
White, Christine
Woodhams, Sue (p)
Forrest, Jackie (pso, mags. crt)
Newman, Roger (pso, mags. crt)

Young Adult Supervision (18-26)
Skinner, Corinne (p, spo)
Ager, Jackie
Bird, Adrian (p)
Burns, Angela
Coffey, Michael
Deveney, Sheila (p)
Dollimore, Pauline (p)
Sammes, Sue

Resettlement (not YAO)
Mikulski, Antoni (spo)
Blake, John
Cameron, Don (p)
Sharp, Sue
Smith, Chas
Welch, Yasmin
Ball, Jackie (pso report scheme)
Holbrook, Jo (pso breach)
Morgan, Trevor (pso report scheme)
Pitman, Sarah (pso breach)
Podmore, Ann (pso crown crt)

Crocker, Silvia (support services off)

15. **Family Court Welfare Service (South)**
from 1.4.01 part of Children & Family Court Advisory & Support Service
35 Guildhall Walk Portsmouth P01 2RY
Portsmouth 023-9261 1061
fax 023-9261 1060

Meritt, Pam (practice mgr)
Cole, Graham
Haunton, Andrew
Nash, Karen (p)
Phillips, Pam
Restall, Angela
Sampson, Phil (p)
Scoins, Joyce
Young, Sue

Martin, Penny (support services off)

16. 70 London Road
Southampton S015 2AJ
Southampton 023-8063 5011
fax 023-8023 1801

Court Team
Barrett, Niki (spo)
Arnold, Andrea (pso)
Forrow, Bev
Glew, David
Lashmar, Sheila
McAllen, Marie
Saunders, Rachel
Southern, Rob
Taylor, Diane
Webb, Georgia
Hill, Joanne (pso)

Supervision Team
Wiseman, Bernard (spo)
Barrett, Lin
Barrett, Sally
Brider, Heather
Couzens, Alison
Jones, Peter
Moulding, Andrea
Tarr, Caroline
Tovey, Adele
Woodward, Sybil
Chaloner, Jennifer (pso)
Cleeve, Katherine (pso)
Maidment, Michael (breach pso)
Pett, Jayne (breach pso)

Programme Team
Mitchell, Chris (spo) (19)
Beck, Mike
Cato, Len
Robinson, Jenie
Turkington, Genny

Hickman, Lynne (support serv off)
Jones, Lesley (support serv off)

17. **Community Service Office**
Old Bank House
66-68 London Road
Southampton S015 2AJ
Southampton 023-8033 9992
fax 023-8023 5778

Carruthers, George (cs service mgr)
Renouf, David (unit mgr)

Emery, Denis (cso)
Keites, H (cso)
Martin, K (cso)
Smythe, Patrick (cso)
Sutton, Gillian (cso)
Thorndyke, M (cso)
Crouch, Liz (project supvr)
Hansford, Tony (project supvr)
Lodge, M (project supvr)
Nobes, David (project supvr)
Parker, Bill (project supvr)
Peart, Kevin (project supvr)
Adhikary, A (admin asst)
Hassall, C (admin asst)
Webb, R (admin asst)

Northern Unit
Glen, Ray (unit mgr)
Chambers, S (ch, cso)
Fisher, P (ch, cso)
Hesketh, T (2) (cso)
Starr, B (ch, cso)
Wade, P (2) (cso)
Combes, T (project supvr)
Dipper, K (project supvr)
Steele, R (project supvr)
Thompson, D (project supvr)
Bremble, L (admin asst)
Doublet, S (admin asst)
Offield, J (admin asst)

Bramhall, Beryl (support services off) (11, 13)

18. **Community Resources Unit**
The Court House, Leigh Road
Eastleigh S050 9ZP
023-8065 2561
fax 023-8065 0294

Russell, David (drugs work devpt off)
Waldman, Keith (emplt, training, educn mgr)
Hibberd Chris (esf finance officer)
Hopper, Chris (emplt, training, educn team leader)

19. **Young Adult Offenders Team**
25 Queens Terrace Southampton S014 3PR
Southampton 023-8033 1157
fax 023-8033 6592

Mitchell, Chris (spo) (16)
Bantink, Celia (po)
Bawa, Sikander (po)
Burt, Julie
Gregory, Claire
Tyson, Lisa (clo)
Yates, Carole

Goodchild, Nicola (pso)

Hickman, Lynne (support services off)

20. **Family Court Welfare Service**
from 1.4.01 part of Children & Family Court Advisory & Support Service
Meridians Cross
7 Ocean Way, Ocean Village
Southampton S014 3TJ
Southampton 023-8063 0996
fax 023-8023 5597

Lock, Jo (service mgr)
Massey-Chase, Ruth (practice mgr) (22)
Butler, Jackie
Chapman-Adams, Norman (p temp)
Davies, Sandy
Kilsby, Tim
Middleditch, Linda
Moore, Robin
Unwin, Mike
Wood, Carol

Martin, Penny (support services off)

21. 9 Testwood Lane **Totton**
Southampton S040 3BT
Totton 023-8086 2287
fax 023-8066 0314

Pascoe, Tony (spo) (13, 7)
Cook, Ann
Youl, Jonathan
Stevens, Patricia
Pearce, Elaine (pso/clo)

22. Cromwell House
3rd Floor, Cromwell House
Andover Road **Winchester** S023 7EZ
fax (01962) 866228

Family Court Welfare
from 1.4.01 part of Children & Family Court Advisory & Support Service
Winchester (01962) 850012
fax (01962) 851770

Birtwistle, Liana (p)
Chidgey, April (p)
Derbyshire, Sue (p)
Krist, Mrs Pam (p)
Poingdestre, Angela
Taylor, Ann

Martin, Penny (sup services off)

Community Service
Winchester (01962) 861323

Fisher, Peter (cso)

Pitman, Sarah (cso)
Hesketh, Terence (cs supvr)

Bramhall, Beryl (support services off)

23. **Winchester Combined Court Centre**
The Law Courts
Winchester S023 9EL
Winchester (01962) 849256
fax (01962) 870405

Caswell, Paul (spo) (4)
Lobb, Andy
Laird, Sharon (pso)

24. **Wessex Project**
8 West End Close, Winchester S022 5EW
Winchester (01962) 877664
fax (01962) 877670

Swyer, Barbara (service mgr)

Youth Offending Teams

25. **Wessex Youth Offending Team**
85 High Street, Winchester
SO23 9AE (01962) 876100
fax (01962) 876109

Sutton, Phil (services mgr)
Tomlinson, Dale (development mgr)
Walker, Carole (support services)

26. **Wessex Youth Offending Team**
North East Team
180 Culver Road, Basingstoke RG21 3NL
Basingstoke (01256) 46403
fax (01256) 327210

Lambert, Mary (area mgr)
Powell, Grace
Woods, Marion (acting senior pract)
Campbell, Margaret (admin officer)
Groves, Janice (admin officer)

North West Team
180 Culver Road, Basingstoke RG21 3NL
Basingstoke (01256) 46403
fax (01256) 327210
Langley, Ian (mgr)
Griffiths, Ceri (seconded po)

27. **Wessex Youth Offending Team**
(Portsmouth & SE)
South East Team
Darby House, Orkney Road
Cosham, Portsmouth P06 3LU
Portsmouth 023-9237 0013
fax 023-9220 0374

Wade, Sue (team mgr)
Baynham, Carole
Earles, Richard

Portsmouth Team
Quaid, Kate
Williams, Lyn (admin off)

28. **Wessex Youth Offending Team**
(Southampton & SW)
33 Selbourne Avenue
Harefield, Southampton S018 5TZ
Southampton 023-8046 3336
fax 023-8047 0060

Southampton City
Morse, Sue (temp mgr)
Pegler, Barbara
Johnson, Don
Manning, Chrissie (support services clerk)

South West Team
Lewis, Zara

29. **Isle of Wight Youth Offending Team**
62 Crocker Street, Newport
Isle of Wight P030 5DA
Newport (01983) 522799
fax 01983 523175

Abbott, Margaret (mgr)
Snell, Patricia

Hostels

30. **Dickson House Bail Hostel**
77 Trinity Street
Fareham P016 7SL
Fareham (01329) 234531
fax (01329) 284523

O'Driscoll, Paul (unit mgr)
Jones, Joanna (res services off)
Chuter, Samantha (res services off)
Kitching, Peter (res services off)
Pearce, Lesley (res services off)
vacancy (res services off)
Aird, David (night wk sup)
Clarke, Christopher (p, night wk sup)
Goffin, Eric (night wk sup)
Sanders, Deborah (res admin sup off)
Paradise, Erika (hostels comm links off)

Brockwell, Pam (support services off)

31. **The Grange Probation Hostel**
145 Stakes Road, Purbrook P07 5PL
Waterlooville 023-9236 3474
fax 023-9236 3481

Carruthers, George (service mgr
Hampshire hostels)

Pearce, Melanie (unit mgr)
Baynham, Myra (dmin sup off)
Buss, Greg (night wk cover)
Dickson, Leonard (p, night wk cover)
Jennings, Trevor (res service off)
Kamara, Ros (res service off)
Logan, Susan (res service off)
Ross, Jean (res service off)
Taylor, Stephen (res service off)

Mazzetelli, Dianne (support services off)

32. **Landguard Road Bail Hostel**
32 Landguard Road
Shirley, Southampton S015 5DJ
Southampton 023-8033 6287
fax 023-8033 6290

Morris, Peter (unit mgr)
MacDonald, Jim (peripatetic hostel mgr)
Daniels, Julie (res services off)
Fargher, Christine (res services off)
Howell, Jan (res admin sup off)
Langlois, Sarah (res services off)
Paul, Debbie (res services off)
Pickering, Darren (night wk cover)
Reid, Bill (night wk cover)
Stanton, Marion (res services off)

Davis, Kate (support services off)

Institutions

33. H M Prison **Albany**
Newport, Isle of Wight P030 5RS
Newport (01983) 524055
fax (01983) 825827

Special visits ext 253
Discipline ext 312
Parole clerk ext 259
SOTP throughcare ext 331

Turtle, Stephen (spo) ext 289
Christie, Stephen ext 304
Heppenstall, Katherine ext 300
Newman, Mark ext 301
Noakes, Sarah ext 300
Jenkins, Su (pso) ext 317
Strong, Lynne (p/t) ext 305
Tovey, Adele ext 302
Thomson, Alan (admin off)

34. H M Prison **Camp Hill**
Newport, Isle of Wight P030 5PB
Newport (01983) 527661
fax (01983) 520505

Cox, Nigel (spo)
Pilbeam, Mary
Poingdestre, Estelle
Vacancy
Vacancy

35. H M Prison **Parkhurst**
Newport, Isle of Wight P030 5NX
Newport (01983) 523855
fax (01983) 524861

Discipline ext 305
Special visits (pm only) 381
Jackson, Chris (spo)
Hollands, Mary
Janvrin, Jane
Mussell, Doug
Stevens, Patience
Corkingdale, Sam (pso)

36. H M Prison **Kingston**
Milton Road, Portsmouth P03 6AS
Portsmouth 023-9289 1100
Direct dial 023-9289 1+ ext
fax 023-9289 1181

Dixon, Tom (spo) ext 217
Devereux, Jan ext 236
Eyers, Eileen ext 236
King, Andrea ext 270
Ledger, Ian ext 222
Roberts, Pam ext 218

37. H M Prison, Romsey Road
Winchester S022 5DF
Winchester (01962) 854494
fax (01962) 849873

Probn clerks ext 301/302
Discipline ext 308
Parole ext 405
Special visits ext 285

Clist, Terry (spo) ext 300
Colquhoun, Peter ext 443
Gray, Caroline ext 258
Reeves, Danie ext 299
Somerville, Jennifer ext 297
Townsend, Sindi ext 258
Earles, Pat ext 295
Boddy, Pat (p/t)
Beatson, Jennifer Qs, psa bail info) ext 296/294
Carter, Judith Qs, psa bail info) ext 296/294

Petty Sessional Areas

3 Alton
4 Andover
5 Basingstoke
8 Droxford

7 Eastleigh
8 Fareham
8 Gosport
10, 11 Havant
12 Hythe
13 Lymington
2 Odiham
14 Petersfield
14, 15 Portsmouth
13 Ringwood
18 Romsey
17 Southampton
21 Totton and New Forest
12 Isle of Wight
4 Winchester

Crown Courts

15 Portsmouth
17 Southampton
23 Winchester

Area Code 26

HEREFORD & WORCESTER PROBATION SERVICE from 1.4.01 amalgamating with Shropshire Probation Service

Out of hours emergency contact point
Braley House Hostel
(01905) 723975

Offices

1. **Head Office**
3/4 Shaw Street
Worcester WR1 3QQ
Worcester (01905) 723766
fax (01905) 29057

Roberts, Mrs Jenny (cpo)
Johnson, Barry (acpo)
Masters, Julie (acpo)
Taylor, Robert (aco, mgmnt services) (based at 8)
Thomson, Malcolm (specialist team mgr)
Bawler, Tim (property services mgr) (based at 8)
Jones, Sandra (personnel officer) (based at 8)
Bury, Shirley (finance mgr)
Jones, Jeff (info officer) (based at 8)
Cooper, Phillip T (system admin)

2. Castle Street
Worcester WR1 3ZB
Worcester (01905) 723601
fax (01905) 619256

Family Court Welfare
from 1.4.01 part of Children & Family Court Advisory & Support Service
Barnes, Chris (mgr)
Bean, Liz
Brown, Pat
Carver, Gillian (p) (3)
Cochrane, Mary (p) (7&8)
Ford, George
Gowenlock, Fred
Hurley, Pauline
Stephens, Maggie (p)
Symes, Alison (p)

Asha Women's Centre
Worcester (01905) 619669

Saunders, Val (p)
Sheath, Jan

3. **Probation Programmes**
30-32 Loves Grove
Worcester WR1 3BU
Worcester (01905) 613822
fax (01905) 724833

Farebrother, Jim (specialist mgr)
Carver, Gillian (p)
Edwards, Janet
McGreal, Mick
Morris, Linda
Stevens, Dave
Whatley, Heather

South Worcestershire

4. 3/4 Shaw Street
Worcester WR1 3QQ
Worcester (01905) 723591
Crt Office (01905) 723747
fax (01905) 20516

Archer, Colin (area mgr)
McLeod, Karen (pract dvpt, th'care, women offenders)
Wain, John (pract dvpt, pub protection, hostel)
Allott, Amanda (resources mgr) (1-3, 5, 6)

Supervision
Lee, Martin (case mgr)
Ashworth, Julie (case mgr, women's specialist)
Cox, Jane (acting case mgr, Hereford supvn)
Bishop, Mandi
Knowles, Veronica (p)

Williams, Pete
McLean, Paula (psa)

Youth Offending Team
Tooke, Susanah

Throughcare
Haywood, Jonathan (case mgr)
Russell, Chris
Wassell, Steve

Courts
Sinclair, Margaret (case mgr, crown crt)
Bamford, Kate
Kendall, Julie (p, victims' off)
Ramsay, Sheena
Roberts, Glyn (p)
Weston, Michael (enforcement)
Dhiman, Anita (psa)

Community Service
Doherty, Marie (case mgr)
Lane, Anna (psa)
Schwab, Richard (psa)

Trainees
Baynton, Glen
Turner, Robert

Trade Union single-filter (for amalgamation & modernisation)
Windows-Yule, Ian

4a. **Youth Offending Team**
Tolladine Road
Worcester WR4 9NB
Worcester) (01905) 732200
fax (01905) 732220

Tooke, Susanah

5. County Buildings, Swan Lane
Evesham WR11 4DE
Evesham (01386) 765689
Crt Office (01386) 442562
fax (01386) 47158

Pearson, Chris (case mgr)
Brandon-White, Chris (p, women's specialist)
Gill, Janet
Lindsay, Sue (psa)

6. Langholme, 50 Albert Road North
Malvern WR14 2YG
Malvern (01684) 892141
fax (01684) 576238

Archer, Colin (area mgr, S Worcs) (based at 1)
Pimpernell, Pamela (area mgr prisons/th'care)
Baker, Paul (area mgr Hereford & N Worcs) (based at 9)

Staff & Practice Devpt
Smith, Linda (practice devpt admin crts)
Bentley, Mike (practice devpt cs/effective supvn)
Smith, Ursula (practice devpt, effective supervn)
Gilmore, Avril (practice devpt, women offenders/effective supvn)
Wain, John (practice developer)
Fuller, Catherine (training mgr)

North Worcestershire

7. 1-4 Windsor Court
Clive Road, **Redditch** B97 4BT
Redditch (01527) 585152
fax (01527) 596459

Baker, Paul (area mgr) (based at 9)
Aust, Avril (pract devpt trainees)
Godfrey, Maureen (practice devpt cts/admin)
Blake, Barbara (resources mgr) (8, 9)

Supervision
Moran, Paula (case mgr & cs)
Ashcroft, Carole
Concannon, Ignatius
Fergus, Paul
Morgan, Jane
Sealey, Claire (psa)

Youth Offending Team
Vacancy

Throughcare
George, David (case mgr)
Bertram, Cleveland
Tham, Samuel

Courts
Jenkins, Neil (case mgr) (based at 8)
Fraser, Margaret
Hammes, Anthony
Harding, Emma (enforcement) (& at 8)
Cochrane, Mary (p, victim's officer) (based at 2)
Grant, Desmond (psa)

Community Service
Moran, Paula (case mgr supvn)
Arnott, Teresa (psa)
Beard, Richard (psa)
Ellis, Ashley (p, cs sup) (8)
Harrison, Ian (p, cs sup)
Riley, Julie (p, cs sup)
Sikanartey, Ninam (p, cs sup)

Trainees
Chung, Dawnn
Daly, Maggie
Emmett, Rebekah
Williams, Tina

7a. **Youth Offending Team**
c/o Smallwood Health Centre
Church Green West
Redditch B97 4DJ
Redditch (01527) 593645

Dawson, Louise

8. Stourbank House, 90 Mill Street
Kidderminster DY11 6XA
Kidderminster (01562) 820071
fax (01562) 862425

Supervision
Skelton, Dave (case mgr & cs)
Davis, Hyacinth
Vacancy (p, women's specialist)
Akhtar, Azeem
Chadwick, Jayne (psa)

Throughcare
George, David (case mgr) (based at 7)
Mamos, Lynn

Courts
Jenkins, Neil (case mgr) (7)
Cochrane, Mary (p, victims' off) (2)
Greenwood, Richard
Harding, Emma (enforcement) (based at 7)
Berry, Nick (psa)

Community Service
Skelton, Dave (case mgr & supvn)
Bassral, Anna (psa)

TSSU Team
Kidderminster (01562) 748375
fax (01562) 748407
Taylor, Robert (p, aco, mgmnt services)
Bawler, Tim (admin services officer)
Jones, Jeff (info off)
Jones, Sandra (personnel off)

Hereford

9. Shirehall Annexe
Hereford HR1 2HX
Hereford (01432) 272521
fax (01432) 350408

Baker, Paul (area mgr) (7, 8)

Supervision
Cox, Jane (acting case mgr)
Hill, Debbie (case mgr)
Hair, Ann
Taylor, Paul
Chilton, Barbara (psa)

Throughcare
Smith, Liz (p, case mgr)
Bennett, David
Douglas, Sandra

Courts
Powell, John (case mgr)
Holland, Anne
Issacs, Patricia
Wall, Peter (enforcement)
McFarlane, Anthony (psa)

Community Service
Stephenson, Jenny (case mgr)
Mills, Sue (psa)
Wildig, Sarah (psa)

10. 37 Etnam Street
Leominster HR6 8AE
Leominster (01568) 611482
fax (01568) 610672

Wed & Fri only (for pre-arranged appts)
all correspondence to Hereford (office 9)

Hostel

11. **Braley House**
89 Ombersley Road
Worcester WR3 7BT
Worcester (01905) 723975
fax (01905) 617687

Rijnenberg, Liz (case mgr)
Wain, John (pract devpt mgr) (based at 1)
Duggal, Pam (asst warden)
Coleman, Neil (asst warden)
Crouch, Carole (asst warden)
Paul, Paramita (asst warden)
Koser, Rozwana (asst warden)
Walker, Fiona (asst warden)

Voluntary Hostel (100% funded)

12. **Iris House,** 68 Bath Road
Worcester WR5 3EW
Worcester (01905) 353884

Murgatroyd, Sue (mgr)

Institutions

13. H M Prison **Brockhill**
Redditch B97 6RD
Redditch (01527) 550314
fax (01527) 550169

Williams, Jane (spo prison team mgr) ext 300

van Toller, Sandra ext 473
Jenkins, Maureen (psa) ext 473/370
Kaur, Ranjit (psa) ext 216

14. H M Prison **Hewell Grange**
Redditch B97 6QQ
Redditch (01527) 550843
fax (01527) 550178

Williams, Jane (spo mgr) (13) ext 207
Hutchins, Katherine ext 207

15. H M Prison **Blakenhurst**
Hewell Lane, Redditch B97 6QS
Redditch (01527) 543348
fax (01527) 546382

Probn clerk ext 344
Discipline ext 437/378/400
Special visits ext 238

Clarke, Peter (spo prison team mgr) ext 310
Ashcroft, Carol ext 433
Cartwright, Claire ext 368
John, David ext 368
Roberts, Val ext 381/428 (Warcs)
Wilks, Helen ext 381/428
Darby, Elaine (psa) ext 268/433
Walker, Lesley (psa) ext 268/433
McLeod, Steve (visit centre co-ord) ext 313

16. H M Prison **Long Lartin**
South Littleton
Evesham WR11 3TZ
Evesham (01386) 830101
fax (01386) 832834

Chiverton, Steve (spo mgr) ext 300
Belshaw, Lisa ext 413
Clydesdale, Hilary ext 729
Hill, Eddie ext 729
Cramp, Phil ext 413
Foster, Andy ext 729
Grove, John ext 729
Webb, Bob ext 414
Crump, Carol (visit centre co-ord) ext 295

Petty Sessional Areas

8 Severnminster
9, 10 Herefordshire
7 North Worcestershire
4, 5, 6 South Worcetershire

Crown Courts

4 Worcester
4 Hereford

Area Code 27

HERTFORDSHIRE PROBATION SERVICE

Offices

1. **Head Office**
Graham House
Yeoman's House
Ware Road
Hertford SG13 7HJ
Hertford (01992) 504444
fax (01992) 504544

Dobson, Geoffrey (cpo)
McDougall, Carole (acpo)
Allen, Glynis (acpo)
Archer, Mary (acpo)
Ball, Rosie (training mgr)
Kelly, Matthew (acpo)
Vacancy (finance mgr)
Richards, Maggie (p, press & pub)
Moses, Sandra (hr mgr) (p/a)
Riccardi, Lisa (service resources mgr)

East Herts Probation Centre
fax (01992 516900)
Clarke, David (spo)
Baker, Jill
Crawford, Anthony
Fitzgibbon, Wendy p, pract devpt assessor)
O'Connell, Mick
Savery, Ann
Smith, Margaret
Spriggs, Pippa
Smith, Richard (p, dtto)

Trainees
Martindale, Clare
Thompson, Michelle

PSAs
Gordon, Shanti (p, crt)
Hester, Maria (p, group)
Jackson, Ian (crt)
Jones, Cheryl (group)
Spencer, Sandra (group)

Community Service
Dickens, Peter (cso)

2. **Mid Herts Probation Centre**
62-72 Victoria Street
St Albans AL1 3XH
St Albans (01727) 847787
fax (01727) 848892

Tsioupra, Fotini (spo)
Woodhams, Janet (spo)
Bushell, Sue
Cumming, Dennis

Fielding, Kay
Hussey, Caroline
Jeffrey, Peter
Murphy, John
Newing, Michael
Osbourne, Julie
Poulter, Pat
Rissen, Susan
Sakai, Barbara
Urwin, Sue
Wilson, Jenny (p)
Wood, Dilys (p)

Stratford, Jenny (spo, dtto)
Evans, Lisa (p, dtto)

Family Court Welfare
from 1.4.01 part of Children & Family Court Advisory & Support Service
Thomas, Pam (spo)
Adams, Steve (p)
Calvert, Jill
Libberton, Christine
Savage, Margaret (p)
Sivills, Janet
West, Rosemary (p)

Sex Offender Group
Woodhams, Janet (spo)
Adams, Steve (p)
Baker, Jill (p)
Bushell, Sue (p)
Jarvis, Phil (p)
Wilson, Jenny (p)

Trainee
Clarke, Sue
Morgan, Nicola

PSAs
Cundall, Jane (p, crt)
McGovern (group)
Pugh, Lisa (crt)
Rembrandt, Bianca (group)
Sheedy, June (crt)
Straker, Susan (p, psa)
Tuvey, Malcolm (group)

Community Service
Gardiner, Barbara (cso)
Hills, Kim (cso)
Johnston, Di (cso)

Allen, Ann (service resources mgr)

3. **North Herts Probation Centre**
Swingate House, Danestrete
Stevenage SG1 1XH
Stevenage (01438) 747074
fax (01438) 314891

Moore, Marilyn (spo)
Mulvie, Catherine (spo until 31.3.01)
Armitage, Lesley (p)
Cochrane, Graham
Cook, Alan
Holloway, Tony
Holmes, Alex
Jarvis, Phil
Moss, Nik (p, dtto)
Oliver-Blais, Merle
Rowlandson, Vikki
Russell, Rosemarie (p)
Slade, Hilary
Sobek, Ann
Whitehead, Xanthe (p)

Family Court Welfare Service
from 1.4.01 part of Children & Family Court Advisory & Support Service
Mulvie, Catherine (spo)
Farmer, Mary
Sharp, Judith
Taylor, Hazel
Turner, Deborah (p)
Watkins, Phil
White, Judith (p)

Trainees
Majabin, Bibi
Nicholas, Kathryn

PSAs
Ganatra, Anjana (group)
Hook, Douglas (group)
Johnston, Anne (p, group)
Sheedy, June (p, crt)
Southgate, Terence (group)
Toofail, Jacqueline (group)

Community Service
Ross, Hal (spo, cs)
Chaney, Jane (p, cso)
Hayward, Robbie (cso)
Hoy, Paul
Hillhouse, Lynne (p, cso)

Tomlin, Jenny (service resources mgr)

4. **South & West Herts Probation Centre**
16-22 King Street
Watford WD1 8BP
Watford (01923) 240144
fax (01923) 221563

Frayne, Jonathan (spo)
Napier, Mike (spo)
Beare, Alan (p, pract devpt assessor)
Cooper, Sandy (p, pract devpt assessor)
Conway, Judy
Harvey, Kate (p)

Hitchcock, Ralph
Hodgson, James
McClure, Tracey (p)
McNicholas, Katharine (p)
Millard, Jean
Oliver, Cookie
Penn, Linda
Viner, Sarah (p)
Webster, Steve
White, Wendy (p)

Parkes, Lesley (p, dtto)

Trainees
Forde, Verona

PSAs
Ashard, Laura (p, crt)
Cleary, Loredana (group)
Hollis, Bryony (crt)
Isaacs, Susan (crt)
Laws, Joy (crt)
Thompson, Bridget (group)
Woolmer, Paul (group)

Community Service
Egglesfield, John (cso)
Pearson, Tony (cso)
Waite-Gifford, Donna (cso)

Pettiford, Beverley (service resources mgr)

5. **Crown Court Probation Office**
Bricket Road, **St Albans** AL1 3JW
St Albans (01727) 753290
fax (01727) 868276

Woodhams, Jan (spo)

6. **Youth Offending Team**
S&W, Watford
(01923) 229012
Paterson, Shirlaw

N Herts, Stevenage
(01438) 723113
Meah, Janet

S&W, Hemel Hempstead
(01442) 230123
Smith, Nicola

E Herts, Hatfield
(01707) 263686
Perkins, David

Institution

7. H M Prison **The Mount**
Molyneaux Avenue, Bovingdon
Hemel Hempstead HP3 0NZ
Hemel Hempstead (01442) 834363 ext 215

Vacancy (spo)
Brooks, Dawn (p)
Lewis, Nick
Maylam, Chris (p)
Parkes, Lesley (p)
Spencer, Maureen

Petty Sessional Areas

1 Hertford and Ware
1 Bishop's Stortford
1 Cheshunt
2 Mid Herts
2 South Mim
2 St Albans
3 North Hertfordshire
3 Stevenage
4 Dacorum
4 Watford

Crown Court

5 St Albans

Area Code 28

HUMBERSIDE PROBATION SERVICE

Offices

1. **Head Office**
21 Flemingate, Beverley
E Yorks HU17 0NP
Beverley (01482) 867271
fax (01482) 864928

Geraghty, Jane (cpo)
Brown, Pete (acpo)
Pettit, Peter (acpo)
Wright, Peter (acpo)
Wardell, R J (acpo)

Siddy, Brian (aco corporate services)
Bannister, Richard (personnel mgr)
Emberton, Mike (info mgr)
Davidson, Val (ext relations mgr)

Community Justice NVQ Team
Neary, Mrs Joy (spo, nvq co-ord policy devpt off)
Corden, Ms Janet (progs devpt assessor) (9)
Walker, Ms Delyse (nvq assessor) (9)
Jahoda, Paul (progs devpt assessor) (8)

2. **East Yorkshire Team**
54a Saturday Market Place
Beverley N Humberside HU17 8AA
Beverley (01482) 869292
fax (01482) 864936

Scargill, Vicki (spo)
Shaddick, Brian
Zobkiw, Ivan

2a. 4 St Johns Avenue
Bridlington N Humberside YO16 4NG
Bridlington (01262) 672512
fax (01262) 400336

Clarke, Mike
Owen, Mark
Timperley, Mary
Stephenson, Ms Lesley J (pso)

2b. Greenawn, 1 Airmyn Road
Goole North Humberside DN14 6XA
Goole (01405) 767177
fax (01405) 720983

Scargill, Vicki (spo) (also at 2)
Evans, Adrian
Fraser, Bob
Marrino, Donna (p, pso)
Wilson, Sue (p, pso)

3. New Cross Street
Kingston upon Hull
North Humberside HUl 3DU
Hull (01482) 323049
fax (01482) 320880

Resource Centre
Goligher, Marcella (spo)
Margetts, Tony (spo)
Burney, Ericka (p)
Dawson, Mrs Pat
Harris, Brian
Hewitson, Mrs Carol
Kiney, Brighid
Mitchell, Nick
Robb, Hayden
Tolan, Ian
Warner, Ian
Wilkinson, Andrea
Wilson, Gill
Atkinson, Eve (pso)
Billam, Lesley (pso)
Lee, Diane (p, pso)
Sambrook, Mark (pso)

Brown, Jane (sup services mgr, north)

Court Services
Clare, Phil (spo)
Atkin, Sarah
Binns, Alison
Boyne, Linda
Brown, Paul
Carter, Tony
Edwards, Julie
Littlecott, Janet
Tolan, Ian
Woods, Mrs Carol
Elias, Annie (prosecutions officer)
Nix, John (prosecutions officer)
Beeson, Ray (pso)
Burton, Lisa (pso)
Green, Sharon (pso)
Guy, Elaine (pso)
Moody, Geoff (pso)

Drug Treatment & Testing Orders
Redfern, Kate

Youth Offending Team
Ramsden, Rosie
Woodcock, Sally
Harding, Mike (pso)

4. Bean Street
Kingston upon Hull
North Humberside HU3 2PR
Hull (01482) 223072
fax (01482) 225653

Intensive Supervision Team
Beaumont, Mrs Celia (spo)
Adams, Pat
Campbell, Tara
Deakin, Michelle
Hoar, John
Lee, Stephen
McCartney, Sarah (p)
Oliver, Anita
Pearson, Rob
Simpson, John
Westmoreland, Chris
Dent, Pamela (victim support officer)
Gowland, Paul (pso)
Oyston, Sam (pso)

Programmes Team
Neary, Paul (spo)
Brookes, Chris
Oliver, Anita
Daykin, Glynis (trainee)
Billam, Lynne (pso)

5. **Crown Court Liaison Office**
Hull Combined Courts Centre
Lowgate, Hull HU1 2EZ
Hull (01482) 585044

6. **Community Service Office**
Clarence House, Clarence Street
Kingston upon Hull
North Humberside HU9 1DN
Hull (01482) 228456
fax (01482) 588040

McNichol, Ian (spo, cs & dtto) (11)
Morton, Dave (cs co-ord north)
Bahn, Steve (cso)
Hickson, Stuart (cso)
Postill, Bill (cso)
Spaven, Eric (cso)

7. Queen Street
Grimsby
South Humberside DN31 1QG
Grimsby (01472) 357454
fax (01472) 355572

Intake Team
Smith, Sue (spo)
Bolton, Wendy (crt)
Earle, Mrs Maureen (crt)
O'Hare, Sam (assessment)
Shepherd, John (assessment)
Ward, Roger (assessment)
Frith, Linda (pso)
Terry, Marie (pso)

Resource Unit
McHugh, Bill (spo)
Cadd, Lorraine
Hipperson, Sarah
Martland, Arthur
Ratcliffe, Mrs Enid
Troup, Ian (burg action team off)
Berni, Jane (trainee)
Coleman, Sarah (trainee)

Intensive Supervision
Smith, Sue (spo)
Jackson, Robert
McMahon, Paul
Parnell, Mrs Diane
Smith, Janet

Programmes Unit
Neary, Paul (spo) (based at 5)
Beresford, Robert
Evans, Mrs Sue M (pso)

Youth Offending Team
Gibson, Steve

Community Service
Duffield, Paul (cso)
Jackson, Linda (cso)
Stephenson, Patricia (p, cso)

Matson, Mrs Mary (prosecutions officer)
Thorpe, Paul (support services mgr, South Bank & cs)

Grimsby Crown Court
Grimsby (01472) 357454

8. 76 Oswald Road
Scunthorpe
South Humberside DN15 7PF
Scunthorpe (01724) 844806
fax (01724) 289301

Intake Team
Ryan, Sue (spo)
Coulton, Alan
Haith, Ms Andrea
Smith, Mark
Bearne, Ann (pso)
Jarvis, Tina (pso)
Henry, Mrs Sue (p, psa crts)

Intensive Supervision
Ryan, Sue (spo)
Boyd, Christine
Godley, John
Grant, Daniel
Doherty, Carole (pso)

Programmes Unit
Neary, Paul (spo) (based at 5)
Walker, Ms Delyse (p)
Doherty, Mrs Carole (p, pso)

Youth Offending Team
Gordon, Les

9. 98/100 Oswald Road
Scunthorpe
South Humberside DN15 7PA
Scunthorpe (01724) 861222
fax (01724) 289301

Resource Unit
Fridlington, Kevan (spo)
Butterworth, Ms Alison
Chung, David
Harding, Keith
Martin, Julia
Thrower, Keith
Corkhill, Kirsty (trainee)
Middleton, Karen (trainee)
Anderson, Shaun (pso)

10. **Community Service Office**
94 Oswald Road, Scunthorpe
South Humberside DN15 7PA
Scunthorpe (01724) 852220
fax (01724) 858020

Alexander, Voni (spo cs & dtto) (6)

Armstrong, Rob (dtto)
Wilson, Ann (cs co-ord south)
Archer, Kevin (cso)
Benson, Dot (cso)

11. **Family Court Welfare Service**
from 1.4.01 part of Children & Family Court Advisory & Support Service
90 Finkle Street, Cottingham
North Humberside HU16 4AU
Hull (01482) 842153
fax (01482) 876478

Young, David (scwo)
Chessman, David
Clark, Gill
Hamlyn, Cynthia
McCartney, Alan
O'Flynn, Maggie
Sheppard, Christine (p)
Sleightholme, Helen
Wilson, Gill (p)

11a. **Family Court Welfare Service**
21 Dudley Street
Grimsby DN31 2AW
Grimsby (01472) 251999
fax (01472) 251397

Fitzsimmons, Maureen
Jahoda, Paul (p)
Tustin, Mary

11b. **Family Court Welfare Service**
96 Oswald Road, Scunthorpe
South Humberside DN15 7PA
Scunthorpe (01724) 271033
fax (01724) 289302

Little, Mrs Jane
Scott, Mrs Susan

12. **Domestic Violence Project**
Preston Road Resource Centre
Flinton Primary School
Preston Road Estate
Hull HU9 5SN
(01482) 789680
fax (01482) 714011

Hahn, Gill (spo proj mgr)
Johnson, Dawn (p)
Sambrook, Mark (p, pso)
Samuel, Mel (prog wrkr)

13. **Youth Offending Team**
Mylton Centre
Porter Street, Hull HU1 2RE
(01482) 609991

14. **East Yorkshire YOT**
Council offices
Main Road, Skirlough
Nr Hull HU11 5HN
(01482) 885924

Harvatt, Diane

Hostel

15. **Probation and Bail Hostel**
41 Queens Road
Kingston upon Hull HU5 2QW
Hull (01482) 446284
fax (01482) 470704

Vacancy (spo warden) (based at 14)
Goss, Chris (po dep)
Pearson, Rob (po dep)
Card, Jean (asst warden)
Taylor, Donna (asst warden,
Whiteley, Miss Viv (asst warden)

16. **Scunthorpe Probation and Bail Hostel**
Victoria House
31 Normanby Road
Scunthorpe DN15 6AS
Scunthorpe (01724) 289124
fax (01724) 289126

Vacancy (spo warden)
Garrett, Tony (dep warden)
Smith, Kerry
Ogden, David (trainee)
Adams, John (asst warden)
Hartley, Mrs Christine (asst warden)
Murray, David (asst warden)

Institutions

17. H M Prison, Hedon Road
Kingston upon Hull
North Humberside HU9 5LS
Hull (01482) 320673
fax (01482) 229018

Probn clerk ext 301
Discipline ext 308
Special visits ext 284

Wright, John (spo) ext 300
Baldwin, Moira ext 304
Baker, Sue ext 363
Eardley, Ms Yvonne (js) ext 303
Flynn, John ext 364
Haynes, David ext 302
Jackson, David (js) ext 303
Naylor, Leroy ext 364
Winters, Chris ext 365
Burns, June (pso) ext 298

Holmes, Elaine (pso) ext 302
Ware, Ian (pso) ext 363

18. H M Prison
Moor Lane
Full Sutton
York YO41 1PS
Full Sutton (01759) 375100
fax (01759) 371206

Probn clerk ext 028
Parole clerk ext 016
Discipline ext 020/012/016
Sentence mgment ext 152/153/155
Special visits ext 044

Mellor, Adrian (spo) ext 013
Barnes, Alison
Jarvis, Mrs Val
Kelly, Paul
Mowforth, John
Warner, Ian
Palmer, Rachel (pso)
Wintringham, Wendy (pso)

19. H M Prison
Everthorpe Brough
North Humberside HU15 1RB
North Cave (01430) 422471

Ryan, Mike (spo)
Biddle, Graeme
Brookes, Mike
Burton, Alan
Turgoose, Josie

20. H M Prison **Wolds**
Everthorpe, Brough
North Humberside HU15 2JZ
North Cave (01430) 421588
fax (01430) 421589

Sellors, Rupert (spo)
Biddle, Miranda
Cotterill, Alan
Munson, Mrs Kate
Swallow, Ken
Kiddle, Jo (trainee)
Robinson, Sylvia (pso)

Petty Sessional Areas

2a Bainton Beacon
2b, 8 Barton on Humber
2 Beverley Beacon
8 Brigg
2a Dickering
2b Epworth and Goole
7 Grimsby (Borough)
7 Grimsby (County)
2 Holme Beacon
2b Howdenshire
3, 4 Kingston upon Hull
2a North Holderness
3 Middle Holderness
8 Scunthorpe
2a South Holderness
2a South Hunsley
2a Wilton Beacon

Crown Courts

5 Beverley
7 Grimsby

Area Code 29

KENT PROBATION SERVICE

Out of hours emergency contact point
Fleming House (01622 755918)

Kent has the following specialised posts

(vlo)	victim liaison officer
(pso)	probation service officer
(probn crt rep)	probation court representative
(pract devpt assessor)	practice development assessor
(om)	office manager
(csdev/dep man)	CS Development/Deputy Manager
(cs un man)	CS Unit Manager
(gp wk)	groupworker

Offices

1. Head Office
58 College Road
Maidstone ME15 6SJ
Maidstone (01622) 687521
fax (01622) 688004

Lawrie, Christine (cpo) ext 135
James, Hilary (dcpo) ext 136
Carter, Chris (acpo information, courts & community service division) ext 152
Spencer, Nigel (acpo prisons & residential services) ext 144
Verity, Robert (acpo programmes & external services) ext 139
Karen Page (acpo case management division) ext 130
Hopkins, Joy (aco human resources/administration) ext 132
Johnson, Maurice (treasurer) ext 134
Oldfield, Mark (research/info) ext 151

McCarthy, Anne (property/admin mgr) ext 145
Chambers, Pauline (personnel mamager) (p) ext 126
Newberry, Elaine (asst personnel officer) ext 148
Pizani Williams, Linda (acop /Euro Devpt off) (01622 673388) mobile 0802 733657
Homewood, Brian (Health & safety officer) 01795 423321

2. **Employment, Training & Education Team**
Creasey, David (mgr) ext 146 (office 1)
Maidstone (01622) 687521

Haddon, Sally (admin)

Hinde, Jill (emplt off) (Ashford) (01233) 633223

Gardner, Iris (emplt off) (Medway) (01634) 846520

Grant, Jane (emplt off) (Maidstone) (01622) 687521

Hijazi, Hasan (emplt off) (Thanet) (01843) 227479

Saxby, Lynn (emplt off) (Faversham) (01795) 591071

Walter, Justine (emplt off) (Sheerness) (01795) 423321

3. **Training Unit**
Ralphs Centre, 24 Maynard Road
Canterbury CT1 3RH
Canterbury (01227) 459564
fax (01227) 785946
email: steve-kps-tran@freezone.co.uk

Rogers, Stephen (training mgr)
Doherty, Sean (training off)
Vacancy (training admin/co-ord)
Crocker, Alan (pract devpt assessor) (p) (19)
Menhennet, Matthew (pract devpt assessor) (p) (19)
Mackey, Heather (pract devpt assessor) (16/15)
Peall, Jeanne (pract devpt assessor) (p) (21)
Kenny, Joanne (pract devpt assessor) (15)

Programmes and External Services
Verity, Rob (acpo) (01622) 687521 ext 139 (groupwork programmes, public protection, child protection, contracts/ptnshp accom, volunteers, drugs, alcohol, mental health, fcw, equal ops, inter-agency provn)

4. **Programmes Unit**
Ralphs Centre, 24 Maynard Road
Wincheap Estate
Canterbury CT1 3RH
Canterbury (01227) 785944/5
fax (01227) 785946

Ensor, Bobbie (spo/prog. mgr)
Hennessy, Penny (dep spo)
Halvorsen, Celia (prog.admin)
Hollins, Sue
Jones, Peter
O'Hagan, Melanie (p)
Rootes, Ros
Russell, Marilyn
Curtin, Heather (gp wk)
Derbyshire, Leigh (p) (gp wk)
Doherty, Fiona (gp wk)
Holloway, Suzanne (gp wk)
McLean, Carol (gp wk)
Pearce, Debbie (gp wk)
Sharpe, Kerry (gp wk)

5. **Drink Drive Rehabilitation Unit**
58 College Road
Maidstone ME15 6SJ
Maidstone (01622) 687521
fax (01622) 688004

Collins, Pauline (mgr)
Delve-Roberts, Rebekah (p, adin)
Gibson, Catherine (p, admin)

6. **Public Protection Unit**
(inc. Sex Offender Resource Team)
address as office 4
Canterbury (01227) 478508
fax (01227) 785946

O'Reilly, Maurice (spo/mgr)
Sampson, Jackie (p, admin)

7. **Resource Development Unit**
PO Box 212
Ashford TN27 0ZY
Ashford (01233) 840931 phone/fax
~~*fax (01233) 191290*~~

Morss, Pat (spo/mgr)
Treharne, Janet (admin)

8. **Kent Drug Action Team**
c/o Kent Area Health Support Agency
11 Station Road
Maidstone ME14 1QH
Maidstone (01622) 655019
fax (01622) 6550022
e mail: johnjolly@btconnect.com

Jolly, John (strategy co-ord)

9. **Family Court Unit (West)**
from 1.4.01 part of Children & Family Court Advisory & Support Service
9 New Road Avenue
Chatham ME4 6BB
Medway (01634) 815855
fax (01634) 811262

Machen, Peter (mgr)
Wallace, Viv (om)
Barker, Paul
Barton, Janice
Fewins, Gill
Glencross, Lesley (p)
Green, Phyll
Hawkins, Julia (p)
Holleyman, Graham
Milne, Richard
West, Peter

10. **Family Court Unit (East)**
from 1.4.01 part of Children & Family Court Advisory & Support Service
Lesser Knowlesthorpe, Barton Mill Road
(off Sturry Road)
Canterbury CT1 1BP
Canterbury (01227) 763263
fax (01227) ~~764339~~ 763 818

mgr at office 9
office mgr at office 9

Clark, Teresa
Johnson, Margaret
Kearney, Jennifer
Sinclair, Mary
Smart, Tony
Trow, Pauline
Watson, Janet (p)

Thanet at office 18
Thanet (01843) 228727
fax (01843) 291527

11. **Contracts & Partnership Unit**
Elwick House, Elwick Road
Ashford TN27 1NR
Ashford (01233) 660471
fax (01233) 660472

Darby, Marjorie (spo/mgr)
Melrose, Joy (admin)

11a. **KPS Volunteer Unit**
address as office 11
Ashford (01233) 634647
fax (01233) 650187
e mail: kpsvu@hotmail.com

Clark, Robert (mgr)
Greenway, Margaret (co-ord)

Information, Courts and Community Service Division
Carter, Chris (acpo) (01622) 687521

12. **Information Systems Unit (ISU)**
27/35 New Road, Chatham ME4 4QQ
Medway (01634) 310099
fax (01634) 812331

Dowie, Alan (spo/mgr)
Roberts, Sarah (p, info asst)
Wickens, Julie (database mgr)
Wright, Julie (it mgr)

13. **Court Services Team**
Probation Office
Maidstone Crown Court
The Law Courts, Barker Road
Maidstone ME16 8EQ
Maidstone (01622) 202121
fax (01622) 677312

James, Nick (mgr)
Ratledge, Paula
Furlong, Helen (admin)
Kelly, Janet (probn crt rep)
Stevens, Julie (probn crt rep)
Lindsay, Brenda (probn crt rep)
Wilson, Susan (probn crt rep)

Victim Liaison Service
Maidstone (01622) 202120
fax (01622) 677312

Nick, James (mgr)
Furlong, Helen (admin)
Clarke, Terri (vlo) (18)
Saunders, Norma (vlo) (21)
Smith, Di (vlo) (16)

13a. **Canterbury Crown Court**
Liaison Probation Office, The Law Courts
Chaucer Road, Canterbury CT1 1ZA
Canterbury (01227) 819299/819301
fax (01227) 764961

mgr at office 13
admin at office 13

Crabb, Deborah
Stead, Pat (probn crt rep)
Watson, Valerie (probn crt rep)

13b. **Magistrates' Courts Canterbury/Thanet**
Wheeler, Andy (Thanet)
Cover, Tania (p, probn crt rep, Canterbury)
Harrison, Sophie (probn crt rep, Thanet)
Williams, David (probn crt rep, Canterbury)

Channel Ports/Ashford
all based at Channel Ports
Robbins, Janet
Austen, Louise (probn crt rep)
Baldwin, Susan (probn crt rep)
Neve, Susan (probn crt rep
Newsam, Holly (probn crt rep)
Rickwood, Helen (probn crt rep)

Gravesend/Dartford
all based at Dartford
Knowles, Jackie
Blake, David (probn crt rep)
Low, John (probn crt rep)

Maidstone/Tunbridge Wells/Sevenoaks
all based at Maidstone
White, Nick
Baker, Angela (probn crt rep)
Beer, Karen (probn crt rep)
Knowles, Kim (probn crt rep)
Randall, Kirsty (probn crt rep)

Medway/Swale
Medway
Samuda, Evonne
Armer, Sue (probn crt rep)
Ravate, Dawn (probn crt rep)

Swale
Thornton, Emma (probn crt rep)

14. **County Community Service**
Ralphs Centre, 24 Maynard Road
Wincheap Estate
Canterbury CT1 3RH
phone & fax (01227) 780420

Taylor, Anne (mgr)
Adelsberg, Sarah (cs dev/devpt mgr)
Lee, Carol (admin)

Canterbury/Thanet
Canterbury
Salisbury, Tim (cs unit mgr)
Mitchell, Wendy (cso)
Nicholas, Bill (pso)

Thanet
Onions, John (pso)
Stacey, June (pso)

VQ Co-Ordinator
Jefferies, John
Thanet (01843) 227479

Channel Ports/Ashford
Channel Ports
Cullen, Stuart (cs unit mgr)
Almond, Derek (cso)
Howes, Winston (cso)
Ledley, Graham (pso)

Ashford
Medlock, Pam (cso)

Dartford/Gravesham/Tonbridge
Dartford
Vacancy (cs unit mgr)
Bailey, Vic (cso) Dartford
Cowell, Ernie (cso) Dartford

Tonbridge
Farrall, Joan (cso)
Jenkinson, Linda (cso)
McLaren, Kenneth (pso)

Maidstone/Swale
Maidstone
Fox, Chris (cs unit mgr)
Berry, Jayne (cso)
Walmsley, Chris (pso)

Swale
Hughes, Jerry (cso)
Foster, Gary (pso)

Medway
all based at Medway
Hockley, Rita (cs unit mgr)
Reeves, Tim (cso)
Waters, Trevor (cso)
Youseman, Janice (p, cso)

Case Management Division (CMD)
Karen Page acpo (01622) 687521
Cook, Mike (p, dep.acpo, cmd) (01795) 423321/2

15. 24 Maynard Road
Wincheap Estate,
Canterbury CT1 3RH
Canterbury (01227) 769345
fax (01227) 764339

McCarthy, Jim (spo)
Tinkler, Phyl (office mgr)
Callister, Andy
Eyre, Colin
Fyles, Susan
Gillon, Anne (p, sort)
Hartley, Alan
Kenny, Joanne (pract devpt assessor)
Raho, David
Williams, Sue
Birkin, Lavinia (p, pso)
Buckett, Karen (pso)
Curteis, Michael (pso)
Groves, Val (pso)
Lucas, Liz (pso)

16. **Channel Ports Team**
Folkestone and Dover offices have been amalgamated. All administrative work is based at Folkestone. All telephone calls for officers covering Dover should be routed through the Channel Ports Admin Centre at Folkestone, although faxes should be sent direct on the numbers given.

The Law Courts, Castle Hill Avenue
Folkestone CT20 2DH
Folkestone (01303) 851140
fax (01303) 248379 or (01303) 221277

Maybrook House, Queens Gardens
Dover CT17 9AH
Dover (01304) 851140
fax (01304) 215561

Down, Christine (spo)
Barry, John (dep.spo)
Morton, Susie (dep.spo)
Redman, Julia (om)
Ashmore, Susan
Atterton, Wendy
Beed, Andrea
Bratton, Jane (p)
Gough, Johanna
Knapton, Christina
Lane, Anne
Laslett, Jim
Mackey, Heather (p, pract devpt assessor)
Martin, Pam
Connolly, Jennifer (trainee)
Goring, Stephen (trainee)
Rhodes, Kerry (trainee)
Young, Stephanie (trainee)
Smith, Diane (vlo)
Batts, Finola (p, pso)
Cadby, Linda (pso)
Graham, Robert (pso)
Hayward, Anna (pso)
Smith, Amanda (pso)
Sprinks, Jill (pso)
Stabler, Jim (pso)
Stringer, Robert (pso)
Robbins, Janet (po, mag crt)

17. **Swale Team**
Sittingbourne, Faversham & Sheerness teams have been amalgamated. All admin work is based at Sittingbourne. All telephone calls and faxes should be routed through the Admin Centre at Sittingbourne.

Thames House, Roman Square
Sittingbourne ME10 4BJ
Sittingbourne (01795) 423321/2
fax (01795) 474251

118a West Street
Faversham ME13 7UE
fax (01795) 530454

46 High Street
Sheerness ME12 1NL
fax (01795) 663240

Cook, Mike (spo)
Johnston, Mark (dep.spo)
Homewood, Cindy (om)
Bywater, Elizabeth
Cormack, Lynda
Gillon, Anne (p, sort)
Myles, Bridget
Smith, Georgina (p)
Topsom, David
Walmsley, Tina
Brown, Deborah (pso)
De Caires, Christine (pso)
Dummott, Karen (pso)
Shaw, Liz (pso)
Thorpe, Donna (pso)

18. **Thanet Probation Office**
38/40 Grosvenor Place
Margate CT9 1UW
Thanet (01843) 228727
fax (01843) 291527

Baumbach, Sue (spo)
Sahagian, Karen (om)
Goldfinch, Sandra (p) (admin)
Cox, Deborah (p)
Dalby, Carol
Gilbert, John
Goulbourne, Theresa (p) (sort)
Lister, Jane
Puce, Eriks
Rees, Sarah (p)
Treacy, Ann
Clarke, Terry (vlo)
Brackley, Amanda (pso)
Evenden, Colin (pso)
Kane, Sarah (pso)
Keeling, Siobhan (pso)
Neaves, Michelle (pso)
Smith, Lorraine (p, pso)

19. **Medway Team**
27-35 New Road
Chatham ME4 4QQ
Medway (01634) 849284
fax (01634) 812331

Hawkins, Hugh (spo)
Edgar, Jeanette (dep.spo)
Morgan, Ian (dep.spo)

Quadling, Hazel (om)
Beighton, Robin
Boulton, Chris (p)
Crocker, Alan (pract devpt assessor)
Glen, Andrew
Griffiths-Moore, William
Hurwitz, Liz (p)
Jefferies, Roy
Kelsey Bourne, Cherith
Kramer, Julie
Louch, Debbie
Loughran, Pamela
Lovell, Christine (p)
Menhennet, Matthew (pract devpt assessor)
Metcalfe, Julie
Morgan, Gail
Stockle, Anthony
Thorne, Tracy
Ball, Clare (trainee)
Blaker, Sarah (trainee)
Dare, Christopher (trainee)
Thomson Kelly (trainee)
Alderson-Rice, Nicholas (pso)
Eva, Diane (pso)
Fennell, Jill (p) (pso)
Galvin, Patricia (pso)
Hunter, Karen (p) (pso)
Jemmett, Trudie (pso)
Tremain, Julie (pso)

20. **Maidstone Team**
56 College Road
Maidstone ME15 6SJ
Maidstone (01622) 687521
fax (01622) 661653

Penny, Simon (spo)
Smith, Jan (om)
Binning, Suki
Channon, Jim
Craven, Tim (sort)
Derby, Ann
Leigh, John
Mead, Henry
Nicolaides, Michael
O'Donoghue, Mike
Sawyer, Michael (p)
Willis, Sue
Hill, Ram (trainee)
Tindall, Pam (trainee)
Birdy, Eimear (pso)
Collier, Helen (pso)
Massey, Christine (pso)
Robinson, Carol (pso)
Town, Heather (pso)

North West Kent

21. St Lawrence House
48a West Hill, Dartford DA1 2EU
Dartford (01322) 289616
fax (01322) 292651

spo at office 22
office mgr at office 22

Brown, Stuart
Campbell, Henry (sort)
Harris, Sonia
Peall, Jeanne (pract devpt assessor)
Ralph, Susan
Thomas, Francella
Oliver, Trudie (trainee)
King, Matthew (trainee)
Langridge, Claire (pso)
McDonald, Iris (pso)
Povey, Ginny (pso)

22. 6/11 High Street
Gravesend DA11 0BQ
Gravesend (01474) 569546
fax (01474) 335146

Carr, Susie (spo)
Imison, Carol (om)
Dold, Gavin
Goldspring, Joanne
Ilyas, Sarah (trainee)
Goddard, Julie (pso)
Lloyd, Nicola (p, pso)

Weald

23. Olwen House, Quarry Hill Road
Tonbridge TN9 2RH
Tonbridge (01732) 351244
fax (01732) 770546

Vacancy (spo)
Preston, Helen (dep spo)
Gain, Tracy (om)
Cairns, Sarah
Coley, David
Knight, Jane
Nettleton, Terry
Prevost, Josephine
Bassett, Linda (pso)
Kilhoffer, Delphine (pso)
Sutherland, Alison (pso)

24. Elwick House, Elwick Road
Ashford TN23 1NR
Ashford (01233) 656500
fax (01233) 647459

spo at office 23

office mgr at office 23
dep spo at office 23

Bainbridge, Sue (p)
Bennett, Peter
Owen, Vicky
Stevens, Jane (p)
Williams, Colin (sort)
Grace, Hedley (pso)
Jones, Romi (pso)
Rasmussen, Nichola (pso)

25. **SORT**
Top Floor, Ralphs Centre
24 Maynard Road, Wincheap Estate
Canterbury CT1 3RH
Canterbury (01227) 478508
fax (01227) 785946

O'Reilly, Maurice (spo/mgr)
Sampson, Jackie (p, admin)
Campbell, Henry (Dartford) (21)
Craven, Tim (Maidstone/Medway) (19,20)
Croft, Colin (Channel Ports) (16)
Gillon, Anne (Canterbury/Swale) (15,17)
Goulbourne, Theresa (Thanet) (18)
Williams, Colin (Medway) (19)

26. **Youth Offending Teams**

East Kent

a. Apollo House, Chapel Place
Ramsgate CT11 9SA
Thanet (01843) 587976
fax (01843) 590009

Fisher, Louise

b. Avenue of Remembrance
Sittingbourne ME10 4DD
Sittingbourne (01795) 473333
fax (01795) 420016

Cockell, Richard

Mid Kent

c. Bishops Terrace, Bishops Way
Maidstone ME14 1LA
Maidstone (01622) 691640
fax (01622) 663928

Darling, Jane

d. Queen's House, Guildhall Street
Folkestone CT20 1DX
Folkestone (01303) 253476
fax (01303) 224329

Conway, Annette

West Kent

e. Joynes House, New Road
Gravesend DA11 0AT
Gravesend (01474) 544366
fax (01474) 544569

Vacancy

f. Social Services Dept,
Croft House, East Street
Tonbridge TN9 1HP
Tonbridge (01732) 362442
fax (01732) 352733

Richmond, Isobel

Medway Area

g. The Family and Adolescent Centre
67 Balfour Rd, **Chatham** ME4 6QU
Medway (01634) 818753
fax (01634) 849660

Birkin, Andy
Manktelow, Melanie (pso)

27 **Effectiveness Unit**
address as office 12
Medway (01634) 310073
fax (01634) 812331

Coupland, David (mgr)
Crozier, Sonia (p, 1 day pw)

Prisons & Residential Services
Spencer, Nigel (acpo) (01622) 687521

28. **Fleming House Probation & Bail Hostel**
32 Tonbridge Road
Maidstone ME16 8SH
Maidstone (01622) 755918
fax (01622) 674809

Walsh, Cynthia (spo mgr)
Wreford, Kevin (dep. mgr)
Robinson, Danny (sup.svcs.mgr)
Burlton, Joanne (asst mgr)
Campbell, Glenna (asst mgr)
Curtis, Joanne (asst mgr)
McGrath, Richard (ass mgr)

29. HM Prison/Detainee Centre,
1 Fort Road
Rochester ME1 3QS
Medway (01634) 838100
fax (01634) 838101

Probn fax (01634) 826653
Probn clerk (01634) 838273
Discipline (01634) 838211
Special visits (01634) 838237

Revis, Malcolm (spo) (01634) 838267
French, Barbara (01634) 838269
Knight, Kathy (01634) 838268
Harris, Steve (bail info off) (01634) 838297

30. HM Prison **Standford Hill**
Church Road, Eastchurch
Sheerness ME12 4AA
Eastchurch (01795) 880041
fax (01795) 880041

Probn clerk ext 298
Discipline ext 309

spo at HMP Swaleside
Cunningham, Mike ext 278
Peel, Steve ext 278
Moon, Donna (pso) ext 300

31. HM Prison, County Road
Maidstone ME14 1UZ
Maidstone (01622) 755611
fax (01622) 691021

Throughcare Clerks ext 269/302

Crozier, Sonia (spo)
Bailey, Ross
Dance Matsutani, Ken
Flay, Helen
Weeks, Barry
Jackson, Vanessa (pso)
Ling, Teena (pso)
Rollinson, Jane (pso)

32. HM Prison & Young Offenders' Institution **East Sutton Park**
Sutton Valence
Maidstone ME17 3DF
Maidstone (01622) 842711
fax (01622) 842636

Probn clerk ext 304
Legal Visits ext 254

spo at HMP Cookham Wood
Dix, Jacqueline
Fairhurst, Jandy (pso)

33. HM Prison
46 Longport **Canterbury** CT1 1PJ
Canterbury (01227) 762244
fax (01227) 785520

Probn Clerk ext 301
Discipline ext 309
Legal Visits 01227 477071

Gray, Colin (spo th'care mgr) ext 300
Bourne, Sandra ext 254
O'Grady, Jo ext 328
Scott, Raymond (p, bail info off) ext 435
bail info fax (01227) 785520

Kent Area Prisons Drug Team
based at HMP Canterbury
Cooke, Geoff (area drug co-ord) ext 204

34. HM Young Offenders' Institution
The Citadel, Western Heights
Dover CT17 9DR
Dover (01304) 203848
fax (01304) 215165

Probn clerk ext 404
Special visits booked through units:
Deal Unit ext 384
Hastings Unit ext 379
Romney Unit ext 375
Sandwich Unit ext 372
Rye Unit ext 389

Gorringe, Radley (spo) ext 435
Ryder, Anne
Duncan, Lynn (pso)

35. HM Prison **Blantyre House**
Goudhurst, Cranbrook TN17 2NH
Goudhurst (01580) 211367
fax (01580) 211060

spo at HMP Maidstone
Harper, Willie

36. HM Prison **Cookham Wood**
Rochester ME1 3LU
Medway (01634) 814981
fax (01634) 828921

Discipline ext 308
Special visits: switchboard

McGarry, Kevin (spo) ext 296
Emes, Jenny ext 299
Kirk, Johanna ext 285
Turner, Janet (p) (temp)

37. HM Prison **Swaleside**
Eastchurch, Sheerness ME12 4AX
Eastchurch (01795) 884100
Direct dial (01795) 88+ ext
fax (01795) 884200

Probn clerk ext 4103
Discipline ext 4154
Special visits ext 4028

Fearns, Frank (spo) ext 4102
Allinson, Barry (p) ext 4137
Chilton, Chris ext 4183
Costen, Sheelah ext 4137
Hooker, Michaela ext 4137

38. HM Prison **Elmley**
Church Road, Eastchurch
Isle of Sheppey ME12 4AY
Eastchurch (01795) 880808
fax (01795) 880536

Th'care clerks inmate's surname:
a-c ext 221
d-h ext 220
i-m ext 278
n-s ext 317
t-z ext 288
All visits 01795 880442

Kadir, Tracey (spo) ext 206
Batchelor, Gillian
Cox, Martin
Hooper, Laura
Parsons, Andrea
Croucher, Hazel (pso)
Ince, Donna (p, bail info off) ext 371
bail info fax (01795) 880140

39. **Canterbury Prison/KPS Partnership**
The Visitors Centre
15 St Martin's Terrace
Canterbury CT1 1PJ
Canterbury (01227) 479105
fax (01227) 479102

Joint project managed by Kent Probation Service
HMP Canterbury & HMP Elmley

Gray, Colin (spo) (based at 33)
Kadir, Tracey (mgr) (based at 38)
Pizani-Williams, Linda (proj mgr) (based at 1)
Baber, Heidi
Swallow, Stuart
Richardson, Cathy (p, admin)

Petty Sessional Areas

Canterbury	Canterbury (15)
	Thanet (18)
Channel	Weald (Ashford) (23)
	Dover & Folkestone (16)
North Kent	Dartford (21)
	Gravesend (22)
	Medway (19)
West Kent	Tunbridge Wells, Sevenoaks (23)
Mid Kent	Maidstone (20)
	Sittingbourne (17)

Crown Courts

13a Canterbury
13 Maidstone

Area code 30

LANCASHIRE PROBATION SERVICE

Central Bail Referral no: (01254) 582381

Offices

1. **Head Office**
99-101 Garstang Road
Preston PR1 1LD
Preston (01772) 201209
fax (01772) 884399

Crawforth, John D (cpo)
Dearden, Colin (dcpo)
Dyer, Peter (aco, finance & admin)
Crooks, Philip (acpo, com supvn)
Mallabone, Theresa (acpo, hostels, prog's, partnerships, operational support)
Phillips, Ian (acpo, prisons, resettlement)
Simpson, Peter (acpo, courts)
Webb, John (acpo, cs)
Whyham, Mrs Mary C (acpo, human resources)
Hennessy, Annette (spo training)
Thompson, Robin (acting spo crams)
Matthews, Anne (communications)
Ridpath, Dr David (info unit mgr)
Mellor, Eileen (area admin mgr)
Ollerton, Julie (admin mgr)

2. **Lancs Probn/NSPCC Partnership Project**
Meadow House, 127 Oxford Street
Preston PR1 3QY
Preston (01772) 200765
fax (01772) 200768

Clark, Paul (mgr)
Blything, Sue
Gray, Bill
Simpson, Rosie

3. **The Crown Court**
The Law Courts
Ring Way, Preston PR1 2LL
Preston (01772) 832404/5
fax (01772) 832413

Kenny, Mick (spo)
Buckley, Brian 832408
Fox, Teresa
Robinson, Janet 832407
Calvert, Mrs Barbara (psa) 832410
Green, Heather (psa)

4. **Crown Court**
Hamerton Street
Burnley BB11 1XD

Burnley (01282) 457443
fax (01282) 455211

Norton, Keith
Bromley, Mrs Shirley (p, psa)

5. 84 Burnley Road
Accrington BB5 1AF
Accrington (01254) 232516
fax (01254) 396160

Community Supervision
Davies, Mary (pract devpt ass)
Crawshaw, Ms Chris
Green, Julie
Parkinson, Christopher
Williams, Diane
Shouib, Kanwal (p, psa)

Court Services
Cummins, Julie
Emmott, Pauline (p)
Przybysz, Linda (psa)

Resettlement
Boydell-Cupit, Mrs Susan (spo)
Wardleworth, Ms Georgina
Willetts, Rachel Ann
Brodest, Chris (psa)

Community Service
Bradshaw, Dave (cso)
Tanswell, Ken (p, cso)
Keogh, John (p, proj sup)

6. 13/15 Wellington Street
St Johns, **Blackburn** BB1 8AF
Blackburn (01254) 265221
fax (01254) 697852

Community Supervision
Ward, Ms Helen (spo)
Cahill, Catherine
Holden, Frank
Kett, Alison
Kimberley Gayle
Scott, Ian
Dunston, Susan (psa)
Melling, A Ruth (psa)

Court Services
Lock, Michael J (spo)
Ainsworth, Susan
Drummond, Shona Anne,
Emmott, Pauline (p)
Jackson, Shona
Scott, Ian
Whittaker, Pamela
O'Sullivan, A (psa)
Przybysz, Linda (psa)

Resettlement
Booth, Lynda
Byrom, Ruth
Ramsay, Norman
Banks, Bernadett (psa)

Community Service
Coates, Priscilla (cs mgr)
Lawson, Susan (cso)
Swindells, Garth (cso)
Shouib, Humayun (cso)
Daly, Michael (proj sup)
Holmes, Veron (proj sup)
Houldsworth, Phil (proj sup)
Shaw, Brian (proj sup)

Programmes
Bentley, Glenys
Harrison, Phillipa (psa)
Tomlinson, Fiona (psa)

Trainees
Rosthorn, Lisa (trainee po)
Wilson, John (trainee po)

Admin
Gildea, Peter (admin mgr)

7. **Probation Centre**
55 Preston New Road
Blackburn BB2 6AY
Blackburn (01254) 261764
fax (01254) 53603

Programmes Team
Bentley, Glenys
Kirk, Ms Christine
Lambert, Jeremy
Lawson, Amanda
Harrison, Phillipa (psa)
Smith, Louise (psa)
Smith, Raymond (psa)
Tomlinson, Lindsey (psa)

8. 1st Floor, Stephen House
Bethesda Street, **Burnley** BB11 1QW
Burnley (01282) 425854
fax (01282) 838947

Community Supervision
Lock, Mrs Linda (spo)
Fletcher, Graham
Morgan, Richard
Mullinder, Lynne (p)
Pollard, Michelle (Dordrecht initiative)
Shackleton, Barry
Smith, Pauline
Eatough, Geoffrey (psa)
Fraser, Sally-Anne (psa)
Lee, Judith (psa)

Court Services
Sunderland, Marcus (spo)
Brown, Judith (p)
Matson, David
Munrow, Anne
Powell, Ruth
McGrow, Margaret (psa)

Resettlement
Grimbaldeston, Ms Doreen
Pilling, Nick
Whalley, Neil
Pollard, Mrs Barbara (psa)

Drug Treatment & Testing Orders
Watson, Ms Pauline
Bird-Stephen, Gillian (psa)
Higgs, Cormack (psa)
Utley, Catherine (psa)
Simmons, Ruth (psa)

Community Service
Martin, Geraldine (cs mgr)
Evans, Duncan (cso)
Pye, John (cso)
Smith, Loraine (cso)
Tebbutt, Russel (cso)
Preston, Stephen (proj sup)
Wilson, Bryan (proj sup)

Accommodation Unit
Burnley (01282) 832299
fax (01282) 838616

Galbraith, Ian (spo) (based at 10)
Armer, Pam (p, psa)
Desai, Rukshana (p, psa)
Faulds, Trish (p, psa)
Maudsley, Tom (p, psa)
Ormerod, Anthony (psa)

Admin
Richardson, Pauline (admin mgr)

9. 25 Manchester Road
Nelson BB9 9YB
Nelson (01282) 615155
fax (01282) 619693

Community Supervision
Ford, Terry
Marc, Michaela (Dordrecht initiative)
Mullinder, Lynne (p)
Waterworth, John
Baguley, Heather (trainee)
Entwistle, Steven (trainee)
Johnson, Wendy (trainee)

Court Services
Belfield, Eddie
Kiernan, Michael

Resettlement
Shinks, Elaine (spo)
Riley, Pauline
Wells, Owen C

Community Service
Baxter, Samantha (cso)
Smith, Lorraine (cso)
Johnson, Cathy (proj sup)
Sargeant, Michael (proj sup)

10. 1 North Street **Rawtenstall**
Rossendale BB4 7LX
Rossendale (01706) 217577
fax (01706) 221973

Community Supervision
Fletcher, Graham
Genders, Bob
Hayman, Vic
Lonsdale, Barry (p)

Court Services
Waide, Walter
Smith, Lynne (psa)

Resettlement
Horrocks, Kath

Community Service
Loughlin, Will (cso)
Bowling, Mark (proj sup)
Lupton, Barry, (proj sup)

Accommodation
Galbraith Ian (spo)

11. Leigh Street
Chorley PR7 3DJ
Chorley (01257) 260493
fax (01257) 233177

Community Supervision
Brooks, Sharon
Okunowa, Ms Modupe
Walton, Diane
Holden, Elizabeth (p, psa)

Court Services
phone & fax to Mag Crt
(01257) 278240

Fiddler, Sue (spo)
Chadwick, Roy
Moore, Bernard
Pace, Lynne (p, psa)

Resettlement
Barwick, David

Community Service
Bentley, Stephen (cso)

Hardisty, Carole (cso)
Roberts, P (proj sup)
Williams, Gary (proj sup)

Admin
Galligan, Hazel (admin mgr)

12. 107 Towngate
Leyland Preston PR5 1LQ
Leyland (01772) 621043
fax (01772) 435090

Thompson, Lesley (rdac mgr)
Costello, Margaret (admin mgr)

Community Supervision
Clegg, B A
Horsley, Mrs Vivian
Brooker, Martin (trainee)
Freeman, William (cs proj sup)
Powell, Shirley (p, psa)

Court Services
phone & fax to Mag Crt
(01772) 431808

Foster, Ms Jane
Costello, Peter
Powell, Shirley (p, psa)

Resettlement
Brotherstone, Rob (spo)
Brewer, Ms Lynn
McLean, Janice
Sweeney, Sharon (psa)

13. 50 Avenham Street
Preston PR1 3BN
Preston (01772) 552700
fax (01772) 552701

Community Supervision
Bailey, Graham (spo)
Bent, Sarah
Chester, Eve
Da Costa, Louise
Holder, Cathy
Koowaroo, Natasha
Lindow, Bill
McCarthy, John
Stanforth, Fiona
Bradley, Janet (psa)
Southworth, Alincia (psa)

Court Services
Boothman, Phil
Davies, Marion
Nagy, Mrs Sheila
Parkin, Ms Susan
Atkinson, Freda (psa)
Wright, Linda (p, psa)

Resettlement
Warburton, Dave (spo)
Greatorex, Ms Pam
Lamba, Manjeet
Livesey, Bet
Kenyon, Jim
Faulds, Trish (psa)
Fisher, Joanne (psa)

Programmes
Graham, Jed (spo programmes)
Berry, Susan (temp spo)
Miller, Mark (spo)
Harker, Jane
Hesketh, Phiona
Sargent, Adam
Young, Rita
Gee, Wendy (psa)
Johnrose, Peter (psa)
Slater, Nadine (psa)
Wasilewski, Mark (psa)
Wilson, Sandra (psa)

Community Service
Troughton, David (cs mgr)
Da Costa, Ms Louise (cso)
Nyland, Patricia (cso)
Rocks, Ms Helen (cso)
Albers, Michelle (proj sup)
Appleby, Roy (proj sup)
Booth, Robert (proj sup)
Harrison, Mike (proj sup)
Houghton, Andrew (proj sup)

Practice Devpt Assessors
Bannister, Sally
Dacre, Michelle

Trainees
Sheridan, Esther (trainee)
Yates, Louise (trainee)

Admin
O'Neill, Brigid (admin mgr)

14. Probation Office, High Street
Skelmersdale WN8 8AP
Skelmersdale (01695) 720248
fax (01695) 556579

Equality & Diversity
Perry, Bobbie (team mgr)

Community Supervision
Kidd, Roland (spo)
Cheshire, Cath
Shaw, Allan

Court Services
phone & fax to Mag Crt
(01695) 579416

Trout, Adrian
Roberts, Alyson
Carr, Patricia (psa)

Resettlement
Leyland, Brian

Community Service
Ashton, Tony (cso)
Masheter, Diane (cso)
Houghton, Mary (proj sup)
Roberts, Richard (p, proj sup)

Trainees
Canning, Helen (trainee)

15. 384 Talbot Road
Blackpool FY3 7AT
Blackpool (01253) 394031
fax (01253)305039

Community Supervision
Javed, Anna (spo)
Barrow, Margaret (p)
Bellamy, Mary
Bennett, Dorothy
Elliott, Pat (p)
Fish, Lesley
Graydon, Lindsey
Horsfall, Jane
Johnson, Lisa
Padley, Pamela
Proud, John (p)
Pye, Joan
Williams, Jo
Westrop, Wendy (trainee)
Turner,Sonia (trainee)
Connelly, Sharon (psa)
Andrews, Tracey (psa)
Major, Angie (psa)

Court Services
Whitehouse, Martin (spo)
Brooks, Karen
Cairns, Ralph
Rickard, Carolyn
Sleightholme, Malcolm
Whiteley, Annette
Charnley, Ann (psa)
Chamberlain, Julie (psa)
Liversidge, Lesley (psa)

Resettlement
Burrough, Rebekah
Clark, Alistair
Pay, Laurie
Greenwood, Christopher (psa)

Community Service
fax (01253) 391881

Ingram, W (cs mgr)
Chambers, Ann (ps)
McCullough, Dennis (ps)
Brown, Iain, (p, cso)
Brownwood, John (cso)
Darvill, Judith (cso)
Khan, Asif (cso)
Moran, Peter (cso)
Stansfield, Julie (cso)
Allwood, Rowland (proj sup)
Chambers, Richard (proj sup)
Clayton, Peter (proj sup)
Weber, George (proj sup)

Admin
Cree, Chris (admin mgr)

15a. **DTTO Unit**
Unit 8
Metropolitan Business Park
Preston New Road
Blackpool FY3 9LT
(01253) 798725

Kerans, Richard (spo)
Mackintosh, Anne (snr pract)
Hamnett, Dawn
Leek, Alex
Costello, Judith (psa)
Joynes, Nicola (psa)
Leefe, Melanie (psa)
Varley, Shirlee (psa)
Foster, Sue (admin mgr)

Accomodation Officer
Bretherton, Dee (psa)

16. **Probation Centre**
11/13 Cookson Street
Blackpool FY1 3ED
Blackpool (01253) 752030
fax (01253) 752103

Programmes Team
Bailey, Lindsey
Robinson, Bryan
Anderson, Lauran (psa)
McElwee, Norma (p, psa)
Winterbottom, Barbara (p, psa)
Wycherley, Samantha (psa)

17. 9 The Esplanade
Fleetwood FY7 6UW
Fleetwood (01253) 874369
direct dial (01253) 879 + ext
fax (01253) 776581

Community Supervision
Gosney, Derek ext 507

Leek, Alex
Howard, Lesley (psa)

Court Services
Nye, Marjorie ext 511
Proud, John
Nixon, Graham (psa) ext 504

Resettlement
Poole, Sue (spo)
Bailey, Su ext 509
Richardson, Elizabeth ext 502
Ferguson, Diane (psa) ext 510

Community Service
Greaves, Jane (cso)
Stott, Andrea (cso)
Green, Ian (p, proj sup)

18. 41 West Road
Lancaster LA1 5NU
Lancaster (01524) 63537
fax (01524) 848519

Community Supervision
Jolly, Allan (spo)
Frankland, Roger
Holbrook, Fiona
Ralston, Cath
Young, Lyn (psa)

Court Services
Kenny, Mick (spo)
Preston, Roger
Thompson, Alan
Darwen, Natalie (psa)
Morris, Isabel (psa)

Resettlement
Boothman, Barbara
Owen, Joy
Smith, Doug
Cullen, L B (psa)

Community Service
Clifton, Val
Edmondson, Mrs Pat (cso)
Webster, Dave (cso)
Green, Barry (proj sup)
Lumb, Roger (proj sup)

Roger Peel (pract devpt assessor)

Trainees
Christian, Diana
Durkin, Elaine
Smith, Anthony
Barrass, Sherry (psa)

19. 2 Kensington Road
Morecambe LA4 5LX
Morecambe (01524) 416171
fax (01524) 832154

Community Supervision
Toms, Ashley
Loxley, Ms Sarah
Thompson, Donna

Court Services
Hopwood, Peter

Family Court Welfare Service
from 1.4.01 part of Children & Family Court Advisory & Support Service

20. **Family Court Welfare Service**
18 Winckley Square **Preston** PR1 3TU
Preston (01772) 203999
fax (01772) 204999

Derby, Colin (spo)
Hubbard, Mike (spo)
Booth, Andrew
Carroll, Richard
Hall, Beverly
Master, Fatema (p fcw, p ext funding off)
Weller, Eileen
Wilson, Carole
Sanderson, Anne (psa)
McEwan, Linda (admin)

21. **Family Court Welfare Service**
1st floor, Darwen Health Centre
Union Street **Darwen** BB3 0DA
Blackburn (01254) 771321/2
fax (01254) 761792

Fogarty Patrick
McCann, Anne
Sumner, Margaret
Worsh, Peter

22. **Family Court Welfare Service**
241 Church Street **Blackpool** FY1 3PB
Blackpool (01253) 294780
fax (01253) 292553

Alexander-Graham, Ms Cassy
Ripley, Joyce
Roberts, Susan
Webster, Kath

Youth Offending Teams

23a. 2/4 Newton Drive
Accrington BB5 2JT
(01254) 389456
fax (01254) 872614

(inc Hyndburn, Rossendale, Clitheroe, Ribble Valley)

Brindle, Neil

b. Bank House
44 Wellington Street
St Johns
Blackburn BB1 8AF
(01254) 299800
fax (01254) 299801

Brindle, Neil

c. Devonshire Centre
307/309 Church Street
Blackpool FY1 3PF
(01253) 392323
fax (01253) 302060

Storey, Mary (team leader)

d. Rokeby Centre
316 Colne Road
Burnley BB10 1XJ
(01282) 456620
fax (01282) 459706

Cigan, Mirelle

e. Halliwell House
15/17 Halliwell Street
Chorley PR7 2AL
(01257) 516051
fax (01257) 516053
(inc Skelmersdale)

Collum, Seamus

f. 15 North Albert Street
Fleetwood FY7 6DW
(01253) 772761
fax (01253) 771328

Cayton, Louise

g. 108 St Leonardsgate
Lancaster LA1 1NN
(01524) 63458
fax (01524) 842467

Bower, Neil

h. Brindle Road
Bamber Bridge
Preston PR5 6RT
(01772) 904690
fax (01772) 335364

Patel, Amita

Hostels

24. **Highfield House Probation Hostel**
Lydia Street, Wood Nook
Accrington BB5 0PX
Accrington (01254) 395997
fax (01254) 398536

O'Donnell, Phil (mgr)
Bentley, Richard (dep mgr)
McCloy, Ms Kirsten (po)
Bailey, J A (asst mgr)
Evans, Duncan (asst mgr)
Marsh, A (asst mgr)
Mayers, Jane (asst mgr)
Johal, Gurjit (supr)
Passmore, Ken (supr)

25. **Haworth House**
St Peters Street
Blackburn BB2 2HL
Blackburn (01254) 59060
fax (01254) 672062

Dewhurst, John (mgr)
Williams, Peter (dep mgr)
McCloy, Ms Kirsten (po) (based at 23)
Bassindale, John (asst mgr)
Hallett, Peter (asst mgr)
O'Connor, Alan (asst mgr)
Shingleton, Ian (asst mgr)
Baines, Gillian (supr)
Dennett, Terence (supr)
Hallett, Heather (supr)
Marshall, Anthony (supr)
Wilkinson, Julie (admin mgr)

Institutions

26. H M Prison **Garth**
Ulnes Walton Lane
Leyland, Preston PR5 3NE
Leyland (01772) 622722
fax (01772)622276

Probn general office ext 46
Flynn, Jeanette (spo) ext 460
Bartley, M
Bond, Terry (p, devpt off)
Fox, Roger
McEvoy, Jean
Parr, Pam
Whalley, B (psa)

based at visitors' centre
Leyland (01772) 622756

27. H M Prison **Kirkham**
Preston PR4 2RN
Preston (01772) 684343

fax (01772) 682855

Probn clerk/special visits ext 369
Prison admin/temp release enquiries ext 310

Bennett, Ms Andrea (spo)
Allison, Stuart
Bray, Nick
Draper, Elaine
Fitzgerald, Sharon
Harrington, Steve
Walsh, Jane

28. H M Prison
The Castle **Lancaster** LA1 1YJ
Lancaster (01524) 385100
Direct dial (01524) 385 + ext
fax (01524) 385101

Probn clerk ext 233
Special visits ext 215
Parole clerk ext 218
Gate 385228
A wing ext 241
B wing ext 244
C wing ext 243

Vacancy (spo)
Giddings, Joan ext 231
Lucas, Esther
Prior, Ralph ext 232

29. H M Young Offenders' Institution
Lancaster Farms
Stone Row Head, off Quernmore Road
Lancaster LA1 3QZ
Lancaster (01524) 848745
fax (01524) 849308

Probn admin officer ext 390
Visitor's centre ext 256
Discipline office ext 308
Parole clerk ext 287
Special visits 242

Bennett, Nigel (spo)
Hartwell, Susan
Hill, Chris ext 379
Weigh, Steve
Towers, K J (psa)

Visitors' Centre
Dixon, Pauline (psa)
Edwards, Ms Julie (psa)
Brew, Ms Pat (psa)

30. H M Prison
2 Ribbleton Lane **Preston** PR1 5AB
Preston (01772) 257734
Special visits (01772) 887342
fax (01772) 556643
bail info fax (01772) 200528
reception fax (01772) 886810
hospital fax (01772) 202143

Probn clerk ext 303

Weetman, John (spo) ext 300
Shooter, Philippa ext 301
Pugh, Joanne (bail info) ext 449

31. H M Prison **Wymott**
Ulnes Walton Lane, Leyland PR5 3LW
Leyland (01772) 421461
fax (01772) 455960

Deasha, Greg
Endicott, Coleen
Fisher, Louise
Hopkinson, Stuart
Hopewell, Keith
Leach, Marilyn
McKean, Geraldine
Whitfield, Darren
Woodall, Janet
Bewley, Caroline (psa)

Petty Sessional Areas

6 Blackburn
15, 16 Blackpool
8, 9 Burnley & Pendle
11 Chorley
8 Darwen
19 Fylde
5 Hyndburn
18, 19 Lancaster
14 Ormskirk
13 Preston
8 Ribble Valley
10 Rossendale
12 South Ribble
17 Wyre

Crown Courts

4. Burnley
3 Lancaster
3 Preston

Area Code 31

LEICESTERSHIRE & RUTLAND PROBATION SERVICE

Out of hours contact nos: Kirk Lodge 0116-270 8327, Howard House 0116-254 9059

Central Hostels referral no: 0116-244 8028

Offices

1. **Head Office**
2 St John Street
Leicester LE1 3BE
0116-251 6008
direct dial 0116-242+ext
fax 0116-242 3250
e mail LRPS@dial.pipex.com

Raban, Tony (acting cpo) ext 3200
Munro, Heather (acpo) ext 3204
Pinfold, Colin (acpo) ext 3202
Findley, Krystyna (acpo) ext 3203
Herbert, Mike (aco) ext 3206
Naylor, Camille (spo pathfinder) ext 3260
Worsfold, Trevor (spo area training) ext 3252
Bolas, Chris (po area training) ext 3253
Bearne, Bob (p, pract devpt assessor) ext 3251
Clarke, Alan (p, pract devpt assessor) ext 3254
Marriage, Ghislane (p, pract devpt assessor) ext 3251
Owens-Rawle, Marilyn (p, pract devpt assessor) ext 3254
Kennedy, Paul (info mgr) ext 3265
Akers, Linda (personnel) ext 3225
Rose, Sue (finance) 3220
Thomas, Mandy (premises) ext 3221

2. Victoria Buildings
29 Bowling Green Street
Leicester LE1 6AS
0116-285 4444
fax 0116-285 3425

Family Court Welfare Service
from 1.4.01 part of Children & Family Court Advisory Service
Poynton, Wendy (scwo)
Cain, Mike
Coe, Steve
Davey, Sandra (p)
Hassall, Sue (p)
Hazelwood-Morris, Carole
Middleton, Anne
Mosley, Sheila (p)
Nightingale, Harvey
Putt, Colin
Wilkins, Jo (p)

3. Victoria Buildings
31 Bowling Green Street
Leicester LE1 6AS
0116-253 6331
fax 0116-247 0329

Magistrates' Court/Bail Info Team
Tregoning, Jane (p, spo) (5)
Chadwick, Liz (p)
Evens, Sally
Houghton, Paul
Pugh, John
Garratt, Bob (p, pso)
McEnteggart, Annette (pso)
McIntosh, Pam (pso)

Records Office
(Central Index)
0116-285 3400
fax 0116-285 3407

4. 49 Millstone Lane
Leicester LE1 5JN
phone: to be announced
fax: to be announced

Drug Treatment & Testing Orders
Flannery, Sharon (spo)
Cassie, Louise
Simpson, Chris
Dhokia, Sheetal (pso)
Ford, Mark (pso)

5. 38 Friar Lane
Leicester LE1 5RA
0116-253 6331
fax 0116-242 4511

Leicester West
Gray, Alan (spo)
Adams, Ed
Barber, Pam (p)
Bellingham, David
Clark, Alan (p)
Gardner, Martin
James, Glynis (p)
Mason, Claire
Maxwell, Margaret
Smillie, Philip
Wynter, Colin
Acton, Sue (pso)
Hanley, Avril (pso)
Illston, Suzanne (pso)

Leicester East
Frost, Andy (spo)

Bearne, Bob (p)
Cripps, Ian
Guru, Sam
Henry, Jenny
Marshall, Peter
Pearce, Jo
Samuel, Pauline
Sansom, Pam
Singh-Bains, Peter
Vernon, Jane (p)
Leyland, Keeley (pso)
McKenzie, Mo (pso)
O'Callaghan, Joe (pso)

City Throughcare Team
Macdonald, Stuart (spo)
Courtney, Nigel
Gregory, June
Jordan, Sue
Karby, Christine
Lawler, Linda
Payne, Claire
Price, Arlene
Roscoe, Gordon
Warmington, Christine
Wilson, Nicky
Fisher, Joy (pso)
Kilpatrick, Andy (pso)
Neckles, Julian (pso)
Wood, Debbie (pso)

Victim Contact Team
Gray, Alan (spo)
Barber, Pam
Courtney, Nigel
O'Donnell, Linda (psa)

Accommodation & Resettlement Unit
Mattson, Neil
Fleck, Julie (p, pso)
Lawrence, Angie (p, pso)
Newberry, Sarah (p, pso)
Taylor, Stephanie (pso)

6. **Crown Court Team**
90 Wellington Street
Leicester LE1 6HG
0116-253 6331
fax 0116-254 1437

Tregoning, Jane (p, spo) (3)
Chadwick, Liz (p)
Whitford, Penny

7. **Probation Centre**
7 Haramead Road
Leicester LE1 2LH
0116-262 0400
fax 0116-253 0819

Sex Offender Unit
Hindson, Paul (spo)
Modi, Panna (p)
Weaver, Lestroy
Wisniewska, Dreda

Programme Provision
Hindson, Paul (spo)
Bradley, Stephen
Chivers, Andrew
Cusack, Steve
Kirby, Arlene (p)
Lawrence, Diana
Middleton, Glynis
Scott, Eric
Walworth, John
Anderson, Lisa (pso)
Baumber, Luke (pso)
Breslin, Constance (p, pso)
James, Brillheart (pso)
Paul, Ellis (pso)

Community Service Office
Holt, Caroline (spo)
Curran, Martin
Chenery, Margaret (cso)
Dhokia, Anita (cso)
Duncan, Mykel (cso)
Griggs, Alex (cso)
Hammond, Alison (cso)
Hextall, Sylvia (cso)
Holmes, Richard (cso)
Lockwood-Jones, Liz (cso)
Lo Galbo, Sal (cso)
Martin, Carole (cso)
Rogerson, Julie (cso)
Ward, Ann (cso)
Watson, Paul (cso)
Whelan, Claire (cso)
Wilkinson, Colin (cso)
Killick, Peter (wkshp mgr)

8. 27 London Road
Coalville LE67 3JB
Coalville (01530) 836688
fax (01530) 834136

Scotson, Tim (p, spo) (9)
Ball, Margaret
Hurd, Stephanie
Quinn, Steve
Bonser, Paul (pso)

9. 35 Station Road
Hinckley LE10 1AP
Hinckley (01455) 615645
fax (01455) 891147

Scotson, Tim (p, spo) (8)

Gardner, Mark
Teasdale, Jackie
Berridge, Jane (p, pso)
White, Suzanne (p, pso)

10. 12 Southfield Road
Loughborough LE11 2UZ
Loughborough (01509) 212904
fax (01509) 218954

Reynolds, Sean (p, spo) (10)
Brown, Jenny
Green, Tom
Hill, Pauline
Jacobs, David
Keeling, Rita
Owens-Rawle, Marilyn (p)
Mooney, Jane (pso)

11. County Council Area Office
Leicester Road
Melton Mowbray LE13 0DA
Melton Mowbray (01664) 410410
fax (01664) 480042

Reynolds, Sean (p, spo) (9)
Gray, Chrissie (p)
Langridge, Tony
Vega, Jane
Barney, Fran (p, pso)
Robson, Tony (pso)

12. 28 Station Road
Wigston Leicester LE18 2DH
0116-257 3800
fax 0116-257 0240

Leicester South
Sisodia, Bijal (p, spo)
Doran, Simon (p, acting spo)
Aley, Brendan
Costello, Maxine
Cullen, Michael
Marriage, Ghislaine (p)
Strong, Grace
Kassam, Shiraz (pso)
Whittam, Linda (pso)

13. **Public Protection Panel Manager**
Hamilton Police Station
Colin Grundy Drive
off Keyham Lane
Leicester LE5 1FY
0116-248 4832
fax 0116 248 4827

Petrie, Bob (spo)

14. **Youth Offending Teams**

a. Eagle House
11 Greyfriars
Leicester LE1 5QN
0116-299 5830
fax 0116 233 6003

Hulait, Jaspal
Ivankovic, Lucy
Taylor, Jane
Fox, Julie (pso)
Kaur, Baldish (pso)

b. 674 Melton Road
Thurmaston LE4 8BB
0116-260 6000

Howden, Caroline
Quinn, Brian (pso)

c. 4 Druid Street
Hinckley LE10 1QH
(01455) 636068
fax (01455) 613129

Green, Tracy
Eldred, Srah-Jane (pso)

15. **Peripatetic Staff**
Hyde, Nick
Vacancy
Vacancy

Hostels

16. **Howard House Bail Hostel**
71 Regent Road, Leicester LE1 6YA
0116-254 9059
fax 0116-254 0303

Jones, Malcolm (spo mgr)
Cusack, Steve (po deputy)
Beckford, Roy (probn hostel off)
Dennett, Julie (p, probn hostel off)
Donald, John (probn hostel off)
Higgins, Lyn (probn hostel off)
Jeggo, Steve (probn hostel off)
Patel, Amita (p, probn hostel off)

17. **Kirk Lodge**
322 London Road
Leicester LE2 2PJ
0116-270 8327
spo direct line 0116-270 6681
fax 0116-244 8696

Jones, Malcolm (spo mgr)
Jones, Tim (po deputy)
Scott, Rose (po deputy)

Bone, Sudeep (probn hostel off)
Duncan, Jude (probn hostel off)
Jones, Sarah (probn hostel off)
Lay, Matthew (probn hostel off)
Marquis, Pauline (probn hostel off)
Thompson, Kevin (probn hostel off)
Wildin, Karen (probn hostel off)

Institutions

18. H M Prison **Ashwell**
Oakham, Rutland LE15 7LF
Oakham (01572) 774100
Direct dial (01572) 77+ ext
fax (01572) 774101

Probn clerk/Probn visits ext 4274
Lifer/Parole clerk ext 4215
Discipline ext 4213

Vacancy (p, spo) ext 4271
Duncan, Nicky ext 4272
Hodge, Alan ext 4273
Smith, Jeff ext 4273
Clegg, Ann (pso) ext 4216
Wright, Barbara (p, pso) ext 4216
Satchwell, Annette (pso) ext 4272

19. H M Prison **Gartree**
Leicester Road
Market Harborough LE16 7RP
Market Harborough (01858) 410234
fax (01858) 410808

Piper, David (spo)
Baines, Carrie
Barnett, Geoff
Pearce, Jan
Robbins, Rena

20. H M Prison
116 Welford Road
Leicester LE2 7AJ
0116-254 6911
fax 0116-247 1753

Doran, Simon (p, spo)
Parmar, Asit
Charters, Elisabeth (pso)
Cousins, Nicola (pso)

21. H M Young Offender Institution
Glen Parva Saffron Road
Wigston LE18 4TN
0116-264 3100
fax 0116-264 3000

Probn clerk ext 3320
Discipline ext 3392/3291
Special visits ext 3260

Sheasby, Liz (p, spo) ext 3336
Coleman, John ext 3321
Griffiths, Richard ext 3318
Patel, Kusum ext 3308
Yorke, Tina ext 3317
McArdle, Fiona (pso)

22. H M Prison **Stocken**
Stocken Hall Road, Stretton
Nr Oakham LE15 7RD
Stamford (01780) 485100
Direct dial (01780) 48+ ext
fax (01780) 410767

Probn clerk ext 5208

Vacancy (p, spo) ext 5308
Cartwright, Trevor ext 5308
Hodge, Alan (p) ext 5309
Keens-Soper, Vicky ext 5309
Li, Joseph ext 5309
Parker-Leehane, Freda ext 5308
Bailey, Becky (pso)
Chessum, Debbie (pso)

Petty Sessional Areas

4, 5 Leicester City
4, 5, 12 Leicester County
8 Ashby-de-la-Zouch
9 Market Bosworth
10 Loughborough
11 Melton and Belvoir
11 Rutland
12 Lutterworth
12 Market Harborough

Crown Court

6 Leicester

Area Code 32

LINCOLNSHIRE PROBATION SERVICE

Out of hours emergency contact point
Wordsworth House
(01522) 528520

Offices

1. Head Office
7 Lindum Terrace
Lincoln LN2 5RP
Lincoln (01522) 523308/520776
fax (01522) 527685

Minshull, Sheridan (cpo)

Higson, Ms Sharon (acpo)
Nicholls, Graham (acpo)
Hollands, David (aco admin)
Gregory, Mrs Melanie (snr admin)
Burke, Tony (info support officer)

2. 8 Corporation Street
Lincoln LN2 1HN
Lincoln (01522) 510011
fax (01522) 514369

Dilley, Claire (spo)
Lane, Eddie (spo) (3, 4)
Marsden, Lynne (spo)
Alty, Jo
Burton, Julie (p)
Dersley, Ian
Gillard, Martin
Hallam, Mrs Pat
Hawley, Sarah
Johnson, Lynn
Loffhagen, Ms Jane (p)
Mead, Jo
McCarthy, Mrs Suzanne
Mountain, Mrs Angela
Plant, Kim
Robertson, Mrs Kim
Rose, Mrs Sue
Spurden, Stephen
Birch, Miss Diane (psa)
Buttress, Clive (psa)
Milnes, Fiona (p, psa)
Murphy, Mrs Lindsay (vco/psa)
Crook, David (trainee)
Dannatt, Sarah (trainee)
Virr, Lesley (trainee)

Community Service
Goude, Tony (cs div org)
Havercroft, Tony (p, csa)
Hough, Quin (csa)
Newborn, Clare (csa)

Groupwork
Bull, Mrs Chris (p, spo) (7a)
Walker, Mrs Janet
Garnett, Hilary (psa)

Basic Skills
O'Meara, Tricia (psa)

Staff Devpt & Training Unit
fax (01522) 579096

Snowden, Ann (spo)
Burton, Julie (p, pract devpt assessor)
Vacancy (p, pract devpt assessor)
Vacancy (psa)

3. **Lincoln Magistrates' Court Office**
The Courthouse, High Street
Lincoln LN5 7QA
Lincoln (01522) 533352/560063
fax (01522) 546332

Lane, Eddie (spo) (2, 4)
Phillips, Martin (crt service off)
Shaw, Maureen (crt service off)

3a. **Lincoln Crown Court**
The Castle, Castle Hill
Lincoln LN1 3AA
Lincoln (01522) 526767
fax (01522) 528779

Lane, Eddie (spo)
Carson, Stephen
Gilkison, Mrs Irene (p)

4. Burbury House, 2 Morton Terrace
Gainsborough, DN21 2RF
Gainsborough (01427) 612260/613867
fax (01427) 612975

Lane, Eddie (spo) (2, 3)
Pollard, Simon
Reed, Ms Sarah
Nolan, Mrs Linda (p, psa)

5. The Town Hall, North Parade
Skegness PE25 1DA
Skegness (01754) 763906
fax (01754) 760202

Connell, Tony (spo) (6)
Atkinson, Miss Wendy
Dring, Mrs Jane (p)
Sarin, N K Raish
Steel, Mrs Linda
Wallace, David
Adderton, Andy (cs div org)
Attwood, Lizelle (psa off support)
Delderfield, Richard (crt service off)
Green, Lorraine (csa)
Hoffman, Mrs Kathryn (p, psa)
Hoy, Caroline (p, crt service off)
Rushby, Teresa (psa)
Nicholls, Alan (vco/psa)
Whitelam, Sandra (trainee)

6. 14 Upgate
Louth LN11 9ET
Louth (01507) 604427
fax (01507) 608642

Connell, Tony (spo) (5)
Donoghue, Terry
Jeffrey, Mrs Di
Barlow, Mrs Gretta (p, psa)

Sellick, Mrs Cynthia (fam crt welfare)

7. The Annexe
The County Hall
Boston PE21 6LX
Boston (01205) Day 310010
evening 310245/310246
fax (01205) 354051

Laughton, Keith (spo)
Cooke, Amanda (p)
Costello, Mike
Gilbert, Mike (p)
Oak, Peter
Oliver, Mrs Joanne (p)
Williams, Eric (fam crt welfare)
Downs, Tony (p, crt service off)
Lee, Kathy (psa)
Wattam, Robin (csa)

7a. Probation Centre/Groupwork
Colley Street, off Wormgate
Boston PE21 6NT
Boston (01205) 354851
fax (01205) 354614

Bull, Mrs Chris (p, spo) (2)
Booth, Mrs Chris
Crisp, Stewart (psa, proj off)
Hancock, Paul (psa)

8. Broadgate House
Westlode Street
Spalding PE11 2AF
Spalding (01775) 722078/767708
fax (01775) 713936

Eyres, Tony (spo) (9, 10, 11)
Crowe, Mrs Elaine
Byrnes, Martin
Stacey, Krystyna (p, psa)
Thomas, Tish (crt service off)

9. Grange House, 46 Union Street
Grantham NG31 6NZ
Grantham (01476) 561061 (daytime)
(01476) 563940/561512 (evening)
fax (01476) 579654

Cope, Denise (spo)
Eyres, Tony (spo) (8, 10, 11)
Downey, Tony (p)
Miller, Mrs Barbara
Naysmith, Mrs Norma (fam crt welfare)
North, Mrs Julie (p, fam crt welfare)
Norton, Nicole
Porter, Angela
Sylvester, Mrs Doreen
Cann, Mrs Jean (p, psa)
Leivers, Beverly (csa)
Simpson, Mrs Yvonne (psa)
Woodhouse, Mrs Sandra (crt service off)
Jones, Angela (trainee)
Gooderson, Steve (trainee)

10. Reporting Centre, The Foyer
81 Eastgate
Sleaford NG34 7EA
Sleaford (01529) 304411
fax (01529) 304574

Eyres, Tony (spo) (8, 9, 11)
Bright, Jenny
Cann, Mrs Jean (p, psa)
Keller, Phil (p, vco)
King, Trish (csa)
Payne, Chris (cs div org)

11. Town Hall, St Maryís Hill
Stamford PE9 2DR
Stamford (01780) 762068
fax (01780) 481176

Eyres, Tony (spo) (8, 9, 10)
Michelson, Sally
Pycock, Mrs Janet (psa)

12. **Family Court Welfare Office**
from 1.4.01 part of Children & Family Court Advisory & Support Service
35 Orchard Street
Lincoln LN1 1XX
Lincoln (01522) 554812/554814
fax (01522) 533209

Stringer, Malcolm (spo)
Burgess, Ms Bev
Marshall, Steve
White, Mike

12a. **Lincoln County Court**
Combined Court Centre
360 High Street
Lincoln LN5 7RL
Lincoln (01522) 510435
fax (01522) 534654

Attenborough, Wilfred
Scott, John

13. **Multi Agency Public Protection**
Lincolnshire Police HQ
PO Box 999
Lincoln LN5 7PH
Lincoln (01522) 558255
fax (01522) 558056

Lewis, Sally (spo)

14. **Youth Offending Service (East)**
Lime House, Foundry Street
Horncastle LN9 6AQ
Lincoln (01522) 554737
fax (01522) 554731

Gilbert, Mike (p)

15. **Youth Offending Service (South)**
6 St Catherine's Road
Grantham NG31 6TS
Grantham (01476) 591522
fax (01476) 569166

Downey, Tony (p)

16. **Youth Offending Service (West)**
Development House
64 Newland **Lincoln** LN1 1YA
Lincoln (01522) 554550
fax (01522) 554552

Campbell, Andy

Hostel

17. **Wordsworth House**
205 Yarborough Road
Lincoln LN1 3NQ
Lincoln (01522) 528520
fax (01522) 526077

Deller, Andrew (spo mgr)
Vacancy (po dep mgr)
Allnutt, Steve (res prog asst)
Hone, Mark (res prog asst)
Jones, Mrs Maureen (res prog asst)
Shortland, Carole (res prog asst)
Knipe, John (res sup wrkr)
Lockwood, Velda (res sup wrkr)
Roberts, Chris (res sup wrkr)

Institutions

18. H M Prison, Greetwell Road
Lincoln LN2 4BD
Lincoln (01522) 533633
fax (01522) 532116

Probn clerk ext 296/300
Discipline ext 310
Special visits ext 221

Price, Miss Avril (spo)
Cope, Phil
Humphries, Gail
Jackson, Angela
Walker, Ian
Harrison, Mrs Tracey (bail info off)
Thynne, Marilyn (psa)

19. H M Prison **Morton Hall**
Nr Swinderby LN6 9PS
Lincoln (01522) 866700
probn direct line (01522) 866730
fax (01522) 866750
probn fax (01522) 866730

Parole/lifer clerk ext 6706
HDC clerk 6709
Discipline ext 6707
Special visits ext 6745
Chapman, Libby (p)
Chisholm, Elizabeth (psa)

20. H M Prison **North Sea Camp**
Frieston, Boston PE22 0QX
Boston (01205) 760481
fax (01205) 760098

Simpson, Graham

Petty Sessional Areas

7 Boston
9, 11 Bourne
4 Caistor
8 Elloe East
8 Elloe West
4 Gainsborough
9 Grantham
5, 6 Horncastle
2 Lincoln County
6 Louth
4 Market Rasen
9, 10 Sleaford
5, 6 Skegness & Spilsby
9, 11 Stamford

Crown Court

3a Lincoln

Area Code 33

LONDON

Until 1.4.01 London is divided into five probation areas

Inner London (incorporating City of London)
City of London, London Boroughs of Camden, Greenwich, Hackney, Hammersmith & Fulham,Islington, Kensington & Chelsea, Lambeth, Lewisham, Southwark, Tower Hamlets,Wandsworth, Westminster.
NOTE this area does not comprise all the London postal districts. Those within other areas are shown below.

North East London
London Boroughs of' Barking, Havering, Newham, Redbridge, Waltham Forest, E4 (part), E6, E7, E10 (part), E11, E12, E13, E15 (part), E16, E17, E18

South East London
London Boroughs of Bexley, Bromley, Croydon, SE2 (part), SEl9 (part), SE20, SW16 (part), SE25.

South West London
London Boroughs of Kingston, Merton, Richmond and Sutton, SW13, SW14, SWl9 (part), SW20. Surrey postal addresses: Carshalton, Cheam, Chessington, Hampton Wick, Kingston upon Thames, Mitcham, Morden, New Malden, Richmond upon Thames (inc. Ham and Kew), Surbiton, Sutton, Wallington, Worcester Park, Middlesex postal addresses: Hampton, Hampton Hill, Hounslow (part), Teddington, Twickenham, Whitton.

Middlesex
London Boroughs of Barnet, Brent, Ealing, Enfield, Haringey, Harrow, Hillingdon, Hounslow. N2, N3 N4 (part), N6, N8, N9, N10, N11, N12, N13, N14, N15, N17, N18, N20, N21, N22, NW2 (part), NW3 (part), NW4, NW6 (part), NW7, NW9, NW10, NW11, W3, W4, W5, W7, W13.

From 1.4.01 London will be one unified Probation Service

INNER LONDON PROBATION SERVICE from 1.4.01 part of the London Probation Service

Offices

1. **Head Office**
71/73 Great Peter Street, SW1P 2BN
020 7222 5656
fax 020 7960 1188

Harding, John (cpo)
Sleightholm, David (dcpo staff management, equal opps, pr, fam crt wk, staff devpt & training, industrial relations, prison liaison and contracts, domestic violence, hostels, housing, partnership support unit, London Action Trust, ciso info systems, research & intelligence, crams, internal inspections, health & safety)
Leach, Tony (dcpo crime prevn, pre-trial services, services to crts, psr's, community orders, probn centres, Resettlement, victims)
Whelan, Ms Dianna M (cao finance, accom services, data protection, legal & insurance)

Administrative Departments
Barton, Ms Heather (hd of human resources)
Hinton, Mrs Dawn (personnel mgr, staffing services/specialist functions)
Turner, Mrs Carole (personnel mgr, staffing services/specialist functions)
Ayton, John E (personnel mgr, policy devpt)
Harrison, Sue (head of internal audit)
Goonawardena, L Kumar S (head of finance)
Piddington, Glen (head of accom services)
Stanton, Ms Kathryn (health and safety officer)

Building Services Department
Pinto, Neville (building services mgr)
Engleman, Phil (building services mgr)
Jukes, Sarah
Thompson, Rosemary

Headquarters Relief Officers
Boyle, Liz (spo)
Okine, Emmanuel (spo)
Jones, Kate
Palmer, Patricia
Thompson, Lorna

Peripatetic Staff
Baines, Ms Viv
Ball, Ms Trinidad
Bernhardt, Andrew
Hopton, Dennis
McKay, Mrs Janet (js)
Morgan, Walter
Nicholson, Rita
Quigley, Mrs Olive (js)
Sydow, Mrs Anita (js)
Weeden, Gillian

Secondments

Home Office
50 Queen Anne's Gate, SW1H 9AT
020 7273 3000

Pitts, Steve (spo,crim policy directorate)

HM Inspectorate of Probation
Hutchings, John (Inspector of Probation)
Cabinet Office
Reardon, David (acpo)
Bail Hostel Development Advisor
Cox, Sebert (acpo)
Race Equality Unit
Douglas, Jennifer
London Training Consortium
Jones, Mike (spo)
Development Manager
Fairweather, Laura
DTTO Project
Battye, June
Transitional Steering Management Group
Harraway, Peter

HM Prison Service
Hogarth Elizabeth (drugs treament mgr)

London NAPO Branch
217a Balham High Road
Balham, London SW17 7BP
020 8682 9356
fax 020 8682 2087

Padgett, Derek (p, branch chair)
Dunkley, Ms Charlotte (p, branch secy)
Cole, Mrs Beverley (p, office secy)

Youth Offending Team Secondments

Lewisham Youth Offending Team
1-3 Ashby Road, Brockley, SE4 1PR
020 8314 7474
Cohen, Keith
Mackenzie, Yannick

Hamersmith & Fulham Youth Offending Team
145 Hammersmith Road, W14 0QZ
020 7371 4886
Mahaffrey, Helen

Westminster Youth Offending Team
6a Crompton Street, W2 1ND
020 7641 5422
Vacancy

Kensington & Chelsea Youth Offending Team
36 Oxford Gardens, W10 5UG
020 7598 4705
Walker, Jennifer

Lambeth Youth Offending Team
1st Floor, 1-9 Acre Lane, SW2 5SD
020 7926 2557/2635
Onibuju, Kemi
Roberts, Leslie

Southwark Youth Offending Team
90 Blakes Road, SE15 5EL
020 7525 7875
Roberts, Emma
Meredith-White, Joanne
Shepherd, Andrea

Wandsworth Youth Offending Team
177 Blackshaw Road, SW17 0DJ
020 8672 1664/7074
Obadai, Jacqueline

Greenwich Youth Offending Team
Well Hall Project, Well Hall Road
Eltham SE9 6SU
020 8859 4492
Ford, Mark
McDonald, Betty

Tower Hamlets Youth Offending Team
Bow Training Centre
KitKat Terrace, E3 2SA
020 7364 1144
Gibson, Rosy

Camden Youth Offending Team
SSD Centre 3, 115 Wellesley Road
Gospel Oak, NW5 4PA
020 7413 6666
Karim, Sheik

Hackney Youth Offending Team
Vacancy

Islington Youth Offending Team
Vacancy

2. **Public Relations Department**
71/73 Great Peter Street, SW1P 2BN
020 7222 5656
fax 020 7960 1117

Stanley, Stephen J (intelligence off)
Lord, Mrs Susan (hd of pr)

Research and Intelligence
Durrance, Pauline (research off)
Asamoah, Ms Audrey (central database mgr)

Computer Systems Team
Mortimer, Ms Sarah A (systems mgr)
Hague, John (project mgr)
Wright, Mrs Hermione (project mgr) (js)
Fawzi, Fawzi (dep systems mgr)
Lardi, Mrs Mary (dep systems mgr)
Kaye, David (project mgr)
Khan, Gulzeb (network infrastructure sup & devpt off)
Milosevic, Drazen (asst netwk info support & devpt off)
Cevidalli, Ms Anna (i.t. trainer)
McKee, Mrs Sue (i.t. trainer)
Tomesims, Ms Manuella (i.t. trainer)

3. Mitre House
223-237 Borough High Street
London SE1 1JD
020 7740 8500
fax 020 7740 8448

Training Department
Vacancy (spo, training mgr)
James, Ms Linda (spo, training mgr)

Administrative Department
Moore, Mrs Pat (bldg mgr)

Community Service & ETE

4. Mitre House
223-237 Borough High Street, SE1 1JD
020 7740 8500
fax 020 7740 8447

Snelgrove Barry (acpo) (offices 4-9)
Conalty, Julie (ete devpt mgr)
Geary, Claire (ete devpt off)
Mayhew, Brian (peripatetic po cs)

5. **Community Service Office**
3a Alexander Road
Islington, London N19 3PG
020 7272 5727
fax 020 7263 9985

Cooke, Ms Pamela (spo)
McEvoy, Ms Jean (po)
Clarke, Mrs Anastasia (scso)
Davis, Keith (scso)
Akib, Roman (cso)
Boutel, Ms Helen
Carroll, James (cso)
Driver, Ms Carol (cso)
Lewis-Lilly, Ms Sharon (cso)
Scott, Michael (cso)
Gibbs, Don (wkshp mgr)

6. **Community Service Office**
Harpenden House
248-250 Norwood Road
London SE27 9AJ
020 8766 5700
fax 020 8766 5772

Wells, Sylvia (spo)
Ashley, Ms Valerie
Thomas, Ms Barbara (po)
Parker, Ms Yvonne (scso)
Turner, Mrs Lesley (scso)
Beverton, Mrs Christine (cso)
Boreland, Mrs Audrey M (cso)
Boyle, Robert (cso)
Deans, Derrick (cso)
Gordon, Ms Annette (cso)
Hamilton, Ms Gemmer (cso)
Newbold, Erica (cso)
Ubaka, Joseph (cso)

7. **Community Service Office**
210 Chiswick High Road, W4 1PD
020 8994 9393
fax 020 8994 0961

Dixon, Mrs Liz (spo)
Dal Pozzo, Ms Magnolia (po)
Desjardins, Miss Tracey (scso)
Clarke, Eric (cso)
Floyd, Peter (cso)
Ford, Mrs Dominique (cso)
Kirton, Mrs Mary (cso)
Matthews, John (cso)
Milosevic, Mrs Valentina (cso)
Perkins, Noel (cso)
Thorley, Miss Christine (cso)
Shearsby, Ted (cs work proj sup)

8. **Community Service Office**
32-34 Greenwich High Road, SE10 8LF
020 8692 7123
fax 020 8694 1957

Allman, Sam (spo)
Mayhew, Brian (peri po)
Smith, Ms Janet (po)
Johnson, Mrs Deborah (scso)
Moheeputh, Rajend (scso)
Bansal, Saarbjit (cso)
Driver, Mrs Carol (cso)
George, Mrs Rita (cso)

Johnson, Mrs Deborah (cso)
Levy, Miss Dahlia (cso)
Mckoy, Fitzroy (cso)
Marsh, Jim (cso)

9. **Community Service Office**
292 Camberwell Road, SE5 0DL
020 7708 0375
fax 020 7252 6492

Larose-Jones, Lloyd (spo)
Scarsbrook, Ms Julie (js)
White, Jacqueline (scso)
Charles, Gregor (cso)
Chin, Mrs Lorna (cso)
Pierre, Kenneth (cso)
Ubaka, Anselm (cso)

FIELD SERVICES

10. **191a Askew Road**
Shepherds Bush, London W12 9AX
020-8743 1987 (acpo only)
fax 020-8743 4921 (acpo only)

Mitchell, Ms Darian (acpo Hamersmith & Fulham, probn centres)

Probation Centres

11. **Women's Probation Centre**
199 Arlington Road
Camden Town, London NW1 7HA
020 7267 2646
fax 020 7284 1967

Ablitt, Ms Frances (spo)
Bloice, Thirza
Mullen, Veronica
Springer, Angela
Walker, Lorna

12. **Sherborne House Probation Centre**
34 Decima Street, SE1 4QQ
020 7407 2264/403 5027
fax 020 7378 6701

Papworth, Jeff (spo)
Davis, Ms Patricia
Donohoe, Ms Paula
Fejzagic, Boris
Phillips, Stewart
Siley, Ms Joan
Hickman, Mrs Irene (admin)

13. **Camberwell Probation Centre**
123 Grove Park, Camberwell
London SE5 8LB
020 7733 0972
fax 020 7737 7857

Norman, Adrian (spo)
Delaney, Ms Monica
Dennison, Mark
Jones, Stuart
Lansiquot, Anthony
Riley, Ms Debbie
Stewart, Miss Lorraine (p)
Teft, Paul
Cross, Alan (educn & training off)
Allan, Stuart (craft instr)
Stratton-Woodward, Edward (prog tutor)
Little, Miss Patricia L (probn centre admin)

14. **191a Askew Road**
Shepherds Bush, London W12 9AX
020 8746 0999
fax 020 8740 5238

Community Supervision Team
Hearne, Tony (spo)
Brown, Ms Peggy
Browne, Ms Eithne
Creighton, Ms Beverly
Dixon, Ms Elizabeth (js)
Hartley, Mrs Beverley
Kay, Ms Pamela
King, Neil
Louison, Trevor
McKenna, Ms Kathryn (js)
Wheeler, Graham (practice devpt assessor)
Wilde, Michael (prog tutor)
Grihault, Suzanna (trainee)
Hall, Christopher (trainee)
Jarvis, Fiona (trainee)
McCarthy, Kerry (trainee)
Moule, Catherine (trainee)
Shannon, Kathryn (trainee)
Ward, Jonathan (trainee)
Wilde, Michael (trainee)

Youth Team
Taylor, Ms Susan (spo)
Cann, Ms Nicola
Dunbar, Ms Sharon
Hosten-McDavid, Ms Norma
Winter, Ms Sal L

Resettlement Team
Crossick, Ms Bettina (p, spo)
Bartlett, Julian
Hardy, George
Mullen, Ms Hayley
Reason, Ms Vilas
Vassallo, David

W London Magistrates' Court
Miller, Ms Heather (spo)

Bastian, Mrs Sylvia (psco)
Ephson, Ms Elizabeth (psco)
Field, Ms Celia (pcso)
Lanzer, Ms Susan (pcso)
Lee, Ms Jennifer (pcso)
Bradford, Ms Christine (money advice off)

DETR Rehabilitation Courses
Miller, Ms Heather (spo organiser)
Ingram, Mrs Valerie (admin)
King, Sean (admin)

15. **71-73 Great Peter Street**
Victoria, London SW1P 2BN
020 7222 5656
fax 020 7960 1188

Monk, David (acpo Westminster, Kensington & Chelsea, offices 16-18)
Tarzi, Ayesha (foreign offenders co-ord)

16. **143 Notting Hill Gate**
Notting Hill Gate, London W11 3LE
020 7727 9491
fax 020 7221 4954

team moving to Office 13 during 2001

PSRs,Community Supervision, Gpwk
Niechcial, Steve (spo)
Bram, Mrs Vicky
Davidson, Laura
Falk, Ms Chloe
Senior, Deleita
Tipping, Ms Karen

17. **1-5 Dorset Close**
Marylebone, London NW1 5AN
020 7724 1531
fax 020 7723 9329

Adult Resettlement/Sex Offenders
Whiteley, Ms Lesley (spo)
Ademulegan, Adewale
Bartley, Jacqueline
Foster, Ms Nikki
Pittalis, Ms Irma
Curran, Ms Clair (based at 16)
Turgoose, Peter (based at 16)

Young Adult Team
team will move to 75 Marsham Street during 2001
Turner-Nash, Neil (spo)
Gray, Sheila
Inniss, Omar
Kitchen, Robert
Nash, Katie
Newlyn, Ms Patricia

Community Supervision, Gpwk
Robertson, Ms Liz (spo)
Rouse, Martin (pract devpt assessor)
Guilfoyle, Michael
Metz, Paul
Penny, Tom
Thomas, Ms Carol
Vanbemmel, Nikolas
Finn, Sandie (prog tutor)

Marcolongo, Deborah (trainee)
Mitchell, Rebecca (trainee)
Okoh, Christopher (trainee)

18. **West End Probation Office**
10 Rathbone Place
London W1P 1DE
020 7631 0535
fax 020 7323 3567

Central London Courts Operations
Ferguson, Kathy (spo)

PSR & Court Team
Maloney, James (spo, psrs & enforcement)
Delahunty, John
Gordon, Sylvia
Hillman, John
Jolly, Ms Melanie
Linton-Smith, Aiden
Quashie, Ms Sandra
Yacobi, Arik
Crellin, Ms Linda (breach off)
Helm, Ms Joanna (breach off)

Allwood, Timothy (psco)
Alexander, Mrs Daphne (psco)
Coke, Ms Faye (psco)
Flynn, Paul (psco)
Hemmings, Ms Susan (psco)
Williams, Carmel (pcso)
Wood, Ms Janet (psco)

18a. **28 Bow Street**
WC2E 7AS
020 7379 4713

18b. **21 Great Marlborough Street**
W1A 4EY
020 7287 4525 (ask for probn)

18c. **59/65 Wells Street**
W1A 3AE
020 7436 8600

Offices 18a-18c not permanently staffed. Letters to office 18. West End Courts served by Rathbone Place Office

19. **53 Holloway Road**
Highbury, London N7 8JD
020 7609 8909
fax 020 7700 0615

Brown, Ms Amanda (acpo Camden & Islington, offices 20-22)

Court Team enquiries to Office 22

20. **Camden House**
199 Arlington Road
Camden Town, London NW1 7HA
020 7267 9231
fax 020 7267 5037

Resettlement & Sex Offenders
Herson, Ms Karen (spo)
Baker, John
Beddis, Ms Anna
Fletcher, MsCharmaine
Hopwood, Joseph

Community Supervision Team
Carruthers, David (spo)
Chambers, Miss Rosemary
Coulter, Theresa
Fisher, Simon
Roome, Ms Sîan
Sutton, Oliver
Turner, Jenny (js)
Walker, Ms Stephanie (js)
Valero, Ms Brigitte
Ward, Martin

21. **401 St John Street**
Finsbury, London EC1V 4RW
020 7837 9223
fax 020 7278 2872/8747

Camden & Islington Young Adult Team
Walker, Sean (spo)
Clough, Ms Alison
Evans, Leighton
Krickler, Ms Tracy (js)
Krivine, Nathalie
Rees, Ms Helen
Reid, Ms Rosemarie
Scotia, Alex
Wilson, Terry
Wiseman, Guy

Resettlement & Sex Offenders
Tate, Alex (spo, th'care)
Gollan, Mrs Julia
Leech, Malcolm
Libby, Ms Alison
Michelson, John
Moir, Ms Elizabeth
O'Meara, Therese
Ruff, Chris

Adult Community Supervision & PSRs
Godfrey, John (spo)
Bertram, Joanne
Bodden, Ava
Grant, Anita
Joseph, Tessa
Virgin, Ms Julie
McGarrigle, Ms Francesca (practice devpt assessor)
Dennison, Alexandra (trainee)
Lynch, Kieran (trainee)
McLean, Jenny (trainee)
Thompson, Georgia (trainee)
Thomas, Candy (trainee)
Pardoe, Jill (trainee)
Stapleton, Jacinta (trainee)

Chris Hignett (spo)
Atkin, Mrs Joanne (js)
Black, Ms Linda (js)
Davies, Chris
McCalman, Ms Barbara
Muhammed, Winston
Pryce, Paul
Myatt, Sarah (prog tutor)

Drug Treatment & Testing Orders
Dodd, Charles (spo)
Devlin, John R A (drug/alc specialist)

22. **53 Holloway Road**
Highbury, London N7 8JD
020 7609 0913
fax 020 7700 2553

Highbury Court & PSR Team
Lloyd, Michael (spo)
Dalrymple, Peter
Nicholson, Rita (js)
Page, Martin
Smith, Ms Kate
Anderson, Karen (psco)
Goddard, Ms Annette (psco)
Gordon, Ms Jacqueline (psco)
Howard, Blanche (psco)
Thomson, Ms Sally (psco)
Maginley, Miss Yvonne (breach off)
Kufeji, Jimi (breach off)
Connolly, Mrs Theresa (money adv off, Camden & Islington)

23. **53 Holloway Road**
Highbury, London N7 8JD
020 7607 3001
fax 020 7700 0615

Parker, Robin (acpo Hackney offices 23-25, crime prevn, victim's service)

Victim's Service
020 7609 2535
fax 020 7609 2503
Barnish, Ms Mary (spo)
Dench, Ms Alison (js)
Glennie, Ms Katrina
Matondo, Ms Panaka
Shrier, Ms Linda (js)

24. **34 Englefield Road**
Hackney, London N1 4EZ
020 7254 8772
fax 020 7275 7627

Young Adult Team
Bartram, Ms Diane (spo)
Agana, Ms Carol
Bartlett, Gary
Christina, Ms Chistina
Mackmurdie, Ms Debra (js)
Sielman, Ms Maruie
Simela, Aggrey
Davies, Ms Anna (prog tutor)
Moseley, Mrs Yvonne (psa)

PSR/Community Sentences Team
Morrison, Ms Ros (spo)
Crew, Mrs Sue
Illingworth, John
Lanjri, Mohamed
O'Hagan, Ms Marianne
Parrott, Phillip
Spence, Richard V H
Krige, Ms Libby

25. **Reed House**
2-4 Rectory Road
Stoke Newington, London N16 7QS
020 7923 4656
fax 020 7923 4084

Resettlement Team
Elliott, Ms Helen M (spo) (js)
Ward, Ms Lyla (spo) (js)
Clifford, Mrs Andrea
Garvey, Ms Judy
Lescombe, Ms Anne
McLeod, Derek
Stevens, Peter
Stableford, Paul (money advice off)

PSR/Community Sentences Team
Joels, Jonathan (spo)
Balfour, Ms Clare
Demisse, Yaregal
Gleeson, Ms Celine
Harris, Phillip
Ofutu, John
Park, Ms Rosalind (p)
Rose, Ms Caroline (p)
McGowan, Ms Valerie (pract devpt assessor)
Bradbury, Christine (trainee)
Sculley, Joanne (trainee)

26. **87a Whitechapel High Street**
Aldgate East, London E1 7QX
020 7375 0419
fax 020 7426 0276

Wyman, Ms Mary (acpo Tower Hamlets, City of London, offices 26-30)

Adult Throughcare
020-7375 0696
Martins, Ronke (spo)
Elliott, Martyn
Sinclair, Norma
Withers, Brent
Taylor, Clive (pso)

27. **50 Mornington Grove**
Bow, London E3 4NS
020 8980 1818
fax 020 8983 0020

Court & PSR Team
Francis, Ms Viv (spo)
Bishop, Mrs Carol
Blac, Nick
Walker, John
Adeyemi, Ms Tunde (psco)
Audain, Ms Elaine (pcso)
Goulbourne, Miss Corrol (psco)
Hayton, Ms Lynn (psco)
Cole, Ms Maxine (breach off)
Llewelyn-Pace, Trefor (breach off)
Parker, Miss Fiona (trainee)

Young Adult Team
Romanes, Alastair (spo)
Davids, Winston
Grant, Ms Valerie
Hoxby, Ms Anne
Knaggs, Ms Belinda

Drug Treatment & Testing Orders
Blackburn, Mick (spo)

28. **1a Alfred Street**
Bow, London E3 2BA
020 8980 4678
fax 020 8980 1260

Community Orders (21+)
Raeside, Dominic (spo) (js)
Morton, Ms Fiona (spo) (js)
Brooks, Mrs Noreen
Daley, Mrs Shirley

Dickens, Mrs Christine
Fitch, Ms Olivia (p)
Dragu, Ms Marianna
Lightburn, Mrs Marilyn
Linfoot, Rebecca
Morris, Christopher
Wilson, David
Blackwood, Velma (gpwrkr)
Serugo-Lugo, Mrs Sarah (pract devpt assessor)
Athwal, Harrinder (trainee)
Clarke, Ms Barbara (trainee)
Haywood, Sophie (trainee)
Jenkins, Andrew (trainee)
Valmas, Catherine (trainee)

29. **377 Cambridge Heath Road**
Bethnal Green, London E2 9RD
020 7739 7931
fax 020 7613 4909

Office closed for refurbishment

30. **City of London Probation Office**
65 Basinghall Street
EC2V 5DA
020 7332 1190/1192
fax 020 7600 0433

Court, PSRs & Groupwork
McNaughton, Mrs Vivienne (spo)
De Boer, Ms Polly (effective pract devpt)
Devlin, Mick
Evans, Nigel
Williams, Ms Susan-Ann

31. **217a Balham High Road**
Balham, London SW17 7BP
020 8767 5905
fax 020 8682 4241

Lewis, Ms Susan (acpo Wandsworth 32-33)

32. **79 East Hill**
Wandsworth, London SW18 2QE
020 8871 2711
fax 020 8877 3342

Adult Resettlement Team
Northmore, Peter (spo)
Graham, Miss Rose
Heerah, Ms Marie
Hepworth, Jonathan
Norville, Ms Perpetua
Ovenden, Richard
Wilson, James

Young Adult Team
Whibley, Ms Marilyn (p, spo)
Gardner, Michael
Gyimah, Raphael
Roebuck, Ms Jo
O'Connor, Richard

Court & Community Work
Johnson, Ms Pru (spo, community team & dtto)
Ayerst, Ms Caroline (dtto)
Geliot, Mrs Diana
Long, Ms Laurie
Moule, Catherine
Orrin, Richard
Parrott, Ms Thelma (money advice off)

Programme Devpt & Delivery
Rance, Ms Sally (spo)
Kirton, Ms Sandrine (prog tutor)

33. **124 Latchmere Road**
Wandsworth, London SW11 2JT
020 7223 2991
fax 020 7924 4775

McLean, Mrs Rita (spo)
Isaacs, Ms Ava
Makin, David
Uzosike, Ms Sandra
Wilson, Mrs Pauline (pract devpt assessor)
Annesley, Mrs Augusta (trainee)
Askew, Honora (trainee)
Hannan, Jo (trainee)
Law, Miss Nicola (trainee)
Makin, David (trainee)
Shemar, Jagdish (trainee)
Thompson, Ms Sharon (trainee)
Daly, Mrs Allison (psco)
Green, Miss Jodi (psco)
Healy, Anthony (psco)
Middleton-Stewart, John (breach off)
Turner, John (breach off)

34. **117 Stockwell Road**
Stockwell, London SW9 9TN
020 7274 7854 (acpo only)
fax 020 7738 4562 (acpo only)

Pagan, Timothy (acpo Lambeth, race issues, offices 34-37)

35. **117 Stockwell Road**
Stockwell, London SW9 9TN
020 7738 5894
fax 020 7738 4720

Adult Community Supvn 2.
Jones, Ian (spo)
Carby, Ms Maisie
Farmer, Brendan

Gordon, Ms Alison
Hardy, Mark
Orlebar, Ms Diane
Tuitt, Ms Eunice
Blades, Dene (trainee)
Defriend, Nat (trainee)
Devlin, James (trainee)
Felix, Victor (trainee)
Ellner, Dawn (trainee)
Read, Thomas (trainee)
Wright, Joanne (trainee)
Barker-McKure, Sharon (prog tutor)
O'Donovan, Caroline (prog tutor)
Robinson, Sara (pract devpt assessor)
Sandhu, Miss Kuljit (effective pract devpt)

Adult Community Supervision (West)
Matas, Maria (spo)
Agbenu, Kwaku
Dix, Angela
Harding, Ms Yvonne
Montrose-Francis, Ms Sharon
Stevenson, Doug
Vakis, Michelle

Young Adult Team
Cox, Lisa (spo)
Conway, Malcolm
Deas, Ms Jacqueline
Lynch, Christine
Norton, Ms Sandra
Onibuje, Ms Kemi
Peters, Ms Elizabeth
Rhone, Ms Avis
Samuels, Ms Kay
Siderfin, John
Blake, Nicholas (psa)

Think First Centre
Rance, Sally (spo)
Clarke, Ms Sharon (po prog tutor)
Ramsay, Ms Joanne (po prog tutor)
Cavuoto, Ms Wilma (po prog tutor)
Coker, Ms Evelyn (po prog tutor)
Reed, Ms Jan (po prog tutor)
Shepherd, Ms Andrea (po prog tutor)

36. **Harpenden House**
248-250 Norwood Road, SE27 9AJ
020 8766 5700
fax 020 8766 5746

Adult Community Supvn 1.
Grealish, Peter (spo)
Barrett, Ms Sharon
Devlin, Eamann
Choudary, Mrs Ingrid
Game, Samuel
Gill, Ms Tajinderjeet
Ogunnaike, Bola (p)
Brooks, Robert (mao)

Adult Resettlement 1
Jappy, Al (spo)
Ashley, Ms Val
Drayton, Edmond
Hayward, Lynda
Jeffcott, Ms Alison

Adult Resettlement 2.
Holland, Sheila (spo)
AcQuah, Gladys
Clark, Mrs Liz J (js)
Douglas, Ms Doreen
Sone, Mrs Mary C

37. **Mitre House**
223-237 Borough High Street
London SE1 1JD
020 7740 8500
fax 020 7357 8315

McFeeley, Ms Mary (acpo Southwark, offices 38-39)

38. **2 Kimpton Road**
Camberwell, London SE5 7UW
020 7703 0822
fax 020 7703 8319

Community Team
Haines, Ryan (spo)
Boyes, Miss Jo
Farrer, Steve
Havard, Ms Tirion
Muir, Ms Jane
O'Brien, Ms Gillian (p)
Small, Yvonne
Thubron, Mrs Jane

Community Team
Reilly, Mrs Sigrun (spo)
Jabbari, Nick
Kerr, Roz
McCullough, Ms Barbara
McLaughlin-Mohammed, Ms Marlene
Trew, Ms Kim
Waterman, Ms Pat
Granata, Miss Judith (prog tutor)

Court Team
Yasmin, Lakhi (spo)
Allen, Mike (psco)
Babudoh, Alex (psco)
Darling, Robert (psco)
Durrant, Valerie (p, psco)
Flockhart, Mrs Wendy (psco)
Mulligan, Ms Janet (p, psco)
Parris, Joan (psco)

Tutt, Carol (psco)
Benjamin, Miss Akhita (breach off)
Roach, Elaine (breach off)
Wojtczak, Nickolas (breach off)
Murphy, Mrs Joan (money adv off) (based at 44)

Resettlement Team
Kerr, Adam (spo)
Butler, Jennifer
Middleton, Susan
Turner, Ms Ambrozine
Webb, Ms Siobhan

39. **North Southwark Teams**
2 Great Dover Street
The Borough, London SE1 4XW
020 7740 8400
fax 020 7740 8449

Community Team
Gulley, Mrs Jean (spo)
Ashdown, Ms Deirdre
Bartrum, Ms Ann
Donegal, Mrs Judith
Ferguson, Alf
Edge, Jill (p)
McGeehan, Georgina
Radcliffe, Dan

Davies, Keith (practice teacher)
Allen, Michael (trainee)
Crews, Roy (trainee)
Folawiyo, Miss Toyin (trainee)
McBean, Angela (trainee)
Martin, Ms Heather (trainee)

Young Offenders Team
Forbes, Ms Michelle(spo)
Anderson, Sylvia
Barker, Allison
Briscoe, Ms Angela
Brosnan, Sean
Carter, Jill
Duffus, Ms Lorraine
Edwards, Ms Paulette V
Morris, Ms Rachel
Russo, Angela

Resettlement Team
Hubbard, Ms Louise (spo)
Chattoe, Mrs Angela
Culey, Emma
Kacsprzak, Ms Adela
Muliindwa, John
Thubron, Jo
Wisdom, Andrew

40. **208 Lewisham High Street**
Lewisham, London SE13 6JP
020 8297 2766
fax 020 8297 2826

Barry, Kevin (acpo Lewisham, internal inspections, offices 40-41)
020 8297 2894 (acpo only)
fax 020 8852 7312 (acpo only)

Resettlement Team
Brennan, Robin (spo)
Adjin-Tettey, Thomas
Dubé, Ms Sibongile
Eastham, James
Ekland, Terence
Jager, Ms Anette
Nunn, Susan
Phipps, Alan

Community Supervision
020 8297 2895
Henderson, William (spo)
Bah, Ms Hawah
Denham, Miss Rachel
Grogan, Ms Marie-Therese
Hall, Kevin
Smith, Ms Nina
Wilson, Ms Deborah
Knight, Ms Deborah (prog tutor)
Smith, Ms Annell (prog tutor)

Adult Team
Slaven, John (spo)
Anderson, David
Benjamin, Joseph
Pollard, Mrs Corinne (js)
Schmidt, Ms Esther

Programme Development
Wilson, Ms Jacqueline (spo)
Burston, Andy
Dalrymple, Derek
Weldon, Elaine
James, Ms Susan (money adv off)

Barling, Lisa (trainee)
Dennis, David (trainee)
Forrester, Sally (trainee)
Small, Eugenie (trainee)

41. **39 Greenwich High Road**
Greenwich, London SE10 8JL
020 8692 6364
fax 020 8694 2173

Coupe, Peter (spo)
Asabre, Ms Veronica
Gill, Jeffrey
Grindley, Ms Tina

Nelson, Olive
Sibson, Ms Claire
Tully, Martin
Barton, Miss Diane (psco)
Lee, Dominic (psco)
Suttle, Brian (psco)
Thomas. Mrs Bobbie (pcso)
Bowie, Mrs Eleanor (breach off)
Okugbeni, Ms Barbara (breach off)
Oduwole, Ola (breach off)

42. **208 Lewisham High Street**
Lewisham, London SE13 6JP
020 8297 5347 (acpo only)
fax 020 8852 7312 (acpo only)

Powell, Norman (acting, acpo Greenwich offices 43-44, internal inspections, volunteers)

43. **130 Powis Street**
Woolwich, London SE18 6NN
020 8855 0266
fax 020 8316 5502

Resettlement Team
Reid, Al (spo)
Costello, Joe
Devo, Ms Sue
Feeney, Ms Julie
Harris, Francis
Lauchlan, Neil
Padgett, Derek
Ukwuoma, Uchendou
Boutel, Helen (trainee)
Braham, Laura (trainee)
Cantello, Ms Laura (trainee)
Hall, Ms Janet (trainee)
Hardy, Ruth (trainee)
Welch, Mrs Brenda (psa)
West, Ms Lisa (money adv off)

Adult Community Supvn Team
Brown, Ms Janett (spo)
Dunne, Ms Adrienne
Court, David
Otuoya, Ms Patricia
Spencer, Ms Caroline
Pilinski, Ms Krystyna (practice devpt assessor)

Young Adult Team
Slaven, John (spo)
Allen, Ms Sharon
Collyer, Ms Lynne (js)
Erskine, Ms Eleanor
Howell, Ms Alex
Mead, Ms Hannah
Ofori, Daniel

44. Riverside House
Beresford Street Woolwich
London SE18 6DH
020 8855 5691
fax 020 8855 6147

Community Supervision
Hennigan, Ms Linda (spo)
Henderson, Mrs Kathryn
Hill, Ray
Scott, Ms Fiona
Thomason, David
Miller, Ms Michelle (trainee)

Family Court Welfare Service
from 1.4.01 part of Children & Family Court Advisory & Support Service

45. **71/73 Great Peter Street**
London SW1P 2BN
020 7222 5656
fax 020 7960 1112

Jeffries, Peter (acpo, offices 45-49)

46. **Principal Registry of the Family Division**
Family Court Welfare Service
5th Floor, First Avenue House
42-49 High Holborn
WC1V 6NP
020 7947 6054
fax 020 7430 1232

Mellor, John (scwo)
Aldridge, Ms Jillian
Clarke, Stephen
Hartley, Malcolm
Hayes, Mrs Janet (js)
Howes-Walters, Ms Orwin (js)
Morris, Ms Aviva (js)
Neill, Ms Gail
Raleigh, Mrs Muriel
Reilly, Dermot
Vassell, Ms Nicola
Walsh, Michael

47. **Family Court Welfare Service**
3rd Floor, 217a Balham High Road
Balham, London SW17 7BP
020 8672 2682
fax 020 8682 3093

Crawley, Ms Claudia (scwo)
Compton, Ms Elizabeth
Demery, Ms Kay
Dunstan, Ms Karen
Greensmith, Mrs Elspeth
McGowan, Mrs Jackie
Sarpong, Mrs Ashiya

Warren, Ms Katie
Werner-Jones, Mrs Marion

48. **Family Court Welfare Service**
7 Percy Road
Shepherds Bush, London W12 9PX
020 8746 1416
fax 020 8740 5291

Hunt, Steve (scwo) (49)
Bruce, Mrs Diana (js)
Flynn, Ms Catrina
Johnstone, James
Kemmis-Betty, Mrs Sally L (js)
Todd, Mrs Ruth
Wilkinson, Miss Sara

49. **Family Court Welfare Service**
195 New Kent Road
London SE1 4AG
020 7403 0115
fax 020 7403 6384

Hunt, Steve (scwo) (48)
Cohen, Ms Esther (js)
Israel, Ian
Johnson, Ms Elizabeth
Ryan, Ms Linda
Smith, Ms Penny (js)
Stirling, Mike

Crown Courts

50. **71/73 Great Peter Street**
Victoria, London SW1P 2BN
020 7222 5656
fax 020 7960 1114

Harris, Mark (acpo crown courts, offices 50-57)

51. Probation Office
Central Criminal Court
Old Bailey, EC4M 7EM
020 7248 3277
fax 020 7236 6692

Morris, Mrs Marian (spo)
Dixon, Miss Kathy
Hope-Wynne, Tim
Kirwin, Kevin
Innis, Ms Cheryl
Lenton, Tony
Moran, Mrs Sylvia (ccpa)

52. Probation Office
Court of Appeal Criminal Division
Room E303, Royal Courts of Justice Strand, WC2A 2LL
020 7936 6066/6092/6865
fax 020 7936 6704

Morris, Mrs Marian (spo)
Gardner, Ken

53. Probation Office
Middlesex Guildhall Crown Court
Broad Sanctuary, Parliament Square
SW1P 3BB
020 7799 2131
fax 020 7233 2215

Day, Ms Liz (spo)
Banton-Douglas, Mrs Glasmine
Gonord, Ms Zoe
Rugen, Oliver
Martin, Jill (ccpa)

54. Probation Office
Inner London Crown Court
21 Harper Road SE1 6AW
020 7407 7333
fax 020 7403 8637

Mavunga, Peter (spo)
Burkett, Michael
Dalrymple, Mrs Melody
Dunkley, Ms Charlotte (p)
Spring, Ms Pamela
Sutherland, Clive
Vaughan, Ms Justina
Wilson,Ms Deborah
Wright, Ms Susan (p)
Phillips, Ms Marva (ccpa)

55. Probation Office
Blackfriars Crown Court (sitting at Pocock Street)
Mitre House, Unit 4 & 5
223-237 Borough High Street, SE1 1JD
020 7740 8550
fax 020 7740 8588

operates from a split site, all mail and admin enquiries to above address

Connolly, Michael (spo)
Benker, Ms Theresia
Brooks, Peter
Gorbutt, Ms Karen (p)
Minhinnick, Ms Frances
Komey, Ms Adelaide (ccpa)

56. Probation Office
Southwark Crown Court
1 English Grounds, SE1 2HY
020 7403 1045
fax 020 7403 8602

Worthington, Rory (spo)
Coad, Mick
Flemming, Ms Rhonda
Johnson-Buchanan, Ms Alice
Kedney, Ms Teresa
Kelly, Mick
Rowe, Mrs Antoinette
Tilly, Mrs Wendy (ccpa)

57. Probation Office
Woolwich Crown Court
2 Belmarsh Road
Western Way, Thamesmead, SE28 0EY
020 8312 7000
fax 020 8317 1605

Dancer, Mike (spo)
Banfield, Mrs Shakun
Brown, Ms Gay
Bryant, Ms Josephine
Woolstone, Ms Diane
Lori, Ms Anne (ccpa)

58. **Mitre House**
223-237 Borough High Street
London SE1 1JD
020 7740 8500
fax 020 7740 8447

Gilbert, Kate (acting acpo partnerships & women offender policy)

The Partnership Support Unit
Cameron, Angus (spo mentally disordered offenders)
Vacancy (spo partnerships & income/service generation)
Brennan, Robin (spo drugs/alc devpt)
Fry, Sarah (info off)
Binding, Diana (p, po ptnrshps)
Boyd, Ms Sandra (administrator)

Hostels

59. **Mitre House**
223-237 Borough High Street SE1 1JD
020 7740 8500
fax 020 7740 8450

Gavin, Ms Geraldine (acpo hostels, offices 59-63)
Noon, Ms Chis (spo sex offender policy)

Purchased Accommodation Services
Stocker, Fil (housing devpt mgr)
Tooth, Amanda (housing devpt off)

Central Referral & Monitoring Unit
020 7407 7293
fax 020 7357 7140
Kelly, Ms Jessica (referrals off)
Skinner, Ms Madeleine (referrals off)

60. **Camden House Bail Hostel**
199 Arlington Road, Camden Town
London NW1 7HA
020 7482 4288
fax 020 7284 3391

Hillas, Andrew (spo mgr)
Nasrudin, Feisal (po deputy mgr)
Cullinane, John G (asst mgr)
Hobart, Keith (asst mgr)
Mullahy, Ms Susan (asst mgr)
W. Central PSA

61. **Tulse Hill Bail Hostel**
147 Tulse Hill, London SW2 2QD
020 8671 4086
fax 020 8671 8546

Sawyer, Mrs Cicely (spo mgr)
Montgomery, Dave (po dep mgr)
Barrett, Adam P (asst mgr)
Reid, Vernon (asst mgr)
Scott, Ms Nadine (asst mgr)
S. Central PSA

62. **Canadian Avenue Bail Hostel**
7 Canadian Avenue
Catford, SE6 3AX
020 8690 3234
fax 020 8314 0650

Tuhill, Ms Louise (spo mgr)
Foot, David(po dep mgr)
Clarke, Ms Clare (asst mgr)
Miles, Leon(asst mgr)
Mitchell, Ms Sandrene (asst mgr)
Weise, Pauline (asst mgr)
S. Central PSA

63. **Ellison House Probation & Bail Hostel**
370 Albany Road, Camberwell
London SE5 0AJ
020 7703 3332
fax 020 7252 6327

Howitt, Mike (spo mgr)
Hutt, Robert (po dep mgr)
Blades, Dene (asst mgr)
Parsons, Don (asst mgr)
Sandford, William (asst mgr)
S. Central PSA

Voluntary Approved Hostels

64. **Katherine Price Hughes**
28 Highbury Grove, N5 2EA
020 7226 2190
fax 020 7354 3221

West, James (mgr)
Bream, Simon (dep mgr)
Worrall, Marta (snr asst mgr)
Duquemin, Tracy (asst mgr)
E. Central PSA

65. **Kelley House** (women only bail hostel)
18-20 Royal College Street
NW1 0TH
020 7388 3945
fax 020 7383 7211

Vacancy (mgr)
McWilliams, Elaine (dep mgr)
Johnson, Cheryl (admin)
Cayrole, Sylvianne (duty proj wrkr)
Ducent, Cleo (proj wrkr)
Fowles, Deby (proj wrkr)
Lawson, Thelma (proj wrkr)
Russell, Dione (proj wrkr)
Smith, Susan (proj wrkr)
Stanwy, Gillian (proj wrkr)
Williams, Jackie (drug wrkr)
Amao, Remi (night proj wrkr)
Mitchell, Sheena (night proj wrkr)
W. Central PSA

66. **HESTIA Streatham Hostel & Housing Assn**
298 Leigham Court Road, SW16 2QP
020 8769 8096
fax 020 8677 1230

Owen, Ted (mgr)
Jones, Simon (dep mgr)
Cusworth, Sarah (asst mgr)
Dyer, Katherine (asst mgr)
Kelly, Eddie (asst mgr)
Williams, Morris (asst mgr)
Williams, Wyn (asst mgr)
S. Central PSA

67. **HESTIA Brixton Hostel & Housing Assn**
9 Cologne Road SW11 2AH
020 7223 3006
fax 020 7924 2156

Owen, Ted (gp mgr)
Bundyford, Paul (mgr, pract teacher)
Brown, David (asst mgr, pract teacher)
Campbell, Sue (asst mgr)
Foster, Jo (asst mgr)
Heffernan, Majella (asst mgr)
Hopwood, Diane (asst mgr)

Prisons

68. 71/73 Great Peter Street
London SW1P 2BN
020 7222 5656
fax 020 7960 1114

Reaich, David (acpo prisons, offices 69-75)

69. H M Prison
Jebb Avenue
Brixton SW2 5XF
020 8674 9811
Special Visits 020 8671 6150
fax 020 8674 6128 (prison)
fax 020 8678 0600 (probn)
fax 020 8674 4456 (bail info)

Probn clerk ext 299
Discipline ext 313/244

Quinn, Ms Anne (spo) ext 295
Bild, Ms Sally
Collins, Miss Eileen
Gorman, Mike
Love, Mrs Joy (p)
Moodie, Ike
Wyatt, Mrs Susan (p)

70. H M Prison
Parkhurst Road
Holloway N7 0NU
020 7607 6747
fax 020 7700 0269 (prison)
fax 020 7700 6518 (probn)

Shipley, Di (spo) extn 2306
Alphonse, Mrs Yvonne
Best, Ms Wendy
Crosby, Josephs, Ms Andrea
D'Arcy, Ms Mary
Garry, Ms Annie (js)
Haggett, Ms Sarah
Redhouse, Ms Elizabeth
Whittaker, Ms Anne-Marie

72. H M Prison **Belmarsh**
Western Way, Thamesmead
Woolwich SE28 0EB
020 8317 2436
fax 020 8317 2421
probn fax 020 8317 8719

Probn clerk ext 403
Discipline ext 300/301/313

Atkin, Ms Margaret (spo) ext 400
Ashby, Ms Jackie ext 333

Baulch, Clive
Howson, Ms Yvette
Guise, Ms Louise

73. H M Prison **Pentonville**
Caledonian Road N7 8TT
020 7607 5353
fax 020 7700 2386 (probn)
fax 020 7700 0244 (prison)

probn clerk ext 306
HDC clerk ext 391
parole/rotl/sentence planning ext 356

special visits 020 7607 6515
fax 020 7609 6745

Owens, Ms Jackie (spo until 31.3.01) ext 302
Tate, Alex (spo from 1.4.01) ext 302
Edwards, David
Hatton, Andrew (D wing) ext 371
Thomas, Mrs Lee-Ann (A/C/E wing) ext 441
Walker, Mrs Diane (hospital, R wing, rule 45) ext 334

74. H M Prison, Heathfield Road
Wandsworth
SW18 3HS
020 8874 7292
fax 020 8875 1648 (probn)
fax 020 8877 0358 (prison)

Probn clerk ext 297

Biggar, Ms Kathleen (spo) ext 384
Bhui, Hindpal
Bryson, Veronica
Dymond, Mrs Jan
Froggatt, Roger
Morgan, Rhys
Nevill, Ralph
New, Mrs Sue
Wood, Alastair

75. H M Prison
Wormwood Scrubs
Du Cane Road, W12 0AE
020 8743 0311
fax 020 8740 1955 (probn)
fax 020 8749 5655 (prison)

Probn clerk ext 296
Discipline ext 309
Special visits ext 289

Fearnley, Janet (spo) ext 299
Aryee, Eric ext 467
Barber, Diane ext 579
Butler, Ms Michelle ext 619
McEvoy, Larry ext 323
Meeson, Terry ext 363
Milton, Mrs Janet ext 484
Prevatt, Petra ext 302
Wiggs, Ann ext 288
Vacancy ext 618
Vacancy ext 382
Baker, Briony (bail info) ext 579

Borough	**PSA Offices**
City of London	City of London 30
Camden	West Central 21, 22
Greenwich	South Eastern 42, 44
Hackney	East Central 24, 25
Hammersmith	West London 14
Islington	East Central 21, 22
Kensington & Chelsea	West London 16, 17
Lambeth	South Central 35, 36
	South Western 35, 36
Lewisham	South Eastern 38-40
Southwark	South Central 38, 39
Tower Hamlets	Thames 26-30
Wandsworth	South Western 32, 33
Westminster	South Westminster 18
	North Westminster 16

Courts
Balham Youth Court 33, 36
Bow Street Magistrates 18
Camberwell Green Magistrates 38
Camberwell Green Youth Court 38
Central Criminal Court 51
Clerkenwell Magistrates 21
Greenwich Magistrates 43
Guildhall Justice Room (City of London) 30
Highbury Corner Magistrates 22
Horseferry Road Magistrates 18
Inner London Crown Court 54
Knightsbridge Crown Court 55
Marlborough Street Magistrates 18
Marylebone Magistrates 17
Middlesex Guildhall 53
Principal Registry of the Family Division 46
Royal Court of Justice (Criminal Division Court of Appeal) 52
Southwark Crown Court 56
South Western Magistrates 33
Thames Magistrates 26
Thames Youth Court 26
Tower Bridge Magistrates 38
West London Magistrates 18
West London Youth Court 18
Woolwich Crown Court 57
Woolwich Magistrates 41

Area Code 62

NORTH-EAST LONDON PROBATION SERVICE from 1.4.01 part of the London Probation Service

London Boroughs of Barking, Havering, Newham, Redbridge, Waltham Forest, E4, (part), E6, E7, E10 (part), E11, E12, E13, E15, E16, E17, E18.

Out of hours emergency contact point
Westbourne House
020 8534 0673

Offices

1. **Head Office**
4th Floor, Olympic House
28/42 Clements Road,
Ilford Essex IG1 1BA
020 8514 5353
fax 020 8478 4450

Lockwood, Howard (chief exec & cpo)
Baldwin, Richard (dcpo)
Baker, Paul (aco)
Carrie, Sue (aco)
Cheston, Len (aco)
Dawes, Lucy (aco)
Appleby, Sally (aco, human resources)
Akerman, Joe (treasurer)
McFarland, Marrianne (hr unit mgr)
Deslandes, Maxine (snr acct)
Weston, Alan (spo partnership)
Smith, Alex (systems off)
Evans, John (properties, supplies, services)
Giles, Kevin (r&i systems mgr)
Matthews, Lisa (service devpt mgr)
Spiegler, Barbara (it trainer)
Matthews, Tracey (research officer)

Robinson, Jim (cttee secy)
fax 020 8478 4450

Youth Offending Team
Anderson, Pauline 020 8270 6462

Staff Development & Training Unit
McVey, Mary (spo)

2. **Crown Court Liaison Office**
Crown Court, Hollybush Hill
Snaresbrook, E11 1QW
020 8530 7561
fax 020 8530 1399

Osborne, Soroya (spo)
Atherton, Sue (p)
Beamish, Edie (p)
Brotherton, Sandra
Davis, Morna
Headley, Andrea (p)
Smith, Steve
Stuart, Malcolm
Franco, Linda (exec off)

3. **Community Service (West)**
15 Belton Road
Forest Gate E7 9PF
020 8472 5412
fax 020 8471 6673

Atherton, Gary (spo)
Flower, Rob (snr supvr)
Khan, Nabila (supvr) (peripatetic at 3 & 4)
Carlton, John-Baptiste (supvr)
Copp, Michael (supvr)
Hinde, Pat (supvr)
Michael, Sherlie (supvr)
Pearce, Colin (supvr)
Rendell, Harvey (supvr)
Rix, Katherine (supvr)
Walcott, Patsie (supvr)
Capy, Jan (admin mgr)

4. **Community Service (East)**
29/33 Victoria Road
Romford RM1 2JT
(01708) 753555
fax (01708) 752096

Howell-Ives, Nick (spo)
Padden, Eddie (snr supvr)
Assi, Suki (supvr)
Grainger, Brian (supvr)
Henderson, Barry (supvr)
Price, Carmel (supvr)
Sherry, Anita (supvr)
Stack, Martin (supvr)
Yarde, Trevor (supvr)
Waters, Pat (admin mgr)

5. 1b Farnan Avenue
Walthamstow E17 4TT
020 8531 3311
fax 020 8531 1319

Community Supervision Team
Rock, Hilary (p, spo)
Browne, Jomo (spo)
Brotherton, John
Cameron, Jeremy
Collins, Caroline
Forbes, David
Hawkes, Colin (p)
Johnson, Michael
Vanderputt, Layton

Woodman, Judith
Bolden, Cheryl (psa)
Foot, Jackie (psa)
Mara, Belinda (p, admin mgr)
Brient, Pat (p, admin mgr)

Victims & Domestic Violence
Riley, Brian (spo)
Imo, Linda (psa)

6. **Resource Centre Team**
Burghley Hall
809/813 High Road
Leytonstone E11 1HQ
020 8 558 2112
fax 020 8 558 5861

Keever, Lourdes (spo)
Maughan, Stephen (pract devpt assessor)
Afridi, Zaheer (p)
Applequist, John
Melville, Pete
Moss, Jo-Anne
O'Neil, Kathy
Robertson, Neil
Stevenson, Christina
Whitehall-Smith, Steve (psa)
Oakman, Maria (admin mgr)

7. 20 Romford Road
Stratford E15 4BZ
020 8534 5656
fax 020 8534 8285

Austin, Richard (spo)
Pilgrim, Mary (spo)
Turley, Kevin (spo)

Community Supervision Team
Hartley, Carol
Headley, Andrea (p)
Lewin, Alphonso
Lewis, Gill (p)
Mumford, Nana
Peart, Paul
Stewart, Sonia
Turner, Haley

Resource Centre Team
Prempeh, Stephanie
Dajani, Basil
Dean, Andrew
Downton, Deborah
Kiil, Karen (p)
Paul, Nick
Storer, Kate
Taylor, Emma-Jane
Tulloch, Lenford
Turkington, Robbie
Dowsett, Kim (psa)
Martin, Jan (admin mgr)

8. Stratford Magistrates' Court
389-397 High Street
Stratford E15 4SB
020 8522 5000

Court Team
Kilbey, Graham
Field, Debbie (psa)
Matwala, Kiran (psa)

9. NELPS Probation Centre
277 High Road
Ilford Essex IG1 1QQ
020 8478 8500
fax 020 8478 8518

Community Supervision & Resource Centre Team
Denton, Claude (spo)
Grizzle, Hope
Husband, Hazel
Moonoosamy, Krishna
Stuart, Malcolm
Taylor, David
Thomas, Penny
Ruparell, Padma (psa)
Shield, Jackie (psa)
Clements, Pat (admin mgr)

Groupwork Team
fax 020 8553 1972
Head, Mike (spo)
Boyde, Pam
Gunn, Ann
Loughnane, Tar-Mischa
Maister, Jane (p)
Scott, Emma
Thomson, Julie (p)
Ward, Shirin
McFarland, Kathy (psa)
Dunkling, Marilynne (psa)

Sex Offenders Project
fax 020 8553 1972
Head, Mike (spo)
Kennerson, Shirley
Martin, Sally
McSharry, David
Rose, Yvonne (p)

Legal Proceedings Team
fax 020 8553 1972
Porter, Alan (lpt mgr)
Cleary, Cyril (lpt off)
Fitzpatrick, Alan (lpt off)
Latham, Lynda (lpt off)

Padden, Pam (lpt off)

Housing & Welfare Rights Unit
fax 020 8478 8518
Cash, Helen (housing & welfare mgr)
Enemuwe, David (hwro, based at 6)
Rana, Aruna (hwro, based at 7)
Coolican, Hilary (hwro, based at 11)
Holman, Simone (hwro, based at 10)

Home Detention Curfew Unit
fax 020 8553 1972
Birthwright, Doreen (hdc wrkr)

Drug Treatment & Testing Orders
fax 020 8553 1972

Findlay, Joan (spo)
Boyd, Sarah
Wogan, Vince

10. **Havering**
1 Regarth Avenue, South Street
Romford Essex RM1 1TP
Romford (01708) 742453/726063
fax (01708) 753353

Resource Centre Team
based at Community Service East (office 4)
Charles-Vincent, Donna (spo)
Ajayi, Grace
Knight, Selina
Kochinky, Manfred
Newman, Linda (psa)

Community Supervision Team
Hawthorne, Maureen (spo)
Tuddenham, Robin (spo)
Drayton, Felecia (pract devpt assessor)
Amartey, Amarh
Bowers, Terry
de Vries, Christa
Ezeigbo, Ibironke
Flynn, Olivia
Groce, Leonie
Heckroodt, Carina
Sefa-Bonsu, Jane
Smith, Jacqueline (p)
Kemp, Jackie (psa)

Pudney, April (admin mgr)

11. **Family Court Welfare Office**
from 1.4.01 part of Children & Family Court Advisory & Support Service
2nd floor, 450 High Road
Ilford, Essex IG1 1QF
020 8553 0535
fax 020 8478 6031

Walker, Richard (sfcwo)
Breeze, Paul
Burrett, Liz
Darling, Beryl
Ferguson, Judith
Harmer, Madeline (p)
Lemonides, Christina
Lubell, Joyce
Lumsden, Barbara
Morrison, Pat
Poyser, Pauline
Stanley, Dolores
Weir, Ian
Browne, Pat (admin mgr)

Hostel

12. **Westbourne House Probation & Bail Hostel**
199 Romford Road, Forest Gate E7 9HL
020 8534 0673
fax 020 8534 8286

Divine, Ann (spo warden)
Treasure, Sarah (po deputy)
Stewart, Nancy (po deputy)
Bailey, Maureen (asst warden)
Barron, Clive (asst warden)
Kane, Germaine (asst warden)
Raison, Peter (asst warden)
Ross, Jenny (asst warden)
Howard, Hilary (temp admin mgr)

Petty Sessional Areas

10 Barking
10 Havering
7 Newham
9 Redbridge
5, 6 Waltham Forest

Crown Court

2 Snaresbrook

Area Code 63

SOUTH EAST LONDON PROBATION SERVICE from 1.4.01 part of the London Probation Service

London Boroughs of Bexley, Bromley, Croydon, SE2 (part), SE 19 (part), SE20, SW16 (part) SE25, SE28 (part).

Offices

1. **Head Office**
Crosby House, 9/13 Elmfield Road
Bromley BR1 1LT
fax 020 8466 1571

Hayes, Paul (chief exec) 020 8464 3430
Withington, Brian (director hr) 020 8464 3436
McDonald, David (director operations) 020 8464 3437
Hodges, Stephen (director finance) 020 8464 3433
Kinnersley, Bronja 020 8460 2740
Miller, Beverley (personnel mgr) 020 8464 3436
Turnbull, Graham (snr research/info) 020 8464 3435
Thomas, Bernadette (staff devpt) 020 8464 3431
Pasquale, Virginia (divnl mgr) 020 8464 3433

Community Devpt Office
020 8460 2740
Horne, David
Taylor, Graham
Heal, Rosanna

2. Norwich Place
Bexleyheath Kent DA6 7ND
020 8304 5521
fax 020 8301 5737

office covers Abbeywood SE2 (pt), Barnhurst, Belvedere, Bexley, Bexleyheath, Blackfen, Crayford, Erith, Footscray, North Cray, Northumberland Heath, Sidcup, Slade Green, Thamesmead SE2 & SE28 (pt), Welling, New Eltham SE9 (pt)

Bransby, Lynn (divnl mgr)
Thornton, Claire (snr pract)
Haycox, Michael (snr pract)
Edwards, Tamara (seconded Greenwich dtto)
Fisher, Jean (p)
Forsyth, Ian (p)
Gabnel, Maria
Nicholas, Malcolm
Phillips, Bruce
Sinclair, Joanne
Marani, Pat (pso)

Community Service Office
Bishop, Karen (cso)
House, Peter (cso)
Tinham, Ann (cso)

3. Magistrates' Court
1 London Road
Bromley Kent BR1 1BY
020 8290 6255
fax 020 8466 6217

Court Duty Officer ext 101

Public Protection Team
Lusk, Ann (spo)
Barnett, Jane
Carr, Diane
Choy, Hilary
de Waal, Michael
Hogg, Jean
Seaton, Wendy

4. 6 Beckenham Road
Beckenham Kent BR3 4LR
020 8658 3511
fax 020 8658 8678

office covers Anerley, Beckenham, Bickley, Bromley (pt), Clock House, Downham (pt), Eden Park, Elmers End, Hayes, Penge (SE20), Shortlands, Sydenham SE26 (pt), Upper Norwood SE19(pt), West Wickham

Costello, Peter (divnl mgr)
Tomlin, Patsy (snr pract)
Craig, Jenny
Quinn, Lee
Vasseur, Anick
Sharp, Jim (effective pract)
Newman, Colin (drug wrkr)

Offender Programme Team
Porter, Nick (spo)
Behr, Andrew
James, Sally (p)
Leighton, Michelle
O'Kelly, Catherine (p)
Morrow, Neal (pso)
Noxon, Rachel (pso)
Osborne, Emma (pso)

Community Service Office
Aling, Jackie (cso)

Hicks, Kerry (p, cso)
Holland, Bernadette (p, cso)
Mather, Andy (cso)

5. 6 Church Hill
Orpington Kent BR6 0HE
Orpington (01689) 831616
fax (01689) 875253

office covers Biggin Hill, Bromley (pt), Chelsfield, Chislehurst, Cudham, Downe, Farnborough (Kent), Green Street Green, Keston, Mottingham SE9 (pt), Orpington, Petts Wood, St Mary's Cray, St Paul's Cray

Humfress, Valerie (pract devpt assessor)
Grandison, Selene (snr pract)
Barnard, Mark
Spare, Sue
Seddon, Phillip
Catling, Sarah (trainee)
Thomas, Jerry (trainee)
Warnock, Mauricia (trainee)

Resettlement Team
Anderson, Iain (spo)
Batchelder, Marion
Hiscock, Lynda
Murray, Ann
Jarvest, Fiona (pso)
O'Connor, Linda (pso)

6. Church House, Old Palace Road
Croydon Surrey CR0 1AX
020 8686 6551
fax 020 8688 4190

Croydon and New Addington offices cover Addington, Addiscombe, Coulsdon, Croydon, Forestdale, Kenley, Monks Orchard, New Addington, Norbury SW16 (pt), Old Coulsdon, Purley, Sanderstead, Selhurst, Selsdon, South Norwood SE25, Shirley, Upper Norwood SE19 (pt), Thornton Heath, Waddon, Whyteleafe, Woodside. Responsibility for particular areas may vary

Williams, Anne (divnl mgr)
Felix, Lorna (p, spo)
Gorf, Richard (spo)
Elliott, Nigel (snr pract)
O'Donnell, Teresa (snr pract)
Teesdale, Mick (snr pract)
Mills, Karen (p, practice devpt assessor)
Allen, Ruth (p)
Harris, Felix
Hunt, Jacqueline (p)
Hutchinson, Ian
Gilchrist, Beryl
Hurcomb, Marion
Jahangir, Fozia
Jones, Mechelle
Kotei, Charles
Lilley, Annabel
Lloyd, Liz
Moore-Cosbert, Coleen
Patterson, Anne (p)
Robinson, Sharon
Jefferson, Emily (pso)
Joseph, Paulina (pso)

O'Connor, Mark (trainee)

Drug Treament & Testing Orders
Allen, Dyanne
Cox, Samantha
Dickinson, Barry
O'Halloran, Gill

7. **Resettlement Team**
Wandle Road
Croydon CR0 1DF
020-8686 4441
fax 020-8686 4442

Gorf, Richard (spo)
Northmore, Helen (p)
Samuel, Sandra
Robinson, Sharon
Ibrahim, Jenny (pso)
Roberts, Amy (pso)
Terry, Angela (pso)

Lockett, Anne (victim liaison off)
020-8686 8642

8. **Community Service Office**
111 Chertsey Crescent
New Addington, Surrey CR0 0DH
(01689) 844735
fax (01689) 840192

Marshall, Trevor (spo)
Austen, Nigel (snr cso)
McCubbin, Madeline (snr cso)

8a. **Community Service Centre**
St Martin's Hall, 47c Dartnell Road
Croydon CR0 6JF
020 8656 8561
fax 020 8656 2587

Chinery-Hesse, Emlyn (cso)
Chapple, Paul (cso)
Hunt, Peter (cso)
Spooner, Pam (cso)
Ryan, Martin (cso)

9. **Crown Court Probation Office**
The Law Courts, Altyre Road
Croydon CR9 5AB
020 8681 5039
fax 020 8667 0178

Glaister, Alice (spo) (9)
Benamaisia, Stephen
Harkins, David (p)
Harris, Grace
Nicholls, Eunice (pso)
Norman, Kate (pso)
Smith, Jenn (pso)

9a. Old Town Hall, Woodcote Road
Wallington SM6 0NR
020 8669 9331 ext 30

Correspondence to office 8

10. **Magistrates' Court Probation Office**
Magistrates' Court, Barclay Road
Croydon CR9 3NE
020 8688 0739
fax 020 8681 7325

Glaister, Alice (spo) (8)
Pearce, Ray (pso) (2)
Shallow, Chireal (pso)
Martin, Rosie (pso)

Legal Proceedings Team
020 8680 5039
Clarke, Robert (pso)
Moore, Lissa (pso)
Burston, Michael (pso)

11. **Family Court Welfare Service**
from 1.4.01 part of Children & Family Court Advisory & Support Service
5 Upper Park Road
Bromley Kent BR1 3HN
020 8460 4606
fax 020 8466 6572

Taylor, Peter (spo)
Barnes, Sharon
Biffin, Denise
Derrick, Maggie
Hale, Nicola
James, Sally (p)
Radigan, Diane
Stringer, Patricia
Tredinnick, Andrew
Ford, Elleen (pso)
Kelly, Muriel (administrator)

12. **Youth Offending Team**
14 Whitehorse Road
Croydon CR0 2JA
020 8665 5588
fax 020 8665 7010

Benjamin, Joe
Pinnock, Paulette

Bromley YOT
Bromley Civic Centre
Stockwell Close
Bromley BR1 3UH
020-8313 4318

Eastham, Esther

Bexley YOT
2 Nuxley Road
Belvedere, Kent DA17 5JF
020-8284 5555
fax 020-8284 5560

Anderson, Lesley

Think First Secondment
Read, Jan

Hostel

13. **4 Beckenham Road**
Beckenham, Kent BR3 4LR
020 8658 3515
fax 020 8663 6244

Stainton, Ann (spo mgr)
Hewitt, Liz (po deputy)
Hills, Susan (admin)
Blair, Ian (asst mgr)
Mariner, Robert (asst mgr)
Pascal, Karen (asst mgr)
Frater, Diana (asst mgr)

Petty Sessional Areas

2 Bexley
3, 4, 5 Bromley
6, 7, 8 Croydon

Crown Court

9 Croydon

Area Code 64

SOUTH WEST LONDON PROBATION SERVICE from 1.4.01 part of the London Probation Service

London Boroughs of Kingston, Merton, Richmond and Sutton, SW13, SW14, SW19 (part), SW20. Surrey postal address: Carshalton, Cheam, Chessington, Hampton Wick, Kingston upon Thames, Mitcham, Morden, New Malden, Richmond upon Thames (inc. Ham and Kew), Surbiton, Sutton, Wallington, Worcester Park (part). Middlesex postal addresses: Hampton, Hampton Hill, Hounslow (part), Teddington, Twickenham, Whitton.

Offices

1. **Head Office**
45 High Street
Kingston upon Thames KT1 1LQ
020 8546 0018
fax 020 8549 8990

Long, Alan P (dir policy &resources) (acting cpo)
Rofey, Derek (dir of operations)
Felgate, Chris (dir personnel & staff devpt)
Citron, Mrs Mary (spo training)
Pick, Mrs Tricia (strategic resources mgr)
Cropper, Mrs Jenny (finance mgr)
Lynch, Eamonn (premises off)

Kingston & Richmond Magistrates' Courts Team
020 8939 4130
Leyne, Ms Breda (crt services mgr)
Broderick, Ms Ann
Cassalls, Craig
Champion, Miss Brenda
Lowe, Ms Tracey
McHugh, Ms Claire
Tucker, Andy (pso)

2. **Kingston Crown Court**
6/8 Penrhyn Road
Kingston upon Thames KT1 2BB
020 8240 2500
fax 020 8240 25525

Nelson, Andy (crt services mgr)
Blake, Les
Walton, Mrs Jane (p)
Badhen, Ms Asha (temp pso)
Costello, Ms Isobel (office mgr)

3. 16 High Street
Hampton Wick
Kingston upon Thames KT1 4DB
020 8977 0133
fax 020 8943 3467

Hampton Wick Community Supvn Team (covers Boroughs of Kingston & Richmond)
McMahon, Mrs M (spo Kingston)
Wilson, Mrs Mary (spo Richmond)
Pitman, Ms Dafna (snr practitioner, sex offenders)
Smith, Keith (snr practitioner, comm safety)
Alexander, Ms Julie
Bartlett, Mrs Hilary
Carvenec, Ms Fiona
Colnbrook, Lee
Freeman, Ms Anna
Gerrard, Jacob
Goodyear, Mrs Lis
Gray, Jim
Henderson, Mrs Sharon
Lindsay, Jane (po lecturer)
Madanayake, Senaka
Walton, Mrs Jane (p)
Wood, Ms Shirley
Shahin, Ms Yvette

Greif, Mrs Judith (asst office mgr)

4. Newton House
1 Commonside West
Mitcham Surrey CR4 4HA
020 8685 0075
fax 020 8646 6353

Merton Magistrates' Court Team
Aiello, Mrs Jan (crt services mgr)
Corrin, Ms Jane
Joseph, Ms Liz
Thorne-Jones, Mrs Angela
Tekin, Ms Sue

Merton Community Supvn Team
Martin, Johm (mgr)
Ahmed, Shamsul
Cooper, Richard
Donovan, Paul
Duck, Michael
Hogarth, Ms Claire
Jones, Ms Lucy
O'Flynn, Ms Frances
Munchin, Ms Susan
McFadden, Mrs Philomena (psa)

Godfrey, Mrs Sue (pract devpt assessor/domestic violence)
Harambee, Mrs Sharon (proj mgr, racially

motivated offenders proj)

Pinkerton, Nina (office mgr)

5. 103 Westmead Road
Sutton Surrey SM1 4JD
020 8643 7211
fax 020 8770 3592

Sutton Magistrates' Court Team
Austen, Andrew (crt services mgr)
Armstrong, Ms Jenny (p)
Idusohan, Ms Vicki (pract devpt assessor)
Shanahan, Mike

Sutton Community Supvn Team
Walpole, Ms Emma (mgr)
Brady, Dermot
Elliot, Mrs Diane (p)
Leeming, Ms Bridget
McDermott, Ms Jennifer
Porter, Ms Jennifer
le Garst, Michael (practice teacher co-ord)

Barnett, Ms Lyndsay (trainee)
Faber, Ms Linda (trainee)
Reid, Ms Beverley (trainee)

Vatin, Ms Michelle (office mgr)

6. **Family Courts Unit**
from 1.4.01 part of Children & Family Court Advisory & Support Service
125 Richmond Road
Kingston upon Thames KT2 5BX
020 8541 0233
fax 020 8547 0915

Thomas, Rod F (sfcwo)
Ahier, Ms Brigitte
Beckendorff, Mrs B
Casey, Mrs Pat
Drummond-Roe, Mrs Peggy
Irwin, David
Thurgood, Mrs Jakki

7. **Probation Resource Centre**
Martin Harknett House
27 High Path
Wimbledon SW19 2JL
020 8545 8500
fax 020 8543 1178

Giles, Chris (mgr)
Marsh, Gordon (snr pract)
Jones, Ms Linda
di Francescomarina, Mrs Tracey
Ramsey, Ms Joanne
Simpkins, Ms Susan
Mellish, Paul (ptnrshp devpt off)

Bondswell, Ms Lorraine (psa)
Fallows, Samantha (psa)
Glynn, Jennifer (psa)
Lawrence, Ms Kim (psa)

Community Service Unit
Dempsie, Mrs Cheryl (snr cso)
Stone, Christopher D (snr cso)
Birkett, Darryl (cso)
Brown, Alistair (cso)
Cruickshank-Faiman, Ms Donna (cso)
Flowers, John (cso)
Leary, Mrs Jan (cso)
Loye, Peter (cso)
Powell, Ms Christine (cso)
West, Ms Sue (cso)
Waugh, James (projects sup)

Drug Treatment & Testing Orders
Palmer, Rob (spo)

Hall, Mrs Avril (office mgr)

8. **Chase Training Centre**
296a Kingston Road
Wimbledon SW20 8LX
020-8543 9110
fax 020-8543 3236

Weijman, Hans (devpt off)

Hostel

9. **Probation & Bail Hostel**
96 North Road, Kew
Richmond upon Thames
Surrey TW9 4HQ
020 8876 6303/4
fax 020 8876 7402

closed for refurbishment

Institution

10. H M Prison
Latchmere House
Church Road, Ham Common
Richmond upon Thames
Surrey TW10 5HH
020 8948 0215
fax 020 8332 1359

Probn clerk ext 416
Th'care dept ext 324
Selection unit ext 321/323
Parole clerk ext 308

Convisser, Ms Sharon (mgr)
Beresford, Graham

Petty Sessional Areas

3 Kingston upon Thames
3 Richmond upon Thames
4 Merton
5 Sutton

Crown Court

2 Kingston

Area Code 65

MIDDLESEX PROBATION SERVICE from 1.4.01 part of the London Probation Service

London Boroughs of Barnet, Brent, Ealing, Enfield, Haringey, Harrow, Hillingdon, Hounslow. N2, N3, N4 (part), N6, N8, N9, N10, N11, N12, N13, N14, N15, N17, N18, N20, N21, N22, NW2 (part), NW3 (part), NW4, NW6 (part), NW7, NW9, NW10, NW11, W3, W4,W5, W7, W13. The London postal areas covered by each office are shown in *italic* after each office address. The majority of offices cover only part of a postal district.

Offices

1. **Head Office**
Glen House, 4th Floor
200 Tottenham Court Road
London W1T 7PL
020 7436 7121
fax 020 7436 9827
cpo, dcpo, co's fax 020 7436 9879
personnel dept fax 020 7637 5492

Walters, J (cpo)
McCulloch, C (dcpo)
Reid, Ms C (co finance)
Steiger, Ms U E (co human resources)
Frost, M (co quality assurance)
Ogbonna, Mrs J (human resources mgr, training, staff devpt)
Webb, Ms T (human resources mgr, personnel)
Mastris, A M (principal finance officer)
McKay, J (facilities mgr)
Brazier, W (info systems & research mgr)
George, Ms E (communications officer)
Logan, A (info tech support mgr)
Cutt, Mrs J (senior admin officer)

1a. **Outstationed Divisional Managers**

Vacancy (Harrow, hostels & central crt team)
DM office at office 6
020 8427 2323
fax 020 8424 2602

Cerfontyne, Ms R (Enfield)
DM office at office 4
020 8363 2261
fax 020 8367 1624

Davies, Ms I (Haringey & east crt team
DM Office, Marlborough Hall
96 Lansdowne Road, London N17 9XX
020 8801 6373
fax 020 8885 4233

Jenkin, M (Ealing)
DM office at office 3
020 8840 6918
fax 020 8579 7835

Jones, W (Brent)
DM office at office 15
020 8830 4393
fax 020 8830 2502

Renau, Mrs C M (Hounslow, prisons & west crt team)
DM Office, 41a Cross Lances Road
Hounslow, Middlesex TW3 2AD
020 8577 7615
fax 020 8570 6127

Rooney, Ms D (Hillingdon & fam crt welfare)
DM office at office 26
(01895) 230035
fax (01895) 271966

Bland, M (Barnet)
DM office at office 7
020 8205 1885/1838
fax 020 8205 5462

2. 4 Birkbeck Road
Acton London W3 6BE
020 8992 5863
fax 020 8993 5942

office covers W3, & pts of W4, W5, NW10

Gallagher, Ms J S (spo)
Barnett, Ms M (p)
Fitzgerald, Ms A
Roberts, Ms J
Sewell, A (p)
Woods, Ms L (pso)

Sex Offender Unit

Roberts, M J S (spo)
Barnfather, Ms J (p)
Cook, D
King, Mrs J A (p)
Roberts, Ms B
Terry, M
McLeod, Ms S (devpt wrkr for adolescent srvs)

Partnerships Dept
020 8993 8613
Chater, C (partnerships mgr)

Young, Mrs B (admin mgr) (based at 3)

3. Leeland House, Leeland Road
Ealing London W13 9HH
020 8840 6464
fax 020 8579 8165

office covers W7 & pts of W5, W13, Northolt, Perivale & Greenford

Stevenson, B (spo)
Diamond, Ms K
Lamont, Ms E
Maycock, J
Tully, S
Reynolds, Ms T (p)

Dunn, Ms M (spo)
Carr, D
Coxall, Ms C (p)
Crane, Ms S
Renn, P
Riddell, L
Rocke, Ms S
Platt, Ms S (pso)

Young, Mrs B (admin mgr)

4. The Old Court House, Windmill Hill
Enfield Middx EN2 6SA
020 8366 6376
fax 020 8367 1624

Harwood, Ms H (spo)
Cobbing, Mrs P (p)
David, Mrs C
Headey, Mrs S (p)
Hemmann, Ms P
Keyte, B
Vacancy
Nunez-Fantie, Ms M (p)
Vacancy
Treble, F T (p)
Wheybrew, Ms J (p)
Roberts-Twinn, Ms S (pso)

Clark, Ms V (admin mgr)

5. 6 Alexandra Grove
Finchley N12 8NU
020 8445 1623
fax 020 8445 1618

office covers N3, N20 & pts of N2, N10, N11, N12, N14

Vacancy (spo)
Akin, Ms M
Lewis, J
Rupra, P
Stapleton, Ms J
Stevens, Mrs H (p)
Vacancy

Koch, Mrs Shula (admin mgr) (based at 7)

6. Rosslyn Crescent
Harrow Middx HA1 2SR
020 8427 7246
fax 020 8424 2101

Upcott, Dixon (spo)
Beecroft, John (p, temp)
Bolton, Mrs Mary (p)
Cawte, Ms Julia
Colley, Mrs Jeanette (p)
Depass, Mrs Rema (p)
Eugene, Ms M
Gordon, P
St Louis, Ms Mitchelle (p)
Wood, A

Johnson, Ms G (p, spo)
Chadder, Philip (pract devpt assessor)
Ostrowski, Ms Elizabeth
Akin, Catherine (trainee)
Brackley, Lorraine (trainee)
Good, Philippa (trainee)

Epie, Ms P (pso)
Sellwood, Ms K (pso)

Thakur, Ms Shaila (admin mgr)

7. **Hendon Probation Office**
Allied House (1st floor)
3 Burnt Oak Broadway
Edgware, Middx HA8 5LT
020 8205 2561 & 3003
fax 020 8205 5462

office covers LB of Barnet, NW4, NW7, NW11, pts of NW2, NW3, NW9, N12

Vacancy (spo)
Johnson, Ms G (p, spo)
Headland, Mrs M (pract devpt assessor)
Brown, D
Carew, Ms R
Dervish, Ms J

Donkin, V R
Downie, WA
Hind, R
Layzell, Mrs J A
Moore, Ms B
Thompson, Ms J
Francis, J (trainee)
Vacancy (trainee)
Vacancy (trainee)
Kyprianou, Ms A (pso)

Contingency Team
Cohen, J B (spo)
Field, C
Lewis, B
Moulson, Ms J
Muller, Ms L
Walcott, Ms C
Williams, A

Home Detention Curfew Team
Laichena, E (hdco)
May, Ms L (hdco)
Pearce, Mrs M (hdco)

7a. **Barnet Youth Offending Team**
Churchfield House
45/51 Woodhouse Road
North Finchley
London N12 9ET
020 8446 9996
fax 020 8446 9998

McDonald, L (mgr)
Malleson, K (mgr)
Berry, D (pract mgr)
Yates, P

8. Telfer House, Church Road
Highgate London N6 4QJ
020 8341 9060
fax 020 8341 4260

Resettlement Team (Haringey & Enfield)
Foy, A (spo)
Forrester, Ms J
Peazer, Ms R
Polius, Ms Y
Walbank, Ms S
Williams, D

Garbutt, Ms C (psr writer)
Millward, J (pract devpt assessor)
Taylor, Ms D (dtto)

Burch, Mrs E (asst admin mgr)

9. Banklabs House
41a Cross Lances Road
Hounslow Middx TW3 2AD
020 8570 0626
fax 020 8814 1238 (com supvn team)
fax 020 8570 1190 (pre & post release team)

office covers pts of W4

Community Supervision Teams
Shaw, Ms J (spo)
Barnes, Ms J
Bimpson, Ms L
Buttress, K
McLean, Ms D
Royle, Ms J
Weale, Ms B
Williams, K
Lamptey, Ms S (pso)
Whiting, Ms S (pso)

Cross, G (spo)
Ashley, M
Belford, Miss A
Horton, Ms J
O'Neal, D
Pendlebury, Ms L (p)

Pre & Post Release Team
Palmer, S (spo)
Bull, Mrs M
Morgan, C
Piedot, Miss V
Keenoy, Ms E (pso)

Fuller, Ms R (admin mgr)

10. **90 Lansdowne Road**
London N17 9XX
020 8808 4849
fax 020 8365 0981

office covers N9, N11(pt), N13, N18

Edmonton Team
Parr, Roger (spo)
Fairbank, Ms Sally
Gilchrist, Ms Telma
Forrester, Ms Jennifer
Lonsdale, Ms Dawn
McLeod, Ms Geraldine
Senverdi, Ms Nalan
Walbank, Ms Sarah
Williams, David

Clark, Ms V (admin mgr) (based at 4)

Admin Contingency Team
Coverdale, Mrs Jae (admin mgr)

11. 71 Lordship Lane
Tottenham London N17 6RS
020 8808 4522

fax 020 8885 5946

office covers, N15, N17, N22

Ferguson, C (spo)
Baggott, M
Carey, Ms C
di Pino, Ms M
Gordon, Ms J
Sharpe, A
Soalla-Bell, D
Stevens, B (p)
Wiliams, Ms F

Bolton, Geraldine (trainee)
O'Sullivan, Tracey (trainee)
Stewart, Mark (trainee)
Worthington, Harriet (trainee)

Community Reintegration Team
McGeown, Ms M (spo)
Laffan, Ms K
Wright, Ms C
Cheetham, Ms R (pso)
Coleman, Ms J (pso)
Fleming-Hodge, Ms W (pso)
Gamanga, D (pso)
Griffiths, Ms E (pso)
Preston, Ms F (pso)
Smith, Ms R (pso)

Carron, Ms S (admin mgr)

12. lst floor, King's House
The Green **Southall**
Middlesex UB2 4QQ
020 8574 1071
fax 020 8813 9124

Griffiths, D R (spo)
Banse, A S
Griffiths, D (p)
McMillan, S
Scullard, Ms P (pract devpt assessor)
Ranger, Ms P
Gough, Ms A (trainee)
Kumar, P (trainee)
Rice, J (trainee)
Rocke, Ms S (trainee)
Gill, Mrs K (comm liaison asst)

Jadunandan, Mrs Z (asst admin mgr)

13. The Court House, Harefield Road
Uxbridge Middx UB8 1PQ
Uxbridge (01895) 231972
fax (01895) 257972

Opong, B (spo)
Barnfather, Ms J (p)
Brown, Ms A (p)
Dalton, Ms R (yot)
Locke, Mrs C E
Lennon, Ms M
Ryan, Mrs C S (pract devpt assessor)
Adams, Ms K (trainee)
Stephens, Ms V (trainee)
Williams, Ms R (trainee)
Shaw, Ms F (pso)

Martin, Ms P (spo)
Auld, Ms S
King, J
Morgan, T
Hay, Ms M (pso)
Mackness, Ms E (pso)
Williams, Ms A (pso)

Foreign Nationals Unit
Abernethy, Mrs R
Hammond, N
Gordge, Ms J (pso)

Manning, Mrs A (admin mgr)

14. 402/408 High Road
Wembley Middx HA9 6AL
020 8903 4921
fax 020 8795 0472

Whyte, Ms M (spo)
Brown, Ms S
Butcher, M
Cover, Ms G
Davies, Ms F
Edwards, Ms S
Lewinson, Ms M
Mills, R
Dottin, Ms D (pso)
Briance, Ms F (asst admin mgr)

14a. **Brent Youth Offending Team**
1 Craven park
London NW10 8SX
020 8965 6020
fax 020 8961 5181

Williams, Ms P

15. 440 High Road
Willesden London NW10 2DW
020 8451 6212
fax 020 8451 3467

office covers pts of NW2, NW6, NW10, W9, W10

Leckey, Mac (spo)
Devine, Ms Kerry
Essen, Mick
Morris, Simon

Oyebola, Kelly
Russo, Ms Angela (p)
Seall, Clive
Meikle, Ms Sandra (trainee)
Carr, Ms Nicola (trainee)

Rambarath, Joe (spo)
Alstrom, Ms Alyson
Barnard, Ms Diane
Johnson, Ms Patricia
Tuitt, Ms Cynthia

Green, Charles (spo)
Clark, Ms Lesley
Fernandez, Ms Lavinia
Lehane, Gerry
Mulowoza, Ms Christine
Nowell, Ms Libby
Steenberg, Christian
Sudds, Allan (p)

Seeley, Ms Kay (admin mgr)

16. **Central Court Team**
(Barnet, Brent & Harrow)
Crown Court, Hailsham Drive
Harrow HA1 4TU
020 8424 2294
fax 020 8424 9346

NB: for results and enquiries at the following Courts
please ring and ask for the Court Officer
Brent Mag Crt 020-8451 6212
Harrow Mag Crt 020-8427 7246
Hendon Mag Crt 020-8205 2561

All other calls (inc breach)
ring Harrow Crown Crt Office (above)

James, Mrs Gloria (spo)
Butterly, Andrew
Davies, Mrs Althea
McDonnell, Patrick
Vacancy (p)
Abbott, Ms Danielle (crt off)
Barlow, Ms Anne (p, crt off)
Bellchambers, Zarina (crt off)
Catmull, Ms Marion (crt off)
French, Beverley (crt off)
Ibbott, Ms Marie (crt off)
Smith, Beverley (crt off)
Thomas, Heather (p, crt off)
Whitten, Ms Catherine (crt off)
Bruno, Sarah (breach off)
Jones, Ray (breach off)
Connage-Hamilton, Mrs B (admin mgr)

17. **West Court Team**
(Ealing, Hillingdon & Hounslow)
Crown Court
36 Ridgeway Road
Isleworth, Middx TW7 5LP
020 8568 8811 ext 272
fax 020 8758 9650

NB: for results and enquiries at the following Courts
please ring and ask for the Court Officer
Acton/Ealing Mag Crt 020-8840 6464
Feltham Mag Crt 020-8890 8747
Uxbridge Mag Crt (01895) 231972

All other calls (inc breach)
ring Isleworth Crown Crt Office (above)

Collins, Miss B (spo)
Baker, Mrs J (p)
Franklin, Mrs C (p)
Milne, R
Singh, Ms A
Backshall, Ms G (crt off)
Batchelor, K (crt off)
Bew, Ms B (crt off)
Booker, Mrs S (crt off)
Bouri, Ms C (crt off)
Desscan, Ms V (crt off)
Freeman, Mrs J (crt off)
Hoque, A (crt off)
Kenyon, J (crt off)
Ryan, Mrs P (crt off)
Mirza, Mrs K (breach off)
Knott, D H (breach off)

Connage-Hamilton, Mrs B (admin mgr)
(based at 16)

18. **East Court Team** (Enfield & Haringey)
Crown Court, Woodall House,
Lordship Lane
Wood Green, London N22 5LF
020 8881 1400 ext 2189/92
fax 020 8881 2665

NB: for results and enquiries at the following Courts
please ring and ask for the Court Officer
Haringey Mag Crt sitting at Tottenham
020-8808 4522
Haringey Mag Crt sitting at Highgate
020-8341 9060

All other calls (inc breach)
ring Wood Green Crown Crt Office (above)

Hughes, Mrs A (spo)
Braithwaite, J (p)
Ellis, Ms J
Khan, Mrs S
Waghorn, Ms H (p)
Benwell, Mrs D (crt off)

Cordwell, Mrs B (crt off)
Humes, Ms D (crt off)
Reeves, Ms M (crt off)
Scanlon, Mrs K (crt off)
Spinks, Ms L (crt off)
Charlemagne, P (breach off)
Elias, M (breach off)

Connage-Hamilton, Mrs B (admin mgr) (based at 16)

19. **Special Programmes Unit**
1st Floor, Allied House
3 Burnt Oak Broadway
Edgware, Middx HA8 5LT
020 8205 2561/3003
fax 020 8205 5462

Bailey, Ms M (spo)
Borgen, Ms D
Hinckley Ms B (seconded as reg trainer for 'R&R')
Obong, B (seconded as reg trainer for 'Think First')
Sawyer, M
Lovett, M (prog devpt off)
Mills, Ms S (pso gpwk officer)
Teasdale, Ms K (pso gpwk officer)

Community Service Offices

20. 1st Floor, King's House
The Green **Southall**
Middlesex UB2 4QQ
020 8843 1828
fax 020 8813 9124

Ealing & Hounslow CS
Wells, M (spo)
Allen, Ms A (temp cso)
Bagot, M (temp cso)
Montag, Mrs B (cso)
O'Kane, A (cso)
Power, Ms J (cso)
Rozwadowska, Ms E (cso)
Russell, Mrs H (cso)
Wilder, Ms A (temp cso)
Chandler, Ms B (prof supvr)

Jadunandan, Mrs Z (asst admin mgr)

21. 402-408 High Road
Wembley Middx HA9 6AL
020 8903 8551
fax 020 8795 0472

Barnet & Brent CS
Sullivan, Ms E (spo)
Fagan, B (cso)
Gibbs, A (cso)
Hewitt, G (cso)
MacDermott, P J(cso)
McKay, P (cso)
Mulloy, P G (cso)
Sutton, K (cso)
Wilkings, P (cso)
Harral, S (proj org)

Briance, Ms F (asst admin mgr)

22. The Old Court House, Windmill Hill
Enfield Middx EN2 6SA
020 8366 6376
fax 020 8367 1624

Enfield & Haringey CS
Davis, Ms J (spo)
Gurrey, Ms K (cso)
Jones, B (cso)
Last, C E (cso)
Malone, J (cso)
Parkin, R I (cso)
Prager, Ms A (cso)
Smith, Ms E (cso)
Tills, A (cs proj co-ord)

Clark, Ms V (admin mgr)

23. The Court House, Harefield Road
Uxbridge Middx UB8 1PQ
Uxbridge (01895) 231972
fax (01895) 257972

Harrow & Hillingdon CS
Flynn, Ms M (spo)
Fairclough, Ms H (p, cso)
Sagoo, Mrs M (cso)
Saunders, Mrs R (cso)

Manning, Mrs A (admin mgr)

based at office 6
020 8427 7246
fax 020 8424 2101

Flynn, Ms M (spo)
Cassidy, M (cso)
Hanson, B (cso)
Marchant, I (proj org)

Thakur, Ms Shaila (admin mgr)

Family Court Welfare Service
from 1.4.01 part of Children & Family Court Advisory & Support Service

24. 8 Alexandra Grove
Finchley N12 8NU
020 8445 1637
fax 020 8445 1041

Walsh, S (scwo)

Castle, Mrs L
Clarke, Ms T
Hughes, Ms L
Payne, Mrs C
Rhoden, Ms S
Symes, G
Watts, Ms M
Yam, Mrs N

25. 75 High Street
Uxbridge Middx UB8 1JR
Uxbridge (01895) 251398
fax (01895) 236299/270237

Burns, Mrs C (p, acting scwo)
Mervin, Mrs L A (p, acting scwo)
Cochrane, Mrs G
Corrigan, Ms B
Farooqi, Ms R
Freeman, Ms A
Gravett, J
Holmes, Mrs P
Knott, Mrs C A
Montserin, W (p)
Scourfield, Mrs M
Smith, Ms B

Jannaway, Ms L (admin mgr)

Hostels

26. **Seafield Lodge Probation Hostel**
71/73 Shoot Up Hill, London NW2 3PS
020 8452 4209
fax 020 8450 2037

referrals 020-8997 9977

Campbell, Ms D (spo mgr)
Ifedoria, Miss A (dep mgr)
Lee, P (hostel officer)
Glenn, Ms C (hostel officer)
Keane, Ms P (hostel officer)
Callender, Ms J (temp hostel officer)
Lehane, G (liaison po) (15)

27. **Ealing Hostel**
2 Corfton Road, Ealing
London W5 2HS
020 8997 7127
fax 020 8810 6213

Holland, Alan (spo mgr)
Djaba, Mrs Hilda (dep mgr)
Philbert, Vivian (temp dep mgr)
Ahmed, Kamron (hostel officer)
Baker, Mark (hostel officer)
Collins, Roy (hostel officer)
Nash, Ms Semona (hostel officer)
Spence, Patrick M R (hostel asst)
Kumar, Ms Rani (finance/admin asst)

Institution

28. H M Young Offender Complex
Bedfont Road **Feltham**
Middlesex TW13 4ND
020 8890 0061
prison fax 020 8844 7496

YOI & Remand Centre
020 8890 0061
probn fax 020 8893 2809
probn admin ext 299

Dalkin, Ms J (spo) ext 300
Heath, Mrs C (admin mgr) ext 299
Charles, D
Davies, T
Stewart, P
Tosso, Ms I
Ashton, Ms N (pso)
Benge, Ms P (pso)
Vacancy (pso)

Bail Information Unit ext 295/296
Penny, Mrs R ext 220
Dominique, Mrs S (pso)
Marshall, Mrs S (pso)

Home Detention Unit ext 236
Brown, Mrs K
Prother, Mrs H

Petty Sessional Areas/ London Boroughs

5, 7 Barnet
14, 15 Brent
2, 3, 12 Ealing
4, 10 Enfield
8, 11 Haringey
6 Harrow
13 Hillingdon
9 Hounslow

Crown Courts

16 Harrow
17 Isleworth
18 Wood Green

Area Code 66

GREATER MANCHESTER PROBATION SERVICE

Offices

1. **Head Office**
6th floor, Oakland House
Talbot Road, Manchester M16 0PQ
0161-872 4802
fax 0161-872 3483

Knott, Ms C M (cpo)
Mathers, R B (dcpo)
Underdown, A W (acpo policy support & info services)
Hindson, M G (acpo family crt welfare, partnerships)
Collett, S J (acpo operations, resettlement, accom)
Davies, M (acpo staff devpt, anti discrim practice)
McMullan, P (acpo operations, comm sentences, sex offenders)
White, Mrs D (acpo prisons, youth justice, crts)
Cook, S (implementation mgr)
Kelly, P J (spo policy inspection & monitoring)
Cotgreave-Jammeh, Ms C (partnerships mgr)
Jones, Ms P A (spo equal opps)
McDonald, Mrs K (spo, dtto)

Jackson, G W A (secy/solicitor)
Millington, J (treasurer)
Baiyee, S (info services mgr)
Wildman, Ms S (head of pr & communications)
Griffiths, K R (head of personnel)
Scott, Ms J (pa to cpo/cttee clerk)
Barkley, Ms D (housing devpt officer)
Vacancy (librarian/info officer)
Vacancy (offender emplt devpt officer)

2. **Manchester Crown Court**
Crown Court Buildings, Crown Square
Manchester M3 3FL
0161-954 1750
fax 0161-839 3856

Minshull Street Crown Court
Courts of Justice
Minshull Street
Manchester M1 3FS
0161-954 7661/2
fax 0161-954 7664

Beddow, D (spo)
Ali, Mrs S
Ashworth, Ms A
Bernard, Ms J
Critchley, D
Driver, Ms S
Entwistle, Ms S
Goodfellow, J
Griffiths, Ms Y
Jenks, Ms A
Mackenzie, Ms C
Daniels, Ms M (psa)
Edwards, Ms C
Hollinworth, Ms A (psa)
Jones, Ms F (psa)
Unsworth, Ms C (psa)

2b. **Bolton Crown Court**
1st floor, Black Horse Street
off Deansgate, Bolton BL1 1SU
Bolton (01204) 372119
fax (01204) 380963

3. **Magistrates Court Building**
Crown Square, Manchester M60 1PP
0161-228 3681
fax 0161-834 3064

Cohen, M (spo)
Davies, H
Ledder, Mrs J
Nelson, Mrs T
Sharpe, J
Anderson, Mrs P (psa)
Bailey, Mrs D (psa)
Everton, Mrs S E (psa)
Finney, Mrs M (psa)
Lomax, M J (psa, bail info)
Naylor, Ms L (psa)
Taylor, Ms C (psa)
Ward, S (psa)

Bolton

4. St Helena Mill
St Helena Road, **Bolton** BL1 2JS
Bolton (01204) 387699
fax (01204) 382372

Bate, Mrs B (district mgr)
Fox, Mrs M (spo)
Holt, Mrs S (spo)
Metcalfe, I (spo)
Rothwell, Ms A (spo)
Taylor, Ms L (spo)
Andrews, Mrs C M
Aslam, H
Bannister, Ms S
Butler, Ms G
Carter, Ms S

Clarke, Ms T
Commissiong, M
Copeland, Ms S
Hagan, Ms U
Harris, Ms B
Johnston, T
Keith, Ms L
Lee, P
Machin, M
Maddix, Ms L
Marginson, Ms L
Maurizi, J
Milne, B
O'Hagan, Ms G
Pickering, R C
Prince, A
Rowlands, D
Scott, Mrs G
Rose, S (drug resource wrkr)
Bailey, Mrs L (psa)
Conway, Ms A (psa)
Davies, Mrs E (psa)
Ducker, Ms S (psa)
Hardman, J (psa)
Hinchcliffe, A D (psa)
McDonald, Mrs S (psa)
McGill, Ms J (psa)
Redding, Mrs D I (psa)
Roberts, Ms N (psa)
Walker, Ms H (psa)
Wright, Mrs W A (psa)

Community Service
Seddon, P (cs mgr)
Duckworth, Mrs P (cso)
Featherstone, J (cso)
Hunter, Mrs P (cso)
Julien, G (cso)
Stroud, Ms A (cso)
Sullivan, J (cso)
Clarke, B (css)
Thomason, A (css)

Bury & Rochdale

5. Argyle House, Castlecroft Court
Castlecroft Road **Bury** BL9 0LN
0161-764 9514
fax 0161-761 2638

Hulse, A P (spo)
Ramos, Ms C (spo)
Baggoley, M
Bancroft, J S
Brown, Ms T
Byrne-Thompson, Ms G
Campbell, R M
McGuffog, Ms S
Riches, Ms I
Straughn, K
Weale, Mrs L
Broadbent, Ms S (psa)
Egan, Mrs J (psa)
Garton, J (psa)
Sherlock, Ms R (psa)

6. St Michael's House, Oldham Road
Middleton M24 2LH
0161-643 0826
fax 0161-643 2414

Boyd, Mrs C (dist mgr Bury/Rochdale)
Butterworth, V (dist admin mgr)

Buckley, Ms A (spo)
Bakshi, Ms N
Belton B
Cunningham, G
Leeming, Miss J
Murphy, Mrs L
Ormerod, S
Perry, Mrs H
Schofield, J
Sharples, Ms Chris
Smith, Mrs C
Briddon, Ms J (psa)
Dixon, Ms J (psa)
Gibney, Mrs G (psa)
Simpson, Ms A (psa)

7. 193/195 Drake Street
Rochdale OL11 1EF
Rochdale (01706) 653411
fax (01706) 713524

Boulter, Mrs M (spo)
Culkin, P (spo)
Robinson, C (spo)
Arrowsmith, J (p)
Heyes, Ms R A
Holden, Mrs J B
Jackson, D
Kay, Ms W
McClintock, Ms T
Murphy, Mrs A
Noall, J M
O'Keefe, I
Stratton, Ms S
Thom, Ms L
Thomas, Mrs A M
Whittaker, Mrs R
Woods, Ms C
Carney, Mrs A M (psa)
Chadwick, Mrs A (psa)
McCorriston, Mrs P (p)
Sidderley, C (psa)

Starkie, Mrs V (psa)
Taylor, Mrs M (psa)
Ward, Ms P (psa)

8. **Community Service**
151 Green Lane
Heywood, Lancs OL10 2EW
Heywood (01706) 620702
fax (01706) 368951

Duddle, A (cs mgr)
Pickering, Ms Y (cs mgr)
Brooks, W (cso)
Connor-Crookes, Ms W (cso)
Howarth, M (cso)
Kennell, Mrs E (cso)
Rimmer, C (cso)
Smith, Mrs P M (cso wkshp)
Yates, S (cso)
Grant, S (css)
Kershaw, J P (css)
Shaw, T (css)

Manchester

9. 87 Moss Lane West
Moss Side Manchester M15 5PE
0161-226 3515
fax 0161-232 0649

Manchester City Management Unit
0161-232 7523
Gillbard, P (dist mgr)
Noah, Ms C (dist mgr)
Owen, Mrs G (dist admin mgr)
Midgley, Mrs G (dist admin mgr)
Shepherd, Mrs A (dist admin mgr)

Clark, Ms E (spo)
Tumelty, J (spo)
Bell, M
Campbell, Ms C
Campbell, Ms F
Christopher, O
Cropper, Ms M
Doyle, Ms A
Foster, Ms S
Hyland, Ms J
James, Ms C
Mattis, Ms D
Mayers, M
Morris, C
Reynolds, T H
Smith, Ms M
Young, Mrs C
Alderson, Ms P (psa)
Jones, Ms A (psa)
Naylor, Ms L (psa)

10. 20 Humphrey Streeet
Cheetham Hill
Manchester M8 7JR
0161-795 1777
fax 0161-720 6707

Vacancy (spo)
Thomas, Mrs J (spo)
Black, M
Bulman, K
Burton-Francis, Ms S
Casey, Ms S
Croall, D
McGinn, D
Mears, V
Murphy, Ms A
Phillips, Ms L
Ross, Ms E
Short, Ms D
Smith, I
Suleman, Ms L
Thompson, L
Totten, J
Williams, Mrs H
Loney, Miss J (psa)
Mansell, Mrs V A (psa)
Read, Ms T (psa)

11. **Longsight District Centre**
521 Stockport Road
Manchester M12 4NE
0161-248 6273
fax 0161-248 8679

Gwenlan, Mrs C (spo)
Johnson, Ms D (spo)
Bhamber, Ms K
Dodson, Ms E
Grant, Ms M
Hill, R
Hudson, Ms S
Johnston, P J
Johnson, Ms H
Kenyon, Ms T
Waugh, Ms S
Wickstead, Mrs L B
Armitage, Ms C (psa)
McLoughlin, Ms M (psa)
Ricketts, Ms C (psa)

12. **Varley Street**
Miles Platting, Manchester M10 8EE
0161-205 7444
fax 0161-205 7563

Corstorphine, Mrs B (spo)
Wood, N (spo)
Brewer, Ms L
Coyle, R

Critchlow, Ms B
Dransfield, Ms L
Lever, Ms A
Saunders, P
Schall, E
Shah, Ms A
Taylor, P
Fairburn, Ms D (psa)
Worrall, Ms S (psa)
Pilkington, K (victim liaison)
Seymour, B (trainee)

13. 258 Brownley Road
Wythenshawe
Manchester M22 5EB
0161-436 1919
fax 0161-498 8304

McGlade, D (spo)
Ward, J (spo)
Briggs, Ms C
Brown, Ms J
Cullinan, B S
Dutton, B J
Graham, P
Kneale, Miss E
McNorton, B W
Ollerton, Ms L
Treherne, Ms N
Williams, B
Williams, R
Merchant, Ms M (psa)
Moore, T J (psa)

14. **Community Service**
Victoria Park
Laindon Road, Longsight
Manchester M14 5YJ
0161-224 0231
fax 0161-248 5378

Mir, A (cs mgr)
Shenton, Mrs J (cs mgr)
Cresswell, A (acting cs mgr)
Atcha, S (cso)
Austin, A (cso)
Barker, Ms S M (cso)
Boyle, F (cso)
Clarke,H J (cso)
Crellin, Mrs J (cso)
Francis, Mrs J (cso)
Graham, Ms D (cso)
Halliwell, P (cso)
Johnson, P S (cso)
Nixon, K (cso)
Shorthose, P (cso)
Simister, C H (cso)
Skidmore, G (cso)

15. **Community Service**
Laindon Road, Longsight
Manchester M14 5GW
0161-224 8181
fax 0161-248 5378

Goode, B C (css)
Hayden, J (css)

16. **Community Service**
43 Carnarvon Street
Cheetham Hill, Manchester M1 1EZ
0161-839 5032

Cardwell, Ms H (css)
Dyer, Ms C (css)
Ricketts, W (css)

Oldham

17. 128 Rochdale Road
Oldham OL1 2JG
0161-620 4421
fax 0161-628 2011

Brierley, D (dist mgr)
Johnson, Ms S (spo)
Samson, Mrs B (spo)
Bywater, Mrs M (dist admin mgr)
Carling, D
Daybank, Mrs K
Fox, M
Hanley, Ms P
Hawley, P
Hill, M
O'Grady, L
Ogunleye, Ms O
Pilkington, Mrs P
Rogers, M
Stevenson, N W
Boardman, Ms P
Jarvis, S (psa)
Marsden, Mrs L (psa)
Ward-Hilton, Mrs S (psa)

18. **Oldham Probation Centre**
Bridge Street
Oldham OL1 1ED
0161-620 4421
fax 0161-628 9970

Crofts, R (spo)
Wright, Mrs M (spo)
Ali, S
Gibbon, M
Hacking, C
Heap, J
Howison, J
Litting, Ms D
O'Brien, Ms M

Paterson, Mrs P
Renshaw, P
Worsley, A
Gartside, Ms L (psa)
Taylor, Mrs J

19. **Community Service Oldham**
Bridge Street
Oldham OL1 1ED
0161-665 3460
fax 0161-628 9970

Finch, Mrs L (cs mgr)
Burton, F (cso)
Edge, Mrs M (acting cso)
Grizzle, E (cso)
Humphries, M (cso)
Newton, Mrs T (cso)
Phillips, Mrs B (cso)
Rimmer, D (cso)

Salford

20. 2 Redwood Street
Pendleton **Salford** M6 6PF
0161-736 6441
fax 0161-736 6620

Wegrzyn, R (dist mgr)
Groves, N (spo)
Homewood, R (spo)
Power, Ms A (spo)
Cain, Ms D (dist admin mgr) (js)
Lyons, Mrs P (dist admin mgr) (js)
Adam, J
Blake, Ms V
Bullough, Mrs R
Davidson, Ms K
Fearon, A
Fletcher, Mrs A
Froggatt, C
Highland, A
Manning, J G
Mason, Ms C G
Morley, J
Prokofiev, Ms A
Reddington, T
Sharples, Mrs C
Wilde, Ms S
Austin, H (psa)
Chow, Ms A (psa)
Egan, Ms K (psa)
Milner, Ms H (psa)
Sackfield, Ms J (psa)
Taylor, Ms S (psa)
Walker, Ms V (psa bail info)
Mills, Ms L (psa dtto)

21. Haysbrook Avenue
Little Hulton M28 6AY
0161-703 8873
0161-702 0611

Hanley, Ms A (spo)
Adams, S
Cotter, Ms G
Doody, Mrs O
Glover, C
Turner, Ms S
Duncan, Miss J (psa)

22. **Community Service**
2 Redwood Street
Salford M6 6PF
0161-736 6441
fax 0161-736 6620

Buckley, J (cs mgr)
Anderson, P (cso)
Copeland, Ms P (cso)
Gee, K F (cso)
Harding, M (cso) (temp)
Holden, T (cso)
Hudson, Ms C (cso)
Worton, M (cso)

Stockport

23. 19/37 High Street
Stockport SK1 1EG
0161-429 0010
fax 0161-476 2709

Davidson, J (dist mgr)
Houghton, I (dist admin mgr)
Nicholls, S R (spo)
Ross, Ms J (spo)
Bryant, Mrs G M
Bunting, D R
Greaves, S H
Hasted, Ms A J
Hilton, Mrs H
Hindmarch, H C
Kaczynska, Ms N
Kennington, T
Oskooi, Mrs L S A
Penny, Ms D
Phillips, Ms M
Ritchie, Ms A
Saxon, Ms D C
Shallcross, Ms M
Tonge, A K
Welford, Mrs E
Wilkinson, J
Allen, Ms F (psa)
Bluff, Mrs D M (psa)
Broadhurst, Ms Z (psa)
McCall, C (psa)

Community Service
Redston, R (cs mgr)
Burrows, G (cso)
Dawson, Mrs J (cso)
Jones, L (cso)
Francis, D (css)

Tameside

24. Francis Thompson Drive
off Water Street
Ashton-under-Lyne OL6 7AJ
0161-330 3695
fax 0161-343 7475

Hamilton, Ms R (dist mgr Tameside)
Hartley, J (dist admin mgr)
Cavanagh, P (spo)
Ashworth, Mrs C
Buckley, Mrs E
Burton, Mrs S
Dawson, P
Mackenzie, I
Pipe, T
Ready, Mrs A
Sayers, A
Gritt, Ms M (psa)
Hackney, M (psa)
Lingard, Mrs J (psa)
March, M (psa)

Community Service
Walker, Mrs S (cs mgr)
Carter, Ms D (cso)
Dippnall, G P(cso)
Fletcher, R (cso)
Upton, Ms C (p, cso)

25. 2 Simpson Street
Hyde SK14 1BJ
0161-366 7344
fax 0161-368 6552

Johnston, Ms F (spo)
Lewis, Ms S (spo)
Assinder, Ms C
Clarke, Ms M
Cutts, B
Eastwood, D
Green, S
Holmes, Ms D
Parkes, G
Plackett, R
Poulson, Ms A
Stott, Ms J
Westby, Ms N
Daley, Ms S M (psa)
Hackney, M (psa)
Johnstone, Ms R (psa)
Scott, L A (psa)
Heath, Ms N (ete)

Trafford

26. Newton Street
Stretford Manchester M32 8LG
0161-865 3255
fax 0161-864 4791

Davidson, J (dist mgr Trafford)
Houghton, I (dist admin mgr)
Hume, C (spo)
Kierc, Ms L (spo)
Clarke, M
Evans, Ms A
Evans, Ms M
Greenstreet, G A
Gibson, J
Kerr, Ms L
Kirk, M
McCaughan, Ms S
McLaughlin, P
Mayo, E
Mills, N B
Robertson, Ms M
Shaw, H
Wastell, Mrs E
Barber, Ms D (psa)
Hearne, P (psa)
Holmes, D (psa)
Scott, Ms A (psa)
Thompson, Ms V (psa)
Wiaktor-Urch, Ms S (psa)

Community Service
Johnson, Ms S (cs mgr)
Bates, E (cso)
Bennett, J (cso)
Murphy, L (cso)
Royle, S (cso)

Wigan

27. 81 Gloucester Street
Atherton M29 0JU
(01942) 876889
fax (01942) 886109

Bowman, D (dist mgr)
Donlan, M (acting spo)
Long, J (spo)
Meakin, Mrs M (spo)
Martlew, Mrs J (dist admin mgr)
Burke, M S
Carpenter, Ms M
Carr, J
Cole, F
Edwards, L

Feeney, K
Foy, R
Hanley, Ms M
Heale, Mrs J
Hunt, M
Ireland, A
McDonagh, Mrs M
Nelson, P
Perkins, T
Piotrowski, W
Royle, Ms L
Smith, Ms C
Smith, Mrs P
Stephenson, A
Walton, Ms D
Walton, Mrs P
Whitehill, P
Bretherton, Miss J (psa)
Duke, Ms K (psa)
Hill, Mrs J H (psa)
Kyte, Ms D (psa)
Morrison, H (psa)
Price, Ms L (psa)
Shearman, Ms C (psa)
Smith, P (psa)

28. **Youth Offending Team**
93 Victoria Road
Platt Bridge WN2 5DN
(01942) 866507
fax (01942) 867422

Foster, Mrs J
Phillips, Ms D

29. **Community Service**
81 Gloucester Street
Atherton M29 0JU
(01942) 876889
fax (01942) 886109

Anchor, Ms P (cs mgr)
Cashmore, Mrs A (cso)
Downham, C (cso)
Horrocks, Mrs F M (cso)
Johnson, Mrs C (cso)
Oliver, G (cso)
Rowe, H (cso)

Units

30. **Administrative Offices**
Kearsley Town Hall, Bolton Road
Kearsley, Nr. Bolton BL4 8NL
Farnworth (01204) 792015
fax (01204) 862940

Proctor, Ms A (training mgr)
Bramwell, Ms A (staff devpt off)
Marland, Mrs A (staff devpt off)
Scholar, Mrs H (staff devpt mgr)
Trinder, A (accred progs implementation mgr)
Hoyes, Mrs J (divnl admin off)

31. **Homeless Offenders Unit**
12 Minshull Street
Manchester M1 3FR
0161-236 7621
fax 0161-228 6745

Humphreys, R (spo)
Hawthorne, Ms E
Lees, Mrs A
McLennan, J
Metcalf, M S
Owen, R G
Rawlinson, N A
Johnson, Mrs P V (psa)
Orwin, Ms C (psa)
Regan, J (psa)
Bailey, Mrs C (day centre mgr)

Probation Programmes Team
0161-237 5173
fax 0161-226 6745

Cope, Mrs A (spo) (38)
Seale, Ms M (spo)
Armstrong-Burns, Ms J
Connolly, A
Doherty, K
Gazdecki, D
Hampson, Ms L
Lavelle, Mrs K
Maddix, Ms J
Patel, N
Reading, N
Tomlinson, Ms S
Anders, Ms S (psa)
Dearing, E (psa)
Hilton, P (psa)
Kershaw, S (psa)
Morgan, M (psa)
Nixon, D (psa)
Stanley, Ms T (psa)
Fletcher, P (gen supvr)
Mirza, I (gen supvr)

32. **Probn Programmes & Devpt Unit (SORT)**
53 Peel Street
Eccles, Manchester M30 0NG
0161-789 2429
fax 0161-707 9370

Cope, Mrs A (spo) (37)

Bradshaw, Ms H
Houton, Mrs J
Sharples, J
Wright, Ms L

Family Court Welfare Service
from 1.4.01 part of Children & Family Court Advisory & Support Service

33. **Family Court Welfare Service Bolton/Wigan**
Great Moor Street
Bolton BL1 1NS
Bolton (01204) 370831
fax (01204) 382385

Griffiths, R B (spo)
Blyth, A J
Cartlidge, Ms R
Collier, J
Mottershaw, Ms J
Packham, R
Piotrowski, W
Steele, Mrs V Y
Thornton, Mrs S
Ward, Ms C A
Wilkinson, Ms S
Wood, B H J
Talbot, Mrs D I (psa)

34. **Family Court Welfare Service Manchester City**
4 Candleford Road
Withington, Manchester M20 9JH
0161-445 8221
fax 0161-445 2887

Cohen, Mrs J (spo)
Bramwell, H
Carpenter, Ms S
Collins, Ms P
Collins, M
Garbett, P J
Holmes, G
Pickering, Mrs J H
Quinn, Ms C
Ransom, J
Reilly, M
Sotomayor-Sugden, Ms R
Swain, S
Watters, Ms J

35. **Family Court Welfare Service Bury/Rochdale/Oldham**
87/89 Manchester Road
Rochdale OL11 4JG
Rochdale (01706) 341529
fax (01706) 713527

Bentley, Mrs M (spo)
Field, G
Galpin, P
Griffiths, Ms S
Hill, Ms S
Hyland, Ms J
Kempster, Ms H
McDonald, N
Morrison, Ms J (p)
Pickering, M
Stafford, Mrs L J (p)
Whittaker, Mrs H

36. **Family Court Welfare Service Stockport/Tameside**
Court Welfare Service, 1st floor
Edward House, Edward Street
Stockport SKl 3DQ
0161-480 5450
fax 0161-476 1522

Harrison, J P (spo)
Barrie, Ms E
Black, Mrs J
Butt, Mrs S C
Cordwell, Ms L
Fantom, Ms J
Garvey, Ms M
Hagan, G
Hill, Ms L
Kelly, J P
Kirkwood, Ms T
Moxham, Mrs E
Schofield, Mrs M
Shanahan, P J
Thorley, J
Smith, Mrs B (p, psa)

Hostels

37. **Hostels Management Unit & Central Admissions Unit**
64 Manley Road
Whalley Range
Manchester M16 8ND
0161-226 1179
fax 0161 227 9052

Central Referrals 0161-226 8465

Kilbane, M (dist mgr)
McGartland, (admin & finance mgr)
Vaughan, Mrs J (central referral off)

38. **Bradshaw House Probation & Bail Hostel**
147/151 Walmersley Road
Bury BL9 5DE

0161-761 6419
fax 0161-763 4353

Elliott, N (spo mgr) (44)
Chambers, L (po deputy)
Nicholls, Ms S (po deputy)
Colton, A (asst mgr)
Davies, S (asst mgr)
Hamer, J (asst mgr)
Yianni, J (asst mgr)

39. **St Joseph's Probation & Bail Hostel**
Miller Street, Patricroft, Eccles
Manchester M30 8PF
0161-789 5337
fax 0161-707 9085

Gordon, P (spo mgr)
Langan, P (po deputy)
Edge, S (asst mgr)
Jeffers, F (asst mgr)
Kluj, P (asst mgr)

40. **Withington Road Probation & Bail Hostel**
172/174 Withington Road
Whalley Range, Manchester M16 8JN
0161-226 1179
fax 0161-227 9052

Shaw, Mrs S (spo mgr)
Sharples, J (po deputy)
Holton, Ms J (relief po/dep mgr)
Brownjohn, Ms J (asst mgr)
Diamond, D (asst mgr)
Lyons, Miss J (asst mgr)
Maloney, M (asst mgr)

41. **Chorlton Probation & Bail Hostel**
10/12 Oswald Road
Chorlton cum Hardy
Manchester M21 1LH
0161-862 9881
fax 0161-862 9554

Devaney, J (spo mgr)
Orr, C (po deputy)
Bernard, T (asst mgr)
Lord, Mrs C (asst mgr)
Mason, V (asst mgr)
Milton, Miss J (asst mgr)

42. **Hopwood House Probation & Bail Hostel**
104 Manchester Street
Heywood, Lancs OL10 1DW
Heywood (01706) 620440
fax (01706) 625927

Elliott, N (spo mgr)
Riley, Ms K (po deputy)
Brown, D (asst mgr)
Dunn, R J (asst mgr)
Lohan, Mrs I (asst mgr)
Lunness, Ms M (asst mgr)

43. **Wilton Place Probation & Bail Hostel**
10/12 Edward Street
Werneth, Oldham OL9 7QW
0161-624 3005
fax 0161-628 6936

Beattie, Mrs K (spo mgr)
Samson, Mrs B (po deputy)
Helire, Ms S (asst mgr)
Cottam, P (p, asst mgr)
Ford, Ms L (p, asst mgr)
Ravey, A (asst mgr)
Stevenson, D (asst mgr)

44. **Ascot House Probation & Bail Hostel**
195 Wellington Road North
Heaton Norris, Stockport SK4 2PB
0161-443 3400
fax 0161-432 9739

Allen, Mrs H (spo mgr)
McDonagh, Mrs M (po deputy)
Cook, C R (asst mgr)
Jones, Mrs J E (asst mgr)
Wright, Ms S (asst mgr)
Knight, P (relief asst mgr)

Hostels for Men

Ascot House, Stockport
Bradshaw House, Bury
Chorlton House, Manchester
St Joseph's, Salford (specialist MDO hostel)
Wilton OPlace, Oldham
Withington Road, Manchester

Hostel for Women

Hopwood House, Heywood

Institutions

45. H M Prison, Southall Street
Strangeways
Manchester M60 9AH
0161-834 8626
special visits 0161-834 7303
fax 0161-832 0074

Probn clerk ext 555
Discipline ext 309/322

Franklin, R (spo)

Bellamy, Ms C
Coulson, J
Fuller, Ms C
Jiacoumi, Ms M
King, Ms C
Mannion, Ms C
Wilson, Ms J
Wood, Ms E
MacLeod, Ms K (psa)

46. H M Young Offender Institution
Hindley Wigan WN2 5TH
Wigan (01942) 866255
fax (01942) 867442
probn fax (01942) 863742

Brimley, J (spo)
Hunt, S
O'Mara, Ms J
Roberts, A
Thompson, E
Thompson, Ms H
Kyte, Ms D (bail info)

47. H M Prison
Buckley Hall
Buckley Hall Road
Rochdale OL12 9DP
Rochdale (01706) 861610
fax (01706) 711797

Parole clerk ext 290
Special visits ext 312

Kennedy, Ms S (spo) ext 245
Bramhall, T ext 442
Hargreaves, B ext 423
Kay, T ext 461
Shkandrij, A ext 461
Venet, Ms S ext 390

48. H M Prison **Forest Bank**
Agecroft Road
Pendlebury
Manchester M27 8FB
0161-925 7000
fax 0161-925 7001

Bail info fax 0161-925 7091
booking visits 0161-925 7029/7030
Healthcare Centre 0161-925 7065
Healthcare Centre fax 0161-925 7055

Macpherson, Ms S (spo)
0161-925 7020
Bryan, R
0161-925 7073
Chambers, D
0161-925 7069
Hayworth, Ms R
0161-925 7071
Holmes, M
0161-925 7088
Lee, G
0161-925 7078
Roberts, Ms A
0161-925 7075
Grundy, Ms J (psa bail info) 0161-925 7000 ext 2019

Petty Sessional Areas

24 Ashton
27 Ashton in Makerfield
4 Bolton
5 Bury
20 Eccles
27 Leigh
9-16 Manchester
6 Middleton
17-19 Oldham
7 Rochdale
20-22 Salford
25 South Tameside
23 Stockport
26 Trafford
27 Wigan

Crown Courts

2 Manchester
2b Bolton

Area Code 34

MERSEYSIDE PROBATION SERVICE

Offices

1. **Head Office**
Burlington House
Crosby Road North
Waterloo, Liverpool L22 0PJ
0151-920 9201
fax 0151-949 0528

Stafford, J W (cpo)
Bradbury, DA (dcpo)
Sproul-Cran, Ms K (secretary /admin)
Hall, I M (Treasurer)
Murray, P J (aco, information services)
Hill, J (personnel officer)
Moss, K (solicitor)
Atherton, Ms L (cttee clerk / admin officer)

Gray, T A (property services officer)
Wood, W J (health & safety officer)
Steele, R I (spo, npsiss)

ACPO Management Units

2. Curtis House,1d Derby Lane
Liverpool L13 6QA
0151-281 0832
fax 0151-281 0866

Eastham, T H (acpo, pre & post release)
Metherell, D C (acpo, cs)
Cottle, G T W (admin asst, cs)
McLoughlin, Mrs P (admin asst, pre & post release)

3. Wirral Probation Centre
40 Europa Boulevard
Birkenhead, Wirral CH41 4PE
0151-666 0400
fax 0151-666 0401

Pakula, Mrs A (acpo, com supervn)
Chung, Mrs S (admin asst, com supervn)

Partnerships
Beckett, T E (mgr)
Halpen, Mrs H (admin asst)

4. Suite 405, Cotton Exchange Building
Old Hall Street, Liverpool L3 9LQ
0151-476 7166
fax 0151-476 7170

Chambers, S (acpo, Com supvn)
Sadler, D A (admin asst, com supvn)

Stelman, A E (acpo, crt services)
Harrington, Mrs L (admin asst, crt services)

Administrative Units

5. **Staff Development**
Rainford Hall, Crank Road
St Helens, Merseyside WA11 7RP
St Helens (01744) 755181
fax (01744) 454671

Murray, D J (acpo, fcw & staff devpt)
Cathcart, E V (admin asst, staff devpt)

Staff Development
Kelly, P J (spo)
Cooper, Mrs J C (staff devpt off)
Padmore, Mrs J (staff devpt off)

6. **Research & Information Unit**
1st Floor, State House,
22 Dale Street Liverpool L2 4TR
0151-236 7128
fax 0151-236 3740

Evans, M W (spo)

7. **Information Systems Unit**
3rd Floor, 10/12 James Street
Liverpool L2 7PQ
0151-236 0611
fax 0151-236 5267

Thwaite, Mrs B (mgr)

8. **Effective Practice**
597 Princess Drive
Liverpool L14 9NE
0151-480 4544
fax 0151-480 3618

Hamilton, Mrs E (spo)

9 **Learning Resource Centre**
63 Argyle Street, Birkenhead
Merseyside CH41 6AB
0151-647 2922
fax 0151-650 0129

Burke, L (mgr)
Fright, P (prog co-ord)
Sweeney, S (pract devpt assessor)
McPaul, M

Community Service Division

10. Belle Vale District Centre
Childwall Valley Road, Liverpool L25 2RJ
0151-487 0123
fax 0151-487 0101

Knowsley/St Helens
Roach, R J (spo) (also Sefton)
Whiteside, A
Donohue, P (operations mgr)
Adams, Mrs I (cso)
Francis, Ms L (cso)
Hoggins, Mrs K (cso)
Hollywood, Ms L (p, cso)
Melia, C (cso)
O'Toole, K (cso)

11. 1b Derby Lane, Old Swan
Liverpool L13 6QA
0151-281 8655
fax 0151-281 8688

Liverpool North
Brown, Miss S F (spo) (also Liverpool South)
Jones, H M
Lynch, J J (operations mgr)

Atherton, B (cso)
Dougan, W J (cso)
Roberts, Mrs M R (cso)

12. Liverpool Community Probation Centre
180 Falkner Street, Liverpool L8 7SX
0151-706 6644
fax 0151-708 5044

Liverpool South
Patton, Ms D
Sinden, D R (operations mgr)
Carroll, B (cso)
Crone, D W (cso)
Losh, Mrs J (cso)
Malvern, W H (cso)
Mathison, D (cso)
Morris, Mrs D (cso)
Parkinson, J J (cso)

13. Sefton House, 1 Molyneux Way
Old Roan, Liverpool L10 2JA
0151-531 6737
fax 0151-527 2534

Sefton
Wyke, G S
Dermott, Mrs J C (operations mgr)
Allen, D (cso)
Cowley, B (cso)
Davies, Mrs K (cso)
Eglin, Ms C (cso)
Owens, D R (cso)

14. 40 Europa Boulevard
Birkenhead, Merseyside CH41 4QE
0151-666 0400
fax 0151-666 0401

Wirral
Vacancy (spo)
Power, F L
Houghton, A (cso)
Loughran, Mrs J A
Turpin, W T (cso)
Williams, Miss J G (cso)

Community Supervision Division

15. **Wirral Probation Centre**
40 Europa Boulevard
Birkenhead, Wirral CH41 4PE
0151-666 0400
fax 0151-666 0401

Cole, A R (spo)
Hamilton, R A (spo)
Bethell, Ms B J
Cameron, Miss J
Craven, Ms P C
Hay, Ms V M
Hunter, Ms V R
Lambert, Ms D
Loram, R
O'Mahony, Mrs C M
Peters, Ms C J
Phillips, H A
Smith, M A
Snell, G R
Tillston, Ms M M
Worgan, D
Haseldon, Mrs P M (psa)
Kennedy, P C (psa)
Webb, Mrs J (psa)

Fresh Start Scheme
Christian, D W (mgr)
Perry, Ms J (operations mgr)
Cummins, Miss S M (psa mentor)

16. 4 Trinity Road **Bootle**
Merseyside L20 7BE
0151-286 5667
fax 0151-286 6900

Barron, Mrs C M (spo) (17, 17a)
Aney, Ms J
Cassidy, P
McGibbon, D
Manley, Ms N
Phillips, Mrs D J
Smerdan, Ms S A (psa)
Smith, J M (psa)
Trout, Ms S (psa)

17. 188 Lord Street **Southport**
Merseyside PR9 0QQ
01704 534634
fax 01704 501845

Aindow, Ms G
Seel, D

17a. 25 Crosby Road South
Waterloo Liverpool L22 1RG
0151-920 4444
fax 0151-928 9143

Chambers, Mrs J A
Hayes, M T
Sarkanen, J V

18. **East Liverpool Probation Centre**
1b Derby Lane
Old Swan, Liverpool L13 6QA
0151-281 8655
fax 0151-281 8688

Kuyateh, Mrs J (spo)
Atkinson, Ms J L
Barnes, R
Burnell, Ms W
Carroll, Ms J C
Guinness, Mrs R
Joyce, B L (hostel liaison)
Kenwright, Ms K
Lynch, V
Cooke, Mrs E H (psa)
Kelley, Miss J (psa)
Prayle, Mrs M F (psa)

Fresh Start Scheme
Jones, Ms A (psa, ops mgr)
Morley, Miss S C (psa mentor)
Riley, Miss S M (psa mentor)

19. 142/148 Stanley Road
Kirkdale Liverpool L5 7QQ
0151-286 6159
fax 0151-284 7847

Tonks, Mrs S (spo)
Chadwick, J A
Clarkson, D J
Dean, Mrs M
Eisner, J
Gay, M R
Humphreys, B P
Macaulay, R G
Ragonese, Ms E L
Rees, Miss A
Roots, Ms S C
Totty, Miss S M
Li, Ms A L (psa)
O'Doherty, B (psa)
Sinkinson, Mrs J M (psa)

20. Liverpool Community Probation Centre
180 Falkner Street Liverpool L8 7SX
0151-706 6688
fax 0151-708 5044

Liverpool South/Central
Edwards, J (spo)
Bell, N G
Goulding, D
Kimber, Ms C P
Lynskey, Ms P F
Minhas, A
O'Neale, S
Adekanmbi, M (psa)
Dunn, Mrs S L (psa)
Kirby, D (psa)
McKenzie, Mrs L M (psa)
Woodford, J (psa)

20a. 14 South Parade
Speke Liverpool L24 2SG
0151-281 0610
fax 0151-281 0710

Jameson, Mrs D E
Jones, G D
Oldham, P N K
Shaw, Mrs E
Torres, G A

21. **South Knowsley Probation Centre**
597 Princess Drive
Liverpool L14 9NE
0151-480 4544
fax 0151-480 3618

Aubrey, Ms C V (spo)
Bilsborough, Ms V
Dent, D J
Gill, Mrs C
Morris, Ms J
Reynolds, C
Sawyer, S
Cheers, R S (psa)
Lloyd, Mrs J A (psa)
Ward, K M (psa)

Fresh Start Scheme
Banton, J (psa mentor)
Pyper, Miss C P (psa mentor)

22. St Helens Probation Centre
St Mary's House
50 Church Street
St Helens Merseyside WA10 1AP
(01744) 630229
fax (01744) 606224

Cunliffe, J (spo)
Collett, S C
Hanley, Ms M
Isherwood, Mrs C
Nicholson-Jones, Ms D
Perkins, A D
Stamper, Miss L M
Shaw Mrs, C M (psa)
Wood, Mrs J E (psa)

Court Services Division

23. **Crown Court**
PO Box 69, Queen Elizabeth II Law Courts,
Derby Square Liverpool L69 6NE
0151-236 5302
fax 0151-255 0682

Crawley, J (spo)
Collins, S C
Daley, Ms J

Dunn, S
Fowlis, Ms N J (p)
Green, Ms P R
Hughes, Mrs M W (p)
Owen, J M
Vellacott, Mrs S (p)
Wolfarth, P J
Kirkpatrick, Ms H (psa)
Pendleton, C (psa)
Reil, Miss S (psa)

24. **Wirral Probation Centre**
40 Europa Boulevard
Birkenhead, Wirral CH41 4PE
0151-666 0400
fax 0151-666 0402

Goodwin, Mrs R (spo)
Adams, Mrs H
Baird, TA
Golby, Mrs P R
Lloyd, Ms S
Ross, S R
Walsh, Mrs J
Murphy, Mrs A M (psa)
Purvis, Mrs W (psa)
Wilson, Mrs A (psa)

25. **Liverpool Magistrates' Court**
1st Floor, State House,
22 Dale Street Liverpool L2 4TR
0151-236 0603
fax 0151-236 5417

England, J F (spo)
Bingham, DW (p)
McCullough, J
Sherlock, Mrs V (p)
Aston, Mrs B A (psa)
Carroll, Ms E (psa)
Pilkington, Mrs B (psa)
Surridge, A J (psa)
Williams, Mrs K A (psa)

25a. **Liverpool Court Services Unit**
6/8 Temple Court Liverpool L2 6PY
0151-286 6226
fax 0151-286 6227

Buchan, Miss E
Callaghan, P B
Lindon-Richey, Ms R
Loughran, P D
Phillips, A M
Robarts, S M
Wake, Ms G H

26. St Helens Probation Centre
St Mary's House
50 Church Street
St Helens Merseyside WA10 1AP
01744 630229
fax 01744 606224

Rutherford, C D (spo)
Briggs, Mrs D T
Edgar, Mrs J
Healey, B T
Riley, Ms L

26a. **South Knowsley Probation Centre**
597 Princess Drive Liverpool L14 9NE
0151-480 4544
fax 0151-480 3618

Holliday, J S
Kerfoot, J J
Loyden, F
Markland, Ms K E
North, Ms C A
Cleary, F (psa)
Jones, Ms M (psa)

27. 188 Lord Street
Southport Merseyside PR9 0QQ
(01704) 534634
fax (01704) 501845

Sloman, R W (spo)
Edwards, Mrs M J
Hypolite, Mrs D
Suddrick, D E

27a. **North Sefton Magistrates' Court**
The Law Courts
Albert Road, Southport PR9 0LJ
(01704) 544277
fax (01704) 545840

Arnold, R J (psa)

27b. 4 Trinity Road
Bootle L20 7BE
0151-286 5667
fax 0151-286 6900

Lewis, Ms K
Kibbey, Mrs R
Piert, A G

27c. **South Sefton Magistrates' Court**
The Court Building
29 Merton Road, Bootle L20 3BJ
0151-933 6999 ext 236
fax 0151-933 8602

Hilton, Mrs B (psa)
Owens, Ms A (p, psa)

Family Court Welfare Service
from 1.4.01 part of Children & Family Court Advisory & Support Service

28. **Family Court Welfare Service**
9-31 Barrow Street, St Helens
Merseyside WA10 1RX
(01744) 630245
fax (01744) 630246

Knowsley/St Helens
White G H (scwo)
Brown, Miss K L
Clarke, Mrs T A
Cooklin, Mrs C R (p)
Douglas, Ms B W
Kay, Ms S J (p)
Lyons, Miss W E
Martin, Mrs K P
Rafferty, M
Wilson, Ms M A (psa)

29. Family Court Welfare Service
3rd Floor, State House
22 Dale Street, Liverpool L2 4TR
0151-286 6464
fax 0151-286 6466

Liverpool/Sefton/Wirral
Ravey, M A (scwo)
Bruggen, Mrs L M (p)
Cribb, G H
Druery, Mrs K A
Finegan, F
Hackett, P F
Ormersher, Mrs E
Rourke, M E
Sherlock, Mrs V H
Shilling, J
Wigmore, R J
Malone, R J (psa)

Pre & Post Release Division

30. Kirkby Probation Centre
Oatlands Road **Kirkby**
Liverpool L32 4UH
0151-547 3160
fax 0151-547 2244

Dickinson, Mrs A T (spo)
Bennett, A J
Cleworth, G C
Dauphin, C J
Fellows, R A
Foster, I G
Hewstone, R G
McGee, E J
Sterry, D E
Stott, J A
Harrison, Mrs C (psa)

31. **Liverpool North Pre & Post Release**
137/139 Breckfield Road
North Anfield, Liverpool L5 4QY
0151-284 4487
fax 0151-284 8683

Harrison, J L (spo)
de Gale, H
Haigh, C
Lennon, Ms B A
Lloyd, H G
Mansaram, R R
Milsom, J
Oluonye, Ms S M N
Rose, Ms F
Seddon, A R (p)
Basley, Ms J (psa)
Powell, Mrs A J (psa)

32. **Liverpool South Pre & Post Release**
Liverpool Community Probation Centre
180 Falkner Street, Liverpool L8 7SX
0151-706 6666
fax 0151-706 6694

Kayani, N S (spo)
Armstrong, P
Birch, Mrs J (p)
Hamlin, Ms J
Holleran, J F
Kennedy, Mrs I
McEllin, Ms B
Muldoon, Ms L A
Price ,G W
Thomas, Mrs M M
Woodruff, Miss J
Lucas, I A (psa)
Richards, Mrs M (psa)
Smith, G (psa)

33. **Sefton Pre & Post Release**
25 Crosby Road South, Waterloo
Liverpool L22 1RG
0151-920 4444
fax 0151-928 9143

Rimmer, D (spo)
Chadwick, Mrs P M (p)
Gough, Mrs L
Gowan, S J
Maguire, Ms J A (p)
Morrison, A

Penn, M R
Sheridan, Mrs D (psa)

34. **Wirral Pre & Post Release**
Wirral Probation Centre
40 Europa Boulevard
Birkenhead, Wirral CH41 4PE
0151-666 0400
fax 0151-666 0401

Sherlock, V G J (spo)
Beggs, J H
Evans, Ms M
McCabe, P T
O'Donnell, S C
Ross, Ms B C
Smeda, M
McGinty, Mrs N P (psa)
Pickstock, Ms K A (psa)

Specialist Services Division

35. **Edge Hill Specialist Unit**
13 North View, Edge Hill
Liverpool L7 8TS
0151-281 1245
fax 0151-281 1246

Garner, P J (housing officer)
Brennan, Mrs N (psa, services to women offenders)

36. **Merseyside Development Unit**
5 Derby Lane, Old Swan
Liverpool L13 6QA
0151-252 0123
fax 0151-252 1117

Nottage, J R (spo)
Anderson, Mrs C A
Balchin, Ms S
Brundell, P
Caton, B P
Green, Ms C E
Hamill, Ms U M
Robertson, J
Wynn, R P

37. **Merseyside Programmes Unit**
Liverpool Community Probation Centre
180 Falkner Street, Liverpool L8 7SX
0151-706 6622
fax 0151-708 5044

Best, Ms J (spo)
Bradbury, Mrs B M
Joel, J J
Kimmance, Ms P
Wright, N E

Car Offender's Programme
Adeniyi, Ms DA
Moss, E
Young, Ms K

Think First' Liverpool
Davies, Mrs C A
Baker, C (psa)

37a. **'Think First' Sefton**
0151 286 6900

Andrews, M A
Daelman, Miss L (psa)

37b. **'Think First' Knowsley**
0151 480 4544
fax 0151-480 3618

Davies, Ms L
Dryhurst, J

37c. **'Think First' St Helens**
(01744) 630229
fax (01744) 606224

Jeffrey, Miss M L (psa)

37d. **'Think First' Wirral**
0151 666 0400
fax 0151-666 0401

Taylor-Watson, Miss S
Chambers, Miss C L (psa)

38. **Substance Misuse**
Liverpool Community Probation Centre
180 Falkner Street
Liverpool L8 7SX
0151-706 6611
fax 0151-708 9687

Crawley, Mrs G L(spo, dtto)
McIlveen J (spo)
Beesley, Mrs P M (dtto)
McKinlay, Ms S J
Lock, P (dtto)
Smith, D (dtto)
Gosling, S J (psa, dtto)
Jennings, K (psa, dtto)
McLean, I (psa, dtto)
Sharples, Ms A E (psa, dtto)
Tubb, Mrs E (psa, dtto)
Whieldon, E V (psa)

38a. **Substance Misuse - St Helens**
(01744) 630229
fax (01744) 606224

Sloan, A F

38b. **Substance Misuse - Sefton**
0151-928 8441
fax 0151-928 3406

Fisher, J J

38c. **Substance Misuse - Wirral**
0151-666 0400
fax 0151-666 0401

Howard, A J (psa)

Hostels

39. **Canning House Probation Hostel**
55 Canning Street, Liverpool L8 7NN
0151-709 4959
fax 0151-707 0813

Mahony, R J (spo, mgr)
Grunhill, P (po, deputy mgr)
Dunleavy J A (probn res officer)
Edwards, J D (probn res officer)
Freeman, J (probn res officer)
Patterson, G C (probn res officer)
Spicer, Miss L (probn res officer)

40. **Merseybank Hostel**
26 Great Howard Street, Liverpool L3 7HS
0151-255 1183
fax 0151-236 4464

Jenkinson, H C (spo, mgr)
Vacancy (po, dep mgr)
Gee, A (probn res officer)
Jordan, M (probn res officer)
Roberts, J J (probn res officer)
Sofia, Ms N (probn res officer)
Warren, G (probn res officer)

41. **Southwood Probation Hostel**
24 Southwood Road, Liverpool L17 7BQ
0151-280 1833
fax 0151-280 3027

Griffiths, Ms C (spo, mgr)
Thomas, P E (po dep mgr)
Hurst, S (probn res officer)
Kennedy, P (p, probn res officer)
O'Neill, P (probn res officer)
Robinson, Mrs S (probn res officer)
Wright, G A (probn res officer)

42. **Adelaide House Probation/Bail Hostel**
115 Edge Lane, Liverpool L7 2PF
0151-263 1290
fax 0151-260 4205

Earlam, Ms C(warden)
Mannion, Ms W (dep warden)

Youth Offending Teams

43a. **YOT - Knowsley**
Youth Justice Section
54/56 Huyton Lane
Huyton, Liverpool L36 7XC
0151-443 3770

Edwards, G G

43b. **YOT - St Helens**
Youth Offending Team
5a Bickerstaff Street
St Helens WA10 1DH
(01744) 25171

Hughes P D

43c. **YOT - Liverpool**
Youth Justice Section
Liverpool Social Services
Millbank, Liverpool L13 0BW
0151-228 6541

Young, Ms K

43d. **YOT - Liverpool Central**
Sefton Grange, Croxteth Drive
Liverpool L17 3AL
0151-233 1912

Byrne, P J M

43e. **YOT - Liverpool South**
Youth Justice Section
Liverpool Social Services
89 St Marys' Road, Garston
Liverpool L19 2NL
0151-494 3627

O'Brien, Mrs D S

43f. **YOT - Sefton**
Supervision Assessment/Court Services
Sefton Youth Offending Team
Police Station, Marsh lane
Liverpool L20 5HJ
0151-934 2785/6
fax 0151-934 2779

Halpen, P J
Patterson, E

43g. **YOT - Wirral**
The Youth Justice Centre
Wirral Social Services
4 Cavendish Road, Birkenhead
Merseyside CH41 8AX
0151-670 1315
fax 0151-653 8446

Mechan, C H

Institution

44. H M Prison **Altcourse**
Higher Lane
Fazakerley, Liverpool L9 7LH
0151-522 2000
fax 0151-522 2121

Redman, Martin (spo)
O'Hanlon, Ms C M
Pinnington, T
Rushton, Ms H

45. H M Prison
Hornby Road **Liverpool** L9 3DF
0151-525 5971
fax 0151-524 1941

Probn clerk ext 2357/8/9
Parole clerk ext 2247
Discipline ext 2229/2241
Special visits 0151-524 0639

Furniss, Peter (spo) ext 2333
McGrath, Ms Karen
Milnes, Mike
Munro, Sandy
Needham, Peter
Pond, Mrs Hazel
Porter, Miss Liz
Pyman, Malcolm P
Clow, Ms J (psa)
Henshaw, Mrs N (psa)

Petty Sessional Areas

21, 26a, 28, 30 Knowsley
20, 20a Liverpool (South)
18, 19, 31 Liverpool (North)
22, 26 St Helens
16, 27, 27a, 33 Sefton North
17, 17a, 27b, 27c, 33a Sefton South
16, 24, 34 Wirral

Crown Court

23 Liverpool Queen Elizabeth II

Area Code 35

NORFOLK PROBATION SERVICE

Out of hours emergency contact point
John Boag House
(01603) 429488

Offices

1. **Head Office**
4th Floor, St James Yarn Mill
Whitefriars, Norwich NR3 1SU
Norwich (01603) 220100
fax (01603) 664019

Reed, Mary (cpo)
(01603) 220105
Blackman, Judith (aco)
(01603) 220106
Graham, Martin (aco)
(01603) 220107
Collyer, Hilary (aco)
(01603) 220108
Rayner, Karen (secy to cttee)
(01603) 220125
Sendall, Robbie R (prop & contracts mgr)
(01603) 220128
Wade, Belinda (finance mgr)
(01603) 220111
Vaughan, Graeme (it mgr)
(01603) 220119

Partnerships/DTTO
(01603) 220123
Attfield, Clive (spo)
Cuell, David (dtto)
East, Paul (dtto)
Fenn, Sharon (dtto)
Latos, Sarah (dtto)

Personnel & Training
Burrage, Amanda (mgr)
(01603) 220120

2. Whitefriars
Norwich NR3 1TN
Norwich (01603) 724000
fax (01603) 768270

Westrop, Jacqueline (spo)
Hornby, Stephen (spo)

Community Supervision
Cummins, John
Feeney, Michael
Leaberry, David
Medhurst, Ian
Michelmore, Sue (p)
Phayre, Lorna

Ryan, Liz
Wilson, Dot
Wivell, Bill
Bedward, Leroy, (psa)
Farendon, Kathy (psa)

Court Services
Walker, Brian (pract devpt assessor)
Davis, Eileen
Hussein, Steve
Pooley, Gill (p)
Singleton, Joy
Smith, Peter
Whadcoat, Gillian (p)
Winchester, Claire
Alden, Beverley (psa)
Clarke, Valerina (psa)
Cocker, Nicky (psa)
Duvall, Jeni (psa)
Jones, Mike (psa)

Crown Court Office
(01603) 728268
Wright, Andrew

Gill, Martin (peri psr writer)

2a. **Sentence Planning & Resettlement**
68 Bishopgate
Norwich NR1 4AA
Norwich (01603) 221600
(01603) 221615

Caton, Margaret
Gray, Karen (p)
Lanaway, Paul M
Martin, Linda (p)
Upton, Sue
Buck, Diana (seconded asw)
Blackman, Paul (psa)
Mitchell, Jayne (psa)
Rix, Terry (psa vict liaison)

3. 1-3 Hamilton Road
Cromer NR27 9HL
Cromer (01263) 512593
fax (01263) 513348

Westrop, Jacqueline (spo) (2)
Lane, Vivien
Morrison, Dave

4. Rampart Road
Great Yarmouth NR30 1QZ
Great Yarmouth (01493) 855525
fax (01493) 332769

Hartland, Andy (spo)
Whitehead, Annette (pract devpt assessor)
Brogan, Rachel
Cook, Maggie
Grimson, Linda
Jefferson, Ruth (p)
Pearce, Sandra
Tricker, Clive
Bruce, Scott (psa)
Craske, Sue (psa)
Doherty, Patricia (psa)

Sentence Planning & Resettlement
Davidson, Ken
McNelly, John

Gill, Martin (peri psr writer)

5. Purfleet Quay
King's Lynn PE30 1HP
Kings Lynn (01553) 669000
fax (01553) 776544

Faulconbridge, Jennifer (spo)
Bertram, David
Butterworth, David
Compton, Jeff
Loosley, Suzanne
Moulton, Bob
Wells, Judith
Carter, Anita (psa)
Harto, Geoff (psa)
Longstaff, Susie (psa)

Sentence Planning & Resettlement
Dewsnap, Chris
McDonald, Denys
Tansley, Richard

6. 12/14 Raymond Street
Thetford IP24 2EA
Thetford (01842) 754071
fax (01842) 751089

Hough, Lansley (spo)
Leibrick, Martin
Martin, Terry (p)
Mayne, Jean
Peaford, Linda
Sweeting, Bill
Young, David
Crewdson, Val (psa)
Pollard, Liz (psa)

7. **Community Service Offices**
68 Bishopgate
Norwich NR1 4AA
Norwich (01603) 221600
fax (01603) 221615

Ramshaw, Charles (spo)
Bennett, Pauline (divnl mgr east)

Burton, Jim (cso)
Chaplin, Bill (cso)
Hayes, Roger (cso)
Toovey, Bryan (cso)
Brown, Roger (cs pathfinder off)
Cocker, Nicky (crt off)

Cromer
East, Paul (cso)
Payne, Stephen (cso)

Kings Lynn
(01553) 669000
fax (01553) 776544
Mainwaring, David (cso)

Thetford
(01842) 766502
fax (01842) 751089
Dawson, Annetta (divnl mgr west)
Kerrigan, Allan (cso)
Smith, Bill (cso)

18 Deneside
Great Yarmouth NR30 3AX
Great Yarmouth (01493) 844991
fax (01493) 332670
McKinnell, Duncan (cso)
Pamment, Mike (cso)

8. **Family Court Welfare Service**
from 1.4.01 part of Children & Family Court Advisory & Support Service
Suite A, St Clement's House
St Clement's Alley, Colegate
Norwich NR3 1BQ
Norwich (01603) 226600
fax (01603) 226619

Arthur, Simon (spo)
Langham-Fitt, Sue (p)
McGilvray, Celia (p)
Parsons, Sarah (p)
Rae, Yvonne (p)
Rowlands, Les
Salmon, Anne (p)
Wright, Ron

9. **Youth Offending Team**
Norwich
(01603) 877500
Curl, Tracey (p)
Phillips, David (p)

Great Yarmouth
(01493) 847400
Wales Andy

Kings Lynn
(01553) 819400
Martin, Richard

Hostel

10. **John Boag House**
1 Drayton Road, Norwich NR3 2DF
Norwich (01603) 429488
fax (01603) 485903

Fitzsimmons, Heather (spo mgr)
Payne, Barbara (po deputy)
Caron-Mattison, Joe (asst warden)
Francis, Michelle (asst warden)
Nicholas, Peter (asst warden)
Pietocha, Mia (asst warden)
Perrett, Andrew (asst warden)
Hardesty, Bernadette (asst warden)

Institutions

11. H M Prison and Remand Centre,
Mousehold **Norwich** NR1 4LU
Norwich (01603) 437531
fax (01603) 701007
probn fax (01603) 706534

Probn clerks
Smith, Anne (p) ext 304
Cowles, Frances ext 404/346
Discipline ext 308
Special visits ext 407

Gosling, Martin (spo) ext 300
Allerhand, Ruth (programmes) ext 394/307
Beale, Peter ext (B/C/M wings) ext 290
O'Byrne, Jon (programmes) ext 394/405
Millard, Tom (A wing, health care) ext 296/343
Parker, Margaret (yoi) ext 301/402
Player, Bob (hdc & sent mgmnt) ext 395
Boulton, Liz (bail info) ext 387
Bayles, Ray (psr writer) ext 305/298

12. H M Prison **Wayland**
Griston, Thetford IP25 6RL
Watton (01953) 858100
Direct dial (01953) 858 + ext
fax (01953) 858077

Probn clerk (visits, gen enquiries) ext 073
Probn typist (sch 1, temp release) ext 071

Cranna, Bob (spo) ext 072
Dada, Lisa ext 057
Docking, Sheila ext 032
Fowler, Mike ext 163
Gale, Marie ext 022
Needham, George ext 168
Parker, Marsha ext 056
Perlmutter, Anthea ext 042
Wilcock, Tony ext 070

Petty Sessional Areas

2, 3 Norwich
5 Great Yarmouth
4 North Norfolk
7 South Norfolk
7 Central Norfolk
6 West Norfolk

Crown Courts

2 Norwich
6 King's Lynn

Area Code 36

NORTHAMPTONSHIRE PROBATION SERVICE

Central Bail Referral no:

Bridgewood Hostel
(01604) 648704

Out of hours emergency contact point
Bridgewood Hostel
(01604) 648704

Offices

1. **Head Office**
53 Billing Road
Northampton NN1 5DB
Northampton (01604) 635274
fax (01604) 231730

Bernard, Ms Carol (cpo)
Ghumra, Rashid (acpo north, cs, high risk, in-service training, info unit)
Kay, Peter (acpo, workforce planning, equal opps, support services,training, personnel, fcw, yot, HMP YOI Onley, HMP Ryehill)
Pearse, Roger (acpo south, pre-release, HMP Wellingborough, hostel, ptnrships, crts, dtto)
Jeffery, Ms Shirley (support services mgr)
Walker, Ms Gill (info mgr)
Cornhill, Alan (systems support & evaluation officer)
Farrow, Mrs Marion (p, accountant)

2. 52 Billing Road
Northampton NN1 5DB
Northampton (01604) 626765/636473/4/5
fax (01604) 604229

Family Court Welfare Team
from 1.4.01 part of Children & Family Court Advisory Service
Rawden, Ms Sue (spo, training, inspections, complaints, p.r., crams)
Fitzgerald, James
Cooper, Graham
Harper, Ms Janice (p)
Hegarty, Mrs Geraldine
Murphy, Ms Deb (p)
Woods, Clive

3. 173 Bridge Street
Northampton NN1 1QF
Northampton (01604) 628231
fax (01604) 232498

Hamson, Chris (spo)
Bromwich, Mrs Rosemary (spo)
Goodman, Quentin (pract devpt assessor)
Walters, Ms Michelle (pract devpt assessor)
Boor, Ms Rebecca
Bowers, Ms Anne
Clowes, Ms Jessica
Cragg-James, Ms Kirsty
Clancy, Ms Glenys
Doran, Paul
Gabriel, Ms Gail
Gill, Dave
Griffiths, Paul
Harmston, Edwin
Heyworth, Ms Sophie
Jay, Ms Valerie
Nichols, Dave
Sheppard, Ms Diana
Smith, Dennis
Bray, Ms Caroline (psa)
Donoghue, Ms Denise (p, psa)
Laing, Ms Claire (psa)
Lansberry, Ms Denise (psa)
Newbold, Andrew (psa)
McPherson, Ms Tracy (p, psa)
Woodward, Ms Teresa (psa)

4. **Crown Court**
85/87 Lady's Lane
Northampton NN1 3HQ
Northampton (01604) 637751
fax (01604) 603164

Jones, Courtney
Shorley, Ms Cate
Wilson, Ms Anne (psa)

5. 37-43 Regent Street
Northampton NN1 2LA
Northampton (01604) 604707
fax (01604) 602650

Community Service
Lambert, Ted (cs mgr)
Ashworth, Alan (cso)
Curtis, Dale (p, cso)
Thomas, Peter (cso)
Lishman, Ms Stevie (cs breach officer)

6. Edinburgh House
7 Corporation Street
Corby NN17 1NG
Corby (01536) 203513/4
fax (01536) 406607

Doel, Mike (spo)
Adams, Ms Rachel
Bromhall, Mrs Christine
Davidson, Tom
Leverton, Martin
Holmes, Mrs Elsebeth
Panter, Ms Lesley (p)
Rogers, Ms Carol
Thwaites, Ms Emma
Gardner, Chris (psa)
Russell, Ms Karen (psa)
Sanders, Ms Cheryl (psa)

Community Service
Barr, Fred (cs officer)
Preskey, Tony (cso)
Tallett, Ben (cso)

6a. Reporting Centre
12a Market Place
Kettering NN16 0AJ
phone & fax (01536) 521740

7. 20 Oxford Street
Wellingborough NN8 4HY
Wellingborough (01933) 276141
fax (01933) 441547

Chapman, Ms Liz (spo)
Lansford, Chris (spo)
Woolley, Ms Julie (comb order care mgr)
Brown, Ms Sadie
Crate-Lionel, Pat
Fergusson, Ian
Hayat, Ms Zareen
Matthews, Ms Doreen
Meanwell, Kevin
Pratt, Joe
Walker, Ms Viv
Cox, Ms Debbie (psa)
Dobson, James (psa)
Hobbs, Ms Joanne (psa)

Community Service
Daft, Ms Nicola (p, cso)

Accomodation
Mattock, Ms Patricia (p, ptnrshp mgr)

8. **Youth Offending Team South**
198 Kettering Road
Northampton NN1 4BL
Northampton (01604) 601241
fax (01604) 601648

Frith, Simon
Wyatt, Ms Christine

9. **Youth Offending Team North**
73 London Road
Kettering NN15 7PQ
Kettering (01536) 533800
fax (01536) 417546

Archer, Chris

Hostels

10. **Bridgewood Adult Probation Hostel**
45-48 Lower Meadow Court
Northampton NN3 8AX
Northampton (01604) 648704
fax (01604) 645722

Horsefield, Ms Judith (spo mgr)
Pratt, Ms Liz (dep mgr)
Carr, Ms Pat (asst warden)
Driver, Ms Tracy (asst warden)
Hunt, Steven (asst warden)
Mason, Ms Michelle (asst warden)
Rice, ms Sharon (night supr)

Institutions

11. H M Young Offender Institution
Onley Rugby
Warwickshire CV23 8AP
Rugby (01788) 522022
fax (01788) 522260

Probn clerk ext 314
Discipline/special visits ext 284

Meylan, Ms Denise (spo) ext 431
Brown, Ms Gloria ext 206
Woodward, Ms Jennifer ext 473
Mangili, Ms Francesca ext 302
Stephens, Christopher
Grimmett, Ms Sally (psa)

12. H M Prison
Millers Park, Doddington Road
Wellingborough NN8 2NH
Wellingborough (01933) 224151
fax (01933) 273903
probn fax (01993) 227898

Probn clerk ext 299
Parole clerk ext 310

Sorley, James (spo)
Hegarty, Eamon ext 411
Lawson, Ms Sue (p) ext 298
Willetts, Ms Janis (p)
Banks, Glen (psa) ext 300

13. H M Prison **Ryehill**
Willoughby, Rugby
Warcs CV23 8AN
(01788) 817269
fax (01788) 521654

Brimble, Ms Pat
Morris, Ms Sarah
Setchell, Ms Helen

Petty Sessional Areas

6 Corby
3 Daventry
6 Kettering
3 Northampton
3 Towcester
7 Wellingborough

Crown Court

4 Northampton

Area Code 37

NORTHUMBRIA PROBATION SERVICE

Offices

1. **Head Office**
Lifton House
Eslington Road, Jesmond
Newcastle upon Tyne NE2 4SP
0191-281 5721
Direct dial 0191-240+ number
fax 0191-281 3548

Murphy, S C (cpo, chief exec) 7312
Winfield, Mrs S M (dcpo, director of service delivery) 7308
Williamson, Mrs P (director of resources) 7309
Melia, P (asst director, resources/treasurer) 7352
Mackie, C (asst director, support services/cttee secy) 7351
Fiddes, Mrs C (qual ass mgr) 7347
Morton, Ms G (spo) 7348
Barron, V (area mgr info tech) 7346
Dunn, J (financial services mgr) 7326
Jackson, I (personnel/payroll mgr) 7328
Taylor, S (property/technical services mgr) 7349
Burns, L (suppt services mgr) 7333
Williams, Mrs P (hq admin mgr) 7332
Stockley, R (health & safety) 7331
Cairns, Ms J (p.r.o.) 7327
Hayes, F (seconded to gov. office)

2. **Training Centre**
Dene House, Durham Road
Low Fell, Gateshead
Tyne & Wear NE9 5AE
0191-491 1693
fax 0191-491 3726

McIntosh, R A (training mgr)
Smith, Ms M (training off)
McElderry, J (pract devpt assessor)

Newcastle

3. Divisional Head Office
6 Lansdowne Terrace
Gosforth
Newcastle upon Tyne NE3 1HW
0191-213 0611
fax 0191-213 1361

Dale, Ms Wendy (divnal director)
Howson, Mrs M (divnal admin mgr)

4. 5 Lansdowne Terrace
Gosforth
Newcastle upon Tyne NE3 1HW
0191-213 1888
direct dial 0191-2468 + number
fax 0191-213 1393

North Team
Fiddes, J (spo, mgr) ext 230
Maughan, Ms J (pract devpt assessor) ext 224
Bates, Ms A ext 212
Clark, M ext 216
Halpin, A (dtto) ext 229
Higgins, R ext 228
Marley, S ext 219
Miles, Ms S ext 208
Norwood, Ms C ext 210
Watson, R ext 211
Badhan, Miss S (trainee) ext 218
Bowers, Miss T (trainee) ext 218
Graham, Miss T (trainee) ext 220
Masendeke, Miss S (trainee) ext 221
Mulvenna, T (psa) ext 215

5. **70-78 St James' Boulevard**
Newcastle upon Tyne NE1 4BN
0191-261 9091
direct dial 0191-2418 + number
fax 0191-233 0758

City Team
Mills, J (spo mgr) ext 112
Caveille, Ms L ext 106
Collins, Mrs D ext 103
Doonan, J ext 105
Elliott, Ms M (p)
Flynn, A G
Gammell, Mrs C (p) ext 102
Mynott, Ms C ext 100
Solan, Ms C ext 114
Wilkes, Mrs G ext 101
Campbell, G (trainee) ext 117
Butt, H (psa) ext 104

6. 6th Floor **Collingwood House**
3 Collingwood Street
Newcastle upon Tyne NE1 1JW
0191-232 3368
fax 0191-233 0760

Court Services Team
Vacancy (spo mgr) (7, 8)
Holland, Mrs M
Parkinson, G
Smith, Mrs M (psa)
Wood, Mrs J (psa)

7. **Victim Liaison Unit**
6th Floor, Collingwood House
3 Collingwood Street
Newcastle upon Tyne NE1 1JW
0191-261 2541
fax 0191-221 1438

Cornick, Ms J
Mantey, Mrs J
Reid, Mrs G (psa)

8. **The Law Courts** Quayside
Newcastle upon Tyne NE1 3LA
0191-230 1737
fax 0191-233 0759

Court Services Team
Davies, J
McLaren, Ms C
Shaw, Miss R
Wilcox, C (psa)

9. **717 West Road**
Newcastle upon Tyne NE15 7PS
0191-274 1153
fax 0191-275 0963

West Team
McLean, Mrs W (spo mgr)
Dale, P
Nesbit, D
O'Farrell, P
Pulle-Rao, Mrs R
Sharpe, I
Wilks, Ms E (p)
O'Neill, M (psa)

10. Glendale Terrace **Byker**
Newcastle upon Tyne NE6 1PB
0191-276 6666
fax 0191-224 2878

East Team
McCartney, J (spo mgr)
Armstrong, Ms A (p)
Cox, Ms J
Dixon, J
Jarvis, Mrs L
Kemmish, J
Loxley, Ms F (p)
Singer, S
Taylor, Mrs C
Truscott, Mrs S
Wilkinson, P
Wright, A
Tatum, M (trainee)
Richardson, Mrs C (psa)

Northumberland & North Tyneside

11. Divisional Head Office
39 Esplanade
Whitley Bay Tyne & Wear NE26 2AE
0191-253 3236
fax 0191-252 7713

Gardiner, J D (divnal director)
Bavidge, Mrs A (p, divnal admin mgr)
O'Hara, Mrs M (divnal admin mgr)

12. **Drug Treatment & Testing Orders**
14 Pitt Street
Newcastle upon Tyne NE4 5SU
0191-261 9515
fax 0191-261 1548

Turner, Mrs M (spo)

13. Former Employment Exchange
South View **Ashington**
Northumberland NE63 0RY
Ashington (01670) 813053
fax (01670) 814858

County Team
Pooley, G (spo mgr) (14)

Downing, Ms D (pract devpt assessor)
Brabbins, P (dtto)
Dunne, L
Foster, C
Randall, Mrs B
Brown, Miss D (trainee)
Hart, Ms C (trainee)
Morris, Miss V (trainee)
Thompson, Ms V (psa)

14. 27 Bondgate Without
Alnwick
Northumberland NE66 1PR
Alnwick (01665) 602242
fax (01665) 605184

Evans, B
Dawson, L (+ Berwick)

15. 38 Beaconsfield Street
Blyth
Northumberland NE24 2DR
Blyth (01670) 352441
fax (01670) 352921

Kelly, Mrs E (spo mgr) (16)
Bennett, Ms V (p)
Hardington, G
Johnstone, Mrs C (p)
Pollard, Ms C (p)
Slater, P
Smith, Miss A (trainee)
Flisher, Mrs E (psa)
Scott, M (psa)

16. 4 Wentworth Place **Hexham**
Northumberland NE46 1XB
Hexham (01434) 602499
fax (01434) 606195

Hearn, Mrs J M (p)
Rickelton, D

17. Lovaine House, 9 Lovaine Terrace
North Shields
Tyne and Wear NE29 0HJ
0191-296 2335
fax 0191-257 6170

Lloyd, P E (spo mgr)
Candon, Ms C
Gallagher, P
Gilbert, S
Graham, H
Mirfin, Ms A
Robson, Ms J
Shiels, Ms J
Ward, Ms C
Seebohm, Ms L (trainee)
McBeth, Mrs P (psa)
Tose, G (psa)

18. 13 Warwick Road **Wallsend**
Tyne and Wear NE28 6SE
0191-262 9211
fax 0191-295 4824

Clarkin, Ms E (spo mgr)
Johnstone, Mrs C (p, dtto)
Currie, I
Deary, Ms K (p)
Kelly, Ms J
MacDonald, Ms C
Suleman, M
Thompson, Ms K
Wallwork, C
Wylie, Mrs K (trainee)
Beare, G (psa)

Wearside

19. **Divisional Head Office**
45 John Street, Sunderland
Tyne and Wear SR1 1QU
0191-510 1859
fax 0191-565 7596

Knotek, Miss H (divnal director)
Donkin, Mrs J (divnal admin mgr)

20. Hylton Road **Pennywell**
Sunderland SR4 8DS
0191-534 5545
fax 0191-534 2380

Ord, Ms M (spo mgr)
Booth, R
Chappill, F
Heron, W
Oxley, Ms A
Singh, S
Turner, Ms M
Harrison, Mrs V (psa)
Holmes, M (psa)

21. Mainsforth Terrace West
Hendon Sunderland SR2 8JX
0191-514 3093
fax 0191-565 1625

Ferguson, L E (spo mgr)
Emeka-Oyolu, Ms C
Speight, Ms L
Stube, Ms L
Sinclair, N
Sweeting, T
Murphy, Miss S (trainee)

Towns, A (trainee)
Robertson, Mrs T (psa)

22. Kings Road **Southwick**
Sunderland SR5 2LS
0191-548 8844
fax 0191-548 6834

Corbett, Ms V (spo mgr)
Baker, Mrs P (p)
Cliff, Mrs M (p)
Findley, Mrs A
Hardy, P
Kavanagh, M
Locklan, Mrs M
McQuillan, S
Murphy, S
Walker, P (trainee)
Mooney, Mrs L (psa)
Stobbart, Miss S (psa)

23. Old Police Buildings
Spout Lane **Washington**
Tyne and Wear NE37 2AB
0191-416 8574
fax 0191-415 7943

Rees, D (spo mgr) (24)
Green, P
Grimes, M
MacQueen, A
Middleton, Mrs L (trainee)

24. 10 Newbottle Street
Houghton-le-Spring
Tyne and Wear DH4 4AL
0191-584 3109
fax 0191-584 4919

Bellamy, P
Cutter, Ms A M
Haran, Ms M
Richardson, Ms L (p)
Houghton, Mrs K (psa)

South Tyneside & Gateshead

25. **Divisional Head Office**
5/8 Cornwallis Street
South Shields
Tyne and Wear NE33 1BB
0191-456 1000
fax 0191-427 6922

Cullen, P F (divnal director)
Falcon, Mrs S (divnal admin mgr)

26. Homer Villa, St John's Terrace
Jarrow Tyne and Wear NE32 3BT
0191-489 7767
fax 0191-483 3961

Love, Mrs A (p, spo mgr)
Bunney, C
Carr, R
Cunningham, Mrs A
Duggan, R
Wilson, T
Anderson, Ms S (trainee)
Frame, Miss K (trainee)
O'Neill, Ms M (psa)

27. Secretan Way, Millbank
South Shields
Tyne and Wear NE33 1HG
0191-455 2294
fax 0191-427 6919

Vacancy (spo mgr)
Groves, Mrs G
Peggie, A (p)
Randall, K
Storrie, R
Stratford, Ms M
Allison, Mrs P (psa)
Davison, Mrs S (psa)

28. Wesley Court **Blaydon**
Tyne and Wear NE21 5BT
0191-414 5626
fax 0191-414 7809

Kelly, Ms J (spo mgr)
Clinton, R
Crowther, Ms L (p)
Franciosi, Ms H
Jacques, Ms D
Lawrence, R
Murphy, P
Parkinson, C (p)
Peaden, Ms K
Saddington, Mrs D

29. Warwick Street **Gateshead**
Tyne and Wear NE8 1PZ
0191-478 2451
fax 0191-478 1197

Taylor, B (spo mgr)
Fisher, Ms P (dtto)
Albiston, Miss K
Coward, Ms W
Cusack, Ms R
Davidson, Mrs P
Jarvis, R
Jones, M
Murphy, Mrs C

Raine, Mrs E
Bateman, Mrs G (psa)
Carter, A (psa)
Cole, Mrs E (psa)

Groupwork & Community Service

30. Lifton House
Eslington Road, Jesmond
Newcastle upon Tyne NE2 4SP
0191-240 7350
fax 0191-281 3548

North, J (divnl director)

31. 14 Pitt Street
Newcastle upon Tyne NE4 5SU
0191-261 9515
fax 0191-261 1548

Practice Development Unit
Mackintosh, Mrs J (eff pract mgr)
Francis, Ms A (eff pract po)

Sex Offender Team
Dodds, Mrs M (risk mgt mgr)
Harrison, K (sex off team)
Ineson, Mrs L (sex off team)
Strachan, I (sex off team)

Sexual Behaviour Unit
0191-260 2540
Kennington, R

Groupwork

32. **70-78 St James Boulevard**
Newcastle upon Tyne NE1 4BN
0191-261 9091
direct dial 0191-2418 + number
fax 0191-233 0758

Coulthard, Mrs G (gpwk & cs mgr) ext 113
Bailey, D ext 115
Hull, Ms M ext 107
Jaimin, D
Graham Mrs H (psa) ext 111
Hodgson, Mrs K (psa) ext 108
Trembath, J (psa)

33. YMCA Building, Church Way
North Shields
Tyne & Wear NE29 0AB
0191-258 0713

Sammut-Smith, I (gpwk & cs mgr)
Gow, Mrs S
Hill, Ms L (p)
Miles, Ms S
Rice, V (p)
Morren, Mrs A (psa)
Patterson, Ms E (psa)
Potts, G (psa)

34. 45 John Street
Sunderland
Tyne and Wear SR1 1QU
0191-510 1859
fax 0191-565 7596

Gavin, Mrs M (gpwk & cs mgr)
Lamb, M
McLeod, Ms A
Walton, P
Boyne, Mrs S (psa)
Cutting, A (psa)
Green, S (psa)

35. 5-8 Cornwallis Street
South Shields
Tyne and Wear NE33 1BB
0191-456 1000
fax 0191-427 6922

Walter, D (gpwk & cs mgr)
Grant, P
Talbot, J
Willan, Mrs K
Edwards, I (psa)
Froud, R (psa)
Smyth, Ms S (psa)

Community Service

36. **70-78 St James' Boulevard**
Newcastle upon Tyne NE1 4BN
0191-261 9091
direct dial 0191-2418 + number
fax 0191-233 0758

Coulthard, Mrs G (gpwk & cs mgr) ext 113
Cockburn, F (cs co-ord) ext 110
Humphries, J (cs co-ord)
Baker, Mrs M (css)
Gray, R (css)
Harrison, R (css)
Lowther, J (css)
O'Farrell, E (css)
Park, K (css)
Paterson, W (css)
Roach, B (css)

37. YMCA Building, Church Way
North Shields
Tyne & Wear NE29 0AB
0191-258 0713

Sammut-Smith, I (gpwk & cs mgr)
Conlon, P (cs co-ord) (18)
Lockwood, P (cs co-ord) (13)

Aitchison, G (css) (17)
Alderson, Ms J (18)
Bolland, D (css) (18)
Burt, F (css) (13)
Clough, R (css) (13)
Stratford, P (css) (17)

38. 45 John Street
Sunderland
Tyne and Wear SR1 1QU
0191-510 1859
fax 0191-565 7596

Gavin, Mrs M (gpwk & cs mgr)
Kelly, G (cs co-ord) (22)
Harper, Ms K (cs co-ord) (20)
Green, A (css) (20)
Hewitt, G (css) (21)
O'Neill, G (css) (21)
Russell, M (css) (22)
Turner, J (css) (23)
Welsh, W (css) (23)

39. 5-8 Cornwallis Street
South Shields
Tyne and Wear NE33 1BB
0191-456 1000
fax 0191-427 6922

Walter, D (gpwk & cs mgr)
Camphuis, J (cs co-ord) (27)
Penfold, K (cs co-ord) (29)
Arnell, P (css) (29)
Coates, G (css) (27)
Close, M (css) (29)
Dingwall, E (css) (29)
Harvey, M (css) (27)
Redford, P (css) (29)
Stimpson, H (css) (29)
Wright, R (css) (27)

Family Court Welfare Service
from 1.4.01 part of Children & Family Court Advisory & Support Service

40. **Family Court Welfare Team**
592 Welbeck Road, Walker
Newcastle upon Tyne NE6 3AB
0191-276 6060
fax 0191-224 2876

Lee, Mrs L (area mgr) (41)
Robson, D (snr pract)
Anderson, C
Astill, Mrs M (p)
Bradley, Mrs M (13)
Conlon, Mrs J
Davison, Mrs L (p)
Fletcher, Mrs V (p)
Gibson, Mrs M
Ibsen, Mrs M
Roberts, Ms S (p)
Roshier, Mrs M
Stanley, Ms E (p)
Todd, Ms D (p)
Walsh, E

41. **Family Court Welfare Team**
Campbell Park Road
Hebburn Tyne and Wear NE31 2SS
0191-483 4611
fax 0191-428 4404

Wild, Mrs A (snr pract)
Alderson, Ms M
Bell, Miss V
Borsberry, Mrs J
Elgie, Mrs A
Gooch, Mrs T
Marsham, I
Russell, Ms T

Youth Offending Teams

42. **Northumberland YOT**
The Riverside Centre
North Seaton Industrial Estate
Ashington, Northumberland NE63 0YB
(01670) 852225

Ford, Miss L

43. **N Tyneside YOT**
153 Tynemouth Road
North Shields
Tyne & Wear NE30 1ED
0191-200 6001

Austin, Ms L (p)
Gill, Ms N

44. **Newcastle YOT**
1 St James Terrace
Newcastle upon Tyne NE1 4NE
0191-261 7583

Bridgeman, Ms N
Pyle, C

45. **Gateshead YOT**
224-230 High Street
Gateshead, Tyne & Wear NE8 1AQ
0191-440 0500

Firth, Ms J

46. **S Tyneside YOT**
30 Commercial Road
South Shields
Tyne & Wear NE33 1RW
0191-427 2850

Vipond, Miss L

47. **Wearside YOT**
11 John Street
Sunderland
Tyne & Wear SR1 1HT
0191-553 7370

McAllister, Ms M J
Roberts, G
Turnbull, J
Wilkinson, Miss J

Hostels

48. **Pennywell House Bail Hostel**
Hylton Road, Pennywell
Sunderland, SR4 8DS
0191-534 1544
fax 0191-534 1049

Willoughby, Mrs H (spo mgr)
Airey, A (deputy mgr)
Baker, Miss D (hostel asst)
Murton, M (hostel asst)
Roberts, Ms A (hostel asst)
Wilkins, J (hostel asst)

49. **Cuthbert House Bail Hostel**
Derwentwater Road, Bensham
Gateshead NE8 2SH
0191-478 5355
fax 0191-490 0674

Teasdale, J (spo mgr)
Seddon, Ms A (deputy mgr)
Douglas, J (hostel asst)
Hannen, Ms H (hostel asst)
Johnston, Mrs C (hostel asst)
Wareham, Ms H (hostel asst)

50. **Ozanam House Probation Hostel**
79 Dunholme Road
Newcastle upon Tyne NE4 6XD
0191-273 5738
fax 0191-272 2729

Gelder, C (mgr)
Yoxall, Ms G (deputy)

51. **St Christopher's House Bail Hostel**
222 Westmorland Road
Cruddas Park
Newcastle upon Tyne NE4 6QX
0191-273 2381
fax 0191-272 4241

Faill, P (mgr)
Familton, Ms B (po deputy)

Institutions

52. H M Prison **Acklington**
Nr. Morpeth
Northumberland NE65 9XF
Morpeth (01670) 760411
fax (01670) 761362

Probn clerk ext 287
SOTP treatment mgr ext 288
Sentence mgmnt clerk ext 310
Sentence mgmnt officers ext 294/319
Probation Officers ext 291

Marshall, Ms D (spo, th'care mgr) ext 293
Brunger, Mrs S
Connor, G
Devine, Ms E
Flynn, A
Graham, Mrs B
Jennings, Ms C
Loughrey, Mrs T
McGovern, M
Mackin, P
Pringle, Ms L

53. H M Young Offender Institution
Castington Nr Morpeth
Northumberland NE65 9XG
Morpeth (01670) 762100
fax (01670) 762101

Parole clerk ext 2033/2034
HDC clerk ext 2032/2034
Discipline ext 2121
Special visits ext 2018

Gibson, N (spo mgr) ext 2013
Cook, F
Jamieson, J ext 2033/2051
Hunter, C ext 2033/2051
Bleanch, G (psa) ext 2023
Hamilton, Mrs A (psa) ext 2102
Smith, Mrs B (psa) ext 2102
Yates, Mrs M (psa) ext 2033/2051

Petty Sessional Areas

14 Berwick on Tweed
28, 29 Gateshead
16 Tynedale
24 Houghton-le-Spring
3-10 Newcastle-upon-Tyne
17, 18 North Tyneside

15, 16 South East Northumberland
26, 27 South Tyneside
19-22 Sunderland
14 Coquetdale

Crown Courts

8 Newcastle upon Tyne

Area Code 38

NOTTINGHAMSHIRE PROBATION SERVICE

Offices

1. **Head Office**
Marina Road
Nottingham NG7 1TP
0115-840 6500
fax 0115-840 6502

Chief Officer/Cttee Secy
0115-840 6462
fax 0115-840 6453

Asst Chief Officers
0115-840 6454
fax 0115-840 6452

Bldgs & Gen Services
0115-840 6471
fax 0115-840 6469

Central Resources &Enquiries
0115-840 6494

Finance
0115-840 6471
fax 0115-840 6469

IT Services
0115-840 6476

Personnel
0115-840 6482
fax 0115-840 6480

Press & PR
0115-840 6492

Research & Devpt
0115-840 6488

Staff Devpt
0115-840 6509

Hancock, David (cpo)
Delves, John (acpo) ext 6461
Finn, Mrs Sue (acpo) ext 6458
Goode, Alan (acpo) ext 6459
Kay, John (acpo) ext 6460
Owen, Derek A (secy to cttee) ext 6451
Taylor, Ed (spo, dtto) ext 6450
Taylor, Brian (spo, staff devpt) ext 6508
Palmer, Rob (staff devpt) ext 6510
Gordon, Stuart (personnel) ext 6485
Newbold, Miss Shirley (finance) ext 6468
Lathall, Glenn (buildings & gen services) ext 6473
Francis, Miss Gill M (research/devpt) ext 6490
Smith, Howard (i.t.) ext 6478
Warrior, Mrs Jude (communications) ext 6492

2. **Groupwork Unit**
88 Carlton Hill, Nottingham NG4 1EE
0115-910 6400
fax 0115-910 6401

Jasper, Ms Heather (spo)
Douglas, Ms Jane
Dyjasek, Ms Marie
Haq, Ms Nasima
Muller, Matt
Murphy, Patrick
Clarke, Ms Julie (dom violence wrkr)
Whittaker, Mrs Audrey (team asst)
Cockram, Mrs J (office admin)

3. **Throughcare Unit**
5 East Circus Street
Nottingham NG1 5AF
0115-952 0322
fax 0115-952 0481

Hill, Nigel (spo)
Wright, Mrs June (spo)
Bernard, Miss Juliette
Fothergill, Trevor
Fryer, John
Gerty, Miss Ann
Harris, Charlie
Mitchell, Rob
Moss, David
Vaites, Mrs Joan
Wheeler, David
Wilson, Ms Chris
Nicholson, Miss Sue (team asst)
Johnson, Ms Cathy (team asst)
Jones, Mrs Maggie (team asst)
Boothe, Ms Carole (psa)
Gatt, Mrs Barrie (unit admin mgr)

Criminal Work (City)

(a) Combined Courts Team

4. **The Crown Court**
Canal Street
Nottingham NG1 7EJ

0115-910 3540
fax 0115-958 6135

Dhindsa, Hardyal (spo)
Boggild, Mrs Brenda
Bolla, Ms Kashmir
Chapman, Mrs Ros (unit admin mgr)

5. **Magistrates' Court Office**
50 Carrington Street
Nottingham NG1 7FG
0115-840 6030 (crt team)
0115-840 6031 (admin)
0115-840 6351 (liaison office in mag crt)
fax 0115-924 2336

Dhindsa, Hardyal (spo)
Coyle, Ms Jane
Holden, Ms Liz
Hyatt-Butt, Tariq
Martin, Ms Susan
Brickell, Mrs Linda (team asst)
Brown, Mrs Anne (team asst)
Hammans, Mrs Gloria (team asst)
Hewitt, Miss Jane (team asst)
McCaffrey, Mrs Pauline (team asst)
Short, Mrs Diane (team asst)
Stapleton, Mrs Mary (team asst)
Dyer, Ms Maxine (p, team asst)
O'Dare, Mrs Helen M (team asst)
White, Ms Rosie (p, team asst)
Young, Mrs Pam (team asst)
Chapman, Mrs Ros (unit admin mgr)

6. **Youth Offending Team**
2 Isabella Street
Nottingham NG1 6AT
0115-841 3008

Graham, Miss Barbara
Lockwood, Ms Penny
Nicholls, Ms Shelley
Shewell-Cooper, Mrs Heidi
Walker, Mrs Angela
Zieba, Miss Helena

(b) Community Service

7. **Community Service Office**
Traffic Street
Nottingham NG2 1NU
0115-956 0956
fax 0115 96 0900

Pratt, David (spo)
Johnson, Steve
Khan, Mrs Abirjan
Mack, Ms Carolyn
Metcalfe, Mrs Gail (p)
Stafford, Mrs Linda
Steele, Ms Carole
Tickner, Mike
Anderson, Mrs Jacqui (team asst)
Morrison, Mrs Jean (team asst)
Webb, Ms Liane (team asst)
Britt, George (csa)
Cockell, Bob (practical proj off)
Fletcher, Mrs Janet R (csa)
Medcalf, Mrs Jackie (projects)
Cooper, Ms Janet (unit admin mgr)

Mulhare Advice Service
0115-956 0939

Hare-Duke, Ms Hilary
Mulrenan, Mrs Una

Access Team
(CS/Probation Workshop)
0115-956 0919
fax 0115-956 0900

Cooke, Steve B (mgr)
Bee, Ms Elaine (emplt)
Elson, Ms Stella (emplt)
Rodgers, Jed (emplt)
Rothwell, Roger (emplt)

(c) City Criminal Work (East)

8. 9 Musters Road
West Bridgford
Nottingham NG2 7PP
0115-914 4333
fax 0115 914 4334

Meade, Ms Jenny (spo)
Balmer, Mrs Claire (p)
Carter, Mrs Sheila
Davies, John
Hanford, Mrs Karen
Hooper, John
Rawlins, Miss Alison
Standing, Oliver
Young, Mrs Elspeth
Brown, Ms Judith (team asst)
Wheeldon, Mrs Margaret (team asst)
Towlson, Mrs Hilary (unit admin mgr)
(based at 9)

9. 38 Robin Hood Chase
St Ann's Nottingham NG3 4EZ
0115-910 5470
fax 0115-910 5471

Lambert, Mrs Beverley (spo)
Johnson, Andrew
Marshall, Ken
Marriott, Paul

Meakin, Ms Tanya
Mulrenan, Jim
Hooker, Miss Ginnie (team asst)
Unwin, Mrs Margaret (team asst)
Phillips, Ms Deborah (emplt)
Towlson, Mrs Hilary (unit admin mgr)

(c) City Criminal Work (West)

10. **177 Forest Road West**
Nottingham NG7 4EL
0115-916 9500
fax 0115-916 9505

Goode, Ms Linda (spo)
Adas, Ms Rebecca (p)
Butcher, Colin
Clare, Mrs Jan (p)
Green, Ms Heather
Green, Stephen
Jacobson, Steve
Peake, Nick
Singh, Gurdev
Weaver, Paul
Bal, Mrs Sita (team asst)
Smith, Miss Belinda (team asst)
Mee, Mrs Marion (unit admin mgr) (based at11)

11. **6 The Ropewalk**
Nottingham NG1 5DT
0115-910 5400
fax 0115-910 5404

Burnage, Colin (spo)
Bryson, Ms Beverley
Caesar, Ms Beverley
Green, Paul (p)
Green, Ms Pauline
Hardy, Graham
House, David
Hudson, Judy (pract devpt assessor)
Lambert, Chris
Raban, Mrs Deirdre (p)
Smith, Adge
Bernasconi, Mrs Loraine (team asst)
Rowe, Mrs Julie (team asst)
Slack, Mrs Miriam (team asst)
Millard, Ms Maxine (emplt)
Mee, Mrs Marion (unit admin mgr)

City Peripatetic Probation Officers
Cina, Ms Eve
Macarthur, Ian T

Criminal Work (County West)

12. 46 Nottingham Road
Mansfield NG18 1BL
Mansfield (01623) 460800
fax (01623) 460801

Thompstone, Ms Annette C W (spo)
Clough, Mike
Etherington, Keith (cs)
Fletcher, Reg
Green, Ms Judy
Holt, Mrs Heather M
McTighe, Arthur
Perry, Ted
Rudkin, Mrs Carole
Sweeney, Paul
Turner, Delhorne
Victor, Andy
Waddingham, Paul (p)
Wade, Pete
Wilkinson, John
Flint, Mrs Anne (team asst)
Hathaway, Ms Paula (team asst)
Mitchell, Mrs Val (team asst)
Moore, Mrs Doreen (team asst)
Nisbet, Mrs Cheryl (team asst)
Andrews, Mrs Cathy M (csa)
Stanford, Mrs Anne (csa)
Gravestock, Miss Diane (p, projects/accom)
Fox, David (emplt)
Shaw, Mrs Wendy (unit admin mgr)

13. Sherwood Court, Sherwood Street
Mansfield NG18 1ER
Mansfield (01623) 468850
fax (01623) 468851

Austin, Ms Shelley (spo)
Scaife, Paul (spo)
Boynton, Tim
Downing, Mrs Beth
Goulder, Mrs Jenni
Maurer, Fergus J
Palmer, Ms Vicki (yot)
Phillips, Dave (pract devpt assessor)
Reilly, Ms Susan
Urquhart, Ms Jane
Wray, Ms Corrina
Wheetman, Ms Ros
Ainsworth-Chester, Ms Nicola (team asst)
Copley, Mrs Christine (team asst)
Sargison, Ms Michelle (team asst)
Dangerfield, Mrs Margaret (team asst)
Maxwell, Mrs Karen (p, proj/accom)
Wallace, Ms Carole (emplt)

North East Unit

14. 11 Newcastle Street
Worksop S80 2AS
Worksop (01909) 473424

fax (01909) 530082

Kelly, Ms Chris (spo)
Hagen, Mrs Gill (dtto)
Hancock, Mike M D
Hemingway, Ms Sarah
Liegis, Ed
Smillie, Rupert
Soar, Ms Sheila
Szulc, Chris
Stafford, Philip
Woodward, Mrs Caroline
Coates, Ms Tracy (team asst)
Doughty, Mrs Janice (team asst)
Richardson, Miss Jennifer (team asst)
Lowbridge, Ms Deborah (emplt)
Mason, Terry (psa)
Flynn, John E (csa)
Taylor, Ms Anita (p, unit admin mgr)

15. 11 Appleton Gate
Newark NG24 1JR
Newark (01636) 652650
fax (01636) 652651

Taylor, Mark (spo)
Davies, Pete (yot)
Jefferies, Mike
Johnson, Terry
Leak, Stewart
Pettit, Ms Sylvia
Saddington, Miss Marion
Walker, Colin (cs)
Lee, Mrs Lorraine (team asst)
Turton, Mrs Candy (crt wrkr)
Green, Robert (csa)
Crossland, Mrs Jo (p, unit admin mgr)

County Peripatetic Probation Officers
Jones, Mark
Robinson, Nick

16. 8-10 Pelham Road
Sherwood
Nottingham NG5 1AP
0115-840 5730
fax 0115-840 5731

Drug Treatment & Testing Orders
Taylor, Ms Steph (spo, dtto)
Amory, Chris
Carri, John
Faulkener, Ms Diane
Williams, Tony
Bush, Mrs Suzanne (team asst)
Calder, Kate (team asst)

Family Court Welfare Service
from 1.4.01 part of Children & Family Court Advisory & Support Service

17. 8-10 Pelham Road
Sherwood
Nottingham NG5 1AP
0115-840 5730
fax 0115-840 5731

Wood, Miss Gay (spo)
Clifford, Mrs Ann (p)
Cork, Mike (p)
Kavanagh, Tony
McLeod, Ms Maggie
Messam, Ms Hyacinth
Price, David
Payne, Mrs Di
Saunders, Miss Sandy
O'Hagan, Ms Cheryl (unit admin mgr)

18. Clumber House
7 Clumber Street
Mansfield NG18 1NU
Mansfield (01623) 466880
fax (01623) 466881

Wood, Miss Gay (p, spo) (based at 6)
Creedon, John
Davids, Miss Maureen
Langford, Mrs Kate (p, Worksop)
Peach, Mrs Kathy
Stanton, Andy K
O'Hagan, Ms Cheryl (unit admin mgr)

Hostels

19. **5 Astral Grove**
Hucknall, Nottingham NG15 6FY
0115-840 5720
fax 0115-840 5721

Holdaway, Sue (spo warden)
Green, Mrs Chris M (asst to warden)
Amos, Mrs Sue E (p, res sw)
Hefford, Terry G (res sw)
Mackenzie, Chris (res sw)
McMeel, Miss Biddy (res sw)
Palmer, Mrs Paula (res sw)
Pates, Miss Gloria (secy)

20. **Trent House**
Woodborough Road, Alexandra Park,
Nottingham NG3 4JB
0115-841 5630
fax 0115-841 5631

Spencer, Derek (spo warden)
Tribe, Ms Sue (po deputy)
Brown, Ms Avis (res sw)

Conway, Ms Bridget (res sw)
Johnson-Harvey, Ms Margot
Storer, Brian (res sw)
Vine, Ms Ngaire (res sw)
Brady, Ms Margaret (intake off) (0115-841 5632)
Rawson, Mrs Gina (secy)

21. **106 Raleigh Street**
Nottingham NG7 4DJ
0115-910 5450
fax 0115-910 5451

Wharrick, Ms Julie (spo warden)
Feather, Mrs Budd (deputy)
Bentley, Ian (res sw)
Brown, Michael (p, res sw)
David, Mrs Marcia (p, res sw)
Harris, Keith (res sw)
Rose, Miss Maxine (p, res sw)
Thurley, Ben (res sw)
Collins, Mrs Pat (hostels admin mgr)
Worley, Ms Prue (secy)

22. **Basford House** (Second Base)
40-42 Isandula Road
Nottingham NG7 7ES
0115-978 5851

Bannister, John (po warden)

Institutions

23. H M Prison, Perry Road
Sherwood **Nottingham** NG5 3AG
0115-962 5022
fax 0115-960 3605

Buckley, Karen (p, spo)
Metcalfe, Mrs Maggie (p, spo) (25)
Abdullah, Ms Malika
Hyatt-Butt, Tariq
Goddard, Miss Pat (team asst)

24. H M Prison **Ranby**
Near Retford DN22 8EU
Retford (01777) 706721
fax (01777)702691

Yates, Paul (spo)
Hodges, Ms Adrienne
Hunt, Mrs Christine
Jepson, Ms Hazel
Maidens, Ms Karen
Odysanya, Ms Judith
Storer, Simon

25. H M Prison **Whatton**
Nottingham NG13 9FQ
Whatton (01949) 850511
fax (01949) 850124

Probn clerk ext 277/309
Discipline ext 308/309
Special visits ext 309

Hodgett, Ms Victoria (spo) ext 277
Lathlane, Mrs Margaret
O'Mara, Ms Ruth
Wright, Peter ext 205
Cloughley, Ms Wendy (team asst)

26. H M Prison **Lowdham Grange**
Lowdham, Nottingham NG14 7DA.
0115-966 9200
fax 0115-966 9220

Crookall, Ms Jean (p, spo) (22)
Carter, Mrs Pam
Wells, Tony A W

Petty Sessional Areas

8-12 Nottingham
13, 14 Mansfield
15, 16 Worksop
16, 17 East Retford
17 Newark and Southwell

Crown Court

2 Nottingham

Area Code 39

OXFORDSHIRE & BUCKINGHAMSHIRE PROBATION SERVICE from 1.4.01 amalgamating with Berkshire Probation Service

Out of hours emergency contact point
Contact any Oxfordshire & Buckinghamshire hostel

Offices

1. **Head Office**
Kingsclere Road
Bicester Oxon OX6 8QD
Bicester (01869) 255300
fax (01869) 255355

Fishbourne, Ray (acting cpo)
Davison, Bruce (director, service delivery adults)
Hudson, Lesley (p, director, staff devpt, cs)
Mackenzie, Ms Gaynor (director, service

estates, facilities, personnel)
Marshall, Gerry (director, service delivery, effectiveness)
Myatt Maxine (acting director, service delivery youth justice, family crts)
Wilson, James (director, finance)

Baker, Veronica (p, snr personnel off)
Barrett, Sarah (personnel off)
Peck, Jayne (personnel off)
Widlake, Stephen (health & safety off)
Durrant, Julia (p, snr facilities off)
Gearey, Diane (snr facilities off)
Clayton, Julie (p, admin asst facilities)
Harvey, Susie (p, snr finance off)
Hardy, Ian (snr finance off)
Chapple, Wendy (finance off)
Unwin, Terri (snr off, finance)

Services Devpt Unit
King, Linda (service devpt mgr)
Brodie, Nicky (devpt off housing)
Martin, Elizabeth (devpt off ete)
Butler, Joe (p, mentor co-ord)
Welters, Brian (p, mentor co-ord)

Staff Devpt Unit
Reynolds, Mike (training & devpt mgr)
Burne, Philippa (staff & pract devpt off)
Singh, Avtar (staff & pract devpt off)
Boylan, Tracey (training off)
Downs, Carol (p, training off)

Research Unit
Vacancy (snr off, research & evaluation)
Belton, Emma (research & info off)

Management Support Unit
Dodds, Christine (sup service mgr)
Youens-Walden, Gwen (personal asst)
Taylor, Keeley (p, personal asst)
Trevor, Julie (personal asst)
Wood, Irene (personal asst)

2. 1/3 Ock Street
Abingdon, Oxon OX14 5AL
Abingdon (01235) 535619
fax (01235) 554511

Adult Court & Community Supvn
Adamczyk, Elizabeth (spo)
Capes, Wendy
Cleverly, Michael
Glassock, Karen
White, Debra
Mott, Andrea (psa)
Ward, Margaret (psa)

Throughcare
Forrest, Linda (p, spo)
Trotman, Rick
Nelson, Sarah (trainee)

Community Service
McIntyre, Shuna (p, spo) (based at 12)
Hedge, John (p, spo) (based at 12)
Humphreys, Fran (snr cso) (based at 12)
Farrington, Lisa (cso)
Wendon, Lois (p, cso)
Davison, Kerry (csa)

Norris, Susan (ete adv)
Quinlan, Beryl (sup services mgr)

3. 2A Wynne-Jones Centre
Walton Road **Aylesbury** Bucks HP21 7RL
Aylesbury (01296) 483174
fax (01296) 415212

Adult Court & Community Supvn
Mulvihill, Anthony (spo)
Adams-Rimmer, Jane (p)
Brown, David
Evans, Robert
Johnson, Ann
Weir, Dermot
Yaworsky, Candace (p)
Claxton, Naomi (trianee)
Hazael, Suzannah (trainee)
Afilaka, Olatunde (psa)
Ballard, Pauline (p, psa)
Beck, Jacqueline (p, psa)
Throup, Lesley (psa)

Youth Team
Butt, Denise (spo)
Aldred, Julie
Elflain, Lynne
Vacancy

Throughcare
Butt, Denise (spo)
Elmore, Nicola

Community Service
Power, Janet (spo) (based at 9)
Coffey, Mike (snr cso)
Butler, Terry (cso)
Grimes, Julie (cso)
Morgan, Elizabeth (cso) (based at 6)
Rogers, Adrienne (p, csa)

Dodds, Christine (sup services mgr)

Information Unit
(01296) 393925
Reynolds, Frankie (info mgr)
Hearn, Danny (info & computing off)
Spayne, Chris (p, info asst)

IT Unit
(01296) 393925
Steadman, Julie (it projs & devpt mgr)
Baker, Ralph (systems mgr)

4. 5 Church Street
Aylesbury Bucks HP20 2QP
Aylesbury (01296) 431000
fax (01296) 431004

Groupwork Team
Morton, Jane (gpwk mgr)
Drake, Paul
Williams, Dominic
Campbell, Melissa (psa)
Cunningham, Bruce (psa)

Drug Treatment & Testing Orders
Walls, David (drug services devpt mgr)
Oliver, David (based at 6)
Simpson, Simon (based at 10)

5. Ivy House, 23 South Bar
Banbury, Oxon OX16 9AF
Banbury (01295) 268436/7
fax (01295) 268120

Adult Court & Community Supvn
Jameson, Pat (spo)
Chapman, Margaret
Eason, Susan
Hanks, Rosemarie
Honeysett, Clare (p)
Kenna, Karen (p)
Masonde, Kabel
Sullivan, Karen
Campbell, Lucinda (psa)
Forbes-Laird, Andrina (psa)
Guerry, Theodore (psa)
McLeary, Lorriane (psa)

Throughcare
Forrest, Linda (p, spo)
Neal-Morrison, Zandra

Community Service
McIntyre, Shuna (p, spo) (based at 12)
Hedge, John (p, spo) (based at 12)
Swift, Erica (based at 9)
Goddard, Bob (cso)
Kirtley, Jane (cso)
Wilson, Patricia (p, csa)

Butler, Maurice (ete adv wrkr)
Everton, Luc (dtto psa)
Quinlan, Beryl (sup services mgr) (based at 2)

6. Easton Court, 23a Easton Street
High Wycombe, Bucks HP11 1NT
High Wycombe (01494) 436421
fax (01494) 450132

Adult Court & Community Supvn
Smith, Greg (spo)
Anderson, Marilyn (p)
Downes, Dick
Houston, Isabel
McFarlane, Jane
Munrow, Gill (p)
Ross, Marilyn (p)
Titley, Carol (p)
Morris, Bernard (trainee)
Court, Dennis (psa)
Bowell, Lynda (psa)

Throughcare
Butt, Denise (spo) (based at 3)
Deans, Tony
Wilson, Sandy

Youth Team
Butt, Denise (spo) (based at 3)
Alkinson, Julie
Hawksworth, Sarah
Lebeanya, Uche
Morris, Sally (p)
de Jongh, Caroline (trainee)

Community Service
Power, Janet (spo) (based at 9)
Coffey, Mike (snr cso) (based at 3)
Dixon, Jean (cso)
Lutter, Simon (cso)
Morgan, Elizabeth (cso)
Taylor, Zoe (psa)
Barkes, Liz (p, csa)

Dodds, Christine (sup services mgr) (based at 3)

7. Bridge House, Bridge Street
High Wycombe, Bucks HP11 2EL
High Wycombe (01494) 436622
fax (01494) 444931

Family Court Welfare Service
from 1.4.01 part of Children & Family Court Advisory & Support Service
(responsible for civil work in areas of Aylesbury & Wycombe offices)
Swan, Jennifer (spo)
Asafo-Agyei, Herman
Dallimore, Judith
Kitson, Sally (p)
Shaheed, Fareena

8. Magistrates' Court
301 Silbury Boulevard
Witan Gate East

Central Milton Keynes
Bucks MK9 2YH
Milton Keynes (01908) 679734
fax (01908) 230050

Adult Court & Community Supvn
Khan, Lorraine (p, spo)
Bosworth, Sue
Cohen, Marise
Crook, Terry (p)
Johnston, Jo-Anne
Oke, Emmanuel
Rees-Jones, Nicola
Sesay, Carol
Jerome, Sally (psa)
Patterson, Sandra (psa)
Stratford, Deborah (psa)

Youth Team
Cook, Pauline (spo)
Brown, Andy
Enfield, Clare
Fitzpatrick, Samantha
Martey, Sandra

Throughcare
Chantler, Sue (p, spo)
Crook, Terry (p)
Foster, Karen
Gateley, Margaret (p)
Honour, Mike
Radford, Anne (p)
Rose, Dawn
Shahi, Kilvinder
Bond, Sarah(trainee)
Scarle, Jane (psa)

Family Court Welfare Service
Swan, Jennifer (spo) (based at 7)
Bairstow, David
Fisher, Val
Smith, Susan
Webster, Fred

Dobson, Ann (ete advice worker)
Mafham, Val (sup services mgr)

9. 20 Market Square
Stony Stratford
Milton Keynes, Bucks MK11 1BE
Milton Keynes (01908) 564812
fax (01908) 262846

Community Service
Power, Janet (spo)
Swift, Erica (snr cso)
Doolan, Mike (cso)
Gibson, Ron (cso)
Stafford, Ruth (cso)
O'Brien, Sandra (p, csa)
Fletcher, Karen (cty cs admin)

10. Albion House
Littlegate Street
Oxford, Oxon OX1 1JN
Oxford (01865) 240750
fax (01865) 240780

Oxford Crown Crt Duty Officer
0780 323 7061
Oxford Mag Crt Duty Officer
(01865) 202039
fax (01865) 200078

Adult Court & Community Supvn
Toner, Michael (spo)
Emberson, Gill
Haskell, Katharine
Lee, Tim
Miles, Julia
Powell, Richard
Solomon, Gail
Thompson, Lisa
Baldauf-Clark, Beatrix (p, psa)
Gannon, Sophia (psa)
Jarvis-Aitoro, Megan (psa)
Partridge, Elizabeth (psa)
Yde-Poulsen, Nicole (psa)
Wild, Julie (psa)

Throughcare
Gill, Ros (p, spo)
Guthrie, Lydia
Loveday, Marian
Vacancy

Partnerships
Benson, Robin (housing advice advocacy & placement proj)
Walmsley, Paul (housing advice advocacy & placement proj)
Morgan, Mike (ete)

Aziz, Kathy (sup service mgr)

11. **Family Court Service**
from 1.4.01 part of Children & Family Court Advisory & Support Service
1st Floor, 2 Cambridge Terrace
Oxford Oxon OX1 1TP
Oxford (01865) 728421
fax (01865) 245938

Bretherton, Harriet (p, spo)
Aldridge, Linda (p)
Bennett, Elizabeth
Kendal, Val
Waite, Loran
Waterston, Harriet
Williams, Ann

Aziz, Kathy (sup services mgr) (based at 10)

12. Unit 8, Kings Meadow
Ferry Hinksey Road
Oxford OX2 0DP
Oxford (01865) 247088
fax (01865) 247092

Community Service (Oxford City)
Hedge, John (p, spo)
McIntyre, Shuna (p, spo)
Humphreys, Fran (snr cso)
Moores, Derek (cso)
Turner, Sheila (cso)
Walker, Sarah (cso)
Davison, Kerry (also at 2)
Henry, Jackie (cty cs admin)

13. 164 Oxford Road, Cowley
Oxford Oxon OX4 2LA
Oxford (01865) 775482
fax(01865) 770311

Youth Team
McCartney, Graham (spo)
Cartwright, Gillian (p)
Jones, Linda
McQueen, Katy
Nimmo, Stuart
Powell, Lesley
Scott-Denness, Bernard
Sheridan, Chris
Smith, Sheila (p)
Welch, Pam

Aziz, Kathy (sup services mgr) (10)

Youth Offending Teams

14. Youth Offending Team
County Hall, 1 Tower Crescent
Oxford OX1 1LX
(01865) 815029
fax (01865) 246614

Elgey, Ros

15. Youth Offending Team
Walton House, Walton Street
Aylesbury Bucks HP21 7QQ
(01296) 434624
fax (01296) 486321

Brierley, Amanda

16. Youth Offending Team
25/26 Easton Street
High Wycombe HP11 1NT
(01494) 463443
fax (01494) 472638

Waterston, Rob

17. Youth Offending Team
Manor Road Centre
Oakwood Drive
Bletchley **Milton Keynes** MK2 2JG
(01908) 271562
fax (01908) 374642

Johnston, Anita

Secondments to other organisations

18. **Thames Valley Project**
17 Park Road
Didcot Oxon OX11 8QL
(01235) 819162
fax (01235) 812596

Faux, Mary (proj mgr)
Marshall, David (po)
Ricks, Linda (po)
Wilson, Chris (po)
Saunders, Rebekah (psa)
Annetts, Trudi (sw)
Bates, Andrew (forensic psychologist)

19. **Thames Valley Partnerships**
Townhill Barn, Dorton Road
Chilton **Aylesbury**
Bucks HP18 9NA
(01844) 202001
fax (01844) 202008

Townsend, Patsy (p, com safety dir)

Reporting Centres

Amersham
(01494) 732273
fax (01494) 732286

Berinsfield
07714 159104 & 07803 237067

Bicester (01869) 324117
fax (01869) 324605

Faringdon
(01367) 241112

Wallingford
(01491) 825332
fax (01491) 828641

Witney
(01993) 704574
fax (01993) 708246

Hostels

20. Probation & Bail Hostel
1 Haddon, Great Holm
Milton Keynes Bucks MK8 9AL
Milton Keynes (01908) 569511
fax (01908) 265949

Czajewski, Steve (spo warden)
Newall, Jo (po deputy)
Cohen, Daniel (asst warden)
Cox, Geoffrey (asst warden)
King, Monica (asst warden)
Norman, Alan (asst warden)
Passant, Rebecca (asst warden)
Jones, Alan (p, night care asst)
Young, Sam (p, night care asst)

21. Probation Hostel
112 Abingdon Road **Oxford**
Oxon OX1 4PY
Oxford (01865) 248842
fax (01865) 794680

Fraser, Simon (spo warden)
Perry, Sheila (po/dep warden)
Adams, Sue (asst warden)
Elliott, Marion (asst warden)
McCalmon, Colin (asst warden)
Macrae, Ron (asst warden)
Phillips, Lynette (p, night care asst)

22. **Clark's House Bail Hostel**
Clark's Row, Oxford, Oxon OX1 1RE
Oxford (01865) 248841
fax (01865) 790756

Warner, Helen (spo warden)
Ratner, Sukey (po/dep warden)
Berni, Natalie (asst warden)
Dhiman, Anita (asst warden)
Faulkener, Sam (asst warden)
Page, Kelly (asst warden)
Webb, Jan (asst warden)
Brown, Vincent (night care asst)
Ward, Kieran (night care asst)

Institutions

23. H M Young Offender Institution
Bierton Road **Aylesbury**
Bucks HP20 1EN
Aylesbury (01296) 424435
fax (01296) 434139

Probn clerk ext 254
Discipline ext 309
Legal visits ext 434

Ball, Brenda (p, spo) ext 300
Bland, Madeleine ext 314
Green, Rosemary ext 277
Harvey, Julian ext 336
Pawley, Polly ext 267
Thorpe, Rodney ext 336
Hoskins, Elaine (psa) ext 254
Ody, Bill (psa) ext 254

24. H M Prison **Bullingdon**
PO Box 50
Patrick Haugh Road
Arncott, Bicester, Oxon OX25 1WD
Bicester (01869) 322111
Special visits (01869) 323876
fax (01869) 243383

Probn clerk ext 459
Discipline ext 310

Emerson, Geoff (spo) ext 205
Brown, Kit (p) ext 390
Eastwood, John ext 389
Morrison, Donald ext 454
Tarkover, Julie (p) ext 390
Wheatley, Dorothy (p) ext 278
Wickham, Tania ext 279/354
Wilson, Belinda ext 359
Chapman, Amanda (bail info) ext 477
Starbuck, Kim (p, bail info) ext 455

25. H M Young Offender Institution
Huntercombe
Huntercombe Place
Nuffield, Henley-on-Thames
Oxon RG9 5SB
Nettlebed (01491) 641711
fax (01491) 641902

Probn officers answerphone ext 397
Discipline ext 309/311
Special visits ext 213

Jeffrey, Stewart (spo) ext 405/407
Bell, Charlie ext 463
Foot, Lyn ext 405
Haigh, Ms Alex ext 463

26. H M Prison **Grendon**
Grendon Underwood
Aylesbury, Bucks HP18 0TL
Grendon Underwood (01296) 770301
fax (01296) 770756

Probn clerk ext 302
Special visits book through Wings

McGovern, Donald(spo) (27) ext 470
Anthony, Rosemary F Wing ext 334
Cohen, Stan D Wing ext 387
Gomersall, Mrs Ann, A Wing ext 370

Grogan, Paul, B Wing ext 376
Heron, Kath G Wing ext 468
Shimeld, Irene C Wing ext 381
Stead, Jenny G Wing ext 398

27. H M Prison **Spring Hill**
Grendon Underwood
Aylesbury, Bucks HP18 0TH
Grendon Underwood (01296) 770301
fax (01296) 770756

Probn clerk ext 296
Special visits ext 236

McGovern, Donald (spo) (26) ext 300
Cooper, Bridget ext 425
Johnson, Debbie (p) ext 415
Prittie, Francis ext 426

28. H M Prison **Woodhill**
Tattenhoe Street
Milton Keynes, Bucks MK4 4DA
Milton Keynes (01908) 501999
fax (01908) 505417

Probn clerk ext 298
Discipline ext 313/311
Special visits (01908) 507832

St Amour, Paul (spo) ext 300
Vacancy (spo)
Devine, Deborah ext 298
Garner, Theresa ext 298
Webb, Alan ext 298
Myers, Rebecca (p, psa)
Staff-Lonie, Sue (psa)

Petty Sessional Areas

2 Abingdon
3 Aylesbury
5 Bicester
3 Buckingham
6 Chiltern
2 Didcot & Wantage
2 Henley
8 Milton Keynes
5 North Oxon
10-13 Oxford City
10 Thame
5 Witney
6 Wycombe

Crown Court

10 Oxford
3 Aylesbury

Area Code 40

SHROPSHIRE PROBATION SERVICE from 1.4.01 amalgamating with Hereford & Worcester Probation Service

Out of hours emergency telephone number
(limited availability)
0802 781190 (8.30am-6.00pm Mon-Fri, 8.30am-noon Sat & Bank Holidays)

Offices

1. **Head Office**
Abbeydale House
39 Abbey Foregate
Shrewsbury SY2 6BN
Shrewsbury (01743) 235013
fax (01743) 236172

Ford, Roger G (cpo)
Brewerton, Anthony R (acpo)
Hunt, Mrs Gail F (acpo)
Taylor, Robert F (aco admin)
Ritson, Miss Catherine A (spo practice devpt)
Preston, David (dep finance & corporate support mgr)
Sweeney, Mrs Sarah (admin)
Hayward, Mrs Trish (asst personnel off)
Cotton, Miss Louise (trainee)
Mapp, Fiona (trainee)
Proctor, Mrs Anne (trainee)

2. 1 Quarry Place
Shrewsbury SY1 1JU
Shrewsbury (01743) 231525
fax (01743) 244914

Shrewsbury & N & S Shropshire
Currie, Tom (spo) (2-7)
Bench, Mrs Ros (p)
Heaven, Keith
Hilder, Ms Sarah
Morgan, David
Southwell, Mrs Debra (p)
Smith, Ms Sue (p)
Harvey, Mrs Carrie (psa)
Crowhurst, Mrs Lee (p, psa)
Konkel, Mrs Carolyn (office mgr)

Programme & Practice Devpt Unit
(01743) 231525
fax (01743) 241062
Law, Tom (spo)
Bywater, T Reg
Gaffney, Ms Jane (dtto)
Smith, Ruth (p)
Willetts, Miss Diane

Norfolk, Ms Gael (psa)

Addison, Ms Sharon (admin off)

3. 12a St Mary's Street
Whitchurch SY13 1QY
(01948) 667111
fax (01948) 667123

Parish, Mrs Gwyneth
Prince, Mrs Lis (psa)

4. 22a Bailey Street
Oswestry SY11 1PX
Oswestry (01691) 656343
fax (01691) 662499

Havers, Laurence
Parish, David

5. 10 Wilkinson Walk, Cheshire Street
Market Drayton TF9 1PW
Market Drayton (01630) 653879

Correspondence to office 3

6. WhitburnStreet
Bridgnorth WV16 4QT
Bridgnorth (01746) 764109

Correspondence to office 2

7. 2nd Floor, 58 Broad Street
Ludlow SY8 1GQ
Ludlow (01584) 875109
fax (01584) 877291

Bufton, Mrs Ailsa M (p)
Hankinson, Ian C H

Telford Team

8. Telford Square
Malinsgate **Telford** TF3 4HX
Telford (01952) 214100
fax (01952) 214111

Warren, John (spo) (8-9)
Barcham, Miss Anna
Batham, Angie C
Bisp, Ms Marilyn D
Briscoe, Mark
Collin, Miss Christine
Cope, Ron
Driver, Mrs Rachel
Gandon, Mrs Michelle
Heywood, Mrs Sue
Horner, Jim
Larkin, Dave
Lord, Mrs Christine G
Williams, Brian
Stokes, Mrs Katie (psa)
Morrow, Mrs Ann (psa)

Nicholas, Mrs Marilyn (office mgr)

Telford Magistrates' Court
tel/fax (01952) 210074

9. **Crown Court Office**
The Law Courts, Shirehall
Abbey Foregate
Shrewsbury SY2 6LU
Shrewsbury (01743) 252934
fax (01743) 252936

Marshall-Clarke, Vincent (cclo)

10. **Youth Offending Team**
24 Victoria Road, Wellington TF1 1LQ
Telford (01952) 257477
fax (01952) 242926

Barlow, Ms Angela
Pready-James, Andrew

11. **Community Service Office**
Telford Square
Malinsgate **Telford** TF3 4HX
Telford (01952) 214160
fax (01952) 214111

Davies, Glyn (spo) (13)
Gorse, Derek (cso)
Johnson, J Colin (cso)
Riley, John (cso)
Broome, Mrs M Ann (office mgr)

12. **Community Service Office**
1 Quarry Place
Shrewsbury SY1 1JU
Shrewsbury (01743) 344303
fax (01743) 244914

Aston, Rob (cso)
Horobin, Colin (cso)
Kelly, Doug (cso)
Swann, Wayne C (cso)

13. Flora Dugdale House
27 Wrockwardine Road
Wellington **Telford** TF1 3DA
Telford (01952) 240172
fax (01952) 255442

Family Court Welfare Service
from 1.4.01 part of Children & Family Court Advisory & Support Service
Stephens, David (scwo)
Barrow, Mrs Pat

Bissitt, David (p)
Little, Peter
McCourt, Mrs Jeanette M
Reid, Ms Susan (p)
Moore, Mrs Lorraine (office mgr)

Institutions

14. H M Prison, The Dana
Shrewsbury SY1 2HR
Shrewsbury (01743) 352511
fax (01743) 356926

Bushell, Miss Julie
Horne, Miss Susan

15. H M Young Offender Institution
Stoke Heath
Market Drayton TF9 2JL
Market Drayton (01630) 654231
fax (01630) 638875
hdc fax (01630) 639590

Discipline ext 309
HDC Unit ext 305
Sentence planning ext 308
Special visits ext 414

Hatfield, Mrs Michele (spo) ext 465
Kramer, Anthony (spo) ext 300
Adams, Mrs Carol ext 286
Baker, Mrs Sybil ext 286
Cummings, John ext 461
McGinity, Miss Emma (psa) ext 286
Noble, Mrs Helen ext 286
Roberts, Alan (psa) ext 253
Weaving, Jayne (psa) ext 460
Dean, Mrs Ruth (psa) ext 286

Petty Sessional Areas

2 Bridgnorth
2 Ludlow
2 Shrewsbury
3 Drayton (Whitchurch)
4 Oswestry (Ellesmere)
4 Oswestry
5 Drayton
8 Telford

Crown Court

9 Shrewsbury

Area Code 41

SOMERSET PROBATION SERVICE from 1.4.01 amalgamating with Avon Probation Service

Out of hours emergency contact point

Glogan House (01278) 424165

Offices

1. **Head Office**
6 Mendip House, High Street
Taunton TA1 3SX
Taunton (01823) 259474
Direct dial (01823) 340+ ext
fax (01823) 332740

Clitheroe, David (cpo) ext 214
Cotgrove, Jill (acpo) ext 203
Stopard, Paul (acpo) ext 215
Wiseman, John (acpo) ext 216
Lowe, Robin (spo, devpt mgr drugs service) (mobile 07855 632058)
Dawe, Andrew (property & finance mgr) ext 204
Jones, Jacqueline, (personnel off) ext 228
Heyworth, Elaine (spo training & devpt) ext 205
Fennings, Jean (office mgr) ext 223

2. 10 Canon Street
Taunton TA1 3SN
Taunton (01823) 330202
fax (01823) 323821

Family Court Welfare Service
from 1.4.01 part of Children & Family Court Advisory Service
Loughlin, Anne (sfcwo)
Barclay, James
Dixon, Lyn
Keedwell, Rob
Mason, Carol
Moy, David

Practice Devpt Team (based in teams)
Ashton, Richard (4)
Elliott, Jennifer (9)
Mercouris, Paula (9)
Skinner, Carrie (8)

IT & Information Unit
(01823) 251351
fax (01823) 323821

Meadows, Frank (i.t. mgr)
(01823) 346439

3. The Lonsdale Centre
Blake Street
Bridgwater TA6 3NB
Bridgwater (01278) 423977
fax (01278) 453941

Court & Individual Interventions Team
Foy, Thomas (spo)
Carver, Adrian
Clark, Roger
Darbin, Steve
Hamilton, Mike
Little, Di
Perkins, Simon
Smyth, Lynda
Tomlinson, Jane
Way, Lynn
Carver, Aileen (crt admin)
Denslow, Shelley (fin & admin mgr) (5)

Community Service
Palmer, Tracey (cso)
Taylor, Philip (cso)
Bennett, Sharon (cs admin)

Accommodation
Price, Carol (accom off)

4. 11 Canon Street
Taunton TA1 1SN
Taunton (01823) 251351
fax (01823) 321724

Court & Supervision
Hamilton, Liz (acting spo until 31.3.01)
Ashton, Richard
Evans, Mike
Grover, Maggie
Hamilton, Michael
Penelhum, Margaret (js)
Powell, Angela
Roberts, Paul
Vinnicombe, Peter
Waugh, Nicky
Baker, Jane (crt admin) (js)
Rawles, Colette (crt admin) (js)
Hunter, Cheryl (trainee
Wright, Sara (trainee)
Fensom, Pat (fin & admin mgr) (2)

Programmes
Seaton, Jackie (spo)
Cartwright, Faith
Chin, Mike
Kelly, Philip

Sex Offender Programme
Brandt, Peter

Community Service
Gardner, Pauline (cso)
Penn, David (cso)

Accommodation
Sanchez, Paula (accom off)

5. The Old Stables
Alexandra Road
Minehead TA24 5DP
Minehead (01643) 706561
fax (01643) 705251

open Tues pm, Thurs to 7 pm, Fri
Foy, Thomas (spo) (based at 3)

Court & Individual Interventions Team
Lewis, Lis
Harman, Roy (cso)
Searle, Daniel (css)

6. **Crown Court Unit**
Shire Hall, Taunton TA1 1EU
Taunton (01823) 338599 & 335972
fax (01823) 338946

Hamilton, Liz (based at 4)
Radford, Kathy (admin) (js)
Smith, Maxine (admin) (js)

7. Northover House
North Parade **Frome** BA11 1AU
Frome (01373) 462385 & 463606
fax (01373) 452535

Court & Individual Interventions Team
McLaughlin, Jane (spo) (8)
Jones, Kevin
Rymell, Alison

CS & Reintegration Team
Corry, Sylvia

8. St Lawrence Lodge
37 Chamberlain Street
Wells BA5 2PQ
Wells (01749) 677779
fax (01749) 672169

Court & Individual Interventions Team
McLaughlin, Jane (spo) (9)
Bradley, Stephen
Carrie, Skinner (p)
Hardman, Howard
Jones, Kevin
O'Gorman, Sean
Flower, Joan (crt admin)

CS & Reintegration Team
Corry, Sylvia

Practice Devpt Team
Carrie, Skinner (p)

Programmes
Bradley, Stephen

Community Service
Bristow, Kath (spo)
Greaves, Judy (cso)
Gulliford, Wendy (cs admin)

9. Court Ash House
Court Ash **Yeovil** BA20 1AG
Yeovil (01935) 476461/2
fax (01935) 475290

Court & Supervision
Whiley, Nicola (spo)
Elliott, Jennifer
Geraghty, Dominic
Jones, Mark
Mercouris, Paula
Newbery, Nigel
Pittam, Jenny
Pring, Graham
Rixon, Anna
Robinson, Shirley
Mikshick, Jock (secondment)
Hextall, Nigell (trainee)
Miller, Bob (trainee)
Squire, Tom (trainee)
Stewart, Alison (crt admin)

Kingsbury, Marion (fin & admin mgr) (7, 8)

Programmes
Jerzykowski, Ernie
Willett, Nicole

Sex Offender Programme
Adley, Pat

CS & Reintegration Team
Mason, Steve (spo)
Tanner, Andrew

Community Service
Ellery, Joy (cso)
Cooper, Mike (cso)
Vacancy (cs admin)

10. **Youth Offending Team**
5-7 West End
Street BA16 0LG
Street (01458) 440820
fax (01458) 449100

Edmonds, Marie (team ldr)
Nightingale, Jill

Hostel

11. **Glogan House**
59 Taunton Road, Bridgwater TA6 3LP
Bridgwater (01278) 424165
fax (01278) 446054

Gunby, Gary (spo, mgr)
Barford, Ann (po)
Bridgwater, Caroline (asst mgr)
Derrick, Richard (asst mgr)
Foxwell, Anton (asst mgr)
Greenway, karen (asst mgr)
Murkin, Robert (asst mgr)
Horn, Sheldon (asst mgr)

Institution

12. H M Prison, Cornhill
Shepton Mallet BA4 5LU
Shepton Mallet (01749) 343377
fax (01749) 345256

Mason, Stephen (p, spo) (9)
Porter, Richard
Sawyer, Ian (ets treatment mgr)
Webster, Robin

Petty Sessional Areas

7 Mendip
3 Sedgemoor
9 South Somerset
4 Taunton Deane
5 West Somerset

Crown Court

6 Taunton

Area Code 42

STAFFORDSHIRE PROBATION SERVICE

Out of hours: please note that Staffordshire Police retain a list of all managers home telephone numbers.

Offices

1a. **Head Office**
University Court
Staffordshire Technology Park
Beaconside, Stafford ST16 0GE
Stafford (01785) 223416
fax (01785) 223108

Walton, David (cpo)
Fieldhouse, Peter (acpo county services divn)

Forrester, Mrs Sandra (acpo southern divn)
Lawrence, Mrs Muriel (acpo north divn)
Mandley, Rob (acpo mgment services divn)
Clewlow, Mrs Linda (temp financial services mgr)
Bowden, Mrs Sandra (personnel services mgr)
Quinn, Jim (cttee accountant)
Hewitt, Ian (buildings services mgr)

1b. **Information Services Unit**
Beckwith, John (info services mgr)
Massey, Phil (research off)
Sheehan,Mrs Sue (systems/training off)
Parekh, Mohamed (computer services off)
Stanley, James (asst computer services off)
Armour, Wendy (p.r. off)

1c. **Employment & Training Devpt Unit**
Jolley, Mike J (offender emplt & ext resources mgr)
Reeves, Rob (offender emplt off)
Cameron, Miss Beverley (educn off)
Morse, Mrs Vivienne (p, educn off)

1d. **Training & Devpt Unit**
Jones, Mrs Barbara (spo training & devpt unit)

Practice Devpt Assessors
(based at office 22)
Stafford (01785) 212625
fax (01785) 228708
Burrows, Mrs Lesley
Dawson, Mrs Ann
Elks, Mrs Barbara

1e. **Effective Practice**
Trenery, Mrs Alison (spo)

1f. **Housing Development Unit/ Partnerships**
Scott, Peter (partnerships mgr)

Accommodation Officers
at office 17 (Hanley)
Stoke (01782) 212608
fax (01782) 286265
Walton, Bernard (accom off)

at office 12 (Lichfield)
Lichfield (01543) 258185
fax (01543) 419361
Austin, Blair (accom off)

2. Town Hall, High Street
Biddulph Stoke-on-Trent ST8 6AR
Stoke (01782) 518070
fax (01782) 523082

Bailey, Andrew (p, acting spo)

3. Eaves Lane **Bucknall**
Stoke-on-Trent ST2 8JY
Stoke (01782) 261961
fax (01782) 287459

Gough, Mick (spo)
Dehal, Ms Rupinder (p)
Garner, Mrs Maureen
Hayes, Mrs Shirley
Walsh, Ms Elizabeth (p)
Williams, Andrew
Yarwood, Mrs Ellen

4. Horninglow Street
Burton-upon-Trent DE14 1PH
Burton (01283) 564988
fax (01283) 567978

Williams, Sam (spo)
Hine, Miss Sue (spo dtto devpt)
Blakemore, Mrs Gill (p)
Devlin, Patrick
Garrison, Keith
Hinds, Colin
Kean, Mrs Frances
Shaw, Miss Judith
Woolhouse, John
Crouch, Ms Zoe (pso)
Kidd, Ms Sharon (pso)

5. 200a Wolverhampton Road
Cannock WS11 1AT
Cannock (01543) 506112/3/4
fax (01543) 501029

Atkins, Jim (spo)
Amer, Bob
Cairns, Ms Esther
Francis, Ms Susan
Grimshaw, Martin (js)
Singham
Wood, Tony
Young, Miss Lesley
Burgess, Mrs Val (pso)

6. District Council Office
Leek Road **Cheadle** ST10 1JB
(01538) 754484
fax (01538) 751287

Bailey, Andrew (p, acting spo)

7. **Crown & County Court**
Bethesda Street Hanley
Stoke-on-Trent ST1 3BP
Stoke (01782) 286831
fax (01782) 287994

Gough, Mick (spo)

Booth, Ms Jane (p)
Eckersley, Rod
Hill, Jeff W
Norris, Ms Lisa (pso)

8. **Crown & County Court**
Victoria Square
Stafford ST16 2QQ
Stafford (01785) 223433
fax (01785) 224156

Gough, Mick (spo)
Fieldhouse, Mrs Kathryn (p)
Poulter, Mrs Kath
Carwardine, Ms Sarah (pso)

9. **Magistrates & Youth Court Team North Division**
Ryecroft
Newcastle-under-Lyme ST5 2DT
Newcastle (01782) 719036
fax (01782) 715998

Gough, Mick (spo)
Boulton, Mrs Jenny
Kent, Mrs Helen
Ryan, Robert
Steer, Mrs Jean
Barker, Mrs Jackie (pso)
Birt, Mrs Lynne (p, pso)
James-Harford, Mrs Tina (p, pso)
Thurlow, Bernard (p, bail info asst)

10. Broom Street
Hanley Stoke-on-Trent ST1 2EN
Stoke (01782) 286836
fax (01782) 286685

Staplehurst, Ms Angela (spo)
Bettany, Kevin
Cooper, Mrs Linda
Dunne, Steven
Holloway, Trevor
Johnson, Mrs Virginia
Vacancy (p)
Nixon, Mrs Susan
Stokes, Mrs Elizabeth
Whitmore, Andrew
Brookes, Mrs Anne (pso)
Moayedi-Azarpour, Ms Rachel (pso)

11. Kidsgrove Town Hall
Liverpool Road **Kidsgrove** ST7 4EH
Stoke (01782) 776181
fax (01782) 776249

Woolgar, Geof (spo)

12. Cross Street
Leek ST13 6BT
Leek (01538) 399355
fax (01538) 399245

Bailey, Andrew (p, acting spo))
Flowers, David (p)
Pointon, Tim
Sproston, Mrs Stephanie
Wood, Gerard
Heath, Ms Pam (p, pso)
Whealdon, John (pso)

Chadwick, Ms Jean (p, mentally disordered offenders,
based at St Edward's Hospital, Cheddleton)

13. Stowe Court, Stowe Street
Lichfield WS13 6AQ
Lichfield (01543) 251423
fax (01543) 419361

Corcoran, Mrs Lynne (spo)
Esty, Lloyd
Patterson, Rob
Wakeham, Ms Trudi
Yendale, Ms Jo (pso)

14. Marlborough Road
Longton ST3 1EJ
Stoke (01782) 599690
fax (01782) 598562

Hartley, Trevor (spo)
Boucher, Ms Shelley
Cooper, Mrs Claire (js)
Shaw, Jeff
Stanyer, Mrs Joy
Terry, Mrs Lindsey
Vacancy (p)
Hughes, Ms Kim (pso)
Skelton, Kenneth (pso)

15. 26 Sandon Road **Meir**
Stoke-on-Trent ST3 7DL
Stoke (01782) 321521
fax (01782) 598763

Hartley, Trevor (spo)
Dalgarno, Ms Claire
Robins, Jonathan
Wilson, Ms Clare
Weaver, Mrs Tina (pso)

16. Ryecroft
Newcastle-under-Lyme ST5 2DT
Newcastle (01782) 717074
fax (01782) 713374

Kosh, Mike (spo, risk & victim liaison)

Woolgar, Geof (spo)
Alexander, Ms Barbara
Armstrong, Mrs Ann (p)
Bennett, Ms Judith
Boyle, John (p)
Eyre, Ms Michelle
Jones, Richard
Mills, Michael
Proctor, Ms Wendy
Pye, Terry
Stockall, Steve (prolific offender project)
Stone, Martin
Litherland, Mrs Sylvia (pso)
Lowndes, Mrs Sandra (pso)

17. Bryan's Lane
Rugeley WS15 2JN
Rugeley (01889) 574730
fax (01889) 577478

Atkins, Jim (spo)
Bentley, Robin
Clarke, Philip
Bains, Ms Herminder (pso)

18. South Walls
Stafford ST16 3BL
Stafford (01785) 223415
fax (01785) 224159

Boult, Chris (spo)
Dodgson, Paddy
Hall, Ms Margaret
Hughes, Mrs Gill
Kirkland, Ms Pam
Oldacre, Ray (p)
Powell, Mrs Eleanor
Caddick, Mrs Janice (p, pso)
Reeves, Mrs Julie (pso)

19. Spinning School Lane
Tamworth B79 7AP
Tamworth (01827) 66906
fax (01827) 69152

Corcoran, Mrs Lynne (spo)
Gibbs, Ms Catherine
Harrison, Ms Stephanie
Leitch, Bob
Turner, Ms Laura
Khwaja, Shawez (pso)
Maddox, Mrs Lynda (pso)

20. Uttoxeter Report Centre
Red Gables, 59 High Street
Uttoxeter ST14 7JQ
(01283) 564988
fax (01283) 567978

Williams, Sam (spo)

21. **Programmes Team**
Broom Street **Hanley**
Stoke-on-Trent ST1 2EN
Stoke (01782) 283488
fax (01782) 283661

Birkett, Mike (spo, progs mgr)
Almond, Robert J
Cooper, Mrs Sally
Davis, Clive A
Grant, Mrs Diane (p)
Hodgkinson, Ian
Burdon, Ms Julie (pso)

22. **Programmes Team**
Bryans Lane
Rugeley WS15 2JN
Rugeley (01889) 574730
fax (01889) 577478

Birkett, Mike (spo, progs mgr)
Dwight, Ms Ellie
Flynn, Barry
Gray, Mrs Philippa (p)
Robotham, Mrs Sue
Sutton, Mrs Heather
Torr, Mrs Sue (pso)

Community Service Offices

23. **Stafford Community Service Office**
Dorrington Drive
Dorrington Industrial Park
Common Road, Stafford ST16 3DG
Stafford (01785) 228608
fax (01785) 228708

Cartlidge, John (cs org) (23-26)
Darnbrough, Philip
Hartill, Bill (proj off)
Malone, Oliver (proj off)
Roberts, Peter (proj off)

24. Broom Street **Hanley**
Stoke-on-Trent ST1 2EN
Stoke (01782) 213324/5
fax (01782) 286265

McLoone, Mrs Chris
Keeling, Neil (snr proj off)
Lowndes, Chris (proj off)
vacancy (proj off)
Lowndes, Tony (proj off)
Tams, George (proj off)
Harrison, Mrs Gail (pso)

25. 200a Wolverhampton Road
Cannock WS11 1AT
Cannock (01543) 501000/3
fax (01543) 501029

Seavers, Mike

26. Unit 1, Crossfields Industrial Estate
Lichfield WS13 6RJ
Lichfield (01543) 263299
fax (01543) 419360

Corns, Bill
Bradley, Mrs Shirley (proj off)
Thorndyke, John (proj off)
Harries, Marc (proj off, temp)

Civil Courts Family Welfare Service
from 1.4.01 part of Children & Family Court Advisory & Support Service

27. 13 Hartshill Road
Stoke on Trent ST4 7QT
Stoke (01782) 747127
fax (01782) 745106

Mason, John (spo) (26-28)
Bebbington, Miss Hazel
Cumberlidge, Mrs Pat
Gilmore, Simon G
Kenney, Miss Nicola
Pugsley, Ms Judith (p)
Thorogood, Mrs Carolyn A
Wadsworth, Mrs Ingrid (p)
Walton, Mrs Alison (p)

28. Tillington Street
Stafford ST16 2RE
(Stafford (01785) 785816
fax (01785) 785817

Bader, Adrian E (based at 4)
Elliott, Mrs Lynne
Parsons, Clive
Pegg, Mrs Andrea
Simpson, Ms Jane
Watson, Stanley (p)

29. Moor Street **Tamworth** B79 7QZ
Tamworth (01827) 55549
fax (01827) 69533

Boyd, Miss Jane
Trigg, Terry
Vacancy (p)

Youth Offending Team

30. Unit C, Metro Business Park
Clough Street **Hanley**
(01782) 235858

Breen, Ms Helen
Breaze, Stuart

30a. Seabridge Youth & Community Centre
Newcastle under Lyme
(01782) 297615

Downing, Mrs Moyra

30b. Priory House
Friars Terrace **Stafford**
(01785) 277022

Martin, Ms Lisa

30c. The Old House
Eastern Avenue **Lichfield**
(01543) 510103

Preston, Andrew

Hostels

31. **Wenger House Probation & Bail Hostel**
21a Albert Street
Newcastle-under-Lyme ST5 1HJ
Newcastle (01782) 717423
fax (01782) 714332

Butler, Chris J (hostel mgr)
Charlesworth, Mrs margaret (dep mgr)
Rogers, Ms Emma (asst warden)
Dedic, Michael (asst warden)
Gordon, John (asst warden)
Hare, Ms Karen (asst warden)
Weaver, Peter (asst warden)

32. **Staitheford House Probation & Bail Hostel**
14 Lichfield Road, Stafford ST17 4JX
Stafford (01785) 223417
fax (01785) 224153

Allerton, Clive (hostel mgr)
Hay, Ms Catherine (dep mgr)
Butler, David (asst warden)
Burke, Richard (asst warden)
Richardson, Ms Jacqueline (asst warden)
Saville, Mark (asst warden)

33. **Wharflane House Bail Hostel**
Rectory Road, Shelton
Stoke on Trent ST1 4PW
Stoke (01782) 205554
fax (01782) 205552

Singleton, Mrs Sylvia (hostel mgr)

Vacancy (deputy mgr)
Bell, Ms Jacqueline (asst warden)
Forrester, Mrs June (asst warden)
Walters, Ms Sandra(asst warden)
Pennant, Anthony (asst warden)

Mounfield, Ms Diane (p, central bail referral off)

Institutions

34. H M Prison, 54 Gaol Road
Stafford ST16 3AW
Stafford (01785) 254421
fax (01785) 249591

O'Connor, Mike (spo)
Bonser, Ms Jane (js)
Brereton, Simon
Cavanagh, Ian
Hibbs, Ms L
Holloway, Trevor
Milnes, Ms Patricia
Pointon, Tim
Vacancy
Wherry, Ian L (js)

35. H M Prison **Drake Hall**
Eccleshall, Nr Stafford ST21 6LQ
Eccleshall (01785) 858100
fax (01785) 858010

Poulter, Michael (spo)
Leadbetter, Mrs Jo
Vacancy (p)
Smith, Ms Jenny (p)

36. H M Young Offender Institution
Swinfen Hall 18 The Drive
Swinfen, Nr Lichfield
Staffordshire WS14 9QS
Shenstone (01543) 481229
special visits (01543) 483305
fax (01543) 480138

Johnson, Nigel (spo)
Bignell, Mrs Janice
Carpenter, Mrs Sheelah
Clayton, Ms Ros

37. H M Prison, New Road
Featherstone Wolverhampton
West Midlands WV10 7PU
Wolverhampton (01902) 790991
fax (01902)791843

White, Mark (spo)
Esty, Lloyd
Gilbride, Miss Susan (p)
Hibbert, Ms Sharon (p)
Lawton, Stephen
Sgroi, Gerald (p)
Vacancy
Withington, Mrs Amanda

38. H M Young Offender Institution
Werrington House
Werrington, Stoke-on-Trent ST9 0DB
Ash Bank (01782) 303514
fax (01782) 302504

Large, Malcolm (spo)

Petty Sessional Areas

4 Burton-upon-Trent
5 Cannock
13 Lichfield
18 Mid Staffordshire
16 Newcastle-under-Lyme & Pirehill North
17 Rugeley
2, 6, 12 Staffordshire Moorlands
3, 10, 14, 15 Stoke-on-Trent
29 Tamworth

Crown Courts

7 Stoke-on-Trent
8 Stafford

Area Code 43

SUFFOLK PROBATION SERVICE

Out of hours emergency contact point
The Cottage (01473) 408266

Offices

1. **Head Office**
Foundation House
34 Foundation Street
Ipswich IP4 1SP
Ipswich (01473) 408130
fax (01473) 408136

Barrow, Arnold (cpo)
Garside, Martin (acpo)
Mortimer, Peter (acpo)
Merriam, Robin (acpo)

Sharpe, Don (acting spo subst misuse)
Walsh, Mrs Daria (p, spo community prtrnshps)
Porter, Steve (spo it)

Jones, Glyn (info mgr)

Stephens, Mrs Siobhan (finance)
Lewis, Mrs Gill (p, personnel off)

Training and Development Team
Vicary, Mrs Jill (acting spo training/devpt)

2. **The Marland Centre**
64-70 Foundation Street
Ipswich IP4 1BN
Ipswich (01473) 408160
fax (01473) 408169

Burlinson, Bob (spo operations)
Sykes, Tim (spo practice devpt)
Pestell, Mrs Sari (p, spo practice devpt)
Maudsley, Richard
Castell, Ms Julie (p)
Clements, Paul
Dyde, Ms Clare
Fildes, Ms Lyndsay (p)
Jay, Ms Nicky
McLelland-Brown, Mark
Maddock, Ms Debbie
Mallows, Mrs Glynis
Milner, Rob
Patel, Julie
Turnbull, Miss Christine (p)
Wallace, Miss Shariffa
Westlund, David
Winters, Terry
Cook, Andrew (psw)
Crawford, Mrs Nicky (accom psa)

Court Liaison Team
Farrow, Bob
Gilbert, Terry
Vacancy
Mendham, Mrs Dene
Minhas, Mrs Kalvinder (psw)
Brame, Miss Rachel (psw)

Intensive Probation Programmes
Low, Gordon
Greenhalgh, Ms Karen
Walsh, Ms Cathy
Gladden, Mrs Angela (psw)

Community Service Office
Parker, Mrs Kelley (spo)
Morrison, Kevin (cso)
Pender, Tom (cso)
Hale, Tony (cso)

Youth Offending Team
(01473) 583570
Shields, Ms Sue (yot)

Key, Mrs Kerry (office mgr)

3. Old Nelson Street
Lowestoft NR32 1EG
Lowestoft (01502) 501800
fax (01502) 539363

Doylend, John (spo operations)
Rainton, Mrs Pauline (spo pract devpt)
Cant, Joe
Curtis, Miss Sally
Davis, Shayne
Everton, Dennis
Farrow, Miss Maria
Hipperson, Sarah
Mitchell, Mrs Christine (p)
Moreno, Rene
Mortlock, Mrs Sian (p, crt psw)
Stannard, Miss Anne (crt psw)

Alden, Graham (trainee)
Hacon, Catherine (trainee)
Steel, David (trainee)

Norris, Mrs Juliet (office mgr) (4)

4. Police Station Road
Lowestoft NR32 1NY
Lowestoft (01502) 519990
fax (01502) 580092

O'Hanlon, Mrs Jane (grpwk off)
Chaplin, Mike (cso)
Brinded, Peter (cso)
Chapman-Wright, Ian (psw)
Roberts, Miss Lucy (gpwk psw)

5. **West Suffolk Probation Centre**
Dettingen Way
Bury St. Edmunds IP33 1RS
Bury St. Edmunds (01284) 716600
fax (01284) 716606

List, Ms Sally (spo operations) (8)
Joscelyne, David (spo pract devpt)
Fitchett, Graham (gpwk)
Aylward, Mrs Ali
Connelly, Mrs Jean (p)
Flath, Mrs Alison
Guthrie, Mrs Susan (p)
Lindsell, Mrs Issi
Lowe, Rik
Marshall, Mrs Christine
Meiklejohn, Jamie (p, yot)
Plumb, Alan
Preston, Jay (p)
Reuben, Mrs Cathy
Snodgrass, Andrew
Vacancy
Sykes, Hayley (psw)
Staines, Ms Lesley (cso)

Hobden, Richard (cso)
Key, Martyn (cso)

Bergdahl, Miss Joanne (trainee)
Fontenay, Miss Nathalie (trainee)
White, Colin (trainee)

Coopoosamy, Mrs Ruby (office mgr) (6-8)

6. 14 Market Place
Stowmarket IP14 1DP
Stowmarket (01449) 615121
fax (01449) 672410

7. Crowland House, Withersfield Road
Haverhill CB9 9LA
Haverhill (01440) 702375
fax (01440) 703413

8. 6a Old Market Place
Sudbury CO10 6SZ
Sudbury (01787) 372003
fax (01787) 883080

9. **Family Court Welfare Team**
from 1.4.01 part of Children & Family Court Advisory & Support Service
6 Merchants Court
74 Foundation Street
Ipswich IP4 1BN
Ipswich (01473) 408120
fax (01473) 408127

Sorrell, Peter (scwo)
Brown, Rod
Compton, Alan (p)
Compton, Rosemary (p)
Eadon, Nick

North at office 6
Fisher, Brian

West at office 7
Ames, Mrs Emma (p)
Stuart, Mrs Pat

Hostels

10. **Lightfoot House**
37 Fuchsia Lane, Ipswich IP4 5AA
Ipswich (01473) 408280
fax (01473) 408282

Heath, Richard (spo warden) (13)
Aylward, Graeme (po deputy)
Green, Miss Mandy (po deputy)
Murray, James (asst warden)
Stock, Ms Corinna (asst warden)
Williams, Richard (asst warden)
Thelwell, Tom (asst warden)

11. **The Cottage**
795 Old Norwich Road
Ipswich IP1 6LH
Ipswich (01473) 408266
fax (01473) 408268

Heath, Richard (spo warden) (12)
Aylward, Graeme (po deputy)
Green, Miss Mandy (po deputy)
O'Dwyer, Mrs Pat (asst warden)
Partridge, Neil (asst warden)
Stroh, Jim (asst warden)
Wogan, Chris (asst warden)

Institutions

12. H M Prison **Blundeston**
Lowestoft NR32 5BG
Lowestoft (01502) 730591
fax (01502) 730138

Probn clerk ext 301
Discipline ext 308
Special visits ext (01502) 732565

Comyn, Mrs Diane (spo) ext 300
Vacancy ext 341
Harrison, Mrs Sue ext 297
Harte, Mike ext 402
Rushmore, Alan (p, probn health co-ord) ext 341

13. H M Prison **Highpoint**
Stradishall, Newmarket CB8 9YG
Wickhambrook (01440) 823100
fax (01440) 823099

Dennis, Roger (spo) ext 3071
Brinkley, David ext 3067
Goddard, Mrs Lynne ext 3038
Hewitt, Mrs Marilyn ext 3280
Meadows, Ms Karen (p) ext 3281
Siddaway, Mrs Elizabeth ext 3054
Stewart, Ms Annette (p) ext 3048
Wood, Peter ext 3175
Williams, Mrs Anne (probn health co-ord) ext 3077
Webster, Mrs Philippa (psa) ext 3076
Smeeth, Ms Sarah (psw) ext 3079

14. H M Young Offender Institution
Hollesley Bay Colony
Hollesley, Woodbridge IP12 3JS
Shottisham (01394) 411741
fax (01394) 411071

Probn clerk ext 299
Discipline (open) ext 311
Discipline (closed) ext 309
Special visits phone unit concerned

Taylor, Barbara (spo) ext 296
Moore, Paul (closed yoi) ext 294
Dugdall-Marshall, Ruth ext 296
Pratt, Melvin ext 291
Vacancy
Marsh, Mrs Barbara (probn health co-ord) ext 298

Petty Sessional Areas

2 Deben
2 Ipswich
3 Lowestoft
3, 4 NE Suffolk
7 Haverhill
5 St. Edmundsbury/NW Suffolk
6 Stowmarket
8 Sudbury

Crown Courts

2 Ipswich
2 Bury St Edmunds

Area Code 44

SURREY PROBATION SERVICE

Out of hours emergency contact point:
St Catherine's Priory
(01483) 571635

Offices

1. **Head Office**
Bridge House, Flambard Way
Godalming GU7 1JB
Godalming (01483) 860191
fax (01483) 860295

Varah, Michael (cpo)
Lockhart, Lyn (pa to cpo)
Ball, Yvette (aco)
Gritton, James (aco)
Hake, Sarah (aco)
Herring, Pauline (aco)
Jolly, Penni (hr mgr)
Fripp, Clare (admin off, personnel)
Rowley, Julie (p, admin off, personnel)
Russell, Pam (personnel admin)
Barclay, Mandy (staff devpt off)
Hazell, Kylie (training & personnel admin)
Fruer, Tony (principal i.t. off)
Kellett, James (snr tech advisor)
Hone, James (its off)
Lawrence, Julie (it off)
Slee, Chris (i.t. off)
Asokkumar, Immacula (eval & insp off)
Lovebakke, Jorgen (eval & insp off)
Mitchell, Janet (finance mgr)
Danks, Pauline (p, finance asst)
Garrod, Valerie (p, finance asst)
Green, Valerie (admin asst)
Windless, Kate (receptionist)

2. Probation Centre
White Rose Court, Oriental Road
Woking GU22 7PJ
Woking (01483) 776262
fax (01483) 727244

Assessment & Supervision
Sanders, Roger (mgr)
Belnavis, Ingrid (p, case mgr)
Paterson, Lorna (case mgr)
Pedrick, Linda (p, case mgr)
White, Stella (p, case mgr)
Dennis, Mark (assessmt off)
Tonks, Tony (assessment off)
Jobson, Angela (assessmt sup off)
Delaney, Carol (p, case mgmnt off)
Glover, Debbie (case mgmnt off)
Taylor, Elaine (case mgmnt off)
Baker, Melanie (case co-ord)
Lawlor, Karen (case co-ord)
Cameron, Viviene (trainee)

Court & Customer Services
Rickinson, Sam (mgr)
Beck, Amy (vict liaison off)
Tanner, Terry (vict liaison off)
Duncombe, Emily (crt co-ord)
Husbands, Joanna (crt liaison)
Sharp, Dea (crt liaison)
Bateman, Lee (customer services off)
Hall, Carl (customer services off)
Haleena, Arif (admin)
Watts, Julie (p, receptionist)

Programmes Team
Sauze, Simon (mgr)
Güven, Jenny (prog off)
Large, Candida (prog off)
Levett, Richard (prog off)
Parkinson, Ann (prog off)
Winstone, Lisa (prog off)
Large, Candida (prog off)
Parkhouse, Tim (prog off)
Derbyshire, Gordon (prog sup off)
Rees, Lauren (prog co-ord)

Drug Treatment & Testing Team
Pedrick, Lyn (proj mgr)
Fairbrass, Rosalind (substance misuse)

Community Service
Critchlow, Phil (mgr) (3)

Collins, Kim (snr cso)
Black, Lucy (cso)
Oates, Colin (cso)
Whittle, James (cso)
Bland, Phil (p, css)
Clark, Michael (p, css)
Edsall, Edward (p. css)
Phillip, Joanna (p, css)
Rees, Tony (p, css)
Keane, Ann (p, admin asst)
Pilsworth, Linda (data input)

Staff Devpt
Ainsworth, Carole (staff devpt off)
Aiers, Diane (p, staff devpt off)

Crime Prevention
Golder, Christine (director)

Surrey Springboard Trust
O'Malley, Karen (snr devpt off)
Boyd, Sally (devpt off)
Kirpalani, Nigel (devpt off)
Wilson, Sally (new deal co-ord)

3. Probation Centre
College House, Woodbridge Road
Guildford GU1 4RS
Guildford (01483) 534701
fax (01483) 453702

Assessment & Supervision
Higgis, Brian (acting mgr)
Adams, Michael (case mgr)
Mitchell, Colin (case mgr)
Warnke, Sally (case mgr)
Browning, Lesley (p, assessmt off)
Chapman, John (assessmt off)
Higgs, Brian (p, assessmt off)
MacKenzie, Gus (case mgmnt off)
Moore, Margaret (case mgmnt off)
Fraser, Naomi (p, case co-ord)
Maiden, Michelle (P, case co-ord)
Silvester, Jo (case co-ord)
Baldwin, Eunace (assessment sup off)
Patten, Margaret (p, assessmt sup off)
Braim, Ginny (trainee)
Cornish, Alyson (trainee)
King, Ena (trainee)
Warriner, Nicola (trainee)

Court & Customer Services
Lane, Brenda (mgr)
Lunnon, Sally (crt co-ord)
Jackson, Charlotte (customer services off)
Mussell, Alexandra (customer services off)
Banner, Judith (crt liaison)
Hathaway, Jenny (crt liaison)
West, Janet (crt liaison)
Crossley-Lees, Christine (admin)
Smith, Freya (p, receptionist)

Programmes Team
Myers, Fran (prog relivery off)
Stone, Alan (prog delivery off)

Family Court Welfare Service
from 1.4.01 part of Children & Family Court Advisory & Support Service
Stowe, Pat (mgr)
Dunford, Meg (fcw off)
Evans, David (fcw off)
Nelson, Roma (fcw off)
Quinn, Valerie (fcw off)
Verity, Mark (fcw off)
Wilson, Geraldine (fcw off)
Smith, Freya (fcw co-ord)
Gentry, Anne (p, sup off)
Holland, Clare (sup off)
McClan, Jill (p, sup off)
Sanders, Cynthia (p, sup off)

Drug Treatment & Testing Team
Ferns, Glyn-Anne (subst misuse off)

Community Service
Critchlow, Philip

Staff Devpt
Millar, Randall (peripatetic po)

Surrey Springboard Trust
Lee, Adrian (devpt off)
O'Malley, Dave (accom adv)

4. Probation Centre
Allonby House
Hatchlands Road **Redhill** RH1 6BN
Redhill (01737) 763241
fax (01737) 765688

Assessment & Supervision
Little, Ray (mgr)
Harvey, Emma (case mgr)
Jones, Sally (p, case mgr)
McLean, Marion (case mgr)
Wilson, Adrian (p, case mgr)
Worrall, Catherine (case mgr)
Coltofeanu, Ruth (assessmt off)
Kirk, Valerie (assessmt off)
Bratcher, Mary (case mgmnt off)
Cannon, Sarah (case mgmnt off)
Class, Pam (case mgmnt off)
Clay, Maribel (case mgmnt off)
Mariner, Lynda (p, case mgmnt off)
Norman, Lynn (p, case mgmnt off)
Scourfield, Tracey (case mgmnt off)
Harrison, Katherine (case co-ord)
Waghorn, Margaret (case co-ord)

Deacon, Kay (p, assessmt sup off)
O'Brien, Lin (p, assessmt sup off)
Hardy, Sarah (p, assessmt sup off)
O'Brien, Lin (p, assessmt sup off)
Clark, Brian (trainee)

Court & Customer Services
Dobson, Barbara (mgr)
Edit, Martin (crt liaison off)
Mitchell, Wendy (p, crt liaison off)
Revell, Colin (crt liaison off)
Tucker, Matthew (crt liaison off)
Scoffham, Barbara (crt co-ord)
Henson, Brenda (customer services off)
McConnell, Pauline (p, customer services off)
Prosser, Clare (p, customer services off)
Ward, Catherine (admin)

Programmes Team
Conaboy, Chris (prog delivery off)

Drug Treatment & Testing Order
Wood, Richard (subst misuse off)

Community Service
Critchlow, Philip (mgr) (3)
Ramsbottom, Jim (snr cso)
Cooper, Nick (cso)
Ditzel, Nick (cso)
Ratcliffe, Dave (cso)
Spiller, Susan (cso)
McKiernan, Keith (p, cs supvr)
West, Nick (p, cs supvr)

Staff Devpt
Butcher, Maureen (staff devpt off)

Surrey Springboard Trust
Smith, Claire (snr devpt off)
Collins, Andy (p, devpt off)

5. Probation Centre
Swan House
Knowle Green **Staines**
Middlesex TW18 ~~1XR~~
Staines (01784) 459341
fax (01784) 449932

Assessment & Supervision
Turner-Samuels, Hilary (mgr)
Barrand, Joanne (case mgr)
Bowes, Kirsten (case mgr)
Matthews, Gerry (p, case mgr)
Davis, Mike (assessment off)
Greenhill, Margaret (assessment off)
Hardy, Peter (assessmt off)
Carson, Veronica (case mgmnt off)
Sandiford, Victoria (case mgmnt off)
Sharma, Monica (case mgmnt off)
Stanbridge, Freda (case mgmnt off)
Percy, Gayle (case co-ord)
Potts, Sarah (case co-ord)
Clarkson, Carol (assessmt sup off)
Mookherji, Hanna (p, assessmt sup off)
Fletcher, Tamsin (trainee)

Court & Customer Services
Jackson, Isobel (mgr)
Kay, Stuart (crt liaison off)
Smart, James (crt liaison)
Wilson, Lisa (crt liaison off)
Jennings, Jenny (crt co-ord)
Irving, Morine (customer services off)
Marshall, Anita (customer services off)
Matthews, Katy (admin)
Lake, Vivien (p, receptionist)

Programmes Team
Bishop, Carol (prog delivery off)
Sanders, Lee (prog delivery off)

Drug Treatment & Testing Order
Clark, Jane (subst misuse off)

Community Service (see office 4)

Staff Devpt
Tonks, Jill (p, staff devpt off)

Surrey Springboard Trust
Boyd, Sally (devpt off)
Powell, Christine (p, devpt off)

6. **The Crown Court**
Bedford Road, Guildford GU1 4ST
Guildford (01483) 568561
fax (01483) 306724

Lane, Brenda (mgr) (3)
Thomas, Rosalind (crt off)
Lane, Lynda (crt liaison off)
Brady, Christine (crt co-ord)

7. **Youth Offending Team (West)**
Churchill House
Mayford Green
Woking GU22 0PW
Woking (01483) 723922
fax (01483) 771786

Wells, Toby (cty mgr)
Hibbert, Geoff (mgr west)
Humphreys, John
Reid, Janice

8. **Youth Offending Team (East)**
Pippbrook House
Reigate Road
Dorking RH4 1SJ
Dorking (01306) 742273

fax (01306) 742452

Wells, Toby (cty mgr) (7)
Patchett, Mark (mgr east)
Pickles, Robert

9. **Surrey Springboard Trust**
Hamilton House, Bridge Street
Leatherhead KT22 9AD
Leatherhead (01372) 360370
fax (01372) 376520

Vacancyy (director)
Netley, Julia (pa to director)

10. **Surrey Care Trust**
1 Old Elstead Road
Milford GU8 5EE
phone & fax (01483) 426990

Calvert, Gerard (director)
Egerton, Katie (asst to director)
Thomas, Christopher (devpt mgr)

Surrey Resource Information Service
(01252) 622229
Reeder, Margaret (proj mgr)

Hostel

11. **St Catherine's Priory**
Ferry Lane, Portsmouth Road
Guildford GU2 5EB
Guildford (01483) 571635
fax (01483) 454130

Stacey, John (mgr)
Evenden, Ros (po deputy)
Gitens, Amelia (hostel off)
Kean, Johan (hostel off)
Saville, Jane (hostel off)
Sexton, Sean (hostel off)
Wainwright, Jo (hostel off)
Butcher, Jason (night supvr)
Gregory, Ian (night supvr)
Vacancy (p, finance & admin off)
Vacancy (p, secy)
McGuckian, Jennifer (p, dom supvr)

Institutions

12. H M Prison **Coldingley**
Shaftesbury Road
Bisley, Woking GU24 9EX
Brookwood (01483) 476721
fax (01483) 488586

Parole clerk ext 309
Special visits ext 253

Jones, Simon (th'care mgr) ext 358
French, Deborah (th'care off) ext 221
Newport, John (th'care off) ext 205
Perkins, Clare (th'care off)
Stoves, Bill (th'care off) ext 278
Yeoman, Kevin (th'care off) ext 205

13. H M Prison **Send**
Ripley Road, Send
nr. Woking GU23 7LH
Guildford (01483) 223048
fax (01483) 223173

Probn visits ext 301
Parole clerk ext 304
Discipline ext 308

Keitch, Val (th'care mgr) ext 300
Garrard, Roche (th'care off) ext 305
Page, Lesley (th'care off) ext 302
Vacancy (th'care off) ext 307

14. H M Prison **Downview**
Sutton Lane
Sutton, Surrey SM2 5PD
020-8770 7500
fax 020-87707673

Probn clerk ext 389
Discipline ext 299
Special visits ext 285

Ball, Liz (p, th'care mgr) ext 300
Ayers, Carol (th'care off) ext 388
Etienne, Eddie (th'care off) ext 358
Neubert, Catherine (p, th'care off) ext 257
Green, Clare (th'care off)
Ysart, Louise (p, th'care off)

15. H M Prison **High Down**
Sutton Lane
Sutton, Surrey SM2 5PJ
020-8643 0063
fax 020-8643 2035

Probn clerk ext 217
Custody office ext 462
Special visits ext 385

Bazlington, Pepi (th'care mgr) ext 491
Kenealy-Fox, Denise (resettlement mgr)
Carlile, Catherine (th'care off)
Eastham, Elizabeth (th'care off)
Jansen, Julie (th'care off)
Knight-Sinclair, Joanne (p, th'care off)
Skeens, Gordon (th'care off)
Tester, Roger (th'care off)
Vaughan-Phillips, LouiseTester, Roger (th'care off)
Ysart, Louise (p, th'care off)
Robinson, Brian (th'care co-ord)

Surrey Springboard
Moody, Karen (probn sup wrkr)
Perkins, Neil (probn sup wrkr
Sahi, Nuzzat (probn sup wrkr)

Petty Sessional Areas

2 North West Surrey
3 South West Surrey
4 South East Surrey
5 North and East Surrey

Crown Court

6 Guildford

Area Code 45

EAST SUSSEX PROBATION SERVICE from 1.4.01 amalgamating with West Sussex Probation Service

Offices

1. **Head Office**
6 Pavilion Parade
Brighton BN2 1RA
Brighton (01273) 669966
Direct dial (01273) 669+ext
fax (01273) 620581
e mail esps.hq@dial.pipex.co

Buller, Miss Penny S (cpo) ext 960
Clark, Brian E (acpo) ext 961
Haynes, Peter T (acpo) ext 962
Rogers, Peter M (acpo) ext 963
Godfrey, Jim (head of resources) ext 964
Lyon, Ms Alison (human resources & training mgr) ext 968
Saunders, Ms Chris (finance off) ext 972
Grover, Ms Sarah (finance off) ext 970
Boucher, Ms Yvonne (personnel off) ext 969
Ades, Ken (spo, info services mgr) ext 974

2. **Family Court Welfare Service**
from 1.4.01 part of Children & Family Court Advisory & Support Service
12 Old Steine
Brighton BN1 1EJ
Brighton (01273) 666960
Direct dial (01273) 666+ext
fax (01273) 672308

Mortimer, Bob E B (spo) ext 965
Bridger, Keith J (Hastings)
Brook, Paul ext 963
Donne, Toni (p) ext 968
Hamza, Mrs Patricia ext 962
Jacobs, Mrs Barbara M (p, Eastbourne)
Rhoades-Eggby, Mrs Gill (p) ext 967
Roberts, Ms Fiona J (p) ext 966
Robichon, Mrs Julia M ext 964

Public ProtectionTeam (Throughcare)

3a. **West**
11 Queen Square
Brighton BN1 3FD
Brighton (01273) 224200
Direct dial (01273) 224+ext
fax (01273) 747307

Jones, Mrs Judith O (spo) ext 204
Austin, Ms Tracy J (p) ext 212
Bauermeister, Ms Fiona M ext 209
Cooper, David ext 206
Kent, Paul ext 213
McCrae, Ms Jenny ext 205
Rogers, Leighe ext 207
Vass, Cliff ext 208
Hutchins, Kevin (p, pso, vict liaison off) ext 211

3b. **East**
32 Wellington Square
Hastings TN34 1PN
Hastings (01424) 448180
fax (01424) 440232

Richardson, Martin (spo) ext 181
Cox, Ms Sally E ext 182

35 Old Orchard Road
Eastbourne BN21 1DD
Eastbourne (01323) 746200
fax (01323) 640424

Crouch, Gordon ext 225
Freemand, Jon M ext 227
Warrick, Ms Judith ext 225

Community Supervision Team (West)

4. 9/10 Queen Square
Brighton BN1 3FD
Brighton (01273) 224200
Direct dial (01273) 224+ext
fax (01273) 747307

Smart, Nick (spo) ext 224
Brook, Mrs Jo (p) ext 228
Cook, Stephen ext 231
Davis, Ms Helen ext 234
Deards, Chris J (p) ext 218
Fish, Mrs Sylvia A (p) ext 233

Marsh, Ms Christine (p) ext 229
Miller, Mrs Carole I ext 226
Vacancy ext 232
Tye, Peter L ext 227
Earnshaw, Ms Claire (p, pso) ext 235
Pyper, Mrs Christina (pso) ext 225

Probation Programmes
Wade, Andy (p, spo) ext 216

5. William Street
Brighton BN2 2RG
Brighton (01273) 669500
Direct dial (01273) 669+ext
fax (01273) 620582

Court Team
Element, Ms Jane (p, spo) ext 501
Celano, Tony D ext 507
Donnelly, Sue ext 505
Fitzsimmons, Frank ext 510
Shaw, Chris ext 511
Stroud, Ms Jean ext 508
Wood, Mrs Joanie E ext 509
Nunn, Rachael (trainee) ext 506
Stephansen, Lisa (trainee) ext 506
Carr, Miss Catherine (pso) ext 502
Hamza, Kaz (p, pso) ext 503
Furlong, Ms Michaela (pso) ext 503
Vincent, Colin (pso, bail info) ext 512

6. **Crown Court**
The Law Courts, High Street
Lewes BN7 1YB
Lewes (01273) 487608
fax (01273) 487610

Cowley, Paul C (p, spo)
Evident, Gary J
Brett, Ms Daphne

7. The Court House
Friars Walk
Lewes BN7 2PG
Lewes (01273) 477117/486460
fax (01273) 483843

Cowley, Paul C (spo)
Browne, Ms Jane
Richards, Jonathan (p)
Smale, Ms Pat (p)
Wilsdon, Mrs Jo M
Hinks, Paula (pso)

Community Supervision Team (East)

8. The Law Courts
Bohemia Road
Hastings TN34 1EX
Hastings (01424) 458000
fax (01424) 420504

West, Ms Helen (spo)
Hill, Richard E
Moors, Matthew
Palmer, Chris E
Saunders, Andrea
Taylor, Malcolm
Thompson, Ms Clare M
Warner, Ms Johanna
Bridger, Keith (fcwo)
Wells, Mrs Anne (pso)
Tipper, Miss Tracy (pso)

9. 35 Old Orchard Road
Eastbourne BN21 1DD
Eastbourne (01323) 746200
fax (01323) 640424

Tomlinson, Mrs Mandy J (spo)
Barnes, Geoff (p)
Vacancy
Browning, Ms Nicola
Franks, David
Whitney, Ann
Jacobs, Mrs Barbara (p, fcwo)
Saunders, Rita (trainee)
Munro, Mrs Gillian F (pso)
Robinson, Charles (pso)

Community Service

10. 1 St Leonards Road
Eastbourne BN21 3UH
Eastbourne (01323) 749555
fax (01323) 738484

Rimmer, Paul (spo)
Ferguson, Derek J (unit mgr)
Toni, Paul V (cso)
Wright, Peter S (cso)
Wagstaff, Mrs Esther (admin) (p)

11. 45 Grand Parade
Brighton BN2 2QA
Brighton (01273) 669600
fax (01273) 675790

Youngs, Martyn (dm)
Cairns, Rob A (cso)
Downes, Richard (p, cso)
Moore, Nick (cso)
Westbrook, Paul (cso)
Reed, Chris (cso)

12. 32 Wellington Square
Hastings TN34 1PN
Hastings (01424) 448180
fax (01424) 440232

Harris, Mrs Pat (cso)
Price, Ms Julie (cso)
West, Colin W (cso)

13. **Community Service Workshop**
Unit 8, Bell Tower Industrial Estate
Arundel Road, Kemp Town
Brighton BN2 5RU
Brighton (01273) 696576
fax (01273) 600237

Timson, Bill G (cso)
Apthorpe, Colin A (csa)
Green, Shane (csa)

Hostel

14. **Bail Hostel**
162 Marine Parade
Brighton BN2 1EJ
Brighton (01273) 622300
fax (01273) 623486

Wade, Andy (spo mgr)
Goldhill, Ms Rachel A (po dep mgr)
McMinnies, Abi (asst warden)
Collins, Frank (asst warden)
Reid, Stephen (asst warden)
Wood, Ms Ruth (asst warden)
Bridges, Melanie (admin)

Institution

15. H M Prison, Brighton Road
Lewes BN7 1EA
Brighton (01273) 405100
Direct dial (01273) 40 + ext
prison fax (01273) 405101
probn fax (01273) 405237

Bishop, Ms Yvonne (spo, th'care mgr) ext 5287
Galpin, Phil C J ext 5261
Harbane, Ms Jean (p) ext 5249
Harcombe, Ms Samantha ext 5309
Montero, Ms Rosemary (p) ext 5249
Stevens, Tim ext 5249/5511
Munro, Ms Morag (pso) ext 5249

Petty Sessional Areas

4, 5 Brighton and Hove
7 Lewes and Crowborough
9 Eastbourne and Hailsham
8 Hastings and Rother

Crown Court

6 Lewes

Area Code 46

WEST SUSSEX PROBATION SERVICE from 1.4.01 amalgamating with East Sussex Probation Service

Offices

1. **Head Office**
61 North Street
Chichester PO19 1NB
Chichester (01243) 788299
fax (01243) 532076

Vagg, Mrs Kathy (cpo)
Smith, Adrian (acpo)
Wing, Arthur (acpo)
Pike, David (amalgamation proj mgr)
Seagrove, Martin (temp acpo, business services)
Harbroe-Bush, Mrs Chrissy (human resources mgr)
Beeby, Mrs Susan (p, h.r. off)
Porcas, Mrs Sarah (finance & admin)
Jolley, Roderick (pso, hdc co-ord)

2. 8 Market Avenue
Chichester PO19 1YF
Chichester (01243) 787651
fax (01243) 781151

Criminal Court Services
Bristow, Mrs Candida
Cole, Mrs Claire (p)
Fricker, Mrs Susan
Davies, Mrs Bridget (crt pso)
Mitchener, Mrs Gillian (p, crt pso)
Walsh, Ms Teresa (p, crt pso)

Case Management (Community Supvn)
Dawkins, Ms Heather
Moore, Mike
Padfield, Joseph

Chrystal, Ms Christine (admin off)

3. County Buildings, East Street
Littlehampton BN17 6AP
Littlehampton (01903) 713041
fax (01903) 723022

Criminal Court Services
Morrison, Mrs Jill
Grenier, Mrs Lesley (crt pso)

Case Management (Community Supvn)
Pointon, Mrs Mandy (spo)
Judge, Mrs Claire
Slatter, Mrs Katherine (trainee)
Parker, Ashley (trainee)

Turner, Mrs Claire (trainee)

Case Management (Resettlement)
Parker, Mike (p)
Rasmussen, Ms Siri
Reed, Paul
Townsend, Mrs Margaret (p)

Community Service
Littlehampton (01903) 721857
Barzdo, Ms Lara (cso)
Gear, Mrs Beverley (cso)

Buss, Mrs Catherine (admin off)

4. 4 Farncombe Road
Worthing BN11 2BE
Worthing (01903) 216321
fax (01903) 204287

Criminal Court Services
Berry, Mrs Amanda
Denison, Peter (p)
Whitehead, Mrs Alison (p)
Exton, Ms Jackie (p, pso)
Mustchin, Mrs Suzie (p, pso)

Case Management (Community Supvn)
Arscott, Ms Louise
Booth, Ms Sally (p)
Geall, Ms Julie
Hoskin, Mrs Ros
Priest, Mrs Kate
Rennison, Mrs Pauline (p)
Walker, Mrs Julie p, temp)
Walker, Mrs Sharon (p)
de Sancha, Mrs Rebecca (trainee)
Oldfield, Ms Rebecca (trainee)

Case Management (Resettlement)
Dixon, Ms Cath (p)
Morrissey, Michael
Newton, Mrs Christine

Groupwork & Addictions
Martin, Mrs Claire (spo)
Andrews, Ms Claire (subst misuse)
Gibson, John (subst misuse - options)
Ayliffe, Mrs Glenda
Dixon, Ms Cath (p)
Miles, Peter
Richards, David

Community Service & Community Re-integration
(01903) 201064
Jones, Allan (spo)
Philip, Mrs Cathy (accom off)
Bradley, Mrs Jan (cso)
Turner, MrsAndrea (cso)

Educn Training & Employment
Muir, Mrs Eve (co-ord)
le Cappelain, Mrs Linda (ptnrshp)
Wentworth, Ms Sally (p, ptnrshp)
le Fouili, Mrs Glenys (clerical)

O'Neill, Ms Karen (admin off)

5. Goffs Park House, Old Horsham Road
Crawley RH11 8PB
Crawley (01293) 525216
youth offending team 551717
fax (01293) 525215

Criminal Court Services
Fordham, Colin
Beck, Mrs Marianne (p)
Budden, Mrs Claire (p)
Derring, Ms Sue (p, temp)
Fagan, Mrs Janet (p)
Stewart, Neil (crt pso)

Case Management (Community Supvn)
Barber, Mrs Emma
Fairbrother, Mrs Margaret
McGarvey, Mrs Julia
Watson, Mrs Barbara (p, temp pso)
Arnold, Ms Sally (trainee)
Barraclough, Steve (trainee)
Kennard, Ms Emily (trainee)

Case Management (Resettlement)
(01293) 511376
Jones, Peter (spo)
Goodchild, Mrs Heather
Parker, Mike (p)
Pearce, Ms Corinne (p)
Wilson, Mrs Susan

Groupwork & Addictions
Dew, Stuart (substance misuse)
Thomas, Ms Patricia
Tierney, Mrs Joanna

Community Service & Community Re-integration
(01293) 614806
Frater, Mrs Bettine (cso)
Hobbs, Ms Olive (cso)
Jones, Mrs Carol (cso)

Educn Training & Employment
Maher, Mrs Anne (ptnrshp)
Tohill, Ms Tracey (ptnrshp)

Allen, Mrs Angela (admin off)

6. The Law Courts, Hurst Road
Horsham RH12 2DZ
Horsham (01403) 265445/6
cs tel (01293) 614806
fax (01403) 272903

Case Management (Community Supvn)
Rennison, Mrs Pauline (p)
Weir-Wilson, Ms Maggie

Criminal Court Services Team
Hull, Terence
Doyle, Mrs Francesca (temp, p, crt psa)

Family Court Welfare Team
Coote, Mike
Davies, Ms Mary (p)
Watson, Mrs Harvinder (p)

Fiddaman, Mrs Pat (admin off)

6a. **Haywards Heath Probation Room**
(01444) 416128
fax (01444) 416317

7. **Family Court Welfare Service**
from 1.4.01 part of Children & Family Court Advisory & Support Service
38 Southgate, Chichester PO19 1DP
Chichester (01243) 531764
fax (01243) 531767

Jolley, Mrs Ann (spo)
Dawson, John
McComiskey, Mrs Lynne (p)
Rushmere, Mrs Sarah
Rutt, Peter

8. **Substance Misuse Projects**

a. **Substance Misuse Project**
Crawley Hospital
West Green Drive
Crawley RH11 7DH
Crawley (01293) 600340

Dew, Stuart

b. **Options Project**
24 Grafton Road
Worthing BN11 4QP
Worthing (01903) 204539
fax (01903) 209416

Gibson, John

c. **The Summit**
22 Sudley Road
Bognor Regis PO21 1ER
Bognor Regis (01243) 869234
fax (01243) 824023

Vacancy

9. **Youth OffendingTeams**

a. County Buildings
East Street
Littlehampton BN17 6AP
(01903) 718739
fax (01903) 718740

Cordery, Miriam (spo)
Burden, Mark
Mann, Simon (p)

b. Goffs Park House
Old Horsham Road
Crawley RH11 8PB
(01293) 551717 (direct)
fax (01293) 552522

Clark, Ms Gillian
Powley, Ms Dean

Institution

10. H M Prison **Ford**
Arundel BN18 0BX
Littlehampton (01903) 717261
fax (01903) 726060
probn fax (01903) 731943

Hoskin, Geof(spo)
Chance, Martin
Dean, Ms Vivien
Mason, Mrs Janet
Nelmes, Geoff

Petty Sessional Areas

3 Arundel
2 Chichester & District
5 Crawley
6 Horsham & Mid Sussex
4 Steyning
4 Worthing

Crown Court

2 Chichester & District

Area Code 47

TEESSIDE PROBATION SERVICE

Out of hours emergency number
0850 772068

Offices

1. **Head Office**
Probation House
2 Longlands Road
Middlesbrough TS4 2JL
Middlesbrough (01642) 230533

fax (01642) 220083

Statham, Roger (cpo)
Hadfield, Peter (acpo, cs)
Lumley, Elaine (acpo, com supvn)
Morrison, Alistair (acpo, crts)
Saiger, Lucia (acpo, res)
Holdhusen, Barbara (aco-hr/secy to probn cttee)
Craig, Philip (finance mgr/treasurer)
Henry, Kevin (hr devpt mgr)
Bewley, Mary (er officer)
Coyle, Margaret (pa to cpo)

2. 160 Albert Road
Middlesbrough TS1 2PZ
Middlesbrough (01642) 247438
fax (01642) 244651

Criminal Courts Services
Bolton, Janet (spo)
Edwards, Juliet
Evans, John
Gill, Barbara (p)
Goldby, Eric
James, Lawrence
Johnson, Gill
Miles, Sara
Smith, Lynn
Smith, Peter
Townsend, Isobel
Warden, Simon
Michna, Jan (mdo diversion team)
Burden, Joan (psa)
Gorbutt, Jane (psa)
Grey, Stuart (psa)
Langford, Alison (psa)
Smithyman, Susan (psa)

Community Supervision Middlesbrough West
Whitfield, Joyce (spo)
Gray, Jane
Kitching, Caroline (p)
Shakespeare, Martyn
Taylor, David
Bell, Emma (offender supr)
Davies, Christine (offender supr)
Warrior, Joan (offender supr)
White, Barbara (offender supr)

Community Supervision Middlesbrough East
King, Peter (spo)
Bateman, Jan
Hall, Maureen
Whitehead, Tony
Holden Janet (offender supr)
Knight, Pamela (offender supr)
McMillan, Ellen (offender supr)
Wood, Andrea (offender supr)

2b. **Partnerships Unit**
1 Milbank Street
South Bank, Middlesbrough TS6 6DD
Middlesbrough (01642) 440046

Portues, Russell (ptnrshps mgr)
Whelan, Viki (dep ptnrshps mgr)
Croft, Sue (psa, volunteer co-ord)
Armstrong, Helen(ete devpt wrkr)
Peskin, Sona (ete devpt wrkr)
Williams, Linda (ete devpt wrkr)
Taylor, Sharon (new deal gateway off)
Watson, Richard (victim liaison off)
Pritchard, Nick (housing sup wrkr)
Wilson, Pat (housing sup wrkr)
Dewhirst, Wendy (tenancy/training sup wrkr)
Shaw, Jan (tenancy/training sup wrkr)

3. **Teesside Crown Court**
Russell Street
Middlesbrough TS1 2AE
Middlesbrough (01642) 250469
fax (01642) 230541

Sam-Drysdale, Sandra (spo)
Bailey, John
Bake, Andrew
Tomasetti, David
Smith, Joan (p, psa)

4. Mowlam House, 1 Oxford Street
South Bank
Middlesbrough TS6 9DF
Eston Grange (01642) 452346
fax (01642) 466021

Resettlement
Allan, Julie (spo)
Scott, Lizzie
Spillane, Margaret
Walker, Ashley
Flannagan, Kathleen (offender supr)
Hall, Annette (offender supr)
Menzies, Maria (offender supr)
Smith, Alison (offender supr)
Watkins, Mark (offender supr)
Wileman, Sarah (offender supr)

5. 8 Lindsay House, High Street
Stockton on Tees TS18 1SJ
Stockton (01642) 606111
fax (01642) 607764

Community Supervision
Hunneysett, Elaine (spo)

Kendall, Elizabeth (spo)
Abreu-Hernandez, Frieda
Hall, Pat
Millward, Gavin
Moody, Nicky
Bennett, Maree (offender supr)
Byrnes, Alison (offender supr)
Hewerdine, Lynne (offender supvr)
McAndrew, Kathryn (offender supr)
Nicolson, Kay (offender supvr)
Westbrook, Andrew (offender supr)
McShane, Julie (offender supr)

Resettlement Unit
Burnett, Peter (spo)
Hadfield, Daphne (spo)
Campion, Sue
Keay, Julie (offender supr)
Pawson, Julie (offender supr)

6. 38 Station Road
Redcar TS10 1AG
Redcar (01642) 480611
fax (01642) 489424

Community Supervision
Parker, Richard (spo)
Castleton, Lisa
Hazell, Robin
Whitehead, Philip
Devitt, Vicky (offender supr)
Fryett, Russell (offender supr)
Moore, Claire (offender supr)
Ramsay, Linda (offender supr)
Whitaker, Elaine (offender supr)

7. Avenue Road
Hartlepool TS24 8BL
Hartlepool (01429) 265101
fax (01429) 231854

Community Supervision
Jones, Trevor (spo)
Nicholson, David
Wilkinson, Julie
Wilkinson, Pauline
Armstrong, Ian (offender supr)
Cooke, Sally (offender supr)
Hill, Lesley (offender supr)
Smith, Valerie (offender supr)

Court Team
Roy, Rosana (spo)
Brennan, George
Bullen, Carolyn
Buckton, Geoffrey (psa)
Clarke, Caroline (psa)
Kinnersley, Jackie (psa)

Resettlement
Winn, Lesley
Davies, Peter (offender supr)
Lowes, Sarah (offender supr)

8. **Woodlands Probation Centre**
18 Woodlands Road
Middlesbrough TS1 3BE
Middlesbrough (01642) 225021
fax (01642) 252215

Robinson, Kevin (spo)
Beckett, Tina
Devon, Alan
Phillips, Joe
Moule, Kay (psa)
Gavaghan, Dave (psa)

9. **Community Service**
Milbank House
1 Millbank Street
South Bank
Middlesbrough TS6 6DD
Middlesbrough (01642) 515315/6
fax (01642) 290677

Thomas, Brian (operations mgr)
Smith, Paul (dep mgr)
Bell, Simon (cso)
Brunskill, Fred (cs task supvr)
Emmerson, Harry (cs task supvr)
Gilbey, Alan (cs task supvr)
Norrie, George (cs task supvr)
Patterson, Donald (cs task supvr)
Payne, Bob (cs task supvr)
Pearce, Peter (cs task supvr)
Simmonds, Tony (cs task supvr)
Smith, Debbie (cs task supvr)
Storr, Frank (cs task supvr)
Turnbull, Brian (cs task supvr)
Thomas, Jeffrey (cs task supvr)
Vaughan, Brian (cs task supvr)

10. **Family Court Welfare Service**
from 1.4.01 part of Children & Family Court Advisory & Support Service
2nd Floor, Prudential House
31/33 Albert Road
Middlesbrough TS1 1PE
Middlesbrough (01642) 251555
fax (01642) 211582

Cornwell, Stuart (spo)
Blatchford, Margaret
Connelly, Anne (p)
de Graff, Frances
Firth, Geoff
Platt, Marilyn
Robinson, Sue

Shiel, Jim
Town, Antonia

11. **Student Unit**
154 Borough Road
Middlesbrough TS1 2EP
(01642) 210717

Megan, Sarah (pract devpt assessor)
Brittain, Tracey (trainee)
Brown, John (trainee)
Parry, Kevin (trainee)
Whitelock, Donna (trainee)

DTTO Implementation Manager
West, Doug

Youth Offending Teams

12. **Middlesbrough YOT**
14 Farndale Road
Middlesbrough TS4 2PL
(01642) 501500
fax (01642) 501800

Mitchell, Sarah

13. **Stockton YOT**
52-54 Hartington Road
Stockton TS18 1HE
(01642) 393399
fax (01642) 393380

Whitehead, Sheila

Hostels

14. **Probation Hostel**
13 The Crescent
Linthorpe, Middlesbrough TS5 6SG
Middlesbrough (01642) 826606
fax (01642) 829782

Eves, Wendy (spo)
Gallant, Julie (dep warden)
Davis, Glen (referrals)
Pearson, Annette (snr rsw)
Brown, Dennis (snr rsw)
Faye, Jeremy (snr rsw)
Findlay, Pamela (rsw)
Knox, Alison (rsw)
Menzies, Russell (rsw)
Philips, Ian (rsw)
English, Stephen (rw wkends)
Foggin, Hilary (rw wkends)
Spence, Angie (finance bursar)

15. **Nelson House Probation Hostel**
1 Milbank Street
Southbank, Middlesbrough TS6 6DD
EstonGrange (01642) 456811
fax (01642) 468671

Goldstraw, Ted (spo)
Stratton, Terry (dep warden)
Peel, Debbie (snr rsw)
Beard, Phil (rsw)
Cairns, Jenny (rsw)
Gallagher, Elaine (rsw)
McGowan, Stuart (rsw)
Sowerby, Andrea (rsw)
Turver, Andrew (rsw)
Keighley-Smith, Lynn (rw weekends)
Atkinson, Ivy (rw weekends)

Institutions

16. H M Prison Kirklevington
Kirklevington Grange
Yarm TS15 9PA
Eaglescliffe (01642) 781391
fax (01642) 790530

Discipline ext 201
Special visits (via communications office) ext 230

Turvey, Neil (spo) ext 323
Ford, Dot ext 324

17. H M Prison **Holme House**
Holme House Road
Stockton on Tees TS18 2QU
Middlesbrough (01642) 673759
Probn Office ext 357
fax (01642) 674598
probn fax (01642) 670189

Waddington, Mike (spo) ext 215
all Probn Officers on ext 357
Davy, Virginia
Moppett, Sylvia
Nolan, Mike
Stoddart, Steve
Storey, Hugh
Toyne, Margaret
Davison, Andrea (psa)
Foster, Tracey (psa)
McSween, Katie (psa)
Sellars, Joanna (psa)

Petty Sessional Areas

7 Hartlepool
6 Langbaurgh
2-5 Teesside

Crown Court

3 Middlesbrough

Area Code 17

WARWICKSHIRE PROBATION SERVICE

Out of hours emergency contact point
Kenilworth Road Hostel (01926) 339331

Offices

1. **Head Office**
2 Swan Street
Warwick CV34 4BJ
Warwick (01926) 405800
Direct dial (01926) 405+ ext
fax (01926) 403183

Robson, Philip (cpo) ext 850
Fulbrook, Mrs Diana (acpo) ext 812
Lacey, Wes (acpo) ext 813
Insley, Anne-Marie (finance mgr) ext 841
Richards, John L (staff devpt off) ext 818
Robinson, Karen (external services) ext 817
Jewsbury, Tricia (hr mgr) ext 821
Parn, Barbara (effective pract mgr) ext 828
Vacancy (info manager) ext 808

Family Court Welfare Service
from 1.4.01 part of Children & Family Court Advisory & Support Service
Direct dial (01926) 405834
fax (01926) 405801

Turner, Mike (fcw mgr)
Procter, Suzanne
Wyburn-Powell, Ann

Crown Court Unit
fax (01926) 405801

Surtees, Carol
Chambers, Rosey
Lewis, Wendy

2. 1 Euston Square
Leamington Spa CV32 4NB
Leamington Spa (01926) 331860
fax (01926) 887808

Thompson, Chris (area probn mgr)
Chand, Sarah (snr practitioner)
Duncombe, Jo (snr practitioner)
Burns, Roy
Donnelly, Jim
Evans, Bev
Lawson, Neil
Macleod, Ros
Noon, Nina
Duffy, Peter (psa)
James, Rachael (psa)

Pearson, Ian (snr cso)
Baxter, Susan (cso)
O'Sullivan, William (cso)
Wallis, Steven (cso)

3. Grove Road
Stratford-upon-Avon CV37 6QR
Stratford (01789) 299520/267032
fax (01789) 298264

Frampton, Lesley (area probn mgr)
Gartner, Kate
Mannion, Danny
Stevens, Adrian
Caudell, Edna (sao)

4. The Courthouse, Newbold Road
Rugby CV21 2LH
Rugby (01788) 534900
fax (01788) 547576

McGovern, Donald (area probn mgr/prog mgr)
Chappell, Sharon (snr practitioner)
Windsor, Sybil (snr practitioner)
Cook, Val
Holden, Susan
Farthing, Mark
Lockington, James
Mohammed, Mike
Peaston, Jolie
Sheppard, Diana
McGeoghegan, James (psa)
Marsella, Linda (psa)
Standing, Catherine (psa)

5. 4th Floor Warwick House
Bondgate **Nuneaton** CV11 4DU
Nuneaton 024-7635 1234
fax (01926) 413098

Baxendale, Nadine (area probn mgr)
Measom, Jack (snr practitioner)
Aldridge, Andrea
Birchall, Daphne
Davies, Janice
Hallam, Claire
Haynes, Michele
McReynolds, Sylvia
Roberts, Kay
Mawby, Chris (psa, snr cso)
Fowler, Desmond (psa cso)
Plummer, Clive (psa, cso)
Machin, Gerald (psa emplt)
Adams, David (psa)
Duggan, Tara (psa)

6. 1 Market Street
Atherstone CV9 1ET

Atherstone (01827) 722950
fax (01827) 722970

Lee, Niki (snr practitioner)
Crunkhorn, Sue
James, Barbara
Kiggell, Jackie
Newell, Diane
van der Molen, Mrs Jenny
Bhogal, Jatinder (psa)
Willis, Heather (psa)
Lewis, Linda (sao)

Family Court Welfare Service
from 1.4.01 part of Children & Family Court Advisory & Support Service
Barratt, Gerry
Davies, Helen
Sullivan, Ralph

Warwickshire Youth Offending Team

7. 2 Swan Street
Warwick CV34 4BJ
Warwick (01926) 405842
fax (01926) 403183

Johnson, Diane (yot mgr)
Downing, Gail (pract devpt mgr)
Bonehill, Rob (yot practnr)
Fincham, Melvyn (yot practnr)
Weatherall, Brian (yot practnr)

Hostels

8. **33 Kenilworth Road**
Leamington Spa CV32 6JG
Leamington (01926) 339331
fax (01926) 312518

Johnson, Pat (area probn mgr)
Maitland-Hudson, John (po deputy)
Abbott, Paul (asst warden)
France, Monica (asst warden)
Furnival, Mrs Monika (asst warden)
Kettyle, Susan (asst warden)
Webb, Russell (asst warden)

9. **McIntyreHouse**
125 Edward Street
Nuneaton CV11 5RD
Nuneaton 024 7638 2889
fax 024 7635 3982

Wibberley, Steven (manager)
Ghaiwal, Kanwal (po deputy)
McGrath, Sean (asst warden)
Pickard, Mrs Rosanna (asst warden)
Power, Joy (asst warden)
Verajee, Nasser (asst warden)

Petty Sessions Areas

6 Atherstone & Coleshill
2 Mid Warwickshire
5 Nuneaton
4 Rugby
3 South Warwickshire

Crown Court

1 Warwick

Area Code 48

WEST MIDLANDS PROBATION SERVICE

Offices

1. **Head Office**
1 Victoria Square, Birmingham B1 1BD
0121-248 6666
fax 0121-248 6667

Thompsom, Hilary (cpo)
Marsh, Rick (dcpo)
Steer, Richard (secretary/solicitor)
Nelson, Andy (treasurer)
Hanley, Susan (acpo human resources/partnerships)
Cardin, Enid (equality of opportunities officer)
Newing, Susanna (hd of personnel)
Stafford, Elizabeth (research & info mgr)
Madders, Michael (computer services mgr)
Daly, William (facilities mgr)
Brannigan, Anne (spo inspections)
Habens, Ann (spo external resources)
Young, Keith (po, p.r.)

Dudley & Sandwell Districts

2. Laurel Lane
Halesowen B63 3DA
0121-550 1496
fax 0121-585 5539

Gill, Stephen (acpo)
Westwood, Christine (admin mgr)

Drug Treatment & Testing Order Implementation
Roche, Adrian

2a. **Dudley Youth Offending Team**
Brindley House
Hare Street, Dudley DY2 7DT
(01384) 813265
fax (01384) 813270

Sparkes, Peter
Gould, Ian

3. The Court House, The Inhedge
Dudley DY1 1RR
Dudley (01384) 455351
fax (01384) 235680

Dudley & Tipton Team
Nash, Tim W (spo)
Davies, Steve
Dhillon, Surrinder K
Hamilton, Carol
Higgit, Gary
Jordan, Hazel
Langstone, Diane
Welfoot, Annette
Williams, Morene
Young, David
Zihni, Jeremy
Delaney, Audrey (psa)
Jones, Chris (psa)
Spitari, Paula (psa)

4. 44 New Road
Stourbridge DY8 1PA
Stourbridge (01384) 440682
fax (01384) 441354

Stourbridge & Halesowen Team
Dunbar, Janet (spo)
Brecknell, Davina
Claridge, Mike
Hawley, Anne
Hotchkin, Barbara
Ingram, Sandra
Platt, Andy
Stearn, Stephen M
Taylor, Barbara
Vickers, June

5. 16 Church Square
Oldbury B69 4DX
0121-544 5599
fax 0121-552 9233

Smethwick & Oldbury Team
Norford, Herman (spo)
Burton, Carol
Charmling, Swaroop
Collins, Yvonne
Feesey, Emma
Holt, Paul
Kaye, Peter
Price, John
Woodvine Philippa
Westwood, Rita (psa)

6. 27 High Street
West Bromwich B70 8ND
0121-525 5225
fax 0121-525 2450

West Bromwich & Wednesbury Team
Stevenson, Jackie (spo)
Dubidat, Marion
Fowler, Louise
Glean, Janice
Littlehales, Sue
Mair, Patsy
Pickering, Elaine
Shirgill, Daljit
Smith, Paul
Wiliams, Matthew
Alexander, Marion (psa)
Meredith, Nina (psa)
Smith, Karen (psa)

7. **Mediation & Reparation Unit**
79 Birmingham Road
West Bromwich B70 6PX
0121-525 4659
fax 0121-525 4672

8. **Sandwell Youth Offending Team**
102 Ocker Hill Road
Tipton DY4 0UW
0121-502 0063
fax 0121-556 8122

Batchelor, Sharon
Pickering, Beverley

9. 67/8 Rolfe Street
Smethwick Warley B66 2AL
0121-565 4411
fax 0121-555 5717

Progress Centre
Watson, Janet (spo)
Blake, Sonia
Driscoll, Steve
Morgan, Paul (psa)
Riley, Paul (psa)

Drug Treatment & Testing Orders
Finucane, Gabe (spo)
Hoskin, Trevor (spo)

Coventry & Solihull District

10. 70 Little Park Street
Coventry CV1 2UR
Coventry 024-7663 0555
fax 024-7663 1531

Taylor, Richard (acpo)
Chapman, Janette (admin manager)

Courts & Reports Team
Hird, Maria (spo)
Belgrave, Hugh (cclo)
Hunter, Eileen (cclo)
Cosser, Mike
Herbert, Carole
Meir, Janice
O'Neil, Jim
Lee, Jennifer (psa)
McChleery, Cath (psa)

Throughcare Team
Burnham, Dolores (spo)
Clarke, Brian
Gamble, Alan
Georgiou, Jason
Hammond, Val
Maltam, Lesley
Palmer, Caroline
Savage, Carole
Tamlyn, Carole
Freemantle, Mel (psa)
Nembhardt, Osbourne (psa)

Coventry Field Team
Killeen, Chris (spo)
Almquist, Debbie
Brownbill, Jenny
Gheent, Harvi
Green, Bev
Mason, Stephanie
Nugent, Dennis
Purdy, Lynn
Robinson, Megan

Community Safety
Gravenor, Frank

Coventry Youth Offending Team
Coventry 024-7653 9031
fax 024-7653 9149
Badasha, Dalbir
Laidler, Karen
Robertson, Helen

11. The Old Post Office, Bosworth Drive
Chelmsley Wood
Birmingham B37 5EX
0121-770 9090
fax 0121- 779 6528

McNulty, Adrian (spo)
Wride, David (spo)
Ashley, Wendy
Buckley, Jane
Carpenter, David
Coldrick, Ralph
Darn, Stuart
Edwards, Cheryl-Ann
Gissey, Sharon A
Glennie, Karin
Kirby, Martha
Toor, Harinder
Young, Therese
Thorpe, Alan (psa)

12. **Solihull Youth Offending Team**
Craig Court
Chelmsley Wood
Birmingham B37 7TR
0121-788 4200
fax 0121-779 7974

McCauley, Chris

13. **Solihull Magistrates' Court**
Homer Road
Solihull B91 3RD
0121-711 7331
fax 0121-711 7050

McCarthy, Terry
Lambden, Anne (psa)

Walsall & Wolverhampton District

14. Union Street
Horseley Fields
Wolverhampton WV1 3JS
Wolverhampton (01902) 576000
fax (01902) 455180

Administration Unit
Sahota, Nav (acpo)
Williams, Jenny (admin manager)

Community Team
Vacancy (spo)
DFurbin, Ray
Hughes, Marilyn
Hunter, Colin
Johnson, Janet
Joslyn, Jean
Lever, Kate
Littleford, Frank
Martin, Val
Pahal, Rashpal
Saunders, Ivor
Steventon, Jason

Public Protection Team
Ashby, Ted (spo)
Brownsword, Andrew
Caudwell, Jim
Easthope, Norma
Osbourne, Annette
Stephens, William
Wallace, Clare
Whitehouse, Sally
Wilson, Jean

Progress Centre
Evans, John
Pearson, John
Dee, Jill (psa)
Matthews, Ann (psa)

Walsall & Wolverhampton Partnership
Thompson, Viv (spo)

Victim Offender/Community Safety Unit
Beckford, Audrey
West, Jackie (psa)

15. **Wolverhampton Magistrates' Court**
Law Courts, North Street
Wolverhampton WV1 1RA
Wolverhampton (01902) 711449
fax (01902) 426186

Whinya, Pascal (spo)
Martin, Val
White, George
Dyke, Marjorie (psa)
Jones, Pauline (psa)
Lockley, Sheila (psa)

16. **Wolverhampton Crown Court**
Pipers Row
Wolverhampton WV1 3LQ
Wolverhampton (01902) 481108/9
fax (01902) 713355

Whinya, Pascal (spo)
Bryan, Elaine
Gerrard, Joyce
Storer, Jim

17. **Wolverhampton Youth Offending Team**
c/o Social Services Dept
Beckminster House
Birches Barn Road
Wolverhampton WV3 7BJ
Wolverhampton (01902) 553722

Oliver, Sue (spo)
Patel, Shanta
Payne, Cecilia
Lay, Janet (psa)
Winstone, Diane (psa)

18. Walsall Probation Complex
Midland Road, **Walsall** WS1 3QE
Walsall (01922) 721341
fax (01922) 725616

Community Team
Reed, Lyn (spo)
Brown, Vassel
Coyle, John
Husted, Alan
McGovern, Kathy
Minto, Sharon
Mitchell, Carol
Morris, Sam
Vose, Janet
Walker, Steve

Public Protection Team
Driver, Matthew (spo)
Beckfoot, Audrey
Clark, Mandy
Greensill, Carol
Matile, Lesley
Morgan, Clarabell
Murdoch, Mike
Norton, Denise
Ormsby, Janet

Progress Centre
Sockett, John (spo)
Allison, Una
Rees, Paul
Robertson, Les
Bull, Martin (psa)
Darlow, Malcolm (psa)
Moore, Merna (psa)

Walsall/Aldridge Magistrates' Court Team
Whinya, Pascal (spo)
Elwell, Malcolm
Stapleton, Christopher
Ford, Lesley (psa)
Tonkinson, Sandra (psa)
Wood, Malcolm (psa)

19. **Youth Offending Team**
c/o Social Services Dept
104 Essington Road
New Invention
Willenhall WV12 5DT
Walsall (01922) 493006
fax (01922) 493035

Fletcher, Sandra
Fox, Valerie

Birmingham District

20. **Birmingham ACPO & Admin Unit**
18-28 Lower Essex Street
Birmingham B5 6SN
0121-248 6400
fax 0121-248 6450

Matthews, Judith (acpo, Birmingham South)
Vann, Barbara (admin mgr, B'ham South)
Skidmore, David (acpo, B'ham North)
Brown, Steve (admin mgr B'ham North)
Cave, Jane (spo, partnerships)

Birmingham South Division

21. 12 High Street
Saltley Birmingham B8 1JR
0121-248 6150
fax 0121-248 6151

Vacancy (spo)
Treacy, Laura (spo)
Abrams, Pat
Blackman, Gwyllym
Brydson, Davlin
Burt, Tanya
Cansfield, Karen
Hoo, Marcus
James, Donna
Jordan, Patricia
Kanda, Pushpa
Kaur, Pinda
Leach, Margaret
Mickle, Caron
Myers, Paul
Powell, Simon
Purewal, Manjinder
Silvera, Sharon
Smith, Keith
Vassallo, Carmela
Woods, Pat
Bansal, Amarjit (psa)
MacPherson, Stuart (psa)

22. Greencoat House
259 Stratford Road
Sparkbrook Birmingham B11 1QS
0121-248 5611
fax 0121-248 5613

Hill, Colin (spo)
Taylor, Owen (spo)
Altaf, Samina
Augustine, Ann Marie
Ayee, Jackie
Campbell, Joan
Davis, Gill
Dronfield, Julie
Kedge, Roland
McEvoy, Niall
Mardenborough, Milford
Minott, Marcia
Morris, Paulette
Prideaux, Katrina
Turnbull, Adam
Wigget, Spencer
Vernon, Maureen
Williamson, Zoe
Aziz, Zanfar (psa)
Braithwaite, Kevin (psa)
Makepeace, Pam (psa)

23. **Victoria Law Courts**
PO Box 4081
Corporation Street
Birmingham B4 6QU
0121-248 6080
fax 0121-248 6081

Magistrates' Court Team
Wall, Chris (spo)
Beckford, Christine
Dooley, Phil
Kyle, Suzanna
Tarry, Marion
Ware, Peter
Adam, Betty (psa)
Alexander, Sue (psa)
Brown, Shirley (psa)
Dore, Barbara (psa)
Nixon, Peter (psa)
Ram, Sodhi (psa)
Russon, Janet (psa)

24. **QE 11 Law Courts**
1 Newton Street
Birmingham B4 7NA
0121-248 0099
fax 0121-233 0980

Crown Court Team
Goss, Diana (spo)
Gittins, Jean
Miller, Dick
Thomas, Wyn F
Wilson, Mick

Peripatetic Team
Goss, Diana (spo)
Geddes, Louise
Harragan, Candy
Hodcroft, Felix
Queeley, Claudine

Youth Offending Service

25a. **Youth Offending Service (North)**
Pype Hayes Hall
Pype Haye Park
Birmingham B24 0HG
0121-303 8558
fax 0121-313 1737

Norman, Roger

25b. **Youth Offending Service (South)**
Halescroft Square
off Shenley Hill
Birmingham B31 1HD
0121-476 5111
fax 0121-411 2198

Delaney, Sara
Dyer, John

25c. **Youth Offending Service (East)**
15 Commons Lane
Washwood Heath
Birmingham B3 2US
0121-327 2727
fax 0121-327 3182

Kaur, Inderbir
Wood. Louise

25d. **Youth Offending Service (West)**
All Saints Street
Birmingham B18 7RJ
0121-554 6201
fax 0121-523 8231

Davies, Mike
Hazell, Liz

25e. **Youth Offending Service (Central)**
157-159 St Lukes Road
Deritend, Birmingham B5 4DA
0121-464 1570
fax 0121-464 1595

Pymm, Lesley (spo)
Nesbitt, Paula
Parchment, Lorna

25f. **Youth Offending Service (B'ham Youth Court)**
c/o 52 Newton Street
Birmingham B4 6NF
0121-233 3600
fax 0121-236 0828

Iacopucci, Jo
Read, Sarah
Whitehurst, John

26. 826 Bristol Road **Selly Oak**
Birmingham B29 6NA
0121-249 7900
fax 0121-249 7949

Community Supervision Team (inc licencees)
Power, Sue (spo)
Barzado, Veronica
Brown, Carolyn
Eason, Marie
Francis, Aaron
Garton, Kashmir
Houston, Sally
Peynado, Fenton
Philippides, Toni
Taylor, Wayne
Williams, Cathrine

Progress Group
Farrow, Kathryn (spo)
Whitehead, Christine (spo)
Flyn, Val
Kyne, Chris
Davis, Roy (psa)
Woolley, Malcolm (psa)

Pre Release Throughcare
Farrow, Kathryn (spo)
Whitehead, Christine (spo)
Drayton, Joseph
Lotay, Sarbjit
Martin, Bryan
Sewell, Jean

Birmingham North

27. United Friendly House
76 Walsall Road
Perry Barr Birmingham B42 1SF
0121-248 6680
fax 0121-248 6681

Matill, Miles (spo)
Bassi, Hardeep
Blakeman, Sarah
Cox, Sharon
Davidson, Floyd
Faulkner, Dione
Fellowes, Richard
Francis, Ireka
Jan, Araf
Jones, Roderick

Resource Centre Team
Bailey, Claudette (spo)
Hyman, Joy
Singh, Jaspal
Turner, Hilary
Bachra, Narinder (psa)

Chahal, Rajinder (psa)
Forde, Noel (psa)

28. Stuart Court, 73/75 Station Road
Erdington Birmingham B23 6UG
0121-248 5600
fax 0121-248 5605

Griffiths, Ray (spo)
Blood, Jean
Boulten, Peter
Campbell, Rosemarie
Gilbert, Sylvia
Golding, Sandra
Jones, Martin
Morris, David
Peterkin, Dawn
Thompson, Angela
Larman, Karon (psa)

29. **Homeless Offenders Resettlement Unit**
11-15 Lower Essex Street
Birmingham B5 6SN
0121-248 6460
fax 0121-248 6461

Geach, Mary
Keeley, Patrick
McGhee, Joan
McLeish, Gillian
Martin, Clive
Teale, Ian
Tyler, Annie
Watkins, Laurence

30. 326/328 Hamstead Road
Handsworth Birmingham B20 2RA
0121-248 6500
fax 0121-248 6501

Smith, Liz (spo)
Caesar, Yvette
Coad, Lorna
Edwards, Althea
Knowles, Ann
McLeish, Gillian
Manning, Paul
Marchant, Mel
Mullis, David
Walters, Beverley

31. 4 Albany Road
Harborne Birmingham B17 9JX
0121-248 6230
fax 0121-248 6231

Spearman, Jill (spo)
Chaudrhry, Geet
D'Ippolito, Angela
Edgar, Karen
Frati, Catherine
Hanley, Richard
Lindo, Elizabeth
Mendez-Brown, Gloria
Rees, David

County Victim Liaison Unit

32. 52 Newton Street
Birmingham B4 6NF
0121-248 6100
fax 0121-248 6101

Brown-Richards, Pat (spo)
Astley, Denise
Reynolds, Gill
Williams, Sarah
Yeap, Christine
Preedy, Karen (psa)

33. 70 Little Park Street
Coventry CV1 2UR
Coventry 024-7655 3268
fax 024-7663 1531

Tudor, Barbara (victim liaison devpt off)
Debrens, Marlene
Ferron, Lynn (psa)
Patton, Brian (psa)

34. Union Street
Horseley Fields
Wolverhampton WV1 3JS
Wolverhampton (01902) 576001
fax (01902) 455180

Connelly, Jane (based at 5)
Jacques, Jan
Lay, Janet (based at 28)
West Jacqui (psa)

Residential, Sex Offenders & Pre Trial Services Division

35. 11-15 Lower Essex Street
Birmingham B5 6SN
0121-248 2828
fax 0121-248 6490

Vacancy (acpo)
Morgan, Ms Chloris (admin manager)
Burdett, Sue (housing issues off)

36. **Sex Offenders Unit**
826 Bristol Road **Selly Oak**
Birmingham B29 6NA
0121-249 6730
fax 0121-249 6749

Middleton, David (spo)
Canicle, Jakki
Fincher, Jenny
Halawin, Kath
Holden, Peter
Leyland, Mary
Thomas, Jenny
Tregaskis, David

37. **Pre Trial Services Units**
52 Newton Street
Birmingham B4 6NF
0121-236 0636
fax 0121-212 0108

Short, Mike (spo)
Kelly, Tony
Bebbington, Christine (psa)
Chapasuka, Judith (psa)
Fitzsimmons, Elaine (psa)
Smith, Les (psa)

37a The Court House, The Inhedge
Dudley DY1 1RR
Dudley (01384) 458417
fax (01384) 455691

Jones, Brian
Bhatti, Shahida (psa)

37b Law Courts
Lombard Street West
West Bromwich B70 8ED
0121-525 5381
fax 0121-525 6751

Balu, Amarjit (psa)

37c. Warley Magistrates' Court
Court House, P O Box 5
Oldbury Ringway
Warley B69 4SN
0121-533 3448
fax 0121 544 2037

Barrett, Ann-Marie (psa)

37d. 70 Little Park Street
Coventry CV1 2UR
Coventry 024-7655 1446
fax 024-7655 3393

Hedderick, Beverlety (psa)

37e. 7 Herbert Road
Solihull B91 3QE
phone & fax 0121-711 3143

Fitzsimmons, Elaine (psa)

37f. The Law Courts
North Street **Wolverhampton**
Wolverhampton (01902) 426793
fax (01902) 772361

McGerty, Mike (psa)

37g. The Court House
Stafford Street **Walsall** WS2 8HA
Walsall (01922) 635418
fax (01922) 635422

Kendrick, Carol (psa)
Malone, Angela (psa)

37h. Sutton Magistrates' Court
The Court House, Lichfield Street
Sutton Coldfield B74 2NF
phone/fax 0121-355 8984

Boulton, Marilyn (psa)

Community Service, Combination Orders & Employment Division

38. 67/8 Rolfe Street
Smethwick B66 2AL
0121-565 4411
fax 0121-555 5717

Byford, Nigel (acpo)
Ainsbury, Robert (admin mgr)
Huckerby, Keith (health & safety off)

Community Service Unit
Brown, Barry (spo)
Latham, Ian
Mantle, Nick
Woodgates, Margaret
Garcha, Daive (cso)
Loft, Lesley (cso)
Mullett, Alan (cso)
Sinar, Keith (cso)

39. **Community Service Unit**
162 Halesowen Road
Netherton **Dudley** DY2 9TS
Dudley (01384) 456482
fax (01384) 457441

Brown, Barry (spo)
Fitzgerald, Kevin
Fullwood, Betty
Rawlings, Jim

Cookson, Geoff (cso)
Woolridge, John (cso)

40. **Community Service Unit**
Bishop Street, **Coventry** CV1 1HU
024-7625 8485
fax 024-7663 0183

Vacancy (spo)
Duke, Roger
Duffy, Kitty
Gold, Bill
O'Donoghue, Dee
Smith, Ian
Farmer, Terry (cso)
Killeen, Mick (cso)
Lee, Mark (cso)
McLaughlin, Eddie (cso)

41. **Community Service Unit**
The Old Post Office, Bosworth Drive
Chelmsley Wood
Birmingham B37 5EX
0121-770 9090
fax 0121- 779 6528

Vacancy (spo) (based at 40)
Allder, Marian
Al-Moghraby, Mazen (cso)
Jackson, Trevor (cso)

42. **Community Service Unit**
Minerva Wharf
Horseley Fields
Wolverhampton WV1 3LX
Wolverhampton (01902) 351518
fax (01902) 452496

Patel, Lalita (spo)
Dossett, Kath
Hargreaves, Richard
Jones, Barry
Pejatta, Jas
Stringer, Angela
Wilson, Kath
Cox, Ira (cso)
Hill, Geoff (cso)
Tomkys, Marlene (cso)
Wakely, Tony (cso)

43. **Community Service Unit**
Walsall Probation Complex
Midlands Road
Walsall WS1 3QE
(01922) 720661
fax (01922) 725616

Patel, Lalita (spo) (based at 42)
Ahmad, Pratima
Tracey, Danny
Tonkinson, Sandra (cso)
Walton, Martin (cso)
Watton, Ian (cso)
Wood, Malcolm (cso)

44. **Community Service Unit**
United Friendly House
76 Walsall Road
Perry Barr Birmingham B42 1SF
0121-248 6348
fax 0121-248 6341

Mitchell, Tessa (spo)
Clarkson, Ransford
Dickman, Sue
Rowley, Pat
Dainty, Glynn (cso)
Orbell, Bill (cso)
Worrall, Frank (cso)

44a. **Community Service Unit**
12 High Street
Saltley Birmingham B8 1JR
0121-248 6200
fax 0121-248 6151

Mitchell, Tessa (spo) (based at 44)
Heslop, Mike
Slater, Malcolm
Foster, Maria (cso)
Tulloch, Tony (cso)

45. **Community Service Unit**
Greencoat House
259 Stratford Road
Sparkbrook
Birmingham B11 1QS
0121-248 5620
fax 0121-248 5613

Briscoe, John (spo)
Alden, Andy
Ward, Marie
Ahmed, Shaheen (cso)
Gordon, Patrick (cso)
Reeves, Max (cso)

45a. **Community Service Unit**
826 Bristol Road
Selly Oak Birmingham B29 6NA
0121-248 6700
fax 0121-248 6681

Briscoe, John (spo) (based at 45)
Dee, John
Morton, Jon

Cox, John V (cso)
Hyatt, Basil (cso)
Storm, John (cso)

46. **Community Service Unit**
18-28 Lower Essex Street
Birmingham B5 6SN
0121-666 7301/7388
fax 0121-622 5493

Briscoe, John (spo) (based at 45)
Bishop, Sue (wkshp mgr)
Gee, Alan (wkshp mgr)

47. **Employment Training Unit**
1 Victoria Square
Birmingham B1 1BD
0121-248 6572
fax 0121-248 6667

Russell, Peter (spo)
Gardiner, Coral (mentoring devpt off)
Blow, Adrian (elo) (based at 14)
Braithwaite, Kevin (elo) (based at 22)
Gaughan, John (elo) (based at 11)
McCarthy, Sinead (elo) (based at 10)
Stevens, Christine (elo) (based at 18)
Sutton, Sandra (elo) (based at 9)

Human Resources & Partnership

48. **Training Centre**
826 Bristol Road
Selly Oak Birmingham B29 6NA
0121-249 6700
fax 0121-249 6729

Hanley, Mrs Susan (acpo) (1)
Armstrong, Kim (training admin)
Clare, Jan (spo lecturer)
Plunkett, John (nvq mgr)
Octigan, Mike (spo trainer)
Paris, Alison (spo, joint appt with Univ Birmingham)
Brown, Eve (training off)
Baker, Dorothy (course admin)
Kerslake, Mike (pract devpt assessor)
Aston, Jeff (pract devpt assessor) (9)
Ayriss, Debbie (pract devpt assessor) (10)
Ricketts, Louison (pract devpt assessor) (21)
Beattie, Kath (pract devpt assessor) (14)

Programmes Division

49. ACPO/Admin Unit
326/328 Hamstead Road
Handsworth Birmingham B20 2RA
0121-248 6540
fax 0121-248 6541

Green, Richard (acpo)
Allcott, Rosaleen (admin mgr)
Tennant, Mike (spo effective practice)

50. **Public Protection**
1 Printing House Street
Birmingham B4 6DE
0121-248 6314

Middleton, David (spo)

51. **Bishop Street Programme Unit**
Bishop Street
Coventry CV1 1HU
024-7655 5638
fax 024-7663 0183

Johnson, Eric (spo)
Appleton, Jane
Ford, David

52. **Bordesley Programme Unit**
1a Adderley Road South
Saltley, Birmingham B8 1AD
0121-772 3708
fax 0121-766 7657

Hughes, Phillip (spo)
Fergus, Michael
Hilyer, Rob
Brown, Lloyd (psa)
Jones, Thomas (psa)
Kelley, Stephen (psa)
Williams, Charles (psa)

53. **Lower Essex Street Programme Unit**
18/28 Lower Essex Street
Birmingham B5 6SN
0121-248 6400
fax 0121-248 6401

Grant, Cassell (spo)
Elphick, Bronwen
Hall, Kobina
Haining, Beth
Rogers, Marjorie
Thompson, Jacque
Byron-Scott, Sharlene (psa)
Campion, Sally (psa)
Kane, Pat (psa)
Rowley, Glenda (psa)

54. **Rolfe Street Programme Unit**
67/68 Rolfe Street
Smethwick B66 2AL
0121-565 4411
fax 0121-555 5717

Brown, Len (spo)

Ellis, Philip
Mills, Judith
Rhynie, Janet
Jobber, Howard (psa)
Richardson, Andy (psa)

55. **Sex Offender Unit**
826 Bristol Road
Selly Oak Birmingham B29 6NA
0121-248 6760
fax 0121-248 6761

Farmer, Mark (spo)
Canicle, Jakkie
Clarke, David
Fincher, Jenny
Halawin, Kathryn
Holden, Peter
Thomas, Jenny
Tregaskis, David
Vacancy

56. **Walsall Programme Unit**
Walsall Probation Complex
Midland Road **Walsall** WS1 3QE
Walsall (01922) 721341
fax (01922) 725616

Appleby, Neil (spo) (57)
Patterson, Christopher
Price, Meryl
Darlow, Malcolm (psa)
Garrett, Joan (psa)

57. **Wolverhampton Programme Unit**
Minerva Wharf
Horseley Fields
Wolverhampton WV1 3LX
Wolverhampton (01902) 351518
fax (01902) 452496

Appleby, Neil (spo) (56)
Altaf, Azhar
Neville, Chris
Richardson, Sue
Morris, Mike (psa)
Safi, June (psa)

Family Court Welfare Division
from 1.4.01 part of Children & Family Court Advisory & Support Service

58. **ACPO Unit**
Gough Street
Wolverhampton WV1 3LG
Wolverhampton (01902) 576076
fax (01902) 456473

Fenby, John (acpo)

59. 1 Printing House Street
Birmingham B4 6DE
0121-236 8931
fax 0121-233 2996 (admin)
fax 0121-233 9253 (teams)

Admin Unit
Cochrane, Helen (admin off)

Family Court Welfare Team
Brown, Tom (scwo)
Guymer, Andrew (scwo)
Allen, Brian
Beaulah, Rachel
Bromage, Jan
Chaplin, Mike
Cupper, Steve
Dauncey, Sara
Davis, Mike
Faulkner, Ben
Fisher, Jenny
Gayle, Veronica
Gospel, Jo
Hammerton, Tina
Hazell, Liz
Helliar, Liz
Jones, Carolyn
Mitchell, Carol
Myers, Erica
Peterkin, Dawn
Purfield-Clark, Ria
Rex, Jan
Robbie, Christine
Walton, Jenny

60. **Family Court Welfare Team**
109 Dixons Green
Dudley DY2 7DJ
Dudley (01384) 455123
fax (01384) 455130

Hickman, Grant (scwo)
Blake, Jim
Bourne, Elspeth
Fields, Ruth
Healey, Eric
Jolley, Mary
Noble, Barry
O'Sullivan, Eileen
Pearson, John

61. **Family Court Welfare Team**
Walsall Probation Complex
Midland Road **Walsall** WS1 3QE
Walsall (01922) 720665
fax (01922) 746421

Lisser, Mike (scwo)
Blake, Sonia

French, Ruth
Green, Doreen
Hazeley-Jones, Christopher
Ivett, Carol
West, Carol
Williams, Chris

62. **Family Court Welfare Team**
Gough Street
Wolverhampton WV1 3LG
Wolverhampton (01902) 576076
fax (01902) 453304

Nash, Sally (scwo)
McCann, Sean
McGregor, Jo
Rushton, Hilary
Stephens, Sally
Watson, Albert
White, Carmen

63. **Family Court Welfare Team**
28 Warwick Row
Coventry CV1 1EY
Coventry 024-7655 3601
fax 024-7655 3408

Kennedy, Avril (scwo)
Albutt, Phil
Allder, Marian
Heath, Wendy
McGrady, Linda

Hostels

64. **Central Bail Referral Scheme**
Sycamore Lodge Bail Hostel
Clay Lane, Langley
Oldbury B69 4TH
for male bail referrals only
0121-544 3404
fax 0121-544 3310

Thompson, Maria (referral officer)

65. **Bilston Probation & Bail Hostel**
23 Wellington Road
Bilston, Wolverhampton WV14 6AH
Wolverhampton (01902) 497688
fax (01902) 498150

Brown, Barry (spo mgr)
Benjamin, Audrey

66. **Carpenter House Probation & Bail Hostel**
33 Portland Road, Edgbaston
Birmingham B16 9HS
0121-454 0394
fax 0121-454 7379

Lomas, Simon (spo mgr)
Lawrence, Lynn (po deputy)

67. **Crowley House Probation & Bail Hostel** *(for women & children only)*
31 Weoley Park Road, Selly Oak
Birmingham B29 6QY
0121-472 7111
fax 0121-415 4072

Cox, Sue (spo mgr)
Price, Meryl (po deputy)

68. **Elliott House Probation & Bail Hostel**
(for mentally disordered offenders only)
96 Edgbaston Road, Moseley
Birmingham B12 9QA
0121-440 2657
fax 0121-446 6818

Baker, Jeff (spo mgr)
Boggis, Jan (po deputy)

69. **Welford House Bail Hostel**
31 Trinity Road, Aston
Birmingham B6 6AJ
0121-523 4401
fax 0121-515 1355

Branch, George (spo mgr)
Rhoden, Derek (po deputy)

70. **Stonnall Road Bail Hostel**
85 Stonnall Road
Aldridge, Walsall WS9 8JZ
Walsall (01922) 459574
fax (01922) 455373

Aziz, Naheed (spo mgr)
Gill, Andy (po deputy)

71. **Sycamore Lodge Bail Hostel**
Clay Lane, Langley
Oldbury B69 4TH
0121-552 9930
Brigue, Paveen (spo mgr)
Baker, Barbara (po deputy)

Institution

72. H M Prison, Winson Green Road
Birmingham B18 4AS
0121-554 3838
fax 0121-554 7990

Probn clerk ext 301
Discipline ext 308/309
Special visits ext 285

Sewell, Geoff (spo)
Bezant, Cyril
Coxall, Mary
McConville, Patrick
Simms, Arlene

73. H M Young Offender Institution & Remand Centre
Brinsford New Road
Featherstone
Wolverhampton WV10 7PY
Wolverhampton (01902) 791118
fax (01902) 790889

Sentence planning clerk ext 426
Discipline ext 308
Special visits (01902) 798227

Pymm, Lesley (spo) ext 300
Dudfield, Heather (drug wrkr) ext 305
Farrar, Maggie ext 302
John, Alan ext 301
Jordin, Heather ext 304
Robinson, Angela ext 305
Skellern, Miss Yvonne (psa visitors' centre) ext 331

Petty Sessional Areas

18 Aldrigde and Brownhills
23 Birmingham
10 Coventry
3 Dudley
13 Solihull
2, 4 Stourbridge and Halesowen
28 Sutton Coldfield
18 Walsall
5, 6 Oldbury, Warley & West Bromwich
15 Wolverhampton

Crown Courts

24 Birmingham
10 Coventry
16 Wolverhampton

Area Code 49

WILTSHIRE PROBATION SERVICE

Offices

1. **Head Office**
Rothermere, Bythesea Road
Trowbridge BA14 8JQ
Trowbridge (01225) 713666
Direct dial (01225) + number
fax (01225) 713995

Wheeler, Chris (cpo) 713650
Smith, Philip (aco) 713653
Fox, Paul (aco) 713654
Beech, Graham (aco) 713655
Elliott, Mrs Julie (personnel) 713656
Davis, Mrs Sue (finance) 713658
Hemming, Alan (spo training) 713663
Higgins, Barrie (spo i&d off) 713660
Cork, David (dtto proj mgr)

2. 2 Prospect Place
Trowbridge BA14 8QA
Trowbridge (01225) 763041
fax (01225) 775667

Franklin, Ms Veronica (p, spo)
Morgan, Ms Mary (p, spo)
McGowan, Joe
Minch, Ms Alison
Morris, Keith
Murray, Andrew
O'Pray, Andy
Wyatt, Ms Anne
Ziegart, Ms Jo
Amoroso, Richard (psa, gpwk)
Pleece, Ms Jacquie (psa)

Community Service Office
Trowbridge (01225) 753508
Baker, Derek (cso)
Jones, Ms Chris (cso)
Thornton, Mrs Teresa (cso)

3. 51-52 Parkfields
Chippenham SN15 1NX
Chippenham (01249) 656836
fax (01249) 445497

Ferguson, Peter (spo)
Chapman, Ms Kate
Gooden, Mrs Ellie
Phillips, Mrs Sheila
Powell, Alan
Gillam, Mrs Lynda (psa)
Love, Ms Sandi (p, psa)

Thornton, Mrs Maria (area admin off)

4. The Boulter Centre
Avon Approach **Salisbury** SP1 3SL
Salisbury (01722) 327716
fax (01722) 339557

Sheffield, Mrs Susan (spo)
Dillon, Mrs Monica
Merrick, Geoff
O'Shaughnessy, Ms Debbie (p)
Scott, Ms Penny
Silver, Ms Helen (p)

Taylor, Ms Ann (p)
Woodward, Mrs Sybil
Picton, Mrs Doreen (psa)

Community Service Office
Salisbury (01722) 320897
Ryan, Tony (cs mgr)
Blandford, Ms Beth (cso)

5. Mary Floyd House
15 Milton Road
Swindon SN1 5JE
Swindon (01793) 536612/486823
fax (01793) 541110

Crallan, Ms Katherine (spo)
Rubringer, Stuart (spo)
Denyer, Malcolm
Gray, Ms Jean
Green, Miss Helen
Hickey, Ms Elizabeth
Hoyland, Ms Edana
Ind, Ms Liz
King, Trevor (p)
Maull, Gerald
Phillips, Mrs Jan
Shipp, Derek
Torczuk, Raymond
Weedon, Tom
Baker, Miss Laura (psa)
Phipps, Mrs Sally (psa)
Watson, Miss Karen (psa)

Parker, Mrs Eileen (area admin off)

6. 1/2 Commercial Road
Swindon SN1 5NF
Swindon (01793) 525458/616687
fax (01793) 496468

Groupwork Team
Boocock, Steve (spo)
Baker, Ms Charlie
Henry, Mrs Marilyn (p, psa gpwk)
Webb, Peter (psa, gpwk)

Community Service Team
Swindon (01793) 534259/496622

Jackson, Terry (dep cs mgr)
Fegan, Ms Angela (cso)
Hurford, Richard (cso)
Smith, Miss Abigail (cso)

7. **Family Court Welfare Office**
from 1.4.01 part of Children & Family Court Advisory & Support Service
9 East Street
Swindon SN1 5BU
Swindon (01793) 612299
fax (01793) 613399

all family court welfare enquiries to this office

Angus, David (sfcwo)
Barlow, Ms Jay
Williams, Miss Sally (p)

7a. based at office 2
Trowbridge (01225) 774414
Franklin, Mrs Joy
Morland, Howard

7b. based at office 4
Salisbury (01722) 410357
Kennard, Mrs Judith
King-Li, Richard

8. **Youth Offending Teams**
The Limes, 21 Green Road
Upper Stratton, **Swindon** SN2 6JA
Swindon (01793) 823153
fax (017930) 820578

King, Peter (yjo, secondment)

8a. The Martins, 56a Spa Road
Melksham SN12 7NY
Melksham (01225) 793616
fax (01225) 793556

McClelland, Mike (p, yjo secondment)

8b. 1st Floor, Salisbury Activity Centre
Wilton Road
Salisbury SR2 7GX
Salisbury (01722) 341644
fax (01722) 341655

Silver, Ms Helen (yjo secondment)

Institution

9. H M Prison **Erlestoke**
Devizes SN10 5TU
Devizes (01380) 813475
fax (01380) 818663

Probn clerk/special visits ext 400
Discipline ext 309
Throughcare unit ext 392

Wilcox, Martin (spo) ext 393
Harrop, Jon ext 300
Gregory, Roy ext 396

Petty Sessional Areas

2 West Wiltshire
3 North Wiltshire
3, 4 Kennet,

4 Salisbury
5, 6 Swindon

Crown Courts

4 Salisbury
5 Swindon

Area Code 50

NORTH YORKSHIRE PROBATION SERVICE

Out of hours emergency contact point

York Bail Hostel (01904) 780358

Offices

1. **Head Office**
Thurstan House
6 Standard Way
Northallerton DL6 2XQ
Northallerton (01609) 778644
fax (01609) 778321

Brown, Roz (acting cpo)
Lester, Sally (acting acpo, field services) (2,3,4)
Murphy, Martin (acpo, county services) (6,7,8,9)
Roberts, Tim (aco, operational support & quality assurance)
Briggs, Val (pa to cpo/office manager)
Coates, Jackie (secy to acpos field and county services)
Richardson, Shirley (secy to aco, ism, pm)
Sutton, Gillian (p, head office secy)

Hart, Peter (partnerships mgr)
Richards, Mark (info services mgr)
Ives, Ros (p, communications mgr)
Marginson, Lynda (dtto project mgr)
Coulthard, Helen (finance off)
Hoskinson, Moira (p, info service asst)
Dickson, Karen (snr peronnel admin)
Lucas, Chris (accounts clerk)
Vacancy (p, clerk/wpo)

All family crt referrals to office 6

1a. 108 Lowther Street
York YO31 7WD
Direct Dial York (01904) 526+Ext
fax (01904) 526001

Ives, Ros (p, training mgr) ext 045
Gill, Jenny (p, secy to trg mgr) ext 045
Lomas, Neil (p, local co-ord) ext 045
Bosworth, Susan (p, secy to local co-ord) ext 045
Bourton, John (effective practice mgr) (5) ext 000
Oche-Winn, Ginny (info services asst) ext 057

2. 5/7 Haywra Crescent
Harrogate HG1 5BG
Harrogate (01423) 566764
fax (01423) 565790

Wardley, Sarah (spo) (2a, 2b)
Davies, Penny (practice developer)
Barker, Anne
Chapman, Helen
Edwards, Richard
Hopkinson, Hilary
Jones, Alan
Mackenzie, Sally (p)
Reid, Heather (p, dtto)
Vacancy (p)
Teasey, Marc (trainee)
Barley, Lesley (pso)
Bown, Jonet (p, pso)
Eastwood, Tony (pso)
Ingles, Gillian (office mgr)

Community Service
Harrogate (01423) 709008
covers offices 2, 2a, 2b
Kershaw, Neil (cso)
Terry, Peter (cso)

All fcw correspondence to office 6

2a. Essex Lodge, 16 South Parade
Northallerton DL7 8SG
Northallerton (01609) 772271
fax (01609) 772931

Adams, Jane (incl dtto)
Jones, Wilma
Wilkes, Sue
Bell, John (pso)

2b. The Court House
Bunkers Hill, **Skipton** BD23 1HU
Skipton (01756) 794797
fax (01756) 798614

Hunt, Rebecca
Kirk, Paul (incl dtto)
Thomas, Karen (trainee)
Jenkinson, Lynda (pso)

3. 12 Falsgrave Road
Scarborough YO12 5AT
Scarborough (01723) 366341
fax (01723) 501932

Stokell, Pauline (spo)
Whiteley, Nigel (practice developer)
Ansell, Gillian (incl dtto)
Burke, Alan
Cockerham, Janet
Davidson, Malcolm
Holmes, Geoff (pda + dtto)
Hutchinson, Ian
Vacancy
Pennick, Don
Radley, Amanda
Weatherstone, Paul
Winter, Patrick (p)
Wray, Lesley
Campion, Linda (trainee)
Judd, Marcus (trainee)
Lowde, Sean (trainee)
Bowman, Rachel (p, pso)
Harper, Mal (pso)
Littlewood, David (pso)
Moseley, Susan (p, pso)
Walker, Dave (pso)
Broadbent, David (cso)
Parkin, Karl (cso)
Race, Liz (p, cso)

Lukehurst, Beryl (office mgr)

4. 108 Lowther Street
York YO31 7WD
York (01904) 526000
fax (01904) 526001

Knowles, Liz (spo) (4a, 4b)
Clarke, Richard (practice developer)
Chatters, Sandra (p)
Clapton, Danny
Cooper, Kath (p)
Dawson, David
Griffiths, Gina (dtto)
Hamilton, Elaine (p)
Hughes, Heather (incl dtto)
Littler, Jon
Pavlovic, Michael
Ripley, Ann-Marie
Wilkes, Paddy (pda)
Williams, Anthony
Wright, David
Crossland, Angela (trainee)
Dixon, Joanne (trainee)
Gough, Lesley (p, pso)
Hamling, Tracey (pso)
Langford, Lyn (p, pso)
McKnight, Marilyn (pso)
Moss, Andrew (pso)
Daley, Michelle (cso)
Paterson, John (cso)

Cartwright, Sandra (office mgr)

4a. **York Crown Court**
The Castle, York YO1 9WZ
York (01904) 651021
fax (01904) 652397

Lockley, Simon (cclo)

4b. Union Lane
Selby YO8 4AU
Selby (01757) 707241
fax (01757) 213911

Bean, Elizabeth
Chapman-Gibbs, Petra
Sharples, Henry
Wace, Carol A (p, pso)
Marchant, A R (cso)

Youth Offending Teams

5. **North Yorkshire Youth Offending Team**
Jesmond House, 31/33 Victoria Avenue
Harrogate HG1 5QE
Harrogate (01423) 522880
fax (01423) 522949

Louise Johnson (co-ordinator)
Mark Hughes (p)

5a. **North Yorkshire Youth Offending Team**
Third Floor, Pavilion House
Pavilion Square
Scarborough YO11 2JN
Scarborough (01723) 341367
fax (01723) 361368

Calam, Toni

5b. **York Youth Offending Team**
Mill House, North Street
York YO1 6JD
York (01904) 554565
fax (01904) 554566

Walker, Iain

Family Court Welfare Service
from 1.4.01 part of Children & Family Court Advisory & Support Service

6. 37 Fishergate
York YO10 4AP
York (01904) 641448
fax (01904) 651032

Mozley, Harold (sfcwo) (6a, 6b)
Hill, Helen (p, fcwo)
Scatcherd, Paul (fcwo)
Holt, Richard (fcwo)

6a. *all fcw correspondence to office 6*
1 Westbourne Grove
Scarborough YO11 2DJ
Scarborough (01723) 341083
fax (01723) 341084

Laing, Fiona (fcwo)
Woof, Martin (fcwo)

6b. *all fcw correspondence to office 6*
5/7 Haywra Crescent
Harrogate HG1 5BG
Harrogate (01423) 566764
fax (01423) 565790

Barrows, Christine (p, fcwo)
Kirman, Mark (fcwo)
Wheeler, Barbara (p, fcwo)

Hostel

7. **York Bail Hostel**
Southview, 18 Boroughbridge Road
York YO26 5RU
York (01904) 780358
fax (01904) 780475

Lomas, Neil (spo mgr)
Martin, Jonathan (po dep)
Gledhill, Lisa (hostel wkr)
Legge, Roger (hostel wkr)
Morley, June (hostel wkr)
Vacancy (hostel wkr)

Institutions

8. HM YOI and Remand Centre
East Road, **Northallerton** DL6 1NW
Northallerton (01609) 780078
fax (01609)779664

Probn dept ext 325/290
fax (01609) 760376
Discipline ext 308
Centre Mgmt Unit ext 234/301
Special visits ext 284

Corney, Beverley (spo) ext 372
Gibson, Mark
Vacancy
McBurney, Don (pso)
Minchin, Alison (pso)
Vacancy (pso)

9. HM Prison **Askham Grange**
Askham Richard
York YO23 3PT
York (01904) 704236
fax (01904) 702931
Probn fax (01904) 702865

Watkins, Elaine (spo)
Burns, Frances
Vacancy (p)
Westwood, Marie (pso)
Gough, Lesley (p, pso)

Petty Sessional Areas

2 Claro
4 Easingwold
2a Northallerton
2a Richmond
2 Ripon Liberty
3 Ryedale
3 Scarborough
4b Selby
3 Staincliffe
3 Whitby Strand
4 York

Crown Court

4a York

Area Code 51

SOUTH YORKSHIRE PROBATION SERVICE

Central bail referral no:
0114-278 0075 *fax 0114-278 8520*

Out of hours emergency contact point

Norfolk Park Hostel

0114-275 3054

Offices

1. **Head Office**
11a Arundel Gate
Sheffield S1 2PQ
0114-276 6911
fax 0114-275 2868 & 0114-276 1967

Hicks, John (cpo)
Harker, Heather (dcpo)
Fox, Julian (secretary to the committee)
Kerslake, Brian (treasurer)
Brown, Mrs Rosemary (co personnel)
Vacancy (pr & info off)
Menary, Ian (info tech mgr)
Paul, Ram (partnership unit mgr)

2. 3 West Bar
Sheffield S3 8PJ
0114-272 6477
fax 0114-278 1892

Proctor, Philip (dco)
Daly, Ms Lesley (spo, yot)

Community Supervision
Holmes, Ruth M (spo)
Smith, Ms Jacky (spo)
Came, Mrs Suzanne (p)
Clarke, Dean
Colleyshaw, Ms Julie (p)
Gasper, John
Guiney, Sam
Jackson, Mel
Jones, Ms Paula
Keeton, Ms Jane
Montgomery, Mrs Avril
Murray, Ms Liz
Rejaie, Kaveh
Robson, Mrs Sheila
Scott, Miss Samantha (p)
Shann, Ms Christine
Stocks, Mrs Christine (p)
Turner, Mrs Pat
Williams, Mrs Barbara
Brewitt, Ms Helen (psa)
Davies, Ms Jackie (psa)
Herron, Mrs Janine (psa)
Horbury, John (psa)
Samuels, Milton (psa)

Resettlement Team
Mitchell, Ms Kate (spo)
Broadhead, Julian
Clarke, John
Kerr, Ms Laura
Manifold, Garry
Mylotte, Martin
Parkin, Ms Maxine
Smith, Andrew
Welch, Simon
Wight, Roy
Appleton, Ms Val (psa)
Hawksworth, Mrs Margaret (psa)
Munoz, Ricardo (psa)

Court Team
Adey, Peter (spo)
Bufton, Ms Sally (p)
Cruikshank, Tim
Everitt, Ms Marie (p)
Gupta, Ms Sheila
Hermiston, Paul
Lecutier, Miss Louise (p)
Myers, Andrew
Taylor, Nick
Antcliffe, Ms Cynthia (psa)
Chambers, Mrs Tracy (psa)
Edmunds, Miss Katy (psa)
Everett, Mrs Sue (psa)
Freeman-Keel, Mrs Pam (psa)
Morgan, Mrs Ann (psa) (js)
St Pierre, Mrs Sarah (psa)

2a. **Crown Court**
50 West Bar
Sheffield

all post to office 2

0114-270 1060
fax 0114-275 9816

Bunting, Mrs Kathy (psa)
Gill, Mrs Linda (psa)
Seaman, Mrs Susan (psa)

2b. **Family Court Welfare Service**
from 1.4.01 part of Children & Family Court Advisory & Support Service
3 Dragoon Court
Hillsborough Barracks
Penistone Road, Sheffield S6 2GZ
0114-231 6119
fax 0114-231 6120

Gamble, Andrew (spo dcwo)
Baxter, Alan
Hastings, Gordon
Kemp, Mrs Lynn (p)
Mercer, Tony (p)
Overton, Paul
Strong, Ms Shelagh (p)
Swift, Mike
Young, Clive

3. 8 Eastern Avenue
Sheffield S2 2FY
0114-241 6097
fax 0114-239 4675

Carney, Mike
Bostock, Graham (psa)

4. 7 St Peter's Close
Sheffield S1 2EJ
0114-228 8555
fax 0114-228 8500

Youth Offending Team
Daley, Ms Lesley (spo) (based at 2)
Cotterell, Robert
Glover, Mrs Lynda
Stephens, Ms June
Galton, Mrs Jill (psa)

5. 269 Pitsmoor Road
Sheffield S3 9AS
0114-272 5058

fax 0114-275 4997

Community Service
Wright, Ms Sheila (spo)
Gregory, Mrs Sharon
Jones, Brian
Shorthouse, Richard
Foster, Mark (gpwk co-ord)
Eggenton, Mrs C (cso)
Eyre, L (cso)
MacDonald, Mrs Gwen (cso)
Mosley, Mrs Jenny (cso)
Slack, P J (cso)
Cambell, Neil (csa)
Grubb, David (csa)
Layhe, Ms M (p, csa)
Matthewman, G (p, csa)
Large, Harry (csa)
White, R (csa)
Spowage, Mrs Judith (psa) (js)
Walton, Mrs Christine (psa) (js)

6. **Practice Development Unit**
365 Southey Green Road
Sheffield S5 7QE
0114-231 0754
fax 0114-285 5063

Grapes, Tony (dco)
Holdsworth, Adrian (spo)
Kerr, Ms Janet (p, spo)
Scott, Ms Shelley (p, spo)
Watson, Charlie (p, spo)
Brown, Ms Janice
Hermiston, Mrs Sue

7. Court House
Churchfields **Barnsley** S70 2HW
Barnsley (01226) 243331
fax (01226) 294908
dco fax (01226) 295080

Fox, Julie (dco)
Barker, Mrs Penny (spo)
Allsopp, Ms Sarah (p)
Birkbeck, John
Byerley, Ann
Carlson, Tony
Coghlan-Whyms, Mrs Mary
Curry, John
England, Mrs Sara (p)
Jackson, Phil
Wakefield, Ms Judy
Whitehead, Antony
Knowles, Miss Alexandra (psa)
McDermid, Charlie (psa)
Wright, Mrs Lynne (psa)

8. 6 Victoria Road
Barnsley S70 2BB
Barnsley (01226) 283411
fax (01226) 287441

Forbes, Ms Paulette (spo)
Buckle, Ms Pam (spo)
Barnett, Stephen
Birkbeck, Mrs Barbara
Gregory, Marilyn
Holdsworth, Ms Suzanne
Horridge, Peter
Lavin, Ms Jane
Marsh, Martin
Morris, Ray
Otter, Roy
Quarmby, Ms Linda
Wells, Ms Emma
Edwards, Barbara (psa)
Goodale, Graham (psa)
Gore, Tom (psa)
Hewison, Miss Anna (psa, dtto)
Smith, Ms Cherrylene (psa)
Padgett, Rosemary (psa)
Richardson, Neil (psa)

McNerney, Phil (spo)
Avison, Ms Jackie
Cobley, Peter (gpwk co-ord)
Ellis, Rhys
Ibbotson, Bryan
MacBeth, Ian
Niven, Chris
Pratley, Ms Mary (p)
McDonnell, Ms Colleen (cso)
Steele, Mrs Betty (cso)
Evans, Tony (csa)
Hellewell, Mick (csa)
Morrisroe, Simon (csa)

8a. **Youth Offending Team**
Phase 1/2, County Way
Barnsley S70 2DT
(01226) 774986
fax (01226) 774968

Lavelle, Linda (p)
Meleady, Rosemary
Slimon, Dave

9. The Law Courts
College Road
Doncaster DN1 3HU
Doncaster (01302) 366585
fax (01302) 320853

Court Team
Jones, Graham (spo)
Base, Miss Mandy

Foster, Alan
Mountain, Roger
Thomas, Mrs Pat (psa)
Tottie, John (psa)
Vause, Mrs Pat (psa)
Winstanley, Jacqueline (psa)

10. **Community Service Office**
Yarborough Terrace
Bentley, Doncaster DN5 9TH
Doncaster (01302) 787758
fax (01302) 390865

Coddington, Paul (spo)
McKenzie, Phil (gpwk co-ord)
Barends, David (cso)
Connolly, Jim (cso)
Crookes, Mrs Win (cso)
Doyle, Mrs Brenda (cso)
Murdoch, Scott (cso)
Aimson, John (csa)
Dunnington, Mrs Barbara (p, csa)
Heath, Bob (csa)

11. **Family Court Welfare Unit**
from 1.4.01 part of Children & Family Court Advisory & Support Service
25 South Parade
Doncaster DN1 2EA
Doncaster (01302) 327202
fax (01302) 349641

Brooks, Dave (spo)
Angel, Stan
Arshad-Davenport, Ms Mussaret
Beard, Mrs Claire (p)
Dalrymple, Ms Juliet (p)
Gill, Muriel
Haggart, Mrs Moira (p)
Mosley, Stuart
Sibanda, Mrs Sakhile

12. Bennetthorpe, 34 Bennetthorpe
Doncaster DN2 6AD
Doncaster (01302) 730099
general fax (01302) 730220
dco/dsu fax (01302) 730720

Lloyd, Mrs Pat (dco)

Resettlement Team
Leigh, Mrs Julie (spo)
Fenelon, Mrs Pat
Peat, Mrs Sarah
Sagar-Francis, Ms Maureen
Toole, Mrs Alison
Vernon, Glyn
Vizer, David
Hill, Mrs Jayne (psa)
Thomas, Mrs Janice (psa)

Community Sentences
Jones, Graham (spo)
Dickinson, Mrs Kathryn (spo)
Beckford-Peart, Mrs Marjorie
Cameron, Mrs Roseanne
Crawford, Mrs Angela
Dallas, William
Eyre, Peter
Harrison, Mrs Janet
Kendell, Ms Pauline
Price, Ms Sharon
Reeves, Ms Sheila
Stoddart, Ms Barbara (p)
Wheeler, Mark
Windith, Mrs Adele
Brook, Mrs Ann (psa)
David, Sharon (psa, dtto)
Johnson, Mrs Imelda (psa accom)
McMaster, Mrs Val (p, psa)
Sammut, Miss Melanie (psa)
Talbot, Miss Jackie (psa)
White, Graham (psa)

13. **Doncaster Drug Team**
The Garage, 37 Thorne Road
Doncaster DN1 2EZ
Doncaster (01302) 730956
fax (01302) 361453

Broadbent, Tony
Evans, Ms Nicky (p)

13a. **Thorne Reporting Office**
Middlebrook Lane
Thorne DN8 5DR
(01405) 812738

13b. **Youth Offending Team**
Rosemead Centre, May Road
Balby Doncaster DN4 9AE
(01302) 736100
fax (01302) 736103

Moss, Miss Samantha
Cocker, Glynn (psa)

14. Orsborn House, 1/2 Highfields
Doncaster Road **Rotherham** S65 1EA
Rotherham (01709) 364774
fax (01709) 829172

Whitehead, Mrs Gini (divnl mgr)
Olivant, Mrs Wendy (victim offender off)
Joseph, Ms Glenda

Family Court Welfare Service
from 1.4.01 part of Children & Family Court Advisory & Support Service
Brooks, Dave (spo)
Gooch, Ms Janet (p, spo)
Benavithis, Ms Pat
Clossick, Mrs Margaret (p)
Dyson, Ms Margaret
Rawlinson, Alan
Todd, Mrs Isobel

15. 12 Main Street
Rotherham S60 1AJ
Rotherham (01709) 376761
fax (01709) 838715

Dyson, Mike (spo)
Johnson, Mrs Jennifer (spo)
Turvey, Ms Maryke (spo)
Brennan, Ms Lenday
Burgess, Ms Liz
Clark, Ms Francesca
Crookes, Fraser
Cureton-Fletcher, Andrew
Daglish, Mrs Linda
Deen, Ms Shaheen
Ford, Ms Liz (p)
Gregory, Ian
James, Mrs Lesley (p)
Johnson, David
Johnson, Mrs Sue
Kennedy, Mrs Louise (p)
Lee, Malcolm
Lubienski, Ms May (p)
Kime, Mrs Sheena
Porter, Ms Jennifer
Pullan, Stuart
Robinson, Ms Pat
Saville, Ms Jane (p)
Taylor, Ms Jill
Fogg, Ms Isobel (psa)
Hayes, Mrs Kay (psa)
Houghton, Mrs Michelle (psa)
Lester, Kevan (psa)
McLaren, Miss Lorraine (psa)
Patterson, Mrs Clare (psa)
Rimmer, Mrs Julia (psa)
Turner, Mrs Sheila (psa)
Ward, Miss Donna (psa)
Whyke, Larry (psa)
Yeardley, Mrs Gloria (psa)

Group Programmes Unit
postal address 12 Main Street
visitor's entrance at Westgate Chambers
Westgate, Rotherham
Rotherham (01709) 376806
fax (01709) 821904

Woodgate, Stephen (spo)
Anderson, Mrs Pam
Cosgrove, Mrs Caroline
Doherty, Anthony
Edge, Philip
McCaughey, Ms Chris
Sinclair, Andrew
Tully, Ms Marianne
Walton, Frank
Keyworth, Tony (psa)
Laver, Brian (psa)
Wade, Phil (psa)
Wales, Steve (psa)
Claxton, Mrs Jenny (admin off)
Wragg, Mrs Karen (secy)

16. **Community Service Office**
Masborough Street
Rotherham S60 1HW
Rotherham (01709) 564424
fax (01709) 550952

Nothhelfer-Batten, Ms Sibylle (spo)
Fletcher, Mrs Janet (gpwk co-ord)
Hodgkinson, Michael (cso)
Houghton, David (cso)
Langer, Ms Stella (cso)
Kelly, Tom (csa)
Rhodes, Stephen (csa)
Woodthorpe, Derek (csa)

16a. **Youth Offending Team**
4/6 Moogate Road
Rotherham S60 2EN
(01709) 516999
fax (01709) 836584

Charnley, Ms Anne
Glentworth, John
Henry, Mrs Christina (psa)

Hostels

Central bail referral number
phone 0114-278 0075
fax 0114-278 8520

Taylor, Mrs Stephanie (central referrals off)

17. **Hostel Administrative Support**
at office 19
Rotherham (01709) 361001
fax (01709) 835496

Fox, Ms Julie (dco) (based at office 7)

18. **Norfolk Park Hostel**
100-108 Norfolk Park Road
Sheffield S2 2RU
0114-272 1950
fax 0114-275 3054

Swinden, David (spo)
Edwards, Ms Angela (hostel dep)
Ward, Mick (bursar)
Fox, Mrs Faye (hostel wkr)
Halpin, Mrs Sheron (hostel wkr)
Worthy, Mrs Linda (hostel wkr)

19. **Rookwood Hostel**
Doncaster Road
Rotherham S65 1NN
Rotherham (01709) 361001
fax (01709) 835496

Matthews, Paul (spo)
Platt, Ms Gillian (hostel dep)
Bargh, Alan (bursar)
Bennett, Delroy (hostel wkr)
King, Brian (hostel wkr)
Page, Robert (hostel wkr)
Abbott, Penny (snr admin off)

20. **Town Moor Bail Hostel**
38/40 Christchurch Road
Doncaster DN1 2QL
Doncaster (01302) 739127
fax (01302) 761920

Hannant, Jan (spo)
Nowell, Pete (hostel dep)
Bannister, Graham (bursar)
Berry, Tracy (hostel wkr)
Faulkener, Brian (hostel wkr)
Machin, Mrs Pam (hostel wkr)
Revill, Debbie (hostel wkr)

Institutions

21. H M Prison & YOI **Doncaster**
Marsh Gate, Doncaster DN5 8UX
Doncaster (01302) 760870
Discipline (edr enquiries) ext 308
Discipline (discharge) ext 265
Anti bullying co-ord ext 406
Special visits (01302) 342413
fax (01302) 760851

Probn direct dial (01302) 763+ext
Probn clerk ext 203
Houseblock 1 probn ext 289
Houseblock 2 probn ext 290
Houseblock 3 probn ext 291
Bail info ext 293
Bail info *fax (01302) 368034*

Woffenden, Ms Sally (spo) ext 288
Gayle, Miss Hyacinth
Gordon, Colin
Harley, Bryan
Petersen, Ms Lynn
Phipps, Ms Serena (p, psa)

22. H M Prison **Lindholme**
Bawtry Road, Hatfield Woodhouse
Doncaster DN7 6EE
Doncaster (01302) 848700
fax (01302) 848750

Eastwood, Mick (spo)
Clarke, Monica
Connelly, John
Mockford, Mark
Nixon, Mike
Phillips, Staffel
Greaves, Ms Rita (psa)
Millington, Ms Gill (psa)
Whitworth, Ms Jean (psa)

24. H M Prison & YOI **Moorland**
Bawtry Road, Hatfield Woodhouse
Doncaster DN7 6BW
Doncaster (01302) 351500
fax (01302) 350896

Probn clerk ext 302/303
Discipline ext 308

Pidwell, David (spo) ext 300
Burnett, Ian ext 361
Cartlidge, Mrs Jennie ext 390
Fisher, Darrell ext 303
Marley, Sean ext 357
Skelding, Steve ext 357/371

25. H M Young Offender Institution
Thorne Road **Hatfield**
Doncaster DN7 6EL
Thorne (01405) 812336
fax (01405) 813325

Discipline ext 242/308

Jackson, Ian ext 368
Talbot, Miss Jackie (psa)
Torn, Mrs Shelley (psa)

Petty Sessional Areas

2-5 Sheffield
14-16 Rotherham
7, 8 Barnsley
10-12 Doncaster

Crown Courts

2a Sheffield
9 Doncaster

Area Code 52

WEST YORKSHIRE PROBATION SERVICE

Out of hours emergency contact point
Elm Bank Hostel
(01274) 851551

Offices

1. **Head Office**
Cliff Hill House
Sandy Walk, Wakefield WF1 2DJ
Wakefield (01924) 885300
fax (01924) 382256

Wilson, Paul A (cpo)
Hall, Sue (dcpo)
Barrows, Randel (acpo effective practice)
Mills, Howard (acpo resettlement, accom, prtnrshps)
Thurston, Paul (acpo resettlement, accom, prtnrshps)
McNerney, Val (ete mgr)
Fagg, Caterina (spo, dtto mgr)
Moloney, Neil (spo effective pract mgr)
Johnston, Peter (spo contracts advisor)
Brereton, David (spo staff devpt)
Lorimer, Peter (spo npsiss proj mgr)

Thorpe, Nigel J (secretary)
Pamment, Stuart (treasurer)
Sheard, Jonathan (asst treasurer)
Griffiths, Maureen (aco personnel & staff devpt)
Sykes, Karen (personnel & staff devpt off)
Fisher, Alison (spo, nvq/local co-ord) (js)
Stirum, Vanessa (spo, nvq/local co-ord) (js)
Brown, Imogen (aco info services)
Stephens, Kate (research off)
Robinson, Dave (syst sup off)
Thornton, Janet (info off)
Grazin, Elaine (public rel)
Kettlewell, Derek (housing co-ord)
Clayton, Robert E (property mgr)
Bond, Bob (health & safety off)
Goodale, Chris (snr admin)
Phillips, Eleanor (debts & benefits advisor)

Bradford Division

2. Fraternal House
45 Cheapside **Bradford** BD1 4HP
Bradford (01274) 703700
fax (01274) 703701

Vacancy (acpo Bradford)
Siddall, Mark (area mgr)
Ali, Abid (admin)

Bradford (01274) 703720
fax (01274) 703721

Cameron, Lorna (spo)
Ashcroft, Gillian
Brand, David
Hayes, Rick
Holmes, Rebecca
Juba, Ian
Osman, Paul
Schmitt, Veronica G
Tallant, Christopher
Terrington, Christina D

MacPherson, Stuart J (spo)
Wilson, Margaret (snr pract)
Henney, Tracy A (p)
Lawson, Susan (p)
Milner, Pim
Anwar, Saeed (p, psa)
Bhatti, Shahina (psa)
Thackray, Andrew (psa int probn prog)
Wickham, Ralph (psa)

Bradford Victim & Offender Unit
Cameron, Lorna (spo)
Bailey, Rachael (psa)
Summan, Mukhtar (psa)

3. The City Courts
PO Box 6 **Bradford** BD1 1LB
Bradford (01274) 704500
fax (01274) 721010

Austwick, Martin (spo)
Sheikh, Bushra A (snr pract)
Hala, Bozena
Kubala, Henryk
Lewis, Denis
Miller, Michael J
Mitchell-Clarke, Valari A
Owles, Elayne C H
Small, Sebastian
Begum, Iqbal (psa)
Lamb, Jacqueline (psa)
Peace, Carey (psa)
Viske, Hilary (psa)

Vacancy (spo)
Anjum, Zahida B (p)
Brennan, Debbie (p)
Burke, Maureen A
Cooper, Michael
Goodsell, Evelyn
Khan, Hikmat
Lynch, William
McNulty, Bernard R
Ross, Helen
Suggett, Angela

Cope, Karran (psa)
Fox, Helen (psa)
Long, James (psa)
Todd, Joanne (psa)
Walker, Marcia (psa)
Woolley, Alison (psa)

Myers, Terry (spo)
Bilney, Joanne (p)
Forster, Lynda
Gregory, Gill (p)
Medd, Cathy
Mortimer, Alan L
Oliver, Stephen J
Parker, Catherine
Pinnock, Eugene B F
Sorah, Phil
Stirling, Amanda (p)
Ullah, Ali
Davis, Clare (psa)
Firth, Dannie (psa)
Naheed, Frazana (psa)
Waller, Justine (psa)

4. **The Law Courts** Exchange Square
Drake Street, Bradford BD1 1JZ
Bradford (01274) 742140
fax (01274) 726394

Kenure, Geoffrey J (spo)
Bonfield, Jacquilin M (3)
Brough, Ann M
Doyle, Mary G (p) (3)
Mansfield, Richard M
Plunkett, Michael J
Strachan, Ian B
Timlin, Carol M (3)
Clarke, Christine (psa) (3)
Hardy, Margaret A (psa)
Hirst, Dorota M (p, psa) (3)
Howarth, Leanne (psa)
Wensley, Susan E (psa)

5. 11/19 Cavendish Street
Keighley BD21 3RB
Keighley (01535) 662771/2
fax (01535) 611346

Vacancy (spo)
Anforth, Patricia H
Barraclough, Linda
Bradley, Laura
Foster, Alison
Guy, Jacqui
Maud, Graham
Nazran, Sarah
van der Gucht, Sheila
Bates, John (psa)
Croker, Simon (psa)
Thorpe, Julie (psa)

6. **Community Service**
7 Spring Gardens
Bradford BD1 3EJ
(01274) 301400
fax (01274) 732744

Vacancy (divnl cs mgr)
Ambler, Margaret (dep divnl cs mgr)
Brannan, Judy (cso)
Clarkson, David (cso)
Coe, Diana (cso)
Milczanowski, Richard (cso)
Morley, David (cso)
Pedley, Mike (cso)
Pollard, Rita (cso)
Scott, Graham (cso)
Armstead, Jean (p, css)
Bailey, David (p, css)
Barker, Gillian (p, css)
Blakeley, Carol (p, css)
Brown, Christine (p, css)
Caton, Andrew (css)
Finney, David (css)
Fressner, Shaun (css)
Gilmartin, Sue (p, css)
Hussain, Razeena (css)
Iqbal, Zafer (p, css)
Licence, Paul (css)
Nash, Michael (p, css)
Netherwood, Stuart (p, css)
Page, Richard (p, css)
Partridge, Trevor (p, css)
Proctor, Lesley (p, css)
Rathmell, David (css)
Roberts, Peter (p, css)
Smith, Chris (p, css)

Leeds Division

7. **Waterloo House**
58 Wellington Street
Leeds LS1 2EE
0113-243 0601
fax 0113-234 1951
acpo fax 0113-234 4057

Voakes, Robert W (acpo Leeds)
Culkin, Maggie (area mgr)
Hardie, Hazel (admin)

Clark, Deborah (p, spo)
Pickin, Rod (spo)
James, Peter (spo)
MacDonald, Andrew J P (spo)
Tate, Karen (snr pract)
Allen, Bob (p)

Bankhead, Elizabeth St C
Bentley, Alison V
Blanc, Johny
Bucksun, Margaret
Cantley, Louise
Davies, Ian
Garton, David L
Geeson, Roger
Godley, Simon
Hooson, Cindy A
McAvoy, Jacqueline
McLeish, David
MacPherson, Maria
Metcalfe, Lucy
Mistry, Elaben
Moore, Colin K
Mycock, Pamela
Nolan, Karen
Pettersson, Hakan
Pye, Denise M (p)
Ralcewicz, Liz
Schlaberg, Yvonne
Stenersen, Kristin (p)
Swallow, Rachel
Thompson, John
Turnbull, Louise
Underwood, William
Wilson, Cassy J M
Wilson, Frank
Baz, Shameen (psa)
Botwood, David (psa)
Braithwaite-Vare, Tracey (psa)
Hooson, Chris (psa)
Kilbane, Angela (psa)
Lacy, John (psa)
Leggieri, Anna (psa)
McPhail, Ian (psa)
Masterman, Dorothy (psa)
Westerman, Yvette (psa)

Carless, Susan E (spo)
Rutt, Jennifer S
Weblin, Martin
Potter, Colin (psa)

8. The Basement
Oxford Place, Leeds LS1 3AX
0113-243 5932
fax 0113-242 7336

Leeds' Victim & Offender Unit
Stadward, Christopher (spo) (9)
Armitage, Mark (pso)
Wood, Avril (co-ord)
Wynne, Jean (co-ord)

9. **1 Oxford Row**
Leeds LS1 3BE
0113-243 1107
fax 0113-234 1952

Crown Court
Stadward, Christopher (spo)
Ashford, Rita
Ashton, Melvyn
Barber, Jean
Bruno, Margaret
de Angelis, Maria I
Thackray, Philip C
Gordon, Carole (psa)
Jeffers, Joan M (psa)
Palmer, Hilary R (psa)

10. 28 Westgate
Leeds LS1 3AP
0113-399 5440
fax 0113-245 0967

Magistrates' Court
Minogue, Roderick (spo)
Addlestone, Deborah (p)
Domican, Paul
Falk, Emma
Hannant, Ian
Horsfall, Ruth
Kyle, Jeremy S
Smitheram, Christine A
Town, David
Hunt, Trevor (psa)
Langley, Sue (psa)
Scott, Margaret (psa)
Sheik, Aaliya (psa/interpreter)

11. **379 York Road**
Leeds LS9 6TA
0113-285 0300
fax 0113-285 0301

Ellis, Robert A (spo)
Neal, Elise M (spo)
Wright, Cath (spo)
Melaugh, John J A (snr pract)
Ali, Sajid
Angus, Elise
Bardsley, Jane
Booth, Susan P
Burgess, David V (p)
Dunhill, John
Clarke, David
Hanby, Rachel
Hanson, Phil
Haslewood, Nicholas G D
Hooson, Mick
Horne, Kathy

Hudson, Jennifer M
Hutchings, Tanya
Jarosz, Josephine
Jeffers, Lennie C S
Johnson, Ann-Marie
Klaus, Judith V
Kumaraswamy, Sheila
Lowton, Mark A
McLeod, Mary
Montgomerie, Malcolm
Moody, Linda
Munden, Angharad
Pitchford, William
Quinn, Carol
Scott, Jamie
van Rossum, Hendrikus
Walters-Kelly, Sally
Wattley-Guishard, Calvin R
Bashir, Mohammed (psa)
Bell, Gillian (psa)
Borrill, Steve (psa)
Brown, Alan (psa)
Croft, Daryl (psa)
Cruse, Ann (psa)
Dodson, Pauline (psa)
Giles, Jayne A (psa)
Hills, Jeanifer (psa)
Hudson, Karen (psa)
Keenan, Georgina (psa)
Khan, Zaq (psa)
Silver, Andrea (psa)
Wood, Rita (psa)

Community Service Office
fax 0113-285 0302

Milner, Christine (dvnl cs mgr)
Brett, Marion (dep dvnl cs mgr)
Dugdale, Ian (dep dvnl cs mgr)
Barnett, David (cso)
Bellwood, Irene (cso)
Cannon, Louise (cso)
Dinsdale, Rodney K (cso)
Lawless, Timothy (cso)
Matharu, Jagdish (cso)
Nelson, Richard (cso)
Parrish, Diane (cso)
Smith, Alan K (cso)
Walker, Lorraine (cso)
Walker, Norah (cso)
Wilkinson, Marjorie (cso)
Vacancy (cso)
Ashton, Rose (p, css)
Belton, Steve (p, css)
Bucktrout, Zoe (p, css)
Conway, Martin (p, css)
Farrar, David (p, css)
Harrison, Linda (p, css)
Jeffers, Shammin (p, css)
Jowett, Angela (p, css)
Mahmood, Arshad (p, css)
Nunns, Helen (css)
Oldroyd, James (p, css)
Partridge, Trevor (css)
Robson, Neil (p, css)
Smith, Tom (css)
Turner, Philip (p, css)
Walker, Jonathon (css)
Watson, Roy (p, css)
Wolstenholme, Christine (p, css)
Vaughan, J Anthony (p, css)

Calderdale Division

12. Probation Centre
Spring Hall Lane
Halifax HX1 4JG
Halifax (01422) 340211
fax (01422) 320998

Bagley, Jennifer J (acpo Calderdale)

Charlesworth, Susan M (spo)
Cartwright, Judith
Foster, Sara
Hall, Lynn M
Roberts, Patricia
Kerr, Richard M
Bailey, Kathryn (psa)
Khan, Quaiser (psa)
Kite, Alison (p, psa)
Lister, Georgina (p, psa)
Prescott, John (psa, mediation/reparation)

Branton, Christine (spo)
Ball, Kevin (snr pract)
Foster, Susan (p)
Gardner, Pauline
Gilyeat, David
Lusty, Elaine
Hay, Angela (psa)
Myers, Doreen (psa)
Nicholl, Helen (psa)
Richardson, Hilary (psa)

Probation Programmes Team
Hillas, Deryck (spo)
Chambers, Lynn
Evans, David
Faulkner, Kate
Morris, Mike
Nowell, Fran
Parker, Lisa
Potts, David C
Rudderforth, Jeff (p)
Ruth, Paul
Goodhall, Elizabeth A (psa)

Community Service Office
Brook, Margaret (dep divnl cs mgr)
Jennison, Margaret (cso)
Murgatroyd, Peter (cso)
Waddington, Sue (cso)
Gilmartn, Sue (css)
Hind, Jeannine (css)
Hindle, Edmund (css)
Kavanagh, Karen (css)
Khan, Mansha (css)
Morley, Susan (css)

Kirklees Division

13. West House, Hanover Street
Batley WF17 5DZ
Batley (01924) 479414
fax (01924) 475518

Vacancy (acpo Kirklees)
Dawson, Stephanie (admin)

14. Broadway House
Crackenedge Lane
Dewsbury WF13 1PU
Dewsbury (01924) 464171/3
fax (01924) 453279

Quarmby David (spo)
Thomas, David W (spo)
Gorman, Kevin (snr pract)
Bray, Sheila
Cartledge, Brian
Considine, Tom
Cooper, Sara
Crossley, Elaine (p)
Fielding, Geoff
Firth, Josephine (p)
Grindall, Theresa M
Hattersley, Patricia M (p)
Hines, Janine
Joseph, Elizabeth P
Langton, Christina
Miller, Lynn
Mounsdon, Ian A
Peattie, Katherine (p)
Roberts, Jean
Scott, Robert
Smith, Richard
Trevitt, Joanne
Akbar, Zahir (psa)
Bohanna, Glen (psa)
Brook, Claire (psa)
Gardner, Sandra (psa)
Gavins, Christine (psa)
Lloyd, Tracey (psa)
Newsome, Melanie (psa)
Radcliffe, Nicola (psa)
Sharif, Azar (psa interpreter)
Swithenbank, Shirley (psa)

15. 21 St John's Road
Huddersfield HD1 5BW
Huddersfield (01484) 826100
fax (01484) 422218

Ashton, Julie (spo)
Smallridge, Margaret (spo)
Burns, Janine (snr pract)
Akhtar, Saleem
Barnes, Irena
Barrett, Elaine R
Button, Jeffrey P
Button, Susan
Bramley, Elizabeth (p)
Dewey, Christina M
Hirst, Penelope J
Kilroy, Veronica
Lawrence, Penny
Maffin, Valerie A
Moreton, Gerald
Nicolson, Mike
Parker, Beverley
Romain, Godfrey
Tock, Heather A
Todd, Susan
Williams, Helen
Armitage, Kenny (psa)
Bano, Ifhat, (psa interpreter)
Ducker, Andrew (psa)
Haider, Halima (psa bail info)
Hindle, Debra (psa)
Hussain, Shabaz (psa interpreter)
Khan, Hejaz-ul-Hassan (psa)
Lees, Sharon (psa)
Newton, Belinda (psa)
Simpson, Helen (psa)
Stansfield, Bernie (psa)

Community Service Office
Appleby, Robert A (spo, dvnl cs mgr)
Hall, Brian (dep dvnl cs mgr)
Barrett, David R (cso)
Davies, Elaine (cso)
Denniss, Maria (p, cso)
Fox, Margaret J (cso)
Oldroyd, Philip (p, cso)
Walker, Mandy (cso)
Baptiste, Norris (p, css)
Bartholomew, Bill (css)
Frankland, Gordon (css)
Hargreaves, Julie (css)
Hewitt, Jean (p, css)
Lettice, Jim (p, css)
Milner, Margaret (css)
Thompson, Guy (p, css)

16. 5 Albion Street
Dewsbury WF13 2AJ
Dewsbury (01924) 457744
fax (01924) 458564

Scott, Joan (spo)
Baker, Melvin (comm safety)
Lumb, Jeannie
Roberts, Terrence H
Formby, William A (psa)
Martin, Graham (psa)
Mulla, Nasim (psa)
Moore, Julie (psa)

Wakefield Division

17. 20/30 Lawefield Lane
Wakefield WF2 8SP
Wakefield (01924) 361156
fax (01924) 291178

Lankshear, Ian (acpo Wakefield) (1)
Jones, Margaret (admin) (1)

Parsisson, George H (spo)
Reid, David (snr pract)
Beatson, Maxwell
Brereton, Liz
Cadamarteri, Sharon
Flaherty, Carole (p)
Hill, Phil
Munro, Donald
Razaq, Mohammed
Rollin, Peter B
Sawyer, Sandra
Wood, Susan
Appleyard, Tracey (psa)
Evans, Steve (psa)
Froggatt, Kathleen (psa med/rep)
Palmer, Gail (psa)
Rawlinson, Brian (psa)
Robinson, Christine (p, psa)

Brearton, Julie (spo)
Entwistle, Ben

Community Service Office
Wakefield (01924) 885420

Baxter, Les (dvnl cs mgr)
Brennan, Andrew (cso)
Evans, Steve (cso)
Haigh, Paula (cso)
Johnson, Lynn (cso)
Rainforth, Paul (cso)
Boffin, Anthony (css)
Grason, Daivd (p, css)
Kirrane, Mark (css)
Milner, Margaret (css)
North, Granville (p, css)
Schofield, Nicholas (p, css)
Wales, Granville (p, css)
Ward, Andrew (p, css)

18. Harropwell Lane
Pontefract WF8 1QY
Pontefract (01977) 791357
fax (01977) 602041

Haddrick, David (spo)
Mills, Elizabeth (snr pract)
Basford, Geoff
Brettell, James R
Cartwright, Imogen (p)
Clark, Don
Doonan, Mike
Goodchild, Jenny
Horncastle, Paula
Langford, Angela
Palmer, Gillian E
Spence, Robert
Battye, Patricia (psa)
Johnson, Don (psa)
Lomas, Joyce (psa)
Neto-Claringbold, Ana M (psa)

Court Team
Chandler, Andrew (spo)
Al-Kilani, Yaser
Nelson, Marva
Oliver, Maureen
Charles, Shirley (psa)
Dawson, Christine A (psa)
Nightingale-Clarke, Lorriane (psa)
Tate, Joyce R (psa)

19. Grosvenor House
8-20 Union Street
Wakefield WF1 3AE
(01924) 784999
fax (01924) 781405

Chandler, Andrew (spo) (18)
Shutt, Voirrey
Smith, Miles
Jones, Stephen H (psa)
Walker, Lindsay (psa)

Youth Offending Teams

Lankshear, Ian (acpo) (1)

Bradford Division

20. 1st Floor, Fraternal House
45 Cheapside **Bradford** BD1 4HP
Bradford (01274) 703760
fax (01274) 703761

O'Hara, Paul (yot mgr)
Page, Simon (spo)
Doherty, Eugene P (po)

Hardy, Linda (po)
Jackson, Robert A (po)
Knight, Alice M (po)
Osman, Paul (p, po)
Pickering, Geraldine (po)
Worboys, Anne J F (po)
Forber, Gillian (psa)

Leeds Division

21. 3rd Floor East
Merrion House
110 Merrion Centre
Leeds LS1 8QA
0113-247 7483
fax 0113-247 7228

Harrison, Edwina (yot mgr)

22. The District Centre
Town Street
Chapel Allerton LS7 4NB
0113-214 5663
fax 0113-214 5684

Pickering, John (spo)
Everett, Maggie (po)
Gilmour, Rebecca (po)
Lewis, Denis (po)

23. **Halton Moor Centre**
Neville Road, Leeds LS15 0NW
0113-214 1369
fax 0113-214 1377

Marston, Jack (po)
Sadler, Fiona (po)
Peel, Sarah (psa)

24. 38 Sweet Street
Leeds LS11 9DB
0113-214 5300
fax 0113-214 5299

Bell, Robert (po)
Luty, Angela (po)
Phillips, Leroy (po)

Calderdale Division

25. 3 Trinity Place
Halifax HX1 2BD
(01422) 368279
fax (01422) 368483

Toye, Stephen (yot mgr)
Daniels, Gerrard (po)
Devenport, William (po)

Kirklees Division

26. 1st floor, Somerset Buildings
Church Street **Huddersfield** HD1 1DD
Huddersfield (01484) 226263/4
fax (01484) 226919

Smith, Richard (yot mgr)
Oates, David (po)
Wallace, Mona (po)

Wakefield Division

27. 5 West Parade
Wakefield WF1 1LT
(01924) 304155
fax (01924) 304156

Lawrenson, Steve (yot mgr)
Hesketh, Paul (po)
Smith, Veronica (po)

Family Court Welfare Division
from 1.4.01 part of Children & Family Court Advisory & Support Service

28. 379 York Road
Leeds LS9 6TA
0113-248 1441
fax 0113-285 0303

Melville, Barbara W (area mgr)
Hardie, Hazel (admin) (6)

Leeds Family Court Welfare Team
Bakker, Titia
Brooke, Pauline A
Clark, Corinne A (p)
Higgins, Jennifer C (p)
Jewitt, Fred
Moore, Vera
Page, Jennifer
Pattison, Linda
Pearlman, Debra (p)
Rutt, Stephen J

29. 1st Floor Offices
1046/1060 Manchester Road
Bankfoot, Bradford BD5 8NN
Bradford (01274) 370281
fax (01274) 395519

Bradford & Calder Family Court Welfare Team
Donkersley, Stephen S (spo)
Berry, Ralph (p)
Browne, Jane
Clark, Vicky
Garvey, Brian D
Kilner, Hazel
Maurer, Deirdre M (p)

Middlehurst, Hazel
Pattinson, Catherine A
Powell, Brendan
Riley, Vivian
Sharpe, Hilary
Simpson, Margaret

30. West House, Hanover Street
Batley WF17 5DZ
(01924) 479006
fax (01924) 442403

Kirklees & Wakefield Family Court Welfare Team
Taylor, Alan (spo)
Barrett, Earl
Cooper, Anita
Dilai, Mike
Donkersley, Judith
Main, Jean (p)
Pearce, Kate H
Pollard, Phillip S
Roberts, Christopher
Walker, Julie
Walker, Pamela
Walsh, Graham

Residential Services Division

Thurston, Paul (acpo) (1)
Kettlewell, Derek (housing co-ord) (1)

31. **Holbeck House Probation & Bail Hostel**
Springwell View, Springwell Road
Leeds LS12 1BS
0113-245 4220
fax 0113-245 4910

Heal, Rosemary (mgr)
Rodney, Brian E (dep mgr)
Burnley, Sylvia (res off)
Eggleston, Mark (res off)
Finister, Eddie (res off)
Wales, Sharon (res off)

32. **Elm Bank Hostel**
Bradford Road
Cleckheaton BD19 3LW
Cleckheaton (01274) 851551
fax (01274) 851079

Maw, Stephen S (spo mgr)
Khan, Afzal (po deputy mgr)
Graham, John (res off)
Laidler, Beryl (res off)
Myers, David (res off)
Scott, Alison (res off)

33. **Albion Street Hostel**
30 Albion Street
Dewsbury WF13 2AJ
Dewsbury (01924) 452020
fax (01924) 455670

Brown, Ralph (spo mgr)
Loney, Kathryn (po deputy mgr)
Armitage, Sally (res off) (js)
Battye, Desmond (res off)
Baulk, Karen (res off)
Kirkham, Susan (res off) (js)
Smith, Stuart (res off)

Voluntary Approved Hostels

34. **Cardigan House**
84 Cardigan Road
Leeds LS6 3BJ
0113-275 2860
fax 0113-274 5175

Barker, Tim (mgr)
Marsh, Colin (dep mgr)
Daley, Irvin (res off)
Jagger, Kate (res off)
Lythgow, Ray (res off)
Pugh, Steve (res off)

35. **St John's Hostel**
259/263 Hyde Park Road
Leeds LS6 1AG
0113-275 5702
fax 0113-230 5230

Peaden, Andy (spo mgr)
Vaicekauskas, Kes (po dep mgr)
Berry, Tony (dep mgr)
Braithwaite, David (res off)
Dobbie, Alan (res off)
Rigby, Richard (res off)
Schofield, Bill (res off)

36. **Ripon House**
63 Clarendon Road
Leeds LS2 9NZ
0113-245 5488

Bryan, Jim (mgr)
Ridley, Alison (po dep mgr)
Garrett, Rene (res off)
Flynn, Jackie (res off)
Marriot, Chris (res off)
Naylor, David (res off)

Institutions

Lankshear, Ian (acpo) (1) (yoi only)
Mills, Howard (acpo) (1) (adult prisons)

37. H M Young Offender Institution
York Road **Wetherby** LS22 4NW
Wetherby (01937) 585141
fax (01937) 586488

Pickering, John (spo)
Cave, Malcolm
Wilson, Hilary (p)

38. H M Prison **Wealstun**
Thorp Arch, Boston Spa
Wetherby LS23 7AZ
Boston Spa (01937) 844844
fax (01937) 845862

Probn clerk ext 3268
Parole clerk (open) ext 3310
Parole clerk (closed) ext 3251
Special visits (open) 3268
Special visits (closed) ext 4237

Steed, Mary B (spo) ext 3300
Bissenden, David ext 3267
Burrows, Raymond ext 4299
Clark, Carol E ext 3335
Harrison, Carol A ext 4302
Fell, Theresa (psa) ext 3341
Gibson, Rachel (psa) ext 3304

39. H M Prison **Armley**
Leeds LS12 2TJ
0113-263 6411
fax 0113-279 0151

Probn/Gen Admin ext 296/428

Millinship, Gerald (spo) ext 300
Cody, Christopher ext 457
Dewey, Chris ext 307
Dickinson-Ramsden, Issy ext 302
Gallagher, Anthony ext 226
Lawton, Mary ext 510
Richards, Frances ext 338
Ryan, Mary ext 277
Thomas, Rose ext 391
Ward, Marianne E ext 395
Wilson, Gail ext 411
Evans, Maureen (psa) ext 304
Spenceley, Karen J (psa) ext 352

40. H M Prison, Love Lane
Wakefield WF2 9AG
Wakefield (01924) 378282
fax (01924) 384391

Probn clerk ext 399
Parole clerk ext 310
Special visits ext 502

Turner, Peter J (spo) ext 379
Hanby, Pam ext 481
Roberts, Terry ext 412
Stott, Elaine (p) ext 473/525
Sweeting, Chris ext 480/291
Todd, Vivian (p) ext 405/527

41. H M Women's Prison
New Hall Dial Wood
Flockton, Wakefield WF4 4AX
Wakefield (01924) 848307
fax (01924) 840692
probn fax (01924) 840748

Probn clerk ext 298
Discipline ext 308/309
Sentence planning ext 234/425
HDC clerk ext 479
Special visits ext 394

Akhter, Nasim (spo) ext 485
Forrest, Janet ext 296
Hirst, Penny ext 481
Vacancy (psa)
Senior, Lynda (psa) ext 478
Sheard, Ruth (psa) ext 479

Petty Sessional Areas

2-4 Bradford
5 Keighley
7-11 Leeds
11 Wetherby/Skyrack
7 Pudsey/Otley
7 Morley
12 Calder
14 Batley & Dewsbury
15 Huddersfield
17 Wakefield
18 Pontefract

Crown Courts

4 Bradford
9 Leeds

Area Code 53

DYFED PROBATION SERVICE GWASANAETH PRAWF DYFED from 1.4.01 amalgamating with Powys Probation Service

Offices

1. **Head Office**
   Llangunnor Road
   Carmarthen SA31 2PD
   Carmarthen (01267) 221567
   fax (01267) 221566

   Whitford, Jeanette (cpo)
   Morgan, Caroline R (acpo)
   Pearce, Jan E S (aco)
   John, Jackie (cpo secy, office mgr)
   Davies, Mair (admin & finance off)
   Maguire, Karen (admin & finance off)
   Richards, Mair (acpo's secy)
   Ford, Mike (p, it proj mgr)
   Bale, Shirley (it systems off)
   Glasson, Steve (it systems off)

2. 7a & 7b Water Street
   Carmarthen SA31 1PY
   Carmarthen (01267) 222299
   fax (01267) 222164

   Criminal Division Central
   Eames, Jane (divnl mgr)
   Adams, Gill (p)
   Coleridge, Tom (cclo)
   Brosnan, Mark
   Fisher, Kevin
   Holton, D (p, yot)
   Elliott, Helen (trainee)
   John, Gaye (psa)
   Absalom, Alison (crt admin)
   Saunders, Siân (snr admin secy)

3. Lloyd Street
   Llanelli SA15 2UP
   Llanelli (01554) 773736
   fax (01554) 758491

   Criminal Division East
   Wheatley, Lynn (divnl mgr)
   Brenton, Liz
   Churchill, Janet
   Edwards, Christine
   Hoyles, Lee
   Hussey, Alan
   Lynwen, Lewis (yot)
   Ripley, Carol
   Yih, Mandy
   Hooper, Nicola (trainee)
   Davies, Catherine (psa)
   Harries, Christine (psa)
   Stone, Terry (psa)
   Jenkins, Tim (cso)
   John, Clive (cso)
   Phillips, Heather (snr admin secy)
   Thomas, Janet (p, crt admin)

4. 14 High Street
   Haverfordwest SA61 1DA
   Haverfordwest (01437) 762013
   fax (01437) 765423

   Criminal Division West
   Thomson, Graham (divnl mgr)
   Bennett, Michael (p yot)
   Birks, Sandra
   Evans, Sheila
   Johns, Helen
   Jones, Chris (temp)
   Vacancy
   Culverhouse, Brian (psa)
   Gibbs, Lynn (psa, crt admin)
   James, John (psa)
   Owen, Bob (cso)
   Quinnell, Diane (cso)
   Lewis, Trish (snr admin secy)

5. 23 Grays Inn Road
   Aberystwyth SY23 1DE
   Aberaeron (01970) 612858
   fax (01970) 624713

   Criminal Division North
   Williams, Hugh (acting divnl mgr)
   Llewelyn, Sera (divnl mgr, from July 2001)
   Davies, Bob
   Linck, Jackie
   Wall, Geoff
   Smith, Clive (cso)
   Thomas, Sîan (psa)
   Williams, Harry (psa)
   Morgan, Julie (snr admin secy)
   Lees, Amelia (p, crt admin)

   Family Court Welfare
   from 1.4.01 part of Children & Family Court Advisory & Support Service
   Eames, Jane (dvnl mgr)
   Shephard, Mike
   Starke, Moira
   Wilkins, Bronwen (p)
   Wort, Gill (based at 4)

Petty Sessional Areas

2 Carmarthen South
2 Carmarthen North
3 Dinefwr
3 Llanelli

4 Cleddau
4 South Pembrokeshire
4 North Preseli
5 North Ceredigion
5 Mid Ceredigion
5 South Ceredigion

Crown Court

2 Carmarthen
2 Haverfordwest
2 Lampeter

Area Code 54

MID-GLAMORGAN PROBATION SERVICE GWASANAETH PRAWF GANOL MORGANNWG from 1.4.01 amalgamating with South & West Glamorgan Probation Services

Out of hours emergency contact numbers
Sam Pollock (cpo): (01656) 653834
Allan David (aco): (01656) 667631

Offices

1. **Head Office**
Brackla House, Brackla Street
Bridgend CF31 1BZ
Bridgend (01656) 766336
fax (01656) 767296

Pollock, Sam (cpo)
Jenkins, Teifion (aco)
David, Allan (aco)
Rutter, Ms Frances (aco) (temp)
Williams, Ms Rowena (aco) (temp)
Burridge, Gareth (snr admin officer)
Harry, Robert (spo, staff devpt mgr)
Devonshire, Mrs Sheila (info mgr)

2. Magistrate's Court
Cwmbach Road
Aberdare CF44 0NW
Aberdare (01685) 883505
fax (01685) 882351

Bosward, Ken (spo, dist practice mgr)
Emery, Mrs Eirlys (pract devpt assessor)
Greiner, Ms Sue
McPherson, Robin A
Sabor, Monika (temp)
Banks, Emma (psa)

3. The Law Courts
Glebeland Place
Merthyr Tydfil CF47 8TJ
Merthyr Tydfil (01685) 721131
fax (01685) 370916

Merriman, John (spo, dist operations mgr)
Robertson, Alan (cs mgr)
Brill, Peter (cclo)
Cowan, Patricia (p, yot)
Grant, Patrick (fcwo) (p)
Hegarty, Miss Patricia
Lewis, Ms Cathryn
Mann, Christopher J
Mordecai, Ms Mary (fcwo)
Murphy, Ms Bernadette (p)
Jones, Nicolette (p, fcwo) (career break)
Owen, Richard
Evans, Mrs Paula (p, psa)
Hale, Phil (psa)
Roberts, Margaret (psa)
Shemwell, Mrs Karen (psa)
Jones, Fred (snr cs sup)
Davies, Ms Kirsty (trainee)
Williams, Ms Tara (trainee)

4. Magistrates' Court
Sunnyside **Bridgend** CF31 4AF
Bridgend (01656) 766416
fax (01656) 655089

Linck, Ms Jacqueline (spo, dist pract mgr) (temp)
Smith, Earl (spo, dist operations mgr)
Vacancy (cs mgr)
Olson, Carl (service sup mgr)
Allen, Graham
Apreda, Ms Claire (p)
Bicknell, Ms Helen
Booth, Caroline (p, fcw)
Brady, Ms Claire (4a)
Feniuk, Janet A
Girton, Tracey (case mgmnt off) (4a)
Griffiths, Miss Larraine (fcwo)
Jackson, Ms Jackie
Maddocks, Goodman (yot)
Matthews, Bernard (4a)
Miller, Nigel (4a)
Smith, Len
Brown, Reginald (psa) (4a)
Burridge, Mrs Lynne (p, psa)
Galvin, Mrs Suzanne (psa)
Roche, Mrs Ann (psa) (4a)
Aston, Edward (snr cs sup)
Earle, Ms Maureen (trainee) (4a)
Wybron, Miss Stephanie (trainee) (4a)

4a. **Cae Court Activity Centre**
12 Merthyr Mawr Road
Bridgend CF31 3PG
Bridgend (01656) 767455
fax (01656) 646289

5. Aberrhondda Road
Porth **Rhondda** CF39 0LN
Porth (01443) 687777
fax (01443) 681639

Rees, Nigel (spo, dist operations mgr) (temp)
Collins, Terry (cs mgr)
Andrews, John
Donoghue, Ms Nicola
Evans, Lyn (case mgmnt off)
Harris, Robert
O'Kelly, Ms Frances
Parker, Ms Alison
Rees, Mal
Stewart, Royton
Williams, Katrina
Williams, Keith
Andrews, Mrs Angela (psa)

6. Magistrates' Court
Union Street
Pontypridd CF37 1QT
Pontypridd (01443) 486991
fax (01443) 485994

McGaughey, Angus (spo, dist operations mgr)
Young, Mrs Alison (service sup mgr)
Corcoran, Patrick (fcwo)
Cullen, Robert
Deering, John (case mgmnt off)
Thomas, Robert
Thomas, Mrs Sue (js)
Yarnall, Robert (yot)
Gerrard, David (psa)
Anthony, Ms Sheryn (psa)
Elston, Mrs Diane (psa)
Jones, Mrs Ceri (psa)
O'Brien, Mike (psa, yot)
Watkins, Hywel (snr cs sup)
Burt, Sarah (trainee)
Bush, Andrew (trainee)

Youth Offending Teams

7. Bridgend YOT
c/o Youth Justice Team
23/32a Noltyon Street
Bridgend CF31 1BN
(01656) 657243
fax (01656) 648218

Gay, Mal (mgr)
Maddocks, Goodman (po)

8. Rhonda YOT
Cottage 5, Gareth Olwy
Church Village
Pontypridd CF38 1BT
(01443) 219400
fax (01443) 203443 (North Team)
fax (1443) 219450 (South Team)

Yarnell, Rob (po South Team)
O'Brien, Mike (po North Team)

9. Merthyr YOT
11/12 Pant Morlais
Merthyr Tydfil CF47 8UN
(01685) 389304
fax (01685) 359726

Cowan, Pat (po)

Institution

9. H M Prison **Parc**
Heol Hopcyn John
Bridgend CF35 6AR
Bridgend (01656) 300200
fax (01656) 300201

Lewis, Ms Alison (spo, probn service mgr)
Bray, Anthony
Edwards, Huw L
Jones, Robert
Jury, Ms Caren
Nilsen, Tony
Wieczorkowski, Ms Vanda

Petty Sessional Areas

2 Cynon Valley
3 Merthyr Tydfil
5, 6Miskin
4 Newcastle & Ogmore

Crown Courts

3 Merthyr Tydfil

Area Code 59

SOUTH GLAMORGAN PROBATION SERVICE GWASANAETH PRAWF DE MORGANNWG from 1.4.01 amalgamating with Mid & West Glamorgan Probation Services

Out of hours contact point: Mandeville House 029-20394592

1. **Head Office**
33 Westgate Street
Cardiff CF10 1JE
Cardiff 029-2023 2999
Direct dial 029-2078 5 + ext
fax 029-2023 0384
e mail sglamprobation.hq@cardiff.gov.uk

Trusler, Peter J (cpo)
A'Herne, Jim (aco) ext 008
Brunt, Granville (aco) ext 005
Simpson, Joe (aco) ext 007
Egan, Paul (aco finance & admin & secy to cttee) ext 006
Ferris, Cathryn (principal off, finance) ext 016
Pring, Maxine (admin asst) ext 017

Administration Unit
James, Russell (principal off, admin) ext 020
Lee, Mary (pres admin) ext 071
Summers, Keri (admin asst) ext 021

Information Unit
Brelsford, Pauline (info mgr) ext 011
Keattch, Sue (p, info asst) ext 013
Lamprey, Margaret (systems admin) ext 014
Norman, Beverley (helpdesk asst) ext 015
Mohammed, Shamim ext 013

Research & Quality
Lessels, Melanie ext 070

Offender (Accommodation & Employment) Resources Unit
Barrow, Ian (psa) (Trothwy Housing) ext 041
Mayne, Ruth (psa) (Trothwy Housing) ext 025
Neale Andrea (psa) (Trothwy Housing) ext 025
Wilkinson, Christopher (Careerpaths Ltd) ext 026
Bertram, Sheila (Careerpaths Ltd) ext 027
Smithson Mandy (YMCA) ext 028

Community Supervision West
Barton, A Richard (spo)
Johnston, Terrence (snr pract)
Bickerton, Ian
Harrington, Phil
James, Bryan
Parry, Adele
Propert, Nancy
Short, Cherry
Watkins, Dave
Watkins, Leon
Whelan, Kerry
Williams, Joanne

Community Supervision East
O'Donovan, Gillian (spo)
Beck, Sandra
Brown, Darren
David, Geraldine
Morris, Graham
Pickles, Janet (p)
Pope, Tova
Sheppard, David
Bebb, David (psa)
Vacancy (psa)
Jones, Gill (psa)

Drug Treatment & Testing Orders
Carnuth, Conny
Hopkins, Gareth

Family Court Welfare Unit
from 1.4.01 part of Children & Family Court Advisory & Support Service
Mahoney, Martin (p, spo)
Barry, Daphne
Somerville, Rosemary (p)
Goldsmith, Lesley (p)
Price, Gareth
Roberts, Cath
Smith, Jean (p)
Waller, Trevor

Early Release Supvn Unit
Greenhill, Peter (spo)
Evans, Mike (snr pract)
Atherton, Moira
Vacancy
Coates, Jenny
Hearnden, Alex
Howe, Christine
Jones, Cheryl
Lyons, Amanda
Martin, Anne
Mulligan, Diarmuid
Richardson, Denise
Taylor, Phil

2. **Crown Court**
Cathays Park
Cardiff CF10 3NL
Cardiff 029-2023 2999
Direct dial 029-2078 5 + ext
fax 029-2034 5705

Mahoney, Martin (p, spo) ext 042
Evans, Eirian (snr pract) ext 042
Farrell, David ext 043
James, Beverly ext 048
Lewis, Bernadette (snr crt admin) ext 044
Franklin, Anna (crt admin) ext 049
James, Sara (p, crt admin) ext 049

3. **Magistrates' Court**
Fitzalan Place
Cardiff CF24 1RZ
Cardiff 029-2023 2999
Direct dial 029-2078 5 + ext
fax 029-2049 8587

Mahoney, Martin (p, spo) ext 042
Barker, Leslie (snr pract) ext 050
Williams, Joan ext 054
Smyth, Anne ext 054
Davies, Maxine (snr crt admin) ext 054
Norman, Julie (crt admin) ext 052
Williams, Andrea (p, crt admin) ext 053
Witts, Adrian (crt admin)

4. Probation Office
Greenwood Street
Barry CF6 6JJ
Barry (01446) 740054
fax (01446) 734180

Community Supervision Vale
McLoughlin, Bobbie (spo)
Shellens, Peter (snr pract)
Allen, Mike
Crombie, Moira
Evans, Robert
Jarvis, Barbara
Jones, Karen
Vacancy (psa)
Moyle, Gaynor (psa)

Community Service
Pallister, Sheila (spo) (at office 5)
Arentsen, Honora (cso)
Fraser, Anthony (cso)

5. **Community Service Centre**
2a Lewis Street
Canton, Cardiff CF10 8JX
Cardiff 029-2023 2999
Direct dial 029-2078 5 + ext
fax 029-2066 7870

Pallister, Sheila (spo) ext 029
Martin, Philip (snr cso) ext 030
Bendell, Michael (p, cso) ext 037
Eastman, Charles (cso) ext 035
Lee, Peter (cso)
Rose, Howard (cso) ext 034
Richards, David (cso) ext 040
Taylor, Yvonne (cso) ext 036
Oates, Mark (wkshop cso) ext 040
Boxer, Charles (cs sessional supvr) ext 040
Jones, Paul (cs sessional supvr) ext 040
Sullivan, Stephen (cs sessional supvr wkshop) ext 040

Youth Offending Teams

6. Cardiff YOT
Penhill, The Rise
Cardiff CF11 9PR
029- 2056 0839
fax 0292057 8746

Warner, Courtney
Foulner, Jane
Waite, Leny

7. Vale YOT
91 Salisbury Road
Barry CF62 6PD
(01446) 745820
fax (01446) 739549

Norman, Zarah

Hostel

8. **Mandeville House**
Approved Probation & Bail Hostel
9 Lewis Street, Cardiff CF10 8JY
Cardiff 029-2039 4592 & 2999 ext 4530
fax 029-2023 3857

Tolley, David (mgr warden)
Gibbins, Chantal (po deputy)
Driscoll, Janice (asst warden)
Willis, Sue (asst warden)
Dunleavy, Michael (asst. warden)
Harding, Neil (asst warden)
Lundbech, David (asst warden)
Calnan, Larraine (admin asst)

Institution

9. H M Prison, Knox Road
Cardiff CF24 1UG
Cardiff 029-2043 3100
fax 029-2043 3318

Jones, John (spo)

Somerville, Martin (snr pract)
Cook, Michelle
Evans, Leighton
Jones, Cheryl (p)
Vacancy

Petty Sessional Areas

1 Cardiff
4 Vale of Glamorgan

Crown Court

2 Cardiff

Area Code 58

WEST GLAMORGAN PROBATION SERVICE GWASANAETH PRAWF GORLLEWIN MORGANNWG from 1.4.01 amalgamating with Mid & South Glamorgan Probation Services

Out of hours emergency number
(01792) 299661 (cpo)

Offices

1. **Head Office**
Pearl Assurance House
119 London Road, Neath SA11 1HL
Neath (01639) 639934 & 645393
fax (01639) 641675

Collins, Jeffrey (cpo)
Chaplin, Mrs Janet (acpo divnl mgr)
Richards, Anthony (acpo divnl mgr)
Thomas, Wayne (personnel off)
Dixon, Janis (financial mgr)

Community Service Team
Neath (01639) 631955
fax (01639) 633202

Durgan, Roger (spm mgr)
Wear, Alan (snr cso)
Morse-Jones, Simon (cso)
Francis, Mrs Yvonne (cso)
Matthews, Fred (cso)
Richardson, Darren (cso)

2. 2nd Floor, West Glamorgan House
23 Orchard Street, **Swansea** SA1 5AB
Swansea (01792) 645505
fax (01792) 457809

Supervision Team
Protheroe, Ms Ann (spm mgr
Davies, Mrs Fran (pract suprvr) (2, 7)
Francis, Mrs Ann
Hoare, Ms Rachael
Hunt, William
Jones, Graham
Jones, Mrs Pam
Roberts, Dorian
Richardson, Darren (psa)
Vesuviano, Philip (psa)
Bellis, Miss Jessica (trainee)
Woodroof, Hannah (trainee)

Throughcare Team
King, Mrs Gaynor (spm mgr)
Zammit, Mrs Ingrid (practice supr)
Davies, Gavin
Edwards, Mrs Jeanne
Hughes, David
Hughes, Mrs Gwyneth
Jones, Mrs Jayne
Morgan, Ian
Morris, Mrs Monica
Richards, Keith
Williams, Ken
Kircough, Ann (psa)
Thomas, Peter (psa)
Chandler, William (trainee)

Court Services
Rolt, Mrs Pauline (spm mgr)
Maynard, David (practice supr)
Glennie, Ms Wendy
Mc Donald, Mrs Edna
Cowan, Ms Pippa (psa)
Curtis, Mrs Lorina (psa)
Evans, Mrs Sheila (psa) (7)
Lewis, Mrs Libby (psa) (7)
Poiner, Mrs Beverley (psa)

3. 3rd Floor, West Glamorgan House
23 Orchard Street, **Swansea** SA1 5AB
Swansea (01792) 478178
fax (01792) 459115

Information Unit
Ford, Michael (info & systems mgr)

Training & Staff Devpt
Cowper, Ms Anne (spm mgr)

4. **Induction Centre**
Unifloc Building, Victoria Road
Swansea SA1 1SE
Swansea (01792) 648746
fax (01792) 646080

Johns, Colin (spm mgr) (9)

We

Meredith, Roger (spm mgr)
Colbeck, David (practice supr)
D'Arcy, Mrs Debbie
Davies, Paul
Morgan, Mrs Andrea
Owen, Michael
Reynolds, Mrs Helen
Smythe, Hugh
Budge, Steve (psa)
Fox, Mrs Lyn (psa)
Frudd, Andrew (psa)
McClure, Mrs Irene (psa)
Lewis, Miss Audra (trainee)

5. **Family Court Welfare Service**
from 1.4.01 part of Children & Family Court Advisory & Support Service
3rd floor, 37 The Kingsway
Swansea SA1 5LF
Swansea (01792) 645535
fax (01792) 457876

Cowper, Ms Anne (spm mgr)
Kitaruth, Rishi (practice supr)
Barden, Ms Isabel
Harris, Mrs Marian
Naylor, Robert

6. **Crown Court**
St Helen's Road
Swansea SA1 4PF
Swansea (01792) 459621 ext 210
direct line (01792) 461381
fax (01792) 457783

Rolt, Mrs Pauline (spm mgr) (2)
Reynolds, Michael
Richards, Mrs Claire (psa secy)
Richards, Mrs Susan (psa secy)
Stokes, Mrs Trisha (psa secy)

7. 5/6 London Road
Neath SA11 1HB
Neath (01639) 792200
fax (01639) 632545

Neath & Port Talbot Supervision Team
Protheroe, Miss Ann (spm mg) (2)
Davies, Mrs Fran (practice supr) (2)
Bouleghlimat, Aziz
Hinder, Vic
Loring, Mrs Alyson
Purchase, Mrs Sue
Sheridan, Ms Paula
Jones, Mrs Gillian (psa)
Beckers, Miss Helen (trainee)
McKenzie, Colette (trainee)

8. **West Glamorgan Alternative Scheme**
Green Park Industrial Estate
Port Talbot SA12 6NU
Port Talbot (01639) 895279
fax (01639) 897616

Johns, Colin (spm mgr) (9)
Parry, Mrs Helen (practice supvr)
Jones, Ray
Frudd, Andrew (psa)

9. **Youth Offending Teams**

Swansea YOT
Llwyncelyn Children's Centre
Cockett House, Cockett Road
Cockett , Swansea
Swansea (01792) 522800
fax (01792) 522805

Hoare, Phillip (practice supr)
James, Mrs Jackie
Roberts, Mrs Lillian

Neath/Port Talbot YOT
Cramic Way
Port Talbot SA13 1RU
(01639) 883624
fax (01639) 898244

Stringer, Mrs Sue

Hostel

10. **Emroch House Bail Hostel**
46 Talbot Road
Port Talbot SA13 1HU
Port Talbot (01639) 883551
fax (01639) 890549

Durgan, Roger (spm mgr) (1)
Elliot, Owen (po mgr)
Barker, Clifford (po dep mgr)
Jones, Alan R (asst mgr)
Mizen, John (asst mgr)
Howells, Simon (asst mgr)

Institution

11. H M Prison
Oystermouth Road
Swansea SA1 3SR
Swansea (01792) 464030
fax (01792) 642979

Lewis, Mrs Jill (spm) ext 298
Howells, Wynford ext 298
Thorne, Ms Alicia ext 373
Evans, Viv (psa)
Edwards, Mrs Suzanne (psa)

Petty SessionalAreas

2 Swansea
2 Lliw Valley
7 Neath
7 Port Talbot

Crown Court

6 Swansea

Area Code 60

GWENT PROBATION SERVICE GWASANAETH PRAWF GWENT

Offices

1. **Head Office**
Cwmbran House
Mamhilad Park Estate
Pontypool, Gwent NP4 0XD
Pontypool (01495) 762462
fax (01495) 762461

Regan, Jane (acting cpo)
Langdon, Chris (aco central supp services)
Blease, Adrian (aco operations)
Gotley, Adam (acting aco operations)
Davies, Alan (acting divnl mgr, prtnrshps, fcw)
Jones, Neil (finance off/sao)
Ahluwalia, Satinder (hr off)
Lowe, Allan (research/info)
Ryan, Mary (pa to cpo)
Holland, Susie (pa to aco/css)
Morris, Susan (pa to aco's ops)
Fisher, Bärbel (admin off, personnel)
Whyman, Marsha (admin off, finance)
Phillips, Cherryl (admin off, office/property services)
Clarke, Tony (info systems off)
Humphreys, Gaynor (admin off)

2. 50 Bethcar Street
Ebbw Vale NP23 6HG
Ebbw Vale (01495) 309799
fax (01495)306997

Offender Intervention Unit
Andrews, Ms Chris (dvnl mgr)
Turner, Karen (snr pract)
Brown, Fiona
Carter, Jan
Francis, Shirley
Ilsley, Suzanne
Vincent, Susan
Walters-Moore, Andrew (psa)

Assessment Unit
Bird, Jayne
Davies, Iwan
Pearn, Vernon (p)
Thomas, Fiona (crt off)

Public Protection Unit
Murrell, Maria

Youth Offending Team
Harrison, Susan
based at Abertillery (01495) 216531

Community Service
King, Michael (cs mgr)
Mogford, Mike (cso)
Morgan, Robin (cso)

3. Probation Office
Park Road **Bargoed** CF81 8SP
Bargoed (01443) 875575
fax (01443) 831114

Offender Intervention Unit
Davies, Linda (p)
Lakin, John
Owen, Linda
Powell, Kate
Richey, Linda

Assessment Unit
Hamilton, Jan (crt off)

Public Protection Unit
Walters, Sharon

Community Service
Wilks, Roger (cso)

Giles, Lynn
Rowland, Maria (psa comm supvn)

4. Magistrate's Court
Mountain Road
Caerphilly CF83 2XA
Caerphilly (02920) 885861
fax (01222) 865929

Offender Intervention Unit
Allan, David
Dunne, Jill
Thorne, Stephen

Assessment Unit
Morris, Rhys (dvnl mgr)
Bowkett, Steve (snr pract)
Shaw, Linda
Thomas, Mrs Elizabeth
Solomons, Mrs Gloria (crt off)

Youth Justice Unit
Vacancy

Community Service
Ritchie, Grant (cso)

Affleck, Robert (psa comm supvn)

5. **Groupwork**
The Highway, Croesyceiliog
Cwmbran NP44 2HF
Cwmbran (01633) 872411
fax (01633) 867251

Offender Intervention Unit
Law, Alex (snr pract)
Spacey, Nigel
Brayford, Jo (research off)
Daniel, Peter (psa, oiu)

6. Torfaen House, Station Road
Sebastopol, **Pontypool** NP4 5ES
Pontypool (01495) 755221
fax (01495) 763233

Community Supervision Unit
Ace, Christine (dvnl mgr)
Owen, Peter (snr practitioner)
Bailey, Ann (psa)

Offender Intervention Unit
Smith, Bernard
Thomas-Owen, Mandy
Vernon, Claire

Assessment Unit
Arkell, André
Bell, Nick
Devine, Patricia (p)
Rees, Cellan
Spencer, Susan
Edwards, Sharon (psa)
Price, Marilyn (psa)
Scott, Lynn (psa)

Public Protection Unit
Stacey, Caroline

Youth Justice Unit
Gourlay, Alison (youth justice)
(01495) 768300

Community Service
Axenderrie, Paul (cso)
Brown, Margaret (cso)

7. 19/20 Gold Tops
Newport NP20 4UG
Newport (01633) 213221
fax (01633) 221568

Offender Intervention Unit
Browning, Catherine (snr pract)
Gillard, Karen
James, Shirley
Lewis, Mrs Margaret
Packham, Jill (js)
Pearce, Annette (p)
Pudge, Mrs Lindsey

Assessment Unit
Bell, Doreen
Pearson, Kay
Perry, Reg
Sullivan, Gina
Taylor, Lee (js)
Price, Tony (psa)
Rees, Karen (crt off)
Vaughan, Karen (crt off)

Community Supervision Unit
Edwards Sarah (snr practitioner)
Hosking, Robert (psa)

Public Protection Unit
Clay, Carolyn (dvnl mgr)
Reed, Gail (snr pract)
Bell, Nick
Dunne, Mike
Sullivan, Jane

Youth Justice Unit
Dunley, Karen
(01633) 292900

Community Service
Bidgood, David (cso)
Sims, James (cso)

8. 35 Godfrey Road
Newport NP20 4PE
Newport (01633) 264265
fax (01633) 244072

Family Court Welfare Service
from 1.4.01 part of Children & Family Court Advisory & Support Service
Mason, Colin (snr practitioner)
Hall, Jason
Jackson, Alison
Lamb, Tony
Morgan, Angela
Owen-Winn, Debbie
Roberts, Julia
Rose, Linda
Williams, Christina

Institutions

9. H M Prison
47 Maryport Street
Usk NP5 1XP
Usk (01291) 672411
fax (01291) 673800

Bradley, Mike (spo)
Kidd, Tony
Corkhill, Sarah (psa)
Ruck, Sharon (psa)
Thorpe, Keiron (psa)

10. H M Young Offender Institution
Prescoed
Coed-y-paen
Nr Pontypool NP4 0TB
Usk (01291) 672231
fax (01291) 672197

Bradley, Mike (spo, th'care mgr)
Kidd, Tony
Coleman, Jennifer (psa)
Ruck, Sharon (psa)

Petty Sessional Areas

6 Abergavenny
2 Bedwellty (Tredegar, Blackwood, Ebbw Vale, Brynmawr, Abercarn, Abertillery, Blaina)
6 Cwmbran
6 Chepstow
3, 4 Lower Rhymney Valley
3, 4 Upper Rhymney Valley
6 Monmouth
7 Newport
6 Pontypool
6 Usk

Crown Court

7 Newport

Area Code 55

NORTH WALES PROBATION SERVICE (Counties of Anglesey, Denbighshire, Flintshire, Wrexham, Gwynedd, Conwy) GWASANAETH PRAWF GOGLEDD CYMRU (Siroedd Ynys Môn, Ddinbych, Fflint, Wrecsam, Gwynedd, Conwy)

Out of hours emergency contact point
Ty Newydd Hostel (01248) 370529
Plas y Wern Hostel (01978) 821202

Offices

1. **Head Office**
Alexandra House
Abergele Road
Colwyn Bay LL29 9YF
Colwyn Bay (01492) 513413
fax (01492) 513373

Moore, Carol R (cpo)
Ray, Stephen G (acpo)
Chester, John (acpo)
Barton, Kit (acting aco, corporate support & devpt)
Murphy, Ray (service proj mgr)
Lloyd, Geraint (admin & finance services off)
Pickering, Steve (information support)

2. Llys Garth, Garth Road
Bangor Gwynedd LL57 2RT
Bangor (01248) 370217
fax (01248) 372422

Elis-Williams, Mrs Nia (spo, crt & com supvn west)
Williams, Mrs Rosalie (admin asst)

Court & Community Supervision (West)
Evans, Mrs Jane (snr pract)
Adshead, Mrs Carole (cclo)
Campbell, Ms Glenys (p)
Parry, Mrs Trish
Riou, Ms Jilly
MacDonald, Fergie (psa)
Whatling, Mike (psa)
Vacancy (psa)

Staff Training
Adlam, Doris (snr pract, training off)

Offender Programmes
Jones, Mrs Eryl (p)
Wilson, Ms Sue (p)

Community Service
Conant, Mrs Rebecca (cs unit mgr)
Pritchard, Mrs Vivien (cso)
Thomas, Bob (p, csa)
Thomas, David V (csa)
Wilding, Bob (csa)
Williams, Keith (csa)
Edwards, Mrs Karen (p, admin asst)

All Wales Training Consortium
Jones, Mrs Eirlys (snr pract, pract devpt assessor)

3. 14 Market Street
Caernarfon Gwynedd LL55 1RT
Caernarfon (01286) 674346
fax (01286) 672668

Owen, Llew (spo, pre & post release)
Griffiths, Mrs Mimma (admin asst)

Pre & Post Release
Davies, Ms Lis
Edwards, Ms Meinir
Clark, Mrs Carolyn (psa)
Roberts, Matt (psa)

Court & Community Supervision
Sims, Mrs Georgina (p, cclo)
Williams, Mrs Sîan (psa)

4. Lombard Street
Dolgellau Gwynedd LL40 1HA
Dolgellau (01341) 422476
fax (01341) 422703

Harrison, Mrs Marian (psa clerical asst)

5. 18 Augusta Street
Llandudno LL30 2AD
Llandudno (01492) 875083/876961
fax (01492) 872034

Murphy, Ray (service proj mgr)
Marsh, Ms Sue (admin asst)

Court & Community Supervision (Central)
Jacobs, Rei
Speers, Sam
Dance, Mrs Sheila (psa)
Dickinson, Mrs Roz (psa)

Pre & Rost Release
Gwilym, Ms Ceinwen
Lowe, Mrs Sheila
Roberts, Ms Sue
Roberts, Mrs Jan (psa)

6 13 Princes Drive
Colwyn Bay LL29 8HT
Colwyn Bay (01492) 530600/532692
fax (01492) 532283

Offender Programmes
McIntyre, Mrs Kären
Laing, Ms Angharad (p)
Markwick, Miss Nerys (psa)

Community Service
Hughes, Mrs Liz (cs area mgr)
Gush, Mrs Lynn (admin asst)

7. Epworth Lodge, Brighton Road
Rhyl Denbighshire LL18 3HF
Rhyl (01745) 344521
fax (01745) 356137

Barton, Mrs Gaynor (spo, crt & com supvn central)
Richardson, Ms Judy (admin asst)

Court & Community Supervision (Central)
Roberts, Mike (snr pract)
Balsamo, Mrs Delanie (p)
Green, Dave
Jones, Rhys
Owen, Mrs Lucie Anne
Parry, Glynne
Ryan, Ms Jane
Owen, Mrs Tracey (p, psa)
Vacancy (psa)
Omorogbe, Mark (trainee)
Rattigan, Sylvia (trainee)

Community Service
Evans, Charlie W (cs unit mgr)
Thomas, Graham (cso)
Knowles, Richard (csa)
Roberts, Chris (p, csa)
Roberts, Gordon (p, csa)
Wright, John (csa)
Aristeidou, Cristina (p, admin asst)

8. 10-12 Salisbury Street
Shotton Deeside
Flintshire CH5 1DR
Deeside (01244) 830459
fax (01244) 836833

Catton, Ms Tessa (spo offender progs)
Towers, Mrs Viv (admin asst)

Court & Community Supervision (East)
Henery, Mrs Jill (snr pract)
Davies, John (cclo)
Jones, Peter R
Smith, Ms Jane
Mead, Zam (psa)
Vacancy (psa)

Pre & Rost Release
Evans, Ms Tracey (p)
Seward, Derek (psa)
Vacancy (psa)

9. Ellice Way
Wrexham Technology Park
Wrexham LL13 7YX
Wrexham (01978) 346200
fax (01978) 346206

Griffin, Simon (spo crt & com suprvn east)
Hughes, Mrs Carole (admin asst)
Ellis, Mrs Paula (admin asst)

Court & Community Supervision (East)
Dyment, Mrs Joy (snr pract)
Brett, Ms Emma
Conder, Mrs Jackie
Davidson, Ian B
Eagles, Mrs Jackie (p)
Goodwin, Phil
Magaw, Ms Judith
Rees, Ms Awen Fôn
Roberts, Mrs Carol
Roberts, Ms Pamela (psa)
Sedgwick, Eddie (psa)
Foulkes, Ms Jenny (trainee)
Pawulska, Ms Jacquie (trainee)
Vacancy (psa/clerical asst)

Pre & Rost Release
Evans, Edwyn
Carrison, Mrs Janet
Vacancy (psa)

Offender Programmes
Amirech, Mohammed (snr pract)
Taylor, Mrs Jo (psa)

Community Service
Wrexham (01978) 346207
Davies, Chris (cs unit mgr)
Ellis, Phil (cso)
Mitchell, John (cso)
Vacancy (cso)
Dunning, John (csa)
Hern, Roger (csa)
Lloyd, Dennis (csa)
Poyner, Mike (csa)
Stein, Mrs Pat (csa)
Sedgwick, Mrs Cathy (admin asst)

Family Court Welfare Service
from 1.4.01 part of Children & Family Court Advisory & Support Service
Wrexham (01978) 346208
Harrod, Ms Mari (p)
Norris, Mrs Barbara
Robinson, Peter (p)

10. Heulwen, Glyn y Marl Road
Llandudno Junction
Conwy LL31 9NS
(01492) 581975
fax (01492) 582806

Family Court Welfare Service
from 1.4.01 part of Children & Family Court Advisory & Support Service
Williams, Mrs Jane (spo)
Holmes, Ms Kathryn
Hughes, Ivor (p)
Ifans, Mrs Jonquil
Nolan, Ms Vera
Jones, Miss Sandra (admin asst)

11. **Youth Offending Teams**

Swyddfa Menai
Glan y Mor, Felinheli
Bangor LL56 4RQ
(01248) 679183
fax (01248) 679180

Dafydd, Gareth

3rd Floor, Kelso House
13 Grosvenor Road
Wrexham LL11 1BS
(01978) 267404
fax (01978) 267401

Jones, Mrs Carole

68 Conway Road
Colwyn Bay LL29 7LD
(01492) 523500
fax (01492) 523555

Jones, Andy

Mold Crown Court
Law Courts, Civic Centre
Mold CW7 1AX
phone & fax (01352) 751649

Davies, John (cclo)

Caernarfon Crown Court
Shire Hall Street
Castle Ditch
Caernarfon LL55 2AY
(01286) 675753
fax (01286) 678201

Adshead, Mrs Carole

Hostels

12. **Plas-y-wern**
Ruabon, Nr Wrexham
LL14 6RN
Wrexham (01978) 814949
fax (01978) 810435

Higgins, Chris (spo warden)
Christie, David (po deputy)
Higgins, Gareth (rso)
Jones, Ms Rhian (rso)
Partington, Michelle (rso)
White, Mrs Hilda (rso)
Williams,. Mark (rso)

Garratt, Neil (psa)
Williams, Mrs Margaret (psa)
Griffiths, Mrs Chris (admin asst)

13. **Ty Newydd**
Llandegai
Bangor, Gwynedd LL57 4LG
Bangor (01248) 370529
fax (01248) 371204

Ellis, Dafydd (spo warden)
Farrer, Ms Susie (po deputy)
Mead, Damon (rso)
Parry, Wynne (rso)
Pugh, Richard (rso)
Williams, Emyr (rso)
ap Gruffudd, Gwilym (psa)
Hughes, Ms Lowri (psa)
Cox, Ms Karen (admin asst)

Petty Sessional Areas

5 Aberconwy
2, 3 Arfon
2 Anglesey
5, 7 Colwyn
7 Denbighshire
7, 9 Flintshire
4 Meirionydd
3 Pwllheli
9 Wrexham

Crown Courts

8 Mold
3 Caernarfon
3 Dolgellau

Area Code 56

POWYS PROBATION SERVICE GWASANAETH PRAWF POWYS from 1.4.01 amalgamating with Dyfed Probation Service

From 1.4.01 Head Office will be in Carmarthen

Offices

1. **Head Office**
The Limes, Temple Street
Llandrindod Wells LD1 5DP
(01597) 827700
fax (01597) 827701

Carter, Neil (cpo)
Corbett, Jeremy (acpo)
Insley, Ms Joan (support services mgr)
Powis, Ms Kathleen (operations mgr, s powys)
Davies, Miss Anita (hq team admin)
Grafton, Miss Julie (welsh language devpt off)
Dann, Miss Julie (p, hq admin/health & safety)

2. Probation Office
The Limes, Temple Street
Llandrindod Wells LD1 5DP
(01597) 827700
fax (01597) 827701

Leggett, Jackie (p)
Wooldridge, Jonathan
Livesley, Mrs Julia (trainee, yot, p)
Dodds, Mrs Maureen (snr cso, S Powys)
Smith, Mrs Fay (case load mgr, team admin)
Evans, Mrs Clare (admin asst)

3. Probation Office
Straight Lines House, New Road
Newtown SY16 1BB
(01597) 827700
fax (01686) 611901

Williams, Yvonne (operations mgr, N Powys)
Alman, Mark
Davies, David (p, yot)
Donaldson, Matthew (cclo, fcwo)
Hughes, Renita (p)
Cookson, Patricia (bail & crt duty)
Randle, Brian (bail & crt duty)
Hickman, Miss Tracey (snr cso, N Powys)

Gerrard, Mrs Deborah (case load mgr)
Harvey, Miss Laura (team admin)
Fleming, Christine (info mgr)
Dann, Julie (p, team admin)
Mooney, Nicola (p, admin asst)

4. Probation Office, Captain's Walk
Brecon LD3 7DS
(01597) 827700
fax (01874) 610602

Powis, Kathleen (operations mgr, S Powys)
Burdett, Andrea (p)
Daniel, Darren
Gregory, Ms Janet (p)
Leggett, Jackie (p)
Hughes, Jim (bail & crt duty)
Price, Philip (bail & crt duty)
Scott, Miss Jenny (caseload mgr)
James, Pat (p, team admin)

Williams, Ms Margaret (team admin)

5. **Offender Employment & Housing Unit**
Employment Service, Canal Bank
Brecon, Powys LD3 6HL
phone & fax (01874) 573053

Carter, Charlie (devpts mgr)
Hirst, Neil (devpts off)

6. **Ystradgynlais Office**
all correspondence via Brecon Office

7. **Welshpool Office**
all correspondence via Newtown Office

8. **Machynlleth Court**
all correspondence via Newtown Office

Petty Sessional Areas

2 Llandrindod Wells
3 Newtown, Welshpool, Machynlleth
4 Brecon, Ystradgynlais

Crown Court

3 Welshpool

Area Code 57

NORTHERN IRELAND

Northern Ireland Office
Criminal Justice Services Division
Massey House
Stoney Road
Belfast BT4 3SX
Belfast 028-9052 7530

One of the Division's main responsibilities is funding and monitoring the activities of the Probation Board for Northern Ireland. The Northern Ireland Office is the Board's sponsoring department. Responsibility for managing the relationship between the Government and the Board lies with the Criminal Justice Directorate of the NIO. The Directorate, in conjunction with the department's Financial Services Division, has to ensure that:
the Board carries out its activities within the overall policy and resources framework set by the Secretary of State; and
the Board adheres to the requirements and procedures attaching to its expenditure of public money.

Statistics and Research Branch
Massey House
Stoney Road
Belfast BT4 3SX
Belfast 028-90527 354

The Branch supplies professional statistical and research services to the Northern Ireland Office and other Departments within the criminal justice system. It also assists in answering statistical requests from parliament, research bodies, government publications and the public in general.

Northern Ireland Prison Service
Dundonald House
Upper Newtownards Road
Belfast BT4 3SU
Belfast 028-9052 7356

The Services Directorate is responsible for policy on all aspects of the treatment of prisoners in Northern Ireland. It provides that part of the Probation Board for Northern Ireland budget relating to probation staff who work within prison establishments. In addition it administers the Boards of Visitors and Visiting Committee, which oversee the running of prisons on behalf of the public. It has a responsibility for Home Leave Schemes including the Compassionate Temporary Release Scheme and the Home Visits Scheme and all oversight of life sentence prisoners casework.

Social Services Inspectorate (Criminal Justice Services Group)
Massey House, Stoney Road, Belfast BT4 3SX

In Northern Ireland responsibility for inspection and liaison with the Northern Ireland Probation Board on professional matters rests with the Social Services Inspectorate, which has a discrete section dealing with criminal justice matters. The Social Services Inspectorate provides advice to the Northern Ireland Office about probation service matters.

Chief Inspector 028-9052 0657
Assistant Chief Inspector 028-9052 7513
Inspectors 028-9052 7348

PROBATION BOARD FOR NORTHERN IRELAND

Emergency out of hours contact point: 028-9066 1629

Offices

1. **Head Office**
80/90 North Street
Belfast BT1 1LD
Belfast 028-9026 2400
fax 028-9026 2470

Brannigan, Oliver (chief executive)
Arbuthnot, Mrs Ann (finance mgr)
Doran, Paul (acpo)
Fulton, Brendan, (acpo)
Lamont, Cheryl (acpo)
McCaughey, Brian (acpo)
Curry, Desmond (strategy implementation mgr)
Moss, Peter (secretary to the board)
Hill, Frank (personnel mgr)

Prison Link Team
fax 028-9026 2472
Lappin, Ms Jane (p, spo mgr)
Eyers, Mrs Monica
McSherry, Ms Martina

Assessment Unit
fax 028-9026 2472
Hunter, Ms Christine (p, spo mgr)
O'Neill, Mrs Jean (p, spo mgr)
Arthur, Mrs Liz
Ball, Mrs Rosemary (p)
Barry, Ms Patricia
Brannigan, Miss Mary
Doherty, Ms Mary (p)
Ferguson, Philip
Gaughran, Miss Orlaith
Hopkins, Mrs Shirley (p)
Horgan, Brenda
McRoberts, Mrs Claire (p)
Matthews, Jim
O'Neill, Mrs Noreen
O'Neill, Mrs Oonagh (p)
Parry, John
Peden, Dave
Richardson, Mrs Eileen
Thompson, Paul
Willighan, Stephen
Winnington, Michael
Wylie, David

Training Unit
fax 028-9026 2450
Best, Mrs Pat (spo mgr)

2. **330 Ormeau Road**
Belfast BT7 2GE
Belfast 028-9064 7156
fax 028-9064 1409

McAllister, Mrs Eileen (spo mgr) (9)
Clarke, Roddy
Gillespie, Mrs Barbara
McNally, Ms Carol
Mairs, Ms Julie
Quigley, John
McMillan, Miss Evelyn (psa)

3. 71/73 Bachelor'sWalk
Lisburn BT28 1XN
Lisburn 028-9267 4211
fax 028-9260 4018

Magee, Jack

4. **Youth Justice Unit**
51 Camden Street
Belfast BT9 6AT
Belfast 028-9031 3162
fax 028-9023 5297

Davies, Chris (spo, mgr)
McLaughlin, Mrs Aideen
Moore, Ms Jane
Tracey, Damien
McClenaghan, Joseph (probn community officer)
Martin, Ms Jane (probn community officer)

5. **306 Antrim Road**
Belfast BT15 5AB
Belfast 028-9075 7631
fax 028-9074 3983

Thompson, Mrs Judith (spo mgr)
Cunningham, Miss Carmel
Hughes, Ms Gillian

McClinton, Ms Janet (p)
Pentland, Jim
Roberson, Mrs Brigid
Warren, John
Woods, Ms Geraldine (p)
Potts, Gordon (psa)

6. **93-107 Shankill Road**
Belfast BT13 1FD
Belfast 028-9032 1141
fax 028-9031 3334

Adair, Mrs Yvonne (p, spo mgr)
Cairns, Mrs Kathy (p)
Cummings, Kyle
McCourt, Miss Eileen
McCusker, Paul
Hamill, Mrs Sheila (psa)

7. Glenshane House
202a Andersonstown Road
Belfast BT11 9EB
Belfast 028-9060 2988
fax 028-9061 9313

McKenna, Ms Gloria
Wray, Mrs Harriet (psa)

8. **270-272 Falls Road**
Belfast BT12 6AL
Belfast 028-9023 1763
fax 028-9032 6280

Bourke, John (spo mgr) (3, 7)
Bell, Mrs Lesley (p)
McGlade, Ian
Smith, Ms Helen
Quail, Ms Moira (psa)

9. **297 Newtownards Road**
Belfast BT4 1AG
Belfast 028-9073 9445
fax 028-9046 0119

Dougan, Mrs Carol
McCaughey, Mrs Mary
Best, Colin (psa)

10. 15 Castle Street
Newtownards BT23 3PA
Newtownards 028-9181 7778
fax 028-9181 8905

Darnbrook, Alan (spo mgr) (11)
Cumming, Miss Mary
McAnallen, Martin
Moore, Mrs Donna

11. 2 Church Street
Downpatrick BT30 6EJ
Downpatrick 028-4461 4061
fax 028-4461 2506

Shaw, Stephen

12. 12 Lodge Road
Coleraine BT52 1NB
Coleraine 028-7035 3141 & 7034 3632
fax 028-7035 2442

Kelly, Graham (acpo)
Archibald, Selina
McLister, Mrs Cherry
McQuillan, Mrs Esther (p)
Mullineux, Ms Judith
Pegg, Ms Jackie
Ralph, Chris
Wetherall, Miss Kathleen
McBride, Bernadette (psa)

13. The Bridge House
106 Bridge Street
Ballymena BT43 5EP
Ballymena 028-2565 2549
fax 028-2565 5523

Shiels, Mrs Marlene (spo mgr) (12)
Dempsey, Colin
Dyer, Paddy
Higgins, Ms Caitriona
McCleary, Alan
Nicholson, Mark
MacQuarrie, Andrew (probn community officer)

14. 8 Crawford Square
Londonderry BT48 7HR
Londonderry 028-7126 4774
fax 028-7126 7374

O'Kane, John (spo mgr)
Canning, Mrs Donna
Clifford, Miss Briege
Friel, Ms Breda
Kerrigan, Eileen
McConomy, Martin
Moyne, Terry
Quinn, Peter
Wiseman, Paul

15. 7 Limavady Road
Londonderry BT47 1JU
Londonderry 028-7134 6701
fax 028-7134 1034

Doherty, Terry (spo mgr)
Barr, Mrs Nicola

Cunningham, Mrs Bernie
McEntee, Sean
Nagle, Miss Susan
Quigley, Michael
Tally, Ms Martina
Ferguson Liam (psa)
Fletcher, Mrs Heather (psa)

16. 38 Fountain Street
Antrim BT41 4BB
Antrim 028-9442 8475 & 9446 3519
fax 028-9446 9123

Connolly, Mike (spo mgr) (17, 18, 19)
Brannigan, Miss Oonagh
Graham, Ms Joan
Mawhinney, Miss Anne
Smyth, Ms Julie
Maitland, Michael (psa)

17. Tower House
33-35 High Street
Carrickfergus BT38 7AN
Carrickfergus 028-9336 2088
fax 028-9336 3049

Oliver, Mervyn
O'Neill, Ms Denise (probn community officer)

18. 41 Point Street
Larne BT40 1HU
Larne 028-2827 9231
fax 028-2827 5990

McMillan, Mrs Pauline

19. 123 Doagh Road
Newtownabbey BT36 6AA
Newtownabbey 028-9085 4123
fax 028-9086 4158

Copeland, Ms Jane
McKee, Ms Mary

20. 9 Downshire Place
Newry BT34 1DZ
Newry 028-3026 3955
fax 028-3026 9548

McLean, Mrs Sile (spo mgr) (21, 26)
Doran, Mary (p)
Lamb, Mrs Linda

21. McGredy Buildings
31-33 High Street
Portadown BT62 1HY
Portadown 028-3833 3301
fax 028-3839 4334

Bartlett, Ms Patricia
Sands, Ms Caroline
Weir, Stephanie
Kennedy, Stuart (probn community officer)

22. 11A High Street
Omagh BT78 1BA
Omagh 028-8224 6051
fax 028-8224 8437

Rodgers, Brian (spo mgr) (23-25)
Blaney, Jim
Carty, Selina
Montgomery, Harry
Murphy, John (probn community officer)
McCrory, Thomas (psa)

23. 14 Dublin Road
Cathcart Square
Enniskillen BT74 6HM
Enniskillen 028-6632 4383
fax 028-6632 5988

Mohan, Ms Patricia
Ingram, Jim

24. 58 Loy Street
Cookstown BT80 8PE
Cookstown 028-8676 1211
fax 028-8676 6276

McClintock, Miss Liz

25. 30 Northland Row
Dungannon BT71 6AP
Dungannon 028-8772 2866
fax 028-8775 2318

Devlin, Paul
Calvin, Mrs Marilyn

26. 25 College Street
Armagh BT61 9BT
Armagh 028-3752 5243
fax 028-3752 8530

Murphy, Ms Margaret
McLaughlin, Terry
McCann, Kevin (psa)

27. **40-44 Great Patrick Street**
Belfast BT1 2LT
Belfast 028-9033 3332/9043 8990
fax 028-9023 5295

Programme Delivery unit
Moore, Jimmy (spo mgr)
Boyle, Tom
Burns, Michael

Guthrie, Alan
Malone, Mrs Caitriona (p)
Rainey, Mrs Lindsay (p)
Wylie, Mrs Margaret
Young, Mike
Beattie, Graham (probn community officer)
McVeigh, Ms Josie (probn community officer)

28. **Alderwood House (Integrated Supervision Unit)**
Hydebank Wood
Purdysburn Road
Belfast BT8 4SL
Belfast 028-9064 4953
fax 028-9064 1435

Bailie, Mrs Rosemary (spo mgr)
Owens, Mrs Val (spo mgr)
McGibbon, Gareth
Maguire, Mrs Catherine
Robinson, Ms Lorraine (p)

29. **Ramoan Centre**
The Old Rectory, 11 Novally Road
Ballycastle, Co Antrim BT54 6HB
Ballycastle 028-2076 2835
fax 028-2076 9698

Rodgers, Mrs Brigie (project mgr)
Black, Austin (project worker)
McWilliams, Ms Jacqueline (project worker)
Stirling, David (project worker)
Wilson, Mrs Dorothy (project worker)
Jennings, Michael (project asst)
Walsh, Seamus (project asst)

Institutions

30. H M Prison Welfare Unit
Magilligan
Co Londonderry BT49 0LR
Ballarena 028-7775 0434/5
fax 028-7775 0312

Davies, Shawn (spo mgr)
Christie, Ms Patricia (p)
Hill, Kieran
Lees, Ray
O'Donnell, Noel
McWilliams, Ms Gil

31. H M Young Offenders Centre
Hydebank Wood
Hospital Road, Belfast BT8 8NA
Belfast 028-9049 1015
fax 028-9064 2868

Muldoon, Ms Roisin (spo mgr)
Conlon, John
Ritchie, Jim

32. HM Prison Welfare Unit
Maghaberry
Old Road, Upper Ballinderry
Lisburn BT28 2PT
Lisburn 028-9261 2665
fax 028-9261 9976

O'Hare, Rita (spo mgr)
Cubillo, Bill
Knight, Ms Roisin
McCarthy, Vincent
Patterson, David
Pickering, Mrs Mavis
Reid, Maurice
Robinson-McDonald, Mrs Rosaleen
Sheppard, Paul
Taylor, Mrs Siobhan (p)

On Secondment

Chapman, Mrs Alice (spo mgr)
O'Rourke, Mrs Marion
Breen, Ms Siobhan

On career break

Dillon, Marita
Heery, Gerry
Martin, Ms Eileen
Murphy, Deirdre
Peel, Elaine
Stout, Brian

Area Code 99

CHANNEL ISLANDS, ISLE OF MAN, IRISH REPUBLIC, AND BRITISH FORCES GERMANY

The Channel Islands and the Isle of Man are separate jurisdictions. Community Orders are not formally transferable to or from them. Special procedures exist for the transfer of post custodial Licences. Contact should be made with the relevant Service before any offender moves to the Channel Islands or the Isle of Man.

Area Code 93

GUERNSEY PROBATION SERVICE

Cambria House, New Street
St Peter Port
Guernsey GY1 2PQ
Guernsey (01481) 724337
fax (01481) 710545
e mail probation@gov.gg

Workman, Mrs Barbara (cpo)
Guilbert, Anna (spo)
Crisp, Stuart
Harvey, Greg
Ozanne, Carol
Sisson, Shiralee

ISLE OF MAN PROBATION SERVICE

Government Buildings
Lord Street, Douglas
Isle of Man IM1 1LE
Douglas (01624) 686579/686578
fax (01624) 686569

Sellick David B L (cpo)
Rafferty, Jim (spo)
Cubbon, Dawn (info officer)
Butler, J F G (Claude) (crt welfare)
Bass, John
Dunne, Margaret
Grahame, Pat
Steeples, Mary
Tully, Mick
Walker, Jeff
Wood, Mrs Barbara (psa)

JERSEY PROBATION SERVICE

P O Box 656,13/15 Don Street
St Helier JE4 8YT
Jersey (01534) 733261
fax (01534) 758796
e mail jsy-prob@itl.net
www.gov.je

Heath, Brian (cpo)
e mail b.heath@jersey.gov.je
Cutland, Michael (acpo)
Cooley, Mrs Jenny (office mgr)
Miles, Helen (p, research & info mgr)
e mail h.miles@jersey.gov.je

Jordan, Barry (snr pract)
Ormesher, Adelaide (snr pract)
Trott, David (snr pract)
Bennett, Rachel (crt liaison off - subst misuse)
Brown, Susan
Carré, Marilyn
Lister, Lisa (p)
Pike, Chay
Roche, Kate
Szpera, Deirdre (p)
Tobler, Joanna
Christmas, Jane (p, psa)
da Silva, Sergio (p, psa)
Morgan, Joy (p, psa)
Price, Mel (cs mgr)
Allix, Nicky (p, asst cso)
Banks, Shaun (p, asst cso)
Cauvain, Jerry (p, cs supvr)
Griffin, Sean (p, cs supvr)
Perry, Michael (p, cs supvr)
Thompson, Mark (p, cs supvr)
Houiellebecq, Kevin (trainee)
Le Brocq, Charlotta (trainee)

IRISH REPUBLIC

Probation and Welfare Service
Smithfield Chambers
Smithfield, Dublin 7
Dublin 00 3531 8173600
fax 00 3531 8722737

Tansey, M N (chief probation and welfare officer)

BRITISH FORCES GERMANY PROBATION SERVICE

G1 Division
First Floor, Block 8,
Catterick Barracks
BFPO 39

The unit is based in Bielefeld, Germany
Direct dial from UK 0049 521 9254 3120
fax 0049 521 9254 3221

Smart, George (spo, head of bfg service)
Willis, Sheila

Area of Responsibility
British Forces Germany
British Forces Low Countries
Includes Army, RAF and civilian employees and dependants

YOUTH JUSTICE BOARD FOR ENGLAND & WALES

Youth Justice Board for England & Wales
11 Carteret Street
London SW1H 9DL
020-7271 3033
direct dial 020-7271 + ext
fax 020-7271-3030
e mail enquiries@yjb.gsi.gov.uk
individual e-mail usually
forename.surname@yjb.gsi.gov.uk
www.youth-justice-board.gov.uk

Chair
Norman Warner 3057
Zoe Williams (pa) 3056

Chief Executive
Mark Perfect 3067
Pamela Benjamin (pa) 3066
Marie Davies (general enquiries) 3033

Communications
Rachel Pitkeathley 3075
Alison Morgan (communications mgr) 3076
Susie Brown (press asst) 3014

Managing Director for Community Interventions
Roger King 3061
Tonya Rogers (pa) 3063

YOTs Youth Justice Plans, etc
Adrian Bell 3027
Patrick Benjamin (yots) 3023
Louise Atkin 01746 764080
Kevin White 3022
Kirsten Grace (yot database) 3084
Vacancy (office mgr) 3157
Sue McGinley 3026
Graeme Quinn-Smith 3136

Attendance Centres
Cecilia Claxton-Phillip 3043
Dick Dungay 3041
Christina Houlihan 3044
Vince Sailsman 3042

Development Fund
Louise Bennett 3016
Penny Wilcock (prevention grants) 3010
Joanna Carpenter (youth inclusion) 3012
Alan Jones (positive futures) 3095
Matthew Anderson 3010
Thomas Burnham 3058
Helen Powell (research) 3011
Bhavna Patel (support) 3013
Tim Geldard (support) 3017

Finance
Allan Hutton 3036
Rob Burnand (accounts) 3051
Masood Beg 3037
Ronel Cronjé 3038
Kaushika Vaghela 3035
Ian Spicer 3019
Will Banks 3018
John Belza (procurement) 3039
Eileen Henneberry (info systems) 3069
David Ejoh 3110

Youth Inclusion
Matt Howell 3138
Clive Mitten 3139
Maree Tunny 3147
Lucy Carter
Kate Puntis
Sara Holden
Bernard Rix

Secretariat
Andrew Brown 3031
Lesley Smart (personnel) 3032
Duncan Mitchell 3034
Ellie Greenwood 3077
David Oastler (corporate policy) 3135
Keith Fraser (it/facilities) 3047
Facilities Helpdesk 3048
Michael Hitchin 3046
Lizzie Hayward 3048

Youth Justice System, Tackling Delays, Assessment
Ruth Allan 3112
Alison Holden (tackling delays) 3111
James Banjoko 3054
Fiona Miles (secretary) 3059

Inspections, Restorative Justice
Judy Renshaw 3081
Lionel Smith 3082
Fiona Miles (secretary) 3059

Managing Director Secure Facilities
Jan Dalrymple 3127
Majella Charles (secretary) 3126

Secure Facilities: Policy
Robert Newman 3123
Peter Dunn (standards) 3124
Amanda Pennell (policy devpt) 3134
Desmond French 3122

Secure Facilities: Contracting, Performance Management
Nick Fry (prisons) 3109
Larry Stockton 3148
Louise Gilchrist 3141
Marcia O'Garro (LASUs) 3108

Secure Facilities: Market, Strategic Development

Fiona McGlone	3101
Temp Secretary	3097
Peter Mant	3133
Martin Murphy	3131
Neeraj Kaushal	3142

Secure Facilities: Placements

Call Centre	**020-7271 3121**
fax	*020-7271 3080*
pager	**07623 523523 ref 883 179**

Jon Fayle	3128
Patsy Wood	3132
Peter Minchin	3104
Liz Pannell	3140
Samantha Ankrah	
Evros Agathou	3118
Johanna Anderson	3114
Nick Ford	3116
Samuel King	3113
Katherine Simmons	3115
Simon Surtees-Goodall	3117
Nicola Crooks-Ramgeet	3096
Support	3130
Natalie Closs (support)	3053
Louise Cooper (support)	3096
Raymond Garbah (support)	

YOUTH OFFENDING TEAMS

East

1. **Bedfordshire**
   Bedfordshire County Council
   County Hall
   Cauldwell Street
   Bedford MK42 9AP
   01234 363222 ext 2017
   fax 01234 228137
   mercera@sccd.bedfordshire.gov.uk

   Andrew Mercer

2. **Cambridgeshire**
   74 Burleigh Street
   Cambridge
   Cambridgeshire CB1 1DJ
   01223 718223
   fax 01223 718212
   mike.davey@ceu.camcnty.gov.uk

   Mike Davey

3. **Essex**
   Suite 2, Empire House
   Victoria Road
   Chelmsford CM1 1PE
   01245 265151
   fax 01245 346396
   tanya.gillett@essexcc.gov.uk

   Tanya Gillett

4. **Hertfordshire**
   County Hall
   Pegs Lane
   Hertford SG13 8DP
   01992 556337
   fax 01992 556323
   tom.rees@hertscc.gov.uk

   Tom Rees

5. **Luton Borough Council**
   16 Rothersay Road
   Luton
   Bedfordshire LU1 1QX
   01582 547900
   fax 01582 547901
   thomasm@luton.gov.uk

   Mike Thomas

6. **Norfolk County Council**
   45 Netherwood Green
   Norwich
   Norfolk NR1 2JF
   01603 223615
   fax 01603 223590
   sue.Massey.yot@norfolk.gov.uk

   Sue Massey

7. **Peterborough**
   Community Services
   Bayard Place
   Broadway, Peterborough PE1 1HZ
   01733 742506
   fax 01733 742601
   aac378@peterborough.gov.uk

   Robert Footer

8. **Southend on Sea**
   Floor 7, West Wing
   Baryta House, 29 Victoria Avenue
   Southend on Sea SS2 6AZ
   01702 608500
   fax 01702 335788
   garyskull@southend.gov.uk

   Phillip Robertson

9. **Suffolk County Council**
   Alexandra House
   Rope Walk, Ipswich IP4 1LR

01473 583389
fax 01473 583473
john.gregg@socserv.suffolk.cc.gov.uk

John Gregg

10. **Thurrock Council**
Five Wells, West Street
Grays, Essex RM17 6XR
01375 413900
fax 01375 393376
pkay@thurrock.gov.uk

Peter Kay

East Midlands

11. **Derby City Council**
55 Ashbourne Road
Derby DE22 3FS
01332 717525
fax 01332 369297
sharon.squires@derby.gov.uk

Sharon Squires

12. **Derbyshire**
County Hall
Matlock
Derbyshire DE4 3AG
01629 772164
fax 01629 772009
simon.westwood@derbyshire.gov.uk

Ian Johnson

13. **Leicester City Council**
Eagle House, 11 Friar Lane
Leicester LE1 5RB
0116 299 5830/43
fax 0116 233 6003
sandm001@leicester.gov.uk

Mary Campagnac

14. **Leicestershire County Council**
Floor 3, County Hall
Glenfield LE3 8RL
0116 265 6780
fax 0116 265 6880
phawkins@leics.gov.uk

Philip Hawkins

15. **Lincolnshire**
Development House
64 Newland
Lincoln LN1 1YA
01522 554554
fax 01522 554558
simkjj@lincolnshire.gov.uk

John Simkins

16. **Northamptonshire County Council**
198 Kettering Road
Northampton NN1 4BL
01604 601241
fax 01604 601648

Sandy Pragnell

17. **Nottingham City**
2 Isabella Street
Nottingham NG1 6AT
0115 841 3092
fax 0115 841 3009
Chris.wright@nottinghamcity.gov.uk

Chris Wright

18. **Nottinghamshire County Council**
15 West Hill Avenue
Mansfield NG18 1PQ
01623 476611
fax 01623 476602
phillip.arnold@nottscc.gov.uk

Philip Arnold

London

19. **London Borough of Barking & Dagenham**
5a Parsloes Avenue
Dagenham
Essex RM9 5PA
020 8270 6462
fax 020 8270 6461
fdeadman@barking-dagenham.gov.uk

Fay Deadman

20. **London Borough of Barnet**
Churchfield House
45-51 Woodhouse Road
North Finchley, London N12 9ET
020 8446 9996
fax 020 8446 9998

Kate Malleson

21. **London Borough of Bexley**
2 Nuxley Road
Belvedere
Kent DA17 5JF
020 8284 5555
fax 020 8284 5560

Roger Meredith

22. **London Borough of Brent**
1 Craven Park
Harlesden, London NW10 8SX
020 8965 6020
fax 020 8961 5181
peter.sutlieff@brent.gov.uk

Peter Sutlieff

23. **London Borough of Bromley**
B28 St Blaise
Bromley Civic Centre
Stockwell Close, Bromley BR1 3UH
020 8313 4318
fax 020 8313 4331
alan.doherty@bromley.gov.uk

Alan Doherty

24. **London Borough of Camden**
Social Services
115 Wellesley Road
London NW5 4PA
020 7974 6762
fax 020 7974 1196
peggy.schaffter@camden.gov.uk

Peggy Schaffter

25. **London Borough of Croydon**
14 Whitehorse Road
Croydon, Surrey CR0 2JA
020 8665 5588
fax 020 8665 7010
ray_maguire@croydon.gov.uk

Ray Maguire

26. **London Borough of Ealing**
2b Cheltenham Place
Acton, London W3 8JS
020 8993 9555
fax 020 8993 6292

Ed Shaylor

27. **London Borough of Enfield**
St George's Chambers
23 South Mall, Floor 2
Edmonton
London N9 0TS
020 8345 5557
fax 020 8345 6954

Keith Napthine

28. **London Borough of Greenwich**
The Well Hall Project
Tudor Parade
Well Hall Road
London SE9 6SU
020 8859 4492
fax 020 8859 2706
ray.seabrook@greenwich.gov.uk

Ray Seabrook

29. **London Borough of Hackney**
Hackney YOT
55 Daubeney Road
London E5 0EE
020 8533 7070
fax 020 8986 7446
nbidmade@gw.hackney.gov.uk

Nick Bidmade

30. **London Borough of Hammersmith & Fulham**
145 Hammersmith Road
London W14 0QZ
020 7371 4880
fax 020 7371 4412
youth.offendingteam@lbhf.gov.uk

Larry Wright

31. **London Borough of Haringey**
2-6 Middle Lane
Hornsey, London N8 8PL
020 8489 1146
fax 020 8489 1588
jean.croot@haringey.gov.uk

Jean Croot

32. **London Borough of Harrow**
Social Services Department
PO Box 7, Civic Centre
Harrow HA1 2UL
020 8420 9680
fax 020 8863 0236
richard.segalov@harrow.gov.uk

Richard Segalov

33. **London Borough of Havering**
Portman House
16-20 Victoria Road
Romford, Essex RM1 2JH
01708 436220
fax 01708 436222
dstonehouse.ss@havering.gov.uk

David Stonehouse

34. **London Borough of Hillingdon**
Darren House
65 High Street
Uxbridge, Middx UB8 1JP
01895 812279
fax 01895 812281

Lynn Hawes

35. **London Borough of Hounslow**
Chief Executive's Directorate
Civic Centre
Lampton Road
Hounslow, Middx TW3 4DN
020 8583 2472
fax 020 8583 2466

Christine Pangbourne

36. **London Borough of Islington**
27 Dingley Place
Islington
London EC1V 8BR
020 7527 7050/60
fax 020 7527 7066
sally.gran@islington.gov.uk

Sally Gran

37. **Royal London Borough of Kensington & Chelsea**
36 Oxford Gardens
London W10 5UQ
020 7598 4714
fax 020 7598 4715
socbok@rbkc.gov.uk

Brendan O'Keefe

38. **Royal London Borough of Kingston**
Four Oaks Centre
105a Mount Road
Chessington, Surrey KT9 1JH
020 8397 0156
fax 020 8397 4127

Paul Donaghy

39. **London Borough of Lambeth**
Lambeth YOT
1-9 Acre Lane
Brixton, London SW2 5SD
020 7926 2644
fax 020 7926 2639
LAllman@lambeth.gov.uk

Lambert Allman

40. **London Borough of Lewisham**
1-3 Ashby Road
Brockley, London SE4 1PR
020 8314 9569
fax 020 8691 6383
brendan.finegan@lewisham.gov.uk

Brendan Finegan

41. **London Borough of Merton**
226 London Road
Mitcham, Surrey CR4 3HD
020 8640 8535
fax 020 8646 7226
geofflowry@hotmail.com

Geoff Lowry

42. **London Borough of Newham**
Stratford Police Station
18 West Ham Lane
Stratford, London E15 4SG
07932 050491
fax 020 8217 5490
peter.nicholson@newham.gov.uk

Peter Nicholson

43. **London Borough of Redbridge**
Adolescent Resource Centre
Station Road
Barkingside, Essex IG6 1NB
020 8708 7497
fax 020 8708 7495
kathy.nixon@redbridge.gov.uk

Kathy Nixon

44. **London Borough of Richmond-upon-Thames**
Services for Children & Families
42 York Street
Twickenham, Middx TW1 3BW
020 8891 1411
fax 020 8891 7962
p.battista@richmond.gov.uk

Pietro Battista

45. **London Borough of Southwark**
90 Blakes Road
Peckham, London SE15 6EP
020 7525 7873
fax 020 7525 7876
yvonne.davies@southwark.gov.uk

Chris Domeney

46. **London Borough of Sutton**
Adolescent Resource Centre
717 London Road
North Cheam, Surrey SM3 7DL
020 8337 0095
fax 020 8335 3033

Sandra McGinley

47. **London Borough of Tower Hamlets & City of London**
St Mary's Church Hall
Kitcat Terrace, Bow, London E3 2SA
020 7364 1144
fax 020 8983 9911
stuartj@dial.pipex.com

Stuart Johnson

48. **London Borough of Waltham Forest**
604 High Road
Leyton E10 6RN
020 8496 2151
fax 020 8496 2123
mark.boother@soc.lbwf.gov.uk

Mark Boother

49. **London Borough of Wandsworth**
177 Blackshaw Road
London SW17 0DJ
020 8672 7074/1664
fax 020 8682 4255
sdunkling@wandsworth.gov.uk

Sean Dunkling

50. **City of Westminster**
6a Crompton Street
London W2 1ND
020 7641 7799
fax 020 7641 5311
ebrennan@westminster.gov.uk

Eamon Brennan

North East

51. **Darlington Borough Council**
Central House
Gladstone Street
Darlington DL3 6JX
01325 346226
fax 01325 346846
terry.sharkey@darlington.gov.uk

Terry Sharkey

52. **Durham County**
County Hall
Durham DH1 5UG
0191 383 3982
fax 0191 383 4362
christina.blythe@durham.gov.uk

Christina Blythe

53. **Gateshead**
Former Felling Police Station
Sunderland Road
Gateshead
Tyne & Wear NE10 9NJ
0191 440 0500
fax 0191 440 0501
B.Langley@SocialServices.Gatesheadmbc.gov.uk

Brian Langley

54. **Hartlepool**
Aneurin Bevan House
35 Avenue Road
Hartlepool TS24 8HD
01429 523962
fax 01429 523971

Bridget Gardner

55. **Newcastle upon Tyne**
1 St James' Terrace
Newcastle upon Tyne NE1 4NE
0191 261 7583
fax 0191 261 7591
StapleyRod@Newcastle.gov.uk

Rod Stapley

56. **North Tyneside**
Youth Court Services Team
153 Tynemouth Road
North Shields
Tyne & Wear NE30 1ED
0191 200 5897/6001
fax 0191 200 6009
jen.harrison@northtyneside.gov.uk

Jen Harrison

57. **Northumberland**
Social Services Department
Civic Precinct
Forum Way, Cramlington
Northumberland NE23 6SJ
01670 712925
fax 01670 738685
CLong@northumberland.gov.uk

Carol Long

58. **South Tees**
14 Farndale Road
Middlesebrough TS4 2PL
01642 501500
fax 01642 501800
colin wilson@middlesrough.gov.uk

Colin Wilson

59. **South Tyneside**
30 Commercial Road
South Shields
Tyne & Wear NE33 1RW

0191 427 2850
fax 0191 427 2851
sarah.thompson@s-tyneside-mbc.gov.uk

Phil Bennett

60. **Stockton on Tees**
52-54 Hartington Road
Stockton on Tees TS18 1HE
01642 393399/0
fax 01642 393380
tony.hodgson@stockton-bc.gov.uk

Tony Hodgson

61. **Sunderland**
Sunderland Youth Offending Service
11 John Street, Sunderland SR1 1HT
0191 553 7370
fax 0191 553 7381
Susan.Smith@ssd.sunderland.gov.uk

Helen Watson

North West

62. **Blackburn with Darwen**
Bank House
44 Wellington Street
St John's, Blackburn
Lancashire BB1 8AF
01254 299 800
fax 01254 299 801
Bryan.peake@blackburn.gov.uk

Bryan Peake

63. **Blackpool Borough Council**
The Devonshire Centre
307-309 Church Street
Blackpool FY1 3PF
01253 392323
fax 01253 302060
Steve.cook@blackpool.gov.uk

Steve Cook

64. **Bolton**
Bolton Youth Offending Team
Le Mans Crescent
Bolton BL1 1SA
01204 331 263
fax 01204 331258
Steve.agger@bolton.gov.uk

Stephen Agger

65. **Bury**
Seedfield Resource Centre
Parkinson Street
Bury BL9 6NY
0161 253 6862
fax 0161 253 6944
G.M.Smyth@Bury.gov.uk

Graham Smyth

66. **Cheshire**
St Thomas House
Whitby Road
Ellesmere Port
Cheshire CH65 6TU
01244 615500
fax 01244 615501
sheperda@cheshire.gov.uk

Aileen Shepherd

67. **Cumbria**
5 Brunswick Street
Carlisle
Cumbria CA1 1PB
01228 607380
fax 01228 607094

Yvonne Lake

68. **Halton/Warrington**
Warrington Police Station
Arpley Street
Warrington WA1 1LQ
01925 445006
fax 01925 411656

Rhona Bradley

69. **Knowsley Borough Council**
10 Derby Street
Prescot, Knowsley
Merseyside L34 3LG
0151 443 3872
fax 0151 443 3770
richard.ford.ce@knowsley.gov.uk

Richard Ford

70. **Lancashire County Council**
Social Services Directorate
PO Box 162, East Cliff County Offices
Preston PR1 3EA
01772 261305
fax 01772 262078
anne.brazier@socserv.lancscc.gov.uk

Anne Brazier

71. **Liverpool City Council**
Liverpool Social Services
26 Hatton Garden
Liverpool L3 2AW
0151 225 3924
fax 0151 225 3749
c/o chris.higgs@liverpool.gov.uk

Sue Cook

72. **Manchester City Council**
Grey Mare Lane Police Station
Bell Crescent, Beswick
Manchester M11 3BA
0161 856 3604
fax 0161 856 3605
Phil-lloyd@notes.manchester.gov.uk

Phil Lloyd

73. **Oldham**
Marion Walker House
Frederick Street
Oldham OL8 1SW
0161 620 7546
fax 0161 633 0415

Allan Broadbent

74. **Rochdale**
Dunsterville House
Manchester Road
Rochdale OL11 3RB
01706 643327
fax 01706 758909
yot@rochdale.gov.uk

Rodger Massiah

75. **Salford City Council**
10-12 Encombe Place
Salford, Manchester M3 6FJ
0161 832 5382
fax 0161 832 4306
Tom.McDonald@salford.gov.uk

Tom McDonald

76. **Sefton MBC**
Police Station
Marsh Lane
Bootle, Merseyside L20 5HJ
0151 777 3902
fax 0151 934 2779

Steve Eyre

77. **St Helens Youth Offending Team**
5a Bickerstaffe Street
St Helens, Merseyside WA10 1DH
01744 25171
fax 01744 731541
BobSmith@StHelens.gov.uk

Robert Smith

78. **Stockport MBC**
Chief Executive's Division
Room 125, Town Hall
Stockport SK1 3XE
0161 474 3033
fax 0161 474 3009
steve.brown@STOCKPORT.GOV.UK

Steve Brown

79. **Tameside**
The Old Court Building
Jowetts Walk
William Street
Aston-under-Lyne OL7 0BG
0161 330 3012
fax 0161 330 3149
tina.wills@nxcorp1.tameside.gov.uk

John Whittle

80. **Trafford**
13 Washway Road
Sale M33 7AD
0161 912 3421
fax 0161 912 3429
trafordyot@lineone.net

Helen McFarlane

81. **Wigan Metropolitan Borough Council**
28-29 Bridgeman Terrace
Wigan WN1 1TD
01942 239993
fax 01942 867422

Sharon Bond

82. **Wirral Social Services**
Social Services HQ
63 Hamilton Square
Birkenhead, Wirral CH41 5JF
0151 666 3629
fax 0151 666 3603

Bindy Shah

South East

83. **Bracknell Forest**
76 Binfield Road
Bracknell
Berkshire RG42 2AR
01344 354300
fax 01344 354310
lindsey.bass@bracknell-forest.gov.uk

Lindsey Bass

84. **Brighton & Hove**
Brighton & Hove Youth Offending Team
22 Ship Street
Brighton
East Sussex BN1 1AD
01273 296156
fax 01273 296170
colin.tucker@brighton-hove.gov.uk

Colin Tucker

85. **Buckinghamshire**
Youth Offending Team
Walton House
Walton Street
Aylesbury
Buckinghamshire HP21 7QQ
01296 434624
fax 01296 486321
pcamilleri@buckscc.gov.uk

Pauline Camilleri

86. **East Sussex**
Ridgewood Rise Centre
Highview Lane
Uckfield
East Sussex TN22 5SY
01825 768297
fax 01825 764496
john.hawkins@eastsussexcc.gov.uk

John Hawkins

87. **Kent County Council**
Sessions House
County Hall
Maidstone ME14 1XQ
01622 694773
fax 01622 694909
kumar.mehta@kent.gov.uk

Kumar Mehta

88. **Medway**
The Family & Adolescent Centre
67 Balfour Road
Chatham, Kent ME4 6QU
01634 818753
fax 01634 849660
ian.sparling@medway.gov.uk

Ian Sparling

89. **Milton Keynes**
Manor Road Centre
Oakwood Drive
Bletchley
Milton Keynes MK2 2JG
01908 391000
fax 01908 391031
lee.westlake@milton-keynes.gov.uk

Lee Westlake

90. **Oxfordshire County Council**
1 Tower Crescent
Oxford OX1 1LX
01865 815057
fax 01865 246614
maggie.blyth@oxfordshire.gov.uk

Maggie Blyth

91. **Reading & Wokingham Borough Council**
34-36 Crown Street
Reading RG1 2SE
0118 939 0298
fax 0118 939 0935
Phil.Hutchins@reading.gov.uk

Philip Hutchins

92. **Slough Borough Council**
2a Mildenhall Road
Slough SL1 3JE
01753 522702
fax 01753 572355

Rose Burgess

93. **Surrey County Council**
Churchill House, Mayford Green
Woking, Surrey GU22 0PW
01483 723922
fax 01483 771786

Toby Wells

94. **Wessex Youth Offending Team HQ**
85 The High Street
Winchester SO23 9BL
01962 876100
fax 01962 876109
sshgyjps@hantsnet.hants.gov.uk

Philip Sutton

95. **IOW Youth Offending Team**
62 Crocker Street
Newport, IOW PO30 5BA
01983 522799
fax 01983 523175

Margaret Abbot

96. **NE and NW Hants**
180 Culver Road
Basingstoke, Hants RG21 3NK
01256 464034
fax 01256 327210

Ian Langley

97. **Portsmouth & SE Hants**
Darby House
Orkney Road, Cosham
Portsmouth PO6 3LU
02392 370013
fax 02392 200374

Mark Owen

98. **Southampton & SW Hants**
33 Selborne Avenue
Harefield
Southampton SO18 5DZ
02380 463336
fax 02380 470060

Sue Morse

99. **West Berkshire Council**
c/o Newbury Police Station
Mill Lane, Newbury RG14 5QU
01635 264753
fax 01635 264759
adpearson@westberks.gov.uk

Davy Pearson

100. **West Sussex Youth Offending Team**
County Buildings
East Street
Littlehampton
West Sussex BN17 6AP
01903 718739
fax 01903 718740
terry.bishop@westsussex.gov.uk

Terry Bishop

101. **Royal Borough of Windsor & Maidenhead**
Maidenhead Project Centre
Reform Road
Maidenhead
Berkshire SL6 8BY
01628 683295
fax 01628 778976
pete.dennis@rbwm.gov.uk

Pete Dennis

South West

102. **Bath NE Somerset**
Youth Offending Team
180 Frome Road
Combe Down
Bath BA2 5RF
01225 396966
fax 01225 396969
Sally_churchyard@bathnes.gov.uk

Sally Churchyard

103. **Bournemouth and Poole**
9 Madeira Road
Bournemouth
Dorset BH1 1QN
01202 458018
fax 01202 458129
pauline.batstone@bournemouth.gov.uk

Pauline Batstone

104. **Bristol**
Kenham House
Wilder Street
Bristol BS2 8PD
0117 903 6480
fax 0117 903 6481
paul_burton@bristol-city.gov.uk

Paul Burton

105. **Cornwall**
Chiltern House
City Road
Truro
Cornwall TR1 2JL
01872 274567
fax 01872 242436
youthoffending@ceo.cornwall.gov.uk

Tom Whitworth

106. **Devon**
Ivybank, 45 St David's Hill
Exeter EX4 4DN
01392 384963
fax 01392 384985
MSPRAGG@devon-cc.gov.uk

Martin Spragg

107. **Dorset County Council**
Youth Justice Centre
Southwinds
11 Cranford Avenue
Weymouth
Dorset DT4 7TL
01305 760336
fax 01305 761423
c.r.hawkins@dorset-cc.gov.uk

Clive Hawkins

108. **Gloucestershire**
40 Brunswick Road
Gloucester
Gloucestershire GL1 1HG
01452 547540
fax 01452 551114
Yot@gloscc.gov.uk

Phil Kendrick

109. **North Somerset**
c/o The Police Station
Walliscote Road
Weston Super mare
North Somerset BS23 1UU

01934 638206
fax 01934 638207

Mike Rees

110. **Plymouth County Council**
Old Treasury Building
Catherine Street
Plymouth PL1 2AD
01752 306191
fax 01752 306194

Steve Moore

111. **Somerset County Council**
5-7 West End
Street, Somerset BA16 0LG
01458 440820
fax 01458 449100
LHBarnett@somerset.gov.uk

Linda Barnett

112. **South Gloucestershire District Council**
48-50 Elm Park
Filton, S Gloucestershire BS34 7PH
01454 868558
fax 01454 868560

Steve Waters

113. **Swindon Borough Council**
The Limes, 21 Green Road
Upper Stratton
Swindon SN2 7JA
01793 836652
fax 01793 820578
KevinFisher/SocialServicesCivicOffices@s
windon.gov.uk

Kevin Fisher

114. **Torbay Council**
Abbey House, 75 Abbey Road
Torquay, Devon TQ2 5NN
01803 201655
fax 01803 201721
fred.pethard@torbay.gov.uk

Fred Pethard

115. **Wiltshire County Council**
The Martins, 56a Spa Road
Melksham
Wiltshire SN12 7NY
01225 793616
fax 01225 793556

Bob Ashford

Wales

116. **Bridgend**
32-32a Nolton Street
Bridgend CF31 3BN
01656 657243
fax 01656 648213
gaym@bridgend.gov.uk

Mal Gay

117. **Caerphilly & Blaenau Gwent**
Youth Offending Team
Tiryberth Centre
New Road
Tiryberth
Hengoed CF82 8AU
01443 875536
fax 01443 875371
willis@Caerphilly.gov.uk

Susan Williams

118. **Cardiff**
The Rise
Penhill Road
Cardiff CF11 9PR
029 2056 0839
fax 029 2057 8746
phil.dinham@virgin.net

Phil Dinham

119. **Carmarthenshire**
Ty Elwyn
Town Hall Square
Llanelli SA15 3HF
01554 742276
fax 01554 775369
Rsummers@Carmarthenshire.gov.uk

Richard Summers

120. **Central and Northern Wales**
68 Conwy Road
Colwyn Bay LL29 7LD
01492 523 500
fax 01492 523 555

Joy Kett

121. **Gwynedd Mon**
Menai Office
Beach Road
Felinheli
Gwynedd LL56 4RQ
01248 679183
fax 01248 679180
Theresa Adshead@gwynedd.gov.uk

Gareth Hughes-Jones

122. **Merthyr Tydfil**
Merthyr CBC Youth Justice
47-48 Pontmorlais
Merthyr Tydfil CF47 8UN
01685 389304
fax 01685 359726

Alan Elmer

123. **Mid Wales (Powys & Ceredigion)**
The Park, Newtown
Powys SY16 2PL
01686 627006
fax 01686 626292
bernards@powys.gov.uk

Bernard Steer

124. **Neath Port Talbot**
Cramic Way
Port Talbot SA13 1RU
01639 885050
fax 01639 882809
ingrid@netlineuk.net

Ingrid Masmeyer

125. **Newport**
Helyg Centre
Ringland Circle
Newport NP19 9PJ
01633 292900
fax 01633 290221

Andrew Wallsgrove

126. **Pembrokeshire Unitary Authority**
Social Services Department
Riverside (Old Block)
Woodbine Terrace
Pembroke SA71 4PL
01646 683571
fax 01646 622399

Paul Brecknell

127. **Rhondda Cynon Taff**
Cottage 5, Garth Olwg
Church Vilage
Pontypridd CF39 1BT
01443 219400
fax 01443 219450

Andrew Gwynn

128. **Swansea**
Llwyncelyn Campus
Cocket Road
Cocket, Swansea SA2 0FJ
01792 522815
fax 01792 522805
eddie.isles@swansea.gov.uk

Eddie Isles

129. **Torfaen & Monmouthshire**
Mamhilad House
Mamhilad Park Estate
Pontypool, Torfaen NP4 0NZ
01495 768300
fax 01495 768368

Steve Williams

130. **Vale of Glamorgan Council**
91 Salisbury Road
Barry CF62 6PD
01446 745820
fax 01446 739549
wdcollins@valeofglamorgan.gov.uk

Wendy Collins

131. **Wrexham and Flintshire**
Roxborough House
Hill Street
Wrexham LL11 1SN
01978 298035/6
fax 01978 298029
darren.johnson@wrexham.gov.uk

Darren Johnson

West Midlands

132. **Birmingham**
Head of Youth Offending Services
Kingsmere
18 Gravelly Hill North
Birmingham B23 6BQ
0121 464 0600
fax 0121 464 0609

Graham Fletcher

133. **Coventry**
c/o Little Park Street Police Station
Little Park Street
Coventry CV1 2JX
024 7653 9031
fax 024 7653 9149

Rose Ruddick

134. **Dudley**
6 St James's Road
Dudley
West Midlands DY1 3JL
01384 813060
fax 01384 813270
team.yot@mbc.dudley.gov.uk

Mike Galikowski

135. **Sandwell MBC**
102 Ocker Hill Road
Tipton, West Midlands DY4 0UW
0121 502 0063
fax 0121 556 8122
keith.barham@btinternet.com

Keith Barham

136. **Shropshire & Telford/Wrekin**
24 Victoria Road
Wellington, Shropshire TF1 1LG
01952 257477
fax 01952 242926
c/o socialcare@wrekin.gov.uk

Willie Goodwillie

137. **Solihull**
Craig Croft Centre
8 Craig Croft
Chelmsley Wood
Solihull B37 7TR
0121 788 4217
fax 0121 704 6362
ccroftrec@solihull.gov.uk

Peter Ashplant

138. **Staffordshire County Council**
Priory House
Friars Terrace
Stafford, Staffordshire ST17 4AU
01785 276909
fax 01785 277032
sally.rees@staffordshire.gov.uk

Sally Rees

139. **Stoke on Trent**
Unit C, Metro Business Park
Clough Street, Hanley
Stoke on Trent ST1 4AF
01782 235957
fax 01782 235860
john.tate@stoke.gov.uk

John Tate

140. **Walsall**
104 Essington Road
New Invention
Willenhall
West Midlands WV12 5DT
01922 493006
fax 01922 493035

Ged Campion

141. **Warwickshire**
c/o Warwickshire Probation
2 Swan Street
Warwick CV34 4BJ
01926 405842
fax 01926 403183
dianejohnson@warwickshire.gov.uk

Diane Johnson

142. **Wolverhampton**
Beckminster House
Birches Barn Road
Wolverhampton WV3 7BJ
01902 553722
fax 01902 553733
BULMAN@shirley37.freeserve.co.uk

Andy Bulman

143. **Worcestershire & Herefordshire**
Worcestershire & Herefordshire YOT
Central Administration Office
Tolladine Road
Worcester WR4 9NB
01905 732215
fax 01905 732220
brobinson@whyot.org.uk

Bill Robinson

Yorkshire

144. **Barnsley**
c/o Barnsley Community Safety
Partnership
County Way
Barnsley S70 2DT
01226 774953
fax 01226 774969

Colin Barnes (mgr)

145. **Bradford & District**
Bradford Youth Offending Team
Fraternal House
45 Cheapside
Bradford BD1 4HP
01274 703760
fax 01274 703761
paul.ohara@Bradford.gov.uk

Paul O'Hara

146. **Calderdale**
3 Trinity Place
Halifax
West Yorkshire HX1 2BD
01422 368279
fax 01422 368483

Steven Toye

147. **Doncaster MBC**
Rosemead
May Avenue
Balby
Doncaster DN4 9AE
01302 736119
fax 01302 736103

Mark Summers

148. **East Riding of Yorkshire Council**
Council Office
Main Road
Skirlaugh
East Riding of Yorkshire HU11 5HN
01482 885924
fax 01482 885917
darren.oneill@east-riding-of-yorkshire.gov.uk

Darren O'Neill

149. **Kingston Upon Hull City Council**
Myton Centre
Porter Street
Kingston upon Hull HU1 2RE
01482 609991
fax 01482 609983

Neil Colthup

150. **Kirklees**
Floor 2, Somerset Buildings
10 Church Street
Huddersfield HD1 1LS
01484 226935
fax 01484 226938
richard.smith@kirkleesmc.gov.uk

Richard Smith

151. **Leeds City Council**
Social Services
Merrion House, 110 Merrion Centre
Leeds LS2 8QB
0113 247 7483
fax 0113 247 7228
edwina.harrison@leeds.gov.uk

Edwina Harrison

152. **NE Lincolnshire District Council**
44 Heneage Road
Grimsby
N E Lincolnshire DN32 9ES
01472 325252
fax 01472 325242
youth.justice@nelincs.gov.uk

Neill Martin

153. **North Lincolnshire**
Shelford House
Shelford Street
Scunthrope
N Lincolnshire DN15 6NU
01724 274188
fax 01724 274259
YOT@IC24.net

Mick Gibbs

154. **North Yorkshire County Council**
4 Hawkshill Drive
The Hawkshills
Easingwold
N Yorkshire YO61 3EG
01347 823 177/084
fax 01347 821173
peter.foulsham@btinternet.com

Peter Foulsham

155. **Rotherham MBC**
4-6 Moorgate Road
Rotherham
S Yorkshire S60 2EN
01709 515713/516999
fax 01709 836584
jane.mcwilliam@Rotherham.gov.uk

Pat Booth

156. **Sheffield**
7 St Peter's Close
Sheffield S1 2EJ
0114 228 8555
fax 0114 228 8500

Malcolm Potter

157. **Wakefield Metropolitan District Council**
51 West Mead
Airedale, Castleford WF10 3AF
01977 722010
fax 01977 722021

Steven Lawrenson

158. **York**
PO Box 246, Mill House
North Street
York YO1 9YX
01904 554565
fax 01904 554566
david.poole@york.gov.uk

David Poole

SCOTTISH EXECUTIVE JUSTICE DEPARTMENT

Saughton House
Broomhouse Drive
Edinburgh EH11 3XD
fax 0131-244 8794

Parole and Lifer Review Branch
Functions: administration of parole scheme, review and release of life sentence prisoners, children in custody

Staff
Grade 7 Head of Branch: Mr A Quinn
Higher Executive Officer: Ms L Macdonald (parole), Mrs A Sharp & Mr J T Hislop (life cases)

Enquiries: 0131-244 8530

PAROLE BOARD FOR SCOTLAND

Saughton House
Broomhouse Drive
Edinburgh EH11 3XD
0131-244 8755
fax 0131-244 6974

Secretary to the Board: H P Boyle

General enquiries: 0131-244 8755

ABERDEEN CITY COUNCIL

Central Bail Referral telephone no:
Neil Williamson (ssw, crt services) (01224) 405800

Emergency out of hours contact point:
(01224) 684795

Central Services

1a. St Nicholas House
Broad Street
Aberdeen AB10 1BY
(01224) 522000
fax (01224) 623156

Tomlinson, John (director of social work & com devpt) ext 2529
Dawson, Alisdair (asst director, childcare & criminal justice) ext 3108

1b. Social Work Department
Exchequer House
3 Exchequer Row
Aberdeen AB11 2BW
(01224) 405800
fax (01224) 576109

Bew, Jenny (sw mgr, criminal justice)
Bell, George (asst mgr criminal justice)
Hewitt, Angela (research/info officer)

Specialist Criminal Justice Teams

2. Exchequer House
3 Exchequer Row
Aberdeen AB11 2BW
(01224) 405800
fax (01224) 576109

Court Services Team
Williamson, Neill (ssw)
Brownlee, Linda (p, sw)
Harrison, Jean (sw)
McAllister, Anne (p, sw)
Mair, Joan (sw)
Oram, Helen (sw)
Rutherford, Jean (p)
Smith, Edwina (p, sw, sup attendance) (temp)

Probation Team
Williamson, Sheena (ssw)
MacAulay, Iain (ssw, quality assurance)
Fogg, Noreen (sw)
Fox, Sue (p, sw)
Gillan, Gillian (sw)
Fyffe, Karaina (p, sw)
Halford, Vina (sw)

Hendry, Christine (sw)
Murray, Lorna (sw)
Roach, Philip (sw)
Wood, John (sw)

Th'care, Diversion & Programatic Work Team
Youngson, Nicola (ssw)
Brownlee, Linda (p, sw)
Buchanan, Neil (sw)
Burr, Mary (sw)
Connon, John (sw)
Gillan, Gillian (sw)
MacDonald, Gus (sw)
Rennie, Kate (sw)
Russell, Kevin (sw)
Simpson, Lesley (p, sw)

Community Service

3. 11 Willowdale Place
Aberdeen AB24 3AQ
(01224) 624317
fax (01224) 626544

Community Service Resource Team
Murray, Joan (mgr)
Reid, George (projects officer)
Finnie, Pam (order supving off)
MacAllister, Dennis (order supving off)
Peacock, Carol (order supving off)

Probation Hostels

4. **St Fitticks House**
36 Crombie Road, Torry
Aberdeen AB1 3QQ
(01244) 877910
fax (01224) 894303

(males & females aged 18+)

Dickson, Stewart (unit mgr)
Dawson, Gary (sw)

Penal Establishment

5. Social Work Unit
HM Prison, Craiginches
Aberdeen AB9 2HN
(01224) 876834/876868
fax (01224) 876834

Reith, Kim (ssw)
Morgan, Carol (sw)
Mulvey, Kim (sw)

Health Services

6. St Nicholas House
Broad Street
Aberdeen AB10 1BY
(01224) 522000
fax (01224) 623156

Palin, Fiona (sw mgr, adult care) ext 2469

6a. Social Work Department
Royal Cornhill Hospital
Cornhill Road
Aberdeen AB9 2ZH
(01224) 663131

Hughes, Rob (ssw) ext 57255
Elliot, Sue (sw, forensic unit ext 57415)

Independent Sector

7. **SACRO** (Grampian Office)
18 Little Belmont Street
Aberdeen AB10 1JG
(01224) 625560
fax (01224) 627338

mediation & reparation, supported accommodation

Shackleford, Murray (proj mgr, cs services)
Price, Susan (proj mgr, rep & med)

7a. **APEX Scotland**
27-29 King Street
Aberdeen
(01224) 623141
fax (01224) 623142

supervised attendance orders, employment

Macdonald, Aileen (snr trainer)

7b. **Victim Support (Scotland)**
4 Albyn Place
Aberdeen AB10 1YH
phone & fax (01224) 622478

Third, Jennifer (area co-ord)
Sxcott, Mary (co-ord)
Russell, Sandra (co-ord)

7c. **RLO Monitoring Services**
Premier Monitoring Services
PO Box 18016
Bridge of Don
Aberdeen AB23 8TU
(01224) 708967
fax (01224) 708972

restriction of liberty orders (electronic monitoring)

Marshall, Sharon (responsible officer)

ABERDEENSHIRE COUNCIL

Head Office

1. Woodhill House
   Westburn Road **Aberdeen** AB16 5GB
   Aberdeen (01467) 665490
   fax (01224) 665445

   Wells, Margaret (director of sw & housing)

2. Seafield House
   37 Castle Street
   Banff AB45 1DQ
   Banf (01261) 812001
   fax (01261) 818244

   Mackenzie, Colin (head of sw, responsible for crim justice)

3. 53 Windmill Street
   Peterhead AB42 6UE
   Peterhead (01779) 484224
   fax (01779) 474961

   English, Philip (sw mgr responsible for criminal justice)
   Balme, Jane (info & research off)

4. **Joint Sex Offender Project**
   88 King Street
   Aberdeen AB42 1HH
   (01779) 490904
   fax (01779) 474961
   Watson, Sheena (ssw)
   Matthews, Rory (sw)
   Robertson, Marianne (sw)
   Vacancy (sw)
   Vacancy (p, sw)

Aberdeenshire North Team

5. Winston House
   Castle Street **Banff** AB45 1DQ
   (01261) 812001
   fax (01261) 813474

   Cambridge, Megan (sw)

6. 14 Saltoun Square
   Fraserburgh AB43 9DA
   (01346) 513281
   fax (01346) 516885

   Scott, Bill (sw)
   Smith, Angela (sw, addictions service)
   Watson, Eric (sw)

7. 53 Windmill Street
   Peterhead AB42 6UE
   (01779) 477333
   fax (01779) 474961

   Munro, John (ssw)
   Coffield, Joan (sw)
   Garden, Gillian (sw)
   Gibson, Eileen (p, sw)
   Innes, Corinne (sw)

   Community Service
   Duthie, Barbara (proj off)

   Supervised Attendance Orders
   Black, Celia (proj off)

8. 25 Gordon Street
   Huntly AB54 5EQ
   (01466) 794488
   fax (01466) 794624

   Biggs, Peter (p, sw)

Aberdeenshire South Team

9. 56 Cameron Street
   Stonehaven AB39 2HE
   (01569) 767553
   fax (01569) 767906

   Westland, Fiona (ssw)
   Duncan, Nicola (sw)
   McLean, Lindsey (sw, addictions service)
   Perkins, John (sw)
   Reeman, Julie (sw)
   Rhodes, Jayne (sw)
   Thorn, Doug (sw)

   Community Service
   Westland, Fiona (ssw)
   Holtes, Morag (proj off)

Penal Establishment

10. Social Work Unit
    HM Prison **Peterhead** AB42 2YY
    phone & fax (01799) 473315

    Shirran, Anne (ssw)
    Cooper, Angie (sw)
    Donnelly, Fiona (sw)
    Vacancy (sw)
    McDonald, Kellie (sw)

ANGUS COUNCIL

Emergency out of hours contact point:
(01382) 436430

1. Social Work Headquarters
   County Buildings
   Forfar Angus DD8 3WS
   (01307) 461460
   fax (01307) 473366

Robertson, Bill (director of social work)
Peat, Robert (head of strategic planning, commissioning & criminal justice services)

2. Criminal Justice Services Office
9 Fergus Square
Arbroath DD11 3DG
(01241) 871161
fax (01241) 431898

Hodgkinson, Mark (service mgr)
Peat, Doreen (ssw)
Turnbull, Iain (ssw)
Watt, Dave (ssw)
Smith, Valerie (research/i.t. officer)
Cherrington, Isobel (sw)
Christison, Jacky (sw)
Gall, Stuart (sw)
Holton, Anne (sw)
Melville, Pete (sw)
Menzies, Bill (sw)
Nicolson, Don (sw)
Rae, Kathryn (sw)
Rennie, Diane (sw)
Herbertson, Sylvia (sup att)

Penal Establishment

3. Social Work Unit
HM Prison **Noranside**
Fern, by Forfar, Angus DD8 3QY
(01356) 650217

Anderson, Clive (sw)
Lawrence, Brenda (sw)

ARGYLL & BUTE COUNCIL

1. 16 Church Street
Dunoon PA23 8BG
(01369) 707829
fax (01369) 703641

Criminal Justice Team
Community Service Office
Dunoon Sherif Court Social Work Unit
Filshie, Alex (criminal justice mgr)

2. **Criminal Justice Services & Community Service Office**
Soroba Road
Oban PA34 4JA
(01631) 563068
fax (01631) 566724

all CJ services for Oban & Lorn areas

3. **District Headquarters**
Dalriada House, Lochnell Street
Lochgilphead PA31 8SJ
(01546) 602177
fax (01546) 606589

4. Social Work Department
29 Lomond Street
Helensburgh G84 8TQ
(01436) 673328
fax (01436) 67826

6. Social Work Unit for Helensbugh
Sheriff Court
McLean Place
Dumbarton G82 1PY
(01389) 608484

7. Social Work Department
Old Quay Head
Campbeltown PA28 6ED
Campbeltown (01586) 552659
fax (01586) 55491

CSO & CJ Services for Campbeltown and Kintyre Peninsula

8. Social Work Department
Union Streeet
Rothesay, Island of Bute PA20 0HD
(01700) 503748
fax (01700) 505408

all CJ Services for the Island of Bute

9. Social Work Department
Breadalbane Street
Tobermory Island of Mull
(01688) 302216
fax (01688) 302093

10. Social Work Department
Kilarrow House
Bowmore Island of Islay PA43 7HW
(01496) 810484
fax (01496) 810457

CLACKMANNANSHIRE COUNCIL

1. Housing & Social Services
Lime Tree House, Castle Street
Alloa FK10 1EX
(01259) 452417
fax (01259) 452400

McGeoch, Gerry (service mgr, criminal justice services)
Reid, Anne (clerical asst)

2. 6 Marshill
Alloa FK10 1ED
(01259) 721069
fax (01259) 723998

Criminal Justice Team
Robson, Yvonne (team leader)
Buchanan, June (sw)
Cameron, Douglas (sw)
Grinly, Helen (sw)
Russell, Bobby (sw)
Smillie, Alistair (sw)

Community Service Team
Gibson, Ruth (cso)
Drysdale, Ken (wk supvr)

Admin
McDougal, Marilyn
Noblett, Susan
Williamson, Julie

3. Social Work Unit
HM Prison & YOI
Glenochil King O' Muir Road
Tullibody, FK10 3AD
phone & fax (01259) 767315

Newton, John (team leader)
Boyd, Mae (sw)
Duncan, Fiona (sw)
Goodwin, Anne-Marie (sw)
Hughes, Caroline (sw)
Logan, Carol (sw)
McGuire, Libby (sw)
Hepworth, Susan (admin)
McKenzie, Kelly (admin)

COMHAIRLE NAN EILEAN SIAR Western Isles Council

Out of hours contact: (01851) 701702

1. Social Work Department Headquarters
Council Offices
Sandwick Road
Stornoway
Isle of Lewis HS1 2BW
(01851) 703773
fax (01851) 709532

Smith, Malcolm (director of sw)
Macaulay, Iain (depute director of sw)
Mackay, Mrs Maria (principal officer)

Lewis & Harris
Harper, Keith (team leader, criminal justice services)
Graham, George (p, cs supvr)

2. **North Uist, Benbecula, South Uist & Barra**
Social Work Department
Council Offices
Balivanich
Isle of Benbecula HS7 5LA
(01870) 602425
fax (01870) 602332

Twidale, Pat (team leader)
Macphee, Alasdair (p, cs supr)

DUMFRIES & GALLOWAY COUNCIL

1. Social Services Headquarters
Grierson House, The Crichton
Bankend Road
Dumfries DG1 4ZH
(01387) 260000
fax (01387) 260924

Makin, K (director of social services)

Nithsdale Area

2. 5 Gordon Street
Dumfries DG1 1EG
(01387) 260000
fax (01387) 260824

Arnold, D E (service mgr, crim justice)

3. 79 Buccleuch Street
Dumfries DG1 2AB
(01387) 262409
fax (01387) 267964

MacKenzie, C (team mgr, case mgr)
Desborough, Ms T (sw)
Hall, J (sw)
Sturgeon, J (sw)
Ward, Ms H (sw)

Glynn, J (team mgr, service provn inc. cs)
Abrines, G (sw)
Hannah, Ms J (sw)
Muir, Ms T (sw)

4. **Community Service**
8 King Street
Dumfries DG2 9AN
(01387) 248495

Glynn, J (team mgr) (based at 3)
Fitzpatrick, Mrs E (sw)
Jordan, Mrs S
Nuttal, L (sw)
Ferguson, A (cso)
Smeaton, E (cso)
Stenhouse, Ms N (cso)

5. Main Street
Kirkconnel DG6 4LU
(01659) 67601
fax (01659) 67750

contact office 3

Annandale & Eskdale Area

6. 2 Bank Street
Annan DG12 6AA
(01461) 203411
fax (01461) 205964

MacKenzie, C (team mgr) (based at 3)
MacKay, Mrs F (sw)

7. Council Offices
Dryfe Road **Lockerbie** DG11 2AP
(01576) 203040
fax (01576) 204411

contact office 6

Stewartry Area

8. 1 Academy Street
Castle Douglas DG7 1AP
(01556) 504101
fax (01556) 503553

McKenzie, R (team mgr Stewartry & Penal Establishments)
Knipe, Cathrine (sw)
Usher, Mrs J (sw)

Galloway Area

9. 39 Lewis Street
Stranraer DG9 7AD
(01776) 706167
fax (01776) 706884

Monteforte, A (team mgr)
Moodycliffe, J (sw)
McCallum, A (sw)
Stead, J (sw) (sw)
Watson, Ms E (sw)

Community Service
Hamilton, B (cso Galloway)

10. 23 King Street
Newton Stewart DG8 6DQ
(01671) 403933
fax (01671) 403017

contact office 9

Sheriff Courts

11. Sheriff Court House
Buccleuch Street, Dumfries DG2 7AR
(01387) 262334

12. Sheriff Court House
High Street, Kirkudbright DG6 4JW
(01557) 30574

13. Sheriff Court House
Lewis Street
Stranraer DG9 7AA
(01776) 702138

Penal Establishments

14. HM Young Offenders Institution
Terregles Street, **Dumfries** DG2 9AX
(01387) 261218
fax (01387) 264144

Jones, Yvonne (sw)

DUNDEE CITY COUNCIL

Out of hours contact no: (01382) 436430 *fax (01382) 436435*

1. Friarfield House
Barrack Street
Dundee DD1 1PQ
(01382) 435001
fax (01382) 435073

Baird, Alan (mgr, criminal justice)
Wilson, Ray (snr planning officer, criminal justice)
Wood, G (service mgr, criminal justice)
Mellor, Ms C (snr admin asst, criminal justice)

Team 1
Fenton, J (ssw)
Blair, Rosie (sw, crt off)
Bochsler, J (sw)
Delaney, Fiona (sw)
Dobson, Mrs M (sw)
Hinnrichs, Mrs J (sw)
Isayev, Roman (sw)
Sinclair, R (sw)

Team 2 (Community Service)
Millar, A (ssw)
Howard, Mrs T (sw)
Patterson, Grant (sw)
Vaughan, E (sw)
Willatts, Joanna (sw)
Wilkie, I (sw)

Team 3
Lindsay, S (acting ssw)
Duff, I (sw)
Hutt, Mrs E (sw)
Meldrum, Mrs P (sw, crt officer)

Nail, S (sw)
Titterington, E (sw)
Dunnett, Ms Jeanette (cj asst)

Tay Project
Finnon, K (proj leader)
McDonald, T (sw)
O'Rourke, Mike (sw)
Smith, R (sw,)

Supervised Attendance Order
Garrigan, Mrs H (snr cj asst)
Baxter, Collette (cj asst)
Ogg, Ms A (cj asst)

EAST AYRSHIRE COUNCIL

1. Social Work Headquarters
John Dickie Street
Kilmarnock KA1 1BY
(01563) 576907 & 576969
fax (01563) 576937

Moore, Stephen (head of sw)
Flannery, Donal (service unit mg - criminal justice)

2. Social Work Department
43/49 John Finnie Street
Kilmarnock KA1 1BL
(01563) 539888
fax (01563) 538055

McCarthy, Isobel (team leader - criminal justice)

Community Service Team
(01563) 539809
Turner, Ian (cso)

3. Social Work Department
Barrhill Road
Cumnock KA18 1PG
(01290) 428372
fax (01290) 428380

McRoberts, Grace (team leader - criminal justice)

Penal Establishment

4. Social Work Unit
HM Prison
Mauchline Road
Kilmarnock KA1 5JH
(01563) 548851
fax (01563) 548869

Hart, Gerard (ssw)

EAST DUNBARTONSHIRE COUNCIL

Out of hours standby service: Freephone 0800 811505

1. Social Work Headquarters
William Patrick Library
2/4 West High Street
Kirkintilloch G66 1AD
0141-775 9000
fax 0141-578 3444

Bruce, Sue (strategic director - community)
Moran, Mike (acting head of service, children & families, & criminal justice)
Flemming, John (acting service mgr, criminal justice)

2. **Criminal Justice Unit**
Unit 23, Fraser House
Whitegates
Kirkintilloch G66 1HF
0141-578 0100
fax 0141-578 0101

Jeffrey, Jim (team leader) (temp)
Smillie, Alastair (team leader)

Offender Services
Gemmell, Mae (sw)
Kennedy, Kirsty (sw)
Lynch, Tracy (sw)

Community Service & Supervised Attendance
Sutherland, Neil (cso)
Nixon, Joseph (cs asst)
Wallace, Jack (suprvsd attendance officer)
Barker, James (cs supr)

Administration Section
Bradley, Margaret (admin asst)
Kerr, Laura (p, clerical off)
Woods, Joan (clerical off)
Watt, Karen (sessional clerical off)

Penal Establishment

3. Social Work Unit
HM Prison **Lowmoss**
Crosshill Road
Bishopbriggs
Glasgow G62 2QB
0141-762 1010

Ure, Ian (sw)

EAST LOTHIAN COUNCIL

Out of hours contact: emergency social work service: freephone 0800 731 6969

1. Dept of Social Work & Housing
   9-11 Lodge Street
   Haddington EH41 3DX
   (01620) 825393
   fax (01620) 824295

   Walker, B (director of sw & housing)

2. **Criminal Justice Practice Team**
   6-8 Lodge Street
   Haddington
   East Lothian EH41 3DX
   (01620) 826600
   fax (01620) 826345

   Ramsay, J (practice team mgr)
   Kaminski, P (ssw)
   Coates, G (sw)
   Fawcett, P(sw)
   McFarlane, B (sw)
   Ritchie, K (sw)
   Rooney, G (sw)
   Walsh, W (sw)
   Love, R (cs asst)
   McAlpine, O (cs asst)
   Mackenzie, S (service support)
   Holm, J (service support)

EAST RENFREWSHIRE COUNCIL

1. East Renfrewshire Council Headquarters
   Eastwood Park
   Rouken Glen Road
   Giffnock G46 6UG
   0141-577 3844
   fax 0141-577 3846

   Ross, Dr S (director of sw)

2. Lygate's House
   224 Ayr Road
   Newton Mearns G77 6DR
   0141-577 3382
   fax 0141-577 3377

   Aitken, Doris (crime & public safety mgr)

3. **Criminal Justice Services**
   63 Darnley Road
   Barrhead Glasgow G78 1ED
   0141-881 9267
   fax 0141-881 9974

   McCorquodale, Anne (ssw, criminal justice)
   Craig, D (sw)
   Cunningham, N (sw)
   Kane, S (sw)
   McLean, S (sw)
   Downie, E (csa)
   Milne, H (cs supr)

CITY OF EDINBURGH COUNCIL

Out of hours contact: emergency social work service: freephone 0800 731 6969

1. Social Work Headquarters
   Shrubhill House, Shrub Place
   Edinburgh EH7 4PD
   0131-554 4301
   fax 0131-554 0838

   McEwan, Leslie J (director of social work)
   MacAulay, Duncan (head of operations)
   Brace, Sue (head of planning commissioning)
   Boyle, Monica (head of business services)

   Criminal Justice Services
   Lancashire, Ron (criminal justice services mgr)
   Millar, Don (asst criminal justice services mgr)
   Tyson, John (asst criminal justice services mgr)

Court Liaison Services

2. **Edinburgh**
   (District, Sheriff and High Courts)
   1 Parliament Square
   Edinburgh EH1 1RF
   0131-469 3408/9
   fax 0131-469 3410

District Criminal Justice Practice Teams

3. **Edinburgh North East**
   9-11 Giles Street
   Edinburgh EH6 6DJ
   0131-553 3835
   fax 0131-553 6540

   Robertson, Harry (practice team mgr)

4. **Edinburgh South East**
   40 Captain's Road
   Edinburgh EH17 8HN
   0131-529 5300
   fax 0131-529 5384

   Marshall, Mike (practice team mgr)

5. **Edinburgh North West**
34 Muirhouse Crescent
Edinburgh EH4 4QL
0131-343 1991
fax 0131-315 2172

Sleith, Muriel (practice team mgr)

6. **Edinburgh South West**
5 Murrayburn Gate
Edinburgh EH14 2SS
0131-442 4131
fax 0131-442 4842

Gray, Dominic (practice team mgr)

7. **Central Criminal Justice Services**
21 Market Street
Edinburgh EH1 1BL
0131-469 3408/9
fax 0131-469 3410

Fraser, Rona (acting practice team mgr)

Services include: bail info and assessment, diversion from
prosecution, resettlement team, domestic violence probation project and:

Albrae (supported accommodation facility)
24 Broughton Place, Edinburgh EH1 3RT
0131-556 9969
fax 0131-558 1809

Kaminski, Joe (project mgr)

Penal Establishment

8. Social Work Unit
HM Prison, 33 Stenhouse Road
Edinburgh EH11 3LN
0131-444 3080
fax 0131-444 3036

Youngson, Graeme (practice team mgr)

FALKIRK COUNCIL

1. Social Work Headquarters
Brockville, Hope Street
Falkirk FK1 5RW
(01324) 506400
fax (01324) 506401

Wilkinson, Ms Carole (director of social work)

Criminal Justice Service
(01324) 506464
fax (01324) 506465

Anderson, Margaret (service mgr)
Duncan, Robin (research, training & info off)

Probation & Throughcare Team
Stirrat, Ms Sharon (team mgr) (js)
Burgess, Nick (team mgr) (js)
Brodie, Andrew (sw)
Dobbie, Ms Diane (sw)
Franks, Ms Winifred (sw)
Kent, Mrs Gill (sw)
Vacancy (sw)
Parnell, Ms Anne Marie (sw)
Sewell, Ms Maggie (sw)
Thomson, Jim (sw)

Community Service & Supervised Attendance Team
Ord, John (cs mgr)
O'Neil, Colin (sw)
Marshall, Mrs Kay (sw asst)
Allan, John (cso)
Brockie, Clem (cso)

Administration
McComb, Ms Ginny

Voluntary Organisation

2. **SACRO Intensive Probation Project**
22 Meeks Road
Falkirk FK2 7ET
(01324) 627824
fax (013240 622006

Penal Establishment

3. Social Work Unit
HM YOI **Polmont**
Redding Road, Brightons
Falkirk FK2 0AB
(01324) 711708
fax (01324) 714919

White, Ms Jackie (ssw)
Brownlie, Ms L (sw)
Burgess, Nick (sw)
Devlin, Ms Anne (sw)
McLellan, Ms M (sw) (js)
Vallance, Ms G (sw)

FIFE COUNCIL

Out of hours contact: (01592) 414000

1. **Social Work Headquarters**
Fife House, Glenrothes
Fife KY7 5LT
(01592) 414141
fax (01592) 413044

Sawyer, M (head of social work)
Martin, Ms J (service mgr) (based at 11)

Services to Community Service & Young Offender Strategy
Aitken, T (asst service mgr) (based at 2)

Services to Court District & Court Services
MacGregor, R (asst service mgr) (based at 9)

Administration & Support Services
Stewart, H (support services mgr) (based at 11)

2. **Cupar District & Court Social Work Team**
21 St Catherine Street
Cupar KY15 4TA
(01334) 412015
fax (01334) 412034

Young, J (team leader)
Lucas, R
McArthur, S
Nairn, Ms S
Reid, Ms A
Russell, D

Fairfoul, Ms L (admin support)
Paterson, Ms C (admin asst)

Sheriff Court Social Work Services

3. **Dunfermline Sheriff Court**
Carnegie Drive
Dunfermline KY12 7HJ
(01383) 312950
fax (01383) 312951

O'Kane, Ms J
Keenan, Ms D (admin support)
Simpson, Ms K (admin support)

4. **Kirkcaldy Sheriff Court**
Whytescauseway
Kirkcaldy KY1 1XQ
(01592) 412375
fax (01592) 412378

Hollerin, T
Turner, P (mentally disordered offenders specialist)
Neil, Mrs D (admin support)

5. **Cupar Sheriff Court**
21 St Catherine Street
Cupar KY15 4TA
(01334) 412015
fax (01334) 412034

Nairn, Ms S
Ralph, Ms K (admin support)

Community Service by Offenders Scheme

6. **Main Office**
21 St Catherine Street
Cupar KY15 4TA
(01334) 412015
fax (01334) 412034

Francis, G (sw)
Smith, M (sw asst)
McIlroy, D (snr project officer)
Mitchell, K (admin support)

7. **Kirkcaldy Base**
7a East Fergus Place
Kirkcaldy KY1 1XT
(01592) 412160
fax (01592) 412172

McMurchie, C (snr cso)
Bell, D
Gerrard, Ms M (sw asst)
Green, R (sw asst)
Melville, A (sw asst)
Brass, R (proj off)
Barrett, Ms M (admin support)
Turner, Ms T (admin support)

8. **Dunfermline Base**
Rannoch House
2 Comely Park
Dunfermline KY12 7HU
(01383) 312131
fax (01383) 312134

McMurchie, C (snr cso)
Pearson, B
Horsburgh, Ms A (cjs asst)
Gallo, Ms J (cjs asst)
Dunn, Ms M (admin support)

Services to Kirkcaldy Court District

9. **Kirkcaldy Court District Team**
Wemyssfield
East Fergus Place
Kirkcaldy KY1 1XT
(01592) 412424
fax (01592) 412321

Rodger, A (team leader)
Fernee, Ms P
Fraser, D
Rose, Ms S
Simpson, Ms A
Sutherland, Y
Watson, E

Wedge, Ms A
Turner, C (admin support)

10. **Leven/Glenrothes Court District Team**

a. 96 Wellesley Road
Buckhaven KY8 1HT
(01592) 414488
fax (01592) 414482

Pullar, Ms A (team leader)
Black, Ms N
Campbell, L
Duncan, N
Nicholson, Ms K
Christensen, Ms B (admin support)

b. 390 South Street
Glenrothes KY7 5NL
(01592) 415252
fax (01592) 415278

Hatch, S
Moran, A
Wilkinson, I (p)
Williams, Ms S
Robson, Ms A (admin support)

Services to Dunfermline Court District & Young Offender Strategy

Martin, Ms J (service mgr) (based at 11)

11. **West Fife Team**
Rannoch House
2 Comely Park
Dunfermline KY12 7HU
(01383) 312131
fax (01383) 312134

Myers, R (team leader)
Fraser, G
Millar, Ms D
Mullen, Ms H
Munton, R
Nicholson, A
Ross, Ms S
Sheridan, J
Thompson, Ms S
Barriball, Ms G (admin support)
Harley, Mrs J (admin support)

12. **Intensive Probation Team (Young Offender Strategy)**

a. **Buckhaven Base**
96 Wellesley Road
Buckhaven KY8 1HT
(01592) 414488
fax (01592) 414482

Lister, D (team leader)
Baker, P
Hopton, S
Ramage, Ms M
Butler, Ms E (admin support)

b. **Dunfermline Base**
Rannoch House
2 Comely Park
Dunfermline KY12 7HU
(01383) 312131
fax (01383) 312134

Chalmers, Ms M
Dewar, Ms M
Innes, M
Keenan, Ms D (admin support)

Community Protection Team

13a. **Dunfermline Base**
Rannoch House
2 Comely Park
Dunfermline KY12 7HU
(01383) 312131
fax (01383) 312134

Farrand B (team leader)
Hood, C
Watson, J
Kopec, Ms L (cjs asst)
Paterson, M (admin support)

b. **Kirkcaldy Base**
Broomlea
1 Swan Road
Kirkcaldy KY1 1UZ
(01592) 417966
fax (01592) 412139

Farrand B (team leader)
Kinnear, W
Ricketts, M
Reeves, J (admin support)

c. **Drug Treatment & Testing Orders**
96 Wellesley Road
Buckhaven KY8 1HT
(01592) 414488
fax (01592) 414482

Oghene, G
Blair, R
Emerson, S
Williamson, F
Young, R
King, D (admin support)

GLASGOW CITY COUNCIL

1. Social Work Headquarters
3rd Floor, Nye Bevan House
20 India Street
Glasgow G2 4PF
0141-287 8700
fax 0141-287 8840

O'Connor, R (director of social work services)

Criminal Justice Unit
Direct dial 0141-287 + number
fax 0141-287 8778

Holmes C (head of children & families/criminal justice services)
moving Feb 2001 to
Centenary House
100 Morrison Street
Glasgow G5 8LN
0141-420 5500

Silk, P (principal officer, cj) 8744
Tran, F (principal officer cj)
Muirhead, J (snr officer, south cj) 8748
Sexton, J (snr officer, north east cj) 8747
Smith, C (snr officer, north west cj) 8310
Dunbar, F (research officer cj) 8722
O'Donnell, J (resource wrkr cj) 8746
Jack, M (snr training officer cj) 0141-550 7887

2. **Anniesland Area Team**
1660/70 Great Western Road
0141-959 7457
fax 0141-954 0284

Tolmie, B (ssw cj)

3. **Drumchapel Area Team**
236 Kinfauns Drive
Glasgow G15 7UE
0141-944 0551
fax 0141-944 6931

Tolmie, B (ssw cj)

4. **Maryhill/Partick Area Team**
Unit 8b The Quadrangle
59 Ruchill Street
Glasgow G20 9PY
0141-287 6300
fax 0141-287 6267

Friel R (ssw cj)

5. **Easterhouse Area Team**
36 Westerhouse Road
Glasgow G34 9AE
0141-781 4000
fax 0141-781 4011

Anderson, I (ssw cj)

6. **Ruchazie Area Team**
1 Ruchazie Place
Glasgow G33 5DA
0141-770 8531
fax 0141-770 5058

Anderson, I (ssw cj)

7. **Springburn/Possil/Royston Area Team**
15 Glenbar Street
Glasgow G22 2NN
0141-552 1935/8537
fax 0141-553 2372

Bradley, E (ssw cj)
Remigio, R (ssw cj)

8. **Homeless Persons Team**
118 Osbourne Street
Glasgow G1 5QH
0141-552 7991
fax 0141-552 5460

Kyle, E (ssw cj)

9. **Parkhead/Baillieston Area Team**
The Newlands Centre
871 Springfield Road
Glasgow G31 4HZ
0141-565 0230
fax 0141-565 0614

Brown, N (ssw cj)

10. **Bridgeton/Dennistoun Area Team**
The Newlands Centre
871 Springfield Road
Glasgow G31 4HZ
0141-565 0230
fax 0141-565 0614

Stewart, W (ssw cj)

11. **Castlemilk Area Team**
10 Ardencraig Place
Glasgow G45 9UA
0141-287 6100
fax 0141-287 6127

Bell, D 9ssw cj)

12. **Gorbals/Govanhill Area Team**
187 Old Rutherglen Road
Glasgow G5 9TD
0141-420 8026
fax 0141-420 8004

Bell, D (ssw cj)

13. **Govan Area Team**
7 merryland Street
Glasgow G51 2QG
01451-445 3178
fax 0141-425 1062

Mair, W (ssw cj)

14. **Pollok Area Team**
130 Langton Road
Glasgow G53 5DD
0141-883 2222
fax 0141-883 1033

Mair, W (ssw cj)

15. **Pollokshaws Area Team**
24/34 Shawbridge Arcade
Glasgow G43 1RT
0141-287 1601
fax 0141-287 1602

Vacancy (ssw cj)

16. **Priesthill Area Team**
10 Overtown Avenue
Glasgow G53 6JB
0141-880 7326
fax 01451-880 8034

Vacancy (ssw cj)

17. **Access Project** (Mental Health)
Centenary House
100 Morrison Street
Glasgow G5 8LN
0141-420 5508
fax 0141-420 5505

Vacancy (proj leader)

18. 117/127 Brook Street
Glasgow G40 3AP
0141-550 7808
fax 0141-550 7707

moving Feb 2001 to
Centenary House
100 Morrison Street
Glasgow G5 8LN
0141-420 5500

Probation Resource Unit
McClafferty, B (proj leader)

Clyde Quay Project (Sex Offenders)
Doherty, L (proj leader)

19. **Supervised Attendance Orders**
Social Work Unit
40 Carlton Place (basement)
Glasgow G5 9TW
0141-429 8067
fax 0141-420 8375

20. **Bail Services**
Social Work Unit
Glasgow Sheriff Court
1 Carlton Place
Glsagow G5 9DD
0141-429 6830
fax 0141-420 1703

Social Work Unit
Stipendiary/District Court
68 Turnbull Street
Glasgow G1 5PW
0141-553 0856/7
fax 0141-552 5422

21. **Drug Treatment & Testing Orders**
93 Hope Street
Glasgow G2 6LD
0141-248 9682
fax 0141-248 1686

Ashworth, M (proj co-ord)

22. **Prison Throughcare Team**
82 Gordon Street
Glasgow G1 3BU
0141-222 2141
fax 0141-243 2483

Mazzoncini, P (ssw)

Community Service Orders
from February 2001 CS will be based in the Area Teams (except for Office 26)

23. **South**
Centenary House
100 Morrison Street
Glasgow G5 8LN
0141-420 5509
fax 0141-420 5505

24. **North**
Unit 9, Port Dundas Business Park
100 Borron Street
Port Dundas
Glasgow G4 9XE
0141-353 0277
fax 0141-353 3224

25. **North**
The Quadrangle, 59 Ruchill Street
Glasgow G20 9PY
0141-946 1599
fax 0141-946 1885

26. Community Service (Industry) Team
Centenary House
100 Morrison Street
Glasgow G5 8LN
0141-420 5500

McCann, P (cs org)

Courts

27. **Glasgow High Court**
1 Mart Street
Glasgow G1 5NA
0141-559 4526

Social Work Unit
0141-559 4529

28. **Glasgow Sheriff Court**
1 Carlton Place
Glasgow G5 9DD
0141-429 8888
fax 0141-418 5244

Social Work Unit
0141-429 6830
fax 0141-420 1703

Fyfe, R (unit mgr crts)

29. **Stipendiary/District Court**
21 St Andrews Street
Glasgow G1 5PW
0141-227 5401
fax 0141-552 7895

Social Work Unit
68 Turnbull Street
Glasgow G1 5PW
0141- 552 1671
fax 0141-552 5422

Voluntary Organisations

30. **Glasgow Partnership Project**
(NCH/APEX Scotland/Glasgow City Council)
Intensive Supervision Project
Floor 2, 94 Hope Street
Glasgow G2 6PH
0141-248 7749
fax 0141-243 2483

31. **Motoring Project**
Floor 2, 94 Hope Street
Glasgow G2 6PH
0141-248 7749
fax 0141-243 2483

32. **SACRO** (inc supported accommodation)
93 Hope Street
Glasgow G2 6LD
0141-248 1763
fax 0141 248 1686

33. **Glasgow Council on Alcohol**
9th Floor, Elmbank Chambers
289 Bath Street, Glasgow G2 4JL
0141-226 3883
fax 0141-226 3014

34. **Victim Support (Glasgow)**
19 Bridgegate
Glasgow G1 5HX
0141-553 2415
fax 0141-2405

35. **Victim Support (Strathclyde)**
10 Jocelyn Square
Glasgow G1 5JU
0141-553 1726
fax 0141-552 3316

36. **Probation Hostels**
(Church of Scotland Board of Social Responsibility)
Dick Stewart Hostel
2 Westercraigs, Glasgow G31 2HZ
0141-554 0212

Dick Stewart Hostel
40 Circus Drive
Glasgow G31 2JE
0141-554 0277
fax 0141-554 6646

37. **Talbot Association**
Govanhill Project
75 Coplaw Street
Glasgow G42 7JG
0141-433 9223
fax 0141-433 9255

38. **APEX (Scotland)**
6th Florr, 94 Hope Street
Glasgow G2 6PH
0141-248 4537
fax 0141-248 4542

39. **Turnaround Project**
(Turning Point Scotland)
121 West Street
Glasgow G5 8BA
0141-418 0882
fax 0141-420 6170

40. **Phoenix House** (DTTO)
Unit 4b, Templeton Business Centre]
62 Templeton Street
Glasgow G40 1DA
0141-551 0703

Penal Establishments

41. HM Prison **Barlinnie**
Lee Avenue
Glasgow G33 2QX
0141-770 2000
fax 0141-770 9448

Social Work Unit
0141-770 2123
fax 0141-770 9808

Reid T (unit mgr)

THE HIGHLAND COUNCIL

1. Social Work Headquarters
Kinmylies Building
Leachkin Road
Inverness IV3 8NN
(01463) 703456

Dempster, Ms Hariet (director of social work)
Miller, Len (head of criminal justice)
Paulin, Jeremy (devpt mgr)

Criminal Justice Services

2. **Inverness Area**
Carsegate House
Glendoe Terrace
Inverness IV3 6ED
(01463) 724022

Rainnie, William (area team leader)

3. **Ross and Cromarty**
Caledonian House, High Street
Dingwall IV15 9RY
(01349) 865600

Morris, Ms Lynda (area team leader)

4a. **Lochaber and Skye**
Unit 4B1, Blar Mhor Industrial Estate
Caol **Fort William** PH33 7NG
(01397) 704668

McDermott, Pauleen (ssw)

4b. Social Work Area Office
Top Floor, Resource Centre
Bridge Road **Portree**
Isle of Skye
(01478) 612943

Leaworthy, Ms Jane (psw)

5a. **Caithness and Sutherland**
Unit 27b, Airport Industrial Estate
Wick KW1 4QS
(01955) 603161

MacKenzie, Keith (acting ssw)

5b. Social Work Area Office
Olsen House, Main Street
Golspie KW10 6RA
(01408) 634040

MacKenzie, Keith (acting ssw)

Drug Misuse

6. The Old Schoolhouse Culduthel
Culduthel Road
Inverness IV2 6AE
(01463) 716324

Bolger, Kenneth (ssw)

Community Service & Supervised Attendance

7. 196 Culduthel Road
Inverness IV2 4BH
(01463) 242511

Boyd, David (cso)
Gilmore, Mike (p, sao)
Currie, Alistair (proj off)

7a. Albany Road
Invergordon IV18 0HA
(01349) 853885

Oag, Alistair (cso)

7b. Unit 4B1, Blar Mhor Industrial Estate
Caol **Fort William** PH33 7NG
(01397) 704668

Wilson, John (cso)

7c. Unit 27b, Airport Industrial Estate
Wick KW1 4QS
(01955) 603161

Paul, Francis (projects officer)

Voluntary Projects

8. **APEX (Employment Guidance)**
17 Lotland Street
Inverness IV1 1ST
phone & fax (01463) 717033

MacDonald, Alistair (snr emplt counsellor)

9. **NCH (Intensive Probation)**
2nd Floor, 46 Church Street
Inverness IV1 1EH
(01463) 717227
fax (01463) 236335

Mawby, Mike (proj wrkr)

10. **SACRO (Supported Accomodation)**
The Old Schoolhouse Culduthel
Culduthel Road
Inverness IV2 6AE
(01463) 716325
fax (01463) 716326

Paterson, Lynne (mgr)
Bissett, David (proj wrkr)
Vacancy (proj wrkr)

Probation Hostel

Paulin, Jeremy (devpt mgr, sw liaison)
(01463) 703475

11. John Clark House
Waterloo Place
Inverness IV1 1NB
(01463) 712516

Edmiston, Linda (mgr)

Bail Beds

Paulin, Jeremy (devpt mgr, sw liaison)
(01463) 703475

11. Huntly House
Inverness IV3 6HA
(01463) 234123

Campbell, Alex (officer in charge)

Penal Establishment

12. HM Prison, Porterfield
Inverness IV2 3HH
(01463) 223489
fax (01463) 236595

Paulin, Jeremy (devpt mgr, sw liaison)
(01463) 703475

Barr, Bob (sw)
Graham, Ms Helen (psw)

INVERCLYDE COUNCIL

1. Social Work and Housing Services
Dalrymple House
195 Dalrymple Street
Greenock PA15 1LD
(01475) 714000
fax (01475) 714060

Gethin, Noreen (head of service)

Criminal Justice Services

2. **Court Liaison/Fieldwork**
Larkfield Office
11 Burns Road
Greenock PA16 0SE
(01475) 714500
fax (01475) 714515

McDonald, Stewart (service mgr)
Bradley, John (ssw)

3. **Greenock Sheriff Court**
Social Work Office
1 Nelson Street
Greenock PA15 1TR
(01475) 785321
fax (01475) 785194

4. **Community Service**
Unit 6, Kingston Business Park
Port Glasgow PA14 5DR
(01475) 715791
fax (01475) 715794

Clark, Anne (cs org)

5. **NCH Intensive Probation Unit**
9 Terrace Road
Greenock PA15 1DJ
phone & fax (01475) 727363

Hind, Alan (mgr)

6. **Supervised Attendance Order Scheme**
Unit 6, Kingston Business Park
Port Glasgow PA14 5DR
(01475) 715791
fax (01475) 715794

Darroch, George (sup att off)

Penal Establishments

7. Social Work Unit
HM Prison **Greenock**
Gateside, Greenock PA16 9AH
(01475) 787801
fax (01475) 783154

Miller, Ann (ssw)

MIDLOTHIAN COUNCIL

Out of hours contact: emergency social work service: freephone 0800 731 6969

1. Social Services Division
Fairfield House
8 Lothian Road
Dalkeith EH22 3AA
0131-270 7500
fax 0131-271 3624

2. **Criminal Justice Team**
Dalkeith Social Work Centre
11 St Andrew Street **Dalkeith**
Midlothian EH22 1AL
0131-271 3860
fax 0131-660 6792

Neil, I (practice team mgr)
Gray, M (p, ssw)
Anderson, M (cso)
Dudley, S (sw)
Gray, C (sw)
Vacancy (sw)
Kelly, J (sw)
Lyon, R (sw)

THE MORAY COUNCIL

Out of hours contact no: 0345 565656

Community Services Department

1. Springfield House
Edgar Road **Elgin** IV30 6FF
(01343) 557000
fax (01343) 546367

Martin, Mike (director of community services)
Sullivan, John (Head of Children, Families & Criminal Justice Services)

2. Criminal Justice Team
9 North Guildry Street
Elgin IV30 1JR
(01343) 541111
fax (01343) 550342

Dempsie, Blair (service manager)
Gillies, Ms Mairi (sw)
Keys, Ms Miranda (sw)
Reid, Ron (sw)
Terry, Ms Liz (p, sw)

Other Social Work Teams

3. 1 Gordon Street
Elgin IV30 1JQ
(01343) 552699
fax (01343) 541125

Central Moray Child Care Team
Rizza, Graeme (team manager)

North Moray Childcare Team
Harkins, Gerry (team manager)
Anderson, Peter (sw criminal justice)

4. **West Moray Child Care Team**
Inglewood, Inverene Road
Forres IV36 0DZ
(01309) 674382
fax (01309) 674747

Cotter, Mark (team manager)

5. **East Moray Child Care Team**
13 Cluny Square
Buckie AB56 1AH
(01542) 837200
fax (01542) 837201

Hall, Mrs Trisha (team manager)
Leitch, Robert (sw) criminal justice

NORTH AYRSHIRE COUNCIL

1. Social Work
Elliott House
Redburn Industrial Estate
Kilwinning Road
Irvine KA12 8TB
(01294) 317700

Docherty, Bernadette M (corporate director - social services)
McLean, W R (mgr criminal justice services)

2. **Criminal Justice Services**
20 Bank Street, **Irvine** KA12 0AD
(01294) 273110

Greaves, A (ssw)

3. **Criminal Justice Services**
157 New Street, **Stevenston** KA20 3HL
(01294) 463924

McCrae, J (ssw)

4. **Community Service Order Scheme**
157 New Street
Stevenson KA20 3HL
(01294) 463924

Mooney, J (cs org)

NORTH LANARKSHIRE COUNCIL

1. Social Work Department
Scott House, 73/77 Merry Street
Motherwell ML1 1JE
(01698) 332000
fax (01698) 332096

Dickie, Jim (director of sw)
Fegan, Mary (head of sw services)

Scott, John (principal officer criminal justice)
Scullion, Jim (co-ord, criminal justice)
McGuigan, Sean (resouce wrkr, criminal justice)

2. Social Work Department
Coats House, Gartlea Road
Airdrie ML6 6JA
(01236) 757000

Airdrie Sheriff Court
Walls, Bert (ssw, cj)

Airdrie Area Team
Smith, Owen (ssw, cj)

3. Carron House
Town Centre, Cumbernauld G67 1DP
(01236) 784000

Cumbernauld Area Team
Gardner, Keith (ssw, cj)

4. 8 Emma Jay Road
Bellshill ML4 1HX
(01698) 346666

Bellshill Area Team
O'Neill, Terri (ssw, cj)

5. 122 Bank Street
Coatbridge ML5 1ET
(01236) 622100

Coatbridge Area Team
Smith, Owen (ssw, cj)

6. Kings Centre
King Street
Wishaw ML2 8BS
(01698) 348200

Wishaw Area Team
Bell, Liz (ssw, cj)

7. Scott House, 73/77 Merry Street
Motherwell ML1 1JE
(01698) 332100

Motherwell Area Team
O'Neill, Terri (ssw, cj)

8. **Community Service Team**
Alexander Resource Centre
83 Blair Road
Coatbridge
(01236) 422544

Howie, Mary (cs mgr)
Cairns, Michael (asst cs mgr)

9. **Groupwork Project**
28 Muir Street
Motherwell ML1
(01698) 275944

MacPherson, Alan (proj mgr)

Penal Establishments

10. Social Work Unit
HM Prison **Shotts**
Newmill, Canthill Road
Shotts ML7 4LE
(01501) 824100

Cowan, Tom (ssw)

ORKNEY ISLANDS COUNCIL

Out of hours emergency contact: via Kirkwall Police (01856) 872241

1. Department of Community Social Services
School Place
Kirkwall KW15 1NY
(01856) 873535

Garland, Harry (director of community social services)
McTaggart, Sam (asst director, community care)
Williams, Adrian (asst director, children & families, criminal justice)
Hadley, Angela (snr asst director, suport services)

2. **Criminal Justice Section**
The Strynd
Kirkwall KW15 1HG
(01856) 875733
fax (01856) 875727

Humphreys, Jon (team mgr)
Thomson, Stuart (sw int probn)
Larmouth, John (sw)
MacLeod, Ian (cso)
Vacancy (clerical asst)
Purvis, Maureen (clerical asst)

PERTH & KINROSS COUNCIL

1. Head Office
   Housing & Social Work Service
   Pullar House
   35 Kinnoull Street
   Perth PH1 5GD
   (01738) 476700
   fax (01738) 476710

   Morrison, Gillian (head of sw services)

1a. Criminal Justice Service
   3-5 High Street
   Perth PH1 5JS

   Duncan, Allan (service mgr, cj services)
   (01738) 476836

   Paton, Mary (snr admin asst) (js)
   Patterson, Gillian (snr admin asst) (js)
   (0738) 476915

   Munro, Bill (research & info officer, cj services)
   (01738) 476716

2. 22 Whitefriar Street
   Perth PH1 1PP
   (01738) 444244
   fax (01738) 444250

   Courts & Community Team
   Connell, Paul (ssw)
   Beck, Eddie (sw)
   Fraser, Roxanne (sw)
   Haney, John (sw)
   Nisbet, Elizabeth (sw)
   Winstanley, Alexis (sw)
   Edwards, Paul (cj asst)
   Morgan, Christine (cj asst)
   Pow, Barbara (cj asst)

   Probation & Throughcare Team
   Warren, Alasdair (ssw)
   Brewer, Jeff (sw)
   Duncan, Robbie (sw)
   Egan, Susan (sw)
   Fairlie, Alison (sw)
   Penman, Shirley (sw)
   Thomson, Robert (sw)

   MacKenzie, Trudy (admin support)

3. **Community Service Workshop**
   Glover Street, **Perth** PH2 0JD
   (01738) 445793

   Johnston, Ken (cj asst, cso)
   Spark, John (cs supvr)
   Given, William (cs supvr)

Penal Establishments

4. Social Work Unit
   HM Prison, 3 Edinburgh Road
   Perth PH2 8AT
   (01738) 626883
   fax (01738) 625964

   Bone, John (ssw)
   Blackhall, Leanor (sw)
   Cairns, Michelle (sw)
   Constance, Angela (sw)
   Mahoney, Adam (sw)
   Duncan, Brenda (admin support)
   Harding, Paul (admin support)

5. Social Work Unit
   HM Prison **Friarton**
   Perth PH2 8DW
   (01738) 625885

   McFarlane, Kay (sw)

6. Social Work Unit
   HM Prison **Castle Huntly**
   Longforgan, By Dundee
   (01382) 360265
   fax (01382) 360510

   McIntosh, Heather (sw)
   Walker, Debbie (sw)

RENFREWSHIRE COUNCIL

1. Social Work Headquarters
   4th Floor, North Building
   Cotton Street
   Paisley PA1 1TZ
   0141-842 5957
   fax 0141-842 5144

   Duncan, Sheena (director of sw)
   Crawford, David (head of operations)
   Gorman, Bill (head of strategy & devpt)

   Criminal Justice Section
   0141-842 5130
   Bowie, David (principal officer, criminal justice)
   Connolly, Mike (snr resource officer, criminal justice)

2. **Community Service Team**
   62 Espedair Street
   Paisley PA2 6RW
   0141-840 1001
   fax 0141-849 0715

   McCombes, Kenny (cs org)

Fairns, Robert (cso)
Kane, Thomas (cso)
Paterson, Willie (cso)
Stewart, Mary (cso)
Skouse, John (csa)

3. **Community Alternatives Unit**
Queen Street
Paisley PA1 2TU
0141-887 5470
fax 0141-842 1078

Hawthorn, Dorothy (ssw) (temp)
Gray, Ruth (sw)
Kelly, Julie (sw)
Boylan, John (sw asst)

4. **Paisley Sheriff Court**
St James Street
Paisley PA3 2HW
0141-889 0617
fax 0141-848 9348

Maloney, Liz (ssw)
Pitt, Gordon (sw)
Crichton, John (sao)

5. **Johnstone Area Team**
Floorsburn House
Floors Street
Johnstone PA5 8TL
(01505) 342300
fax (01505) 342380

Leinster, Kenny (area mgr)
Aitken, Gordon (ssw)
Graham, James (sw)
Gray, Ruth (sw)
Hamilton, Kirsten (sw)
McEwan, James (sw)

6. **Paisley Area Team**
Kelvin House
River Cart Walk
Paisley PA1 1YS
0141-842 5151
fax 0141-842 4136

Vacancy (area mgr)
Smith, Iain (asst area mgr)
McLachlan, Yvonne (ssw)
Cloherty, Tom (sw)
Earl, Joyce (sw)
Lockhart, Robert (sw)
McIntosh, Anne-Marie (sw)
McNamara, William (sw)
Prior, Raymond (sw)
West, David (sw)
Wright, Irene (sw)

7. **Renfrew Area Team**
6-8 Manse Street
Renfrew PA4 8QH
0141-886 5784
fax 0141-885 2564

Macleod, Peter (area mgr)
Duffy, John (ssw)
Bryce, Sandy (sw)
McGee, Catherine (sw)
Turner, John (sw)

8. **Renfrew Substance Abuse**
20 Backsneddon Street
Paisley PA3 2DF
0141-889 1223
fax 0141-848 9776

Boyle, Ailsa (project leader)
Swan, Nick (snr project wrkr)
Kell, Valerie (snr project wrkr)
Fitzpatrick, Elaine (project wrkr)
Vacancy (project wrkr)
Vacancy (dual diagnosis wrkr)
Adams, Joan (gp outreach wrkr)

Health Board Trust Personnel
Parkinson, Margaret (snr nurse)
Shields, Connie (snr nurse)
Ferguson, Mandy (clinical nurse mgr)
Glasgow, Moira (nurse specialist, drugs)
Connor, Janice (nurse specialist, drugs)
Gough, Frank (nurse specialist - dual diagnosis)
McCrae, Kirstine (harm reduction nurse)

9. **Renfrew Council on Alcohol**
Queen Street
Paisley PA1 2TU
0141-887 0880
fax 0141-887 8063

Muir, Lorna (sw representative)
Crawford, Dr Alec (director)
McQuat, Margaret (snr counsellor)

SCOTTISH BORDERS COUNCIL

1. Social Work Headquarters
Newton St Boswells
Melrose TD6 0SA
(01835) 825080
fax (01835) 825081

Johnson, Colin (director of sw)
Hawkes, Chris (head of service families & criminal justice)

(01835) 825086

Anderson, Colin (group mgr, criminal justice)

2. Criminal Justice Team
Sheriff Court Buildings
Ettrick Terrace
Selkirk TD7 4LE
(01750) 23383
fax (01750) 23384

Keates, Dorothy (advanced pract/crt officer)
Flynn, Jenny M (sw Duns/Kelso)
Grant, Brian (sw Selkirk/Peebles)
Harte, Stephen (sw Duns/Kelso)
Hunter, Kate (sw Hawick)
Robertson, Toni (sw Galashiels)
Matthews, Angela (admin asst)

Community Service/Supervised Attendance
(01450) 370810
Parker, Ralph (ssw cs)
Wood, Liz (supervised attendance officer)

SHETLAND ISLANDS COUNCIL

Out of hours contact: duty social worker (01595) 695611

1. Department of Community Services
Social Care Services
91-93 St Olaf Street
Lerwick Shetland ZE1 0ES
(01595) 744444
fax (01595) 744460

Miller, Michelle (head of service)

Criminal Justice Social Work Unit
Morgan, Denise (acting criminal justice services mgr)
Vacancy (sw)
Miller, Christine (sw)
Whitelaw, Joy (sw)
Alderman, Andy (cs supvr)
Gilfillan, Frank (cs supvr) (temp)
Halcrow, Julie (snr clerical officer)

SOUTH AYRSHIRE COUNCIL

1. Social Work Headquarters
Holmston House
Holmston Road
Ayr KA7 3BA
(01292) 262111
fax (01292) 264132

Thompson, Mrs J (head of sw)
Hunter, J (criminal justice mgr)

2. **Criminal Justice Team**
2/4 New Road
Ayr KA8 8EX
(01292) 289749
fax (01292) 260065

Court Services, Fieldwork Services
CS Scheme, Supervised Attendance
Administration

SOUTH LANARKSHIRE COUNCIL

1. Social Work Headquarters
Criminal Justice Services
Council Offices
Almada Street
Hamilton ML3 0AA
(01698) 453700
fax (01698) 453718

Cameron, Sandy (exec director social work resources)

Brackenridge, Mairi (head of criminal justice services)
(01698) 453715
McGregor, Hugh (criminal justice services mgr)
(01698) 453716

Area Teams

2. **East Kilbride Local Office**
1st Floor, Civic Centre
Andrew Street, East Kilbride G74 1AD
(01355) 807000
fax (01355) 264458

Finnegan, Hilary (team leader)

3. **Rutherglen & Cambuslang Local Office**
380 King Street
Rutherglen G73 1DQ
0141-613 5055
fax 0141-647 9977

English, Allan (ssw)

4. **Blantyre Local Office**
45 John Street
Blantyre G72 0JG
(01698) 417400
fax (01698) 417428

Johnson, Hazel (team leader)

5. **Hamilton Local Office**
9 High Patrick Street
Hamilton ML3 7ES
(01698) 455466
fax (0698) 283257

McAllister, Marion (ssw)

6. **Clydesdale Local Office**
Council Offices, South Vennel
Lanark ML11 7JT
(01555) 673000
fax (01555) 673401

McKendrick, Alf (ssw)

7. **Larkhall Local Office**
6 Claude Street
Larkhall ML9 2BU
(01698) 884656
fax (01698) 307504

McGregor, Hugh (cj service mgr)

Community Service

8. **Blantyre Local Office**
45 John Street
Blantyre G72 0JG
(01698) 527484/527467/527408
fax (01698) 417428

McGregor, Hugh (cj service mgr)

9. **Community Service Workshop**

2/3a Third Road
High Blantyre Industrial Estate
High Blantyre GT2 0UP
(01698) 829509
fax (01698) 824799

Court Units

10. **Hamilton Sheriff Court**
Beckford Street
Hamilton ML3 6AA
(01698) 282957

Social Work Unit
101 Almada Street
Hamilton ML3 0EX
(01698) 282044
(01698) 427865 (diversion)
(01698) 540362 (supervised attendance)
fax (01698) 457427

Finnegan, Hilary (team leader)

10. **Lanark Sheriff Court**
Hope Stree
Lanark ML11 7NQ
(01555) 661531

Social Work Unit
Council Offices, South Vennel
Lanark ML11 7JT
(01555) 673000
fax (01555) 673401

Tannahill, Andrea (sw)

STIRLING COUNCIL

Out of hours contact: emergency duty team (01786) 470500

1. Community Services
11 Gladstone Place
Stirling FK8 2NN
(01786) 463812
fax (01786) 479172

Criminal Justice Service
Pinkman, Anne (head of cj services)
Donnelly, Mark (team mgr)

Probation, Court & Throughcare Team
Richardson, Marie (ssw)
Brady, Gerry (sw)
Connelly, Kristine (sw)
Davies, Matthew (sw)
Mander, Liz (sw crt)
Millar, Stewart (sw)
O'Donnell, John (sw)

Community Service & Supervised Attendance Orders
Kay, Linda (sw, cs)
Gilmour, Norman (cj asst)
Barron, Claire (cj asst, sao)
Cummings, James (cs supvr)
Davidson, Hugh (cs supvr)

Penal Establishment

2. Social Work Unit
HM Institution **Cornton Vale**
Cornton Road, Stirling FK9 5NY
(01786) 832591
fax (01786) 833597

Corvi, Elaine (ssw)
Carroll, Sadie (sw)
Thomas, Janet (sw)
Vacancy (p, sw)

WEST DUNBARTONSHIRE COUNCIL

1. Social Work & Housing Headquarters
   Council Offices
   Garshake Road
   Dumbarton G82 3PU
   (01389) 737000
   fax (01389) 727751

   Jay, Alexis (director of sw & housing)

2. Department of Social Work & Housing
   Criminal Justice Services
   McLean Place,
   Dumbarton G82 1PY
   (01389) 608484
   fax (01389) 608480

   McQuillan, Raymond (section head, criminal justice)

3. **Community Service Orders**
   Unit 3, Leven Valley Enterprise Centre
   Castlehill Road
   Dumbarton G82 5BN
   (01389) 733726
   fax (01389)733958

   Dady, Philip (cs org)

4. **Assessment Team**
   McLean Place
   Dumbarton G82 1PY
   (01389) 608484
   fax (01389) 608480

   Firth, Norman (ssw)

5. **Community Supervision Team**
   17 Castle Street
   Dumbarton G82 1QS
   (01389) 608070
   fax (01389) 608073

   Scullion, Irene (ssw)

WEST LOTHIAN COUNCIL

1. Community Services
   West Lothian House
   Almondvale Boulevard
   Livingston EH54 6QG
   (01506) 777000
   fax (01506) 777256

   Blair, G (head of sw)
   Quigley, Ian (acting snr mgr)

   Criminal Justice Services
   Rowbotham, D (criminal justice mgr)

   Social Care Emergency Team
   (01506) 777401
   fax (01506) 777403

   Tullis, A (emergency services mgr)

2. Lomond House
   Beveridge Square
   Livingston EH54 6QF
   (01506) 775900
   fax (01506) 775925

   Criminal Justice Team
   Streater, Paul (ssw)

WESTERN ISLES

Now known as Comhairle nan Eilean Siar

Nacro (National Association for the Care and Resettlement of Offenders)

169 Clapham Road, London SW9 0PU 020-7582 6500 *fax 020-7735 4666*

Nacro is an independent voluntary organisation working to prevent crime and resettle offenders.

Nacro provides a wide range of practical services to offenders, ex offenders, those at risk of offending, their families, friends and people working with them; and for communities suffering from the effects of crime. Services include employment, training and work experience; housing; resettlement advice projects; local schemes involving volunteers to provide structured activities, advice services, etc to young people and others; training services and courses for people working with offenders, ex offenders and others with special needs.

Nacro also works with different agencies, organisations and communities to develop more effective approaches to tackling crime and dealing with offenders in the fields of community safety; youth crime; race and criminal justice; mental health. Nacro's development services include reviews and audits; strategic planning and policy development; project development and management; research, monitoring and evaluation; training.

The following address list includes headquarters, regional and local contacts for all Nacro's work. If you have difficulty contacting any Nacro service, please contact the Information Officer at Nacro's head office on 020-7582 6500.

[NCT = New Careers Training]

HEAD OFFICE

1. **Nacro**
169 Clapham Road
London SW9 0PU
020-7582 6500 (switchboard)
020-7840 6464 (resettlement info & advice service)
fax 020-7735 4666
e mail first name.surname@nacro.org.uk
www.nacro.org.uk

all contact via main switchboard unless otherwise indicated

Helen Edwards (chief exec)
Wendy Birch (pa to chief exec)

Policy & Info Directorate
Paul Cavadino (director)
Richard Garside (hd of communications)
Corinne Seymour (training inc training for prison staff)
Melior Whitear (publications)
Cynthia Sutherland (publications sales)
Kingsley Mbajuwa (Easily Accessible Service Info database - EASI)
Events: contact Nicola Fulton on 020-7840 6466

Media: contact Neera Dhingra on 020 7840 6497
e mail media@nacro.org.uk
Resettlement plus helpline: contact duty info officer on 020-7840 6464

Research & Devpt Directorate
Vacancy (director)
Frank Warburton (crime & social policy)
Graeme Sandell (mental health unit)
Chris Stanley (youth crime sectn - England)
Keith Towler (hd of Nacro Cymru & youth crime sectn - Wales) tel & fax (01792) 468400
Cathy McDermott & Pete Aldridge (fundraising)
Carol Hendrickson (supporter services)

Education & Employment Directorate
Craig Harris (director) 0161-860 7444
Selina Corkery (Nacro services publications & info) 020-7840 6455

Housing Directorate
Tim Bell (director) 0115-985 7744
Selina Corkery (Nacro services publications & info) 020-7840 6455

Race & Criminal Justice Directorate
Vacancy (director)
Carol Daly (race & c.j. unit)
Richie Dell (prison devpt - race)
Jackie Worrall (prison devpt - resettlement) (01926) 335576
Jackie Lowthian (prison devpt - women) (01924) 893621

Finance & Resources Directorate
Jane Crumpton-Taylor (director)

Welfare Fund
Sandra McIntosh 020-7840 6494

NATIONAL & REGIONAL OFFICES

2. **Nacro Cymru**
35 Heathfield
Swansea SA1 6EJ

tel/fax (01792) 468480
e mail (name)@Nacrocymru.demon.uk

Keith Towler

3. **Training** (inc. Prisons Link Unit)
Head Office contact: Corinne Seymour
(0976) 715270

Challenge House
148-150 High Street, Aston
Birmingham B6 4US
0121-250 5235
fax 0121-250 5239

Angela Hughes
Judith Ford
Saida Banu Zaman
Maggie Hadley

4. **Crime & Social Policy**

South
237 Queenstown Road
Battersea, London SW8 3NP
020-7501 0555
fax 020-7501 0556

Frank Warburton (section head)

North
567a Barlow Moor Road
Chorlton-cum-Hardy
Manchester M21 8AE
0161-860 7444
fax 0161-860 7555

Sharon Lewis

5. **Education & Employment Directorate**
567a Barlow Moor Road
Chorlton-cum-Hardy
Manchester M21 8AE
0161-860 7444
fax 0161-860 7555

Craig Harris (director)

6. **Housing**
16 Vivian Avenue
Sherwood Rise
Nottingham NG5 1AF
0115-985 7744
fax 0115-962 8948

Tim Bell (director)

South East Regional Office
2nd Floor, Chelmer House
11-21 Springfield Road
Chelmsford CM2 6JE
(01245) 606010
fax (01245) 606011

John Lowery (reg mgr)

London Regional Office
159 Clapham Road
London SW9 0PU
020-7840 6480
fax 020-7840 6481

Julie Ruby (reg mgr)

Midlands Regional Office
1 Hastings Street
Normanton, Derby DE23 6QQ
(01332) 273703
fax (01332) 273910

Helen O'Connor (reg mgr)

NW & N Wales Regional Office
567a Barlow Moor Road
Chorlton-cum-Hardy
Manchester M21 8AE
0161-860 7444
fax 0161-860 7555

Dave McCarthy (reg mgr)

7. **Mental Health Unit**
Head Office contact: Graeme Sandell

South West
Barton Hill Settlement
43 Ducie Road
Barton Hill, Bristol BS5 0AX
phone & fax 0117-955 6971

Dave Spurgeon

8. **Youth Crime Section**
Head Office contact: Chris Stanley

Community Remand Projects
Inner London, Bradford,
Newcastle, Bristol
contact: Chris Stanley (above)

VOCS (Victim Offender Conferencing Service)
contact Ann Tighe at head office

Bail Support, Policy & Dissemination Unit
Sue Thomas (01792) 468400

Midlands
1st Floor, Spencer Court
143 Albany Road, Coventry CV5 6ND
phone & fax 024-7667 0861

Peter Gill

Wales
35 Heathfield
Swansea SA1 6EJ
phone & fax (01792) 468400

Keith Towler

LOCAL PROJECTS

North West

9. **Nacro Housing in G Manchester Area Office**
567a Barlow Moor Road
Chorlton-cum-Hardy
Manchester M21 8AE
0161-860 7444
fax 0161-860 7555

Marie Hurley (area mgr)
Andrew Gray (area mgr)

10. **Nacro Housing on Merseyside**
1st Floor, Wellington Buildings
The Strand **Liverpool** L2 0PP
0151-330 6608/9
fax 0151-474 4526

Vacancy (area mgr)

Nacro Merseyside Education & Employment
address as above
0151-330 6600
Val Metcalfe (area mgr)

Safer Merseyside Partnership
address as above
0151-330 6610
fax 0151-330 6613
Kevin Wong

11. **Nacro Housing in Chester**
16 Canalside
Chester CH1 3LH
(01244) 318232
fax (01244) 314009

Wendy Bailey (area mgr)

12. **Nacro Cumbria Education & Employment**
42 Warwick Road
Carlisle CA1 1DN
(01228) 530002
fax (01228) 534699

Glynis Tuke (area mgr)

Nacro Bolton Education & Employment
Unit 12, No. 3 Mill
Halliwell Industrial Estate
Rossini Street
Bolton BL1 8DL
(01204) 494228
fax (01204) 849066

Anne Gregory (area mgr)

13. **Time Out Project**
10 Richmond Terrace
Blackburn BB1 7BP
(01254) 679828
fax (01254) 675706

Antoinette Harrop

14. **Salford Football Community Link Project**
Deans Youth Activity Centre
Deans Road, Swinton
Salford M27 3JF
0161-794 1088

15. **Oldham Football Community Link Project**
PO Box 40, West Street
Oldham OL1 1XJ
0161-911 4051

Roy Soule

16. **Nacro Resettlement Project**
HMP and YOI Styal
Wilmslow, Cheshire SK9 4HR
(01625) 532141 ext 432

Jan Appleton

North East

Community Remands Project (Newcastle)
contact: Chris Stanley at Head Office
020 7582 6500

17. **Nacro Services in Tees Valley**
Brian Rowcroft (divnl mgr)

123 Marton Road
Middlesbrough TS1 2DU
(01642) 223551
fax (01642) 254244

Hutchinson Street
Stockton-on-Tees TS18 1RW
(01642) 615554
fax (01642) 611050

Waverley Buildings
Mainsforth Terrace
Hartlepool TS25 1TZ
phone & fax (01429) 863335

Teesside Court Help Desk
Teesside Magistrates' Court
Victoria Square
Middlesbrough TS1 2AS
(01642) 247225

Elaine Daglish
Neil Johnson

18. The Old Junior School
Bowman Street
Darlington DL3 0HE
(01325) 282934
fax (01325) 465771

Brian Rowcroft

20. **Nacro Northumbria Education & Employment**
29 Welbeck Road
Byker Village
Newcastle-upon-Tyne NE6 2HU
0191-265 8164
fax 0191-224 1400

Kevin Royston (area mgr)

Sunderland Focused Caution Scheme
Task Force, Radlett Road
Red House, Sunderland SR5 5QZ
0191-516 9959
fax 0191-516 9769

Karen Shaw

Yorkshire & Humberside

Community Remands Project (W Yorks)
contact: Chris Stanley at Head Office
020 7582 6500

21. **Nacro W Yorkshire Education & Employment**
Lovell House, 118 North Street
Leeds LS2 7PN
0113-243 4684
fax 0113-246 1684

Sue Scott (area mgr)

Hull Prison Visitors' Centre
13 Newton Court
Hedon Road, Hull HU9 1JF
(01482) 218503

Valerie Batty

Leeds Football Community Link Project
Head Gardener's Cottage
Parkfield Ave, Cross Flatts Park
Leeds LS11 7NA
0113-277 8369
fax 0113-276 0283

Julie Lund

22. **Safer Communities Partnership**
103 Victoria Street South
Grimsby DN31 1NH
(01472) 311611
fax (01472) 311612

Anne Lawtey

23. **Nacro Services in S Yorkshire**
80 Headford Street
Sheffield S3 7WB
0114-272 2319
fax 0114-275 1503

Eileen Lamb (divnl mgr)

24. Office 7, Acorn Centre
51 High Street, Grimethorpe
South Yorkshire S72 7BB
(01226) 780795
fax (01226) 781156

Linda Finney

25. **Grimethorpe Youth Activities Unit & Training Centre**
Elizabeth Street
Grimethorpe, Barnsley S72 7HZ
(01226) 780961
fax (01226) 711483

Linda Finney (training centre)
Dave Robson (yau)

26. **Young People and Community Safety Project (Sheffield)**
c/o Education Department
Leopold Street
Sheffield S1 1RJ
0114-273 5829
fax 0114-273 5894

Maureen Fair

Wales

27. **Nacro Cymru**
Head Office
35 Heathfield
Swansea SA1 6EJ
tel & fax (01792) 468400
e mail (name)@Nacrocym.demon.co.uk

Keith Towler

28. **Nacro Housing in North Wales**
Cathedral Chambers
202 High Street
Bangor LL57 1NY
(01248) 371192
fax (01248) 371925

Wendy Bailey (area mgr)

29. **Nacro Cymru Education & Employment**
117 High Street
Bangor LL57 1NT
(01248) 354602
fax (01248) 355400

Anne Newhall (divnl mgr)

30. **React Project**
12 Bank Street
Wrexham LL11 1AH
(01978) 314313
fax (01978) 353571

31. **Nacro South Wales Education & Employment**
42-46 Holton Road
Barry CF63 4HD
(01446) 745080
fax (01446) 736148

Steve Ferugia

32. **Youth Crime Section & Bail Support, Policy and Dissemination Unit**
35 Heathfield
Swansea SA1 6EJ
phone & fax (01792) 468400

Keith Towler (youth crime section)
Sue Thomas (bspdu)

Midlands

33. **Nacro Housing in Birmingham & Sandwell**
Challenge House
148-150 High Street
Aston, Birmingham B6 4US
0121-359 8070
fax 0121-359 6528

Andy Humberstone (area mgr)

34. **Nacro Housing in Coventry**
Ground Floor, 1 Broomfield Road
Earlsdon, Coventry CV5 6JW
02476 715113
fax 02476 711693

Andy Humberstone (area mgr)

35. **Nacro Housing in Staffordshire**
Kimberley House, 2-4 Howard Place
Shelton, Stoke on Trent ST1 4NQ
(01782) 272525
fax (01782) 279017

Helen Scatcherd (area mgr)

36. **Nacro Services in Birmingham & Staffordshire**
330 Hospital Street
Newtown, Birmingham B19 2NJ
0121-554 6342
fax 0121-523 6895

Helen Stevenson (divnl mgr)

Challenge House
148-150 High Street
Aston, Birmingham B6 4US
0121-359 8070
fax 0121-359 6528

58 Church Street
Tamworth B79 7DF
(01827) 56420
fax (01827) 564522

Chris Ward (area mgr)

37. **Nacro in Derbyshire**

Nacro Housing in Derby
1 Hastings Street
Normanton, Derby DE23 6QQ
(01332) 273703
fax (01332) 273910

Helen Scatcherd (area mgr)

Osmaston Family Project
28-30 Varley Street
Allenton, Derby DE24 8DE
(01332) 384414
fax (01332) 203679

Helen Scatcherd (area mgr)

38. **Nacro in Nottinghamshire**

Nacro Housing in Nottingham
16 Vivian Avenue
Sherwood Rise
Nottingham NG5 1AF
0115-985 7744
fax 0115-962 8948

Paul Phillips (area mgr)

Nottingham Mediation Service & Nottingham Community Justice Project
25 Vivian Avenue
Sherwood Rise
Nottingham NG5 1AF
0115-962 0035
fax 0115-985 7397

Paul Phillips (area mgr)

The Aspley Youth Club
Melbourne Park

Melbourne Road, Aspley
Nottingham NG8 5HL
0115-942 4555/8
fax 0115-942 4555

Gailyn Groves

39. **Nacro Services in the Black Country**
Marriott House
West Cross Shopping Centre
Oldbury Road
Smethwick B66 1JG
0121-558 1902
fax 0121-558 6909

11 Tan Bank
Wellington
Shropshire TF1 1HJ
(01952) 243689
fax (01952) 245445

Mike Bainbridge (area mgr)

1st Floor, Challenge Building
Hatherton Street
Walsall WS1 1YG
(01922) 653330
fax (01922) 654783

Wolverhampton Youth Activities Unit
26 Waterloo Road
Wolverhampton WV1 4BL
(01902) 422640
fax (01902) 429450

Richard Clarke

East Anglia

40. **Nacro Services in East Anglia**
1 Bridge Street
Wisbech PE13 1AF
(01945) 587898
fax (01945) 582670

Linda Goult (divnl mgr)

Dunlop Road
Hadleigh Road Industrial Estate
Ipswich IP2 0UG
(01473) 288838
fax (01473) 288727

Mandy Cowan

1st Floor, Reunion House
35 Jackson Road
Clacton on Sea CO15 1JA
(01255) 431877
fax (01255) 476976

Chris Luff

Nacro Youth Choices
Room 19, St Francis House
141-147 Queens Road
Norwich NR1 3PN
tel & fax (01603) 665124

Nicola Bennett

41. **Nacro Housing in Lincolnshire**
Brunswick House
86-88 Carholme Road
Lincoln LN1 1SP
(01522) 522213/525383
fax (01522) 567877

Martin Wilson (area mgr)

Housing/supported lodgings referrals
(01522) 514127/522050

42. **Nacro Housing in Essex & Hertfordshire**
2nd Floor, Chelmer House
11-21 Springfield Road
Chelmsford CM2 6JE
(01245) 606010
fax (01245) 606011

Brendan O'Mahony

South

43. **Nacro Dorset Education & Employment**
The Lion Works
543 Wallisdown Road
Poole BH12 5AD
(01202) 539966
fax (01202) 539969

Tom Lund

44. **On Side** (Resettlement project for juvenile offenders)
Grenville Wing
HM YOI Portland
Grove Road
Easton, Portland DT5 1DL
(01305) 820310 ext 253

Hazel Hodder

45. **Nacro Medway Education & Employment**
Newbridge House
18 New Road Avenue
Chatham ME4 6BA
(01634) 818305
fax (01634) 812727

Pauline Box (area mgr)

46. **Nacro Surrey Education & Employment**
1st Floor Offices
11-17 Kingston Road
Staines, Middx TW18 4QX
(01784) 492192
fax (01784) 492101

Nigel Good (area mgr)

47. **Nacro Services in Sussex**
Unit D5, Enterprise Point
Melbourne Street
Brighton BN2 3LH
(01273) 704010
fax (01273) 704028

Hylda Mounsey

Key in Magazine Project
(01273) 683318
fax (01273) 620203

Nicky Jeffery

VOCS Wessex
(Portsmouth, SE Hants, Isle of Wight)
Darby House, Orkney Road
Cosham, Portsmouth PO6 3LU
(01705) 327393
fax (01705) 327389

Debra Clothier
David Bourne

London

Community Remand Project
contact Chris Stanley at Head Office
020-7582 6500

48. **VOCS (Victim Offender Conferencing Service)**

VOCS Westminster
(Westminster, Kensington & Chelsea, Hammersmith & Fulham)
1 Compton Street
London W2 1ND
020-7641 7753
fax 020-7641 5313

Chris Pearce
Stephanie Linn

VOCS Hackney
Unit B2, 3 Bradbury Street
London N16 8JN
tel & fax 020-7690 5088

Mandie Player

VOCS Southwark
(Southwark and young adult work only in Lambeth)
c/o Southwark YOT
90 Blakes Road
London SE15 6EP

Joe McGrane

49. **Kilburn Mediation Service**
21-22 Peel Precinct
London NW6 5BS
020-7372 6544
fax 020-7372 7703

Sonia Reid

50. **London Heatcare**
69 Portland Road
South Norwood
London SE25 4UN
020-8654 6060
fax 020-8654 6363

Gary Weston

51. **Nacro Services in London**

Brixton Prison Information Room
G Wing, HM Prison
Jebb Avenue
London SW2 5XF
020-8674 9811 ext 504
fax 020-8674 6128

Joyce Headley

Nacro Youth Services in London
10 Wynne Road
London SW9 0BB
020-7737 3435
fax 020-7733 0183

Vicky Rhodes

Nacro Greater London Education & Employment
Unit 16, The Windsor Centre
Windsor Grove
London SE27 9NT
020-8761 6242
fax 020-8761 1825

Sam Sykes (divnl mgr)

1st Floor, 230-234 Brixton Road
London SW9 6AH
020-7738 4355
fax 020-7738 4359

Leida Dadkhah

Golden Arrow House
237a Queenstown Road
Battersea, London SW8 3NP
020-7978 3000
fax 020-7978 3001

Nigel Good (area mgr)

Nacro Housing in London
159 Clapham Road
London SW9 0PU
020-7840 6480
fax 020-7840 6481

Southwark Family Mediation Project
10 Wynne Road
London SW9 0BB
020-7326 4055
0958 786334

Jodie Holder

Waltham Forrest YAU
Tennants' Resource Centre
c/o Boundary Road Estate Office
Boundary Road Estate
Colchester Road
London E17 8AL
020-8520 3088
fax 020-8520 3077

Sonya Campbell

SOVA

1. **SOVA Head Office**
1st Floor, Chichester House
37 Brixton Road
London SW9 6DZ
020-7793 0404
fax 020-7735 4410

2. **SOVA Regional Office**
Aizlewood's Business Centre
Aizlewood's Mill
Nursery Street
Sheffield S3 8GG
0114 282 3187
fax 0114 282 3292

Cheshire

3. **SOVA Cheshire Community Mentoring Project**
c/o Crewe Magistrates' Court
The Law Court
Civic Centre, Crewe CW1 2DT
(01244) 614177

Maureen Fleet (co-ord)

4. **SOVA Thorn Cross**
HM YOI Thorn Cross
Arley Road, Appleton Thorn
Warrington WA4 4RL
(01925) 605112
fax (01925) 605013

Karen Henry (snr proj mgr)

5. **SOVA Risley**
HM Prison Risley
Warrington Road
Risley, Warrington WA3 6BP
(01925) 763871 ext 778

Philippa Lyon (mgr)

Derbyshire

6. **SOVA/Derbyshire Emplt & Volunteer Project**
c/o Derbyshire Probation Service
Willow House, 1a Willow Row
Derby DE1 3NZ
(01332) 200127
fax (01332) 204393

Al Murray (mgr)

7. **Derbyshire Community Mentoring**
56 Cobden Road
Chesterfield S40 4TD
(01246) 347629
fax (01246) 347639

Jacqueline Mason (mgr)

8. **SOVA Derby City Youth Offending Service**
55 Ashbourne Road
Derby DE22 3FS
phone & fax (01332) 717525

Sally Tarrant (co-ord)

Essex

9. **SOVA Essex Probation Partnership Project**
4th Floor, Ashby House
Brook Street, Chelmsford CM1 1UH
(01245) 287154
fax (01245) 491321

Graham Furnival (mgr)

Hampshire

10. **SOVA Wessex Youth Offending Team Reparation Partnership**
180 Culver Road
Basingstoke, Hants RG21 3NL

(01256) 475200
fax (01256) 475270

Tom Williams (mgr)

Hertfordshire

11. **SOVA Herts Probation Partnership Project**
25d Alma Road
St Albans, Herts AL1 3AR
(01727) 8678000
fax (01727) 811163

Godfrey Leak (mgr)

Humberside

12. **SOVA Hull Leaving Care Mentoring Scheme**
Interactive
Young People's Support Service
Stonefield House
16/20 King Edward's Street
Hull HU1 3SS
(01482) 331004

Sarah Wortley (proj co-ord)

13. **SOVA Hull Befrienders**
Gleneagles Centre
East Carr Road
Hull HU8 9LB
(01482) 701479
fax (01482) 788399

Joanne Gale (mgr)

Lincolnshire

14. **SOVA Lincoln**
Stonebow Chambers
26 Guildhall Street
Lincoln LN1 1TR
01522 540251
fax 01522 542692

Sue Ford (reg director)

15. **SOVA Lincolnshire Befrienders Scheme**
SOVA Volunteer Centre
Lamb Gardens, St Giles
Lincoln LN2 4EG
tel & fax (01522) 575692

Julie Lawson (mgr)

SOVA Lincolnshire New Deal U2
(01522) 589398
Gary Kernaghan (snr proj mgr)

SOVA MIlenium Volunteers
(01522) 589398
Maureen Keddy (mgr)

16. **SOVA Lincolnshire Befrienders - Louth**
Louth Social Services
Eastfield House
Eastfield Road
Louth LN11 7AN
(01507) 600800 ext. 4452

Rosemary Baxendale (volunteer co-ord)

17. **SOVA Lincolnshire Befrienders - Stamford**
Stamford Social Services
38 North Street
Stamford PE9 2YN
(01780) 751821
fax (01780) 751821

Suzanne Collins (volunteer co-ord)

18. **SOVA Volunteer Scheme**
The Audit & Review Team
17 Francis Street
Scunthorpe DN16 6NS
(01724) 278485
fax (01724) 278486

Sue Scoffin (volunteer co-ord)

19. **Lincolnshire Reparation/Mediation Scheme**
Development House
64 Newland, Lincoln LN1 1YA
(01522) 554580
fax (01522) 554552

Lucy Coleman (co-ord)

6 St Catherine's Road
Grantham, Lincs NG31 6TS
(01476 579205
fax (01476) 559166

Judith Hibble (prog mgr)

Louth Social Services
Eastfield House, Eastfield Road
Louth LN11 7AN
(01507) 600800 ext 4452

Rosemary Baxendale (volunteer co-ord)

20. **SOVA Appropriate Adult**
Youth Offending Team
Lime House. Foundry Street
Horncastle LN9 6AQ
(01507) 522279
fax (01522) 554731

Gillian Round (volunteer co-ord)

Greater London

21. **SOVA/Central London**
292 Camberwell Road
London SE5 0DL
020-7708 1962
fax 020-7708 4384

Kate Slater (mgr)

22. **SOVA Young London**
Noel Lounge, Great Field
Grahame Park, Colindale
London NW9 5TS
020-8200 9966
fax 020-8205 7356

Nick Styles (mgr)

23. **D2W**
1st Floor, Chichester House
37 Brixton Road
London SW9 6DZ
020-7840 0808
fax 020-7840 0860

Mary Geaney (prog director)

24. **SOVA Ealing**
2 Cheltenham Place
Acton, London W3 8JS
020-8896 0042
fax 020-8752 2179

Dominic Dineen (mentoring mgr)

25. **SOVA Hounslow**
Redlees Centre, Redlees Park
Twickenham Road
Isleworth, Middx TW7 7EF
020-8847 1053
fax 020-8847 2838

Martin Talbot (mentoring mgr)

26. **SOVA/Middlesex**
Research House Business Centre
Fraser Road, Perivale
Greenford, Middx UB6 7AQ
020-8537 3431
fax 020-8537 3432

Donna Payne (mgr)

27. **SOVA Croydon Young People's Project**
Cornerstone House
14 Willis Road
Croydon CR0 2XX
020-8665 5668
fax 020-8665 1972

Pauline McGrath (mgr)

28. **Bexley & Greenwich Young People's Mentoring Project**
c/o The Leaving Care Team
Howbury Centre
Slade Green Road
Erith, Kent DA8 2HX
020-8303 7777 ext 3958
fax 020-8319 9602

Steve Hall (mgr)

29. **SOVA Volunteer Supported Basic Education Scheme**
HM YOI/RC Feltham
Bedfont Road
Feltham, Middx TW13 4ND
020-8890 0061 ext 456
fax 020-8844 1551

Pip Deverson (mgr)

30. **SOVA Pathfinder**
HM Prison Wandsworth
PO Box 757, Heathfield Road
London SW18 3HS
020-8874 7292 ext 409
fax 020-7708 4384

Kath Pitt (mgr)

Greater Manchester

31. **SOVA Tameside Project**
19-21 Wellington Street
Ashton-under-Lyne
Tameside OL6 6BG
0161-339 7232
fax 0160-339 9850

Liz Featherstone (mgr)

Nottinghamshire

32. **North Nottingham U2 New Deal**
c/o Acorn Initiative
Dukeries Complex
Whinney Lane
Ollerton NG22 9TD
(01623) 860018

Kerry Knowles (proj co-ord)

Staffordshire

33. **SOVA Staffordshire Leaving Care Mentoring Scheme**
Priory House
Friars Terrace
Stafford ST17 4AU
(01785) 276984
fax (01785) 277032

Alison Perry (mgr)

Yorkshire

34. **SOVA Triumph & Success (Rowntree)**
Aizlewood's Mill
Nursery Street
Sheffield S3 8GG
0114-282 3149
fax 0114-282 3292

Vacancy (snr proj mgr)

SOVA Sheffield New Deal
0114-282 3106
Clare Lupton (mentoring officer)

35. **SOVA Sheffield Volunteer Project**
c/o New Directions
8 Eastern Avenue
Sheffiled S2 2GJ
0114-241 6097
fax 0114-281 2328

36. **STEP/NUYPP**
The 16-25 Shop
123 St Philips Road
Sheffield S3 7JQ
0114-270 6411

Julia Stanley (snr proj mgr)

37. **SOVA Community Support Project**
7 St Peters Close
Sheffield S1 2EJ
0114-228 8545/6
fax 0114-281 2191

Marion Codd (snr proj mgr)

38. **SOVA Sheffield CAST & Befriending Scheme**
Eastbank Children's Centre
83 Eastbank Road, Sheffield S2 3PX
0114 279 8889
fax 0114-276 8666

Thelma Whittaker (mgr)

39. **SOVA Sheffield Young Person's Mentoring**
1st Floor, Carver House
2 Carver Street, Sheffield S1 4FS
0114-241 6097
fax 0114-281 2328

Jane Daniels (proj co-ord)

40. **SOVA Millenium Volunteers**
4 Carver Street
Sheffield S1 4FS
0114-273 9389
fax 0114-275 2357

Joanne Chambers (mgr)

41. **SOVA Manor Mentoring Project**
The Shop, 283 Prince of Wales Road
Sheffield S2 1FH
0114-265 4757

Richard Large (proj co-ord)

42. **SOVA Sheffield Youth Inclusion Project**
9a Teynham Road
Shirecliffe, Sheffield S5 8TT
0114-234 0308
fax 0114-234 2053

Gemma Lock (mgr)

43. **SOVA Projects in Rotherham**
c/o South Yorkshire Probation Service
Main Street
Rotherham S60 1AJ
(01709) 839579
fax (01709) 720250

Paul Whitehouse (dist mgr)

44. **SOVA Barnsley**
2nd Floor, Central Chambers
74-76 Eldon Street
Barnsley S70 2JN
(01226) 215257
fax (01226) 215262

Pauline Stott (snr proj mgr)

45. **SOVA Yorkshire Prisons ETE**
HM Prison Wealstun
Wetherby, W Yorks LS23 7AZ
(01937) 844844 ext 3286
fax (01937) 845862

HM Prison Askham Grange
Askham Richard
York YO2 3PT
(01904) 704236 ext 438

HM YOI Hatfield
Thorne Road
Hatfield, Doncaster DN7 6EL
(01405) 812336 ext 331

Gina Carter (snr proj mgr)

Wales

46. **SOVA Wales**
2nd Floor, Ladywell House
Newtown, Powys SY16 1JB
01686 623873
fax 01686 623875

Chris Arnold (Wales director)

47. **SOVA North Wales New Deal**
Kelso House, 13 Grosvenor Road
Wrexham, Clwyd LL11 1BS
01978 262223
fax 01978 263332

Chis Nordoff (proj mgr)

48. **SOVA South Wales New Deal**
33 Heathfield
Swansea SA1 6EJ
(01792) 463597
fax (01792) 461884

Julia Cook (mgr SE Wales)

49. **SOVA Dyfed Volunteer Scheme**
33 Heathfield
Swansea SA1 6EJ
phone & fax (01267) 229099

Clive Cowley (mgr SW Wales)

50. **SOVA Partneriaeth Ymateb**
Ty Newydd Probation & Bail Hostel
Llandegai, Bangor
Gwynedd LL57 4LG
(01248) 326990
fax (01248) 371204

Sheila Parry (trainer)

51. **SOVA Partneriaeth Ymateb**
Rhyl Probation Office
Epworth Lodge
Brighton Road
Rhyl LL18 3HF
(01745) 343215
fax (01745) 356137

Catherine Sharp (co-ord)

RPS RAINER

1. RPS Rainer (Royal Philanthropic Society incorporating The Rainer Foundation)
Rectory Lodge
High Street, Brasted
Westerham, Kent TN16 1JF
(01959) 578200
fax (01959) 561891
e mail mail@rpsrainer.org.uk

Partnership projects providing services for young people at risk.

Projects in partnership with Probation Services

2. **Break Free**
Unit 1, 4 Factory Lane
Bruce Grove
London N17 9LF
020-8885 5000

includes Education, training, employment

3. **Essex Motor Project**
Unit 9, Winstanley Way
Basildon
Essex SS14 3BP
(01268) 273380

4. **Fresh Start**
2nd Floor, 6 Liverpool Terrace
Worthing, W Sussex BN11 1TA
(01903) 219600

5. **Medway Motor Project**
Unit 28, Castle View Business Centre
Rochester, Kent ME1 1PH
(01634) 811466

6. **New Directions**
8 Eastern Avenue
Sheffield S2 2GJ
0114-241 6097

7. **Rainbow**
Room 4, 1-3 Hylton Road
Worcester WR2 5JN
(01905) 339200

MEDIATION UK

Mediation UK is the umbrella organisation for victim/offender, community and schools mediation services. It publishes guidelines for starting victim/offender and community mediation services, and has a victim/offender mediation network of all those interested in it. Anyone can join Mediation UK and receive its quarterly magazine and newsletter. Mediation UK also runs an annual conference at which victim/offender mediation is featured.

Alexander House
Telephone Avenue, Bristol BS1 4BS
0117 904 6661
fax 0117 904 3331

Tony Billinghurst (director)

Avon

Bristol Mediation VOICES
(Victim Offender Community Conferencing Project)
Alexander House
Telephone Avenue, Bristol BS1 4BS
0117 9043321
fax 0117 907 4097

This multi-agency project runs restorative conferences involving young offenders (10-17), their victims and supporters on both sides.

Right Track
9 Lower Ashley Road
St Paul's, Bristol BS2 9QA
0117-935 1515

A Children's Society project that aims to provide for Black children and young people between 10 and 17 years, who are involved in the criminal justice system.

Stokes Croft Youth Justice Centre (NCH Action for Children)
59/61 Stokes Croft
Bristol BS1 3QP
0117-923 2077
fax 0117-942 5126

Community alternatives to custodial sentences for juvenile offenders. Mediation offered as part of an offending based programme including letters of apology, direct and indirect mediation meetings. All mediation negotiated post sentence.

Bedfordshire

Luton Mediation
6 Cardiff Road
Luton LU1 1PP
phone & fax (01582) 411822

This is a new service, established at the request of local police. Now receives referrals from the local Youth offending Team. Principal client groups are young second and subsequent offenders. Small team of trained mediators available.

Buckinghamshire

Restorative Cautioning
Thames Valley Police
Wendover Road
Aylesbury HP21 7LA
(01296) 396168
fax (01296) 396036

Thames valley Police at Aylesbury use Restorative Cautioning on offenders. This is based around family group conferences and was inspired by the Wagga-Wagga Australian model.

Retail Theft Initiative
Thames Valley Police Milton Keynes
302 North Row, Witan Gate East
Milton Keynes MK9 2DS
(01908) 686000
fax (01908) 686164

The Retail Theft Initiative is designed to educate shoplifters about the consequences and effects of their behaviour and includes meetings between shoplifters and shop managers, contact with prison officers and youth services, and preventive strategies.

Cheshire

Boughton Hall Youth Justice & Young Abusers Service
Boughton Hall
Filkins Lane, Boughton
Chester CH3 5EJ
(01224) 310007
fax (01224) 348870

Recently appointed two sessional workers to provide a victim/offender mediation service and to act as Family Group Conference co-ordinators. This will form part of a wider, mainstream youth justice service.

Devon

Plymouth Mediation
St Peter's Centre
18 Hastings Street
Plymouth PL1 5BA
(01752) 671078
fax (01752) 255854

Community mediation service for neighbours and family members in dispute. Domestic violence addressed by support for victims/survivors; programme for perpetrators; mediation around other issues. Also provides victim/offender mediation ans schools mediation.

Hampshire

The Hampton Trust
ECS House
16 Romsey Road
Eastleigh SO50 9AL
(01703) 902442
fax (01703) 902443

Family Group Conferences in youth justice in Hampshire.

VOCS (Victim Offender Conferencing Service)
Wessex Office
Darby House, Orkney Road
Cosham, Portsmouth PO6 3LU
(01705) 327393
fax (01705) 327389

Kent

Maidstone Mediation Scheme
Community Support Centre
Marsham Street
Maidstone ME14 1HH
(01622) 692843

Funded by grant aid from Maidstone Borough Council, this scheme has 22 volunteer mediators who deal with neighbour disputes. Member of Kent Mediation. Works with the Maidstone Young Offender Team and Victim Support and has been offering Victim/Offender Mediation since January 1993.

Mid-Kent Young Offender Team
Wrens Cross, 2 Upper Stone Street
Maidstone ME15 6EY
(01622) 663927
fax (01622) 663928

A pre/post court service for young offenders who wish to make amends and/or seek offence resolution with the victim. Referrals are made by the Young Offender Team to Maidstone Mediation Scheme who provide the mediation.

Intensive Support & Supervision Programme
Social Services Dept
Sessions House, County Hall
Maidstone ME14 1XQ
(01622) 694855
fax (01622) 694909

Multi-agency initiative dealing with persistent young offenders aged 15-18. Programme includes intensive support and supervision, victim awareness, Family Group Conferences reparation and victim/offender mediation. Kent Mediation provides independent co-ordinators for Family Group Conferences.

London

VOCS (Victim Offender Conferencing Service)
Co-ordinator
NACRO, 169 Clapham Road
London SW9 0PU
020-7840 6441
fax 020-7735 4666

VOCS Westminster
(Westminster, Kensington & Chelsea, Hammersmith & Fulham)
1 Compton Street
London W2 1ND
020-7641 7753
fax 020-7641 5313

VOCS Southwark
(Southwark and young adult work in Lambeth only)
c/o Southwark YOT
90 Blakes Road
London SE15 6EP
020-7525 7929

VOCS Hackney
Unit B2, 3 Bradbury Street
Dalston, London N16 8JN
020-7690 5088

VOCS is working with both young offenders and young adult offenders and the victims of their crimes. VOCS operates two schemes (Wessex and West London) under the pilot phase of the Crime and Disorder

Act 1998 on the provision of reparation linked to Final Warnings and Court Orders. In the other areas offender involvement is non statutory. In all areas mediation (direct and indirect) and wider group conferences are provided tailored to the wishes of the parties together with a case assessment by the service. In the areas where the legislation is being implemented a wide variety of socially inclusive placements giving the opportunity to make reparation to the community are being developed.

The School House
200 Chingford Road, Walthamstow
London E17 5AA
020-8527 2333
fax 020-8529 8344

Offers mediation between young offenders (10-17) and their victims. Hopes to develop, in addition to direct and indirect mediation, 'symbolic mediation' where mediation would be provided between a group of victims and offenders of a particular crime, where one party to the offence is unidentifiable or unwilling.

London Borough of Hackney Youth Offender Team
55 Daubeney Road
London E5 0EE
020-8533 7070
fax 020-8986 7446

Victim Compensation Scheme: work experience as part of IT/specified activities requirement. YTS rates of pay; 50% to victim.
Hackney Mediation Service: dispute resolution 020-356 4794
New crime mediation project

Norfolk

Norwich & District Legal Services
The Advice Arcade
4 Guildhall Hill, Norwich NR2 1JH
(01603) 661779
fax (01603) 616116

A small and dedicated service with a focus on working with the new multi-disciplinary agency that has been set up in response to the Crime and Disorder Act. Welcomes contact with other services.

Northamptonshire

Youth Offender Team
198 Kettering Road
Northampton NN1 4BL
(01604) 601241
fax (01604) 601648

North Northamptonshire Diversion Unit
75a London Road, Kettering NN15 7PQ
(01536) 85854
fax (01536) 417546

The YOT continues to develop its mediation and reparation work with victims and offenders across the whole age range. Referral is predominantly police led.

Shropshire

Mediation & Reparation Course
HM YOI Stoke Heath
Warrant Road, Tern Hill
Market Drayton TF9 2JL
(01630) 654231

Runs groups for eight young offenders and makes them aware of mediation. Also runs a one day course creating scenarios using probation officers as victims. Available for schools and young offender establishments as a voluntary service offering any contributions to Mediation UK.

Suffolk

Ipswich Caution Plus Scheme
Ipswich Youth Justice Centre
Taylor House, 160 Norwich Road
Ipswich IP1 2PT
(01473) 583570
fax (01473) 583578

Runs a Caution Plus Scheme, pre-court diversion, which is voluntary. This runs in conjunction with the youth liaison committee, and involves both offence confronting and mediation/reparation.

West Midlands

Victim/Offender Devpt Officer
West Midlands Probation Service
1 Printing House Street
Birmingham B4 6DE
0121-236 8931
fax 0121-233 2996

Responsibility for developing mediation, reparation and victim enquiry work throughout the W Midlands Probation area.

In-service and external training, development and external liaison.

Birmingham Victim/Offender Mediation
52 Newton Street
Birmingham B4 6NE
0121-236 5001

New victim/offender mediation service in Birmingham.

Coventry Victim Unit
70 Little Park Street
Coventry CV1 2UR
024-7655 3268
fax 024-7663 1531

The mediation and reparation service in Coventry is part of mainstream probation and is for the use of any court user. Referrals are also taken from the Youth Liaison Panel at the point of caution. Offers exchange of information service and mediation post sentence and in victim enquiry work.

Sandwell Mediation
79 Birmingham Road
West Bromwich
B70 6PX
0121-525 4659
fax 0121-525 4672

Community mediation scheme: neighbour disputes, family disputes, interpersonnal disputes. Victim/offender services: pre & post-sentence - youth and adults.

Walsall Victim Offender Mediation Service
42 Upper Rushall Street
Walsall
(01922) 644000
fax (01922) 632886

A service that aims to work with the community to help victims and offenders come to terms with crime and its effect. Offers all forms of mediation/reparation; direct and indirect.

Wolverhampton Mediation and Reparation
West Midlands Probation Service
Union Street, Horsley Fields
Wolverhampton WV1 1RA
(01902) 576001

One of the original Home Office funded reparation schemes (the others being Coventry, Cumbria and Leeds). The project works very closely with the Crown Prosecution Service and the police force in dealing with adults and juveniles and takes referrals from all agencies from offender arrest through to post-conviction. The unit also participates, where appropriate, in the probation service victim enquiry work

Wiltshire

Wiltshire County Council Juvenile Diversion Scheme
The Limes Resource Centre
21 Green Road, Upper Stratton
Swindon SN2 6JA
(01793) 823153

Mediation service primarily as part of diversion, but mediation is also seen as a useful tool to prevent reoffending. The service deals with people in the age range of 10 to 16.

Worcestershire

Service to Victims of Armed Robbery
Psychology Dept
H M Prison Long Lartin
South Littleton, Evesham WR11 5TZ
(01386) 830101 ext 49514
fax (01386) 830991

This mediation service is held in a group forum and allows victims to meet perpetrators of armed robbery to discuss the impact the offence has had on the victim and for the perpetrators to discuss this.

Yorkshire (South)

Doncaster Victim/Offender Mediation Project
PO Box 441, Doncaster DN2 6RE
phone & fax (01302) 366693

Sheffield Victim/Offender Mediation Project
342 Glossop Road
Sheffield S10 2HW
phone & fax 0114-276 9660

Offers mediation to offenders and victims of crime in South Sheffield. The project aims to address the fear of crime, give victims a voice, enable offenders to take responsibility for their actions, and restore people to their positions in the community

Yorkshire (West)

West Yorkshire Probation Mediation and Reparation Service covers the whole area with units at the following locations

Victim Offender Unit
c/o City Courts, PO Box 6
Bradford BD1 1LB
(01274) 682128
fax (01274) 682105
covers Bradford Division

Probation Centre
Spring Hall Lane
Halifax HX1 4JG
(01422) 340211
covers Calderdale Division

20-30 Lawefield Lane
Wakefield WF2 8SP
(01924) 361156
covers Kirklees & Wakefield Divisions

The Basement
Oxford Place Methodist Mission
Oxford Place, Leeds LS1 3AX
0113-243 5932
fax 0113-242 7336
covers Leeds Division

The Service provides an opportunity for voluntary mediation and/or reparation to take place between victims and offenders (from age 10 upwards). It can be instigated at any stage in the criminal justice process from post-caution to post-custodial release and for any type of offender, provided that there is an admission of guilt, that the parties are willing and it is considered safe. Referrals are accepted from individual victims and offenders or any other agency involved with them. Also carries out Victim's Charter enquiry work for victims of serious violent or sexual offences where offenders are serving long prison services. The Service is currently extending its work with young offenders in partnership with leeds Initiative Regeneration Board, Police and Social Services.

Wales

MARVEL Mediation and Reparation Service
12 Salisbury Street, Shotton
Deeside, Flintshire CH5 1DR
(01244) 815490
fax (01244) 836833

A young offender/victim mediation and reparation service covering Flintshire and Wrexham Maelor

NACRO Rhwyd Project
c/o Gwynedd Social Services Dept
Arfon Area Office
Penrallt, Caernarfon LL55 1BN
phone/fax (01286) 682743

Aims to divert young people from prosecution and also provides mediation component as part of a criminal supervision order; provides opportunity for victims to speak their minds, ask questions and receive an apology; arranges direct/indirect contact between victim and offender when appropriate; designs sessions to highlight the effects of offending on victims.

Scotland

Glasgow Motoring Project
Block 14, Unit 1
Clydesmill Drive
Cambuslang Investment Park
Glasgow G32 8RG
0141-646 1652
fax 0141-646 1654

Project offers mediation within the total package. Allows the opportunity for victims of car theft for driving (joyriding) to meet a number of offenders in a group setting. Victims do not meet the person who stole their car, although one-to-one sessions are being considered.

SACRO
1 Broughton Market
Edinburgh EH3 6NU
0131-624 7270
fax 0131-624 7269

SACRO Reparation & Mediation Project (Grampian)
Belmont House
18 Little Belmont Street, Aberdeen AB1 1JG
(01224) 627201
fax (01224) 627338

SACRO Reparation and Mediation Project (Hamilton & Motherwell)
11 Merry Street
Motherwell, Strathclyde ML1 1JJ
(01698) 230433
fax (01698) 230410

Pre-trial diversion schemes, applying to adults and operating through referrals from the procurator fiscal. The project offers victims of crime and those accused the opportunity to resolve conflict through mediated reparative agreements. Prosecution is deferred to allow those accused to make amends according to the victims' wishes.

Interest Networks

Victim/Offender Mediation Network
c/o Mediation UK
Alexander House
Telephone Avenue, Bristol BS1 4BS
0117 904 6661
fax 0117 904 3331

An informal network of victim/offender mediation services, schemes, groups and/or interested people willing for their names and addresses to be circulated. Enables members to contact each other for support, to share problems and discuss practice developments. Holds twice yearly informal meetings organised by the Mediation and Reparation Committee. Contact Tony Billinghurst or Jane Lord at mediation UK for further details.

Positive Justice
124 Montagu Mansions
London W1H 1LE
phone & fax 020-7935 6743

A small organisation campaigning for effective, non-punitive approaches to offender behaviour, including mediation and restorative justice. Currently collecting names of supporters wanting information and/or to help with the campaign. Promoting positive justice through lobbying, media work, seminars, newsletters and the internet. Contact Charmian Bollinger, Philip Priestley

RESTORATIVE JUSTICE

Restorative justice is a process whereby all parties with a stake in a specific offence come together to resolve collectively how to deal with the aftermath of the offence and its implications for the future.

Social Concern and Mediation UK have established a Restorative Justice Consortium that brings together national agencies with an interest in this area of work.

The consortium seeks to establish standards for restorative justice programmes, to influence the formation of policy, and to sponsor conferences for those involved in developing restorative justice projects.

Social Concern has a resource centre available to professionals and together with other agencies offers training.

For further information contact Mark Thrush, Social Concern, Montague Chambers, Montague Close, London SE1 9DA.
020-7403 0977 *fax 020-7403 0799*

ARTS FOR OFFENDERS

The information in this section has been provided by the Unit for the Arts and Offenders

The Unit for the Arts and Offenders
Neville House, 90/91 Northgate, Canterbury, Kent CT1 1BA
(01227) 470629 *fax (01227) 453022*
e mail artsunit@dircon.co.uk

An independent charitable trust that supports the development of creative arts opportunities for people in prisons, special hospitals and secure units or on probation or community service. It provides information, undertakes evaluation, research and advocacy, and provides training and advice. Maintains an archive and database. Publishes a Directory and News Bulletin

Burnbake Trust
PO Box 1839, Bournemouth, Dorset BH9 2ZQ
01202 548139 *fax (01202) 522713*

Supplies artists' materials to prisoners and exhibits their work.

The Theatre in Prison and Probation Centre (TIPP)
c/o Drama Department, Manchester University, Oxford Road, Manchester M13 9PL
0161-275 3047 *fax 0161-275 3877* e mail tipp@man.ac.uk

Uses theatre to explore issues (drugs, anger management, employment, etc) with socially excluded groups; particularly within the criminal justice system. Also provides specialist training.

Geese Theatre Company
Midlands Arts Centre, Cannon Hill Park, Birmingham B12 9QH.

0121-446 4370 *fax 0121-446 5806* e mail mailbox@geese.co.uk www.geese.co.uk

Uses drama and role play to address all types of offending and provides staff training in the use of these methods.

Clean Break Theatre Company
2 Patshull Road London NW5 2LB
020-7482 8600 *fax 020-7482 8611* e mail lucy@cleanbreak,org.uk

Clean Break is the UK's only theatre company for women with personal experience of the criminal justice system. It provides accredited education and training in theatre and the performing arts for women ex-offenders, ex-prisoners, prisoners and those sectioned under the Mental Health Act. The company also produces an annual professional production on the theme of women and crime, and runs vocational training and professional development courses nationally.

Insight Arts Trust
7-15 Greatorex Street, London E1 5NF
020-7247 0778 *fax 020-7247 8077* e mail iat@insightartstrust.demon.co.uk

Innovative courses, theatre productions, multi-arts events, training, videos and filming for offenders, ex-offenders, probation clients and criminal justice staff.

Summit Arts
HM Prison Wolds, Everthorpe, Brough, E Yorks HU15 2JZ
(01430) 424526 *fax (01430) 422233* e mail hedley@summit.u-net.com
www.summitarts.com

Runs projects in prisons using a wide range of art forms including the recording of music and video making.

The Writers in Prisons Network
17 Upper Lloyd Street, Rusholme, Manchester M14 4HY
phone & fax 0161-226 3419 e-mail Chopwood98@aol.com

Writers are placed in prisons to work for 2.5 days a week for a year. The scheme is jointly funded by The Arts Council, Prison Service and Regional Arts Boards.

Koestler Award Trust
9 Birchmead Avenue, Pinner, Middx HA5 2BG
020-8868 4044 *fax 020-8864 8500*

Encourages the whole range of the arts in prisons, YOIs, special hospitals and secure units by way of an annual exhibition with award winning work in London.

Irene Taylor Trust
Unit 114, Bon Marche Centre, 241-251 Ferndale Road, London SW9 8BJ
020-7733 3222 *fax 020-7733 3310* e mail musicinprisons@excite.co.uk

Promotes music in prisons. An active working trust committed to raising the profile of music in prisons across the UK as part of the rehabilitation of prisoners.

Safe Ground
PO Box 11525, London SW11 5ZW
020-7228 3831 *fax 020-7228 3885* e mail safe_ground_productions@compuserve.com

Runs theatre and film programmes in prisons, YOIs and the community.

Escape Artists Theatre Company
42 Woodlark Road, Cambridge CB3 0HS
(01223) 301439 *fax (01223) 522301* e mail esc-arts@dircon.co.uk http://www.esc-arts.dircom.co.uk

Aims to rehabilitate serving and ex-prisoners through arts based activities and employment

The Comedy School
Three Mills Island, Three Mills Lane, London E3 3DU
020-8215 0144

Practical and realistic appraoches to stand-up comedy in prisons nationally.

Being Liberated and Knowledgeable (BLAK)
1 Blake Lane, Bordesley Green, Birmingham B9 5QT
phone & fax 0121-773 7367 e mail james@pogslaw.freeserve.co.uk

Arts projects aimed at addressing the creative and rehabilitative needs of black offenders.

Acting Out
The Rostyn Works, Uttoxeter Road, Longton, Stoke on Trent ST3 1PQ
(01782) 501504

Development and provision of groupwork for young and adult offenders, staff training in drama based groupwork techniques and conducting theatre based residential projects for prisons and probation.

Wolf and Water Arts Company
The Beaford Centre, Beaford, Winkleigh, Devon EX19 8LU
(01805) 603201 *fax (01805) 603202* e mail w+w@eclipse.co.uk

Uses drama creatively and therapeutically to explore all issues of offending.

RELIGIOUS ORGANISATIONS OFFERING SERVICES TO PRISONERS

Chaplain General of the Prison Service, Ven David Flemming, HM Prison Service Chaplaincy, Room 709, Abell House, John Islip Street, London SW1P 4LNH. 020-7217 2066/5685 (admin) *fax 020-7217 5090*

Angulimala, Buddhist Prison Chaplaincy Organisation, The Forest Hermitage, Lower Fulbrook, Nr Sherbourne, Warwickshire CV35 8AS. phone & fax (01926) 624385. Provides visiting Buddhist chaplains for prisons and advises the Prison Service on Buddhist matters.

The Baptist Union of Great Britain, Baptist House, PO Box 44, 129 Broadway, Didcot, Oxon OX11 8RT (01235) 517700. Contact The Ministries Adviser, Ministry Department.

The Church of Jesus Christ of Latter Day Saints (Mormons), Office of Area Presidency, 751 Warwick Road, Solihull, West Midlands B91 3DQ. 0121-712 1200

The Church of Scientology, Saint Hill Manor, East Grinstead, West Sussex RH19 4JY. (01342) 324571. Contact Volunteer Minister Section. Scientology is a non-denominational religion and volunteer ministers offer ministerial services to people of all faiths or none.

The Islamic Cultural Centre, 146 Park Road, London NW8 7RG. 020-7724 3363 *fax 020-7724 0493. e mail: islamic200@aol.com*

IQRA Trust Prisoners' Welfare, 24 Culcross Street, London W1Y 3HE 020-7491 1572 *fax 020-7493 7899.* www.iqraprisonerswelfare.org Promotes better understanding of Islam in Britain. It supports prisoners through its Prisoners' Welfare Directorate by providing books, religious clothing and special foods. It can also train people who are working with Muslim inmates. For their publication 'Practising Islam in Prison' phone 020-7491 1572 or e mail pwdiqra@ compuserve.com

The National Council for the Welfare of Muslim Prisoners, 24 Culcross Street, London W1Y 3HE 020-7659 997. Gen Secretary Salah El Hassan

The Methodist Church Prison Ministry. Contact Rev William J Davies, Superintendent Methodist Chaplain, 1 Central Buildings, Westminster, London SW1H 9NH. 020-7222 8010 ext 236 *fax 020-7233 0323.* In collaboration with the Prison Service Chaplaincy, is responsible for appointing, training and giving pastoral support to Methodist/Free Church chaplains in every prison in England and Wales.

The Pagan Federation, c/o National Manager for Visiting Pagan Ministers, BM Box 7097, London WC1N 3XX. *fax (01706) 718228* Covers all areas of Paganism ancluding Wicca, Druidry and the Northern Tradition. Can supply information and reading lists for inmates as well as providing visiting Ministers

Prison Fellowship, England & Wales, PO Box 945, Maldon, Essex CM9 4EW. (01621) 843232. Northern Ireland, 39 University Street, Belfast BT7 1FY (01232) 243691. Scotland, PO Box 366, 101 Ellesmere Street, Glasgow G22 5QT 0141-332 8870. A Christian ministry providing practical and spiritual support to prisoners. Volunteer based organisation with local groups throughout UK that work closely with prison chaplaincy team and local churches. Second aim is to promote Biblical standards of justice in the criminal justice system.

Prison Phoenix Trust, PO Box 328, Oxford OX1 1PJ. Supports prisoners of any faith or none in their spiritual lives by teaching meditation and yoga. It sends out free books *We're All Doing Time* and *Becoming Free Through Meditation and Yoga* and supports prisoners by regular correspondence and newsletters.

Religious Society of Friends (Quakers), Quaker Prison Ministers Group, QPSW, Friends House, Euston Road, London NW1 2BJ. 020-7663 1000 *fax 020-7663 1001.* The group supports about 100 Quaker prison ministers throughout Britain.

Seventh-day Adventist Church, Search Prison Ministries, 25 St John's Road, Watford, Herts WD1 1PY (01923) 232728 *fax (01923) 250582.*

North England Conference of Seventh-day Adventists, 22 Zulla Road, Mapperley Park, Nottingham NG3 5DB
Welsh Mission, Glan Yr Afon, 10 Heol Y Wern, Caerphilly, South Wales CF83 3EY
Scottish Mission, 'Maylea', 5 Orchilview Road, Crieff, Perthshire PH7 3EJ
Irish Mission Office, 9 Newry Road, Bambridge, Co Down, N Ireland BT32 3HF

SPECIAL HOSPITALS

1. **Ashworth Hospital**
   Park Lane, Maghull
   Liverpool L31 1HW
   0151-473 0303
   fax 0151-526 6603

   Backhouse, Richard (head of sw practice)

2. **Broadmoor Hospital**
   Crowthorne
   Berks RG45 7EG
   (01344) 773111
   fax (01344) 754625

   Social Work Services
   (01344) 754522
   fax (01344) 754421

   King, John (acting head of sw services)
   Ruston, Liz (acting dep head of sw services)

3. **Rampton Hospital**
   Retford
   Notts DN22 0PD
   (01777) 248321
   fax (01777) 248442

   Social Work Office
   Galen Avenue
   Woodeck, Retford
   Notts DN22 0PD
   (01777) 247354
   fax (01777) 247259

   Pam, James (prof head of sw)

   Special Services Directorate
   Parkinson, John (lead sw)
   Bevan, Diane (ssw)
   Briggs, Myra (ssw)
   Hudson, Ingrid (ssw)
   Hutt, Mark (ssw)
   Jones, Jean (ssw)
   Sanderson, Philip (ssw)

   Mental Health Directorate
   Madocks, Rod (lead sw)
   Cochrane, Sarah (ssw)
   Griffith, Mark (ssw)
   Head, Paul (ssw)
   Landa, Janga Singh (ssw)
   Oliver, Sonia (ssw)
   Greeaway, Claire (locum ssw)

NATIONAL SPECIALIST COMMISSIONING ADVISORY GROUP

NHS Executive, Department of Health, Room LG04, Wellington House, 133-135 Waterloo Road,
London SE1 8UG
020-7972 2000

The Severe Personality Disorder Service is a national service funded centrally by the National Specialist Commissioning Advisory Group (NSCAG). There are three therapeutic communities, the Henderson Hospital, which has been designated by NSCAG for some years and two new centres, Webb House and Main House with its associated outreach base, Bridger House.

The NHS therapeutic communities treat adults (17-45 years) suffering from personality disorder characterised by emotional and behaviour difficulties. The model is based on psychotherapeutic principles and does not use any psychotropic medication.

Residents are encouraged to stay for a maximum of one year, and during their stay they will take on responsibility for the running of the community. All residents are free to discharge themselves at any time.

Treatment at each of the communities is entirely voluntary. Residents can be on probation orders, a supervision register, a suspended sentence or parole, but treatment at any one of the therapeutic communities cannot be made as a condition of any such order.

Referrals are accepted from anywhere in the UK, but those from outside England do require identified funding. Henderson Hospital referrals are generally from London and the South East Regions. Webb House has referrals from the Northern and North West Regions. The Birmingham based therapeutic community accepts referrals from West Midlands and South West Regions, referrals should be directed to Bridger House.

A wide variety of leaflets and videos are available from all three units. Further information on the service can be found on www.psyctc.org/hend-hosp Further information on NSCAG can be found on www.doh.gov.uk/nscag

Henderson Hospital
2 Homeland Drive, Brighton Road, Sutton, Surrey SM2 5LT
020-8661 1611 *fax 020-8770 3676*

A free book 'Perspectives on Henderson Hospital' and a referrer's guide can be obtained from Sue Garner (Marketing & Information Manager).

Webb House
c/o Mental Health Services of Salford
Victoria Avenue, Crewe, Cheshire CW2 7SQ
(01270) 580770 fax (01270) 580118

Main House
Hollymoor Way, Northfield, Birmingham B31 5HE
0121-678 3630 *fax 0121-678 3635*

Bridger House
22 Summer Road, Acocks Green, Birmingham B27 7UT
0121-678 3244 *fax 0121-678 3245*

SPECIALIST ACCOMMODATION FOR OFFENDERS

Homes for Homeless People
Whitehill House, 6 Union Street, Luton LU1 3AN (01582) 481426
freephone helpline 0800 243675
e mail: homeline@dircon.co.uk

Provides a freephone helpline for those who are, or who are at risk of becoming homeless. Confidential up-to-date advice and information on all aspects of housing. Helpline 8am-9pm Mon-Fri. The service is used extensively by people in custody (usually by post). It offers details of services in the areas where offenders anticipate settling on their release.

Acomb House Hostel
Raglan Housing Association

141/143 Dickenson Road, Rusholme, Manchester M14 5HZ. 0161-224 7272

Caters for male ex-offenders, 40+ with a range of needs. Application to hostel or Greater Manchester Probation Service, Homeless Offenders Unit, Minshull Street, Manchester M1 3FR, 0161-236 7621

Basford House
in partnership with NACRO Second Base

40-42 Isandula Road, Basford, Nottinghamshire NG7 7ES. 0115-978 5851

6 bed (in single rooms) high support housing for male offenders 25+, with supported move on accommodation in 3 properties nearby. Established contact with Nottinghamshire Probation Service essential.

Carr-Gomm Society
London Region, Telegraph Hill Centre, Kitto Road, London SE14 5TY. 020-7277 6060

A charitable housing association that provides supportive environments for single people with a range of needs.

The Effra Trust
Eurolink Business Centre, Unit 7, 49 Effra Road, Brixton, London SW2 1BZ. 020-7326 1013 *fax 020-7924 0308*

45 Effra Road, London SW2 1BZ.

Specialist organisation offering accomodation and support to ex-offenders with mental health difficulties, epilepsy or other difficulties. 34 places available to men only in small group home settings.

Workshop premises
An arts based workshop open to all residents of the Trust and to potential clients for long term assessments. Variety of art, educational and therapeutic activities.

Heantun Housing Association
3 Wellington Road, Bilston, Wolverhampton WV14 6AA. (01902) 571160

Shared housing for ex-offenders in Wolverhampton, Willenhall, Dudley. Maximum stay 12 months.

Iris House Trust (Worcester City Project)
68 Bath Road, Worcester WR5 3EW (01905) 353884

13 bed, specialist hostel for difficult to place offenders including parolees and bail assessment. 24 hour staff cover, keyworking and

support. Nationwide catchment area. Close links with Hereford and Worcester Probation Service via LPO. Part of Stonham Housing Association. 'We have a proven track record of successful work with serious long term offenders.' Move on to cluster flats available.

Langley House Trust
Head Office: PO Box 181, Witney, Oxfordshire OX8 6WD. (01993) 774075 *fax (01993) 772425*
e mail info@langleyhousetrust.org

Referrals direct to the chosen project or via Witney office

Drug Rehabilitation Centres
Chatterton Hey, Edenfield, Ramsbottom, Lancashire BL0 0QH. (01706) 829895 *fax (01706) 828761*
Murray Lodge, 1 Whitley Village, Coventry CV3 4AJ. 024-7650 1585 *fax 024-7650 5759*

Fresh Start Projects
Ashdene, 29 Peterson Road, Wakefield, West Yorkshire WF1 4DU. (01924) 291088 *fax (01924) 366529*
Box Tree Cottage, 110 Allerton Road, Bradford, West Yorkshire BD8 0AQ. (01274) 487626 *fax (01274) 543612*
The Chalet , 9 Downshire Square, Reading, Berkshire RGl 6NJ. (01734) 572457 *fax (01734) 568536*
The Knole, 23 Griffiths Avenue, Cheltenham, Gloucestershire GL51 7BE. (01242) 526978 *fax (01242) 237504*
Langdon House, 66 Langdon Road, Parkstone, Dorset BH14 9EH. (01202) 747423 *fax (01202) 256718*
Longcroft, 58 Westbourne Road, Lancaster LA1 5EF. (01524) 64950 *fax (01524) 844082*
The Shrubbery, 35 Frindsbury Road, Strood, Rochester, Kent ME2 4TD. (01634) 717085 *fax (01634) 291049*

Residential Training Centres
Elderfield, Main Road, Otterbourne, Winchester, Hampshire S021 2EQ. (01962) 712163 *fax (01962) 711174*
House of St. Martin, 1 Langford Lane, Norton Fitzwarren, Taunton, Somerset TA2 6NU. (01823) 275662 *fax (01823) 352455*
Wing Grange, Wing, Oakham, Rutland LE15 8SB. (01572) 737246 *fax (01572) 737510*

Resettlement Project
Bedford Project, PO Box 395, Bedford MK42 9ZE (01234) 330515
Rothera Project, Bradford (women only) (01274) 575560 mobile 07990 595451

Norman House Trust
15 Aberdeen Park, Islington, London N5 2AN
020-7704 2857

A residential high support hostel for men (25-65yrs) who wish to challenge their past offending and establish new patterns of behaviour. Offers groupwork and individual support. All residents must participate appropriately in the community atmosphere and activities. Not intended as a permanent place to live, but a step between prison and independent living

Penrose Housing Association
Head office: 356 Holloway Road, London N7 6PA. 020-7700 0100 *fax 020-7700 8133*

Chief Executive: Janice Horsman

Specialist housing association providing supported housing and resettlement service for homeless male and female offenders in the London area. Schemes in Inner London, NE London, SE London and Middlesex Probation Areas. All housing is shared ranging from two bedroomed flats to 14 bed hostel. Assured tenancies issued. Move-on to permanent self contained housing achieved for most tenants with resettlement support.

Home leaves: 1 bed space reserved exclusively for home leaves for serving prisoners
Women: women only housing provided in small shared flats and self-contained flats using high care 'floating support'.
Priority: lifers and other long term prisoners

All enquiries to head office. Applications for serving prisoners should be made not more than 12 months prior to release date or parole date (except lifers). Applications can only be accepted from probation officers in the London Area.

Rock House Trust
Beacon House, 27-29 Beaconsfield Road, Hexthorpe, Doncaster DN4 0DL
(01302) 562676

Project manager: Jon Bellfield

Christian home for ex-offenders with medium to high care needs. High level of support, housing up to six men. Referrals via Probation/Chaplaincy. Length of stay up to 18 months.

Stepping Stones Trust
Park View, 51 Clapham Common West Side, London SW4 9AS. phone & fax 020-7228 0863

A supported home providing a 'stepping stone' from prison to the community for Christian male ex-prisoners, with emphasis on preparation for independent living. The hostel also accepts clients on probation.

Bridge House, PO Box 3209, London SW8. 020-7720 6421

Long term accomodation and care for Christian male sex offenders. For the unemployed, rent covered by DSS and Housing Benefit. Residents will usually stay for up to two years and can receive psychiatric assessment and treatment through the NHS. NOTE: before making any referral please contact SPO, 79 East Hill, London SW18 2QE 020-8871 2711.

Stonham Housing Association
235-241 Union Street, London SE1 0LR. 020-7401 2020

The largest provider of housing and support for ex-offenders.

Regional offices:
South East Region
276 High Street
Guildford GU1 3JL
(01483) 300738
fax (01483) 300776

Hampshire & Isle of Wight Region
2nd Floor, Chineham House
Shakespeare Road
Basingstoke RG24 9BW
(01256) 840340
fax (01256) 840235

Midlands Region
Queen's Gate, Suffolk Street
Queensway, Birmingham B1 1LX
0121-643 0084
fax 0121-643 0230

North Region
3rd Floor, 53 The Calls
Leeds LS2 7EY
0113-246 8660
fax 0113-246 8665

West Region
2nd Floor, High Point
Thomas Street, Taunton
Somerset TA2 6HB
(01823) 327388
fax (01823) 327390

Gordon House Association
see section on services for problem gamblers

SERVICES FOR DRUG USERS

The following list is not comprehensive. Further information on local treatment services is contained in two directories from the Standing Conference on Drug Abuse 020-7928 9500

Drug Problems: where to get help lists contact details for 700 residential and community services in England and Wales

Residential drug services: a comprehensive guide to rehabilitation in England and Wales provides information on 100 residential services. Price £20.00 (£16.00 to SCODA members)

National Drugs Helpline 0800 77 66 00

Information, advice and support for anyone worried about their own or someone else's drug use. Also referral to local services

National Organisations and Head Offices

1. **Standing Conference on Drug Abuse (SCODA)**
   32/36 Loman Street
   London SE1 0EE
   020-7928 9500
   fax 020-7928 3343

   e mail info@scoda.demon.co.uk
   web site www.ncvo-vol.org.uk/scoda.html
   Provides specialist advice on local drug services and best practice information on drug treatment and care, prevention and education.

2. **Welsh Drug & Alcohol Unit**
   St Davids House
   Wood Street
   Cardiff CF1 1ER
   (01222) 667766
   fax (01222) 665940

3. **Scottish Drugs Forum**
   5 Waterloo Street
   Glasgow G2 6AY
   0141-221 1175
   fax 0141-248 6414

   e mail enquiries@sdf.org.uk
   web site www.sdf.org.uk
   National centre for information on drug use in Scotland. Publishes a directory of specialist drug agencies in Scotland

4. **Institute for the Study of Drug Dependence**
   (address as SCODA)
   020-7928 1211

Library and information service for interested individuals and professionals

5. **ADFAM National**
Waterbridge House, 32-36 Loman Street
London SE1 0EE
020-7928 8900
fax 020-7928 8923

The national charity for the friends and families of drug users. National telephone helpline, Mon-Fri 10am-5pm. Specialist support for prisoners' families

6. **Release**
388 Old Street
London EC1V 9LT
020-7729 9904 (office)
020-7603 8654 (24 hr emergency service)

Advice on legal drug related problems. Office staffed Mon-Fri 10-6pm

7. **Re Solv**
30a High Street
Stone, Staffs ST15 8AW
(01785) 817885
free national helpline 0808 800 2345 (9am-5pm, Mon-Fri)
fax (01785) 813205

National charity dealing with all aspects of solvent and volatile substance abuse (that currently kills an average of 6 young people a month). Research, dissemination of educational materials, training and community projects

8. **Cranstoun Drug Services**
4th Floor, Broadway House
London SW19 1RL
020-8543 8333
fax 020-8543 4348

Provides a range of residential, day and prison services for drug users

9. **Mainliners**
38-40 Kennington Park Road
London SE11 4RS
020-7582 5434 (admin)
020-7582 3338 (general)
020-7582 5226 (advice line)
fax 020-7582 6999

An agency working with and for people affected by drugs and HIV. Monthly newsletter *Mainliners*, seminars and training courses

10. **Turning Point**
New Loom House, 101 Back Church Lane
London E1 1LU
020-7702 2300

Charity with 90 services (information, counselling, residential) nationwide for drugs and alcohol

11. **Phoenix House**
3rd Floor, Asra House
1 Long Lane, London SE1 4PG
020-7234 9740

Residential rehabilitation services in London, East Sussex, Merseyside, Newcastle upon Tyne, Hove, Sheffield and Glasgow for drug users. Also provides community based services throughout the UK and extensively involved in providing services in prisons.

Drugs And Criminal Justice Organisations

12. **The Substance Advice & Referral Unit**
Kings House, 12 King Street
York YO1 9WP
(01904) 632495
fax (01904) 632 490

Specialist service to prisons in the Yorkshire, Humberside and Nottinghamshire areas offering: one-to-one support/counselling, group work, court and parole reports, release packages. Service HMPs (and YOIs) Askham Grange, Doncaster, Everthorpe, Full Sutton, Hatfield, Leeds, Moorland, New Hall, Ranby, Wakefield, Wetherby, Wealstun, Wolds

13. **Drugs and Criminal Justice Forum**
contact Julie Howlin at SCODA

A national network, meeting four times a year, for those concerned in the criminal justice system and in drug services

Self Help Organisations

14. **Narcotics Anonymous**
PO Box 1980, London N19 3LS
020-7272 9040 (for literature etc)
helpline 020-7730 0009 (10am-10pm)

Selfhelp groups throughout the country.

15. **Families Anonymous**
Doddington & Rollo Community Association
Charlotte Despard Avenue

Battersea, London SW1 5JE
020-7498 4680

Advice and support groups for families and friends of drug users (inc. alcohol). Office staffed Mon-Fri 1-4.30pm. A helpline service available evenings and weekends

16. **PADA (Parents Against Drug Abuse)**
12-14 Church Parade
Ellesmere Port
Cheshire L65 2ER
admin & fax 0152-356 1996
helpline 0345 023867
e mail padahelp@btinternet.com
www./btinternet.com/padahelp

A national network of local support groups offering help and support to parents and families of drug users. Helpline (confidential) staffed 24hrs 365 days a year, calls charged at local rate.

17. **Cocaine Anonymous**
PO Box 16111, Kings Road
Chelsea, London SW3 5SZ
24hr helpline 020-7284 1123

Campaigns

18. **Transform** (The Campaign to Reform Drug Policy and Legislation)
1 Roselake House, Hudds Vale Road
St George, Bristol BS5 7HY
0117-939 8052
fax 0117-939 4425

National campaign to end the prohibition of drugs and replace it with an effective policy that will deal with the underlying issues of drug use and misuse

SERVICES FOR PROBLEM DRINKERS

New Drinkline
helpline 0800 917 822
admin 0151-227 4150

Advice

Alcohol Concern
Waterbridge House, 32-36 Loman Street
London SE1 0EE
020-7928 7377
fax 020-7928 4644
e mail alccon@popmail.dircon.co.uk
http://www.alcoholconcern.org.uk

Library, information service, can refer caller to local agencies, produces a variety of literature and directory of local services. Individual and corporate membership available.

Health Education Authority
Trevelyan House
30 Great Peter Street
London SW1P 2HW
020-7222 5350

Institute of Alcohol Studies
Alliance House
Caxton Street, London SW1M 0QS
020-7222 5880/4001
e mail info@ias.org.uk
www.ias.org.uk

Library, research, information, publications

Self Help Groups & Organisations with Local Projects

Alcoholics Anonymous
PO Box 1, Stonebow House
Stonebow, York YO1 7NJ
(01904) 644026
helpline 0845 7697 555
www.alcoholics-anonymous.org.uk

Al-Anon Family Groups
61 Great Dover Street, London SE1 4YF
020-7403 0888 (24hr helpline)
fax 020-7378 9910
e mail alanonuk@aol.com
website www.hexnet.co.uk/alanon

Offers understanding and support for families and friends of problem drinkers, whether still drinking or not. Alateen, a part of Al-Anon, is for young people aged 12-20 who have been affected by somone else's drinking, usually that of a parent. For details of meetings throughout UK and Ireland, please contact above address.

ACA (Adult Children of Alcoholics)
PO Box 1576, London SW3 1AZ
020-7229 4587

Turning Point
New Loom House
101 Back Church Lane, London E1 1LU
020-7702 2300

Projects nationwide for drug and alcohol problems, information, counselling, residential

Aquarius Action Projects
6th Floor, The White House
111 New Street, Birmingham B2 4EU
0121-632 4727
fax 0121-633 0539
e mail whitehouse@aquarius.org.uk

Drug and alcohol projects in Midlands, providing information, training, counselling, residential and day services. Probation partnerships

SERVICES FOR PROBLEM GAMBLERS

The following information has been supplied by GamCare

National Organisations

GamCare Suite 1, 25-27 Catherine Place, London SW1E 6DU 020-7233 8988, helpline 0845 6000 133. The national centre for information, advice, and practical help regarding the social impact of gambling, providing: a national helpline, telephone and face-to-face counselling, network of (and referral to) local organisations, training, literature, and advice on gambling dependency issues for the probation service.

Parents of Young Gamblers 0121-443 2609 *fax 0121-624 4626* Provides advice, help and support for parents of young gamblers and, in West Midlands area facility for support group for young people with gambling problems. Maintains some contacts nationwide.

Gamblers Anonymous PO Box 88, London SW10 0EU. National helpline number 020-7384 3040. GA is a self help fellowship of men and women who have joined together to do something about their own gambling problem and to help other compulsive gamblers to do the same. Over 200 groups throughout the UK and in many prisons.

Gam-Anon address as GA above. 'Sister' organisation to GA, providing advice and support to the spouses and parents of compulsive gamblers.

National Council for Social Concern Montague Chambers, Montague Close, London SE1 9DA 020-7403 0977 *fax 020-7403 0799*. Produces educational materials for schools and youth clubs. The charity specifically works within the area of Restorative Justice (see section on Mediation UK), and addictions including gambling. Contact Peter Carlin, Director.

Residential/Rehabilitation

Gordon House Association 186 Mackenzie Road, Beckenham, Kent BR3 4SF 020-8778 3331. (13 bed unit) and 83 Blowers Green Road, Dudley, W Mids DY2 8UR (01384) 241292 (9 bed unit) National catchment area providing residential facility for males 18+, including offenders on court orders or ex-prison. Therapeutic environment, individual and group counselling and support whilst at hostel and after. Help given to move on. Contact houses direct or liaison officers at Beckenham and Dudley Probation Offices.

Residential Centre Lincolnshire Probation Service, 205 Yarborough Road, Lincoln LN1 3NQ (01522) 528520. In addition to a range of other opportunities has special provision to address the problems presented by offenders who are compulsive gamblers or whose offending behaviour is linked to problematic gambling.

Groups & Organisations with Local Projects

England in alphabetical order by town

Cumbria Alcohol & Drug Advisory Service (CADAS) 1 Fisher Street, Carlisle, Cumbria CA3 8RR (01228) 544140. Provides a telephone and one-to-one counselling service to problem gamblers and their relatives/friends.

Off The Record Threeways, 138 Purbrook Way, Leigh Park, Hampshire PO9 3SU (01705) 785999. Point of contact for youth counsellors in Hampshire who have been trained in working with a gambling dependency. Contact Teressa Wade.

Youth Access 1a Taylor's Yard, 67 Alderbrook Road, London SW12 8AD 020-8772 9900. Co-ordinating agency for youth counselling, network. Can advise on which youth counselling projects have counsellors trained in gambling dependency. Alternatively contact GamCare.

North East Council on Addiction (NECA) Philipson House, 5 Philipson Street, Walker, Newcastle upon Tyne 0191-234 3486 *fax 0191-263 9908.* Centres in Newcastle, South Tyne, Gatehead, Durham, Consett, Peterlee, Hartlepool, Washington, Stanley, Mid Tyne, Chester le Street. All centres provide telephone and one-to-one counselling to problem gamblers and their relatives/friends. Addresses and phone numbers from Philipson House.

Alcohol Problems Advisory Service (APAS) 36 Park Row, Nottingham NG1 6GR 0115-941 4747 or Lo-call 0345 626 316. Provides advice, information and counselling service to problem gamblers and for people affected by someone else's dependency on alcohol, drugs and gambling

The Matthew Project 24 Pottergate, Norwich, Norfolk NR2 1DX (01603) 626123. 24hr helpline (01603) 764754. Provides an advice, training and counselling service to young gamblers who make contact or who are referred.

Focus Southend Youth House Short Street, Southend on Sea, Essex SS2 5BY (01702) 464315. Provides information, advice, counselling for young people on a wide range of issues including gambling. Contact Kevin Walsh

Wales

Islwyn Drug & Alcohol Project
Markham Miners Welfare Society, Bryn Road, Markham, Nr Blackwood, Gwent. (01495) 229299. Provides information, advice and one-to-one counselling to problem gamblers and their relatives/friends who are affected by a gambling dependancy as part of a community project within South Wales and surrounding districts.

Northern Ireland

Dunleway Substance Advice Centre
226 Stewartstown Road, Belfast Northern Ireland BT17 0LB. 028-9061 1162. Three centres in Belfast. Provides a one-to-one counselling service to problem gamblers and their relatives/friends alongside their non-sectarian work in the field of substance misuse.

Parents Advice Centre Franklin House, 12 Brunswick Street, Belfast, Northern Ireland BT2 7GE. 028-9031 0891. Centres in Belfast, Derry, Dungannon & Ballymena. provides telephone and one-to-one counselling and advice to parents and family members who are affected by gambling dependency as part of the help and support they provide to parents

VOLUNTARY WORK

CSV (Community Service Volunteers)
237 Pentonville Road
London N1 9NJ.
020-7278 6601
fax 020-7837 931
e mail volunteer@csv.org.uk

CSV provides opportunities for people to volunteer in the community. CSV's non-rejection policy means that anyone aged 16-35 can volunteer full time, away from home for up to a year at one of 800 social care projects throughout the UK. Volunteers receive a weekly allowance plus free accommodation and food. CSV also works through service and contract agreements (e.g. with the probation services) to involve volunteers as mentors to young offenders and also places as volunteers in their local area young people at risk of offending.

Of special interest to probation officers based in YOIs and Cat C prisons is CSVs partnership with HM Prison Service. CSV offers, as part of an effective resettlement process, one month full time away from home volunteering opportunities to young people in their last month prior to release.

INSURANCE SERVICES FOR EX-OFFENDERS

When obtaining insurance, non-disclosure, or giving false information about any criminal convictions, will almost certainly mean that the policy will be declared void in the case of a claim. It must be remembered that a criminal conviction is a *material fact* and must be declared. By giving false information another crime is being committed. When disclosing their convictions the majority of ex-offenders will find getting insurance for home, building and contents, motor and business cover, practically impossible.

N.B. The editor accepts no responsibility for any of the statements below. They have been supplied by the companies listed.

Specialist insurance for ex-offenders is available through:

Fresh Start

Bank House, 5 Market Place, Whittlesey, Peterborough PE7 1AB
(01733) 206999 *fax (01733) 208610*
e mail mail@culpeck.demon.co.uk

Fresh Start is supported and recommended by Nacro, the Probation Service, CABs, Banks, Building Societies, Insurance and Mortgage Brokers throughout the UK. Fresh Start believes it is the only company to offer a comprehensive choice of cover from different companies along with premium instalment facilities for buildings, home contents and business insurance packages. A fully comprehensive and supportive service is provided by experienced staff offering the best service and cover at the most competitive premiums. Regulated by the General Insurance Service Council.

Clegg Gifford & Co Ltd

Lloyd's Broker, 1 Hall Street, Featherstone, Wakefield, W Yorks WF7 5LS
(01977) 362436 *fax (01977) 798544*

Clegg Gifford is probably the only Lloyd's Broker with a dedicated facility for the ex-offender, built up from experience working with such organisations as prison and probation services, Nacro and Unlock. Cover can be obtained for motor, building and contents, and business. A specialised and discreet department deals with ex-offenders sympathetically and appreciates their problems despite the requirements for full disclosure. Once this is made and the proposal form completed and details agreed, a Certificate of Acceptance will be issued guaranteeing the offender cover (providing personal circumstances do not change).

Fairplay Insurance Services

Charter House, 43 St Leonards Road, Bexhill-on-Sea, East Sussex TN40 1JA
(01424) 220110 *fax (01424) 731781*
www.fairplayhelp.com

Fairplay guarantees that each applicant will be dealt with in a sensitive, non-judgmental and helpful way. Every proposer is guaranteed to be treated with respect regardless of previous convictions.

Three dedicated schemes aimed at providing 'standard' cover to proposers who have criminal convictions
Fairplay Home Insurance (01424) 220110 Nichola Smith
Fairplay Motor Insurance 08700 774466 Carl Pickett
Fairplay Business Insurance (01424) 220110 Nichola Smith

APPROVED PROBATION AND BAIL HOSTELS

PROBATION/BAIL HOSTELS FOR MEN

Avon	Bridge House 74-78 Filton Road Bristol BS7 0PD	17+ 18 places	Bristol 0117-969 3123
	4 Brigstocke Road, St Pauls, Bristol BS2 8UB	17+ 28 places	Bristol 0117-942 5851
Bedfordshire	36-40 Napier Road, Luton LU1 1RG	17+ 20 places	Luton (01582) 418200
Berkshire	St Leonards Hostel 2 Southcote Road Reading RG3 2AA	17+ 22 places	Reading (01734) 573171
	Manor Lodge 8 Straight Road Old Windsor SL4 2RL	17+ 22 places	Windsor (01753) 868807
Buckinghamshire	1 Haddon Road, Great Holm, Milton Keynes MK8 9AL	17+ 16 places	Milton Keynes (01908) 569511/569536
Cambridgeshire	5 Wesleyan Road Peterborough PE1 3RZ	17+ 32 places	Peterborough (01733) 51678/9
Cheshire	Bunbury House Alswick Drive Ellesmere Port L65 9HE	17+ 22 places	0151-357 3551/4
Cleveland	Southbank Bail Hostel 1 Millbank Street South Bank Middlesbrough TS6 6DD	17+ 20 places	Eston Grange (01642) 456811
	13 The Crescent Linthorpe, Middlesbrough TS5 6SG	17+ 20 places	Middlesbrough (01642) 826606
Dorset	Bournemouth Hostel 11 Cecil Road, Boscombe, Bournemouth BH5 1DU	17+ 18 places	Bournemouth (01202) 391757
Humberside	41 Queen's Road Kingston upon Hull HU5 2QW	17+ 19 places	Hull (01482) 446284/5
	Probation & Bail Hostel Victoria House 31 Normandy Road Scunthorpe DN13 6AS	17+ 19 places	Scunthorpe (01724) 289124
Lancashire	Highfield House, Lydia Street, Wood Nook, Accrington, Lancs BB5 0PX	17+ 18 places	Accrington (01254) 395997

Lincolnshire	Wordsworth House 205/207 Yarborough Rd, Lincoln LN1 3NQ	17+ 18 places	Lincoln (01522) 528520
London (Inner)	147 Tulse Hill London SW2 2QD	17+ 27 places	020-8671 4086
	7 Canadian Avenue Catford, London SE6 3AX	17+ 24 places	020-8690 3234
	Ellison House, Aylesbury Estate 370 Albany Road London SE5 0AJ	17+ 25 places	020-7703 3332
	Camden House 199 Arlington Rd, London NW1 7EY	17+ 26 places	020-7482 4288
	St Edmund's Hostel 298 Leigham Court Rd Streatham SW16 6RZ	17+ 25 places	020-8769 8096
	St Mungos 9 Cologne Rd, Battersea London SW11 2AH	17+ 25 places	020-7223 3006
	Bedford/Shenley Hostel 204 Bedford Hill London SW12 9HJ & 2a-e Shenley Road London SE5 8NN	17+ 25 places	020-8675 2693
London (NE)	Westbourne House (North & South) 199 Romford Road Forest Gate, E7 9HL	17+ 40 places	020-8534 2483/0673
London (SE)	4 Beckenham Road Beckenham, Kent	17+ 20 places	020-8658 3515
London (SW)	96 North Road, Kew Richmond upon Thames Surrey TW9 4HQ	17+ 18 places	020-8876 6303/4
Greater Manchester	Bradshaw House 147-151 Walmersley Rd Bury BO9 5DE	17+ 26 places	0161-761 6419
	St Joseph's Hostel Millers Street, Patricroft, Eccles, Manchester M30 8PF	17+ 29 places	0161-789 5337
	Ascot House 195 Wellington Road North Stockport SK4 2PB	17-25 22 places	0161-443 3400

Merseyside	Canning House, 55 Canning St, Liverpool, L8 7NN	17+ 19 places	0151-709 4959
	Southwood Hostel 24 Southwood Road, Aigburth, Liverpool L17 7BQ	17+ 29 places	0151-727 2401
Middlesex	2 Corfton Road, Ealing London W5 2HS	17+ 19 places	020-8997 7127
Norfolk	John Boag House 1 Drayton Street Norwich NR3 2DF	17+ 29 places	Norwich (01603) 429488
Northamptonshire	Bridgewood Hostel 45-48 Lower Meadow Court, Thorplands, Northampton NN3 1YX	17+ 23 places	Northampton (01604) 648704/645722
Nottinghamshire	5 Astral Grove Hucknall, Nottingham N15 6PY	17+ 14 places	Nottingham 0115-963 2835 all referrals to Trent House 0115-962 3992
Somerset	Glogan House, 59 Taunton Rd Bridgwater TA6 3LP	17+ 18 places	Bridgwater (01278) 424165
Suffolk	The Cottage 795 Old Norwich Road, Ipswich IP1 6LH	17+ 18 places	Ipswich (01473) 47139
Surrey	St Catherine's Priory Ferry Lane, Portsmouth Road, Guildford, Surrey GU2 5EB	18-26 18 places	Guildford (014835) 71635
Warwickshire	33 Kenilworth Road Leamington Spa CV32 6JG	17+ 19 places	Leamington Spa (01926) 39331
	McIntyre House 125 Edward Street Nuneaton CV11 5RD	17+ 18 places	Nuneaton 024-7638 2889
West Glamorgan	Emroch House 46 Talbot Road Port Talbot SA13 1HU	17+ 18 places	Port Talbot (01639) 883551
West Midlands	Carpenter House 33 Portland Rd Edgbaston Birmingham B16 9HS	17+ 21 places	0121-454 0394
	Bilston Hostel 23 Wellington Rd, Bilston, Wolverhampton, WV14 6AH	17+ 22 places	Wolverhampton (01902) 497688

	Elliott House 96 Edgbaston Road Moseley Birmingham B12 9QA	17+ 20 places	0121-440 2657
	Welford House, 31 Trinity Rd, Aston, Birmingham B6 6AJ	17+ 19 places	0121-523 4401
	85 Stonnall Road Aldridge, Walsall WS9 8JZ	17+ 12 places	Walsall (01922) 59574
	Sycamore Lodge Clay Lane, Langley Green Oldbury B69 4TH	17+ 32 places	0121-552 9930
West Yorkshire	Cardigan House, 84 Cardigan Rd, Headingley, Leeds LS6 3BJ	19-25 19 places	Leeds 0113-275 2860
	Elm Bank, Bradford Rd, Cleckheaton BD19 3LW	17+ 22 places (inc 1 disabled)	Cleckheaton (01274) 851551
	St John's Hostel, 263 Hyde Park Road, Leeds LS6 1AG	17+ 28 places	Leeds 0113-275 5702
	30 Albion Street Dewsbury WF13 2AJ	17+ 24 places	Dewsbury (01924) 242748
	Holbech House, Springwell View, Springwell Road Leeds LS121BS	17+ 24 places	0113-245 4220
S Glamorgan	Mandeville House 9 Lewis Street Cardiff CF1 8JY	17+ 26 places	Cardiff 029-2039 4592

PROBATION/BAIL HOSTELS FOR WOMEN

Berkshire	Elizabeth Fry House 6 Coley Avenue, Reading RG3 6LQ	17+ 21 places	Reading 0118-957 2385
Merseyside	Adelaide House 115 Edge Lane Liverpool L7 2PF	17+ 20 places	0151-263 1290
London (Inner)	Kelley House 18/20 Royal College Street London NW1 0TH	17+ 26 places	020-7388 3945
West Midlands	Crowley House 31 Weoley Park Road Selly Oak, Birmingham B29 6RA	17+ (& children) 18 places	0121-472 7111

PROBATION/BAIL HOSTELS FOR BOTH MEN AND WOMEN

County	Address	Age/Places	Telephone
Avon	Ashley House 14 Somerset Street Kingsdown, Bristol BS2 8NB	17+ 22 places	Bristol 0117-924 9697
Bedfordshire	78-80 Chaucer Road Bedford MK40 2AP	17+ 25 places	Bedford (01234) 340501
Cheshire	Linden Bank 40 London Road Sandbach CW11 3BD	17+ 22 places	Sandbach (01270) 759181
Cornwall	Meneghy House, East Hill, Tuckingmill, Camborne TR14 8NQ	17+ 18 places	Camborne (01209) 715050
Cumbria	Bowling Green Hostel 90 Lowther Street, Carlisle CA3 8DP	17+ 24 places	Carlisle (01228) 34024
Derbyshire	Burdett Lodge 6 Bass Street, Derby DE3 3BR	18+ 30 places	Derby (01332) 41324/43906
Devon	Lawson House, 14 Paradise Place Stoke, Plymouth	17+ 19 places	Plymouth (01752) 568791
Dorset	'Weston', 2 Westwey Rd Weymouth DT4 8SU	17+ 25 places	Weymouth (01305) 775742
Essex	Basildon Bail Hostel 1 Felmores, Northlands 4 Housing Area, Basildon SS13 1PN	17+ 26 places	Basildon (01268) 557550/557600
Gloucestershire	Ryecroft Bail Hostel 78 Ryecroft Road Gloucester GL1 4LY	17+ 16 places	Gloucester (01452) 380268
Hampshire	Dickson House 77 Trinity Street Fareham P016 7SL	17+ 26 places	Fareham (01329) 234531/2
	The Grange Hostel 145 Stakes Road, Purbrook Nr Portsmouth P07 5PL	17+ 22 places	Portsmouth 023-9236 3474
Hereford & Worcestershire	Braley House 89 Ombersley Road Worcester WR3 7BT	17+ 21 places	Worcester (01905) 723975

Kent	Fleming House, 32 Tonbridge Rd Maidstone ME16 8SH	17+ 25 places	Maidstone (01622) 55918
Leicestershire	Kirk Lodge 322 London Road Leciester LE2 2PJ	17+ 32 places	Leicester 0116-270 8327
London (Inner)	Katherine Price Hughes House, 28 Highbury Grove, London N5 2EA	17+ 19 places	020-7226 2190
Greater Manchester	Hopwood House 104 Manchester Street Heywood, Lancs OL10 1DW	17+ 18 places	Heywood (01706) 620440
	Wilton Place Edward Street Oldham OL9 7QW	17+ 27 places	0161-624 3005
	172/174 Withington Rd Whalley Range Manchester M16 8JW	17+ 32 places	0161-226 1179
	Chorlton Hostel 10-12 Oswald Road Chorlton cum Hardy M21 1LH	17+ 27 places	0161-862 9881
Middlesex	Seafield Lodge,71-73 Shoot-up-Hill, London NW2 3PS	17+ 22 places	020-8452 4209/4200
Northumbria	Ozanam House, 79 Dunholme Rd, Newcastle upon Tyne NE4 6XD	17+ 26 places	0191-273 5738
	St Christopher's House 220-222 Westmorland Road, Cruddas Park, Newcastle upon Tyne NE4 6QX	17+ 19 places	0191-273 2381
	Pennywell Hylton Road, Pennywell Sunderland SR4 8DS	17+ 18 places	0191-534 1544
North Wales	Ty Newydd Llandegai nr Bangor LL57 4LG	17+ 23 places	Bangor (01248) 370529
Nottinghamshire	Southwell House 106 Raleigh Street Nottingham NG7 4DJ	17+ 18 places	Nottingham 0115-978 1417 all referrals to Trent House
	Trent House Woodborough Road Alexandra Park Nottingham NG3 4JB	17+ 22 places	Nottingham 0115-962 3992

Oxfordshire	Clarks House, Clarks Row Oxford OX1 1RE	17+ 18 places	Oxford (01865) 248841
	112 Abingdon Road Oxford OX1 4PY	17+ 18 places	Oxford (01865) 792026
Staffordshire	14 Lichfield Road Stafford ST17 4JX	17+ 23 places	Stafford (01785) 223417
	Wenger House Albert Street Newcastle under Lyme ST5 1JP	17+ 26 places	Newcastle (01782) 717423
Suffolk	Lightfoot House 37 Fuschia Lane, Ipswich IP1 5AA	17+ 22 places	Ipswich (01473) 728198
Sussex (East)	Brighton Probation/Bail Hostel 162 Marine Parade Brighton BN2 1EJ	17+ 16 places	Brighton (01273) 622300
South Yorkshire	Rookwood Doncaster Road Rotherham S65 1NN	17+ 39 places	Rotherham (01709) 361001
	Norfolk Park 100/108 Norfolk Park Rd Sheffield S2 2RM	17+ 39 places	Sheffield 0114-272 1950
West Yorkshire	Ripon House, 63 Clarendon Road, Leeds LS2 9NZ	17+ 24 places	Leeds 0113-245 5488
North Wales	Plas-y-Wern, Ruabon Nr Wrexham, Clwyd LL14 6RN	17+ 23 places	Wrexham (01978) 814949

BAIL HOSTELS FOR MEN*

Lancashire	Blackburn Bail Hostel 86 Preston New Road Blackburn BB2 6BH	17+ 18 places	Blackburn (01254) 59060
Leicester	Howard House, 71 Regent Rd, Leicester LE1 6YA	17+ 18 places	Leicester 0116-254 9059
Merseyside	Merseybank Hostel 26 Great Howard Street Liverpool L3 7HS	17+ 26 places	0151-255 1183

BAIL HOSTELS FOR MEN AND WOMEN*

Hampshire	32 Landguard Road Southampton SO1 5DJ	17+ 22 places	Southampton 023-8033 6287
Northumbria	Cuthbert House Derwentwater Road Gateshead NE8 2SH	17+ 25 places	0191-478 5355
North Yorkshire	South View Hostel 18 Boroughbridge Road York YO2 5RU	17+ 20 places	York (01904) 780358
SouthYorkshire	Town Moor Hostel 38-40 Christchurch Rd DoncasterDN1 2QL	17+ 39 places	Doncaster (01302) 739127

*BAIL PLACES

All approved hostels will accept persons on bail who are being considered for residence, as a requirement in a probation order. With the exception of Abingdon Road (Oxford), all hostels will accept persons remanded on bail with a requirement to reside as a condition of bail.

PRISON ESTABLISHMENTS IN ENGLAND AND WALES

Information supplied by Prison Service HQ Library, London SW1P 4LH tel. 020 7217 5548
Compiled 10.10.2000

Privately operated prisons are marked *

HMP ACKLINGTON
MORPETH, Northumberland, NE65 9XF
(01670) 760411 *fax (01670) 761362*

HMP ALBANY
NEWPORT, Isle of Wight, PO30 5RS
(01983) 524055 *fax (01983) 825827*

HMP ALTCOURSE *
Higher Lane, Fazakerley,
LIVERPOOL, L9 7LH
(0151) 522 2000 *fax (0151) 522 2121*

HMP/YOI ASHFIELD*
Shortwood Road, Pucklechurch
BRISTOL, BS16 9QJ
(0117) 303 8000 *fax (0117) 303 8001*

HMP ASHWELL
OAKHAM, Rutland, LE15 7LF
(01572) 774100 *fax (01572) 774101*

HMP/YOI ASKHAM GRANGE
Askham Richard, YORK, YO23 3FT
(01904) 704236 *fax (01904) 702931*

HMYOI AYLESBURY
Bierton Road, AYLESBURY,
Bucks, HP20 1EH
(01296) 424435 *fax (01296) 434139*

HMP BEDFORD
St. Loyes Street,
BEDFORD, MK40 1HG
(01234) 358671 *fax (01234) 273568*

HMP BELMARSH
Western Way, Thamesmead,
LONDON SE28 0EB
(020) 8317 2436 *fax (020) 8317 2421*

HMP BIRMINGHAM
Winson Green Road,
BIRMINGHAM, B18 4AS
(0121) 554 3838 *fax (0121) 554 7990*

HMP BLAKENHURST *
Hewell Lane, REDDITCH,
Worcestershire, B97 6QS
(01527) 543348 *fax (01527) 546382*

HMP BLANTYRE HOUSE
Goudhurst, CRANBROOK,

Kent, TN17 2NH
(01580) 211367 *fax (01580) 211060*

HMP BLUNDESTON
LOWESTOFT, Suffolk, NR32 5BG
(01502) 730591 *fax (01502) 730138*

HMYOI BRINSFORD
New Road, Featherstone,
WOLVERHAMPTON, WV10 7PY
(01902) 791118 *fax (01902) 790889*

HMP BRISTOL
19 Cambridge Road, Horfield,
BRISTOL, BS7 8PS
(0117) 980 8100 *fax (0117) 980 8153*

HMP BRIXTON
P O Box 369, Jebb Avenue,
LONDON, SW2 5XF
(020) 8674 9811 *fax (020) 8674 6128*

HMP BROCKHILL
REDDITCH, Worcs, B97 6RD
(01527) 550314 *fax (01527) 550169*

HMP BUCKLEY HALL
Buckley Farm Lane, ROCHDALE,
Lancs, OL12 9DP
(01706) 861610 *fax (01706) 711797*

HMP BULLINGDON
P O Box 50, BICESTER, Oxon, OX6 0PR
(01869) 322111 *fax (01869) 243383*

HMYOI BULLWOOD HALL
High Road, HOCKLEY, Essex, SS5 4TE
(01702) 202515 *fax (01702) 207464*

HMP CAMP HILL
NEWPORT, Isle of Wight, PO30 5PB
(01983) 527661 *fax (01983) 520505*

HMP CANTERBURY
46 Longport, CANTERBURY,
Kent, CT1 1PJ
(01227) 762244 *fax (01227) 450203*

HMP/RC CARDIFF
Knox Road, CARDIFF, CF24 0UG
(029) 2043 3100 *fax (029) 2043 3318*

HMP/YOI CASTINGTON
MORPETH, Northumberland, NE65 9XG
(01670) 762100 *fax (01670) 762101*

HMP CHANNINGS WOOD
Denbury, NEWTON ABBOTT,
Devon, TQ12 6DW
(01803) 812361 *fax (01803) 813175*

HMP/YOI CHELMSFORD
200 Springfield Road, CHELMSFORD,
Essex, CM2 6LQ
(01245) 268651 *fax (01245) 493041*

HMP COLDINGLEY
Bisley, WOKING, Surrey, GU24 9EX
(01483) 476721 *fax (01483) 488586*

HMP COOKHAM WOOD
ROCHESTER, Kent, ME1 3LU
(01634) 814981 *fax (01634) 828921*

HMP DARTMOOR
Princetown, YELVERTON,
Devon, PL20 6RR
(01822) 890261 *fax (01822) 890679*

HMYOI DEERBOLT
Bowes Road, BARNARD CASTLE,
County Durham, DL12 9BG
(01833) 637561 *fax (01833) 631736*

HMP/YOI DONCASTER *
Off North Bridge, Marshgate,
DONCASTER, South Yorkshire, DN5 8UX
(01302) 760870 *fax (01302) 760851*

HMP DORCHESTER
North Square, DORCHESTER,
Dorset, DT1 1JD
(01305) 266021 *fax (01305) 267379*

HMP DOVEGATE* (opening July 2001)
Morton Lane
Marchington, near Uttoxeter
Staffordshire
ST18 8XR

HMYOI DOVER
The Citadel, Western Heights,
DOVER, Kent, CT17 9DR
(01304) 203848 *fax (01304) 215165*

HMP DOWNVIEW
Sutton Lane, SUTTON, Surrey, SM2 5PD
(020) 8770 7500 *fax (020) 8770 7673*

HMP/YOI DRAKE HALL
ECCLESHALL, Staffordshire, ST21 6LQ
(01785) 858100 *fax (01785) 858010*

HMP DURHAM
Old Elvet, DURHAM, DH1 3HU
(0191) 386 2621 *fax (0191) 386 2524*

HMP/YOI EAST SUTTON PARK
Sutton Valence, MAIDSTONE,
Kent, ME17 3DF
(01622) 842711 *fax (01622) 842636*

HMP/YOI EASTWOOD PARK
Falfield, WOTTON-UNDER-EDGE,
Gloucestershire, GL12 8DB
(01454) 262100 *fax (01454) 262101*

HMP ELMLEY
Church Road, EASTCHURCH,
Sheerness,Kent, ME12 4AY
(01795) 880808 *fax (01795) 880118*

HMP ERLESTOKE
DEVIZES, Wiltshire, SN10 5TU
(01380) 813475 *fax (01380) 818663*

HMP EVERTHORPE
BROUGH, East Yorkshire, HU15 1RB
(01430) 422471 *fax (01430) 421351*

HMP/YOI EXETER
New North Road, EXETER,
Devon, EX4 4EX
(01392) 278321 *fax (01392) 214684*

HMP FEATHERSTONE
New Road, Wolverhampton,
Staffs, WV10 7PU
(01902) 790991 *fax (01902) 791843*

HMYOI/RC FELTHAM
Bedfont Road, FELTHAM,
Middlesex, TW13 4ND
(020) 8890 0061 *fax (020) 8844 1551*

HMP FORD
ARUNDEL, West Sussex, BN18 0BX
(01903) 717261 *fax (01903) 726060*

HMP/YOI FOREST BANK*
Agecroft Road, Pendlebury,
MANCHESTER, M27 8FB
(0161) 925 7000 *fax (0161) 925 7001*

HMP FOSTON HALL
Foston, DERBY, Derbyshire, DE65 5DN
(01283) 585802 *fax (01283) 585826*

HMP FRANKLAND
Brasside, DURHAM, DH1 5YD
(0191) 384 5544 *fax (0191) 384 9203*

HMP FULL SUTTON
Full Sutton, YORK, YO41 1PS
(01759) 375100 *fax (01759) 371206*

HMP GARTH
Ulnes Walton Lane, Leyland,
PRESTON, Lancashire, PR5 3NE
(01772) 622722 *fax (01772) 622276*

HMP GARTREE
Gallow Field Road,
MARKET HARBOROUGH,
Leicestershire, LE16 7RP
(01858) 410234 *fax (01858) 410808*

HMYOI/RC GLEN PARVA
Tigers Road, Wigston,
LEICESTER, LE8 4TN
(0116) 264 3100 *fax (0116) 264 3000*

HMP/YOI GLOUCESTER
Barrack Square, GLOUCESTER, GL1 2JN
(01452) 529551 *fax (01452) 310302*

HMP GRENDON/SPRING HILL
HMP Grendon, Grendon Underwood,
AYLESBURY, Bucks, HP18 0TL
(01296) 770301 *fax (01296) 770756*

HMP/YOI GUYS MARSH
SHAFTESBURY, Dorset, SP7 0AH
(01747) 853344 *fax (01747) 850217*

HMP HASLAR
2 Dolphin Way, GOSPORT,
Hampshire, PO12 2AW
(023) 9258 0381 *fax (023) 9251 0266*

HMYOI HATFIELD
Thorne Road, Hatfield, DONCASTER,
South Yorkshire, DN7 6EL
(01405) 812336 *fax (01405) 813325*

HMP HAVERIGG
MILLOM, Cumbria, LA18 4NA
(01229) 772131 *fax (01229) 770779*

HMP HEWELL GRANGE
REDDITCH, Worcs, B97 6QQ
(01527) 550843 *fax (01527) 550178*

HMP HIGH DOWN
Sutton Lane, SUTTON,
Surrey, SM2 5PJ
(020) 8643 0063 *fax (020) 8643 2035*

HMP/YOI HIGHPOINT
Stradishall, NEWMARKET,
Suffolk, CB8 9YG
(01440) 823100 *fax (01440) 823099*

HMP HINDLEY
Gibson Street, Bickershaw, WIGAN,
Lancashire, WN2 5TH
(01942) 866255 *fax (01942) 867442*

HMP/YOI HOLLESLEY BAY
WOODBRIDGE,
Suffolk, IP12 3JW
(01394) 411741 *fax (01394) 411071*

HMP/YOI HOLLOWAY
Parkhurst Road, LONDON, N7 0NU
(020) 7607 6747 *fax (020) 7700 0269*

HMP HOLME HOUSE
Holme House Road,
STOCKTON-ON-TEES,
Cleveland, TS18 2QU
(01642) 673759 *fax (01642) 674598*

HMP HULL
Hedon Road, HULL, HU9 5LS
(01482) 320673 *fax (01482) 229018*

HMYOI HUNTERCOMBE
Huntercombe Place, Nuffield,
HENLEY-ON-THAMES,
Oxfordshire, RG9 5SB
(01491) 641711-15 *fax (01491) 641902*

HMP KINGSTON
122 Milton Road, PORTSMOUTH,
Hampshire, PO3 6AS
(023) 9289 1100 *fax (023) 9289 1181*

HMP KIRKHAM
Freckleton Road, PRESTON,
Lancashire, PR4 2RN
(01772) 684343 *fax (01772) 682855*

HMP KIRKLEVINGTON GRANGE
YARM, Cleveland, TS15 9PA
(01642) 781391 *fax (01642) 790530*

HMP LANCASTER
The Castle, LANCASTER, Lancs, LA1 1YL
(01524) 385100 *fax (01524) 385101*

HMP/YOI LANCASTER FARMS
Far Moor Lane, Stone Row Head,
off Quernmore Road, LANCASTER,
LA1 3QZ
(01524) 848745 *fax (01524) 849308*

HMP LATCHMERE HOUSE
Church Road, Ham Common,
RICHMOND, Surrey, TW10 5HH
(020) 8948 0215 *fax (020) 8332 1359*

HMP LEEDS
Armley, LEEDS, West Yorkshire, LS12 2TJ
(0113) 2636411 *fax (0113) 2790151*

HMP LEICESTER
Welford Road, LEICESTER, LE2 7AJ
(0116) 2546911 *fax (0116) 2471753*

HMP/YOI LEWES
Brighton Road, LEWES,
East Sussex, BN7 1EA
(01273) 405100 *fax (01273) 405101*

HMP LEYHILL
WOTTON-UNDER-EDGE,
Gloucestershire, GL12 8BT
(01454) 260681 *fax (01454) 261398*

HMP LINCOLN
Greetwell Road, LINCOLN, LN2 4BD
(01522) 533633 *fax (01522) 532116*

HMP LINDHOLME
Bawtry Road, Hatfield Woodhouse,
DONCASTER, DN7 6EE
(01302) 848700 *fax (01302) 848750*

HMP LITTLEHEY
Perry, HUNTINGDON,
Cambridgeshire, PE28 0SR
(01480) 812202 *fax (01480) 812151*

HMP LIVERPOOL
68 Hornby Road, LIVERPOOL, L9 3DF
(0151) 525 5971 *fax (0151) 525 0813*

HMP LONG LARTIN
South Littleton, EVESHAM,
Worcestershire, WR11 5TZ
(01386) 830101 *fax (01386) 832834*

HMP LOWDHAM GRANGE*
LOWDHAM
Nottinghamshire, NG14 7TA
(0115) 966 9200 *fax (0115) 966 9220*

HMYOI LOW NEWTON
Brasside, DURHAM, DH1 5SD
(0191) 386 1141 *fax (0191) 386 2620*

HMP MAIDSTONE
36 County Road, MAIDSTONE,
Kent, ME14 1UZ
(01622) 755611 *fax (01622) 688038*

HMP MANCHESTER
Southall Street, MANCHESTER, M60 9AH
(0161) 834 8626 *fax (0161) 832 0074*

HMP/YOI MOORLAND
Bawtry Road, Hatfield Woodhouse,
DONCASTER, South Yorkshire, DN7 6BW
(01302) 351500 *fax (01302) 350896*

HMP MORTON HALL
Swinderby, LINCOLN, LN6 9PT
(01522) 866700 *fax (01522) 866750*

HMP THE MOUNT
Molyneaux Avenue, Bovingdon,
HEMEL HEMPSTEAD,
Herts, HP3 0NZ
(01442) 834363 *fax (01442) 834321*

HMP/YOI NEW HALL
Dial Wood, Flockton, WAKEFIELD,
West Yorkshire, WF4 4AX
(01924) 848307 *fax (01924) 840692*

HMYOI NORTHALLERTON
15A East Road, NORTHALLERTON,
North Yorkshire, DL6 1NW
(01609) 780078 *fax (01609) 779664*

HMP NORTH SEA CAMP
Freiston, BOSTON,
Lincolnshire, PE22 0QX
(01205) 760481 *fax (01205) 760098*

HMP/YOI NORWICH
Mousehold, NORWICH,
Norfolk, NR1 4LU
(01603) 437531 *fax (01603) 701007*

HMP NOTTINGHAM
Perry Road, Sherwood,
NOTTINGHAM, NG5 3AG
(0115) 962 5022 *fax (0115) 960 3605*

HMYOI ONLEY
Willoughby, RUGBY,
Warwickshire, CV23 8AP
(01788) 522022 *fax (01788) 522260*

HMP PARC *
Heol Hopcyn John, BRIDGEND,
Mid-Glamorgan, CF35 6AP
(01656) 300200 *fax (01656) 300201*

HMP PARKHURST
NEWPORT, Isle of Wight, PO30 5NX
(01983) 523855 *fax (01983) 524861*

HMP PENTONVILLE
Caledonian Road, LONDON, N7 8TT
(020) 7607 5353 *fax (020) 7700 0244*

HMYOI PORTLAND
Easton, PORTLAND, Dorset, DT5 1DL
(01305) 820301 *fax (01305) 860794*

PORTSMOUTH see HMP Kingston

HMP/YOI PRESCOED
Address as for HMP Usk
(01291) 672231 *fax (01291) 672197*

HMP PRESTON
2 Ribbleton Lane, PRESTON,
Lancashire, PR1 5AB
(01772) 257734 *fax (01772) 556643*

HMP RANBY
RETFORD, Nottinghamshire, DN22 8EU
(01777) 706721 *fax (01777) 702691*

HMYOI & RC READING
Forbury Road, READING, Berks, RG1 3HY
(0118) 9587031 *fax (0118) 9591058*

HMP RISLEY
Risley, WARRINGTON,
Cheshire, WA3 6BP
(01925) 763871 *fax (01925) 764103*

HMP ROCHESTER
1 Fort Road, ROCHESTER,
Kent, ME1 3QS
(01634) 838100 *fax (01634) 838101*

HMP RUDGATE see HMP Wealstun

HMP RYE HILL*(Opening Jan 2001)
Willoughby, RUGBY
Warwickshire, CV23 8AM
(01788) 817269

HMP SEND
Ripley Road, Send, WOKING,
Surrey, GU23 7LJ
(01483) 223048 *fax (01483) 223173*

HMP SHEPTON MALLET
Cornhill, SHEPTON MALLET,

Somerset, BA4 5LU
(01749) 343377 *fax (01749) 345256*

HMP SHREWSBURY
The Dana, SHREWSBURY,
Shropshire, SY1 2HR
(01743) 352511 *fax (01743) 356926*

HMP SPRING HILL
Grendon Underwood,
AYLESBURY, Bucks, HP18 0TH
(01296) 770301 *fax (01296) 770756*

HMP STAFFORD
54 Gaol Road, STAFFORD, ST16 3AW
(01785) 254421 *fax (01785) 249591*

HMP STANDFORD HILL
Church Road, EASTCHURCH,
Sheerness, Kent, ME12 4AA
(01795) 880441 *fax (01795) 880267*

HMP STOCKEN
Stocken Hall Road, STRETTON,
Nr Oakham, Rutland, LE15 7RD
(01780) 485100 *fax (01780) 410767*

HMYOI STOKE HEATH
Stoke Heath, MARKET DRAYTON,
Shropshire, TF9 2JL
(01630) 654231 *fax (01630) 638875*

HMP/YOI STYAL
Styal, WILMSLOW, Cheshire, SK9 4HR
(01625) 532141 *fax (01625) 548060*

HMP SUDBURY
Ashbourne, DERBYSHIRE, DE6 5HW
(01283) 585511 *fax (01283) 585736*

HMP SWALESIDE
Barbazon Road, EASTCHURCH,
Sheerness, Kent, ME12 4AX
(01795) 884100 *fax (01795) 884200*

HMP SWANSEA
200 Oystermouth Road, SWANSEA,
West Glamorgan, SA1 3SR
(01792) 464030 *fax (01792) 642979*

HMYOI SWINFEN HALL
Swinfen, LICHFIELD, Staffs, WS14 9QS
(01543) 481229 *fax 01543) 480138*

HMYOI THORN CROSS
Arley Road, Appleton Thorn,
WARRINGTON, Cheshire, WA4 4RL
(01925) 605100 *fax (01925) 605101*

HMP THORP ARCH see HMP Wealstun

HMP USK
47 Maryport Street, USK, Gwent,
NP15 1XP
(01291) 672411 *fax (01291) 673800*

HMP THE VERNE
The Verne, PORTLAND, Dorset, DT5 1EQ
(01305) 820124 *fax (01305) 823724*

HMP WAKEFIELD
5 Love Lane, WAKEFIELD,
West Yorkshire, WF2 9AG
(01924) 378282 *fax (01924) 384391*

HMP WANDSWORTH
Heathfield Road, LONDON, SW18 3HS
(020) 8874 7292 *fax (020) 8877 0358*

HMP WAYLAND
Griston, THETFORD, Norfolk, IP25 6RL
(01953) 858100 *fax (01953) 858220*

HMP WEALSTUN
WETHERBY, West Yorkshire, LS23 7AZ
(01937) 844844 *fax (01937) 845862*

HMP WEARE
Rotherham Road, Castletown,
PORTLAND, Dorset, DT5 1PZ
(01305) 822100 *fax (01305) 820792*

HMP WELLINGBOROUGH
Millers Park, Doddington Road,
WELLINGBOROUGH, Northants,
NN8 2NH
(01933) 224151 *fax (01933) 273903*

HMYOI WERRINGTON
Werrington, STOKE-ON-TRENT,
Staffordshire, ST9 0DX
(01782) 303514 *fax (01782) 302504*

HMYOI WETHERBY
York Road, WETHERBY,
West Yorkshire, LS22 5ED
(01937) 585141 *fax (01937) 586488*

HMP WHATTON
14 Cromwell Road, NOTTINGHAM,
NG13 9FQ
(01949) 850511 *fax (01949) 850124*

HMP WHITEMOOR
Longhill Road, MARCH,
Cambs, PE15 0PR
(01354) 660653 *fax (01354) 650783*

HMP WINCHESTER
Romsey Road, WINCHESTER,
Hampshire, SO22 5DF
(01962) 854494 *fax (01962) 842560*

HMP WOLDS *
Everthorpe, BROUGH,
East Yorkshire, HU15 2JZ
(01430) 421588 *fax (01430) 421589*

HMP WOODHILL
Tattenhoe Street, MILTON KEYNES,
Bucks, MK4 4DA
(01908) 501999 *fax (01908) 505417*

HMP WORMWOOD SCRUBS
PO Box 757, Du Cane Road,
LONDON, W12 0AE
(020) 8743 0311 *fax (020) 8749 5655*

HMP WYMOTT
Ulnes Walton Lane, Leyland,
PRESTON, PR5 3LW
(01772) 421461 *fax (01772) 455960*

HEADQUARTER & CENTRAL SERVICES

HM Prison Service
Cleland House, Page Street
London SW1P 4LH
020-7217 6000 *fax 020-7211 7992*

HM Prison Service
Abell House, John Islip Street
London SW1P 4LH
020-7217 6000

HM Prison Service
Lunar House, 40 Wellesley Road
Croydon CG9 2BY
020-8760 1222

HM Prison Service
Calthorpe House, Hagley Road
Birmingham B16 8QR
0121-455 9855

HM Prison Service Coillege
Aberford Road, Wakefield
W Yorks WF1 4DE
(01924) 434100 *fax (01924) 384989*

HM Prison Service College
Newbold Revel, Nr Rugby
Warcs CV23 0TH
(01788) 832666 *fax (01788) 834101*

SECURE TRAINING CENTRES

MEDWAY SECURE TRAINING CENTRE
Sir Evelyn Road
ROCHESTER Kent ME1 2YB
(01634) 823300

HASSOCKFIELD SECURE TRAINING CENTRE
Corbridge Road
MEDOMSLEY Co Durham DH18 6QY
(01207) 5656000

RAINSBROOK SECURE TRAINING CENTRE
Willoughby
RUGBY Warcs CV23 8SY
(01788) 528800

SCOTTISH PRISON SERVICE ESTABLISHMENTS

HMP ABERDEEN
Craiginches, ABERDEEN,
Aberdeenshire AB9 2NE.
(01224) 876868 *fax (01224) 896209*

HMP BARLINNIE
Barlinnie, GLASGOW,G33 2QX
0141-770 2000 *fax 0141-770 206*

HMP CASTLE HUNTLY
Castle Huntly, LONGFORGAN,
Near Dundee, Angus DD2 5HL
(01382) 360265 *fax (01382) 360510*

HM INSTITUTION CORNTON VALE
Cornton Road, STIRLING,
Stirlingshire FK9 5NY
(01786) 832591 *fax (01786) 833597*

HMYOI DUMFRIES
Terregles Street, DUMFRIES,
Dumfriesshire DG2 9AX
(01387) 261218 *fax (01387) 264144*

HMP EDINBURGH
Saughton, EDINBURGH EH1 3LN
0131-444 3000 *fax 0131-444 3045*

HMP FRIARTON
Friarton, PERTH, Perthshire PH2 8DW
(01738) 625885 *fax (01738) 630544*

HMP/YOI GLENOCHIL
King O'Muir Road, TULLIBODY,
Clackmannanshire FK10 3AD
(01259) 760471 *fax (01259) 762003*

HMP GREENOCK
Gateside, GREENOCK,
Renfrewshire PA16 9AH
(01475) 787801 *fax (01475) 783154*

HMP INVERNESS
Porterfield, INVERNESS,
Invernessshire IV2 3HH
(01463) 233320 *fax (01463) 236595*

HMP KILMARNOCK
Mauchline Road, KILMARNOCK KA1 5JH
(01563) 548851 *fax (01563) 548869*

HMP LOW MOSS
Bishopbriggs, GLASGOW G64 2QB
0141-762 4848 *fax 0141- 772 6903*

HMP NORANSIDE
Fern, By Forfar, Angus DD8 2QV
(01356) 650217/8 *fax (01356) 650245*

HMP PERTH
3 Edinburgh Road, PERTH,
Perthshire PH2 8AT
(01738) 622293 *fax (01738) 630545*

HMP PETERHEAD
Invernettie, PETERHEAD,
Aberdeenshire AB42 6YY
(01779) 479101 *fax (01779) 470529*

HMYOI POLMONT
BRIGHTONS, Near Falkirk,
Stirlingshire FK2 0AB
(01324) 71155 *fax (01324) 714919*

HMP SHOTTS
SHOTTS, Lanarkshire ML7 4LE
(01501) 824000 *fax (01501) 824001*

HM UNIT SHOTTS
Scott Drive, SHOTTS,
Lanarkshire ML7 4LF.
(01501) 824140 *fax (01501) 824141*

NATIONAL INDUCTION CENTRE
SHOTTS, Lanarkshire ML7 4LE
(01501) 824120 *fax (01501) 824121*

SCOTTISH PRISON SERVICE COLLEGE
Newlands Road, BRIGHTONS,
Near Falkirk, Stirlingshire FK2 0DE
(01324) 710400 *fax (01324) 710401*

SCOTTISH PRISON SERVICE HQ
Calton House, 5 Redheughs Rigg,
EDINBURGH EH12 9HW
0131-244 8745 *fax 0131-244 8774*

NORTHERN IRELAND PRISON SERVICE ESTABLISHMENTS

HMYO CENTRE HYDEBANK WOOD
Hospital Road, BELFAST BT8 8NA
028-9025 3666 *fax 028-9025 3636 (general)*
028-9025 3711 (secure)

HMP MAGHABERRY
17 Old Road, Upper Ballinderry
LISBURN, Co Antrim BT28 2NF
028-9261 1888 *fax 028-9261 9516*

HMP MAGILLIGAN
Point Road, MAGILLIGAN
Co Londonderry BT49 0LR
028-7776 3311 *fax 028-7776 5931*

HM PRISON SERVICE COLLEGE
Woburn House, MILLISLE,
Co Down BT22 2HS
028-9186 3000 *fax 028-9186 3022*

NORTHERN IRELAND PRISON SERVICE HQ
Dundonald House
Upper Newtownards Road
BELFAST BT4 3SU
028-9052 2992 *fax 028-9052 5284*

ISLE OF MAN, JERSEY, GUERNSEY

ISLE OF MAN PRISON
Victoria Road, Douglas,
Isle of Man IM2 4RD.
(01624) 621306 *fax (01624) 628119*

HMP JERSEY
La Moye, St Brelade, Jersey,
Channel Islands JE3 8HQ
(01534) 44181 *fax (01534) 46875*

STATES PRISON GUERNSEY
Les Nicolles, Baubigny, St Sampson, Guernsey, Channel Islands GY2 4YF (01481) 48376 *fax (01481) 47837*

MISCELLANEOUS ADDRESSES

Descriptions of the organisations are those provided by themselves; the publisher takes no responsibility for these statements. Entries marked * did not reply to a request for information for the 2001 Directory, but are left in as the information may still be correct. Any information about these or other organisations that might usefully be included will be welcomed. Please send it to Owen Wells, 23 Eaton Road, Ilkley LS29 9PU (01943) 602270 *fax (01943) 816732*

*Adult Dyslexia Organisation, 336 Brixton Road, London SW9 7AA. 020-7737 7646 *fax 020-7207 7796* helpline 020-7924 9559

Advisory Service for Squatters, 2 St Pauls Road, London N1 2QN. 020-7359 8814 (phone first, Mon-Fri 2-6pm). Legal and practical advice for squatters and homeless people.

Aftermath, PO Box 414, Sheffield S1 7RT. 0114-275 8520. Support for families of serious offenders.

The Aldo Trust, c/o NACRO, 169 Clapham Road, London SW9 0PU. 020-7582 6500 *fax 020-7735 4666.* Charitable grants to prisoners in England and Wales only, no applications direct from prisoners

Alternatives to Violence Project, AVP Britain, The Old Painswick Inn, Gloucester Street, Stroud GL5 1QG. 01453 756751 *fax (01453) 767823* e-mail avp@waitrose.com. Offers workshops on alternatives to violence in prisons and the community. Also trains AVP workshop facilitators including serving and ex-prisoners and people on probation.

*Apex Charitable Trust Ltd, Head Office, St Alphage House, Wingate Annexe, 2 Fore Street, London EC2Y 5DA 020-7638 5931 *fax 020-7638 5977.* e-mail hq@apextrust.com www.apextrust.com Helps people with a criminal record obtain jobs, self employment, training or further education through its 27 projects around the country providing direct advice and guidance to ex-offenders. Provides employers with information about the best ways of recruiting and retraining preople with a criminal record.

APEX Leicester Project Ltd, 8th & 10th Floor, 60 Charles Street. Leicester LE1 1FB 0116-222 1860/1 Advice, guidance and education for ex-offenders in Leicestershire . Also provides accredited training.

*ARC (Antenatal Results & Choices), 73-75 Charlotte Street, London W1P 1LB phone & fax 020-7631 0280. Offers non-directive, specialised support to parents who discover that their unborn baby is abnormal, gives support to parents making a decision about ante-natal testing and offers ongoing support to those parents that decide to end the pregnancy. Refers parents who decide to continue with the pregnancy to appropriate support organisations.

Asian Family Counselling Service, Church Road, Hanwell, London W7 1LB

*Assist: Assistance Support and Self Help in Surviving Trauma, 27a Church Street, Rugby CV21 3PU (01788) 560800. Offers support, understanding and friendship both to individuals affected by post traumatic stress and the families and friends of those so affected. Nationwide helpline, Mon-Fri 10am-4pm, 01788 560800. One-to-one counselling in Rugby area (service is free and completely confidential)

Association for Shared Parenting, PO Box 2000, Dudley, West Midlands DY1 1YZ. (01789) 751157. Seeks to promote the rights and needs of children following separation or divorce, through promoting view that children have the right to receive love and nurture from both parents.

Black Prisoners' Support Project, c/o POPS Office, Suite 4b, Building 1, Wilson Park, Monsall Road, Newton Heath, Manchester M40 8WN phone/fax 0161-277 9066. The BPSP works with Black people who have a link with the Greater Manchester area. It can assist with advice on coping with imprisonment, personal difficulties arising from imprisonment, drug/alcohol dependency, resettlement, including employment/accommodation, maintaining contact with friends/relatives and statutory/voluntary agencies, welfare and education.

Black Prisoners' Support Scheme, Nottingham Black Initiative, 4th Floor, Fenchurch House, 12 King Street, Nottingham NG1 2AS. 0115-941 0481 *fax 0115-948 3641.* Provides advice and assistance to inmates facing racial, cultural and legal issues within the penal system.

Acts as a referral and training ageny for solicitors, probation and other agencies. Accesses defendants at police stations, courts and post sentence.

British Epilepsy Association, New Anstey House, Gate way Drive, Leeds LS19 7XY. 0113 210 8800 *fax 0113 391 0300* helpline 0808 800 5050 e mail epilespsy@bea.org.uk www.epilepsy.org.uk Advice and information on all aspects of living with epilepsy.

Brook National Office and Book Publications, 421 Highgate Studios, 53-79 Highgate Road, London NW5 1TL. 020-7284 6040 *fax 020-7284 6050* helpline 0800 0185 023. Offers young people free confidential birth control advice and supplies and helps with emotional and sexual problems. Information and educational material available from Education and Publications Unit. For immediate information about contraception (inc emergency), pregnancy testing, abortion, sexually transmitted infections - helpline 0800 0185 023

Campaign Against Double Punishment, c/o POPS Office, Suite 4b, Building 1, Wilson Park, Monsall Road, Newton Heath, Manchester M40 8WN phone/fax 0161-277 9066. Advice and information to those under threat of deportation. CAPD campaigns for the abolition of the use of deportation as a penalty for convicted prisoners. Acts as a referral and training agency for Probation Service and other agencies.

*The Child Bereavement Trust, Brindley House, 4 Burkes Road, Beaconsfield, Bucks HP9 1PB. (01494) 678088 *fax (01494) 678765.* Cares for bereaved families by offering specialised training and support to the professional carer, also offers resources for families and professionals (e.g. videos and books)

Childline, Freepost 1111, London N1 0BR. 0800 1111. 24 hr national telephone helpline for children and young people in trouble or danger. The service is free and confidential.

Child Poverty Action Group, 94 White Lion Street, London N1 9PF. 020-7837 7979 *fax 020-7837 6414* www.cpag.org.uk. For details of CPAG and training courses and membership schemes contact above address. Welfare rights enquiries (advisors only): Citizen's Rights Office 020-7833 4627, 2-4pm Mon-Thurs. Promotes action for relief, directly or indirectly, of poverty among children and families with children. Works to ensure that those on low incomes get their full entitlement to welfare benefits. Aims to eradicate the injustice of poverty.

Children's Legal Centre, University of Essex, Wivenhoe Park, Colchester, Essex CO4 3SQ (01206) 872466 (admin and publications) *fax (01206) 874026.* Free and confidential advice and information service covering all aspects of law and policy affecting young people in England and Wales. Publishes 'Childright' and other publications. Advice line (01206) 873820 Mon-Fri 10.30am - 12.30pm & 2-4.30pm. 24hr answerphone

The Children's Service, Cambridge Family and Divorce Centre, Essex House, 71 Regent Street, Cambridge CB2 1AB (01223) 576308 (info & answerphone) (01223) 576309 (admin & fax). Counselling for under 19s experiencing difficulty as a result of a current or past parental divorce. Offers support rather than therapy

Citizen Advocacy Information & Training, Unit 162 Lee Valley Technopark, Ashley Road, Tottenham Hale, London N17 9LN. 020-8880 4545 *fax 020-8880 4113.* e-mail cait@teleregion.co.uk website www.citizenadvocacy.org.uk Maintains a national database of citizen advocacy schemes and provides information, training & publications on citizen advocacy.

*CLAPA, Cleft Lip & Palate Association, 235-237 Finchley Road, London NW3 6LS. 020-7431 0033 *fax 020-7431 8881* e-mail clapa@cwcom.net website www.clapa.mcmail.com

CoDA (Co-dependents Anonymous), Ashburnham Community Centre, Tetcott Road, Chelsea, London SW10 0SH. 020-7376 8191 (answerphone/helpline). An informal Twelve Step fellowship of men and women, whose common problem is an inability to maintain functional relationships with self and others as a result of co-dependancy in their lives. CoDA uses the Twelve Steps, as a part of its suggested programme of recovery and for building healthy relationships, in a safe and confidential environment.

The Commission for Racial Equality, Elliot House, 10/12 Allington Street, London SW1E 5EH. 020-7828 7022 *fax 020-7630 7605.* e mail info@cre.gov.uk website www.cre.gov.uk CRE has three main duties: (1) to work towards the elimination of racial discrimination and to promote equality of opportunity (2) to encourage good relations between people from different racial backgrounds (3) to monitor the way the Race Relations Act is working and recommend ways in which it can be improved. It is the only government appointed body with statutory power to enforce the Race Relations Act. It has a reference library that is open to the public (by appointment).

*Community Advice Project, Room 9, Winchester House, 11 Cranmer Road, Kennington Park, London SW9 6EJ. 020-7735 6592 *fax 020-7820 1389* This is the charitable arm of the Society of Black Lawyers. It administers advice.

Community Care Enterprises, 1st Floor, Crosby House, 9/13 Elmfield Road, Bromley, Kent BR1 1LT 020-8460 1224. Offers services to support the reconciliation of offenders with their communities who are subject to a supervision order with the Probation Service. Housing case work, housing advice, housing need assessment, resettlement, advocacy networking with specialist projects for adult offenders.

The Compassionate Friend, 53 North Street, Bristol BS3 1EN. phone & fax 0117-966 5202 (helpline 0117-953 9639 9.30am-10.30pm every day). An organisation of and for bereaved parents

Criminal Injuries Compensation Board, Tay House, 300 Bath Street, Glasgow G2 4LN. 0141-3312726 *fax 0141-331 2287.* Administers the government funded scheme to provide compensation to innocent victims of violent crime in Great Britain.

Criminal Cases Review Committee, Alpha Tower, Suffolk Street, Queens Way, Birmingham B1 1TT.

Cruse Bereavement Care, Cruse House, 126 Sheen Road, Richmond, Surrey TW9 1UR. 0870 167 1677 *fax 020-8940 7638*. e-mail info@crusebereavementcare.org.uk. The UKs largest and only national organisation that helps and supports anyone who has been bereaved by death. Since 1959 it has been providing advice, bereavement counselling and information on practical matters for bereaved people entirely free of charge. Cruse's bereavement support is delivered through a network of 180 branches across the UK. It also offers training, support, information and publications to those working to care for bereaved people. Cruse aims to increase public awareness of the needs of bereaved people through education and information services.

*Divert Trust, 33 King Street, Covent Garden, London WC2E 8JD 020-7379 6171 *fax 020-7240 2082*. e mail info@divert.org www.divert.org National charity for the prevention of youth crime that aims to divert vulnerable people between 8-25 at risk of crime or school exclusion by encouraging them to engage in constructive activities. Runs mentoring schemes in the community and schools. Also provides small grants to local voluntary organisations to help them set up community initiatives (for example football teams, homework and computer clubs and bicycle renovation projects)

Down's Syndrome Association, 155 Mitcham Road, London SW17 9PG. 020-8682 4001 *fax 020-8682 4012.* Exists to support parents and carers of people with Down's Syndrome and to improve the lives of those with the condition.

Dyspel, London Action Trust, 88 Clapham Road, London SW9 0JT 020-7793 0842 *fax 020-7820 3577* A project that helps dyslexic offenders.

Eating Disorders Association, 1st Floor, Wensum House, 103 Prince of Wales Road, Norwich, Norfolk NR1 1DW admin only (01603) 619090 *fax (01603) 664915*. helpline (01603) 621414 (weekdays 9am-6.30pm), youth helpline (01603) 765050 (up to 18yrs, weekdays 4pm-6pm), recorded information service 0906 302 0012 (calls cost 50p a minute). e-mail info@edauk.com. www.edauk.com. Provides information, help and support for people affected by eating disorders and, in particular, anorexia and bulimia nervosa.

*The Equal Opportunities Commission, Overseas House, Quay Street, Manchester M3 3HN. tel & minicom 0161-833 9244 *fax 0161-835 1657*.e-mail info@eoc.org.uk website www.eoc.org.uk A public body that works to remove discrimination on grounds of sex and to promote equal opportunities for women and men.

Fairbridge , 207 Waterloo Road, London SE1 8XD 020-7928 1704 *fax 020-7928 6016.* Charity providing personal development through a combination of residential outdoor activities courses and long term support.

Families Need Fathers, 134 Curtain Road, London EC2A 3AR. 020-7613 5060. 0990 502506. www.fnf.org.ukNational network of voluntary contacts. Keeping children and parents in contact after separation or divorce. Regular meetings are held around the country

Family Planning Association, 2-12 Pentonville Road, London N1 9FP. 020-7837 5432. Helpline 020-7837 4044 (mon-fri 9am-7pm) providing information and advice on contraception, sexual health and family planning services.

*Family Rights Group, The Print House, 18 Ashwin Street, London E8 3DL. 020-7923 2628. Telephone advice service: mon-fri 1.30-3.30pm, freephone 0800 731 1696. Provides a phone and written advice service for parents, relatives and carers who have children in care, on the child protection register, or who are receiving services from social services departments.

Family Service Units, 207 Old Marylebone Road, London NWl 5QP. 020-7402 5175 *fax 020-7724 1829.* Provides social work and family support services for families and children experiencing serious problems, through a national network of local projects.

Family Welfare Association, 501-505 Kingsland Road, London E8 4AU. 020-7254 6251 *fax 020-7249 5443.* Provides a range of social care services including community mental health services, activity based resource centres, family centres, grants to people in need, and grants advice for students undertaking vocational courses.

*Federation of Prisoners' Families Support Groups, c/o Save the Children Fund, Cambridge House, Cambridge Grove, London W6 0LE. 020-8741 4578 *fax 020-8741 4505.* National umbrella organisation acting as the voice for, and encouraging the development of organisations that provide assistance for the families of people in prison. Provides details of local support services, publishes a National Directory and other resource material.

Fellowship of Depressives Anonymous, Box FDAI, Self Help Nottingham, Ormiston House, 36-36 Pelham Street, Nottingham NG1 2EG (01702) 433838 *fax (0702) 433843.* A self help association of sufferers (and relatives) to encourage mutual support. Local groups, meetings, pen-friend scheme, newsletter.

Female Prisoners' Welfare Project/Hibiscus, 15 Great St Thomas Apostle, Mansion House, London EC4V 2BB. 020-7329 2384 *fax 020-7329 2385.* e-mail fpwphibiscus@hotmail.com. Charity providing advice and support to women in prison, their children and families. Visits and supports British and foreign national women also group sessions for foreign nationals including Spanish speaking women. Provides Home Circumstance Reports for the Courts via an office in Jamaica. Staff speak a wide range of languages.

Gay Rights in Prison, 82 Barnett Road, Hollingdean, Brighton BN1 7GH. (01273) 708659

Gingerbread (the association of one parent families in England and Wales, 300 local self-help groups), 16-17 Clerkenwell Close, London EC1R 0AN. 020-7336 8183 *fax 020-7336 8185.* advice line 020-7336 8184. e mail office@gingerbread.org.uk

Grubb Institute, Cloudesley Street, London N1 0HU, 020-7278 8061 *fax 020-7278 0728.* e-mail info@grubb.org.uk www.grubb.org.uk Organisational role analysis, consultation, and development for managers and management teams in relation to purpose, vision and values. The Institute is a registered charity

Howard League , 708 Holloway Road, London N19 3NL. 020-7281 7722 *fax 020-7281 5506.* e-mail howard.league@ukonline.co.uk A charity working for humane and effective reform of the penal system

*Institute for the Study and Treatment of Delinquency (ISTD), Centre for Crime & Justice Studies, King's College London, 8th Floor, 75-79 York Road, London SE1 7AW. 020-7401 2425 *fax 020-7401 2436.* e-mail istd.enq@kcl.ac.uk An independent educational charity, offering membership, courses, conferences, seminars, lectures, study visits, research and publications to all with an interest in criminal justice.

Institute of Career Guidance, 27a Lower High Street, Stourbridge, West Midlands DY8 1TA. (01384) 376464 *fax (01384) 440830.* e mail hq@icg-uk.org www.icg-uk.org The largest membership organisation for careers guidance professionals

Institute of Criminology, University of Cambridge, 7 West Road, Cambridge CB3 9DT (01223) 335360. *fax (01223) 335356.* A centre for teaching and research in criminology and criminal justice matters; other activities include Cropwood Fellowship Programme and a biennial senior course for practitioners in the criminal justice system

*Irish Commission for Prisoners Overseas. Dublin Office: 57 Parnell Square, Dublin 1 (353 1) 8722511 *fax (353 1)8723343*. London Office: 50-52 Camden Square, London NW1 9XB 020-7482 4148 *fax 020-7482 4815*. e mail icpuk@ireland.com. ICPO is a subsection of the Bishops' Commission for Emigrants. It cares for all Irish prisoners abroad, regardless of faith, offence or prison status, and their families when requested. ICPO works at an international level to ensure that minimum levels of human rights for Irish migrants, refugees and prisoners abroad are respected and enforced. As an NGO, ICPO operates on a not for profit basis to represent the needs of Irish individuals imprisoned overseas and to improve standards of rights enforcement and service provision.

*Joint Council for the Welfare of Immigrants, 115 Old Street, London EC1V 9JR. 020-7251 8706 (advice) 020-7251 8708 (admin) *fax 020-7251 8707*. The only independent voluntary organisation working nationally in the field of immigration, nationality and refugee law. Publishes 'Immigration Nationality and Refugee Law Handbook', fact sheets, briefings and JCWI Bulletin. Runs training courses.

Justice, 59 Carter Lane, London EC4V 5AQ 020-7329 5100 *fax 020-7329 5055*. Justice is a law reform and human rights group. It cannot deal with individual cases, but has produced 'How to Appeal' a simple guide to the criminal appeal process. The guide is free to prisoners (send sae 9"x6" with 31p stamp). It is available to others at £2.50 inc p&p.

KIDSCAPE, 2 Grosvenor Gardens, London SW1W 0DH. 020-7730 3300. Provides books, posters, videos, teaching materials and training about prevention of child sexual abuse and school bullying. Send sae (A4 60p) for information and leaflets. Helpline for parents of children bullied at school, Mon-Fri 10am-4pm.

Law Society, 113 Chancery Lane, London WC2A

*Look Ahead Housing and Care Ltd, 282-284 Brigstock Road, Thornton Heath, Surrey CR7 7JE. 020-8689 9559 *fax 020-8665 9958* (supportive accommodation and housing management services)

MESSAGE HOME helpline 0800 700 740 a 24 hr national freecall helpline for those who have left home, or run away from home ,to send a message to their familyor carer and get confidential help and advice. See also Missing Persons Helpline (National)

MACA (Mental After Care Association), 25 Bedford Square, London WC1B 3HW. 020-7436 6194 *fax 020-7637 1980*. e mail maca-bs@maca.org.uk A national charity providing a wide range of high quality community and hospital based services for people with mental health needs and their carers; including advocacy, assertive outreach schemes, community support, employment schemes, forensic services, helplines/information, respite for carers, social clubs, supported accommodation including 24 hour care.

MENCAP (Royal Society for Mentally Handicapped Children and Adults), 123 Golden Lane, London EC1Y 0RT. 020-7454 0454. The largest charity for people with learning difficulties.

MIND (Nat Assn for Mental Health), Granta House, 15/19 Broadway, Stratford, London E15 4BQ 020- 8519 2122 *fax 020-8522 1725*
Mind*info*line London 020-8522 1728.
Mind*info*line outside London (0845) 7660163.
Mind is a charity campaigning to improve services for people with mental distress and their families, and with the promotion of increased understanding of mental health issues.
Northern Mind, 158 Durham Road, Gateshead, Tyne and Wear NE8 4EL 0191-490 0109
NW Mind, 28 Ribblesdale Place, Preston, Lancs PR1 3NA (01772) 821734
SE Mind, 1st floor, Kemp House, 152-160 City Road, London EC1 2NP. 020-7608 0881
SW Mind, Pembroke House, 7 Brunswick Square, Bristol BS2 8PE. 0117-903 0937
Trent and Yorks Mind, 44 Howard Street, Sheffield S1 2LA 0114-272 1742
Wales Mind, 23 St Mary Street, Cardiff CF1 2AA (01222) 395123
W Midlands Mind, 20-21 Cleveland Street, Wolverhampton WV1 3HT (01902) 24404

Missing Persons Helpline (National), Roebuck House, PO Box 28908, London SW14 7JE 020-8392 4545 *fax 020-8878 7752*. National helpline 0500 700 700 The charity is dedicated to helping missing people, their families and those who care for them. See also Message Home .

MAMAA (Mothers Against Murder and Aggression), 516 Wickham Road, Shirley, Croydon, Surrey CR0 8DL phone & fax 020-8777 3406, 07930 416391/2 National support group for families of murder victims.

National Association of Bereavement Services, 2nd Floor, 4 Pinchin Street, London E1 1SA. admin & fax 020-7709 0505, referral helpline weekdays 10am-4pm 020-7709 9090, child bereavement project 0115 911 8070 NABS is a co-ordinating body for all those working with the dying and bereaved. The referral helpline aims to put people in touch with their nearest, most appropriate source of support.

National Association of Child Contact Centres, Minerva House, Spaniel Row, Nottingham NG1 6EP. 0115-948 4557 *fax 0115-941 5519* e mail contact@naccc.org.uk www.naccc.org.uk Child Contact Centres exist to provide neutral meeting places where children of a separated family can enjoy contact with one or both parents, and sometimes other family members, in a comfortable and safe environment where there is no viable alternative.

National Association of Citizens Advice Bureau, 115-123 Pentonville Road, London N1 9LZ. 020-7833 2181 *fax 020-7833 4371*.The national organisation of the CAB Service. Local bureaux provide free, confidential, independent and impartial to anyone on any subject. The CAB Service draws on its experience of client's problems to show where services and policies are failing both locally and nationally. www.nacab.org.uk for information about the CAB Service including a UK wide CAB directory. www.adviceguide.org.uk for on-line CAB advice and information.

National Association of Prison Visitors, 29 Kimbolton Road, Bedford MK40 2PB (01234) 359763

National Child Rescue Organisation, Southern Office: 89 Upper Lewes Road, Brighton, East Sussex BN2 3FF phone/fax (01273) 692947. Northern Office: Unit 28, Cleethorpes Enterprise Centre, Wilton Road, Humberston, Grimsby, Lincs DN36 4AS. (01472) 210562. Specialising in Attention Deficit Hyperactive Disorder and all legal aspects of this condition.

National Children's Bureau, 8 Wakley Street, London EC1V 7QE. 020-7843 6000 *fax 020-7278 9512.* Identifies and promotes the interests of children and young people through policy, research and practice development. The Bureau is multi disciplinary, working with professional across all sectors.

National Council for One Parent Families, 255 Kentish Town Road, London NW5 2LX. 020-7428 5400. Information service for lone parents, other organisations, local authorities and the media. Providing consultancy on employment initiatives for lone parents and rights based training for professionals working with lone parents. Campaigning and lobbying to change the law and improve provision for lone parents and their children.

National Institute for Social Work, 5-7 Tavistock Place, London WC1H 9SN. 020-7387 9681. website www.nisw.org.uk Active throughout the UK, and internationally, supporting practitioners and managers, policy makers and their organisations, and users and carers, with a comprehensive range of services aimed at achieving excellence in practice and management in social work and social care.

National Organisations for Counselling of Adoptees and Parents (NORCAP), 112 Church Road, Wheatley, Oxon OX33 1LU (01865) 875000. Provides support, guidance and sympathetic understanding to adult adoptees and their birth and adoptive parents. Telephone counselling service. Intermediary role for those seeking renewed contact. For members, advice on searching and research service, contact Register

National Schizophrenia Fellowship, 28 Castle Street, Kingston-upon-Thames KT1 1SS. 020-8547 3937, advice service 020-8974 6814 (mon-fri 10am-3pm) *fax 020-8547 3862.* A national voluntary organisation that helps people with a severe mental illness, their families and carers and provides training for professionals.

NSPCC National Centre, 42 Curtain Road, London EC2A 3NH. 020-7825 2500 *fax 020-7825 2525*. 24hr child protection helpline 0808 800 5000 e mail infounit@nspcc.org.uk The NSPCC is the UK's leading charity specialising in child protection and prevention of cruelty to children. It exists to prevent children from suffering significant harm as a result of ill treatment; to help protect children who are at risk from such harm; to help children who have suffered abuse overcome the effects of such harm; and to work to protect children from further harm.

National Youth Agency, 17-23 Albion Street, Leicester LE1 6GD. 0116-285 3700 *fax 0116-285 3777* minicom 0116-285 3788. Information, advice and support for those working with young people. Validates qualifying training for youth and community work

New Bridge, 27a Medway Street, London SW1P 2BD. 020-7976 0779. *fax 020-7976 0767* e-mail new.bridge@ukgateway.net
PO Box 2364, Swanage, Dorset BH19 2YT (01929) 425582.
PO Box 123, Shrewsbury, Shropshire SY1 3UW (01743) 357877
Volunteer Centre, Clarence Terrace, Chester le Street, Durham DH3 3DQ 0191-388 6069. New Bridge Voluntary Associates visit and write to prisoners in more than 100 prisons and runs Family matters/Parenting courses in a number of establishments. The Employment Service has a partnership agreement with SW London Probation Service and runs a job finding service in 15 prison establishments. . Also publishes 'Inside Time' the national newspaper for prisoners.

Nurses Welfare Service, Victoria Chambers, 16-18 Strutton Ground, London SW1P 2HP. 020-7222 1563/4 Help for nurses, midwives and health visitors whose right or fitness to practise is being investigated by their regulatory body.

Out-Side-In, PO Box 119, Orpington, Kent BR6 9ZZ. helpline (01689) 835566 e-mail quequeg@globalnet.co.uk Support group for gay/lesbian prisoners.

*Parentline Plus, Third Floor, Chapel House, 18 Hatton Place, London EC1N 8RU. 020-7209 2460, *fax 020-7209 2461* e mail headoffice@parentlineplus.org.uk. helpline 0808 800 2222, textphone 0800 783 6783 Formed by a merger of Parentline and the National Stepfamily Association. Works with adults, children and young people to provide information and support for families. Works to expand what is understood by parenting and to increase the support available to all those who parent and contribute to the welfare of children. Free confidential helpline, accredited parenting courses, information and publications, and training and consultancy.

Partners of Prisoners Families Support Group, Suite 4b, Building 1, Wilson Park, Monsall Road, Newton Heath, Manchester M40 8WN phone/fax 0161-277 9066. e-mail families@surfaid.org www.partnersofprisoners.co.uk Offers a wide range of services to anyone who has a loved one in prison. Advice, information, moral support is available to families from arrest to release. Manchester based, but telephone calls taken from all areas as acts as a referral agency to support groups nationally. Manages the Black Prisoner Support Project that gives support to black people in custody from the Greater Manchester area.

Portia Campaign, The Croft, Bowness on Solway, Carlisle CA7 5AG phone & fax (016973) 51820. e mail ken_portia@onetel.net.uk www.portia.org Counselling and support for women prisoners we believe falsely convicted, non-rational shoplifters, potential baby-snatchers. Publishers of 'The Lynch-Mob Syndrome' which argues that Louise Woodward, Manjit Basuta and many others are most unlikely to have killed children in their care.

The POW Trust, 295a Queenstown Road, Battersea, London SW8 3NP 020-7720 9767 *fax 020-7498 0477.* Founded in 1992 with the specific intention of helping the afflicted in society, including the socially excluded and ex-offenders. Aims to give those who reach it 'that vital extra chance where in other places the door has been firmly shut'.

The Prince's Trust, 18 Park Square East, London NW1 4LH. 020-7543 1234 *fax 020-7543 1200* General enquiries freephone 0800-842842 or visit website www.princes-trust.org.uk Helps 14-30 year olds to develop confidence, learn new skills, move into work and start businesses. It offers training, personal development opportunities, business start up support, mentoring and advice. The Trust particularly welcomes applications from young people who are disabled, from an ethnic minority community, or ex-offenders.

Prison Dialogue, PO Box 44, Chipping Campden, Glos GL55 6YN (01386) 849186 *fax (01386) 840448.* www.prisondialogue.org.uk Relationship based approach to organisational and therapeutic issues in the criminal justice system. Work is targeted across the criminal justice continuum from high security to local prisons and into the community.

Prison Link, 29 Trinity Road, Aston, Birmingham B6 6AJ 0121-551 1207, 0121-523 0965 *fax 0121-554 4894* A black prisoner support scheme providing services to offenders and their families.

Prison Officers Association, Cronin House, 245 Church Street, London N9 9HW. 020-8803 0255

Prison Reform Trust, 2nd Floor, 15 Northburgh Street, London EC1V 0JR. 020-7251 5070 *fax 020-7251 5076.* e-mail prt@prisonreform.demon.co.uk Runs a research and publishing programme, and offers advice and information on all aspects of penal policy, publishes a quarterly magazine 'Prison Report'. Jointly (with HM Prison Service) publishes "Prisoners' Information Book"

Prisoners Abroad, 89-93 Fonthill Road, Finsbury Park, London N4 3JH. 020-7561 6820 *fax 020-7561 6821.* email info@prisonersabroad.org.uk www.prisonersabroad.org.uk The only UK charity providing information, advice and support to Britons detained overseas, to their families and friends, and to released prisoners trying to re-establish themselves in society. Prisoners Abroad makes no moral judgement about its clients: it helps convicted and unconvicted, guilty or innocent, solely on the basis of need.

Prisoners' Advice Service, 305 Hatton Square, 16/16a Baldwins Gardens, London EC1N 7RJ. 020-7405 8090 *fax 020-7405 8045* The PAS is an independent charity that offers free confidential advice and information to prisoners in England & Wales, particulary concerning prisoners' rights and the application of Prison Rules. Publishes a quarterly bulletin "Prisoners' Rights".

Prisoners' Families and Friends Service, 20 Trinity Street, London SE1 1DB. 020-7403 4091 *fax 020-7357 9722.* e mail pffs@btclick.com Advice and information service for prisoner's families. Other facilities available in the London area.

Prisoners Wives and Families, 254 Caledonian Road, London N1. 020-7278 3981 Information, advice and support for prisoners' families. Overnight accommodation for families travelling long distances to London prisons and courts.

*Prison Watch, 24 Rochester Close, Derby DE24 0HS. (01332) 756158 *fax (01332) 756158* mobile 0585 578029. 145 Coronation Avenue, Keysham, 1-3 Brixton Road, London SW18 2QG 020-7582 1313. Support and advise for prisoners at risk from self harm or suicide.

Probation Managers Association, Hayes Court, West Common Road, Bromley, Kent BR2 7AU. 020-8462 7755 *fax 020-8315 8234* e mail s.towe@headoffice.aeeu.org.uk

Reach Out Project, Nottingham Black Initiative, 4th Floor, Fenchurch House, 12 King Street, Nottingham NG1 2AS. Client freephone 0800 731 4090 e mail nbi@nottinghamblackinitiative.org.uk Provides information and advice on drug related issues, sexual health information, and referrals to other drug related services. legal advice and information, counselling and support groups. Support offered to parents and carers.

The Rights Shop (Bethnal Green), 296 Bethnal Green Road, London E2 0AG, 020-7739 4173 *fax 020-7613 3758;* open 9.30am-3.00pm Mon-Thurs; 9.30am-2.30pm. Drop-in welfare rights/housing advice/money advice and habitual residence test support

*Royal National Institute for the Blind (RNIB), 224 Great Portland Street, London W1N 6AA. 020-7388 1266 *fax 020-7388 2034.* General enquiries: RNIB Resouce Centre, London; benefit rights; education; employment and leisure enquiries; services for local societies; health, social and environmental services; reference library; advice on wills and legacies; enquiries on multiple disability; physiotherapy support. Office house 9am-5.15pm Mon-Thurs, 9am-5pm Fri.

Royal National Institute for Deaf People, 19-23 Featherstone Street, London EC1Y 8SL. 0808 808 0123 (voice), 0808 808 9000 (text), *helpline fax 020-7296 8199.* e mail helpline@rnid.org.uk www.rnid.org.uk The RNID is the largest charity representing the 8.7 million deaf and hard of hearing people in the UK. As a membership charity it aims to achieve a radically better life for deaf and hard of hearing people. It does this by campaigning and lobbying, by raising awareness, by providing services and through social, medical and technical research

RSI Associartion, 380-384 Harrow Road, London W9 2HU

*SAMM (Support After Murder and Manslaughter), Cranmer House, 39 Brixton Road, London SW9 6DZ 020-7735 3838. Offers understanding and support to families and friends bereaved as a result of murder and manslaughter, though the mutual support of others who have suffered a similar tragedy.

SANDS (Stillbirth And Neonatal Death Society), 28 Portland Place, London W1B 1LY. Admin 020-7436 7940, *fax 020-7436 3715,* helpline 020-7436 5881 e mail support@sands-uk. org www.sands-uk.org Support and advice for parents and families whose baby dies before, during or after birth

Saneline, 1st floor, Cityside House, 40 Adler Street, London E1 1EE 020-7375 1002 *fax 020-7375 2162* Saneline (helpline) 0845 767 8000 (12 noon-2am every day of year). A national mental health helpline for anyone with a mental health problem, their friends, families, carers and interested professionals. Can offer emotional support and information on local and national services, illnesses, medications, therapies and mental health law.

Schizophrenia Association of Great Britain, The Crescent, Bangor, Gwynedd LL57 2AG. phone & fax (01248) 354048. Special leaflets available for probation officers and magistrates. Free information pack for all enquirers.

Sex Addicts Anonymous, BCM Box 1457, London WC1N 3XX. 020-8442 0026 (12 step fellowship based on model pioneered by AA, meetings open to anyone who feels their sexual behaviour is causing problems either to themselves or others. Newcomers meeting each Monday (inc bank holidays) 6pm, at The Church Hall of St Mary-the-Virgin, Eversholt Street, London NW1, nearest tube Euston

Shelter (National campaign for homeless), 88 Old Street, London EC1V 9HU. 020-7505 2000 *fax 020-7505 2169.* Freephone emergency 24hr advice 0808 800 4444. Runs a network of housing aid centres providing advice and advocacy to people who are, or are threatened with, homelessness, and campaigns on their behalf

SITRA, Bramah House, 65-71 Bermondsey Street, London SE1 3XF. Central services 020-7357 8922, training 020-7357 8955, *fax 020-7357 8824.* e-mail post@sitra.org www.sitra.org.uk Training, advice, policy information and consultancy on all supported housing and supporting people matters. Monthly journal 'SITRA Bulletin' goes to all probation service housing co-ordinators/partnership managers.

*Society of Black Lawyers, Room 9, Winchester House, 11 Cranmer Road, Kennington Park, London SW9 6EJ. 020-7735 6592 *fax 020-7820 1389* e-mail National-Office@sbl_hq.freeserve.co.uk

SOFA (Serious Offenders Families Association), 2 The Chestnuts, Ella Street, Hull HU5 3AR. (01482) 442133

Tavistock Marital Studies Institute, The Tavistock Centre, 120 Belsize Lane, London NW3 5BA 020-7435 7111 *fax 020-7435 1080*

Trauma Aftercare Trust, Buttfields, The Farthings, Withington, Glos GL54 4DF (01242) 890306. Offers training including standards, ethics and experience for trauma counselling qualifications plus skilled help for individuals and families suffering from trauma

*Unlock (National Association of Ex-Offenders), 10 Seymour Grove, Sale, Cheshire M33 3AD phone & fax 0161-969 0725

*Victim Support, National Office, Cranmer House, 39 Brixton Road, London SW9 6DZ 020-7735 9166 *fax 020-7582 5712.* Co-ordinates the work of local Schemes providing services to victims of crime and their families, also co-ordinates the Witness Service which supports witnesses in Crown Courts and a growing number of Magistrates' Courts..

Voluntary Service Overseas, 317 Putney Bridge Road, London SW15 2PN. 020-8780 7200 *fax 020-8780 7300*

Women in Prison, 3b Aberdeen Studios, 22 Highbury Grove, London N5 2EA. 020-7226 5879 *fax 020-7354 8005.* Established as a support and campaigning group for women prisoners, visits women prisoners and offers practical advice on a range of welfare issues, particularly accommodation referrals. Also the Education & Training Connection that provides bursaries for distance learning courses for women prisoners, and links women with education/training centres on release.

Women's Aid Federation of England Ltd, PO Box 391, Bristol BS99 7WS. national co-ordinating office telephone 0117-944 4411 (mon-fri 10am-1pm, 2pm-4pm), national helpline 08457 023468 (mon-fri 10am-8pm, sat 10am-5pm). Public information, publications and training on domestic violence. National helpline for women and children experiencing domestic violence. Co-ordinates work of women's refuges in England.

Workaholics Anonymous, PO Box 11466, London SW1V 2ZQ

Zito Trust, PO Box 265, London WC2H 9JD. 01497 820011

INDEX OF OFFICE NAMES ENGLAND, WALES & NORTHERN IRELAND

INDEX OF OFFICE NAMES SCOTLAND